Cryptology Unlocked

Cryptology Unlocked

Reinhard Wobst
Translated by Angelika Shafir

John Wiley & Sons, Ltd

Other Wiley Editorial Offices

John Wiley & Sons Inc., 111 River Street, Hoboken, NJ 07030, USA

Jossey-Bass, 989 Market Street, San Francisco, CA 94103-1741, USA

Wiley-VCH Verlag GmbH, Boschstr. 12, D-69469 Weinheim, Germany

John Wiley & Sons Australia Ltd, 42 McDougall Street, Milton, Queensland 4064, Australia

John Wiley & Sons (Asia) Pte Ltd, 2 Clementi Loop #02-01, Jin Xing Distripark, Singapore 129809

John Wiley & Sons Canada Ltd, 6045 Freemont Blvd, Mississauga, Ontario, L5R 4J3, Canada

Wiley also publishes its books in a variety of electronic formats. Some content that appears in print may not be available in electronic books.

Anniversary Logo Design: Richard J. Pacifico

Library of Congress Cataloging-in-Publication Data:

Wobst, Reinhard.
   Cryptology unlocked / Reinhard Wobst ; translated by Angelika Shafir.
     p. cm.
   Includes bibliographical references and index.
   ISBN 978-0-470-06064-3
   1. Computers—Access control. 2. Data protection. 3. Cryptography. I.
Title.
   QA76.9.A25W62 2007
   005.8′2—dc22

                                        2007008058

British Library Cataloguing in Publication Data

A catalogue record for this book is available from the British Library

ISBN 978-0-470-06064-3 (PB)

Typeset in 11/13pt Times by Laserwords Private Limited, Chennai, India
Printed and bound in Great Britain by Antony Rowe Ltd, Chippenham, Wiltshire
This book is printed on acid-free paper responsibly manufactured from sustainable forestry
in which at least two trees are planted for each one used for paper production.

Contents

Preface

"Cryptology"—the science of secret writing—is peculiarly fascinating. Its vocabulary alone reminds you of crime thrillers rather than of science: radio reconnaissance, invisible ink, encrypted message exchange, ciphertext attack. . . This fascination begins probably rather early in our lives. I once watched my older son as he zestfully tried to decipher some secret writing in a children's puzzle magazine. When I was a kid I experimented with the legendary invisible ink made of salt solution or lemon juice (which never worked, because as I heated it up the paper would always char instead of magically revealing the secret writing). When my dad later told me about his method for encrypting radio traffic (Section 2.3), I was thrilled and had a dim feeling that there's got to be a bunch of mathematics behind it. I simply couldn't imagine that anybody could ever be able to read such ciphers without knowing the key. And with so many keys around—no way anybody could try them all out!

My next encounter with cryptology happened two decades later. Long after my math studies, I had access to a PDP11 computer and experienced for the first time that computers can be there for people rather than the other way round. I began to test an encryption algorithm I invented on this computer and thought it to be bomb-proof—as always when you don't have enough background knowledge. Ten years later, I further developed this algorithm, studied it to the best of my knowledge, and published it in the German *UNIX Magazine*. The lively readers' response took me by surprise.

Unfortunately, this algorithm was insecure. You will read in Section 3.7 how it can be cracked.

In the years that followed, I dealt with cryptology over and again and increasingly more often. Motivated by a magazine article, Mr Wehren of Addison-Wesley Publishing asked me whether I would like to write a book on this topic. I initially thought it was too daring. After a month of playing with the idea, I agreed, and I haven't been sorry. This book is an English version of the fourth edition of that book, and I hope you enjoy reading it as much as I enjoyed writing it. The book is intended to be fun, but it also has other goals.

Today, as we can't imagine our everyday lives without cryptology, there is a widening gap between modern and hard-to-understand cryptological research on the one hand, and the general state of knowledge on the other hand. The risks from naïve use of bad encryption methods (or—more often—bad use of good methods) mustn't be underestimated. That's not panic-mongering: We first have to get to grips with the new information age. A popular, but not superficial, discussion of this issue is necessary. This book is intended to be easily understandable for non-mathematicians, too, and it should show how exciting, many-facetted, and entertaining cryptology can be. Whether or not I achieved these goals is up to you.

A lot has happened since the first edition of this book (1997). Cryptology has left its mystery-mongering world, and modern society would be unthinkable without it any more. While there were still only a handful of specialists who furthered cryptanalysis actively (i.e., cracked code) in the mid-1990s, it is now a broad field of research that produces interesting results. And while good encryption was subject to tight restrictions, not only in the USA, at the beginning of the 1990s, we now have an encryption standard like the AES that came about by an international challenge, and the USA now use a Belgian algorithm for their own security. Also, we understand much better today that encryption is only a small part of security, and that most errors are made when implementing algorithms. Nevertheless, cryptology has remained one of the hardest subjects in information security to understand.

The developments won't come to a standstill. Additions and corrections to this book will certainly become necessary, though it is already in its fourth edition. This is why you will find current information on the topics discussed in this book and errors that attentive readers will have found at

http://www.wileyeurope.com/go/cryptology

So, if you find wrong or incomplete information, or if you think that one term or the other should appear in the Glossary, please send an email to the address given below.

I welcome every critical comment. **But please don't send me ciphertexts to decrypt, or new 'uncrackable' algorithms.** When you've read the book (and particularly the text in *txt/FAQ/memo.txt* on our Web site!), you'll understand that those are extraordinarily cumbersome tasks, and I normally won't have the time or sometimes the knowledge.

Reinhard Wobst
r.wobst@gmx.de
GnuPG fingerprint:
897A 6984 9C8D FED9 305F 082E F762 909D A28C 4B16

Chapter 1

Introduction

We live in a world where information and its exchange play central roles, and yet it's only the beginning of the information age. It will become increasingly important to protect information which, in turn, requires knowledge in cryptology. **Cryptology** encompasses two fields: **cryptography**, which is, roughly speaking, the science of data protection by encryption, and **cryptanalysis**, which is the art of obtaining information on secret data without knowing the key. Though people have been dealing with cryptology for several thousands of years, it is still somewhat mystery-mongered. It is also a difficult field. First, every cryptologist needs to have sound mathematical knowledge. Second, a cryptologist is often hindered by the fact that he's either bound to confidentiality, or that research findings are kept secret. Cryptology still hasn't rid itself of its reputation of being a playground for national intelligence agencies, diplomats, and militaries, though it has meanwhile made its way into everyday use—think only of your bank card's PIN, or digital cell phones. On the other hand, for example in the United States up into the 1990s, good (secure) encryption algorithms had been banned from export. They were classified as 'ammunition'. In France, cryptography was thought of as the second most dangerous type of weapon, and its use had to be approved by the Prime Minister (explicitly excluding criminals and alcoholics). Meanwhile, the regulations have loosened up in France, too.

Knowledge of good cryptographic methods and mainly their correct use is still not widely disseminated. We often use bad or unpublished algorithms, or

Cryptology Unlocked Reinhard Wobst
© 2007 John Wiley & Sons, Ltd

algorithms whose security we know little or nothing about. 'Security' means almost always: we haven't found a vulnerability so far, but who knows whether somebody found one long ago and just didn't tell us about it. Security that is both theoretically provable and practically usable is still the pipe-dream of all cryptologists today, even though we may quite reasonably trust modern, thoroughly studied algorithms.

In contrast, interested outsiders encounter problems with the large choice of algorithms, theoretical findings from analyses, and difficult cryptographic protocols. The significance of good methods cannot be appreciated enough. The 'information society' needs to have a totally new security awareness; the risks are different and sometimes even much greater than in the physical world. One thing is for sure: not knowing about cryptology can only make things worse. You will find plenty of hair-raising examples in this book.

All the mystery-mongering, the imponderabilities and their particular significance make cryptology very different from other fields of knowledge. Cryptology is an adventure we will try to unlock in this book.

1.1 Should You Read This Book?

This is not a textbook. It is by no means complete, and it isn't particularly mathematical either (at least not more than absolutely necessary). If you have some background knowledge and want to delve deeper into cryptology, I recommend the seminal work of Schneier [SchnCr], but this is a hefty tome of more than 800 pages. Nevertheless, the author refers to the literature frequently enough when it comes to the details (more than 1653 quotations!). Or perhaps you are looking for an easier way to first get to grips with the basics in cryptology: What does it actually research? What is known so far? What is it good for? How can I benefit from it? If you are intrigued by these questions, you may want to have a go at this book. If you make it to the very end, you will hopefully have found answers to these questions. And you should have a rough idea of how the security of methods and protocols is evaluated, and what to think of the findings. You will know how many fields belong to cryptology (and which don't), how much inventiveness cryptanalysts put into their work, and how little we know in spite of it all; many statements in this book are only suppositions.

Cryptological knowledge can prove very useful in practice. With basic knowledge, if somebody tries to talk you into buying a product by simply stating that 'nobody will reveal the data because they are encrypted', you will not buy it. Modern ciphering devices and ciphering programs should have freely usable interfaces for a customer's cryptographic components, or they should at least offer reproducible methods. But only a qualified customer can force vendors to do this. This customer could be you, for example. The triumphant success of the free PGP program shows *one* possible way toward 'cryptological justice'.

You will find reading this book easier if you have some IT knowledge—people who know the C programming language will have a home advantage—and if you are not too hostile toward mathematics. But you don't have to be a professional programmer. *Cryptology Unlocked* is meant to be a book for practitioners who want to get a rough idea of this fascinating field without having to delve deeply into its theory. I'll spare you the nitty-gritty, like formulas, to the widest possible extent. Many things can be explained verbally just as well. Sometimes, however, there is no way around formulas. After all, cryptology is a field where each side uses mathematical ingenuity to trick the other side. This is why not everything can be explained without using some background knowledge. But it's not a math book for sure.

You will find only a few ready-made programs on the Web site to this book (www.wileyeurope.com/go/cryptology). Conversely, you will find plenty of C source texts 'to play' with, and many documents that go far beyond the things discussed here. The Web site to this book, the list of references, and information sources on the Internet will help you if you want to deal with cryptology more deeply.

1.2 Why Busy Ourselves With Cryptology?

1.2.1 'I've Nothing to Hide'

I've heard this sentence over and again and think it's a big mistake. Almost everybody is careful about their physical possessions: people lock their apartment doors, don't leave their wallets lying around unattended, and lock their cars. The fact that information represents an asset doesn't seem to have crossed many people's minds. All right, you wouldn't write everything on postcards, and you don't pass on the personal identification number (PIN) of your bank card. But the problem begins when handling this PIN: people who write their PIN on the card itself are simply unaware of the things unauthorized persons can do with such information! Information often embodies a much greater value than material things. Look at this example: back in the 1990s, Philip Morris bought Kraft Foods for 12.9 billion dollars, including 1.3 billion for material assets. The buyer deemed it worth paying 90 % for know-how, experienced staff, brand name, customer base, and so on—all of this largely representing

---

Example of the value of a company:

- Material assets worth 1.3 billion dollars.
- Miscellaneous (know-how, customer base, brand name, staff, ...) worth 11.6 billion dollars.

Figure 1.1: Information can be more valuable than material assets.

information that could mean added value for a competitor, for example, the know-how and disclosing of the customer base [Peters, p. 27].

Or think of the huge amounts of data from seismographic measurements that could give a clue on the location of a future oil platform and would mean millions in profit for an impostor. The German Chamber of Industry and Commerce (IHK) and industrial associations estimated the damage caused by industrial espionage to be at least 4 billion euros for Germany in 1988. This has remained the only official figure. Estimates from the beginning of the millennium were between 10 and 35 billion euros. The wide range of these estimates shows better than any verbose statement how large the gray zone must be.

Yet another consideration explains the significance of information: according to Peters [Peters], virtual companies will drive other business formats out of the market, because they are much more flexible and efficient. In this context, several companies would merge temporarily and for a specific purpose. Secure exchange of information represents an immediate value-adding potential for such virtual companies.

Underestimating the value of information can have catastrophic consequences. We should have learned this much from history. In both world wars, reading encrypted messages of the adversary played a decisive role, and in both world wars, the parties concerned simply ignored the impact of it. In 1914, when the German cruiser *Magdeburg* ran aground and fell to the Russians, including the *Signalbuch der Kaiserlichen Marine* and other code books, it didn't raise suspicion on the German side; no secret code was changed on this account. A Russian prisoner then even told the Germans that they owned the code books. Obviously the Germans underestimated the significance of cryptanalysis, and they hadn't even gotten suspicious when the activities of British warships made clear that the German intelligence communication had been eavesdropped.

Breaking the German Enigma code by the Poles and British in World War II was most important for the outcome of the war. A large part of Chapter 2 is dedicated to this topic. But in England, too, it took some time until the British admiralty recognized the value of their cryptanalysts, while they had a close shave themselves: according to Kahn [KahnCode], it would have been possible for the German Wehrmacht to land in Great Britain (in fact, things had been going according to plan!)—had the British not changed their own code in time—for the Germans listened in on them. Later on things changed, not only militarily: while the British managed to listen in on the Germans increasingly faster, the German top echelon refused to consider that their Enigma ciphering machine might *not* be infallible. Many insiders think that cryptanalysis was decisive for the outcome of many wars. Kahn [KahnCode] even thinks that cryptanalysis helped gain more information than all espionage activities together. At least four events decisive for the outcome of World War II were possible only by cryptanalysis. Among others, this includes the battle off the Midway Islands, which prevented the dominance of the Japanese in the Pacific, and the shooting down of Admiral Yamamoto's plane by the US air force. However, the best example is the submarine war in the Atlantic. If the Enigma hadn't been deciphered, the USA would probably have dropped nukes over Europe. More about this in Chapter 2.

We may reasonably assume that militaries, national intelligence agencies, and other organizations learned a lot from past errors. Otherwise, there wouldn't be agencies like the NSA (National Security Agency), for example, which specializes in the 'surveillance' of global intelligence communication and cryptology, among other things. Its largest listening-post outside the USA and Great Britain is located in Bad Aibling in the south of Germany. Readers interested in the details should look at Section 8.2.1.

You Have Information Worth Protecting

'I don't wage submarine wars, don't buy companies, and don't drill for oil', you will say, 'What should I protect?' Well, consider the following points.

- Any piece of information obtained in an unauthorized way that gives clues on your financial situation can be dangerous for you. If you have lots of money it will for sure. But even if you have no money it may: it could interest a potential employer, or your landlord. This person doesn't necessarily have to wiretap your line itself. Don't forget that information (as opposed to tape recordings) won't change even after the 15th copying between computers.

- Also your acquaintances and the possibilities for espionage or sabotage given by your work can make you an interesting subject for others—for national intelligence organizations, religious groups, or competitive companies. This is one of the fields with likely the largest percentage of undetected crimes. We don't know the proportions of the 'war behind the scenes'.

- Businesses are particularly at risk. [IHK] describes a case from the textile industry, where a company's major competitor lured away customers from that company's customer base. Address lists of any sort are cash! And people outside the business world shouldn't be indifferent about this either. Information is power, and it's usually the powerful who get to it more easily. This can lead to new types of painful competitive imbalances. The customer will feel it in the form of excessive prices, poor service, and inelastic supply.

- [IHK] points to the fact that scientists in particular see themselves as colleagues rather than competitors, and such circumstances are recklessly exploited by national intelligence organizations.

- Don't forget that some confidential information that may not be of interest to you can acutely endanger your friends or acquaintances. Possessing third-party information can also be dangerous in some situations. In February 1995, when insider information about Scientology became public on the Internet, the sender of this message had used an anonymous remailer. A remailer is a computer that strips off all information about the sender when forwarding emails (which is legitimate and sometimes necessary). On earlier occasions, such messages had been deleted by unknown people due to alleged disclosure of trade secrets. In this case, the Finnish police, called in by the FBI and Interpol, and Scientology themselves called the remailer operator and requested the sender's address be disclosed. While this led to nothing, when the Swedish daily *Dagens Nyheter* connected him with child pornography three days later, the Finnish police waved a search and seizure warrant at him two days later. The alleged child porn was found to be untenable a couple of days later. You can read more about this thriller in [Kunz.ct].

- Cryptology doesn't only deal with data secrecy. It also deals with data integrity and authorship. If your ATM card is stolen and the thief (or his organization) manages to cryptanalyze the PIN (see Section 6.6.8), you might find the money stolen to be the least painful consequence. The bank may claim that you had passed on your PIN with fraudulent intention and sue you. This has happened more than once. In court, your PIN is as good a judicial evidence as your signature.

Poor cryptography allows adversaries to rummage in your name, and you will be held responsible for the damage. Think of unscrupulous nuts with enough capability and a decent budget!

This book is not about national economy and data protection. But it uses examples from these fields to show you how important it is to protect information today. Together with the explosively growing popularity of the Internet, data protection gains unimagined significance. As convenient and beneficial as global communication may be, we have to learn *which* information we have to protect against unauthorized access, and *how* we can protect it. This book deals mainly with the second question.

Have you noticed something? Our real-world examples talked little about national intelligence organizations, and the popularly quoted armchair hacker wasn't mentioned at all. Information has become merchandise, and accordingly it is of interest for business. I recommend the book by Hummelt [Humm] for further reading; he worked with companies specializing in competitive analyses himself and knows what he is writing about. This explains the large number of instructive examples in his book.

Nevertheless, we should by no means underestimate the potential threat from national intelligence organizations. Thanks to rapidly evolving computer technologies, the possibilities of unnoticed surveillance grow just as rapidly. Section 8.2.1 will show you how technology can enable surveillance of our everyday lives, and how much of it has been implemented.

1.2.2 Cryptology: A Special Chain Link

Security is a Very Complex Field

Good cryptological algorithms alone offer no protection at all. Security can only be achieved by a gapless chain of measures:

- All members of staff concerned have to be trustworthy.
- All members of staff concerned have to be security-aware: none of them may write passwords on the bottom of the keyboard, have anyone looking over their shoulders as they type their passwords, let alone mumble them. Unfortunately, this happens quite often in practice.
- Data media with unencrypted information must be stored safely.

- Confidential plaintext (readable text) must never flow through a network others can eavesdrop, such as the Internet or intranets. It is believed that every data packet crossing the Internet in the USA is listened in on with a probability of 10 %. A DFN-CERT employee estimates a similar rate for Germany.

- Your computers have to be secured against illegal access over the network. *IP spoofing* (a technique used to gain unauthorized access to computers, whereby the intruder sends messages to a computer with an assumed IP address) is actually a complicated matter. But thanks to the wealth of software packages on the black market, this type of attack has become 'respectable', in addition to many other ingenious methods. We don't know how many of these attacks are malicious. Firewalls are not impenetrable!

If all of this wasn't scary enough, think of software working as an active spy. For example, the *Promis* program originally designed for criminal investigation had been universally used and might also have helped the NSA (National Security Agency) in accessing a large number of international databases, possibly including those of Swiss banks. I refer readers interested in the details to [SpiegDat] and spies you happen to know. The article referred to mentions, among other things, that every normal computer with a normal screen works like a TV transmitter. The signal can probably be filtered out from a distance of even one kilometer, and the screen contents can be reconstructed from this signal. Automatic teller machines (ATMs) are also computers, by the way. And we don't know how many computers are out there running keyboard sniffers that simply capture keystrokes and then send passwords or other sensitive stuff they recovered over the network.

Don't give up just yet. At the advent of the Industrial Revolution in England, most houses had no door locks, and current security technology wouldn't have meant anything to anybody back then. The current change toward the information society is just as revolutionary, and we'll once more have to learn things from scratch. And it will get dangerous if we fail to understand the threats.

What Cryptology Means for Data Protection

Back to our topic. You have seen that cryptology is not everything, but is something special. Why? Encryption can protect information when it is clear that unauthorized access cannot be prevented. (A classical example are the address lists on your Windows computer at your workplace.) However, I find another aspect much more significant.

Bugging a room, listening over laser mikes, extorting a company's employees, or penetrating a company's perimeters, and similar things are hard work and risky. No wonder spies are well paid. But when a popular encoding algorithm is secretly cracked, and the attack can be 'cast' in reasonably fast software, then data espionage gets much easier. Using this software is easy. Imagine somebody who can just about move a mouse suddenly getting hold of your confidential information and selling it to the brains behind the scenes to replenish his petty cash! This person won't have any hard work to do, because our networks are astonishingly easy to eavesdrop (or computers to tap), and he will normally not leave any traces. Other persons or computers can also use the program: copying the software is cheaper than buying a bug.

Yet another factor illustrates the special role of cryptology: if an eavesdropper can't decrypt encrypted messages, he can at least hoard them. One day either the encryption algorithm or the protocol will be cracked, or the eavesdropper will get access to a faster computer—and here we go, he will read all your messages in arrears. Since some information doesn't lose its value with age, even in our hectic times, you could have an unpleasant surprise after several years. For who knows what methods cryptanalysis will use in five years from now?

Fast and good decryption programs could enable large-scale surveillance the 'needlework spy' can only dream of. This is one of the new-quality risks to the information society. There are parallels to using nuclear power: the probability of an accident is much smaller than with other processes (in cryptology this means that money forging is much easier than finding an exploitable backdoor in the DES algorithm). But *when* an accident happens, the damage can outdo everything known so far.

Not even the leaky software mentioned above could have as many consequences as the fast, unauthorized decryption of a widely used algorithm—if at all possible.

All vulnerabilities mentioned so far have to be exploited individually; in contrast, cryptanalysis can be massware. You will find a small example on the CD that comes with this book: *newwpcrack* is a program that finds the password for an encrypted WordPerfect file on a PC with high probability within 10 ms.

Surprising Simplifications

I admit, I want to scare you a little. Really usable software like the one for WordPerfect doesn't normally come for free, and only the theoretical method is discussed. Almost no program will work as fast as WordPerfect. But don't rely on it, because complex mathematical problems have a peculiarity: once their solutions are found, they often become much simpler. The following examples show just how much simpler.

- You certainly know about Rubik's cube, which challenges you to turn the layered pieces such that each of its six sides has a different color. It took me two weeks of occasional trial and error to get my first two layers in place. The next attempt succeeded after three days, then it took only one—I had grasped the trick. I then felt I had to proceed more systematically. Within a week, I found a sequence of 'pieces' and composed a puzzle out of them. Later I handled the cube without training (but using a crib) within five to ten minutes. I'm convinced that everybody can do this.

- A much more drastic example is the base problem in functional analysis. The problem itself originates from mathematical basic research; I won't explain it here. Anyway, it concerns an assumption expressed in the 1930s which is relatively easy to formulate, as many hard problems are. For decades, leading mathematicians had cut their teeth over it. Nobody was able to prove it, until a Dutchman found a counterexample in the mid-1970s: it was all wrong! The proof that this was a counterexample in the first place was said to have been about 600 pages long—an inconceivable mental achievement. I heard a lecture about this proof, cut down to 'only' 80 pages, in Warsaw. Coryphées in functional analysis I so much admired shook their heads over the complexity of a single theorem. So I wasn't really sad that I failed to understand most of it. Six months later, a Polish mathematician told me that the proof had been cut down to less than five pages and had become readable.

Such stories seem to repeat themselves more often than not in mathematics. The so-called Hilbert problems were very popular at the end of the 19th century. I remember that at least one of them had been solved by an 'outsider', a student from former Leningrad.

So let's summarize:

- Even if great minds cannot solve a problem, an unknown person with unconventional ideas may sometimes be successful.

- Even if a solution initially appears outrageously complicated, it can sometimes be drastically simplified.

Chess programs appear to be subject to such changes, too. The playing strength of current computers is certainly due not only to their computation power, but also to chess theory. These programs have become so efficient because their development is rewarding: they sell well. Conversely, the only vendor of crypt-analytic software I know of is AccessData.[1] Their software makes encrypted files from numerous programs readable again (older versions handled Word-Perfect, Lotus 1-2-3, Excel, Symphony, Quattro Pro, Paradox, and Word; their Web site also mentions Microsoft's encrypted EFSD file system). Confirming what I said above, one of the software's designers said they built wait loops into the software to make sure people wouldn't be shocked by its real speed [Hoff]. You will see for yourself in this book how much the encoding algorithm of WordPerfect is worth.

Normally, cryptanalysts are satisfied with showing the principle and occasionally demonstrating a program. Easily usable and efficient cryptanalytic software for more sophisticated algorithms is developed by somebody who deems it worthwhile—and then the average punter won't get the product. Large corporations and national intelligence organizations pay more and want to keep the goodies for themselves.

However, there is at least one sensational exception: [Hoff] mentions that governmental agencies in the USA use a program to crack the cipher contained in *pkzip*; more details in Section 5.7.1. You can find such a program on the Web site at `www.wileyeurope.com/go/cryptology`.

Don't get me wrong: value addition can be achieved when information is exchanged, and not when it is held back. But carelessly handling the protection of information can destroy these values—faster today than in the near future. On the other hand, thanks to cryptology, not only will our world become more secure, our lives will become more comfortable. Think of electronic payment systems, electronic elections, or digital signatures. Cryptology will perhaps also finally help us to download a brief chapter from a textbook (or a soundtrack) for a few bucks over a computer network rather than having to buy the entire book (or CD).

1.3 What This Book Doesn't Cover—Another Story

Security is an endless topic, and the existing literature is accordingly large: How do I protect my computer/the local area network against unauthorized

---

[1] http://www.accessdata.com. The software is not cheap.

access? What do I have to be particularly careful about when backing up data? What risks can arise from third-party software (particularly operating systems)?

This book doesn't deal with these topics. Readers interested in the security landscape can find plenty of material on the Internet, for example by visiting the DFN-CERT servers, because the information offered there is current.[2] This book deals mainly with encryption algorithms and their analysis in view of the previously explained special role cryptology plays.

Steganography

There is another method for protecting information against unauthorized tapping, in addition to 'open' encryption. This method is called **steganography**, and it hides messages in messages. Its purpose is to hide the existence of information rather than making it unreadable. There is no limit to the wealth of ideas. One example: my father was never allowed to tell anybody of his whereabouts during World War II. So in his army mail, he sort of accidentally underlined a digit in a date, say 5. All my mother needed to do was find the first letter of every fifth word in the message to recover his location. When I heard this as a child, I was sure nobody would ever be able to see through such a smart trick. How wrong I was! Steganography is an art that is thousands of years old, and it had reached totally different heights, as well as the routine of its recovery. Minimal changes to some letters, slightly varying spaces between words, previously agreed templates—everything conceivable had certainly been exploited. You can admire a so-called *semagram* in the seminal book by Kahn [KahnCode, p.523]: the naive pen-and-ink drawing of a brook with bridge, flowers, and houses. The receiver knew that she had to look at the blades of grass along the river bank: a Morse code had been hidden in their different lengths. Invisible ink is also something that belongs here, and microdots—entire A4 pages are accommodated in a single typewriter dot using microphotographic methods. (Kahn explains in detail how to produce microdots. Just this much here: they won't help you against surveillance anymore!) Other methods are discussed in [BauerDS] and [BauerMM].

The usual steganography has a serious drawback: the message is not protected by a secret and changeable key, but by a fixed method. Once the method is

---

[2]http://www.cert.dfn.de, ftp.cert.dfn.de

revealed, all messages are compromised. This is the reason why a message is normally encrypted before you hide it steganographically.

Steganography is still popular today. Encrypted emails must not be sent to some countries (including Russia and Saudi Arabia), which means that one is enormously tempted to hide the very existence of secret messages.

There are free software products for at least two methods intended to help keep emails secret:

The *first method* creates 'artificial words', which behave statistically similar to readable text. The message is hidden in the sequence of these artificial words. Of course, everybody who looks inside the mail itself will see that it doesn't contain normal text (see Figure 1.2). But it helps fool a listening computer.

Nevertheless, I have my doubts. Analyzing written language is by far easier than analyzing the spoken word, and even for the latter research has come a long way. The statistical study alone gives many clues. Surely every software designer will think of letter frequencies (and perhaps frequencies of pairs). As an adversary interested in picking encrypted texts from a data stream, I would definitely select more intelligent functions, at least ones that the popular free programs don't consider.

Only an UFO buff like you would want to have fun with Buster Keaton. You know that Sigmund Freud was Eva Peron's granola supplier in a previous life. Glucose Chips! So ripe that it's the eighth wonder of the world! Gonzo Q! So expensive that it's the eighth wonder of the world! Yo! Burt Reynolds would be Best Actor of the Year if he hadn't evenly got hair all over Dwight Eisenhower. How can you rob Cortez so disappointedly? Having a part-time lover makes you more cannibal prosimian. Wheaty! So nasty that it's the eighth wonder of the world! Have a Lipash-brand hat for your pteranodon! Bless my virtue! Eat tripe—the moth intestines of the earth! Bless my stomach! You're Scotch, my little father. Bozhe moi, your power ties are really amusingly freaky. Frobo brand grape soda is flamboyant and crisp! Roger Bacon is into Scientology. Sugar Pimples, for the people who can't get enough sugar! Possibly L Ron Hubbard and Paul Cezanne get paid a whole lot, but all they ever do is artfully write protest letters to Congress. C'mon, gimme the spiritual renewal.

Figure 1.2: This 'artificial' text hides encrypted information—it is a so-called mimic function by Wayner (more details in the mimic.txt file on our Web site, see A.1).

Compression won't do the trick either, by the way. Compressed text can be decompressed, and those who try to be particularly clever by making encrypted text pass for compressed text forget that compressed data obey certain rules, too. More about this topic in Chapters 2 and 3.

I'm convinced that sufficient testing options can be found, except they aren't generally known.

The *second method* hides information in digitized images. Nope, this time not in the length of a blade of grass: the color of each image dot (pixel) is described by several bits, e.g., 4, 8, or even 24 (accordingly 16 million possible colors). In this method, the first few bits determine the pixel color, while the last few bits serve merely for 'fine tuning'. Changes in these last bits are hardly visible in the presentation; they are often even truncated when output on a screen. These bits are used to hide secret information. Here too, I have my doubts about the method's security. Images are subject to certain well-known rules—otherwise, there wouldn't be effective image compression methods. These rules also apply to the least significant bits. Now, if these bits contain an encrypted message, they are purely random, leaping to the eye exactly because of this, though our naked eye can't recognize anything. Adapting to the statistics of the image would certainly be possible, but costly and never perfect. Rumors have it that every photo (at least the digitized ones) that leaves NASA is previously checked for hidden information. Why shouldn't such programs work in large mail nodes? Basically, all objections made against the first methods apply to this method, too.

'Real' steganography hides information such that its existence cannot be proved lest you know the secret key. This is extremely difficult. You would have to

- filter out 'noise' independent of the actual information from a data stream;
- replace this noise by a secret text with equal statistical properties (not hard with so-called 'white noise', because secret texts created by good methods are equally distributed statistically);
- and finally mix this noise back into the reduced signal.

However, I have to warn you that statistical independence doesn't mean deterministic independence! It means that there might be a very simple test that shows whether or not encrypted messages had been hidden. This is the critical point when using steganography.

Approaches that hide information in *video conferences* or *digitized speech* (audio files) are of particular interest (see [Westf], [Pfitzstego]). Such data are physically created and superimposed by an independent semi-conductor noise. This nourishes hopes for secure steganography, in contrast to cryptography, where we are still searching for a practically *and* provably secure algorithm. Studies conducted by Westfeld [Westf] look promising and show that a GSM phone call can be transmitted behind an ISDN video conference.

I should mention a (former) product of Steganos (*www.steganos.com*), a company based in Frankfurt, Germany, at this point: the product was used to camouflage information about the choice of synonymous formulations. As a side effect, the software was able to improve the style (e.g., avoiding repeated words). This provided an excellent pretense for using the program, and proving that steganography was involved became really difficult. Currently, the company offers only a program for embedding messages in images.

We will discuss another approach that's also secure, but not universally usable, in connection with subliminal channels in digital signatures in Section 6.3.3. This topic will also turn up again in Section 6.7.

Cryptanalyzing steganographic methods doesn't appear to be in advanced development stages in public research (see the next section about digital watermarks). The two methods mentioned above are uncritically praised over and again as a panacea. Prohibiting the free use of cryptography would encourage research and perhaps encourage the discovery of practically usable subliminal channels in methods other than digital signatures.

Steganography has *one* function in any event: It makes surveillance of data communications harder. Though thorough statistical studies are possible, they require sufficient material and considerable computation power. Together with the innumerable data formats commonly used, this can be a problem for eavesdroppers, though we should by no means underestimate the power of current supercomputers. More about this in Section 8.2.1.

Digital Watermarks

Another very young field of research is closely related to steganography. Intellectual property is becoming increasingly available in electronic versions— think of MP3 players, CDs, and DVDs, just to name the most obvious. As the use of these formats rises, so does the amount of piracy. If illegal copying cannot be entirely stopped, then we will at least want to be able to prove fraud.

With this in mind, manufacturers try to accommodate hidden, mostly irremovable information about the author in digital documents; we also speak of **digital watermarks** (copyright marking systems). A digital signature wouldn't help since it can be easily removed. A good example is the protocol by Birgit Pfitzmann described in [Pfitzfinger], which safeguards the anonymity of the honest customer.

However, in this hide-and-seek game, too, there are ways to make hidden information unusable, if it cannot be protected. Perhaps the first attack of this type against steganographic methods is described in [PetAndMark]. The authors are convinced that this type of analysis has helped steganography in making progress just as cryptanalysis has furthered cryptography. I understood from their work that the development of automatic tests for revealing hidden information is still in its infancy—at least in the civilian sector. [Ditt] is a book that thoroughly discusses the possibilities and risks.

Chapter 2

Cryptology from the Romans to World War II

Now that we have talked about the cryptology landscape more than about cryptology itself, let's get to the point. We begin with pretty simple algorithms, which, unfortunately, still play a role. But first, let's define several terms. You will probably be familiar with some of them:

- **Plaintext:** This is the original text to be encrypted.
- **Ciphertext:** This is the encrypted text.
- **Cryptography:** This is the science of designing encryption algorithms.
- **Cryptanalysis:** This is the art of recovering an encrypted text (or at least clues about it) without knowing the key. The process is called **code breaking** or **compromising**. An algorithm that doesn't resist cryptanalysis (except perhaps for an uninteresting special case) is said to have been **broken, compromised**, or **cracked**.

A **plaintext attack** is the cryptanalysis of a ciphertext, where parts of the plaintext are known. This type of attack is generally much more effective than the pure analysis of a ciphertext. Plaintext attacks play a major role in this chapter.

Enough theory for the time being. Just check out the Glossary if you have problems with one term or another. You should find it there (and if you don't,

Cryptology Unlocked   Reinhard Wobst
© 2007 John Wiley & Sons, Ltd

I'd appreciate your letting me know). For, in contrast to the usual textbook style, we will first deal with the practice and sum up a few important things in Chapter 3. At that point, you'll have a pretty good idea what is behind all these terms.

Let me tell you at this point: everything described in this chapter is yesterday's bread. None of the algorithms presented here is secure today (with one exception). They all originate from prehistoric times when computers weren't around. Back then, people looked at plaintext as a sequence of characters (while almost always today we look at it as a sequence of bits). Nevertheless, you can learn a lot about cryptography and cryptanalysis from the methods discussed here. This knowledge will come in handy in the later chapters, because it is more or less the basis of modern cryptology. Moreover, it's simply fitting for a cryptologist to know about the Enigma. And actually it is a very thrilling matter—a pure cryptological adventure.

2.1   The Caesar Method and its Relatives

Even the old Romans wanted to send encrypted messages. Caesar used one of the simplest encryption methods, known as the **Caesar cipher** or Caesar addition. In this method, each letter is substituted by the one three places further behind in the alphabet. We think of the alphabet as if it were written on a ring so that A follows Z. The encryption rule will then look as follows:

```
A -> D
B -> E
C -> F
...
W -> Z
X -> A
Y -> B
Z -> C
```

Blanks are omitted and no difference is made between lowercase and uppercase letters. This can result in ambiguities, and the code writer must pay attention. A quick help can be the use of an agreed division sign (which will always create a vulnerability). By the way, the Romans didn't use 26 letters, but that doesn't change the method.

This method may have represented an insurmountable hurdle for the Roman army and its adversaries. Augustus, Caesar's successor, who was thought to have been less intelligent than Caesar, found the method too complicated. He simply substituted each letter by the next letter in the alphabet, i.e., A became B, B became C, and so on. Since a circularly shifted alphabet must have overstrained his abilities, he replaced the last letter of the Roman alphabet, which was 'X', by 'AA'. In view of this kind of intellectual achievement, the Greek mathematicians and philosophers must have been incredible masterminds.

Is this a cipher at all? What is the key in this cipher? Yes, it is a cipher, and it uses key '3'. Augustus used the same method with key '1'. So the key is the number of steps forward as letters in the alphabet are substituted. This means that there are 25 meaningful keys (key '0' won't change the text). Well, things can't really be simpler than that, and you will find this method at the beginning of almost every cryptology textbook.

Expressed mathematically, this encryption method corresponds to the number-theory addition of a constant in the residual class modulo 26, i.e., adding the remainders when dividing by 26. Let p be the plaintext character, c its cipher (i.e., the ciphertext character created), and s the key (constant), then

```
c = p + s mod 26.
```

We assume that the letters are numbers: 'A' corresponds to 0, 'B' to 1, 'Z' to 25. 'mod 26' means in this context that if $p + s$ becomes greater than or equal to 26, we deduct 26 from the sum. Non-mathematicians will probably think that this is theoretically playing up a simple thing, but we will get back to this later. The method's name, 'Caesar addition', comes from this approach, by the way.

Breaking the method is a kid's game; I won't bore you with a detailed explanation. But try it *without* a computer! You will see that cryptanalysis requires intuition and patience. To make sure we won't leave this statement in dead space, and to prove that cryptology for private use would only foster criminals anyway, as fearful politicians like to argue, I give you a small cryptogram. This is what riddles challenging you to find the plaintext from an encrypted text are called:

```
ZKKFFBWZMVPVRIJLEKZCKYZJSFFBWZERCCPTFLCUSVKIREJCRKVU
```

This ciphertext was created by a Caesar cipher using an unknown key. I won't resolve it for you but tell you just this much: further down in this section, there is a helpful hint for cryptanalyzing it. I encourage you to try it using pen and paper. You will get an idea as to how the cryptanalysts in World War I must have felt.

However, it is shocking to find this ancient method still around. According to [BauerMM], it was introduced to the Russian army in 1915 when it transpired that harder methods had overstrained the top echelon. One could hardly have given the cryptanalysts in Prussia and Austria a nicer present. (Meanwhile, however, Russian cryptology has long been up to date.)

Quite another matter is ROT13, a method widely used in UNIX, which represents nothing more than a Caesar cipher with key '13'. ROT13 was not designed to protect data by encrypting it; it serves to protect data against inadvertent reading—just like newspapers often print the solution to a puzzle upside down underneath the puzzle section. One simply had to think of something different for computers.

There was a simple reason why 13 was chosen of all numbers. Encrypting the ciphertext once more produces the plaintext:

```
ROT13(ROT13(Text)) = Text.
```

2.2 About Gold Bugs and Rhymes: Substitution and Transposition

2.2.1 Simple Substitution

The Caesar cipher is a special case of a much more general method: simple substitution. With this method, each letter of the alphabet is substituted by any other letter. The only side condition is that two different characters must not be substituted by the same letter (e.g., never substitute both A and X by C); otherwise, the ciphertext cannot be decrypted unambiguously. This kind of mapping the alphabet onto itself is called **permutation** (sort of rearranging the alphabet). While the Caesar method uses 25 possible keys, the number of theoretically possible substitutions is astronomically high, namely 26! or

```
403.291.461.126.605.635.584.000.000 (403 quadrillions).
```

Several possibilities can be disregarded though, because they leave excessively large parts of the plaintext unchanged. That leaves perhaps only 400 quadrillions of possibilities. I spare myself the calculation how long the fastest computers in the world would take to test all of these keys.

Nevertheless, this method isn't worth much either. It can be broken effortlessly by statistical analysis. Instructions can be found in Edgar Allan Poe's famous novel, *The Gold Bug*, perhaps the first popular work on cryptanalysis. Poe explains very vividly how cryptanalysts work: revealing information step by step as they exploit every particularity.

I don't want to repeat the passage concerned from the book here in detail. You can either read it there or in [BauerMM, 15.10]. But let's have a quick look at the keys used; it's worthwhile:

Assume we want to decode a ciphertext 203 characters long, consisting of numbers and various typographic special characters. (It doesn't actually matter whether letters are substituted by letters or other characters. The main thing is that the substitution is reversible.)

- Knowing the code writer, the cryptanalyst concludes that he has surely used just a simple substitution. Bear in mind: you *always* have to assume that your adversary knows the method you used.

- First, the analyst will search for the most frequent character—that's '8'—and assume that it corresponds to 'e', which is the most frequent letter in the English, German, and other alphabets (see Table 2.1).

Table 2.1 Frequency analysis for the first chapter of the German edition of this book

The 10 most frequent letters and characters	The 10 most frequent pairs of letters and characters
13.78 % ' '	3.11 % 'e'-'n'
13.17 % 'e'	2.65 % 'e'-'r'
8.09 % 'n'	2.57 % 'n'-' '
6.65 % 'i'	2.35 % 'c'-'h'
5.67 % 'r'	2.18 % 'e'-' '
5.17 % 't'	1.56 % 'e'-'i'
4.39 % 's'	1.54 % 'r'-' '
4.03 % 'a'	1.49 % 't'-'e'
3.77 % 'h'	1.47 % 'i'-'e'
2.99 % 'l'	1.35 % ' '-'d'
total: 66.7 %	total: 20.3 %
average frequency of a letter: 3.85 %	average frequency of a pair: 0.0015 %

- This is a hypothesis, but it is substantiated by the fact that string '88' occurs strikingly often in the text, and 'ee' is most frequent in the English language. So the attacker is already looking at digrams, i.e., two-letter pairs. That's pretty easy with the naked eye.

- If '8' corresponds to 'e', then there could be a pattern composed of three characters and one '8' in several instances at the end—namely the correspondence for the frequent word 'the'. Such a pattern occurs seven times. This means that we might already have recovered three characters. Let's continue testing the hypothesis.

- The cryptanalyst uses the characters recovered and guesses several words and, by using them, recovers more letters. Step by step, but increasingly faster, the cryptanalyst gets closer to his goal. The most important prerequisite is that he knows what that goal should be: the English language.

From Theory to Practice: Automatic Decryption

One would assume that text encoded in this way can be read 'online' thanks to modern computer technology, provided one has a suitable program. Still, you'd spend a lot of time searching the Internet for free software that breaks substitution ciphers *without* human interaction. The only explanation I have is this: the theory is clear, and a simple demonstration program for cryptanalysis can be written quickly, though some manual work will remain in the end. Obviously, no author has been interested in a *fully automatic* cryptanalysis so far. Well, there may have been such authors, but their software has allegedly been locked up. As ridiculous as this may sound, I have actually received serious hints.

I felt it was about time to do away with this deplorable state and tackled the task myself. The frequency analysis described is poorly suitable for programs, because it requires too much understanding of the context and too much text. So my idea was to test for 'forbidden' pairs rather than for particularly frequent ones (which corresponds to negative pattern search, as we will see in Section 3.4.1). The frequency of single characters should serve only to set up an initial substitution scheme. In general, several forbidden pairs will result from the decoding attempt. Optimizing things by slightly varying the substitution from one step to the next should then allow us to continually reduce the forbidden pairs.

So much about a cute theory. However, experiments resulted in catastrophic findings; my idea was simply unusable. (National intelligence agencies are likely to know more about such statistical niceties than cryptologists!)

I was more lucky with *cryptograms*. These are popular crypto-puzzles, especially in the English-speaking world, where you have to guess the plaintext from a given ciphertext. However, the word boundaries are not hidden, i.e., blanks are not removed or encrypted. So most of the solution programs are based on frequency analyses with subsequent dictionary search—useless for our task.

Only one method, the one by Edwin Olson described on the Web site at `www.gtoal.com/wordgames/cryptograms.html`, appeared to be more apt. It uses letter repeat patterns of words taken from a large dictionary. For example, 'BANANA' has the pattern 'ABCBCB', 'ENTER' and 'ESTER' the pattern 'ABCAD', and so on. A code breaker would proceed in a similar way: he would first look for striking patterns.

Olson didn't disclose the source text of his program, and he described the algorithm only roughly (by the way, he also utilized the knowledge of word boundaries). But that was sufficient for me to build on this idea and develop my own program, which you find on the Web site under *subscrack.zip*, including documentation in English and German. It was written in the Python script language, so that it is relatively independent of the operating system you use. Since it is a demonstration program, it is limited to the original task, i.e., the substitution of 26 letters without punctuation marks and blanks. My algorithm shares only the basic idea with Olson's and looks like this:

1. Build a list of letter repeat patterns from a large dictionary. Assign a list of words corresponding to this pattern to each pattern.

2. Search the ciphertext for a long word pattern using a short pertaining word list. Use the first word from the list to obtain substitutions for some letters.

3. Once the first match is found, look for the next pattern in the ciphertext. Check for each word from its list whether or not there are contradictions: identical letters always have to decipher to the same letter, different letters to different ones. Moreover, *subscrack* checks whether there are new letters. If there aren't, it tests for the next word in the list. When the list is exhausted, the program continues with the next pattern. Then a third pattern is found once an attempt was successful, and so on. Once all patterns are exhausted, the program takes the next word in its list from the last pattern but one, and so on. This is called a **tree search**.

4. Once all or almost all characters have been deciphered, the entire ciphertext is tentatively decrypted. Next, the program uses a large dictionary to

recover more words from the parts not yet decrypted. If the percentage of the ciphertext parts decrypted in this way is a given value, then the attempt is deemed to have been successful, and *subscrack* exits by outputting both the key and the plaintext.

5. Otherwise, the last word is discarded, and the search continues.

The program is astonishingly surefire and fast on 'normal' texts. The main problem of this tree search is that it sometimes tests too many possibilities. After all, it is an optimization algorithm, and as such doesn't generally work as a black box:

- A hit is probable, but not guaranteed.

- The computation time can fluctuate heavily.

- The result is not always unambiguous (there can be more than one solution), and it is not always correct (the program doesn't understand context, i.e., it can't make an intelligent choice of words).

Various parameters, such as minimum and maximum lengths of search patterns, permitted percentage of non-decipherable letters, and maximum nesting depth, decide on the success or failure and essentially on the computation time. Let's look at a practical example: we want to decrypt an aphorism by Christian Morgenstern with a length of 260 characters:

```
cmgvgpiimhdtibvgueehxmutmqjfmuzodtvmtrptcmgfqogomubedmgc
umfqogomubimxjibkdoqxbmtfpgqdecumvqtkmcueemgmtbuqxgmzotd
tvvmjqdbuibuibqdzokdvxmuzocmgvgdtcdtigmgfubkuvmtvmcqthmt
fppebcqivqtkmouteqxxmtfdmgcmfmttfugcumqjfmuzodtvmtutmutm
glouxpiplouizomtibgmtvmtmoamtfdmgcmt
```

On an Athlon 1700 PC, *subscrack* takes about four seconds to load the 'predigested' dictionary and then computes for about 1.6 seconds. The following appears to be a clear solution:

```
dergrossekunstgriffkleineabweichungenvonderwahrheitfuerd
iewahrheitselbstzuhaltenworaufdieganzedifferentialrechnu
nggebautististauchzugleichdergrundunsrerwitzigengedanken
wooftdasganzehinfallenwuerdewennwirdieabweichungeninine
rphilosophischenstrengenehmenwuerden
```

In contrast, the program cut its teeth over a short Caesar riddle similar to the one above!

Such games are helpful in learning to understand problems and possibilities of automatic cryptanalysis that have been a classic domain of national intelligence organizations. This is the learning effect. And the aspired Aha effect should have happened when the author's kids dead cert secret writings gradually revealed themselves on the screen. All right, I openly admit, that was my motivation for the entire effort in the first place. Unfortunately, the kids had long left the house before my modest program finally finished.

2.2.2 First Improvement: Homophone Substitutions

We have seen that simple substitution ciphers can be broken by frequency or pattern analysis, even when the messages are relatively short. A trick helps you make this task harder. The trick is the so-called **homophone substitution**, which let's you assign one plaintext character to several ciphertext characters. The ciphertext alphabet includes more than letters; for example, it can also include numbers and special characters. You will want to assign several symbols particularly to the most frequent characters, such as 'e', 'n', 'i', 'r', and 't'. (Blanks are always omitted in classic cryptology.) In the ideal case, all characters would occur more or less equally often in your ciphertext. The homophone substitution is better than the simple substitution, but it still has serious drawbacks:

- First, there are no defined rules for selecting one out of several possible ciphertext characters. The quality of such rules determines the quality of the algorithm. Look at this simple example:

  Assume we want to substitute the character 'e' by either 'b', '4', or '!'. A stupid or unqualified code writer would take his choices cyclically: in the first cycle, he replaces 'e' by 'b', in the next by '4', then by '!', and then by 'b' again. If the adversary is aware of this approach, which is normally the case, then he will search a lengthy text (using a computer) for groups of characters that always occur in the same cyclical arrangement. And the encryption algorithm will quickly have been identified to be simple substitution.

  A random, 'unreliable' selection by hand would definitely be more secure. This is the way the method was used in practice. Living in the computer age, we have different demands.

- Second, the algorithm is extremely vulnerable to the most important cryptanalytic approach, the plaintext attack (see above). Even if an attacker knows nothing but the original (i.e., the plaintext) of an encrypted message, he can recover at least large parts of the key—the remainder results from 'idiomatic experiment', as described above in connection with the Gold Bug example. Of course, this holds true for all substitution methods. We will see later in this chapter that a piece of plaintext is normally known in practice. A good encryption algorithm *must* resist such attacks under reasonable assumptions.

Homophone substitution makes poor use of a language's inner rules. With today's computer technologies, it would surely allow an adversary to mount attacks even without knowing anything about the plaintext and about the key creation. But I think this kind of stuff doesn't interest anybody anymore. The weaknesses of this method are too serious, or are they...?

2.2.3   What If I First Compressed the Text?

... you might ask. Software or hardware compression is matter-of-factly in the computer age, because it cuts down file sizes considerably (e.g., by a factor of 3 or even 10) without losing any of their contents. The files can be decompressed and their contents restored at any time.

Compressed files are distributed pretty much equally, i.e., all characters are more or less equally frequent (that much for a jump into the computer age, talking of the 256 values a byte can have rather than of 26 letters). Frequency analysis doesn't do the trick any more. Does that mean more security? No, for two reasons:

- First, reconstructing the key during a plaintext attack remains as simple as if the beginning of the message were known. You just have to first compress the known beginning of the message and then compare the compressed product with the ciphertext.

- Second, though the compressed product appears to be equally distributed, it is by no means random. To exploit the careless use of combined substitution and compression, I recommend proceeding as follows:

Every compression method places special information—so-called *magic numbers*—at the beginning to identify the method. A poor method would already disclose the first elements of the key.

Naturally, a clever code writer would truncate the fixed part of this beginning, but that doesn't matter much. One of the most effective compression methods, the Ziv–Lempel–Welch compression, creates tables listing the strings in parallel to the text read. Instead of these strings, only the number of the table entry appears in the text. When building the tables, these numbers cannot be arbitrarily large at the beginning; their possible upper limit grows by 1 with each step. This means that you can't decompress any arbitrary byte sequence (in contrast to encryption methods that are supposed to always diligently 'decipher' nonsense). So we can make an assumption for the first character and, using this assumption, consider the probable substitutions for the second character. Not all of them will produce compressed text; we will discard those. Next, we look at possible remaining substitutions for the third character, and so on. We might get stuck proceeding like this, however. If we do, we must have made a mistake in one of the previous steps. We go back a step and start over again from there, using the next possibility. This is like systematically running around in a labyrinth with a very special structure, the **tree structure**.

Sloppy programming would cost us huge amounts of computing power for such a search (as we have seen in the *subscrack* example). In practice, however, we would discard more and more possibilities as we penetrate this labyrinth. At some point along the road, there will only be a few alleys left; one of them leads to the light. Now the key is known. And mind you, we didn't need one single character from the plaintext! Experience has shown that, using appropriate

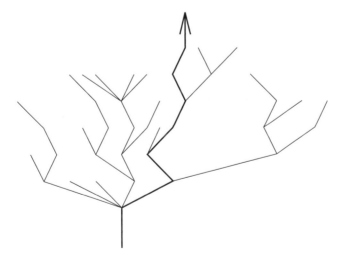

Figure 2.1: Successful search in a tree structure.

programming tricks, the computation time can be cut down dramatically. We will see in Section 3.6.4 that all of this works in the real world.

Compression combined with homophone substitution is a trifle cleverer. Creating a program that breaks this combination is certainly not easy, but it is possible. You'd have to do the work only once—then the method is for ever worthless.

2.2.4   Transposition

While substitution ciphers preserve the order of the plaintext symbols but disguise them, transposition ciphers, in contrast, reorder the letters but do not disguise them. The easiest transposition method is the 'cube'. Using it, you write the message line by line in a rectangle:

```
DELIVE
RTHERA
NSOMTO
MORROW
ASAGRE
EDJOHN
```

and read it column by column:

```
DRNMAEETSOSDLHORAJIEMRGOVRTORHEAOWEN
```

Naturally this method offers no security whatsoever—it uses only the edge length of the square to serve as key. In practice, the code writer would have to use more ingenious transpositions, which depend mainly on keys with a large number of conceivable values. It is, therefore, recommended to transpose the columns of the rectangle once the plaintext is written and only then start reading.

The method is very old. Back in the 5th century BCE, the Spartans had already created this type of transposition (without columnar transposition). They wrapped a parchment strip on which was written a message around a rod, and the receiver would then unwrap the paper. The method was called *Skytale*.

The rod, or more exactly its thickness profile, served as a key [BauerMM, 6.3].

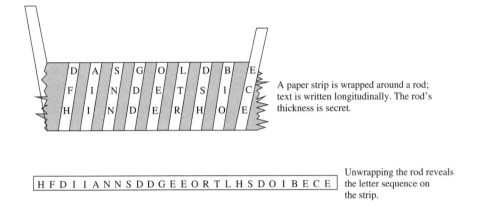

A paper strip is wrapped around a rod; text is written longitudinally. The rod's thickness is secret.

| H F D I I A N N S D D G E E O R T L H S D O I B E C E |

Unwrapping the rod reveals the letter sequence on the strip.

Figure 2.2: Ciphering by use of a rod.

The frequencies of characters don't change versus the original text, but this insight is of little use for us. Only information about the way the transpositions were made will help us further. Unfortunately, this method is also insecure:

- An initial clue to a vulnerability could be supplied by a sloppy user who pads the last line with fillers (e.g., 'X') to bring it to the required length. This reveals parts of the transposition's structure.

- Short messages could contain only a few or none of certain letters. An attacker can draw conclusions as to which messages had definitely *not* been sent. This may be sufficient to launch an attack.

- Sinkov [Sinkov] explains how an attack using a 'probable word' (more about this term in Section 3.4.1) is possible even with transpositions. The idea is very simple, but it can be used only provided the probable word is longer than the block length. In this context, 'block length' means the number of characters in the group in which a transposition occurs.

  Let's go back to the example with the rectangle above to be more specific. (In this case, the block length is 6, i.e., the number of columns in the rectangle.) Assume the word DELIVER occurs in the text, and that the algorithm used is the 'cube' with subsequent columnar transposition. With a block length of 3, there would have to be an 'I' underneath the 'D' in the rectangle, i.e., the string 'DI' would have to occur in the ciphertext. This is not the case, so assuming a block length of 3 was wrong. We will find out by trial and error that the block length has to be 6 (since 'DR' does occur in the ciphertext). We have found the position of the word and can even determine whether a columnar transposition is likely, except for the two columns in which the 'E' of the probable word occurs.

- Consecutive letters statistically depend on one another in a certain way, because language has a structure. In this way, sufficiently long ciphertexts that came into being by transposing equally long groups of characters can be statistically tested for dependent (but now torn apart) pairs. We proceed as follows:

  - To determine the length, N, of the groups, we can use character coincidence (Section 3.6.1), for example.

  - We look at all $N^*(N-1)/2$ possible pairs in positions i and j in the groups ($i, j = 1, 2, \ldots, N$). For each pair of positions, we analyze the common distribution of the pertaining characters in the ciphertext at these places.

  - If the plaintext is normal language, then pairs of successive characters have a typical distribution (see Table 2.1). Non-adjacent characters are statistically less dependent and have a different distribution.

  - We apply this to the pairs of positions mentioned in the previous point. With some pairs, but not with others, we will find the typical digram distribution of the plaintext. We will call pairs with numbers from 1 through N *distinguished pairs*.

  - Among the distinguished pairs, we try to find chains with the following form:

```
(n1,n2),  (n2,n3),  (n3,n4),  ...
```

Such a chain of length N, in which all n_i are different, could already be the permutation (i.e., transposition) we are looking for.

  - If we don't find such a chain, or if no meaningful decryption results are produced, then we try to join chain links; we will have to guess missing members. Digrams that virtually never occur could be helpful.

It is certainly an attractive task to write and expand a corresponding program (that would be an elegant practical training course for high schools).

The major drawback of this method is the large amount of plaintext it requires.

   – Notice that transpositions are very sensitive to differential cryptanalysis.
    We will discuss this topic in Section 3.7.

You can also combine transpositions with substitutions and give the code
breaker a hard time. Rest assured that all simple combinations of both methods
can be broken quickly by use of one of the existing programs, even though
you won't be able to get such a program.

2.2.5 Multiple Encryption

'Two are better than one' is a common saying, but it holds true neither for
medicine nor for cryptology in general. Executing two or more Caesar ciphers
in succession results in a Caesar cipher again: the alphabet is still shifted cyclically; the only difference is that it's shifted by another amount. We have seen
above why this method is also called 'Caesar addition'. Adding two constants,
$s1$ and $s2$, to a plaintext character, p, has the same effect as adding first the
constants and then adding them to the text:

```
(a + s1) + s2 = a + (s1 + s2) mod 26
```

(With such residual classes, you calculate as you would with common natural
numbers.)

Similarly, two or more substitutions produce another substitution. The same
applies to transpositions. Methods that have this property are said to form a
group.

In contrast, if we combine a substitution with a transposition things appear to
look better. In reality, though, we wouldn't gain much, because an attacker will
first run a frequency analysis, probably revealing some parts of the substitution.
At least knowing a little of the plaintext, the attacker can then start reconstructing the transposition. And if you give a cryptanalyst an inch he takes a mile.
(This is probably the reason why an encryption method is sometimes given up
as soon as it gives clues to only one bit of the key at a justifiable cost. This is
always the beginning of the end.)

In general, it is hard to say when double encryption, normally using two different methods, is better than a simple one. It is often hard to say that even
in a specific case. Section 5.2.1 will discuss this topic in more detail, among
other things.

2.3   Combined Substitution: Digram Substitutions

Though 'digram substitution' is a term that sounds rather scientific, it hides something very simple. In Section 2.1, we substituted *single* characters by other characters based on a fixed rule. With digrams, we substitute *character pairs* by other characters or character pairs. According to [BauerMM, 4.1.1], the oldest representation of such a method dates back to 1563, and the inventor was Giovanni Porta. He constructed 625 hieroglyphs for all possible 25*25 pairs of successive letters, where 'J' is substituted by 'I', and blanks were omitted, and lowercase letters were converted to uppercase letters.

This method can theoretically be attacked similar to simple substitution, namely using frequency analysis. However, as we have seen in Table 2.1, the frequencies of single digrams do not differ as much as the frequencies of letters. In this case, it is normally a good idea to consider the characteristic pattern of the language more intensely and, above all, exploit the fact that many digrams virtually never occur. (Even a negative statement can be extremely helpful in cryptanalysis!)

Moreover, the statistical analysis is generally more sophisticated, compared with the Gold Bug example. Since the statistical distribution of digrams is more even than it is with letters (see Table 2.1), we would arrange them by their frequencies and then try to find a match in the digram frequencies of a typical language, where deviations are legitimate to a certain extent. Moreover, we have to pay attention to side conditions, for example, that certain digrams follow one another either almost never or particularly often, and that single frequencies depend on one another. Digrams blur the structure of the language, but don't remove it. Everything together produces a huge puzzle, but it shouldn't pose an insurmountable hurdle for today's computer technology.

My dad, who was a radio operator in World War II, taught me another method, which also uses only 25 uppercase letters. The key consists of two squares arranged next to each other, 5*5. The alphabet is entered in secret sequence in each of these squares:

```
HQEFK        WHSFK
RYBOD        LPDNQ
NUGIS        EIUXY
APCMZ        VBOAM
LWJVX        RCGTZ
```

The code writer divides the text in lines of equal length (perhaps using padding characters at the end). He encrypts superimposed letter pairs as follows: He searches the left square for the upper letter, and the right square for the lower letter. Both points found form the diagonal of a rectangle. The other diagonal of this rectangle is determined by a new letter pair, which the code writer uses as his ciphertext—placing the letter from the left square in the upper line and the other letter in the lower line:

```
HEUTEKEINEBESOND   ->   HQEFK   WHSFK   -> N...
ERENVORKOMMNISSE        RYBOD   LPDNQ      W...
                        NUGIS   EIUXY
                        APCMZ   VBOAM
                        LWJVX   RCGTZ
```

If both letters are in the same line, then the two letters to the right of them form the ciphertext. So 'HS' become 'QF'. Once the last column has been reached, work is continued on the first column—i.e., 'KF' become 'HK'.

The code writer doesn't actually have to tell the line length used. The receiver writes the deciphered pairs one after the other and will notice where a line break should go as he continues reading. What's more, you can change the line length even within the same text, provided that doesn't produce ambiguities. That would make an attack much harder. However, I doubt whether this possibility was ever used in practice where things are usually sloppy. In [Hinstrip], Noel Currer-Briggs, an English cryptanalyst, suggests a fixed line length of 13 or 17 characters.

Notice that 50 letters were rather many for a key at that time. Such permutations (arrangements) of the alphabet are normally pretty easy to create; you put a keyword at the beginning and write the unused letters behind it in alphabetical order:

```
TICKNERabdfghjlmopqsuvwxyz
```

(Wheatstone wrote the permuted alphabet line by line in a box and then read it column by column. That's more secure.) But the German Wehrmacht didn't use this method; I haven't found the principle for constructing the squares.

The method has the remarkable property that the statistical relationship between successive letter pairs doesn't provide any more benefit during the analysis. (I don't think that in German, for example, the 1st, 14th, 27th, and 40th letters of a sentence will still be in a meaningful relationship to each other.) This distinguishes the method, for example, from the **playfair method** mentioned in [BauerMM, 4.2.1], which uses only one single square and looks at pairs of *successive* letters. Also, the method avoids pairs of equal letters, since they won't be converted. To this end, the code writer inserts an 'x':

```
Atxtila, Sexer.
```

Of course, that's dangerous. In our case, equal-letter pairs play no role at all since they are generally not translated into such pairs.

The method described above was broken by the British, by the way, together with the Enigma code at the famous Bletchley Park (we will get back to this in Section 2.5.2). A reader of the first German edition brought an article by Noel Currer-Briggs in [Hinstrip, Chapter 23] to my attention. This article described cryptanalysis in detail. I'd like to briefly mention a few interesting details.

Just like all methods mentioned so far, this method isn't invulnerable to plain-text attacks either. The example above ("keine besonderen Vorkommnisse" (no unusual occurrences)) is rather typical: many messages of this type were sent by the German Wehrmacht. And when a commander passed an encrypted command he wasn't likely to omit a 'HEILHITLER' closing ahead of his name. Of course, the enemy also knew the commander's name (i.e., the last word of the message). After all, numbers had been stiffly translated into words: '1324 = ONETWOTHREEFOUR'. That's what we call a **ciphering error**. More about it in Section 2.5.2.

However, the Germans made it even easier than that for the British. First, they replaced a blank by an 'X' (another ciphering error). Second, umlauts were represented as usual, namely 'AE', 'OE', and 'UE'. Since 'E' is the most frequent letter in German texts anyway, a particularly frequent occurrence of the 'XE' and 'EX' pairs had to be expected. Third, 'J' was replaced by 'II' (more about the impact of this below). And fourth, there were plenty of long words like UNTERGRUPPENFUEHRER and GEFANGENGENOMMEN (DEPUTY GROUP LEADER and CAPTURED) that didn't fit in one cipher line. All these things helped the cryptanalysts to search for specific digrams in a targeted way, such as, for example, 'UU' from the word Untergruppenführer split in a 13th line. In addition, if the 'PP' of UNTERGRUPPENFUEHRER happened to fall in the position above the 'II' of DNIIEPROPETROWSK (such names occurred frequently in radiograms on the eastern front), both 'PI' pairs ciphered into identical digrams. There weren't that many possibilities of this sort that one wouldn't have been able to try them all out—without the help of computers, of course, but lots of intuition, enormous staffing, and huge time pressure. But once the 'magic squares' were constructed, they could be used to decrypt all messages encrypted in this way on the same day at one go. If a radio operator inadvertently used the key of the previous day (which the British already knew) and sent the same, unchanged message again, encrypted with the 'new' key, the British jumped for joy.

2.4 Permanently Changing Tactics: Polyalphabetic Substitutions

A major vulnerability of simple substitutions is the fact that they are reversible: each character in the ciphertext always corresponds to the same plaintext character, no matter where exactly the ciphertext character stands within the text, which means that characteristic patterns are preserved. For example, looking at the encrypted word WLRWJXL and using an electronic dictionary, it shouldn't be too hard to find out that the plaintext probably reads SEASIDE. (We have already learned that word boundaries disappear since blanks are left out, but a computer won't have any problem searching the text for certain patterns.) This statement also holds true for digrams.

The idea behind **polyalphabetic substitution** is to make the substitution rule dependent on the position in the text. Initial thoughts in this direction had been expressed by Alberti in 1466. Some think this was the birth of modern cryptology. Though polyalphabetic methods are broken by computers nowadays, they are still much harder than simple substitution.

2.4.1 The Vigenère Cipher

It is easiest to go back to the above representation of the Caesar addition method to describe the simplest case of polyalphabetic substitution:

```
c = a + s mod 26
```

This time, however, we will not simply select a shift, s, to serve as the key. We will select a keyword, such as ABCD. We write this keyword repeatedly over the plaintext:

```
ABCDABCDABCDABCDABCDABCD...
MEETINGTODAYEVENINGATTHE...
```

Next, we add superimposed pairs:

```
A + M = M
B + E = F
C + E = G
D + T = W
A + I = I
...
```

(Like in the example above, we have to think of letters as numbers: $A = 0$, $B = 1, \ldots, Z = 25$). That's already the ciphertext. So, with this keyword of length 4, we have defined four different Caesar additions, which we will use cyclically. We can already see from the first few characters that the 'EE' in 'MEETING' become 'FG': patterns are generally destroyed. And unless you know the length of the keyword, you can't tell which same plaintext characters correspond to which same ciphertext characters.

This encryption method is called the **Vigenère cipher**, which is not entirely correct, because Vigenère described a more general method in 1585: he took an arbitrary substitution of the alphabet and shifted it cyclically. This, too, is merely a special case of the general polyalphabetic encryption. But let's go back to our example.

How do you break this Vigenère cipher? It is basically simple. Assume we know the key length, which is 4 in the above example. We pick out the ciphertext characters at positions 1, 5, 9, 13, . . . , i.e., each 4 characters apart. This subset of the ciphertext is Caesar-encrypted since, at these positions, there is always the same character above the plaintext line. We determine the frequencies of all characters in this subset and assume that the most frequent character is 'e'. That produces a shift. Similarly, we proceed with the subset formed from the ciphertext characters at positions 2, 6, 10, 14, . . . We may be able to retrieve the plaintext. If we don't, we have to play a little—we might want to guess another frequent character instead of 'e'. In practice, it is better to compare the distribution of all characters in the ciphertext with the distribution in the language; that almost certainly produces the shift.

And how do we determine the key length? By experimenting with different lengths and analyzing the frequency distributions in the subsets mentioned! We will see in Chapter 3 that there are much more reliable methods.

You can see that this approach is easy to program. I actually thought I'd found such a program on the Internet: *solvevig.c* by Mark Riordan, written in 1991. Unfortunately, when I had a closer look I found that the program merely tries a given list of keys and that the cipher tests the character frequency to check whether or not it might be English text. I find this incomprehensible. Apart from the fact that there are other tests for revealing text (including digrams or words, and many more), we know how it's done. Trying many keys is really the very last resort in cryptanalysis. You are likely to experience a similar disappointment with some cryptanalytic programs available for free. Chapter 3 will discuss various possibilities of how to break Vigenère ciphers in detail. Chapter 3 will also introduce a program you can find on our Web site.

The cryptanalyst has to proceed more elaborately even with the general polyalphabetic substitution. Rather than doing Caesar ciphers, he does general substitutions. The method's principle remains unchanged: the substitutions are applied one after the other to the single characters of the plaintext, and once you have used up the last one, you start over again with the first. The number of substitutions used is referred to as the **period** of the method.

We can think of a large variety of rules to be used to form each of the substitutions—they won't change the cryptanalysis much. In principle, it is not much different from that of the Vigenère method, except that we have to find the substitution for each subset. Knowing the rules by which the substitutions are formed from one single keyword can strongly reduce the number of mistrials. We will come back to the cryptanalysis of polyalphabetic substitutions in Chapter 3.

The designer of the algorithm defends himself against this attack by making a huge number of possible substitutions available, i.e., enabling as long a period as possible. The set of the ciphertext to be tested will (hopefully) not be enough for a static analysis. Out of these considerations emerged the rotor machines and particularly the Enigma. We will see this in a moment. First, let's summarize the most important things:

Polyalphabetic methods are simple substitutions dependent on positions. These substitutions really depend only on the position in the text, while their inter-relationships are determined *only* by the key and the method itself. Such a method would be much harder to break if the substitution also depended on the plaintext (naturally such that it could still be decrypted!) but that's not the case here.

The advantage of this property is that methods can be easily synchronized, which means that if some characters are garbled during a transmission then only those few cannot be decrypted. Even if the length of the unclear part is unknown, it is relatively easy to find the connection. We will see in Section 4.5 that there are methods allowing us to encrypt dependent on the plaintext and synchronize at the same time.

2.4.2 Bitwise Vigenère Method: Vernam Cipher

A particularly simple variant of polyalphabetic ciphers is the bitwise Vigenère method, representing the computer-friendly conversion of the characterwise method. So far, we have looked at 26 letters and added modulo 26 (i.e., we looked only at the remainders when dividing by 26). Nowadays we work with bits and bytes. A bit is just a letter in a two-element alphabet (consisting of '0s' and '1s', where '1' is written as 'L'). Adding modulo 2 in this alphabet corresponds to the bitwise XOR (exclusive 'or', often written as $\oplus$):

```
0 + 0 = 0
0 + L = L + 0 = L
L + L = 0
```

The Vigenère key can continue to remain a finite string, but instead of adding characterwise, we now add bitwise (a string can actually be thought of as a bit sequence). The decryption happens simply by re-encryption, since the XOR operation is involutory (doing the XOR transformation twice generates the output data again):

```
(a ⊕ b) ⊕ b = a
```

This different approach doesn't change anything in either the method or its cryptanalysis. Schneier [SchnCr] calls this modified method the *simple XOR method*, while Bauer [BauerMM] calls it the *Vernam cipher*. The latter name, however, often refers to the bitwise one-time pad (see below).

By the way, this section also ends with the sad comment that even the simple bitwise Vigenère method is still in use: up to Version 5, the popular text processor WordPerfect used a slight modification of it (more about this in Chapter 3). And WINCRYPT joined the list of highly insecure methods: it used a 512-byte Vigenère key. According to [SchnCr, 1.3], the Vigenère method is still thought to be heavily used in commercial software.

2.5 Domain of the Militaries: Ciphering Cylinders, Rotor Machines, and the Enigma

Rotor machines have played an important role in the last century, both for militaries and in cryptanalysis. We will first have a brief look at their precursors—ciphering cylinders—and then have a closer look at the Enigma, the most famous rotor machine.

Ciphering Cylinders

Computers have become so matter-of-fact for all of us that we consider some things to be simple while they actually became simple only with the help of computers. One of these things is polyalphabetic substitution. Back when everything was done by hand it was deemed too difficult and error-prone. The first mechanization came in the form of ciphering cylinders. A **ciphering cylinder** is an apparatus consisting of a set of disks with a different alphabet on the edge of each disk, i.e., permuted alphabets in arbitrary sequence. Each disk is responsible for a different permutation. For example, if you have 30 such disks at your disposal, you turn them against each other such that 30 characters of the plaintext appear in one line. The ciphertext is read from the line above or below it, or from an arbitrary line. The code breaker sets 30 ciphertext characters on the cylinder and finds the plaintext in another line. The order of the disks is the key (with 30 disks, that results in 30! or approximately $2.6*10^{32}$ possibilities).

Of course, the method is not secure by current standards, particularly if an attacker has somehow come into possession of such a device, which always happens sooner or later. Frequency considerations (and using other methods; see Chapter 3) would then allow him to easily determine what disk is in which place.

As always, such devices were used for longer than the level of cryptanalysis would suggest. A well-known ciphering machine was the M-94 of the US Army, which was in use at least from 1922 to 1943. It consisted of 25 aluminum

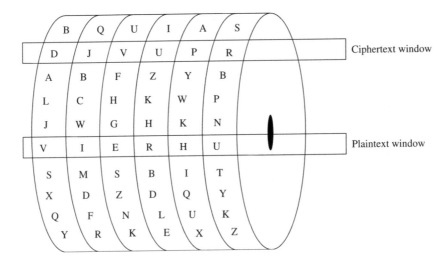

Figure 2.3: Ciphering cylinders.

cylinders. In general, however, both the order of the disks in ciphering cylinders and their selection from a larger set (e.g., 30 out of 100, corresponding to approximately $3*10^{25}$ possibilities) were secret. In World War II, the Japanese failed to break a device known as CSP-642 with 30 sliders (algorithmically equivalent to a ciphering drum), although they were in possession of several sliders. In contrast, the US 30-stick device O-2 was broken by the German Rohrbach [BauerMM, 7.4.3]. On the other hand, the Germans thought their Enigma to be absolutely secure, an opinion the Poles and British didn't share at all—see below! The level of cryptanalysis differed very much from one country to another, and that's still the case today.

Rotor Machines

Rotor machines are based on a much cleverer idea than ciphering drums. With rotor machines, electric power came into play for the first time; they are electro-mechanic encryption devices. Some descriptions of rotor machines are hard to understand, while their principle is very simple. Let's look at it in steps:

- Imagine a thick, electrically insulating disk. Twenty-six contacts are arranged in a circle on its opposite faces. Every contact on the left side is connected to exactly one on the right side, and vice versa, in some secret way. This corresponds to a substitution.

- The left contact surfaces are scanned by 26 sliding contacts, similarly the right ones. The sliding contacts correspond to the letters of the alphabet. Applying voltage to one of the left sliding contacts by the push of a button, this voltage arrives at another right sliding contact and can cause one of 26 small lamps to light up. This approach is nothing but a simple substitution. It offers two minor benefits, compared with rigid schemes: we can replace the disk by another one, and we can specify an arbitrary start position. We already know that the method is one of the most insecure despite this.

- Next, we turn the disk forward by one step after each character. This produces a polyalphabetic substitution with period 26 (the 27th character in the plaintext is then encrypted like the first one). This corresponds to the Vigenère cipher in the historical sense.

- Another idea uses several such disks arranged adjacently, each one with a different inner wiring (i.e., substitution). Between each pair of two disks we attach sliding contacts that connect the right contact surface of the left disk with the opposite, left contact surface of the right disk.

As we know from the section on 'multiple encryption', this won't initially give us anything new: again, only a simple substitution will be produced at the far right.

- Let's combine the last two ideas: after each encrypted character, we turn each disk a little further, but each by a different amount. The substitutions that are permanently wired in the disks will now produce a totally different substitution at the right-hand end each time. This arrangement serves the purpose of keeping the period very large with minimum effort (which makes cryptanalysis much harder).

- For example, we can move three disks like in a counter. After each character, the right disk turns forward by one step; after each 26th character, the middle disk will also turn one step forward, and once the latter has completed one full rotation, the left disk will also turn. In a general case, this results in a period of $26^3 = 17\,576$. Arbitrarily complicated approaches are conceivable to make cryptanalysis as hard as possible.

Whatever the case, the algorithm of the disk movement is fixed, and only the ground settings and the disk arrangement are variable.

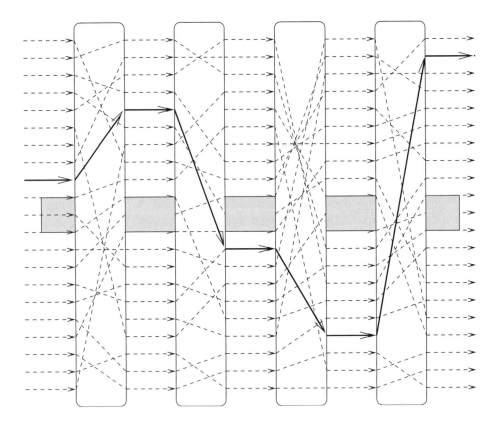

Figure 2.4: Wiring diagram of a rotor machine.

Rotor machines were registered for patent by several inventors around 1920; every country first lists the most patriotic inventor (Arthur Scherbius, 1918, is most frequently quoted in connection with the Enigma). The disks used in these machines are referred to as **drums** or **rotors**.

2.5.1 Structure and Significance of the Enigma

The most famous representative of rotor machines is the **Enigma** machine that was later used in the German Wehrmacht. Some details (such as how the mechanics worked, how the plugboard was built, etc.) are not important for our purposes. We just want to understand its principle, and we mainly want to see how it was cracked.

Incorrect Correction of a Rotor Machine: The Enigma

The first Enigma models were regular rotor machines with four rotors, as described above.

But 'good is not good enough for us', said Willi Korn in 1926 and he went about improving the rotor machine—at least so he thought. His fateful idea was the so-called **reversing drum**, also called a **reflector**: in place of the sliding contacts on the far right, his version featured an additional disk, with contact surfaces on one side only. These contact surfaces were interconnected such that each surface was connected to exactly one other surface. This corresponds to a special substitution, namely one where no letter transforms onto itself.

Voltage is applied to a 'letter' on the far left, and propagates through the rotors toward the right, 'turns around' in the reversing drum, and then traverses the rotors again from right to left over a totally different path (which explains why the reversing drum is also called a *reflector*). 'Two are better than one', cryptologist Korn must have thought. As we will see further below, this was a fateful mistake. This arrangement guaranteed that, during the ciphering process, a letter can never transform onto itself, or there would be a short circuit. I have already mentioned that, in cryptanalysis, even negative statements can sometimes be very helpful, as we will see in Section 2.5.2.

Since the reversing drum made the Enigma 'more secure', Korn must have believed that three rotors and the reversing drum would be sufficient. An additional plugboard was used to swap letter pairs before and after encryption.

The rotors moved roughly like a counter: once a rotor had reached a specific position, the next rotor was turned forward by one step through a catch. This specific position was different for each rotor. They probably believed that this would confuse the adversary. However, it led to the exact opposite: exactly this difference of all things would later allow the British to find out how the rotors were arranged. The Germans detected their error only with rotors VI through VIII and always placed the catches at the same position. (You will find a more detailed description in the file *enigma-wiring.txt* on our Web site).

Rings with consecutive alphabet sets or numbers were fastened to the rotors (the photos show both labeling types). These rings were plugged on only when the rotors were used. Their positions relative to the rotor itself were part of the so-called *basic key*, which will be discussed further below.

The German army used this machine, called Enigma I, in the described configuration. From 1942 onwards, the German navy possessed an Enigma with

Figure 2.5: The Enigma ciphering machine (courtesy of M. Swimmer, IBM).

four rotors, since the positions of submarines had to be kept particularly secret. The first three rotors could be selected from a total of five (changing rotors, however, is said not to have been easy). From 1943 onwards, a sixth rotor was available to the navy, which could take the fourth position. Finally, there was a total of eight rotors, partly with deviating movement properties.

Enigma's key consisted of the selection and arrangement of three or four rotors, their ground positions, and the description of the plugboard.

The army Enigma had 26^3 possibilities for the three rotor positions, multiplied by 10 possibilities to select three rotors out of five, each multiplied by $3! = 6$ possible rotor sequences. This resulted in a total of 1 054 560 possible keys. And we haven't considered the permutations on the plugboard yet. Twenty-six letters could be grouped in pairs in $26!/(13!*2^{13})$ ways, i.e., in roughly eight billion ways. This resulted in a total of about eight trillion ($8*10^{18}$) possible keys for the Enigma (and not 265 749 120 as stated in the file *enigma-wiring.txt*; the author forgot a few multiplications). That's an extremely large number of possibilities, even for current computer technology. By the way, though several reversing drums existed, they were never changed in a permanent machine.

This sort of number-crunching game had impressed the cryptologists and certainly the top Nazi echelon. Anyhow, the German Wehrmacht thought the Enigma was perfectly secure. The Enigma almost gained a monopoly; estimates state that between 40 000 and 200 000 machines were built. It was perhaps the first time that so much depended on one single algorithm. The Enigma was the basis for secure radio communications in the entire Wehrmacht.

And for decades, we've entrusted our 'really important things' (such as banking) again to one single algorithm: DES . . . But more about that in Chapters 4 and 6.

2.5.2 The Cryptanalysis of Enigma

How the Enigma was broken is an unusual story like no other (at least among the cryptanalytic stories that have become known to date). In view of the units produced and the significance of these machines, every effort put into cryptanalyzing them was justified. So, in the Enigma story, we find everything that makes a good spy thriller: spying, most intensive research, ciphering errors, mass deployment of men and material, celebrated successes, utmost secrecy, dramatic backgrounds, and enormous pressure. To get an idea of the human side of it all, I recommend the suspense book by Harris [Harris]. The following presentation is based mainly on [BauerMM]. More details can be found in Kahn [KahnEnig], who documented both the military and political events and backgrounds exactly, and in the Enigma texts on the Web site to this book (including further references).

- It all began with the Poles in about 1927 when their customs authority intercepted an Enigma, which had inadvertently been dispatched to a German company in Poland (incomprehensible mistakes had been made already back then!). Poland even bought an Enigma officially from a German manufacturer later on. Of course, those were 'civilian' machines, but their basic functionality had become known. What does theorem number One in cryptography read again? *The adversary always knows the algorithm.* In this case, it specifically meant that the Poles found a particularity of the Enigma: never ever is a letter transformed onto itself during the encryption. Why is that so important? Because it enables the so-called **negative pattern search**. That's easily explained: imagine we know that the plaintext contains the word

```
oberkommandowehrmacht
```

but we don't know in what position. All we know is that no plaintext character can coincide with a ciphertext character. The word is composed of 21 letters. We write it underneath the ciphertext. Following the known theory, there is a probability of

```
1 - (1 - 1/26)²¹ = 0.5611...    (i.e., 56%)
```

that the ciphertext and the plaintext coincide in some position. If we move along underneath the ciphertext, coincidences will occur in about half of all cases, i.e., we don't have to consider these cases. This is merely statistics; in practice, there may be far fewer possible cases left. Things look even better with longer words. For example, plaintext parts 100 characters long supply forbidden places with a 98 % probability. We will come back to this in Section 3.4.1.

- The Wehrmacht had plenty of training and radioing opportunities with the Enigma in East Prussia before the war. Of course, the Poles listened in on them, and so there was *plenty of material* to study. In addition, a spy delivered instructions and the keys for September and October 1932 to the French, for whom (just as well as for the British) the stuff didn't mean anything at that time, so they passed the material on to Poland.

- So much for the 'material' prerequisites; without them, cryptanalysis is usually impossible (things are totally different with software!). As it happened, there was another logistic difficulty inherent in all symmetric methods (see Glossary): how do you distribute the secret key?

To this end, there was something called 'ground setting' for each day. It was published in a *code book* every month, and specified both the selection and arrangement of the rotors as well as the position of the rings relative to the rotors. Based on this ground setting, the radio operator defined a 'message key' composed of three letters for each radiogram. This key was encrypted with the ground setting, and everything that followed was encrypted with the self-selected message key. This was basically a good idea. Current practice still selects a new key for every secret information exchange for each computer. This approach ensures that the adversary won't be able to collect a sufficiently large number of messages encrypted with the same key which, in turn, prevents statistical analyses. Moreover, the method allowed the knowledge about the key to be split between two persons: a commander switched the machine to ground setting, an operator defined the message key. Neither of the two knew the other's key (to know the commander's key, the operator would have had to disassemble the machine, since changing the rotors was not easy). That was surely very foresighted thinking in the midst of a war.

But when humans define message keys they make mistakes. They often select keystrokes like 'aaa', 'bbb', etc. Though this was forbidden later on, the Poles had already initiated their first cryptanalytic attack. Meanwhile, the operators' reaction to the new rule was that they often selected keys adjacent in one row on the keyboard and similar things. Also, the rotors' positions after the last ciphering session often served as key. Since the Poles had constantly listened in on them, they knew these positions. Bauer [BauerMM] provides a table with 40 message keys used; only three of them were not stereotypical.

As we know, the purpose of the message key was to prevent too much material encrypted with the same key from falling into the adversary's hands, and to increase the security. The outcome was the exact opposite. They hadn't thought of the human insecurity factor.

Which takes us to the next vulnerability: the best method is worth nothing when the keys are drawn from a small value space. We are talking of a **reduced key space**. Prehistoric stuff? Nope. That was an illness that transpired when transmitting credit card numbers via Netscape—a highly topical issue. Once upon a time, people died because codes were broken. Today, you might find your accounts cleared out, though people still die.

- Next ciphering error: the message key was an extremely important piece of information. As mentioned earlier, polyalphabetic methods (and the Enigma implemented one) have the benefit that brief transmission interferences cause little damage. Except for the message key, because if this key is lost the entire message is indecipherable. The receiver's request, 'again please', would naturally also be encrypted—and here you had a neat vulnerability for a plaintext attack. Such a request would often have been out of the question for military reasons: for example, radio silence was ordered for submarines to prevent others from direction-finding their positions. A command sent from the headquarters simply *had* to be decipherable!

Such mishaps caused by transmission interferences were prevented by typing the *message key twice in a row* at the beginning. This became apparent statistically, and the Polish genius Marian Rejewski seemed to have guessed quickly that a string occurred twice at the beginning, and that it was probably a key. Since this concerned only six encrypted characters, it moved only the first rotor in 20 out of 26 cases. So they found the inner wiring of the first rotor. By 1936, the drum position was changed every three months so that each rotor enjoyed once the honor of working at the very front—and the Poles enjoyed analyzing it. Poland built a copy of the Enigma with five possible drums and passed it on to both France and Great Britain.

Exploiting the circumstance that the Enigma doesn't transform any character onto itself, and considering the poorly selected keys, and knowing the rotor wiring, they were able to recover the message key.

The Warsaw-based factory AVA began building a device that tabulated conformities of the Enigma. Again, Rejewski was one of the major players. Using the tables, they were able to find the day keys within 10 to 20 minutes. That was back in 1937.

Putting the same string twice at the beginning was the ciphering error.

- The ring setting, i.e., the positions of the rings on the rotors, could be revealed by mounting a plaintext attack. That was the point where another ciphering error by the radio operators materialized: most of the texts began with ANX, where 'X' stood for a blank (and 'AN' means 'TO').

- In 1938, the Wehrmacht changed the message-key method. The former methods became ineffective, but the leading double message key remained in effect. The Polish cryptanalysts used self-developed machines as their only means to search for plaintext patterns in the form 123123. These machines looked somewhat like iced cakes, called 'bomba' in Polish. This was the reason why their expanded successors carried the misleading name 'bomb' in Great Britain later on. Such a 'bomba' found the key within two hours.

- A little later, still in 1938, the Wehrmacht approved two additional rotors to be used in the Enigma. At this point, the reconnaissance planes owed something important to chance: the military intelligence encrypted each radiogram initially by means of a digram method before they passed it on to the operators for encoding on the Enigma. In Poland, they first thought it to be a method different from the Enigma. Inadvertently, however, the number '1' sneaked into a digram ciphertext. The operator diligently typed it into the machine as a ONE. Poland noticed and understood that this had to be a multiple encryption. It took little effort to break the digram method.

When they introduced the two new drums, the military intelligence didn't change their digram method, which meant that the drums could be analyzed as before. Their structure quickly became known. Again, the attackers knew the adversary's full algorithm.

- In 1939, just before the war broke out, the findings won in Poland traveled to Great Britain. There, the famous mathematician Turing busied himself with the Polish 'bombas' and improved them. (Turing is famous

in information technology, for example, for the Turing machine, a basic
model for a computer.)

- In 1940, the Germans corrected their ciphering error, i.e., the leading double message key. By then it was too late. The British knew many details of
the machine. And they could mount plaintext attacks often enough—recall
the HEILHITLER at the end of a command, or ANX at the beginning of a
text, or the popular KEINEBESONDERENVOKOMMNISSE.

- Another opportunity for recovering plaintext was supplied by floating
mines. The ship that discovered the mines had to issue an encrypted warning to the other ships and submarines very quickly. While the Enigma-
encrypted messages to the submarines flowed over the air, they used simpler methods that had already been broken to warn the other units. Usually
there was no time to rewrite the messages using a different encryption
method and so the adversary also learned the plaintext of the messages
to the submarines. Bauer [BauerMM] refers to this as a **compromised-
ciphertext-ciphertext attack**. The British called it '**kiss**'—they could
have kissed the operators for their ciphering errors.

When the Germans did not make errors, the British were very
inventive. For example, they bombed a light buoy with the
sole purpose of making a German observer send the encrypted
radiogram 'ERLOSCHENISTLEUCHTTONNE' (FLAREWENTOUT),
which he promptly did [BauerMM]. '**Gartenpflege**' (gardening) was the
watchword for mining port entries or previously cleared areas, which
triggered similar stereotype messages, or supplied a kiss. This is how
things can look in practice when one foists plaintext on an adversary
(which is a 'chosen-plaintext attack'; see Chapter 3).

- In 1941, the poorly armed trawler *Krebs* (cancer) fell into the hands of
the British when they attacked an industrial site on the Lofoten Islands
off the western coast of Norway, and the trawler's crew didn't have
time to destroy all secret documents before the British came aboard.
The British found two rotors they knew about already. Most importantly,
however, they found the basic key for February. They could use it to
finally decipher many unknown messages in arrears for the first time.
Among other things, they learned that the German weather ships also used
Enigmas to encrypt their information, and that they had used special code
books that contained what they called a *weather key* for their weather
reports since October 1940. Such weather messages represented strategic
data, so their encryption was justified.

- That gave the British an idea: weather ships often remain at sea for months, so they have to carry code books with ground settings for the entire period afloat. From the military viewpoint, they were weak adversaries. The only problem with their seizure could emerge if the Germans became suspicious. But the Germans had other things to worry about at the time, namely in the east. The coup was successful. The first victim was the *München* northeast of Iceland in May 1941. The British warships fired intentionally past the ship. The crew panicked and abandoned the ship, were taken prisoners by the British and taken below deck immediately for them to see that their ship wasn't sinking (yet). A later British radio broadcast confirmed what the Germans thought, namely that all secret papers sank together with the *München*. And the British held the basic keys for June 1941 in their hands.

- Shortly after that event, the German submarine *U*-110, together with extensive material, fell into the hands of British warships by chance. Again, the Germans didn't become suspicious. The material was so extensive that it had to be documented in photographs and shipped to Great Britain in special containers. It included not only the basic keys for a lengthy period, but also a large number of other code tables and the 'Kleine Signalbuch' (signal reference book) for submarines, which was of particular interest for plaintext attacks.

- When the weather ship *Lauenburg* was fired at north of the Arctic Circle, the British used time-fuse missiles with black-powder charges, among other things, which exploded above the ship without destroying it. The system had an immediate effect; the conquerors again found highly interesting documents on the ship abandoned in panic.

- Those were true successes. Of course, all German crews were strictly instructed to destroy secret documents before they could be captured by the enemy. Code books were printed on absorbent paper with water-soluble ink. Particularly with U-110 submarines, it was difficult to take the material safely to a British warship.

- We already know that the Germans sent encrypted weather reports from submarines. It also transpired that they first compressed the meteorological information using a secret dictionary. The British had such dictionaries. But only the submarines and one single land station possessed an Enigma with four rotors. So when sending a weather report they held the fourth rotor in place. That was a vulnerability for a plaintext attack against the 3-rotor machine and eventually led to the breaking of the

4-rotor Enigma. If the story told in [Harris] is authentic, then thousands paid with their lives for changing the weather report dictionary.

Meanwhile, decryption was practiced with massive input. Roughly 7000 people (other sources, including [KahnCode], mention 30 000) worked against time at the famous Bletchley Park in Great Britain. The book by Harris [Harris] is thought to give an authentic narration of this story.

It hadn't always been like this. In the beginning, about 200 cryptanalysts and employees at Bletchley Park had a hard time getting a response from the conservative English admiralty. The first military disasters and the personal commitment of Churchill changed the situation. Cryptanalysis became 'respectable' at that time.

From 1940 onwards, Great Britain regularly listened in on German air force messages, and from 1941 onwards, they listened in on the navy's, too. To my knowledge, there are unconfirmed speculations connecting this with the fateful air raid on Coventry. Rumors had it that a radiogram was previously intercepted. Churchill was said to have not responded in order to prevent betraying that they had already broken the Enigma. If this was the case, then it must have been awful for Bletchley Park employees originating from Coventry: they knew in advance what was going to happen and couldn't even warn their relatives. Nothing was to be done to prevent the Germans from learning that the Enigma had been broken. If a few details of this story are incorrect, sufficient similarly awful situations can also be found. After all, national intelligence organizations are supposed to do everything to the best of their abilities in order not to disclose the state of their cryptanalysis. Let's memorize this sentence; it will play an important role later on.

- The young mathematician Gordon Welchman improved the principle of the *bombs* decisively with the so-called *diagonal board*, which made the *bombs* dramatically faster; now they required only 11 minutes for one pass. The first batch of these devices was taken into operation in 1940; 200 were operating by the end of the war. Welchman is seen as the actual hero in the Enigma story. He is probably identical to the hero Tom Jericho in the book by Harris [Harris] mentioned earlier.

So this is roughly Enigma's story. If you are interested in more details, I recommend reading the rather thrilling and historically sound book by Kahn [KahnEnig]. Moreover, you will find several texts on the Web site to this book.

- No character is transformed onto itself.

- Each rotor was turned further by the left neighbor in rotor-specific setting and could thus be identified.

- Message keys were written twice successively at the beginning.

- Message keys were stereotypical.

- Many messages began with the same 'ANX' and contained other stereo-typical parts (HEILHITLER).

- Sometimes plaintext was included: 'Gartenpflege' (mining certain areas by the British air force—message sent by German observers).

- Basic keys sometimes became available by military conquests.

- Weather reports were transmitted by using 3-rotor Enigmas only.

- The same message was encrypted with two different methods—mainly in 'Gartenpflege'.

- The Enigma was deemed to be totally secure until the end of the war—almost the entire secret radio communications were based on it: there was sufficient material for analysis!

Figure 2.6: Vulnerabilities for cryptanalyzing the Enigma.

When hearing the words 'Bletchley Park' every insider will think of the greatest cryptanalytic action in history until then. In Great Britain, the project was called 'Ultra', which refers both to the effort and the secrecy. Perhaps some high-ranking cryptologists in Germany had a hunch that their wonder machine had been broken. But who would have admitted it in times like those? So they preferred to limit themselves to gradual improvements that always came a bit too late.

It can be assumed that the current state of computer technology came about thanks to the analysis of the Enigma, at least to some extent. In any event, its code breakers had a major impact on the course of the war and were able to prevent many of the feared submarine attacks. Let's leave a more exact evaluation up to the historians.

Later developments of the 'bombs' worked even faster and were auto-mated to a higher degree. But actually what for? We will learn the answer in the next section.

2.5.3   The Enigma after 1945

So what happened to the Enigma after the end of World War II? The 'Ultra' project continued to be top secret. Nobody knew officially that the Enigma had been broken. Hints about that fact remained unnoticed.

The fact that this machine was compromised probably became officially known in 1974. With the appearance of his book *The Ultra Secret*, Winterbotham let the cat out of the bag. In the second edition of *The Codebreakers* by David Kahn [KahnCode], the author even states that Winterbotham had obtained special approval from the government to write his book. (But the first edition of *The Codebreakers* in 1967 was also a drum-beat. Up to that time, cryptology appeared to still be what it always was: a sort of occult science. By the way, the book by Kahn, especially dedicated to the Enigma, appeared only in 1991 [KahnEnig].)

On October 19, 1993, Sir Harry Hinsley held a seminar at Cambridge University. Hinsley interpreted the German fleet's messages deciphered at Bletchley Park and is considered the official historian of the 'Ultra' project. This seminar was recorded and you can find the highly interesting work on the Web site to this book.

On May 20, 1994, Keith Lockstone posted an article that summarized the most important contents in the *sci.crypt* Internet newsgroup (you can also find it on our Web site):

- According to that article, Germany and Switzerland continued to produce Enigmas after the war and sold them to Africa, the Middle East, and South America for military and diplomatic communications. Germany may still have believed in its marvel, while the Swiss intelligence agencies knew back in 1943 about the adversary's activities and had warned Germany then (!). The Germans turned a deaf ear to this warning. No comment.

- Similarly 'noble' motives appeared to have encouraged the USA to sell Enigmas to third-world countries, according to Zimmermann [ZimmPGP], while the real reason was presumably to be able to listen in on their communications. We will see later on that this tactic is being pursued to this day. Cries of horror (like in a TV program I watched years ago) would be feigned. After all, it's about national intelligence.

- And in the Soviet Union, too, nobody was warned about using the Enigma though cryptanalysis of the Enigma had allegedly been on the same level as in the USA and Great Britain, but thanks to a parallel development rather than to spying. People aware of the strength of Soviet mathematicians won't be taken by surprise.

However, we don't know precise details, for cryptology in the Soviet Union has been locked against the outside.

Actually we don't know many precise details in general—what became of the captured Enigmas, how many machines were built or sold, who produced them, and up to when they were in use.

Hinsley also speculates about what turn the war might have taken had the Enigma texts *not* been deciphered: the invasion of the allied forces would have happened nevertheless, but perhaps in 1946 or 1947. Unless the Soviet Union had ended the war by that time the USA would probably have used nukes in Europe, too (this is one of Hinsley's speculations, but it's worth considering). Well, history cannot be turned back, nor should it be overly simplified. When Willi Korn invented the reversing drum, he had no way of knowing what consequences it was to have for world history.

There is still no end to mystery-mongering. The NSA declassified thousands of documents about World War II on April 4, 1996 (50 years later!). You can find notes and quotations on the Internet; references are also included on the Web site to this book. The British government has not to date declassified many important details about deciphering the Enigma. It became known only in 2000 that ten 'Colossus II' machines, which were superior to the first official ENIAC computer, were in use. More about this on our Web site (*colossus.txt* and *declassif_UK.txt*).

Cryptanalysis Today

Despite it all, I believe that this machine can be broken without using a plaintext attack considering the current state of computer technology. Since it works with only 26 letters, we may reasonably assume that it uses normal plaintext. Its letter distribution is known, and I would launch an attack at this very point. Without considering the plugboard, a 'ridiculous' set of 1 054 560 possible keys remain to be tested at various speeds, depending on the program quality and hardware. Each decryption attempt results in a letter distribution that can be compared with the expected distribution. We select keys with reasonable results and test for other criteria to see whether or not the result could be a language. This trial-and-error process is likely to be fast. But what about the plugboard? The second transposition—before revealing the plaintext—doesn't change anything in the distribution, the first does. Without being able or wanting to substantiate my statement, I think that that's something one could handle.

Another approach is based on computer algebra. Modern computers can process formulas. Though they don't handle them as elegantly as we humans do, they faultlessly master 'tapeworms' millions of members long. Computers can even work with algebraic structures, since operations in such structures meet exactly defined laws. As the Enigma drums and their movements were fixed, the structure of the substitutions was well known. We could try to describe the dependence of the substitutions in consecutive steps with appropriate expressions, and then build a totally different cryptanalysis on that. The only question is then whether or not it would still be worth our while.

One interesting initiative is the 'M4 Project'. (see *m4_project.txt* on the Web site to this book). The challenge is to break three original Enigma messages from World War II that have not yet been deciphered by means of free software. This so-called *hill-climbing method* is a mixture of experimenting with the rotor settings and subsequently 'adapting' the plugboard. At the time of writing, one of the messages has been decrypted. The project shows that Enigma cryptanalysis is still no kid's game today.

Clipped, But Still Secret: UNIX-*crypt*

The UNIX world has always had a command called *crypt*, which can be used to encrypt files. This command runs a kind of Enigma with only one rotor and one reflector (reversing drum). However, the rotor has 256 'contacts', because it's a matter of encrypting bytes and not just letters. The method is insecure, which mightn't come as a surprise after all you've read so far. Things looked different when UNIX emerged in 1970.

To prove the insecurity claimed, Robert Baldwin of the MIT created a program package called *Crypt Breakers Workbench* (*CBW*) in the mid-1980s. The product offers a convenient interface for unauthorized deciphering of files encrypted with *crypt*. The program is freely available; everybody can have a look at it and analyze its functionality. Of course, it is also included on the Web site to this book. The Workbench integrates a program functionally equivalent to *crypt* (by the misleading name of *enigma.c*). Nevertheless, *crypt* is available under UNIX for compatibility reasons. There's nothing unusual about it.

But now hold tight: until well into the 1990s, it was strictly forbidden to export a UNIX system from the USA if it included *crypt*. *crypt* was considered ammunition—you'll probably remember that part from Chapter 1. *crypt* was stripped off every legally exported UNIX. On the UNIX systems SunOS 4.1.3 and on my ESIX V.4.2 (shipped at the end of 1994) I found *crypt* documented, but *crypt* itself was missing. OSF/1 no longer offered *crypt*. Though I found it on another system, I convinced myself to forget it at all cost in order not to bring its vendor to the gallows. Hopefully, no slouch hat will be ringing at my door for mentioning it here.

This unrealistic behavior was typical for NSA's security policies. We will come across this issue at several places in this book.

Nowadays, password security under UNIX and Linux is based on other algorithms, such as Blowfish or hash functions.

2.6   The Only Safe Method: One-Time Pads

So far, we haven't discussed one single encryption algorithm without showing, at least rudimentarily, how it can be broken. Though you are likely to come across statements like 'provably secure method' in publications, don't buy it: rather than proving that their method is secure, the authors normally just attribute it to another one that hasn't been broken yet (and often to the problems of factoring large numbers, or calculating the discrete logarithm; more about these issues in Section 4.5).

'Is there such a thing as a secure encryption method?', you'll probably ask. Yes, there is, and it's called a **one-time pad**. The method is very easy to describe. It's a polyalphabetic cipher with infinite period. In other words, we select a key which is at least as long as the plaintext:

```
ANEXTREMELYLONGANDCOMPLETELYRANDOMLYSELECTEDKEY
THEPLAINTEXTISSOMEWHATSHORTER
```

Superimposed characters are added (as in the Caesar cipher described earlier): A corresponds to 0, B to 1, Z to 25, and if the sum grows larger than 25, we deduct 25 to once more obtain a number that can be translated back into a letter:

```
  ANEXTREMELYLONGANDCOMPLETELYR
+ THEPLAINTEXTISSOMEWHATSHORTER
= TUIMERMZXPVEWFYOZHYVMIDLHVECI
```

The receiver is (hopefully!) the only one who also knows the key and subtracts it from the ciphertext:

```
  TUIMERMZXPVEWFYOZHYVMIDLHVECI
- ANEXTREMELYLONGANDCOMPLETELYR
= THEPLAINTEXTISSOMEWHATSHORTER
```

We encrypt bitwise rather than bytewise nowadays. We no longer add characters modulo 25, but bits modulo 2, which corresponds to the bitwise exclusive OR (XOR, or operator in the C programming language). That's a basic operation for every microprocessor, and it can also be used to encrypt arbitrary data streams.

The important point about this method is that the section of the key concerned may be used once only. Since absolutely nothing is known about the key, any plaintext could have produced a given ciphertext, and all conceivable plaintexts are equally likely. All other symmetric methods (these are encryption algorithms like the ones described in this book so far) have shorter keys, which means that they necessarily contain some rules (the trouble is, we just aren't clever enough to recognize and exploit these rules). There are no such rules with the one-time pad, not even in theory.

Unfortunately, there are two problems inherent in this method.

Problem 1: How can we create a 'truly random' key? Using a computer won't do the trick properly, because every computer output obeys rules, which means that it can be at best 'pseudo-random'. What we need is chaotic input from the real world, which cannot be traced back. How about this for 'chaotic' and 'real world': record whatever an unreliable Geiger counter measures from a radioactive sample in the trunk of your car as you rumble over bumpy roads, then overlay this data stream with the digitized gurgling of a waterfall and the bleating of sheep. Every spy will just give up.

Since there were times when digitizing didn't exist, people selected sections from books for use as keys, for example. Naturally, that's far from being secure. [BauerDS] explains the so-called **zigzag method**, which *does* break this method after all: for a starter, you know a little bit of plaintext, from which you can easily calculate a fragment of the key. This fragment doesn't normally end at word boundaries so that, with some luck, fragments missing in words can be filled in. This, in turn, produces a little piece of plaintext—and so on. Though this cryptanalysis doesn't always work, it can indeed reveal important parts of the plaintext.

Good keys, i.e., non-reproducible keys, were carried around by good spies in printed form. Adversaries would regularly pull them out of the hollow knob of their walking sticks.

Both the sender and the receiver of a message have to carry this individual key with them.

This takes us straight to *problem 2*: handling the key. How does the key get to the receiver? How should it be stored? This is not practical in most cases. If you want to use a one-time pad to encrypt a complete hard disk, you need a second disk only to store the key. How about locking away the critical disk in the first place? Anyway, fast data streams over lengthy periods cannot be encrypted in this way.

The following historical episode should teach us a lesson in this respect: one-time pads were used by Soviet spies in the USA during World War II. They reused the same pads; the KGB must have supplied them in identical batches. That was a fateful mistake. Of course, the adversary listened in on them and copied the messages, although they couldn't initially make sense of them. Using simple statistical tests, they managed in arrears to fish out usable ciphertext pairs. If you use different pads, S_1 and S_2, for two plaintexts, P_1 and P_2, then the results, $C_1 = P_1 + S_1$ and $C_2 = P_2 + S_2$, are independent, and both the sum and the difference of C_1 and C_2 produce equally distributed random numbers. In the case of $S_1 = S_2$, however,

$$C_2 - C_1 = P_2 - P_1$$

holds, and the difference of two texts in the same language is by no means random—it has striking statistical characteristics. One single little piece of plaintext from a message will allow you to apply the zigzag method, using all messages encrypted with the same pad, S_1!

This was how the USA started getting an idea of the entire dimension of Soviet espionage in the USA for the first time after the end of World War II (rumors had it that there were about 200 spies). The cryptanalysis was extraordinarily difficult, because the messages had first been encrypted by means of code books, and not all cover names were revealed. Only part of the ciphertexts had been decrypted. Eventually the NSA gave up on their work in 1980 (!). Still, this enterprise, named the **VENONA Project**, was a success. Famous personalities like Julius and Ethel Rosenberg and the nuke spy Klaus Fuchs fell victims to the project.

This example helps us understand why national intelligence organizations listen in on encrypted texts even when they initially can't make sense of them. And it shows very impressively that even the single most secure ciphering method is not worth a bean if sloppy work is done in the environment—in this example, the key management.

I must refer you to the lion's den if you are interested in more details: visit the NSA homepage at `http://www.nsa.gov` and search the site for 'venona'.

Consequently, the one-time pad is reserved for very special purposes. Rumors have it that the hotline between Moscow and Washington was protected by a one-time pad. Schneier [SchnCr, 1.5] notes with some amusement that even the aliens from Andromeda will never have a chance to decrypt the traffic in arrears, unless they take a time trip into the past. I see things a little differently: cryptology is not everything; politicians tend to write their memoirs sooner or later.

2.7 Bottom Line

You may be a little ill-tempered after reading this chapter. Only one single method is secure, but it's one that goes by the board for most practical interests. Moreover, mystery-mongering is everywhere, and honesty cannot be expected in this business anyway.

Let me reassure you, it's not that bad. Cryptology has made enormous progress during the past twenty years, and it has become important for everyone. There is strong public cryptological research; in particular cryptanalysis has been practiced increasingly since the late 1990s. Still, none of us knows how far we actually lag behind the NSA.

A major weakness of all algorithms discussed in this chapter is that they encrypt entire characters. And an algorithm may be as good as it can get—it will normally always have small statistical dependencies. For this reason, a long time ago, I published an algorithm called *fcrypt* [Wobfcrypt] that works characterwise. It can be used to prove that statistical dependencies are virtually lost during encryption. This was one of my first more serious attempts in cryptology, so, at that time, I didn't see how vulnerable the method was compared with differential cryptanalysis (more about this in Section 3.7). The article found lively echo; hopefully, the algorithm is no longer used. Steer clear of it.

Chapter 3

Cryptanalysis in Detail

Our discussion of cryptography (i.e., the science of designing encryption algorithms) and cryptanalysis have balanced out so far in this book. From this chapter onwards, we will systematically deepen the knowledge gained on cryptanalysis. This is necessary because blindly trusting encryption algorithms without knowing cryptanalytic methods is careless. Though we won't look at modern *algorithms* yet, it doesn't mean that modern *software* doesn't play a role! Moreover, looking at simpler methods makes it easier to understand cryptanalysis.

It is required for this chapter to have read Chapter 2. I can still spare you the mathematics to some extent. However, I will introduce three small C programs. Even if you've never programmed you should try to understand the explanations about these programs. You will learn interesting details about cryptanalysis.

The Web site to this book allows you to try out several things discussed in this chapter. Believe me, even if everything looks pretty simple in theory, there is a fascinating experience to be had just in seeing how a program recovers your really complicated and long password from apparent chaos in no time at all! That gives you a real feeling for real dangers whilst having fun.

Though most of the programs discussed here were developed and tested under UNIX, many of them are described generally so that they'll probably run on any system as long as there is a C compiler. Check out Appendix A.1 for more details.

Cryptology Unlocked   Reinhard Wobst
© 2007 John Wiley & Sons, Ltd

3.1   Aim and Methods. Some Basic Notions

You've already learned what plaintext, ciphertext, cryptography, and cryptanalysis are. And you have heard of a cryptanalytic method, the plaintext attack. It's about time I told you what we want to achieve with cryptanalysis:

Cryptanalysis is aimed at revealing as much information about the plaintext as possible without knowing the secret key.

In the worst case, all we have is a ciphertext without any other information. In this case, we even have to find the encryption method used. Sometimes we succeed. For example, if the ciphertext consists of uppercase letters only, and the character distribution coincides with the usual one in the English language, but it has a shift of its maximum, then chances are that a Caesar cipher was used. If the cryptanalysis produces a readable plaintext, we were right and won everything: the method, the key, and the plaintext.

This sort of success can normally be expected only from classic encryption methods. In the following discussion, we will assume that *the encryption method is known*. This prerequisite is not unrealistic: in information society we deal with massware—encryption programs, chip cards, cell phones, ciphering devices. Every algorithm will be disclosed sooner or later. And critical users will want to know exactly what method they use and how it was implemented anyhow.

Under the prerequisite of knowing the method, winning the key is probably the greatest possible success for a cryptanalyst. It has the benefit that he can replay all encrypted messages just as fast as the receiver with no additional work—as long as the key doesn't change.

The 'next smaller' success is recovering the plaintext. If that can be done fast enough thanks to a weak method, then it will be sufficient; otherwise, it's not bad either.

Another little success is some idea about the plaintext without knowing it entirely. Using the negative pattern search, for example, finding that a certain word is *not* included in the ciphertext can be interesting indeed. Moreover, the length of a message and its addressee can sometimes provide information. But that's not something we deal with in this book. We are only interested in revealing methods, keys, or plaintext.

Four Basic Methods for Cryptanalysis

There are four known methods for cryptanalysis:

Ciphertext-only attack: The key or plaintext is revealed exclusively by means of the ciphertext. This method is the most difficult. If too little is known of the rules of the ciphertext to be able to exploit them, only one obvious thing remains: trying every possible key. This is called **brute-force attack** (exploiting the key space; exhaustion method). Often, however, it is sufficient to try just a few keys; but more about this later.

Known-plaintext attack: Part of the plaintext is known in addition to the ciphertext, and used to reveal the remaining plaintext, normally by means of the key. This is perhaps the most important cryptanalytic method, because it is much more powerful than a ciphertext-only attack and normally possible: the attacker guesses certain words in the text; the beginning of the text is fixed; known, uncritical plaintexts are encoded with the same key as confidential plaintexts, etc.

Chosen-plaintext attack: This is also a plaintext attack, except that the attacker can choose the plaintext so that the attack becomes possible in the first place, or will become easy. In this case, the cryptanalyst is active himself: he needs a James Bond to deliberately introduce some text.

Adaptive-chosen-plaintext attack: This is a repeated attack with selected plaintext, where the plaintext deliberately introduced is selected dependent on the current state of the cryptanalysis. Algorithms used in ciphering devices with permanently burnt-in keys have to be resistant against this sharpest method.

So these are the methods commonly used, but not all conceivable ones. For example, most textbooks don't mention the following method:

Ciphertext-ciphertext attack: This is the method described in Section 2.5.2, where the plaintext is encrypted with two different methods. The attacker can exploit this in different ways. In general, a method is already broken so that

---

- Using stereotype formulations (facilitating plaintext attacks).
- Repeated sending of slightly changed plaintexts.
- Inappropriate, foreseeable selection of keys.
- Using pad characters (e.g., 'X' for blanks, or for padding the text at the end).

Figure 3.1: Some common ciphering errors.

everything boils down to a plaintext attack. Such an attack is always based on a ciphering error. Good cryptographers use a different plaintext for each method.

Later in this book, we will discuss the **chosen-ciphertext attack**, which plays a role with digital signatures. The attacker deliberately introduces a certain ciphertext and gains access to the 'plaintext' generated from that ciphertext. The attacker can use this information to calculate other plaintexts, and the code writer is unable to prove the attack (see Section 4.5.3).

Yet another method is the **chosen-key attack**, which will be discussed in Section 4.4.3. With this type of attack, the attacker exploits known relationships between unknown keys. For example, he might know in what bits the keys differ. Using each of these keys, an attacker encrypts the same plaintext and then studies the results, and finally reconstructs the original key.

Of course, there are many other 'methods' to get hold of a key: vulnerabilities in the security system, extortion, keyword guessing, and many more. The first two methods (i.e., ciphertext-only attack and known-plaintext attack) play the major roles in this book, because using them means the smallest risk for the attacker's cryptanalysis, while the code writer runs the risk of being totally compromised.

Every Cryptographer Has to Be a Good Cryptanalyst

Every cryptographer's aim is naturally to design an algorithm that won't supply any practically usable results when cryptanalyzed. This doesn't necessarily mean that it can't be cryptanalyzed at all. It normally means that it would take too long (the encrypted information might become worthless in the meantime), or that it would be too costly to justify the value of the information.

For instance, the encryption methods used at the fronts in World War I had been estimated by the cryptologists to require at least one day's work for the adversary to recover the plaintext. After one day, the encrypted commands had become worthless—the shells had long hit by that time. The catch in the matter could only have been that the adversary deciphered faster than expected [BauerMM].

Both the time and the cost of a cryptanalysis have to be in a reasonable relationship to its result. Hardly anyone would buy a supercomputer to write a love letter.

Unfortunately, there is no recipe for designing good encryption algorithms. The one-time pad (Section 2.6) is the only method that is theoretically secure (but mostly unusable). To my knowledge, there are still no reliable estimates of the minimum effort a cryptanalyst has to invest to break a certain algorithm. (This is the subject of so-called **complexity theory**.) Consequently, the cryptographer has to test a new algorithm against all current cryptanalytic methods and ideally guess the unconventional thoughts of an attacker. Since the security of an algorithm is in the foreground, its cryptanalysis is the measure of all things. Of secondary importance are criteria like fastness, easy implementation in hardware, etc. *This means that cryptography grows out of extensive knowledge of cryptanalysis.* You have seen enough examples that confirm this statement in Chapter 2. Just like theorem number One in cryptanalysis, '*the adversary always knows your method*', there are two important theorems in cryptography:

1. It is virtually useless to want to develop a good encryption algorithm if you don't have a clue about cryptanalysis.

2. You will never make it on your own to exhaustively analyze an encryption algorithm. An algorithm should first be disclosed and then be discussed worldwide.

So a cryptographer always has to also be a cryptologist, i.e., to master cryptanalysis.

Being more particular, the second point above holds true only for the part of the world that's accessible to us, i.e., public cryptological research. One example is the National Security Agency (NSA), for example. **NSA** is the biggest employer of mathematicians in the world (unconfirmed estimates range between 30 000 and 40 000 employees), and it is totally sealed off against the outside. It goes without saying that the NSA employs the best cryptologists in the world, who mutually review their developments. However, their algorithms normally remain secret. The only exception might be the *Skipjack* algorithm of the Clipper chip (see Section 5.7.5). We have no idea what level the knowledge accumulated there has reached, but it's likely to be an unexpectedly high level.

3.2 Cryptanalytic Approaches

Suppose we have received a ciphertext and know the encryption method, as agreed. How could we proceed?

- We first need information on the plaintext, i.e., the goal to be achieved: what language is the plaintext in (German, English, Chinese?); is it a file created by a word processor (which word processor?); is it a compressed file (which compression program?); is it a piece of recorded voice or images? Each of these plaintexts has specific properties for which we can test (have we achieved the goal?), and which we will exploit as extensively as possible during the cryptanalysis.

Our attack will be much more difficult without this information. All that's generally left to do is to try each of the text formats and see what specific guess would allow us to mount an attack. This approach requires extensive experience and the kind of software that is probably not available on the Internet.

- If we know the structure of the plaintext and find out that the method is not particularly simple (i.e., not really Caesar, substitution, or Vigenère), then we can look at the possible keys. There might not be that many possibilities. For example, there would be approximately 300 million possible keys if, say, passwords were composed of only six uppercase letters. This number won't pose any major problem to a fast PC. However, we have to come up with a few very fast plaintext tests. We will expediently test in several steps:

  - To start with, let's test the first 100 characters of the 'plaintext' created for forbidden characters.

  - If this preliminary test was successful, let's test roughly for letter frequencies.

  - Next, we test for forbidden digrams.

  - Then we run a comparison with a dictionary.

  - Finally, we have to manually test the last 20 variants to see whether or not they are meaningful.

This brute-force method is typically applied against the Caesar cipher. You can test the text by simply looking at it. A statistical method that also supplies the shift right away, and that can be automated would be more elegant.

However, even the worst cryptologist understands so much of his trade today to choose an astronomically large number of possible keys. If fewer keys are used, then it is most likely one of the older methods, or there is some intention behind it (e.g., because NSA so requested, or a crack software vendor wants to make a living).

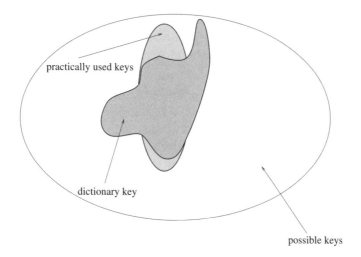

Figure 3.2: Dictionary attack.

It is actually a cryptologist's highest goal to design his algorithm so well that the cryptanalyst has to fall back on the brute-force method, for then the attacker has generally little chance.

- But we might not have to go that far. A dictionary attack might be sufficient. People often take the request 'Enter your password' literally and type a real password. In that case, ten thousand or hundred thousand attempts will do to recover the key. There are plenty of corresponding dictionaries available. This approach is appropriately called **dictionary attack**. We will discuss a qualified attack of this type in Section 3.3.

  Such **reduced key spaces** where the number of keys practically used is much smaller than the number of keys theoretically possible are serious ciphering errors. They are a major vulnerability in the symmetric methods discussed so far.

  This shortcoming can be removed reliably by using random session keys (more about this in Chapter 4), or by crunching a passphrase such as with PGP (see Section 7.1.3).

- With methods working characterwise, which are most of the methods discussed so far, we will often use statistical methods. There were plenty of examples in Chapter 2, and we will come back to this issue in Sections 3.5 and 3.6.

  A prerequisite for such methods is the availability of sufficient statistical material. In view of the 'monster files' that current word processors create, there shouldn't be a lack of material, as opposed to World War II when characters had been typed manually. With a file the size of one Mbyte, it is no longer helpful to change the key regularly—one Mbyte is enough for statistics.

- It might even be possible to mount a plaintext attack. There are many possibilities to do just that. Look at the following realistic approach: the staff in an office produce documents by given guidelines, including the mandatory use of specific style files or macro files. The entries in the file created are considerable; in fact, they can amount to umpteen Kbytes (together with all other style data, my letterhead in WordPerfect is 22 Kbytes long). It's just a question of recovering the remaining Kbytes of confidential text...

   However, the bombing of light buoys (Chapter 2) went out of fashion. There are better methods today.

- Testing for **probable words** is another special plaintext attack. In this case, all we know (or guess) is that a certain word occurs in the text, and perhaps we even know roughly where. We could start a plaintext attack for any possible position to recover the key, or at least part of it. We try to limit the number of possible positions by means of other methods, e.g., the negative pattern search described in Section 3.4.1.

- We could arbitrarily include other information about the plaintext in our analysis. Section 3.6.4 shows several examples.

- Not least, every program that poorly implements a good algorithm offers the cryptanalyst welcome vulnerabilities. Imagine that a 'dead secure' software package for encrypted data communication stores your key on the hard disk of a DOS or Windows computer, perhaps even without you knowing! (Or the encryption is faked. I noticed a curious example under Microsoft Word 6.0, when the text parts themselves obviously remained unchanged by 'protecting the file'.) Such mishaps are bound to happen when a programmer knows nothing about cryptology.

- Finally all kinds of ciphering errors make an attacker's life easier; see Figure 3.1. Since ciphering errors always happen in practice, there is only one way out, namely to prevent them from within the program. Therefore, a good algorithm always has to be resistant to plaintext attacks. Keys should be created by a program.

These are all rather blurred statements. Things will get more specific from the next section onwards. However, there is no general-purpose recipe as to

---

- Information about the plaintext: Created by which program? What striking properties?

- Brute force: Trying the key space, if possible (important: quick testing for correct plaintext).

- Searching a reduced key space (common in practice; dictionary attack).

- Plaintext attack: Fixed byte sequences in word processors; known formats of database files, etc.

- Testing for probable words (special plaintext attack, especially for short files): experimenting, negative pattern search.

- Exploiting additional information about the plaintext: compressed file, ASCII text, ...

- Exploiting any theory: In practice, it is usually a mix of algebra, number theory, and probability theory; the remainder can be handled by experimenting.

- Exploiting vulnerabilities in the implementation: Inept 'improvements' or 'simplifications' of an algorithm, but also keys stored in unsafe places, transmitting a key in plaintext over an insecure network, etc.

Figure 3.3: Potential vulnerabilities for the cryptanalyst to exploit.

how a cryptanalyst should proceed. Even with an algorithm as primitive as the Vigenère method, cryptanalysis depends heavily on the plaintext expected so that one single deciphering program will never cover all practically thinkable cases. Nevertheless, people quite simply say that 'Vigenère was broken'.

The reason is that cryptanalysts may use any theory; the main thing is that it leads to success often enough. Should their crack programs not find a password occasionally—oh well, they can surely explain and get over it. The attacked algorithm remains insecure all the same. In contrast, the cryptographer who designed the algorithm is disgraced by one single successful attack. The cryptographer would actually have to cover himself against *everything* during the design, which is impossible, of course.

As long as complexity theory cannot supply provable minimum estimates of the effort required for cryptanalyzing an algorithm, the 'cryptography versus cryptanalysis' race will continue.

3.3 Example: *Crack* Finds UNIX Passwords

A popular and important example of dictionary attacks is *Crack*, a free program by Alec D. E. Muffett (Great Britain). The program tries to find weak passwords in UNIX systems. A brief digression is necessary to better understand how it works.

How the UNIX Login Works

To log into a UNIX computer you have to enter a name and a password. If you forget the password, you can't work at the computer. How does it work?

Storing passwords in plaintext is extremely dangerous. Once upon a time, I saw this under the RSX-11 operating system on PDP11 computers, the precursor of VMS on VAX computers. Though RSX-11 had cleanly managed access privileges, which guaranteed that not everybody could access all files,[1] it would have been easy to get hold of the passwords had I had bad intentions, since I was often alone at the computer at night, and as things are with hardware, it broke down suddenly now and then. Only restarting the computer helped. I could have interrupted the startup phase by (electric) switch to become a privileged user with access rights to all files.

UNIX developers recognized these risks and stored passwords in encrypted form. That's said rather sloppily, for the plaintext was known (by the way: it consists only of bytes with the numerical values 0 and 1), and the key was the password itself. From the result, i.e., the short ciphertext, the key could no longer be revealed. You would have had to mount a plaintext attack to try and find the key. However, UNIX uses 24 rounds of a modified DES algorithm (see Section 4.3) for encryption, and by the officially known current state of the art, the only meaningful type of attack that remains to reveal the key is the brute-force method (in theory, there are other approaches, but I doubt whether they could be practically used).

This means that not even the UNIX superuser (i.e., the system administrator), who can read and change everything, knows the users' passwords. If one of his sheep forgets its password, he can help out only in one way: he deletes the encrypted password, and the user has to think of a new one. There is nothing wrong with making the password file readable to all users, for it also contains

---

[1]MS-DOS systems and Windows systems up to Windows 98 hadn't known such rights. You could protect your files against unauthorized access only by encryption!

other information of general interest. And new users select their password themselves; taking some care nobody will know it.

All of this was thought out rather cleverly (not only for the level of the 1970s), but two vulnerabilities remain:

1. When two users—a good one and a bad one—accidentally use the same password, then each one of them can log in by the name of the other user and get unlimited access to that user's files. The situation would certainly be noticed and removed soon, but then it would be too late: the bad user might have installed a Trojan horse, i.e., a program he can use to get unauthorized access to the files of the good user, even if he doesn't know the password since it had been changed.

2. There are circuits that implement the DES algorithm at very high speed. This means that an attacker with appropriate hardware could mount a brute-force attack and guess the password.

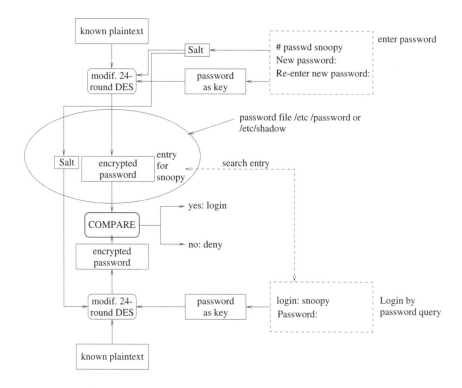

Figure 3.4: Password check during UNIX login.

These are the reasons why a little salt is strewn in: the UNIX login program
(and also the *password* program used to change passwords) modifies the DES
algorithm randomly in one of 4096 ways. This additional information is the
salt that is placed in front of an encrypted password. In the event that two users
actually get the same entry in the password file, then the *password* program can
select a different salt. But the main thing is that the DES ciphering hardware
has become worthless since it cannot map the DES variants mentioned.

How *Crack* Works

UNIX password encryption is still cryptologically very secure. The only vulnerability in the entire process is humans: people use the names of their friends
as passwords, or the official names of their departments or subjects, if they
have no sense of humor. Rumors have it that the password 'fred' has been
used quite often. Have a look at Figure 3.5 and you'll know why.

Crack exploits this fact. It basically runs a brute-force attack, though rather than
doing this at random, it tries many possibilities with the help of a dictionary.
It makes sense that the user of *Crack* is responsible for the dictionary (since
he won't initially find the names of work subjects or names of friends in it).
The entries in the dictionary are selected and modified based on rules defined
by the user. You can see some of these rules in Figure 3.6.

Depending on the planned computing power and the known peculiarities of the
users (who select their passwords themselves!), the *Crack* user can individually
build his search strategy. Once it has guessed the password, *Crack* tells the
program operator about it. Upon request, it also sends an email to the person
concerned!

What *Crack* Is For

The last sentence probably shows best the actual purpose of *Crack*: the program
is not intended to enable breaking a system, but to increase its security. When

Figure 3.5: Part of a computer keyboard—why the password 'fred' is so
popular.

Some modification rules:

- Add characters to the beginning or end: xfred, freddy.
- Convert to uppercase or lowercase letters: FRED, fred.
- Use uppercase for the first letter of the word only: Fred.
- Write the word backwards: derF (or combine the last two possibilities: Derf).
- Write the word twice: FredFred.
- Reflect the word: FredderF.
- Overwrite a certain position with a different character: Frxd.
- Insert a character in a certain position: Fried.
- Replace a character by another one: Frad.
- Use parts of the word: red.
- Use arbitrary combinations of the possibilities above and their negations.

Some selection rules:

- State the minimum and/or maximum length.
- Select or exclude words that include certain characters.
- Select or exclude certain patterns or numbers of vocal-consonant changes.

Crack uses a special high-performing language for these things. The selection options can be formulated much more solidly than their equivalent *regular expressions* in UNIX tools (such as *egrep*).

Figure 3.6: Modification and selection rules of *Crack*.

a user learns that his password was guessed, he will hopefully select a better one. A security-aware system administrator will pay attention to these things, just as well as they will choose a good UNIX *password* program to be used to define or change passwords. (I can think of *goodpasswd* under SCO UNIX which rejects poor passwords. Unfortunately, it is not common to find such an important feature.)

This is a big deal. Imagine a situation where a company fires an employee. Maliciously, our ex-employee secretly copies the password file */etc/password*.

At home, she lets *Crack* run on her PC for a couple of weeks until she finds a password. She logs into her former employer's system over the network. Next, she looks for a vulnerability in the system (which is often easy for insiders), becomes a superuser, and eventually causes immense damage to that company. Don't think things like this can't happen, because 80 % of all known successful attacks to computers originate from current or former employees.

But carelessness dominates. When I got my first Internet access I looked at the password file of the Sun workstation just for fun. Using the UNIX tool *grep*, I quickly found out that among the users who had no password *at all*, there were twenty professors. I knew one of them well. I accommodated a little script in his startup file (*.profile*) that generated the following output:

```
Dear Mr XYZ,
You have no password at all.
Just think of all the bad people out there!
```

When I ran into him the next day, he was all excited and told me: 'Imagine what happened! I logged myself into the Sun yesterday, and this output pops up at me,' and I said 'Dear Mr XYZ, You have no . . .'. He has had a password ever since.

Some time later, the administrator ran *Crack* on this Sun and removed all faults. I was proud that *Crack* hadn't guessed my password.

The successes of *Crack* are surprising. In general, about 20 % of all passwords are guessed. This shows clearly how much a cryptologically excellent method (namely the UNIX password encryption) is worth when there's something wrong in the environment (in the above case, the key selection). The fact that a fast computer may have to work for a week changes nothing in what's been said: such an effort is worthwhile for a criminal attacker.

Crack is popular and performs well. This issue actually belongs to Chapter 7, but it demonstrates very impressively how intelligently one can mount a meaningful brute-force attack.[2]

Current UNIX and Linux systems protect themselves against *Crack* attacks by storing the encrypted passwords in a separate file called */etc/shadow*, which the regular user can't read, and no longer in */etc/password*. In addition, many login

---

[2]We will learn another possibility called 'time–memory tradeoff' in Section 4.4.1.

programs enter a wait loop, e.g., 5 seconds, after each wrong password entry. This prevents the most popular passwords being tried over the network. Rather than DES encryption, other systems use a one-way hash function, e.g., MD5 (more about it in Chapter 6). All these measures are correct, but cryptologically insufficient. Really correct is only the stopping of bad passwords by the *password* command itself. On the other hand, admissible passwords should not be overly complicated, since that would encourage users to write them down.

3.4 Back to Ciphering Cylinders

After this excursion into modern cryptology, let's get back to outdated methods. We will see that cryptanalyzing these methods is still of interest. We begin with the ciphering cylinders introduced in Section 2.5. A little reminder: a ciphering cylinder is a homophone polyalphabetic method with a small period (e.g., 30). The single substitutions are known, only their selection and sequence are secret. Negative pattern search is very useful to cryptanalyze them. It can be deciphered even if the ciphertext is too short for statistical analyses.

3.4.1 Negative Pattern Search

We know that the disks in ciphering cylinders are turned so that the plaintext appears in one line. The ciphertext is read in another line. One of the properties of this method is strikingly similar to the Enigma, namely that a character never transforms onto itself during encryption. While this may seem to increase the method's security, it is actually a rather strong limitation. We saw at the beginning of Section 2.5.2 that this may help somebody to find the position of a piece of plaintext. The following simple (and impractical) example shows how we can utilize it.

An Example (Caesar Cipher)

The task at hand is to decrypt the following Caesar-ciphered message without the help of a computer:

```
GLHVHUWHAWHQWKDHOWHLQZDKUVFKHLQOLFKHVZRUW
```

We know that the text part

```
WAHRSCHEINLICHESWORT
```

```
GLHVHUWHAWHQWKDHOWHLQZDKUVFKHLQOLFKHVZRUW
WAHRSCHEINLICHESWORT
 WAHRSCHEINLICHESWORT
  WAHRSCHEINLICHESWORT
  *WAHRSCHEINLICHESWORT
    WAHRSCHEINLICHESWORT
     WAHRSCHEINLICHESWORT
      WAHRSCHEINLICHESWORT
       WAHRSCHEINLICHESWORT
        WAHRSCHEINLICHESWORT
         WAHRSCHEINLICHESWORT
         *WAHRSCHEINLICHESWORT
          *WAHRSCHEINLICHESWORT
           WAHRSCHEINLICHESWORT
            WAHRSCHEINLICHESWORT
             WAHRSCHEINLICHESWORT
              WAHRSCHEINLICHESWORT
               WAHRSCHEINLICHESWORT
                WAHRSCHEINLICHESWORT
                *WAHRSCHEINLICHESWORT
                 WAHRSCHEINLICHESWORT
                  WAHRSCHEINLICHESWORT
                  *WAHRSCHEINLICHESWORT
```

Figure 3.7: Negative pattern search. The highlighted letters show a coincidence (i.e., a match between the plaintext and the ciphertext in that position). All that remains are the five possibilities marked '*'.

(probable word) appears in the plaintext. We've come across such probable words in Chapter 2. They even play a greater role in the modern data processing world—just think of headers in word processor files.

Back to the probable word. We write it on a piece of paper and move it along underneath the ciphertext, as shown in Figure 3.7. No character transforms onto itself in the Caesar cipher either. So, when two equal characters happen to be superimposed in any place, this position of the paper strip is out of the question.

Based on the theory, only 46 % of all cases will have no such match, but language is not random. In our case, there are only five possible positions of the paper strip.

Next, we pick a letter that occurs at least twice in the probable word; let's select 'R'. Notice that the same character always has to correspond to 'R' in the ciphertext since the text is Caesar-ciphered. The first possibility is no good since a 'W' is above the left 'R', and a 'Z' above the right 'R'. This can't be the right position. Similarly, we find the letters 'K' and 'H', 'D' and 'L' as well as 'Z' and 'V' above the 'R' in the second, third, and fourth positions. They are out of the question, too. The last position remains, where 'R' is always converted into 'U'. We try to determine a shift (here 3) and, running a deciphering attempt, obtain the following:

```
DIESERTEXTENTHAELTEINWAHRSCHEINLICHESWORT
```

All right, so this text was 'originally' Caesar-encrypted (i.e., using shift 3).

Of course, there are other methods we could have used to cryptanalyze this example. For instance, the letter 'H' occurs in the ciphertext with a frequency of 19 %. Assuming that 'H' corresponds to the most frequent letter, 'E', we would also have found the solution. This is actually the way for ciphertext attacks. However, using the negative pattern search on a probable word meant that we didn't have to count up anything. It led to success almost effort-lessly.

Approach for Ciphering Cylinders

The approach for ciphering cylinders is similar: the negative pattern search supplies us with a few possible positions of the plaintext for a starter. What makes this approach more difficult, however, is that the probable word could be torn, and a careful code writer may have selected a different cylinder line for each period. But we're not interested in this right now.

We start a plaintext attack by exploiting each possible position of the probable word as follows:

- For every letter, we know the character it will be transformed to in the ciphertext. This heavily limits the selection of the disks, and even homophony cannot change that (i.e., the fact that we don't know from what row the ciphertext was read), which increases our effort by 26-fold.

- For each assumed disk choice, we look up another period of the cipher-text to see whether or not this choice will produce a fragment of some meaningful plaintext in a row. Only a few possibilities will generally remain.

- We add more and more sections (periods) of the ciphertext as we continue revealing the correct choice for as many disks as there are letters in the probable word.

- In every period, we decrypt the part of the ciphertext determined by the disks we already know. We will hit scraps of words like ORDE, ANNABI, MITTANC, or XPOS, and completing them shouldn't pose a major problem. Having revealed yet another piece of plaintext, we can start all over again, luckily from a better starting position.

- Step by step and piece by piece, we will end up knowing all disks.

The interesting part of this approach is that even homophony—ambiguity in the cipher—does not represent an insurmountable obstacle. Of course, my representation refers to the way we'd have worked before the computer era. Humans are still better than computers when it comes to forming sentences from scraps of words. But when you use a computer you'd proceed differently anyway.

3.4.2 The Viaris Method

The method developed by Viaris represents a refinement of the cryptanalysis discussed above. Again, we use a probable word, except that this time we improve the negative pattern search.

To this end, we hold the row from which the ciphertext had been read (the so-called *generatrix*) on the cylinder for a moment. Under this prerequisite, we analyze the letters that could form at all from the letters of the probable word for all disks. We appropriately build ourselves a table (*matrix*) for this purpose. Each row in the table corresponds to a disk, and each column to a letter of the probable word (see Figure 3.8).

As before, we move the probable word along underneath the ciphertext. We'll know we have hit the correct position when each character of the ciphertext above the word appears at least once in the corresponding matrix column. Positions with coincidences (character matches like above) fall out automatically, but generally other cases do too. If we find no possible position, we have to try all over again using a different generatrix. Notice that the number of possibilities to be analyzed is slightly smaller with this method. Givierge refined the method once more by doing without probable words and using only digram and trigram frequencies. You will find more details and references in [BauerMM, 14.3].

The Attacking Method by Viaris

Let the probable word be CHIFFRE, and the ciphertext VIWSHQTLUFT-WDTZ.

The ciphering cylinder should consist of ten disks with the following settings (to be read from top to bottom; connecting the first row with the last row to form a ring):

```
1 2 3 4 5 6 7 8 9 10    (disk number)

N X F V M S X U T P
B J C X X A I B V M
A E L I T G L J G G
C Q G G Y J F W F Z
R N B D K V C R A X
V P T E D R V V X I
U T R C B D W M E S
H B A T L Q D L L V
D Z D R E O J F U L
Q H V F F L P O K J
W V M Q R H S P J W
M I H S H C R K W C
K G S N Q I E Y Q A
Z A O Z A U G Q S T
P S Z K W E T G Z U
L R U W J Z O A O N
F Y I H U Y A H I D
T K X U I M Y S B O
S F W Y O B N I R B
O O J M G X M C H Y
J C Y J N W B Z C R
G W P A C N U X N K
Y M E P Z K H T M F
X D Q O V F Z N Y E
I U N L S T Q E D Q
E L K B P P K D P H
```

We look at the first generatrix, i.e., the ciphertext is read from one row underneath the plaintext row. This turns 'C' into 'R', 'H' into 'D', 'I' into 'E', and so on, in the first disk. We write this result in the first row of a matrix. We fill the second row analogously for the second disk. We obtain the following 10×7 matrix:

```
1   R D E T T V N
2   W V G O O Y Q
```

Figure 3.8: Using the Viaris method to attack ciphering cylinders.

```
 3  L S X C C A Q
 4  T U G Q Q F C
 5  Z Q O R R H F
 6  I C U T T D Z
 7  V Z L C C E G
 8  Z S C O O V D
 9  N C B A A H L
10  A P S E E K Q
```

The position

```
VIWSHQTLUFTWDTZ
CHIFFRE
```

of the probable word supplies no coincidence (no two superimposed characters are equal), which means that it is theoretically no option. We place the pertaining ciphertext fragment, VIWSHQT, on top of the 10×7 matrix above. Only the 'V' from the first position can be found in the next column (disk 7); the other characters are not in the first generatrix in any other disk. This completes that word position for this generatrix.

The word CHIFFRE is now moved forward and, excluding all positions, we look at the next generatrix until we find a ciphertext fragment in which each ciphertext character happens to be in one of the lower columns at least once. Another exclusion condition is that the ciphertext characters must occur in *different* matrix rows. (If there are multiple occurrences in one column, then we should be able to make the choice so that this condition is met.)

We can now mount a plaintext attack on all positions found.

Figure 3.8: (*continued*)

The method fails when the permuted alphabets on the disks form a Latin square, i.e., when the disks have turning positions that cause each letter to occur at least once in every row.

It is very unlikely that people still use ciphering cylinders today, and nobody implements them in software. So why dedicate a full section to the Viaris method, which is especially tailored to these devices? For a couple of reasons. First, because of the comment on Latin squares in the paragraph above: when you run cryptanalysis yourself, you will begin to understand why this disk property is so important for cryptanalysis. This still doesn't mean that we are able to design secure algorithms: we simply don't know what methods have been or will be used by all the cryptanalysts in the world.

Second, there is one more risk we should be aware of: when designing an algorithm, the developer may be particularly cautious, never letting any character transform onto itself. In doing this, he actually compromises his own method. Bauer [BauerMM] refers to this approach as an *illusory complication*. Endeavoring to design things particularly well often leads to the exact opposite. At this point, you might *not* understand why German cryptologists hadn't seen the risk caused by the Enigma's reversing drum: it enabled negative pattern search.

3.4.3   This is Still Interesting Today!

The ciphering cylinder is history, and so is characterwise encryption. 'So what do we discuss it for?', you will probably ask. We encrypt bitwise nowadays! Well, negative pattern search is still a potential risk, even with algorithms working bitwise. We certainly won't compare superimposed bits any longer. But we might be able to prove a statement like the following:

If byte 1 has even and byte 3 uneven parity in the plaintext block, then there is a 76 % likelihood that bit 26 in the ciphertext block is equal to 1.

Of course, it would be best to have a 100 % probability, for we could then run a negative pattern search, like before. But every value that deviates from 50 % can be helpful.

These kinds of statements are dangerous for all algorithms that are vulnerable to plaintext attacks. Look at this not totally unrealistic example: assume a WordPerfect file was encrypted bitwise using a Vigenère method (more about this in Sections 3.5 and 3.6). We know for sure that it includes the string

```
Lexmark 4039 plus PS2
```

(21 characters), since our security department uses this printer. Moreover, we know the code writer is chronically lazy, i.e., he would never bring himself to use a password with a length of ten characters. We are looking for the position of the probable word; we have a hunch where in the ciphertext it might be found. If the password is four characters long, then 'L' and 'a' have got to be encrypted in the same way. This is written as follows in cryptology:

```
p₁ ⊕ s = c₁
p₅ ⊕ s = c₅
```

Where p_1 represents the plaintext character 'L'; p_5 represents 'a'; c_1 and c_5 denote the pertaining ciphertext characters; s represents the key character for this position; and $\oplus$ denotes the bitwise XOR according to the operation ^ in the C language. We XOR the left and right sides of both equations and obtain

```
p₁ ⊕ p₅ = c₁ ⊕ c₅
```

This is a good criterion for checking a position in the text, since we already know that $p_1 \oplus p_5 = 'L' \oplus 'a'$. We will naturally run this test on the other character pairs, too. If no possible position at all results, we have to try it with a different period length.

Once we've eventually found the correct position of the word, we use it to reveal the correct key, since the Vigenère method is not resistant to plaintext attacks: the plaintext length is greater than the period length so that we can compute the key (plaintext XOR ciphertext) directly. Again, it is remarkable that this approach can do totally without statistic analyses.

3.5 WordPerfect Encryption as a Modern Example

The WordPerfect word processor let's you encrypt your files just like many other application programs. Though the method hadn't been disclosed, it appeared on the Internet nevertheless. First I suspected somebody might have reverse-engineered parts of the program, but then I realized that this effort wasn't necessary. Finding out this method is so unbelievably simple that I want to briefly demonstrate it here without qualifying you for a hacker (after all, I'm not one either). All you need is the right intuition. I once used WordPerfect Version 5.1 under UNIX (it's equivalent to the same version for other operating systems).

3.5.1 The Encryption Method: How to Find It, and How to Break It

Let's first create a simple text in WordPerfect 5.1. For example, we opt for lines composed of 'A's only:

```
AAAAAAAAAAAAAAAAAAAAAAAAAAAAAAAAAAAAAAAAAAAAAAAAAAAAAA
AAAAAAAAAAAAAAAAAAAAAAAAAAAAAAAAAAAAAAAAAAAAAAAAAAAAAA
AAAAAAAAAAAAAAAAAAAAAAAAAAAAAAAAAAAAAAAAAAAAAAAAAAAAAA
...
```

We look at this file to see where we find this text string, using a hexdump program (the first four characters give the hexadecimal address from the beginning of the file, followed by 16 characters both in hexadecimal and ASCII representations).

```
0650   00 e7 27 58 02 50 23 00   01 d1 9f 53 ad 08 23 7c   ..'X.P#....S..#|
0660   00 67 00 00 00 00 00 41   41 41 41 41 41 41 41 41   .g.....AAAAAAAAA
0670   41 41 41 41 41 41 41 41   41 41 41 41 41 41 41 41   AAAAAAAAAAAAAAAA
*
0690   41 41 41 41 41 41 41 41   41 41 41 0a 41 41 41 41   AAAAAAAAAAA.AAAA
06a0   41 41 41 41 41 41 41 41   41 41 41 41 41 41 41 41   AAAAAAAAAAAAAAAA
*
```

Now, let's encrypt this file. The trick to be found here is to again select 'A' as the password. The part of the file considered here now looks as follows:

```
0650   03 e5 22 5c 05 56 2a 08   0a db 92 5f a2 06 32 6c   .."\.V*...._..21
0660   13 75 15 14 17 16 19 59   5a 5b 5c 5d 5e 5f 60 61   .u.....YZ[\]^_'a
0670   62 63 64 65 66 67 68 69   6a 6b 6c 6d 6e 6f 70 71   bcdefghijklmnopq
0680   72 73 74 75 76 77 78 79   7a 7b 7c 7d 7e 7f 80 81   rstuvwxyz{|}~...
0690   82 83 84 85 86 87 88 89   8a 8b 8c c6 8e 8f 90 91   ................
06a0   92 93 94 95 96 97 98 99   9a 9b 9c 9d 9e 9f a0 a1   ................
```

It virtually leaps to your eyes that there are ascending numbers, which is not the case when selecting 'B' for the password:

```
0650   00 e6 21 5f 06 55 29 0b   09 d8 91 5c a1 05 31 6f   ..!_.U)....\..1o
0660   10 76 16 17 14 15 1a 5a   59 58 5f 5e 5d 5c 63 62   .v.....ZYX_\]\cb
0670   61 60 67 66 65 64 6b 6a   69 68 6f 6e 6d 6c 73 72   a'gfedkjihonmlsr
0680   71 70 77 76 75 74 7b 7a   79 78 7f 7e 7d 7c 83 82   qpwvut{zyx.~}|..
0690   81 80 87 86 85 84 8b 8a   89 88 8f c5 8d 8c 93 92   ................
06a0   91 90 97 96 95 94 9b 9a   99 98 9f 9e 9d 9c a3 a2   ................
```

Obviously, the two 'A' characters have somehow 'lifted themselves off', but not by subtraction, for then the last file would look different: the difference between 'A' and 'B' is 1, and this would probably not have had such a big influence. It seems that the plaintext is XORed with the keyword, and an ascending number sequence is additionally superimposed. Let's find out what the outcome would be if we used the password 'AB':

```
0650   02 e1 23 5c 04 5a 2b 08   0b df 93 5f a3 1a 33 6c    ..#\.Z+....._..31
0660   12 71 14 14 16 1a 18 59   5b 5f 5d 5d 5f 63 61 61    .q.....Y[_]]_caa
0670   63 67 65 65 67 6b 69 69   6b 6f 6d 6d 6f 73 71 71    cgeegkiikommosqq
0680   73 77 75 75 77 7b 79 79   7b 7f 7d 7d 7f 83 81 81    swuuw{yy{.}}....
0690   83 87 85 85 87 8b 89 89   8b 8f 8d c6 8f 93 91 91    ................
06a0   93 97 95 95 97 9b 99 99   9b 9f 9d 9d 9f a3 a1 a1    ................
```

We can see that, from address 66*a* onwards, every other character forms an accordingly ascending row, but this time with difference 2:

```
5b 5d 5f 61 63 65 ...
```

Perhaps all that's done here is a simple Vigenère cipher and XORing, like in Section 2.4.2, and then additionally superimposing an ascending number sequence on everything? One can find out pretty quickly that this is actually the case. More specifically, the method in WordPerfect 5.1 looks like this:

- Write bytes with the following numerical values on one row: the first value is larger than the password length by 1; every following value is larger than its predecessor by 1; 0 comes after 255.
- Write the password underneath several times, and
- underneath it, write the bytes of the WordPerfect file again, starting with byte number 16.
- XOR three superimposed characters bitwise. The result is the 'ciphertext' (Figure 3.9).

Let the password be UNIX, i.e., let it have length 4. The WordPerfect file should look like this from byte 16 onwards, for example (doesn't happen in practice):

```
Canon BJ-200 (LQ Mode)
```

The encrypted text is produced by bitwise XORing the following three rows:

```
5  6  7  8  9 10 11 12 13 14 15 16 17 18 19 20 21 22 23 24 25 26
U  N  I  X  U  N  I  X  U  N  I  X  U  N  I  X  U  N  I  X  U  N
C  a  n  o  n     B  J     2  0  0     (  L  Q     M  o  d  e  )
```

Figure 3.9: The encryption method of WordPerfect 5.1.

You can see that the method can be recovered within one to two hours at most when proceeding cleverly. This is not an exceptional case. Vigenère methods or modifications are thought to still be very popular in MS-DOS and Mac software. The manufacturers say that their method 'is almost as secure as DES, only much faster'. Though the second part of this statement may be true, let's show compassion for the first part.

How do you break the WordPerfect encryption? The most obvious method is to simply try all password lengths. There aren't many since the program limits the maximum admissible length to 23. We use the statistical method (as described in Section 2.4.1) to try and find the key for each length. This is not a problem, for there is plenty of material to analyze—almost all WordPerfect files are many Kbytes long—and there are sufficient peculiarities in how the characters are distributed in these files.

But it can be even *simpler* than that. WordPerfect 4.0 is thought to have encrypted only the text itself. In contrast, Version 5.1 'protects' headers, too. The motivation for this expansion may have been to also encrypt the business addresses included in the styles (which are included in the headers). But the header contains plenty of known bytes that can be exploited in a plaintext attack. We will see exactly how this is done in the next section.

3.5.2 The *newwpcrack* Program

WordPerfect encryption is known not only on the Internet; there are lots of programs you can get for free that can break it. One of these programs was written by Ron Dippold in 1991 and is included on the Web site to this book. As usual, nobody will guarantee the software's reliability, but that's not the point. Even a success rate of 50 % would show that the method works.

Unaware of this program, I had developed and published one of my own [Wobsymm]. I'll introduce an improvement in this section. The program is still short (only 70 lines; see listing in Figure 3.10), but it shows how several methods can be combined. Since cryptanalysis is very specific, you should take your time and look at the details, even if you don't think you'll ever use WordPerfect.

How does *newwpcrack* work?

- We first have to identify the bytes that are constant in WordPerfect files. To find these bytes, I used a program called *wph.c*, a program found on our Web site. It compares bytes 17 through 56 of several WordPerfect

```
 1 /* Crack encoded WordPerfect 5.1 files: newwpcrack <encoded_file
 2    (C) R.Wobst (Dresden), @(#) 30.Oct 00:34
 3 */


 4 #include <stdio.h>


 5 #define INVERS   "\033[07m"      /* switch on inverse printing */
 6 #define NORMAL   "\033[0m"       /* return to normal printing */


 7 #define HEADER   16              /* # of header bytes, variable */
 8 #define MAXKEY   23              /* max. keylength (WP specific) */
 9 #define MAXPLAIN 40              /* # of bytes in known plaintext
     */
10 #define PROBE    1024            /* portion of read plaintext */


11 main()
12   {
13   static unsigned int wp[MAXPLAIN] =
14     {
15       0xfb, 0xff, 0x05, 0x00, 0x32, 0x00, 0x100, 0x04,
16       0x00, 0x00, 0x100, 0x00, 0x100, 0x00, 0x00, 0x00,
17       0x42, 0x00, 0x00, 0x00, 0x100, 0x100, 0x100, 0x100,
18       0x00, 0x00, 0x100, 0x00, 0x00, 0x00, 0x100, 0x100,
19       0x100, 0x100, 0x00, 0x00, 0x100, 0x100, 0x00, 0x00
20     };


21   unsigned char b[PROBE];
22   unsigned int key[MAXPLAIN];
23   int len, m, k, bad, N;


24   fread(b, 1, HEADER, stdin);          /* Header: Name etc. */
25   N = fread(b, 1, PROBE, stdin);


26   if(N < MAXPLAIN) exit(1);


27   for(len=1; len <= MAXKEY; ++len)     /* test on keyword lengths
     */
28     {
29     /* construct periodic key from known bytes */
```

Figure 3.10: The *newwpcrack.c* program.

```
30        for(m=0; m < MAXPLAIN; ++m) key[m] = ((len+1+m)^wp[m]^b[m])
   & 0xff;


31       /* test on period */


32       for(m = MAXPLAIN-len; m--; )
33          if(wp[m] != 0x100 && wp[m+len] != 0x100 && key[m] !=
   key[m+len])
34             break;


35       if(m >= 0) continue;


36       /* possible keyword found */


37       printf("len = \%2d: \"", len);


38       /* reconstruct keyword */


39       for(m=0; m < len; ++m)
40          {
41          bad = 0;
42          k = key[m];


43          if(wp[m] == 0x100)     /* not unique, test on another
   known byte */
44             {
45            for(k=m; k < MAXPLAIN; k += len)
46               if(wp[k] != 0x100)
47                  {
48                  k = key[k];
49                  break;
50                  }


51          if(bad = (k >= MAXPLAIN))   /* trial failed, use
   statistics */
52             {
53             int cnt[256];
54             int l, max, indx;
```

Figure 3.10: (*continued*)

```
55                      for(l=256; l--;) cnt[l] = 0;
56                      for(l=m; l < N; l += len) ++cnt[((len+1+1) & 0xff)^
     b[l]];


57                      for(indx=max=0, l=256; l--;)
58                         if(cnt[l] > max)
59                           {
60                             max = cnt[l];
61                             indx = l;              /* '\0' is preferred byte!
     */
62                           }


63                      k = indx;
64                    }
65                  }


66          if(bad) printf(INVERS);


67          if(k < 32) printf("^%c", k+'@');
68          else putchar(k);


69          if(bad) printf(NORMAL);
70        }


71      putchar('"'); putchar('\n');
72     }


73   return 0;
74  }
```

Figure 3.10: (*continued*)

files, where the file names are passed as arguments. When two bytes in two files differ, the program outputs the value 0x100, which corresponds to no character at this place. You can see the result of these tests in the *wp* field (lines 13–20 in the listing in Figure 3.10). Only insiders can check whether or not these assumptions are always valid. No contradiction has been found so far in practice. By the way, the number 40 for the field length was selected relatively at random.

- Next, the encrypted text is read from the standard input *stdin* (lines 24 and 25); the first 16 bytes are discarded.

- The big loop used to try all possible password lengths begins at line 27. The most important calculation is done at line 30, where the ciphertext, the known plaintext, and the 'number sequence' (top row in Figure 3.9) are used to tentatively guess the key. The mathematical background is as easy as it could be:

```
cipher = plain ⊕ key ⊕ number
(where ⊕ stands for XOR) becomes
key = cipher ⊕ number ⊕ plain (1)
```

- We have to test to see whether or not we've been successful. We test in lines 32 through 35: if the key created is not periodic, we certainly weren't successful. We can only test for positions that contain known plaintext. The trial has succeeded if there is no rejection.

- Next, we want to reconstruct as much of the key as possible. The first period alone may not supply enough information, since we normally know only scraps of the plaintext. However, there might be a known plaintext byte that reveals the character we are looking for in another period. This is done in lines 41 through 50.

- Some characters of the key still haven't been found yet. Let's use statistical methods. All right, this sounds high-flown: the thing is I noticed that zero bytes occur in masses in the headers of WordPerfect files. You can see the distribution of the first 1000 characters of this chapter (as a WordPerfect file) in Figure 3.11.

37.50 %	'^@' (zero byte)
20.60 %	'd'
13.10 %	'x'
5.50 %	'<255>'
3.10 %	'P'
2.10 %	'<254>'
2.00 %	'<140>'

Figure 3.11: Distribution of the first 1000 characters in a special WordPerfect file.

In view of such 'exotic' statistics (the zero byte was by far the most frequent in all cases analyzed), let's not deal with the innards of WordPerfect and instead search for the most frequent character in the transformed ciphertext, which was 'cleared' of the disturbing ascending number sequence. This happens in lines 51 through 62. Without that number sequence, only the following remains from equation (1):

```
key = cipher_nonum ⊕ plain
```

However, since the *plain* byte equals 0, we get

```
key = cipher_nonum     !
```

We mark this character as 'unsafe but probable' and output it together with the other ones in lines 66 through 69. The entire 'session' can look like this, for example (under UNIX):

```
$ newwprack <c.wp
$ len = 18: "THIS IT NOT SECURE"
$
```

(The marked characters appear inverted in the output, which means that they have been revealed statistically.)

The program is not flexible—it supplies only one suggestion for each keyword length. Though significant improvements are possible (if there are several characters with approximately equal probability, then all of them should be output), I didn't come across a keyword that *newwpcrack* failed to guess. It is rather striking how surefire this quick-and-dirty method works.

Hopefully you've understood that one can proceed rather heuristically—the main thing is that this path often leads to the goal. The program's computing speed is impressive: calculating a password took 9 ms (0.009 seconds) on a 133-MHz PC Pentium under PC-UNIX (ESIX V.4.2). As mentioned in Chapter 1, AccessData has wait loops built into its software to avoid having to confront customers with the brutal truth. But I'd never have imagined they'd occupy a PC 386-16 for full 60 seconds with the same task that *newwpcrack* handles . . . Certainly, their program is much more reliable than mine (I'm serious).

Had the cryptologists been a bit more careful, they would have encrypted only the text itself to at least prevent plaintext attacks. Even then, however, it would still be easy to break the code: you will see how and by what program in Section 3.6.

3.6 The Vigenère Method Under the Magnifying Glass

The Vigenère method is very simple and (unfortunately) still often used.[3] This is why it is a good and interesting candidate for discussing a few problems in cryptanalysis. Similarly to the previous section, you will learn a specific C program, but one that's much more powerful and universal. Again, we will limit ourselves to using the 'bitwise Vigenère method', also called simple XOR.

3.6.1 The Index of Coincidence Supplies the Period Length. The Kasiski Method

We determined the method's period length experimentally both in the discussion of the Vigenère method in Section 2.4.1 and in deciphering encrypted WordPerfect files in the previous section. But things would be much faster and simpler if we considered the **index of coincidence**, also called **kappa**. Though this sounds very scientific again, it's very simple.

If we write two equally long texts, T_1 and T_2, in two lines one on top of the other, then the kappa of both texts is defined as follows:

$$\kappa = \frac{number\ of\ coinciding\ characters}{number\ of\ characters\ in\ the\ text}$$

More specifically, it looks like this:

```
this is the first text
and this is the second
..........*..........
```

The two texts coincide only in one character (a blank) and are 22 characters long each. Consequently, the kappa of the two texts is 1/22, or 4.5 %. The special thing about this quantity kappa is that it always has roughly the same

---

[3]For example, the *wincrypt* program uses a 512-byte Vigenère key.

value for sufficiently long, different texts in the *same language*. This is quite
amazing, but the reason is clear: in the first approximation, the characters
of long texts have a certain distribution based on probability theory, which
depends on the language used. Moreover, the pairs of letters written above
one another are statistically somewhat independent in long texts. Therefore,
the kappa expected is the square sum of all character probabilities. Whether or
not you can reproduce this in detail is not important—just remember this: *the
kappa results from the common distribution of single characters in two texts.*

We shift the entire text block by four characters to the right and form the kappa
of the shifted text onto itself (and simply cut off ends that jut out):

```
is the first text
this is the first
      *
```

We can see that roughly the same kappa as for long texts occurs here too.
Though superimposed characters are no longer entirely independent (especially
when moved by one position only), the effect is still there. Had I used English
text with all the blanks and line breaks removed from it, I would have obtained
a kappa of approximately 5.5 %.

Let's use this function for a special case: a plaintext, represented by the
character string $(p_i)i = 1, 2, 3 \ldots$, is to be Vigenère-encrypted with a key
$(s_1, s_2, \ldots, s_N)$ of length N, to produce ciphertext $(c_i)i = 1, 2, 3, \ldots$:

```
p₁ p₂ p₃ ... pₙ pₙ₊₁ pₙ₊₂ ...
s₁ s₂ s₃ ... sₙ s₁   s₂    ...
c₁ c₂ c₃ ... cₙ cₙ₊₁ cₙ₊₂ ...
```
$$\text{with} \quad c_1 = p_1 \oplus s_1, \quad c_2 = p_2 \oplus s_2, \quad \ldots$$

We can see instantly that $c_i = c_{N+i}$ exactly when $p_i = p_{N+i}$, since both ciphertext characters were encrypted with the same key characters (whereas different
key characters produce different ciphertext characters). So we conclude:

*The kappa of the ciphertext shifted by N positions against itself equals the kappa
of the plaintext calculated in the same manner.*

If the ciphertext is shifted against itself by an amount smaller than N, then the
result will be a different kappa, namely one in the order of magnitude of a kappa

from truly random text: 1/256 or 0.39 % (how about this compared with a value of 5.5 % for the English language!). Such a small kappa is also to be expected with shifts by amounts larger than N, unless the shift is a multiple of N.

We won't dive into the theory any further at this point. The important thing to remember is that we have found the method for recovering the period of a polyalphabetic cipher:

For all text shifts up to an arbitrary upper limit, we calculate the kappa of the shifted text against itself. When shifting by a multiple of the ciphering period, the kappas should clearly be higher than those for other shift values.

This quantity kappa also played a role in the Enigma, by the way. At one point it was found that the kappa of two Enigma texts encrypted with the same first six characters was near the theoretical value for the German language. The Poles correctly concluded from this that these six characters revealed the rotor setting.

The Kasiski Method

For the sake of completeness, I briefly want to mention yet another method that can be used to reveal the period length. It was introduced by the Prussian army commander Kasiski in 1863. Though this method is much more plausible, it is less universal.

When a ciphertext is fairly 'random', the probability that a character string at least three characters long will occur in the ciphertext more than once is very low (provided there is not 'too big' a distance between the two strings). In normal language, however, multiple occurrences are rather frequent—think of *-tion, -ning, inc-*, etc.

Now, if two identical character strings in the plaintext have a distance between them that corresponds to a multiple of the period length, then we get the same ciphertext in the two places concerned. Using the Kasiski method, we would consequently search for reoccurrences of character strings that are at least three characters long in the ciphertext, and then look at their distances. For example, looking at the distances

```
24, 54, 18, 29, and 66
```

it becomes obvious that the period is 6 (or 2 or 3)—29 is an 'outlier'.

It is pretty easy to program this method, but it requires a certain plaintext structure.

3.6.2 Ciphertext Attack

How do we break a Vigenère cipher using statistical methods? We know from Section 2.4.1 that it's done in two distinct steps: revealing the period length and breaking each of the monoalphabetic substitutions.

We've seen in Section 3.6.1 how the period length can be revealed effectively and reliably. To reveal the substitutions, we only have to find the key character used for XORing.

If the ciphertext is reasonably long, which we initially assume, then we pick out the group of all characters that were encrypted with the same key character. If we use period length N, there are N such groups. In every group, we calculate the frequencies of all characters (to find the character distribution) and try to adapt it to the expected distribution. Let's just briefly assume for our purposes we wanted to encrypt by addition modulo 256 (i.e., a Caesar addition for the 'byte alphabet'), rather than by XOR. The distribution curve of a ciphertext group should then be similar to that of a related plaintext, except that it would be shifted (Figure 3.12).

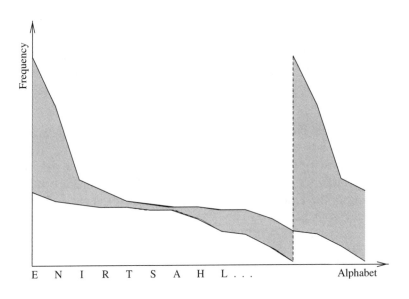

Figure 3.12: Shifted distributions.

The shaded area is a measure of the coincidence of the two curves. The question as to which shift we should define as the 'statistically best' will always be somewhat subjective, so we try to minimize the area content by selecting a suitable shift.

In mathematical terms, we try to make an expression in the form

$$(g_0-p_0)^2 + (g_1-p_1)^2 + \ldots + (g_{255}-p_{255})^2 \qquad (2)$$

as small as possible in dependence on a shift, where g_i are the relative frequencies of a shifted ciphertext, and p_i are the relative frequencies of a related plaintext.[4]

Let's go back to the XOR operation. It doesn't correspond to a shift, but to a permutation of the 'byte alphabet'; anyway, this doesn't basically change anything in our considerations. The only thing is that Figure 3.12 can no longer be represented with this operation as it would be far too big. The so-called objective function remains for minimizing the expression in (2).

So, we try all 256 key characters possible in each group and select the one with the smallest objective function value. This is how we reveal the key.

Notice that there are more sophisticated cryptanalytic methods. But as long as it's a matter of practical use on word processors, spreadsheets, etc., we will have sufficient material for good statistics. That's purely pragmatic. The surprisingly successful cryptanalysis using a program called *vigcrack* introduced in the next section confirms that we can be pragmatic about it.

3.6.3 The *vigcrack* Program

This C program is not particularly long either (122 lines, excluding the comment in the header; see listing in Figure 3.13), but it uses more theory, and it is a lot more universal than *newwpcrack* from Section 3.5.2.

Since we've learned the theoretical background in Section 3.6.2, we can now focus on important details of the implementation. *vigcrack* cracks Vigenère-encrypted files with unequally distributed characters (i.e., readable texts, source

---

[4]For mathematicians: what we basically do here is a kind of Chi-square adaptation test with a distribution over 256 groups. Except that, rather than testing for a hypothesis with given error probability, we select the most favorable, the one that would pass the hardest test, out of several samples. However, the shaded area in Figure 3.12 corresponds to the sum of the absolute amounts of the differences in (2) and not to their squares.

```
 1  /* crack vigenere ciphers by statistical methods
 2     (C) Reinhard Wobst, Dresden (Germany) @(#) 30.Oct 22:57, 1996


 3     Usage: vigcrack distr_file <crypted_file


 4     The 'distr_file' must be generated by the program 'distr' from
 5     a typical plaintext:


 6     distr <plaintext >distr_file


 7     The file plaintext must have typical character frequencies.
 8     Not applicable for equally distributed plaintexts (gzip etc).


 9     Output: One proposed keyword, trust value (the higher, the
    better).
10     A trust value near 1 indicates insecure password detection.
11  */


12  #include <stdio.h>
13  #include <ctype.h>
14  #include <memory.h>


15  #define MAXPERIOD       64       /* max. key length */
16  #define MAXLEN          40960     /* max. portion of read source */
17  #define THRESH          0.1       /* "threshold factor for max.
    probability" */
18  #define PERC            0.01      /* 1% - kappa (coeff. of coincidence)
    */


19  main(argc, argv)
20    char *argv[];
21    {
22    unsigned char buf[MAXLEN], key[MAXPERIOD+1],
23                  *p;
24    register n, m;


25    int n0, c, off, indx, period, kappacnt, N, Np,
26        cnt[256];
```

Figure 3.13: Using *vigcrack* to break a Vigenère cipher.

```
27    double thresh, trust1, trust, min, delta, expkappa, Nd,
28           kappa[2*MAXPERIOD], patt[256], frequ[256];


29    FILE *fp;


30    if(argc != 2 || (fp = fopen(argv[1], "r")) == NULL)
31      {perror(argv[1]); exit(1);}


32    /* read distribution pattern */


33    expkappa = thresh = 0.;


34    for(n=0; n < 256; ++n)
35      {
36       if(fscanf(fp, "%d %le\n", &c, patt+n) != 2 || c != n ||
   patt[n] < 0.)
37            {
38             fprintf(stderr, "error in pattern file, line %d: %d %g\n",
39                    n, c, patt[n]);
40             exit(1);
41            }


42       expkappa += patt[n]*patt[n];


43       if(patt[n] > thresh)
44         {
45          indx = n; thresh = patt[n];
46         }
47      }


48    thresh *= THRESH;
49    printf("expected index of coincidence: %.2f%%\n", expkappa*100.);


50    /* read file probe */


51    N = fread(buf, 1, MAXLEN, stdin);
```

Figure 3.13: (*continued*)

```
52    if(N < 2*MAXPERIOD)
53      {
54       fprintf(stderr, "file too short: %d bytes\n", N);
55       exit(1);
56      }


57    Nd = n;


58    /* compute coincidence index */


59    for(period=1; period <= 2*MAXPERIOD; ++period)
60      {
61       kappacnt = 0;
62       for(n = Np = (N/period-1)*period; n--;)
63          kappacnt += buf[n] == buf[n+period];


64       kappa[period-1] = (double)kappacnt/Np;
65      }


66    /* look at frequency peaks */


67    period = -1;


68    for(min = expkappa-PERC; min > PERC; min-=PERC)
69      {
70       n0 = -1;
71       for(n=0; n < 2*MAXPERIOD; ++n)
72         {
73          if(kappa[n] < min) continue;
74          if(n0 < 0) {n0 = n+1; continue;}
75          else if((n+1)%n0) break;
76         }


77       if(n < 2*MAXPERIOD) continue;
78       period = n0; break;
79      }


80    if(period < 0)
```

Figure 3.13: (*continued*)

```
81        {
82         fprintf(stderr, "no period found!\n");
83         exit(1);
84        }


85     /* compute characters of key */


86     key[period] = '\0';
87     Np = (N/period-1)*period;
88     trust = 1.e+9;


89     for(off=period; off--;)
90        {
91     y   memset(cnt, 0, 256*sizeof(int));


92        /* compute distribution */


93        for(n = Np + off; n >= 0; n -= period) ++cnt[buf[n]];
94        for(n=256; n--;) frequ[n] = cnt[n]/Nd;


95        /* align distribution: get 1 char of key */


96        min = 257.;


97        for(m = 256; m--;)
98           {
99            if(frequ[indx^m] < thresh) continue;


100           delta = 0.;


101           for(n = 256; n--;)
102               delta += (frequ[n^m] -  patt[n])*(frequ[n^m] - patt[n]);


103           if(min > delta)
104              {
105               trust1 = min/delta;
```

Figure 3.13: (*continued*)

```
106              min = delta;
107              key[off] = m;
108            }
109          }
110        if(trust > trust1) trust = trust1;
111      }


112    /* print result */


113    printf("trust value: %.2f\n", trust);
114    printf("key dump (%d characters):\n", period);


115    for(n=0; n < period;)
116      {
117      c = key[n];


118      if(c == ' ')          printf("   ");
119      else if(c == '\n')  printf("\\n ");
120      else if(c == '\r\)  printf("\\r ");
121      else if(c == '\t')  printf("\\t ");
122      else if(isprint(c)) printf("%c  ", c);
123      else if(iscntrl(c)) printf("^%c ", c);
124      else                printf("%02x ", c);
125      if(!(++n%15)) putchar('\n');
126      }


127    printf("\n\nPROPOSED KEY: ");
128    for(p=key; *p != '\0\; ++p)
129      if(*p < ' ') printf("^%c", *p+'@');
130      else putchar(*p);
131    printf("\n");


132    return 0;
133    }
```

Figure 3.13: (*continued*)

texts, word processor files, etc.). Passwords can be up to 64 characters long
(this limit is totally arbitrary).

There's no universal cryptanalysis, not even for the Vigenère method. We
first need to know something about the statistical properties of the plaintext

expected: is it a natural language (German, English?); a programming language
(C, C++, Fortran?); a database; a word processor? To find answers to these
questions, we need pattern files, in which the characters are distributed approximately as we would expect from the plaintext. We use the simple program
distr found on our Web site, to analyze these files. This little program gives
us the relative frequencies of the characters in a file. We save the frequency
profile to a file.

- For a starter, *vigcrack* reads the file, computes the kappa, κ_P, of the
  plaintext expected (appears on the screen), and finds the largest relative
  frequency of a character (lines 30 through 47).

- In line 51, the program reads as much of the ciphertext as possible; the
  maximum is 40 Kbytes.

- Next, the program computes the kappa, κ_n, of the ciphertext shifted
  against itself for each of the 64 possible password lengths, n. It takes
  the result to compute the period duration rather pragmatically:

  - It first minimizes the kappa, κ_P, of the plaintext by one percentage
    point and analyzes to see whether those n with κ_n that exceed this
    threshold are all multiples of the smallest of these n:

    ```
    n, 2*n, 3*n, ...
    ```

  - If so, then *vigcrack* takes this n as a period.

  - Otherwise, it minimizes κ_P again by one percentage point and repeats
    the test.

  If it doesn't find a period, it terminates the cryptanalysis. However, experience has shown that this very sharp test succeeds on this kind of files
  that are usually long (lines 59 through 84).

- Now that the period is known, *vigcrack* can compute the relative frequencies of each of the ciphertext groups (lines 93 and 94).

- Next, the program computes the square deviation of the distribution found
  from the theoretical deviation for all possible 256 key characters. Since
  the deviation is computed in a triple nested loop (the outer loop traverses
  the period length), it requires a lot of computation time, which is the
  reason why it has a pretest built in: if the most frequent character of
  the plaintext transforms into a 'rare' character in the cipher, then the

key character is discarded right away, rather than being included when computing the deviation (line 99). 'Rare' means ten times rarer than expected (as specified by the THRESH constant in line 17). The ratio between the second smallest square deviation and the smallest deviation is called the 'trust level' in this program (just an imaginative word). The more this number deviates from 1, the securer the result.

- Finally, the results from lines 113 through 131 are output in readable form. It cannot be reasonably expected that all key characters are ASCII characters, so the key is shown as a 'dump': ASCII characters are shown as such; line break and tab characters are written with a backslash '\', like in C; and all other characters (including umlauts) are shown as hexadecimal numbers.

The program is astonishingly surefire. On the configuration mentioned above (133-MHz Pentium, PC-UNIX ESIX V.4.2), its computation times range between 150 ms and 600 ms (the latter on very long passwords of about 60 characters). It works on English and German, on *vigenere.c*—WordPerfect files encrypted onto themselves, on C programs—as long as the characters are not distributed equally. Try it.

As a sideline, you can also use *vigcrack* on a 'sophisticated' combination of transposition and subsequent Vigenère cipher. The substitution doesn't change anything in the text's distribution so that *vigcrack* reconstructs the password with the usual certainty. You can then break the transposition, for example, by looking at the frequencies of digrams.

You can see that combining several different methods doesn't always lead to benefits (and sometimes leads to even more insecurity!).

3.6.4 Compression = Compromise

The cryptanalytic programs introduced so far (except *Crack*) are rather simple while still working amazingly fast and secure. A closer look reveals that the theory behind these attacks is not particularly profound, but we can't generalize, of course. This section introduces a problem that's different in every respect: a cryptanalytic approach that totally does away with statistical analyses, and the program used is downright tricky, requiring rather long computation times. But you will find the result more interesting!

More specifically, I'm referring to the claim asserted in Section 2.2 that compression does *not* always increase the security (as opposed to the widely held

0.87 % '^D'	0.17 % '~'
0.86 % ' '	0.17 % '<253>'
0.84 % '^P'	0.17 % '<251>'
0.83 % '^C'	0.17 % '<234>'
0.80 % '^F'	0.17 % '<189>'
0.78 % '^B'	0.17 % '<183>'
0.78 % '4'	0.15 % '<249>'
0.72 % '^@'	0.14 % '<239>'
...	0.14 % '<236>'
	0.14 % '<219>'
0.18 % '<250>'	0.14 % '<219>'
0.18 % '<223>'	0.11 % '<174>'
0.18 % '<221>'	0.10 % '<255>'

Figure 3.14: Character frequencies in a compressed file.

opinion), though it does make cryptanalysis a bit harder. The illusion of more security comes from the fact that the character distribution curve is very flat in compressed files; there are almost no usable maximums and minimums (see Figure 3.14).

In contrast to natural language, however, compressed text obeys fixed rules—something we'll take full advantage of. We try to mount a ciphertext attack against Vigenère-encrypted compressed files, referring to *compress*, a program that once was widely used in the UNIX world.

But first, we have to deal a bit with the plaintext or, more specifically, with the format of files created by *compress*.

How Are Files Compressed?

Most people realize that language is not the shortest form in which we can express ourselves. Compression means that a piece of text is 'summarized' in a way that ensures no information is lost. More specifically, a program is used to convert a piece of text into a much shorter one, which becomes illegible in the process. Another program can be used to retrieve the original text from the compressed text at any given time. There is a large number of compression methods, where the effect (how much a file will shrink) depends on both the file contents and the method. The *compress* program implements a well-known and very effective method based on the **Ziv–Lempel algorithm**. *compress* used to be on every UNIX system, including FreeBSD. (*gzip*, which has become very popular lately, is based on the Deflate algorithm of *zip*; it cannot be used here—see Wikipedia entries on *gzip*.) It's extremely easy to use *compress*. The example below is from a UNIX session (the number in front of the month shows the file length in bytes).

```
$ ls -l vigc_crk.*
-rw-r--r--  1 wobst     other        5211 Nov  6 13:51 vigc_crk.c
$ compress -v vigc_crk.*
vigc_crk.c: Compression: 45.63% -- replaced by vigc_crk.c.Z
$ ls -l vigc_crk.*
-rw-r--r--  1 wobst     other        2833 Nov  6 13:51 vigc_crk.c.Z
$
```

How does this algorithm work? Most importantly, it replaces entire character strings by numbers, which makes the compressed product short. This replacement is done based on a table that stores character strings. At program start, the table has 257 entries, namely all 256 one-element character strings formed from all possible bytes, and an additional abortion code and, sometimes, an additional reset code (depending on the implementation). The table is expanded in every step as the uncompressed text is read. If a character string that has already been saved to the table is encountered in the text, then the algorithm outputs the number of that table entry in its place. This is roughly how the Ziv–Lempel algorithm works. If you are interested in the details, you'll find an exact description in [Welch].

A little trick helps to save even more space: initially, the table includes less than 512 entries, i.e., the numbers of entries can be described using 9-bit numbers. Once 256 9-bit words have been output, we can use 10-bit numbers; after another 512 steps, we can use 11-bit numbers, and so on, till 16-bit numbers are output. The program authors don't generally say what will happen once 16 bits have been exhausted (our example won't reach these spheres). This sort of output with variable word length is called the **adaptive Ziv–Lempel**

algorithm. *compress* places a header composed of these three unchanging bytes in front of this word sequence:

```
1f 9d 90
```

We will refer to the numbers output by *compress* as **compress words** in the following discussion.

Using the *vigc_crk* Program for a Ciphertext Attack

The *vigc_crk* program (see listing in Figure 3.15) uses essentially the fact *that a word written by compress in the nth step cannot be larger than* $256 + n$.(*)

As little as this may actually appear, it is surprisingly sufficient in practice. Yes, we even do without evaluation of the three fixed bytes at the beginning of the text for 'sporty reasons'. This is no kid's game, since a careful cryptographer would truncate these bytes anyway. In detail, we proceed as follows:

- We certainly can't determine the period length using the index of coincidence (see Section 3.6.1) due to the very flat distribution. We have to try the expected period lengths one after another (at this point, the program may still have considerable reserves).

- For every given period length, we now recover the key, proceeding character by character. Suppose we already know n characters. We try all 256 possible values for the $(n + 1)$th character. We store the current value for each period together with all characters collected so far. For example, this could look like this for period 5, $n = 3$ characters already known—'a', 'u', and 'f'—and using 'c' as the $(n + 1)$th character:

a	u	f	c	?	a	u	f	c	?	a	u	f	c	?	a
G	e	h	e	i	m	t	e	x	t	.	.	.	.	.	.

where "Geheimtext" means ciphertext.

We try to decrypt the ciphertext in the known positions, i.e., we XOR the characters shown one on top of the other. We use the resulting part of plaintext to check whether the relation marked with an asterisk (*) above is met in the checkable cases.

```
 1 /* crack vigenere ciphers of compressed files
 2    (C) Reinhard Wobst, Dresden (Germany) @(#) 7.Nov 00:44, 1996


 3    Usage: vigc_crk [max_keylength] <crypted_file
 4 */


 5 #include <stdio.h>
 6 #include <ctype.h>
 7 #include <memory.h>


 8 #define HEADER          3        /* # of bytes in compress-header
    */
 9 #define MAXPERIOD       64       /* max. key length */
10 #define MAXKEYS         64       /* max. # of stored keys */
11 #define MAXLEN          40960    /* max. portion of read source
    */


12 static void tree_search(), print_result();


13 static unsigned char buf[MAXLEN],        /* ciphertext */
14                      key[MAXPERIOD];     /* key field */
15 static N, maxperiod;
16 static tcnt=0;


17 static long bitoff[6], blenmsk[17] =
18   {
19   01, 01, 01, 01, 01, 01, 01, 01, 01,   /* dummy */
20   0x1ff, 0x3ff, 0x7ff, 0xfff, 0x1fff, 0x3fff, 0x7fff, 0xffff
21                                   /* indices 9...16 */
22   };


23 main(argc, argv)
24   char *argv[];
25   {
26   int period, n, blen;
27   long p2, sum;


28   if(argc != 2 || sscanf(argv[1], "%d", &maxperiod) != 1 ||
29       maxperiod < 1 || maxperiod > MAXPERIOD)
```

Figure 3.15: Using *vigc_crk.c* to break a Vigenère-encrypted compressed file.

```
30        maxperiod = MAXPERIOD;


31     printf("maximal keylength: %d bytes\n", maxperiod);


32     N = fread(buf, 1, MAXLEN, stdin);                    /* read
    file probe */


33     /* preliminary computation: bit offsets */


34     p2 = 256; blen = 9; sum = 0;


35     for(n = 0; n < 6; ++n)
36        {
37        bitoff[n] = (sum += blen*p2);
38        ++blen; p2 <<= 1;
39        }


40     /* compute possible keys */


41     for(period=1; period <= maxperiod; ++period)
42        {
43        if(N < 30*period)
44           {
45           fprintf(stderr,
46              "file too short(%d bytes) for period (%d) - search
    stopped.\n",
47                 N, period);
48           exit(1);
49           }


50        fprintf(stderr, " %2d\r", period); fflush(stderr);
51        tree_search(period, 0);
52        }


53     printf("%d recursive calls\n", tcnt);
54     return 0;
55     }
```

Figure 3.15: (*continued*)

```
56 /* ------------------------------------------- */
57 /* recursive tree search
58    input: key - key field
59          len - key length
60          knb - # of known bytes (starting with key[0])
61    print result if path through is found
62 */


63 static void tree_search(len, knb)
64   {
65   int val, k, off, blen, knb0, knb1, knb2;
66   long n, bits, bits0, cnt, cwd;
67   ++tcnt;


68   if(knb == len+1) {print_result(len); return;}        /*
   through */


69   knb0 = knb; while(knb0 >= len) knb0 -= len;
70   knb1 = knb-1; while(knb1 < 0) knb1 += len; while(knb1 >= len)
   knb1 -= len;
71   knb2 = knb-2; while(knb2 < 0) knb2 += len;


72   for(val = 0; val < 256; ++ val)        /* test all values for
   key byte */
73     {
74     if(knb < len) key[knb] = (val+'A') & 0xff; else val = 256;
75     if(!knb) {tree_search(len, 1); continue;}


76       for(n=knb; n < N; n += len)                   /* test val for
   all periods */
77         {
78         if(n < 4) continue;                      /* skip header + 2
   bytes */
79         bits = (n-HEADER) << 3;                    /* compute bit
   offset */
80         bits0 = 0; blen = 9; cnt = 256;


81         for(k = 0; k < 6; ++k)
82           {
83             if(bitoff[k] < bits)
```

Figure 3.15: (*continued*)

```
84                      {
85                        cnt += (1 << (blen++ - 1));
86                        bits0 = bitoff[k];
87                        continue;
88                      }
89                  else
90                      {
91                        cnt += (off = (bits-bits0)/blen);
92                        off = bits0 + (off+1)*blen;
93                        if(bits+8 < off) break;
94                          /* (compress-word not determined yet - test
     next period) */
95                        off = bits+8 - off;


96                        /* compose compress-word (from 2 or 3 bytes) */


97                        if(off+blen <= 16)
98                          {
99                          cwd = ((buf[n] ^ key[knb0]) << 8) |
100                               ((buf[n-1] ^ key[knb1]));
101                          cwd = (cwd >> (16-blen-off)) & blenmsk[blen];
102                          }
103                        else
104                          {
105                          if(n == 4 || (len >= 2 && knb < 2)) break;
106                                      /* next period */
107                          cwd = ((buf[n]    key[knb0]) << 16) |
108                               ((buf[n-1]   key[knb1]) << 8) |
109                               ((buf[n-2]   key[knb2]));
110                          cwd = (cwd >> (24-blen-off)) & blenmsk[blen];
111                          }


112                        if(cwd > cnt) goto next_val;              /* test
     rejected! */
113                        break;                /* next period */
114                      }
115                  }
116              }


117      /* all tests went through for this val, try next key byte
     */
118      tree_search(len, knb+1);
```

Figure 3.15: (*continued*)

```
119 next_val: ;
120      }
121    }


122 /* -------------------------------------------- */
123 /* print result */


124 static void print_result(period)
125    {
126    static unsigned char found_keys[MAXKEYS][MAXPERIOD];
127    static char *kd="key dump: ";
128    static found = 0, periods[MAXKEYS];
129    int n, m, c;


130    /* test if key is of form old_keyold_keyold_key... */


131    for(n=found; n--;)
132       if(!(period%periods[n]) &&
133          !memcmp(found_keys[n], key, periods[n]))
134          {
135          for(m = period/periods[n]; m--;)
136             if(memcmp(found_keys[n], key + m*periods[n],
   periods[n]))
137                break;


138          if(m < 0) return;
139          }


140    /* store key */


141    if(found < MAXKEYS)
142       {
143       memcpy(found_keys[found], key, period);
144       periods[found++] = period;
145       }


146    /* print */
```

Figure 3.15: (*continued*)

```
147    printf("period: %d, PROPOSED KEY: \"", period);


148    for(n=0; n < period; ++n)
149      {
150      c = key[n];
151      if(iscntrl(c)) printf("^%c", c+'@');
152      else putchar(c);
153      }


154    printf("\"\n%s", kd);


155    for(n=0; n < period;)
156      {
157      c = key[n];


158      if(c == ' ')         printf("   ");
159      else if(c == '\n')   printf("\\n ");
160      else if(c == '\r')   printf("\\r ");
161      else if(c == '\t')   printf("\\t ");
162      else if(isprint(c))  printf("%c  ", c);
163      else if(iscntrl(c))  printf("^%c ", c+'@');
164      else                 printf("%02x ", c);
165      if(!(++n&0xf))
166        {
167        putchar('\n');
168        for(m=strlen(kd); m--;) putchar(' ');
169        }
170      }


171    printf("\n\n");
172    }
```

Figure 3.15: (*continued*)

- If this relation for the character is met in all periods, then these first $n + 1$ characters could be the beginning of a valid password. We repeat the last step with all 256 possible $(n + 2)$th characters. (If n is sufficiently large—see below—we'd even have found a password.)

If the relation for the character is not met in at least one period, then we try our luck with the next $(n + 1)$th character.

If the relation was met for no $(n + 1)$th character in no period, then the nth character must have been wrong. We go back one step and increase the key character in the nth position by 1.

- Proceeding like this—always stepping forward and backward in the key—we try all possibilities until we have searched all branches in the tree (see Figure 2.2 and the accompanying text).

- If we are unsuccessful, we increase the period length by 1 and start the procedure all over again.

With a period length, p, we would have to try $256p$ keys in a brute-force attack. The relation (*) reduces this number to a tiny fraction, which will become tinier the longer the ciphertext (for, the more inequalities would then have to be met, i.e., the more dead ends there would be in the tree).

A 'great strategy': in detail, however, we'll have to grapple with some rather nasty problems. I'll use the following listing to explain some of them.

- Lines 34 through 39: We don't even think of the ciphertext as a byte sequence, but as a bit stream. These lines compute the numbers of those bits where the length of the *compress* words printed increases, and save them to the field *bitoff*. (Though we could write these numbers in a table right away, our approach requires only minimal computation time, and errors are easier to catch.)

- Line 63: The actual work is handled by the function *tree_search()*, which is invoked by *main()* once for each period length, and then invokes itself (i.e., recursive calls).

  Similarly to the known *knb* key character, it is responsible for determining the $(knb + 1)$th character. To this end, it looks up all periods to see whether adding the $(knb + 1)$th character would result in a *compress* word that hadn't been tested for yet:

  – If it does, then it computes the word and tests relation (*). This happens in lines 98 through 113 (a major 'bit shifting' job).

  – If it doesn't, then it skips the current period and continues testing in the next.

- If (*) is true in all testable cases, even after character number $knb + 1$ was added, then *tree_search()* calls itself with a *knb* value increased by

1 (line 119). This action corresponds to one step forward in the search tree. If (*) is false for a period, then the program jumps out of the period test loop (going to *next_val*; lines 113 through 120), and tests the next value. Once all 256 values have been processed, the function returns, which corresponds to one step backward in the search tree.

- If *tree_search()* can see from the period length values and the number of bytes already known that all test cases have been analyzed, then it considers the password found to be valid and prints it (line 68).

- There are several particularities about this action:

  - (*) cannot be tested for $knb = 0$, because every *compress* word is at least 9 bits long, and no such word is found in the partially decrypted text for a period length greater than 1 (line 75). Period length 1 is nevertheless dealt with!

  - Even if all key characters have already been fixed, there are *compress* words that haven't been tested for (*) yet: these are the words that reach beyond the period boundary. Therefore, we let *knb* run not only from 0 to *len* − 1, but to *len* + 1, and accordingly replace the *len* and *len* + 1 indices by 0 and 1. Lines 69 through 71 and 74 show that our programming has to be extremely careful.

  - Line 74 reveals a little trick: when searching for the next key character, we start with 'A' rather than '0', since we assume that passwords are composed mainly of letters. Though this little trick doesn't shorten the overall computation time, it helps to get to a correct password faster—even dramatically faster, depending on the tree structure.

- Finally, we have a look at the *print_result()* function, since it is not limited to printing the password. If 'abc' was used to Vigenère-encrypt a plaintext, then trivially enough it is also encrypted to 'abcabc', 'abcabcabc', etc. For this reason, *print_result()* stores up to 64 passwords and checks for 'multiples' of these words.

Doubtlessly the program can be greatly improved, though it is generally quite fast and reliable. No obvious problems occur with long files. On a UNIX-PC (133-MHz Pentium, ESIX V.4.2), *vigc_crk* found the correct solution from a compressed 260-Kbyte file encrypted with a 60-character password within 16 seconds:

```
$ vigc_crk <u1
maximal keylength: 64 bytes
period: 60, PROPOSED KEY:
"0123456789a123456789b123456789c123456789d123456789e123456789"
key dump: 0  1  2  3  4  5  6  7  8  9  a  1  2  3  4  5
          6  7  8  9  b  1  2  3  4  5  6  7  8  9  c  1
          2  3  4  5  6  7  8  9  d  1  2  3  4  5  6  7
          8  9  e  1  2  3  4  5  6  7  8  9
16980 recursive calls
$
```

In contrast, short files could cause problems. When using the program to test a 512-byte file, I observed the following computation times, depending on the password length (on the same Pentium computer).

Up to 5 characters long:	less than 1 second; unambiguous solution
6 characters:	1.8 seconds; 2926 function calls; unambiguous solution
7 characters:	9.4 seconds; 4643 function calls; unambiguous solution
8 characters:	1.5 seconds; 2795 function calls; unambiguous solution
9 characters:	8.6 seconds; 5646 function calls; unambiguous solution
10 characters:	8.3 seconds; 14 553 function calls; 16 passwords

Additional tests are necessary to find the correct password from the passwords proposed in the last example: whether or not the plaintext produced can be decompressed (which is sometimes possible even with 'wrong passwords'), whether or not the decompressed output is something meaningful, and so on. There are cases where *vigc_crk* in the form represented here won't be sufficient: when I encrypted the file with a 15-byte password, it took the program 25 minutes (and almost four million function calls) to come up with about 31 000 possible passwords on the screen (all of which obviously let you guess the correct password: 'abcdefghijklmno').

The program tends to get tangled up particularly with multiples of the period length. While searching it displays the period length currently assumed for controlling reasons. With the correct period length (and its multiples), it can be seen clearly how the search time increases: from 0.1 to 0.2 seconds to several seconds. With wrong assumptions about the period length, the dead ends in the search tree appear to be very short. Additional tests for greater search depth are missing. This is a point where the method could be significantly speeded up.

Conclusions

It is remarkable that the actual encryption method plays a role only in two expressions—see the '^' (XOR) character in lines 99, 100, and 107 through 109. There could be an addition corresponding to the Vigenère method in the classical sense instead. With true polyalphabetic methods, the set of substitutions possible could be limited, at least with long files. However, the program would then have to work more effectively, and it would be much more complex.

compress is not the only compression program around. *pkzip*, which is popular in the DOS world, also implements the Ziv–Lempel algorithm, among other things. Of course, the file format differs from that of *compress*. Nevertheless, the attack remains basically the same. The well-known Huffmann method, implemented in *pack* for UNIX, writes character frequencies to a header and subsequently appends a bit stream. *gzip* is a free and very effective program (available for UNIX and DOS) and is also based on a Ziv–Lempel algorithm. Each one of these methods requires a different approach.

You can see that, for the examples discussed in this section, we don't need any information about the plaintext, except that it was compressed with *compress*. We need to look at the text itself only if there are several possible passwords and we can't guess the right one, *and* if several passwords let us decompress the plaintext. Naturally, the code writer can select a different compression method and add cryptological elements to it, for example, 'disturbing' bits. A prerequisite is that the code writer knows exactly how a cryptanalyst would proceed against his method. This means that he would basically jump out of the frying pan into the fire.

Making a method appear more complicated by previously compressing things can sometimes have the opposite effect. As a sideline, compression also makes a brute-force search much easier. We will get back to this issue in Section 4.4.1.

After all, 'more complicated' doesn't always mean 'more secure'.

3.7 *fcrypt*: How Differential Cryptanalysis Works

The discussion in this section takes us back to *fcrypt*, the encryption method I mentioned at the end of Chapter 2, which is described in detail in [Wobfcrypt] (not to be confused with the faster *fcrypt* DES implementation). To cryptanalyze it, we will use a method totally different from those discussed so far, namely **differential cryptanalysis**. This method was first introduced by the Israeli mathematicians Biham and Shamir in 1990 [Bih.diff] and used for an attack against DES; we will discuss this issue in more detail in Section 4.4.2.

Though my *fcrypt* method should no longer be used for encryption, it is quite interesting for cryptanalysis. As mentioned in the previous section that dealt with compressed files, we won't worry about the probability theory as we mount our attack, because *fcrypt* is immune to statistical methods. We will reach our goal with a particularly simple type of differential cryptanalysis.

The *fcrypt* Method

How does *fcrypt* work? The basic idea is pretty simple: we divide the plaintext in blocks of 256 bytes each (appropriately padding the last block). We take each block and split it into 16 groups of 16 bytes each in a secret way. There are $256!/(16!)^2$ or approximately 10^{192} different ways (so we don't need to consider brute force from the outset). We encrypt each group separately by the following rule:

Replace each byte by the sum of the other 15 bytes of that group.

Let the plaintext bytes of a group be $p_1, \ldots, p_{16}$, then the formula for creating the ciphertext bytes, $c_1, \ldots, c_{16}$, is as follows:

$$
\begin{aligned}
c_1 &= p_2 + p_3 + \ldots + p_{16} &\pmod{256} \\
c_2 &= p_1 + p_3 + \ldots + p_{16} &\pmod{256} \\
&\ldots \\
c_{16} &= p_1 + p_2 + \ldots + p_{15} &\pmod{256}
\end{aligned}
$$

(The decryption is just as easy, but we are not interested in it here.) This method has a remarkable property: if the plaintext bytes are sufficiently random, we might be lucky enough to get equally distributed ciphertext bytes. Even sharp tests didn't show any more statistical dependencies between the ciphertext bytes. However, I found in the first design that the method has a conceptual weakness:

If two plaintexts differ only in one byte, then the ciphertexts (created with the same key) differ in 15 bytes. These 15 bytes all belong to the same group.

This is the reason why *fcrypt* writes the 256-byte plaintext blocks in a 16×16 matrix such that each row contains the elements of one group. (The order of the plaintext bytes written in the matrix is secret!) Once the encryption 'by rows' is complete, we analogously encrypt 'by columns'. This approach introduces yet another considerable improvement to the method's statistical properties, and makes it a bit more secure.

Attacking *fcrypt*

What happens with the improved *fcrypt* if two plaintexts differ in one byte only? You may come to think that the ciphertexts (again created with the same key) differ in all bytes, except for the bytes in positions within the matrix (in columns or rows) that coincide with the position of the changed byte. Let's look at an example: two plaintexts differ in the byte written in row 7, column 4. Writing '.' for changed bytes and '0' for unchanged bytes in the ciphertext, the ciphertext block (written as a matrix) we create would basically look like this:

```
...0............
...0............
...0............
...0............
...0............
...0............
0000000000000000
...0............
...0............
...0............
...0............
...0............
...0............
...0............
...0............
```

Don't forget, the ciphertext doesn't appear in rows in this matrix, since the way the characters are written in the matrix (and read from it) is secret. The only thing we can see is that 31 positions somewhere strewn across the text haven't changed, and we know that they've got to be in the same row or in the same column that the changed byte is in.

An attacker initially won't be able to do much with these 31 numbers. What I (incomprehensibly!) hadn't thought of back then was the following:

If we take an arbitrary plaintext, p_0, and build 17 plaintexts, p_i, that all differ only in one byte of p_0, then there must be at least two p_i in which the differing bytes are in the same row. We select two such texts, p_m and p_n, and encrypt them. Exactly 31 positions of every cipher will *not* differ from the encrypted text, p_0. For example, if we use '0' for the bytes where fcrypt(p_m) does not differ from fcrypt(p_0), and analogously use '1' for the bytes of p_n, things would look like this:

```
...0......1.....
...0......1.....
...0......1.....
...0......1.....
...0......1.....
...0......1.....
XXXXXXXXXXXXXXXX
...0......1.....
...0......1.....
...0......1.....
...0......1.....
...0......1.....
...0......1.....
...0......1.....
...0......1.....
```

The positions marked with 'X' haven't changed in the two ciphertexts. If we were an attacker with access to a ciphering device, we would consequently proceed as follows:

- We take plaintext p_0 and build 17 slightly modified plaintexts, p_i, as described above.

- We have all 18 texts encrypted with the same key and intercept the ciphertexts.

- For each cipher, fcrypt(p_i), we find the bytes that don't differ from fcrypt(p_0). These are always 31 positions. We call the set of all positions of these bytes the 'checkpoint set'.

- Two different checkpoint sets will generally have two common elements. But at least two sets have exactly 16 common elements. This means that we've recovered one row or one column of the secret matrix.

- Using a sufficiently large number of plaintexts and doing some puzzle work, it's relatively easy to recover the secret matrix.

The remarkable thing about this approach is that we haven't bothered about the plaintext *at all* in our cryptanalysis; we were only interested in the positions in which the two plaintexts *differ*. Moreover, we were not interested in the ciphertexts created, but again only in the positions where the bytes changed. In differential cryptanalysis, which will be discussed in detail in Section 4.4.2, you look at the differences of plaintexts or ciphertexts and additionally use probability theory. Well, *fcrypt* is a very simple example indeed.

But that's not all. In the form described so far, the *rfcrypt* plaintext-to-ciphertext mapping suggested by the key is linear. This means that, if we multiply the plaintext bytes by 3, then the ciphertext bytes will also be multiplied by 3; the same applies to additions (everything modulo 256, of course):

```
rfcrypt(n*P)   = n*rfcrypt(P)
rfcrypt(P₁±P₂) = rfcrypt(P₁) ± rfcrypt(P₂)
```

(P, P_1, P_2: plaintexts; n: natural number; multiplication and addition are done bytewise, modulo 256.)

Exploiting this linearity, we'll often be able to recover plaintexts that differ in one byte only from plaintexts that differ in many bytes: we have managed to make a transition from a chosen-plaintext attack to a plaintext attack. However, we need many blocks encrypted with the same key. But this is a security issue not directly related to the algorithm, and, as is well known, security issues are always violated.

Several Problems Remain Unsolved

Unfortunately, things are not as simple as that. The ciphertext created by *fcrypt* has excellent statistical properties provided that the plaintext contains 'a little chance', i.e., it isn't exactly composed of blanks. Since this can't be excluded in practice, I take a few countermeasures:

1. Before the first encryption, a secret key is added bytewise to the plaintext. In contrast, after the second encryption, a secret key is XORed with the result. Addition and XOR are 'incompatible'; it's not easy to get rid of this complication.

2. After each block, the key is modified in a relatively complicated way (depending on the ciphertext of the last block and a key that is not used otherwise).

Point 2 makes it hard to exploit more than the first ciphertext block. Otherwise, a sufficiently long plaintext (perhaps only 18 blocks long, i.e., 4.5 Kbytes) would already be the key to success. However, Point 1 turns *fcrypt* into a non-linear mapping, which means that we are back to having to rely on chosen plaintexts. (Adding or XORing a byte wouldn't change anything in our consideration as to what bytes will or won't change.) On the other hand, we could pick out plaintext blocks that differ little from the beginning of messages to eventually reveal the matrix. As far as the method is concerned, it would certainly be a fascinating and challenging task, but its actual benefit is doubtful.

As a sideline, thanks to the complications under Points 1 and 2, *fcrypt* acquires excellent statistical properties. I encrypted a sequence composed of ten million line break characters ('\n'); the ciphertext showed no cycle whatsoever and behaved like a sequence of very good random numbers in every respect. Also thanks to the two complications, a plaintext attack wouldn't be as easy as one might think. You can see that probability-theoretical statements have to be rated very carefully—if statistics can't be used for cryptanalysis, there are still plenty of other methods. *vigc_crk* from Section 3.6.4 is an impressive example.

Transpositions and Differential Cryptanalysis

Transpositions (see Section 2.2) are even easier to break if we use differential cryptanalysis rather than *fcrypt*. Pure transpositions are linear, regardless of whether they are bitwise or bytewise (with bitwise operations, we compute modulo 2, as usual; otherwise modulo 256). This means that a few plaintext blocks will do; we take them to form linear combinations (see Glossary) that differ only in one bit or byte. Since we can compute the corresponding cipher-texts as linear combinations[5] in the same way, we can see directly which bits or bytes differ there, thus revealing the transposition just as directly. Here, too, we need not know anything about the text's statistics; the only prerequisite is that a sufficient number of plaintext blocks are linearly independent (i.e., none of their linear combinations is zero). This prerequisite is very realistic.

Linear methods such as *fcrypt* (without the addition or XOR modification) and transpositions are rewarding candidates for differential cryptanalysis, since they can be mounted as plaintext attacks in cases like this. Generally, however, they require chosen-plaintext attacks, often even with extremely extensive plaintext, as we will see in Section 4.4 and Chapter 5.

---

[5]This is the simplest linear algebra, except on a finite field.

3.8 Bottom Line

If you've made it through this chapter, you learned a thing or two about crypt-analysis. You have seen that there are no limits to imagination in cryptanalysis (and you will learn more and unusual methods later on). In contrast to the subliminally suggested opinion that cryptanalysis depends only on the method, you know at least since Section 3.6.4 that the plaintext to be expected can also play a role.

There is no such thing as a general 'theory of cryptanalysis'. The cryptanalyst's principle is to exploit available vulnerabilities. This is somewhat chaotic from the outset. The *vigcrack* program discussed in Section 3.6.3, which includes the expected-plaintext spectrum in its considerations, has the only touch of universality in this chapter.

You can surely guess how to give an attacker a hard time: you'd have to combine or modify methods in unusual ways, use exotic plaintext (for example, one you created with your own compression method), and similar things. I intentionally write this in the subjunctive for two reasons:

- First, it could backfire—'improving' a good method almost always means correcting mistakes into it.

- Second, algorithms are used in mass-market products nowadays. There is no longer such a thing as 'individual variation', and attacking an algorithm is always rewarding. Something you could call 'new' would be a user-specific variation and combination of methods, but these methods would then have to be as secure as the original algorithm. And this is the very aspect in which the theoretical background is problematic.

But all complications a cryptanalyst has to deal with are gray theory, because practice still helps him often enough. For example, the radio communications of some US cell phones are encrypted using a 160-bit Vigenère key at the NSA's request. Do you have any idea how it is cracked? More about this sort of 'practice' in Section 6.7.

Chapter 4

Development Milestones: DES, RSA

You may have gained the impression so far in this book that though they have a very difficult task, cryptanalysts eventually have the upper hand over cryptographers. As long as commercial programs make do with simple XOR (i.e., the bitwise Vigenère method) or strapped-down Enigma machines, this impression is true. But there are much better encryption methods, and their best-known representative is the DES algorithm discussed in this chapter. Modern algorithms and implementations should be resistant to ciphering errors like those shown in Figure 3.1. At least plaintext attacks shouldn't have a chance.

Cryptanalyzing the methods discussed from this chapter onwards by use of a freely available program will be an absolute exception.

Discussions about security are always somewhat speculative; some methods can be judged only intuitively. The reason is the nature of the matter, and what's more, we only know about the results of *public* cryptological research.

Historically, we will jump from the end of World War II to the mid-1970s, when the emerging computer technology required good encryption algorithms and cryptology had to come out of its dark corner. It was the beginning of public research in this field. You will have a pretty good grasp of the significance of this change once you've read Section 4.3.1.

First, however, we need to define a few basic terms.

Cryptology Unlocked   Reinhard Wobst
© 2007 John Wiley & Sons, Ltd

4.1 Basic Terms

4.1.1 Bitwise Processing

The methods discussed so far were character-oriented, with the exception of the simple XOR ciphering, which we discussed together with the classic Vigenère method, since it is analogous to this method. When computers are available as ciphering machines, it is no longer meaningful to limit ourselves to bytewise encryption. Computers work with bits, bytes, and words (i.e., groups of bytes). It is much better to work with bits for statistical reasons alone: we know that 'e' is the most frequent character in the English and German languages. But is there also some usable evidence about the distribution of bit 3 of all bytes in a text?

However, the particularities of a text won't be lost when decomposing it into single bits. Think only of the headers in WordPerfect files, where many zero bytes occur successively. This fact alone could be fateful for a weak method.

4.1.2 Confusion and Diffusion

C. E. Shannon, the 'father of information theory', published two basic encryption principles back in 1949: confusion and diffusion. **Confusion** refers to covering up the relationship between the characters in the plaintext and in the ciphertext. **Diffusion** refers to distributing the information contained in the plaintext across the ciphertext. We can use the methods discussed so far to easily explain these two terms.

Both the Caesar cipher and the simple substitution are methods that use confusion. The relationship between a single ciphertext character and the corresponding plaintext character is intentionally blurred; it should be recoverable only by means of a key. Polyalphabetic methods, such as the Vigenère cipher or the Enigma, are other methods that work with confusion only, but the kind of 'blurring' additionally depends on the position in the text.

The *fcrypt* program discussed in Section 3.7 is a good example of diffusion. In this case, every ciphertext character depends on $256 - 31 = 225$ other plaintext characters, and it is impossible to identify these characters. This 'smudging' of information is the basic idea behind *fcrypt*. In addition, it uses confusion, namely when adding a secret key or XORing with a secret key. It wasn't pure chance that we had to fall back on the help of a new cryptanalytic method with *fcrypt*, and that linking diffusion and confusion prevented a plaintext attack (requiring a chosen-plaintext attack instead). Diffusion is the acting principle of transposition, which becomes easily attackable by differential cryptanalysis only.

A stronger term for smudging than described by diffusion is the **avalanche effect** for block ciphers (see also the following section): every bit of the ciphertext block should depend on every bit of the plaintext block *and* every bit of the key. The avalanche effect of *fcrypt* is insufficient: with a fixed key, only some ciphertext characters (i.e., ciphertext bits) depend on a changed plaintext bit. We will use this as a good peg for differential cryptanalysis.

A good block algorithm demands even more: if somebody swaps some plaintext bit or key bit, then every ciphertext bit should change with a probability of exactly 50 %. Differential cryptanalysis exploits any deviation from this value.

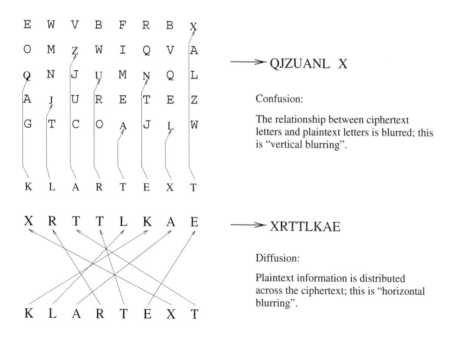

Figure 4.1: Confusion and diffusion.

4.1.3 Stream Ciphers and Block Ciphers

Most current methods work by either one of these two principles:

- Depending on some key, a 'wild' bit sequence is created and normally used as a one-time pad, i.e., it is XORed with the plaintext. The method's entire security lies in creating the bit sequence. For one thing, it has to behave statistically perfectly; second, it must never be possible to recover the entire sequence and certainly not the key from parts of it, or it would be vulnerable to plaintext attacks. These methods are called **stream ciphers**. As the name implies, they are well suited for online encryption of message channels. The one-time pad can even be computed in advance, if need be, to speed up the ciphering process in the event of message bursts.

  A stream cipher is also suitable for encrypting entire hard disks; more about this in Section 7.4. Thanks to the XOR method, the same program or device can be used both for decryption and encryption. This is another aspect that gives XOR an advantage over other methods, such as bytewise addition. RC4, A5, and SEAL are good examples of stream ciphers; see also Chapter 5.

- A method working by the second principle groups bits and encrypts them jointly as a group. This is called a **block cipher**, and used by methods like simple character substitutions, for example: they work with 8-bit blocks. Polyalphabetic methods use larger blocks (according to the period length). My *fcrypt* program (Section 3.7) works with 256-byte blocks. In general, the bits of a block are linked in a complicated way, as we will see in our discussion of the DES algorithm.

In fact, the best-known and most secure algorithms are block ciphers. They have several advantages over stream ciphers:

- Confusion and diffusion can be combined, while stream ciphers normally use confusion only. So block ciphers can be more secure.

- They must never reuse a key bit sequence (see Section 5.1.1; OFB Mode).

- Block ciphers can be faster than stream ciphers.

You will find more information on how block ciphers are implemented in Section 5.1. Examples are DES, IDEA, RC5, and AES.

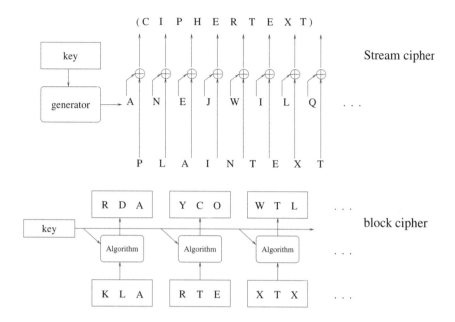

Figure 4.2: Block ciphers and stream ciphers.

Stream ciphers and block ciphers are also told apart by their purposes of use, which are not strictly defined. You can actually use a block cipher similarly to a stream cipher (e.g., in OFB mode; see Section 5.1.1).

We will look only at block algorithms in the following discussion.

4.1.4 Product Algorithms

Most modern block ciphers are **product algorithms**: simple, cryptologically relatively insecure steps are made one after the other. Such a step is called a **round**. You've already come across a seven-round product method. To really confuse you I'll describe it like this:

- The first round is a polyalphabetic substitution with period 26. A fixed substitution scheme is rotated cyclically by 1 in each position of the period, which results in 26 substitutions.

- The second round is similar, except 26 substitutions follow one another (and are rotated only then), which results in a period length of $26^2 = 676$.

- The third round has an analogous period of $26^3 = 17\,576$; 676 identical substitutions follow one another.

- The fourth round is a fixed substitution.

- The fifth round is the reversion of the third round, the sixth round is the reversion of the second round, and the seventh that of the first.

- Moreover, character pairs are flipped before the first round and after the seventh round, which corresponds to a particularly simple transposition. (More specifically, we have nine rounds here.)

You recognize the method? Right, it's the Enigma. You already know that the Enigma is more secure than any substitution. The third round by itself is statistically easy to break: we look only at 676 identical substitutions and derive the other rotor positions from them. But exactly because this third round is combined with the other rounds, the method obtains the large period length of $17\,576$, which is so critical for its security.

So, cleverly combining simple methods increases the security dramatically. That's similar to solving equations:

- Linear equations in the form $ax + b = c$ are trivially solvable.

- To solve quadratic equations, we know the formula from school.

- To solve cubic equations, things are getting a bit more complex: we need several formulas with some kind of case differentiation.

- The solution formulas for fourth-order equations are pretty complex, but still solvable.

- In contrast, it has been proven that there is no *generalized* solution formula (except perhaps using fundamental operations and roots) for fifth-order equations and higher. This is a quality leap. Of course, there are still solution formulas for special fifth-order equations, and it should also be possible to write the general solution in closed form if you also use special, novel functions.

These statements are easily transferable to the cryptanalysis of product algorithms: product formation does not always increase the security; on the other hand, there appear to be 'sound barriers'. For example, the most effective cryptanalyses against the DES algorithm get stuck after eight rounds when things get much harder.

Nobody can prove when and why this is so; all there is are indications (for example, making differential cryptanalysis harder; see Section 4.4.2). Using product formation can sometimes even lead to the opposite. We will discuss an interesting example in the next section.

4.1.5 The Image Is Gone, But We Still See It

The following example of a repeated image transformation was taken from [Crutch]. I wrote an identical program; it is included on our Web site (it's a program called *book/trans/trans.c*; see Appendix A.1) so that UNIX users can experience the same surprise on the screen I had. The program vividly demonstrates the effects of a product algorithm, and how one can get lulled into a false sense of security.

For the sake of simplicity, we take any square image (rectangular formats would also do the job, but they are more clumsy to handle). We take the image and do a simple transformation: the image is right-rotated by 90 degrees and distorted, as shown in Figure 4.3. We cut off the two protruding ends and paste them as follows.

We repeat this transformation until the image appears gray. I used the 'Escher knot' included as bitmap in the X Window system and changed it to 216×216 format. You can see the first few transformations in Figure 4.4.

The image will never turn uniformly gray, but it looks well mixed. Let's continue following up on the image series. We will see blurred rings that will disappear again after 24 rounds. Such diffuse appearances alternate with the

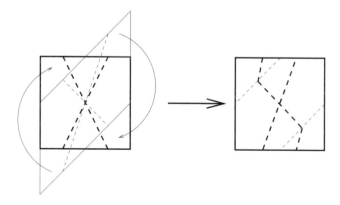

Figure 4.3: A simple image transformation.

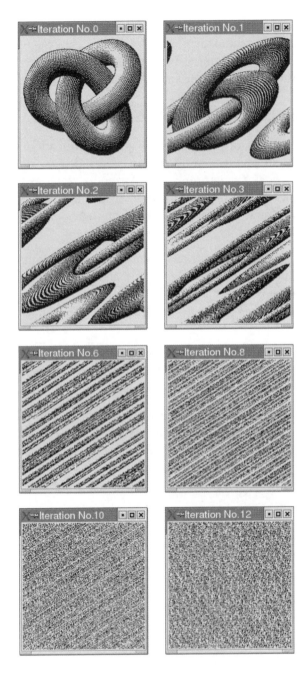

Figure 4.4: Transformation from Figure 4.3, applied to the Escher knot.

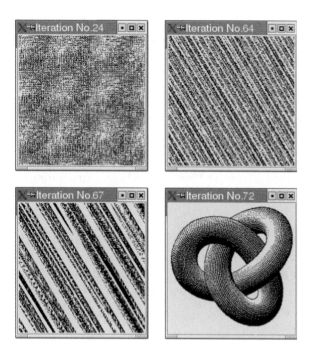

Figure 4.5: The transformation apparently produces the original image after 72 rounds.

'chaos' cyclically. However, you will see a clear structure again after 64 rounds, which becomes gradually clearer to eventually peak in the original image after 72 iterations to our surprise (Figure 4.5).

How is this possible? A closer look at this method reveals that there should actually be chaos—a totally mixed-up image—after 72 rounds. Well, almost totally mixed—except for a raster with 216×216 dots, on which the original image forms again! Mathematically, the image is gray almost everywhere, except in the raster dots, and exactly these dots are represented on the screen. The image is no longer there, but we still see it!

Only thanks to the special property of the human brain to be able to construct an image from adjacent dots can we recognize the risk that could arise out of the use of this type of encryption mechanism. If we had transformed the bits of a text, we would have been deceived by an illusion. When bits within a close neighborhood are strongly correlated (i.e., when only very few randomly depend on one another), then it might be possible to reconstruct the original text...

Of course, this is a malicious, fabricated example. Still, we should bear it in mind. Product algorithms can have excellent properties, but they have to be studied as critically as all others. Mixing things or creating plain 'chaos' is *never* a guarantee for security.

4.2   Feistel Networks

Many of the product algorithms currently used are so-called **Feistel networks**. They were described by Horst Feistel (IBM) and first published in the 1970s [Feistel]. The underlying principle is rather simple, only you don't initially see how it could be useful.

We split each block into two equal halves and denote the left half of the block as L_i and the right half as R_i in the ith round. Depending on a secret key, S, we can compute a function, $f_{S,i}$, that converts half blocks to half blocks. The actual encryption consists in that we swap the two half blocks, and XOR L_i and $f_{S,i}(R_i)$:

```
Li + 1 = Ri
Ri + 1 = Li ⊕ fs,i(Ri)(1)
```

This is graphically represented in Figure 4.6.

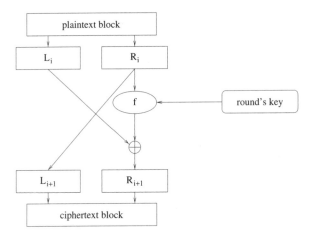

Figure 4.6: A round in a Feistel network.

Why is this principle so useful? Because if you know function $f_{S,i}$ for all i, you can decrypt! The reason is that you get the following from (1):

```
Lᵢ = Lᵢ ⊕ f_{S,i}(Rᵢ) ⊕ f_{S,i}(Rᵢ) = R_{i + 1} ⊕ f_{S,i}(Rᵢ)
```

And from this, you can already derive the decryption for an n-round method:

```
R_{n - 1} = Lₙ
L_{n - 1} = Rₙ ⊕ f_{S,n - 1}(R_{n - 1})
...
R₀ = L₁
L₀ = R₁ ⊕ f_{S,0}(R₀)
```

This means that the $f_{S,i}$ functions don't have to be reversible. To design encryption algorithms, we had to ensure that the key-dependent mapping, f_S, in

```
ciphertext = f_S(plaintext)
```

was reversible only by somebody who had key S. With the method discussed here, we only need to ensure that none of the $f_{S,i}$ functions can be computed without knowing S. This is a much simpler task; we can build 'wild' functions.

Of course, cryptanalysis has adjusted itself to this. But more about this later. Examples of Feistel networks are DES, FEAL, and Blowfish.

4.3 The DES Method

The **Data Encryption Standard (DES)** is probably the best analyzed cryptographic method. We owe many modern design principles and modern cryptanalysis to this algorithm.

Although the suspicion that the NSA might have built a backdoor into DES has never been cleared up, no practically usable vulnerability has been found in it until today to my knowledge. The insecurity of DES is due to the fact that brute-force attacks are technically possible nowadays.

Since DES has played a major role in history and still does today, we will have a closer look at this algorithm.

4.3.1   A Difficult Labor

In 1973, when it identified a need for a governmental standard to encrypt
sensitive information, the National Bureau of Standards (NBS; now named
NIST—National Institute of Standards and Technology) publicly solicited proposals for a secure cipher. Due to the development and proliferation of computer
technology and communication, a generally accessible and secure method was
needed. Though the response to this request showed a strong interest in such
a standard, none of the submissions turned out to be suitable [SchnCr, 12.1]!
This shows very impressively how much cryptology was an occult science
back then.

When a second request was issued in 1974, an IBM workgroup including Horst
Feistel (mentioned in Section 4.2) and the famous cryptanalyst Don Coppersmith, submitted a candidate that was deemed acceptable. It was a cipher based
on the Lucifer project conducted by IBM, after which at least one algorithm
was named.

Supposedly short of expert knowledge, the NBS involved the NSA in evaluating
the security of the algorithm. This involvement—so it was feared—wasn't
limited to evaluating the proposed standard. The suspicion was that the NSA
had shortened the key length from 128 bits, as suggested by IBM, to 56 bits.
IBM developers Tuchman and Meyer said that the NSA had not changed a
single bit in DES. But Coppersmith commented that the so-called S-boxes (see
Section 4.3.2) were all different when they came back from the NSA. This can
be interpreted in two ways: either the NSA built a backdoor into DES, or they
wanted to prevent IBM from building in a backdoor themselves.

In any event, the design criteria of the S-boxes—the security-relevant part
of DES—remained hidden. That gave rise to suspicion, of course. Tuchman
(who claimed the NSA had changed nothing) commented that these criteria had
been kept secret on NSA's request since members of the IBM team '... had
unknowingly rediscovered some of the best-guarded secrets their own [NSA's]
algorithms were based on' [SchnCr, 12.3].

In 1978, a committee that had access to publicly inaccessible documents inves-
tigated the matter and found that DES was completely safe and free from
weaknesses. However, the specific findings underlying this judgment remained
secret.

DES was approved as an official encryption standard at the end of 1976. The
method was authorized for use on 'unclassified' data rather than for the protection of highly confidential information. Of course, this gave rise to doubts

again, but it could have been just a formality—the reason for this restriction might have been its disclosure rather than DES itself.

It is also possible that DES is really very secure, and that it was published only due to misunderstandings between the NBS and the NSA, and the NSA had assumed that DES would be implemented in hardware only. Two reasons speak in favor of this assumption:

- DES was the first algorithm studied by the NSA that became publicly known. The next NSA standard algorithm—Skipjack (see Section 5.7.5)—typically remained secret for many years.

- The design criteria of the S-boxes were published after Biham and Shamir discovered the differential cryptanalysis in 1990. You can read about it in [SchnCr, 12.5]. The S-boxes obviously guarantee maximum resistance to differential cryptanalysis. This is no coincidence, since IBM and the NSA already knew this attack when DES had been in the design phase. Coppersmith wrote in 1992 that differential cryptanalysis would have become known as early as in 1977 had the said criteria been disclosed, and neither IBM nor the NSA wanted this to happen. After the design criteria were published, Shamir asked Coppersmith to admit that there were no attacks more effective against DES to his knowledge. Coppersmith didn't comment. Schneier [SchnCr, 12.4] states 'personal communication' as his source.

You can see that much remains in the realm of speculation. But there is one obvious fact: since the NSA had been aware of differential cryptanalysis long before DES was designed, by their own statements, it can be reasonably assumed that *the NSA was at least 20 years in the lead of public cryptological research in this field*. That was back then—it is likely to be much less today.

4.3.2 The Algorithm

We will discuss the DES method here only to the extent required to better understand it. If you are interested in the specific design of the S-boxes, you'll find all details in [SchnCr, 12.2], or visit the Web site—you will find two DES implementations.

The following characteristics show that DES is a product algorithm, especially a Feistel network:

- It uses a 56-bit key

- to transform 64 bits of plaintext blockwise into 64 bits of ciphertext, and vice versa,

- which is done in 16 key-dependent rounds, where

- a fixed, bitwise transposition (i.e., permutation) is done before the first round and after the last round. The final permutation is the reversion of the first one.

You know from Section 4.2 that the blocks in a Feistel network are split into equally large left and right halves, and that each round has the following form:

$$L_{i+1} = R_i$$
$$R_{i+1} = L_i \oplus f_{S,i}(R_i)$$

So DES looks roughly as shown in Figure 4.7.

How is the round- and key-dependent function, f, structured in DES?

- First, the 56-bit key is modified depending on the round, and 48 bits are selected.

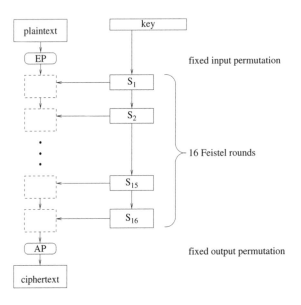

Figure 4.7: Rough scheme of DES.

- Next, the right block half, R_i, is expanded from 32 to 48 bits.
- The two 48-bit sequences are XORed.
- Eight so-called S-boxes are used to transform the result into a 32-bit sequence. (An **S-box** is a table with 4 rows and 16 columns.)
- The 32-bit sequence is permuted, i.e., its sequence is modified. This transformation is described by the P-box. (A **P-box** is simply a certain arrangement of the numbers 1 through 32.)

All that remains to be done is to take the 32-bit block created and XOR it with the left block half, L_i, to produce the right block half for the new round. Decryption works as in any Feistel network—similarly to encryption, except with the round keys in reverse order.

We will look at a few details in the following sections.

Input and Output Permutation

The permutations before the first round and after the last round serve no security purpose. Their use is probably due to the hardware because, in the mid-1970s, it wasn't easy to load 64-bit data into a register. Even 16-bit microprocessors weren't around.

Key Transformation

Before each round, we decompose the 56-bit key into two 28-bit halves and rotate each half by 1 bit or 2 bits, depending on the round number. 'Rotating' by 2 bits means that all bits walk two places to the left, while the two bits pushed out march back in to the two places on the right. Subsequently, we put the two halves together again to make a 56-bit key.

Based on a fixed scheme, we select 48 bits out of the 56 bits and permute them concurrently, i.e., we modify their arrangement. Since this process reduces the number of bits, it is called **compression permutation**.

On account of this (rigid) key transformation, different key bits are used in each round; every bit is used in about 14 rounds, but not distributed equally (which could be exploited in a special attack referred to as related-key cryptanalysis—see Section 4.4.3).

The Half-Block Expansion

A fixed transformation is used to expand the 32 bits of block half R_i to a 48-bit block. Some input bits occur twice in the output (every fourth bit and

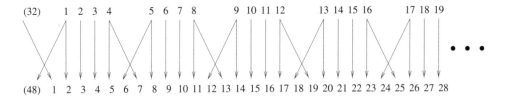

Figure 4.8: Expansion permutation in DES rounds.

the following). This is also a rigid transformation and, analogous to the above transformation, is called **expansion permutation**.

The cryptological background of the expansion permutation is the avalanche effect mentioned earlier: every changed key or plaintext bit should influence all ciphertext bits after as few rounds as possible. For this reason, it is better to reduce the key to 48 bits and expand half the block, rather than XORing half the block right way with a key reduced to 32 bits.

The expansion permutation is shown in Figure 4.8. We will look at it again in Section 4.4.2.

The S-Boxes

The result achieved from the last XOR operation is a 48-bit block. We take these 48 bits and divide them into eight groups of 6 bits each; then we transform each group using another S-box (short for 'substitution box'). These eight S-boxes represent the most critical part of DES. Each S-box is a table consisting of 4 rows and 16 columns, and it converts 6 input bits into 4 output bits. You can see an example of such an S-box in Figure 4.9.

We use this table as follows: if the input consists of six bits, $b_1, \ldots, b_6$, then the number determined from b_1 and b_6 (2 bits $=$ 4 values) denotes the table row, while the number determined from the four remaining bits ($b_2b_3b_4b_5$)

2	12	4	1	7	10	11	6	8	5	3	15	13	0	14	9
14	11	2	12	4	7	13	1	5	0	15	10	3	9	8	6
4	2	1	11	10	13	7	8	15	9	12	5	6	3	0	14
11	8	12	7	1	14	2	13	6	15	0	9	10	4	5	3

Figure 4.9: S-box number 5 of DES.

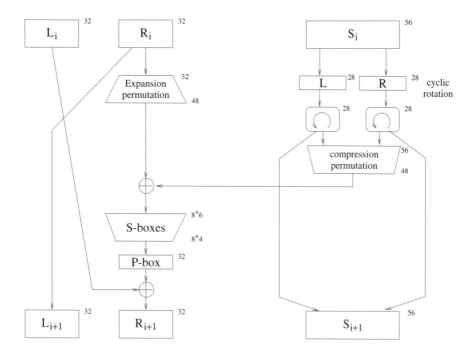

Figure 4.10: A DES round; the numbers to the right of the boxes denote the width in bits.

denotes the table column. The number in the corresponding row and column is the output value. You can see that 4 bits are sufficient for the output: the largest table entry is 15.

Figure 4.10 shows a schematic representation of a DES round.

Design Features of the Algorithm

If you think that the DES algorithm is rather complicated you are right, but it is extremely hardware-friendly: no step involved does additions or multiplications, everything is limited to bitwise shifts, fixed permutations (that are easy to implement in hardware), and XOR operations. There is a system behind the complexity:

- The expansion permutation and the P-box are responsible for diffusion (more specifically, for the avalanche effect).

- In addition, the P-boxes ensure that a plaintext bit traverses another S-box in each round on 'its way through the algorithm'.

- The S-boxes introduce non-linearity and resistance to differential cryptanalysis (see Sections 4.4.2 and 4.4.4).

- As the round keys are created, the rotation and the compression permutation ensure that any change to a key bit can influence all ciphertext bits after only a few rounds.

- As mentioned above, the input and output permutations are probably due to the hardware design; they are meaningless from the cryptology viewpoint.

You may reasonably assume that each detail of DES has its reason. Talented cryptologists have cut their teeth over it. For one thing, it is very difficult to design S-boxes such that the algorithm created is cryptologically secure. Rumors have it that when designing DES the developers put their computers to work on good S-boxes for months.

To an outsider who doesn't know the theory behind them, the S-boxes may seem to be merely an 'arbitrary' collection of numbers. No wonder many users were extremely doubtful about DES and suspected a backdoor. There might be one, or there might not. We'll be smarter in fifty years from now when the secret documents will likely have become accessible.

4.4   How Secure is DES?

We know that there is no exhaustive, officially known answer to this question. Only the types of attacks against DES are known:

- brute-force,
- differential, and
- linear cryptanalysis.

We will discuss all three types below and, on this occasion, learn a new cryptanalytic method.

4.4.1   Brute-Force Attack and the 'Deep Crack' Computer

The only practicable attack against DES is brute force, i.e., trying all 2^{56} possible keys. This is a huge number: the ciphertext has to be decrypted *and* tested for about 72 000 000 000 000 000 or 72 quadrillion keys to produce some meaningful plaintext.

A large number of estimates can be found in the literature as to which computers would be busy for how long and, mainly, how much a special computer that could handle this task within meaningful time would cost. In 1993, for example, the price of a machine used for a 3.5-hour brute-force attack was estimated to be one million dollars [SchnCr, 1.27; GarPGP, Chapter 3, 'DES Cracking']. Of course, this estimate is old hat: a mention at EUROCRYPT '98 reduced this hypothetical time to half an hour (at the same price). A 40-bit DES key could be found in 50 ms.

The RSA Challenge

Since nobody built such a machine, people fell back on available resources, namely idle times of computers on the Internet. To this end, RSA Data Security, Inc. started an initiative called **RSA Challenge**, where a brute-force attack was distributed over innumerable computers. When a DES key was found (the search took from January to June 1997), RSA started a second initiative, which was successful in February 1998 after only 39 days. In this initiative, about 22 000 users all over the world had put to work more than 50 000 processors (CPUs) for this task, and tried 85 % of all possible keys before the correct one came up. You can find all the details on the RSA Web site at www.rsa.com.

'What's all this good for?', you might ask. Brute force is nothing to write home about these days, and all this computer capacity wasted! Not really, for the following reasons:

- First, computers worked at this task only when they were not busy otherwise so that no valuable computation time was wasted. (In fact, most computers are jobless during the largest part of their lives.)

- Second, the initiative gained valuable experience with distributed processing in large projects.

- Third and most importantly, the initiative was able to demonstrate to outsiders, too, that DES is no longer as secure as its supporters claim. This, in turn, had an immediate impact on the US export policies for cryptographic products so that eventually all of us profited.

The initiative's first impact, however, looked more like a backfire: in February 1998, an expert declared before US Congress that, while this RSA Challenge was an impressive proof of how secure DES really was, it also showed that this approach was inappropriate for practical, unnoticed cryptanalysis. All this whereas the initiative's purpose was to show that a DES cracking machine could be built at all if only one had enough financial means.

How Deep Crack Was Born

The **Electronic Frontier Foundation** (**EFF**; www.eff.org) put an end to all speculation and doubts about potential DES cracking machines when it built such a machine. And not only that: the organization published a book [EFF] that describes how it's built, disclosing the chip design and the firmware, printing the listings in scanner-friendly layout, and on top of it all, writing 'Scan This Book!' on the cover (the paper version had its reason in a loophole in the US laws, prohibiting the export over the Internet and on electronic media, but leaving out print media). No doubt this book had been intended to move things, and it really did.

In view of the hardware friendliness of DES, it came as no surprise to experts that such a machine could be built, but the implementation of the idea called **Deep Crack** is interesting nevertheless.

The actual surprise was how inexpensively such a machine could be built: a team of about ten people worked on it for little over 18 months, and not even full-time. The required control software came from voluntary work in less than three weeks. Altogether, the costs for design and testing were roughly 80 000 dollars, and 130 000 dollars were spent on material. The 'total price' of the project is usually stated to amount to 250 000 dollars. Series production of the machine would naturally be much cheaper. Advanced Wireless Technologies (AWT), the developers of the special chips, have started offering the machine for sale. Much faster special computers are no utopia either. An article in the magazine *Information Week* [InfWeekDES] assumes somewhat higher costs and estimates a write-off time of three years for the computer. With the one-million-dollar machine mentioned above (which could find a key within half an hour), the costs would be approximately 20 dollars per DES key. In other words, this could mean, for example, that the DES encryption of an email (for instance using PEM in the current form, which is the PGP counterpart) would be worthwhile if the message were worth 20 dollars at most. But such values are usually underestimated. Cruel irony: the very same magazine had offered free annual subscription (worth 150 dollars) over a lengthy period of time to people who'd fill out a 'harmless' questionnaire. So much for how much people are really willing to pay for information.

The Innards of Deep Crack

What do the parameters of the machine look like? Its core is a 40-MHz special chip with 24 independent search units, each of which manages one DES decryption within 16 clock pulses. Sixty-four such chips are housed on one board. There are 12 such boards, plugged into scrapped Sun 4/470 computer boxes, and two such computers work in parallel. This results in a search speed of approximately 90 billion keys per second, i.e., roughly 2.5 times faster than the entire free capacity on the Internet that had been deployed for the RSA Challenge! Each chip tests concurrently for certain criteria to find whether or not the plaintext created is meaningful, and stops when hitting a success. A control computer running Linux or Windows95 is responsible for further evaluation, and continues the search, if need be. The average search time is 4.5 days.

Of particular interest is the test on plaintext, i.e., whether or not a tested key is the correct one. The hardware doesn't find the correct key itself; it rather tests, for example, to see whether the plaintext created consists only of characters from a certain subset, for instance ASCII characters. If this is true, then a second ciphertext block (consisting of 8 bytes) is decrypted instantly, and the test is repeated. If this test is positive, too, then the search unit stops and informs the controlling PC which, in turn, takes over and runs further analyses. This means that the hardware is not responsible for finding the correct key, but for singling out as many 'bad' keys as possible! As a sideline, the machine also works with texts encrypted in CBC mode (see Section 5.1.1). Remember this 'gradual filtering' of a data stream. National intelligence organizations also work by this principle. We will get back to this issue in Chapter 8.

Meanwhile, there is at least one official successor: Copacobana (www. copacobana.org), which stands for 'Cost-Optimized Parallel Code Breaker', is a machine with an FPGA basis developed jointly by the universities at Kiel and Cologne, Germany. You can buy it for 8980 euros (probably not in the supermarket though). It can handle about 48 billion DES ciphers per second, while consuming only 600 watts. This means that searching the full key space would take about nine days. It can also be used to break other block ciphers programmed in FPGA.

Other Considerations

It may be reasonably expected that DES cryptanalysis will be offered as a service unofficially. So you'll have to strike out the sentence that can still be

Figure 4.11: The Copacobana DES cracking machine (from www. copacobana.org, Gallery, with the courtesy of the authors).

read quite often: *DES is not secure against national intelligence agencies and large organizations.* I tend to rewrite this sentence to read:

Don't use DES for encryption if a party interested in the plaintext would be willing to pay a three-figure or four-figure sum. (The money amounts estimated really include all 'expenses'; otherwise we would have to speak of a two-figure sum.)

Nobody doubts that the key length of 56 bits instead of 128 bits came about at the request of the NSA. We can guess why. However, this corresponded to the situation in place 20 years ago! There is much speculation as to whether and how the NSA cracks DES. Rumors have it that the NSA disposes of devices the size of small suitcases that handle such tasks in a matter of seconds.

Alternative Methods

With everything said above, we could actually shelve the 'DES cryptanalysis' topic. A real vulnerability hasn't been found to this day; all that remains is brute force, and this is something that can be done today. All other attempts at breaking DES merely promoted the theory, and were practically unusable. But the theory is decisive in evaluating new algorithms with slightly larger key lengths, where brute force won't do the trick. For this reason, we'll stay with this topic a bit longer.

For example, it would be possible to use very large optical memories with values computed in advance. In the 'simplest' case, an attacker would have to determine and store all 72 quadrillion ciphertext blocks that can be formed by encrypting a frequent plaintext block. Such a plaintext block could contain eight zero bytes, for example (they certainly occur often enough, e.g., in WordPerfect; see Section 3.5). In this case, the plaintext block assumes the role of the probable word we know from earlier sections. This would be less simple technically: since the ciphertext blocks are 8 bytes long, we need about 850 million CDs to store them. When using 100-GB magnetic tapes, there would 'only' be about five million tapes. The media required can be further reduced when using new (e.g., holographic) methods. But things can be done far more thriftily.

Time–Memory Tradeoff

This is a brute-force method developed by Hellman in 1980 [Hell.troff; Denn83, 2.6.3] with a rather complicated name: it means that we aim at achieving a tradeoff between time and memory. This method is not limited to DES; it can be applied to any encryption method. This means that it is a general cryptanalytic method.

The *time–memory tradeoff* is a refinement of the plaintext attack mentioned earlier. The trick is to store just a small part of the possible ciphertexts of a frequent plaintext rather than all of them. The rest is computed during the analysis. In detail, this looks as follows:

Assume we have a frequent plaintext block, P, the corresponding ciphertext, C, and some (very easy to compute) function, R, which maps the 64-bit blocks to 56-bit blocks. For example, R can be a rule which says that the most significant bits should be truncated from the 8 bytes that form the 64-bit block. The following function is then defined for each 56-bit key, S:

```
f(S) = R(Es(P))
```

where $E_S(P)$ is the encryption of P with key S (E = encryption). We look for all keys, S, in such a way that

```
f(S) = R(C)
```

Such an S can already be the key searched, but not necessarily, since eight bits are not tested. To search for this S, we randomly select m keys, $S_1, \ldots, S_m$, and compute the following table with t columns and m rows for a given width, t:

$$S_1 \quad f(S_1) \quad f^2(S_1) = f(f(S_1)) \ldots f^t(S_1)$$

$$\ldots$$

$$S_m \quad f(S_m) \quad f^2(S_m) = f(f(S_m)) \ldots f^t(S_m)$$

This means that each element comes into being by removing eight bits from an encryption of the fixed plaintext, P, and serves as key for the element to the right of it. But we discard all intermediate results and store only the first and last columns.

Next, we look for our ciphertext, $R(C)$, reduced to 56 bits, in the right-hand column. If we find it there in row k, then $R(C)$ came into being by the encryption of P (and subsequent reduction, R), together with the key located in row k of the table, column $t - 1$. That's how we built the table in the first place. We can compute this key, since we had also stored S_k; we 'only' have to transform it $(t - 1)$ times by using function f.

If we don't find $R(C)$ in the last column, we might find it in the last column but one. If $R(C)$ is there, then $f(R(C))$ should occur in the last column of the table. So, let's look for $f(R(C))$ in the last column. Now we can understand why we built the table in exactly this way. Our approach is then relatively easy in theory:

- Compute the table and store only the first and last columns.

- Search for $R(C)$ in the last column.

- If not found, search for $f(R(C))$ in the last column.

- If not found there either, search for $f(f(R(C)))$ in the last column.

- $\ldots$

- If found, compute the table element in the same row, but one column earlier.

The method doesn't necessarily lead to the goal, but it's very likely that it does. It ranges roughly in the middle between the usual brute-force attack (which tests all possible keys) and the dictionary attack (which tests only probable keys). In practice, we would create many tables in parallel (since the left columns are random) and select the m and t values such that the probability of being successful is sufficiently large, despite potential 'false alarms': after all, we test only 56 out of 64 bits for a match with the ciphertext block. The method can be made faster; see [Denn83, 2.6.3].

We can see that, depending on what we select for m, t, and the number of tables, we can decide ourselves what we want to focus on: if we have plenty of storage available, we can select large m and number of tables; if our computer is very fast, we can work with large t; hence the name of the method.

Hellman suggested one million tables with 100 000 rows each computed in parallel and one million rounds per row (which could cover a maximum of 10^{17} or 100 quadrillion possible values—the key space has 'only' 72 quadrillion entries). All tables together would require a storage space of roughly one Tbyte (terabyte, corresponds to one trillion bytes, or one million Mbytes)—no problem considering the size of current jukeboxes. We would need a 1-Gbit memory, i.e., 125 Mbytes. All PCs will have this capacity before long. Moreover, we would have to deploy 10 000 DES chips. That's a bit harder. In 1980, Hellman estimated 4 µs as the time required per encryption for one DES chip. That would have resulted in a computation time of well over a year.

Of course, current chips are much faster. The VM007 chip produced by VLSI Technology in 1993 can handle 25 million encryptions per second (that's an improvement by a factor of 100 compared with 1980—when using a 32-MHz clock frequency—and by a factor of 10 compared with the *Deep Crack* chips). With a tenfold use of such DES chips (i.e., 100 000 units), the time–memory tradeoff could be done in half a workday. The time required for one-time table computation is twice that amount.

The encryption modes we will discuss in Section 5.1.1 allow us to push up the cost of this attack:

- The time remains the same when using the ECB mode and a known plaintext. The table can be computed once and for all, i.e., this time is negligible.

- In CBC mode, though the plaintext is known, it has to be deemed to be random. A new table has to be created for every attack so that the time involved triples.

- Things are similar with the CFB and OFB modes. However, we need to know *two* consecutive pairs of ciphertext blocks and plaintext blocks.

The purpose of the time–memory tradeoff is, however, to compute the table once (at high cost) for a specific plaintext block and then try to find the key in routine operations relatively quickly. In this constellation, encryption in CBC mode would be hindering.

My considerations about the computing time may even be underestimated. Who do you think can listen in on your DES code?

Visual Cryptanalysis

The heading of this section is the title of a paper published by the well-known cryptanalyst Adi Shamir, who introduced it at EUROCRYPT '98 [Shamvis]. The simplified basic statement might initially seem spooky: throw away all computer technology and buy yourself a high-resolution black-and-white negative film for aerial photographs, a photographic developer, and a black-color spray can. How on earth would anybody be able to run a cryptanalysis with that sort of material?

Photographic films are suitable for parallel processing. Though the development of a film takes ages compared with electronic bit processing, the film contains a very large number of bits. We divide the film's image field into as small areas as possible, which we will call 'dots' for the sake of simplicity. A black dot corresponds to value 1, a non-black dot to value 0. We use this mask to expose a second film, and the inverse bit pattern will form once we've developed this film—where there was a 1, there's a 0 now, and vice versa. Logically, we have executed a NOT operation, but processed all 'film bits' in parallel.

In contrast, if we superimpose two or more films so they are exactly congruent, and use this bunch to expose another film, then a dot on this (bottom) film will turn black, provided there are only non-black dots on top of it. This corresponds to the NOR operation, written as $\sim(a|b)$ expression in C. If we expose consecutively rather than concurrently, we do a NAND operation: $\sim(a\&b)$.

Yes, we could even do a XOR operation by utilizing the solarization effect. This effect says that, when exposing the negative for too long, it will no longer be blackened, but remain white after the development. To do a XOR operation, we prepare two films with dark gray instead of black dots and expose them long enough so that solarization occurs in the transparent places. In contrast, if there is only one gray dot on top, there is still blackening, while there will be almost no blackening in two superimposed gray dots. We may have to additionally use a photographic reducer; amateur photographers who develop their films themselves know such tricks. (This method was not described in the original paper.)

To make a long story short: we can use this method to 'compute' very complex logical expressions. Though the process is slow, we actually process an extraordinarily large amount of bits in each step. The hardware friendliness of DES is vulnerable to this algorithm. If we accommodate all possible keys on 64 sufficiently big films—one film for each bit position—we can create all possible ciphertexts from a known plaintext in many—but a finite number of—steps, again distributed across 64 films, i.e., one film for each bit position. We link these bit levels photographically such that a 0-bit can be only where the eavesdropped ciphertext was created. The position of this (theoretically) single 'light spot' reveals the DES key.

What do we need the spray can for? Well, we can use it to create random bits: we simply spray color on a film substrate such that about 50 % of the dots appear black. We can use the result to generate the 64 bit levels of all possible keys.

This is just a very simplified description of the method. Interested readers will find the details on our Web site or in the Proceedings of EUROCRYPT '98. However, knowledgeable people will already have identified several technical problems:

- Shamir assumes a technically feasible storage density of about one billion bits per square inch. This means that one bit would have an expansion of $1\,\mu$m, i.e., we'd need clean-room conditions for film processing.

- People knowledgeable about chip production processes know of the problems involved in trying to exactly adjust the films, mainly because of their deformation (due to humidity, temperature, and inhomogeneity). This means that we'd have to work with much smaller sections and many adjustment marks and many single steps per exposure.

- Superimposing the films so they can act as exposure masks isn't as easy as it may sound: the light source has to supply parallel beams, and the light diffusion has to remain very small. Interference effects must be expected.

- Photographic layers are not homogeneous; instead, they can have 'holes' (small areas without light-sensitive particles).

- The spraying process works (if at all) only provided the drops are not electrically charged; otherwise, there will be a minimum distance between drops.

It appears more realistic to use small squares with an edge length of 5 to $10\,\mu$m. Also, it is by no means clear whether or not the financial cost for a visual cryptanalysis will remain within the acceptable range at a reasonable execution time. Shamir himself thinks that visual cryptanalysis could be most effective when combined with suitable computer technology. Still, I felt the basic idea behind his method was so original that I shouldn't withhold it from you, just to show how many faces cryptanalysis can have. We will come across more surprising methods further on in this book.

As a sideline, you will find a remarkable note about a press release by CRAY of March 7, 1995 in the literature referenced above. The report praises the special production of a massive parallel bit-slice computer named CRAY-3/SSS—a joint development by CRAY and the NSA. This computer can compute one million bits in parallel, thus achieving a processing speed of up to 32 trillion bits per second—with a price/performance ratio unparalleled by any other computer. The press release says that 'the CRAY-3 system with the SSS option will be offered as an application-specific product'. Think for a moment of who cooperated in the development and you'll know how to interpret this sentence.

Compression = Compromise

Remember Section 3.6.4? It introduced the surprising fact that the prior compression of data doesn't increase security, even though the plaintext is statistically distributed pretty much equally.

This argument holds for DES, too, only the attack is not as simple as against the Vigenère method: you actually should have a DES crack machine in your den before you can think of putting the following idea to work.

The approach against DES looks like this: assume we have a sequence of ciphertext blocks, $C_1, C_2, C_3, \ldots$. They are the DES ciphers of a plaintext created by *compress* (where the three fixed bytes at the beginning should be truncated to make things a bit harder for the attacker). First, we will limit ourselves to encrypting in simple ECB mode.

Now we have our machine try all possible DES keys. We normally decrypt only C_1 tentatively. Since the resulting plaintext block, P_1, is 64 bits long, we can already test to see whether or not P_1 could have been created by *compress*—the equation (*) from Section 3.6.4 will probably be sufficient for an initial test.

In most cases, (*) will *not* be true for a pair of two 9-bit blocks from P_1. In about 0.8 % there is no contradiction. This figure is not hard to check: a plaintext block contains seven 9-bit blocks of this sort. There is a probability of about 0.5 that each of the 9-bit blocks is valid. With a plaintext created randomly (which can be plausibly assumed when using a wrong key), relation (*) will be true for all blocks with a probability of only 2^{-7}, i.e., 0.0078.

In these few cases, we decrypt C_2 tentatively and test for (*), and so on. We will gradually obtain all possible candidates for the plaintext, which we can test with other means, if need be. Practically, however, (*) will be sufficient for unambiguously revealing the key, since, with a random key, there is a probability of

$$2^{-(64*8)/9} = 2^{-56.8...}$$

that eight ciphertext blocks produce a plaintext that might have been created by *compress*. In reality, this probability may even be smaller. In fact, it is $(1 - 257/512)$ for the first 9-bit block, $(1 - 258/512)$ for the second, and generally $(N < 255)$ for N blocks:

$$\prod_{n=1}^{N}\left(1 - \frac{256\,n}{512}\right)$$

We can use a small program to quickly verify that this product will already be smaller than 2^{-56} for $N = 49$, i.e., due to

```
9*49 = 441 < 488 = 7*64
```

seven ciphertext blocks will suffice to recover the key on average. Though there is really no profound mathematics behind it, the result sounds sensational [Wobrump]:

People who compress their plaintext using *compress* before they DES-encrypt it facilitate a ciphertext attack that requires only seven ciphertexts!

The astonishing thing about this finding is that cryptanalysts don't even dare to dream of a ciphertext attack that might be generally mountable against DES. We can see from the procedure that even the encryption mode plays only a subordinate role. But the formulation is not entirely correct. It is not a pure ciphertext attack. Though we don't know the plaintext, we do have an important clue about it. This facilitates the test for correct decryption, as if we already had the plaintext. What you actually want to call this type of attack doesn't really matter. The important thing is to know that compression introduces an additional risk!

Unfortunately, there is *no* Deep Crack in *my* den so that I won't be able to tell you exactly how much computation time is involved. Anyway, I'm convinced that the method is almost as effective as brute force with a given plaintext, for, when 99.2 % of all plaintext blocks fall through the sieve, the search cost increases by less than 1 % compared with a plaintext attack. I find the following facts particularly remarkable:

- As mentioned earlier, it is a *ciphertext attack* against DES-encrypted code; the only one I know of.

- It doesn't matter which ciphering mode is used.

- The findings are by no means limited to *compress*; the process can be applied to any compression method for which an easily checkable test for plaintext, similar to (*) in Section 3.6.4, can be found.

- The process can also be generalized for each block algorithm with too short a key length. I find this alarming, particularly in view of the US export laws that dictate 40-bit keys (which would require six ciphertext blocks).

I don't want to warn of compression in general. If the encryption method is good and the key length sufficient, there won't be any risk. For example, though the PGP program discussed in Section 7.1 compresses a plaintext before it is encrypted, it uses the secure IDEA algorithm, and the 128-bit key length of that algorithm sends any idea about a brute-force attack into the realm of utopia.

4.4.2 Differential Cryptanalysis—The Role of the S-Boxes

No method that could crack DES faster than a brute-force attack was known until 1990. In that year, the Israeli mathematicians Elie Biham and Adi Shamir developed differential cryptanalysis and used it first against DES, then FEAL, LOKI, and other known algorithms. That was a breakthrough in cryptanalysis. We used this method in relatively simple form against *fcrypt* in Section 3.7, and want to have a closer look at it now.

DES Without S-Boxes

Imagine DES were designed without S-boxes. Assume that some fixed compression permutation from 48 to 32 bits were to take their place. We change some single bit in the plaintext block and follow up on the effect this change has on the ciphertext, as shown in Figures 4.7, 4.8, and 4.10.

The only effect permutations have is that the position of the changed bit changes within the block. Also, nothing sensational happens with the XOR operation on the key: though the change to a bit can change the direction, e.g., from 1 to 0 instead of from 0 to 1, the position remains the same. Expressed mathematically: if P and S are bit sequences with equal length (where S stands for 'key'), and if the ith bit (and only this one) is changed in P, then the ith bit (and only this one) will also change in $P \oplus S$.

Things get a bit more interesting when linking the left and right block halves in a Feistel network (Figure 4.7). Though a changed bit in L_i influences only one bit in R_{i+1}, if the bit is in R_i, it changes two bits in the result of that round: one bit each in L_{i+1} and in R_{i+1}. These two bits have the same positions in L_{i+1} and R_{i+1}, i.e., the change does not propagate further.

With the expansion permutation, such a change can 'split itself up'. Figure 4.8 shows that this happens with every fourth bit and each of the following ones. It depends on our fictitious compression permutation (which replaces the S-boxes) whether or not this change will have an impact on all bits after a sufficient number of rounds.

(Bear this method in mind. We will get back to it in Section 4.4.4 and see that it offers no security at all against a plaintext attack despite its complexity.)

Let's summarize: if we change a plaintext bit, then *which* of the ciphertext bits will also change does *not* depend on the key. The reason is that the key is simply XOR-embedded in the round.

DES With S-Boxes

We will now bring the S-boxes back into play. They alone make the interaction of the key with the algorithm complex; they are the non-linear element in DES (see Section 4.4.4) and increase the avalanche effect.

On account of the S-boxes, which of the ciphertext bits will be influenced by one single plaintext bit will now depend essentially on the key. Even more: *for certain well-defined sets of changed bits in block R_i you can observe a statistical dependence of the S-box output on the key.* This statement is inexact; we will formulate it in a more mathematically exact way in a moment.

We have been talking of 'changed bits' so far. In differential cryptanalysis, however, we speak of 'differences'. The meaning is virtually the same, except the first term is more expressive, while the second can be used to compute. If we XOR two equally long blocks, A and A':

```
ΔA = A ⊕ A'
```

then exactly the bits in which A and A' differ are set in ΔA. Since the XOR operation behaves like a usual addition of numbers (except in a number field that consists only of equally long sequences of zeros and ones), we also refer to ΔA as the **difference** of the two blocks.

We denote the transformation defined by the S-boxes as SB and the 48-bit key of an arbitrary DES round as S. For two 48-bit blocks, A and A', which emerged from the expansion permutation, DES computes the 32-bit blocks as

```
C = SB(A ⊕ S) and C' = SB(A' ⊕ S)
```

Again, we denote the difference, ΔC, as $\Delta C = C \oplus C'$. We can now formulate the above statement more exactly as follows:

The values of ΔC depend on the key, S, for certain values of ΔA.

How can this be exploited? There are values, ΔP, for plaintext pairs (P, P'), for which certain differences, ΔC, of the corresponding ciphertext pairs (C, C') have a higher probability than expected. Such pairs of differences are called **characteristics**, and plaintext pairs with the distinguished values for ΔP are called **right pairs**. However, the higher probability mentioned above will decrease as the number of rounds increases.

We can determine the characteristics for a 15-round DES. By encrypting a sufficiently large number of right pairs, we eventually obtain probable values for the key of the last round. This supplies us with 48 bits out of 56 key bits. We find the last 8 bits by brute force (don't take it too literally, though).

This sounds neat and practicable if it weren't for the problem that the chosen plaintext pairs will have to somehow be foisted on the code writer. But as we got worked up we forgot the specific data, for the catch is: 'we eventually obtain probable values for the key of the last round'. How do we determine such probable values? By comparing the frequencies, that's for sure. But we would have to acquire 2^{48} frequencies. They correspond to about 280 trillion numbers, for which we would need a 1000-Tbyte memory. For the time being, that's too much by six orders of magnitude.

Refinements and Results

Biham and Shamir looked at characteristics not for a 15-round DES, but for only 13 rounds. Reducing the number of rounds makes higher probabilities stand out more and leads to success faster. Moreover, they found a method that allowed them to test for the correct key immediately. This meant that the 2^{48} counters for frequencies were no longer required.

Of course, we are mainly interested in practically usable results. Figure 4.12 gives an overview that requires several comments.

The third column shows the number of plaintext blocks *not* especially chosen, but required for a plaintext attack. Only among that many plaintexts will we find a sufficiently large number of right pairs (i.e., pairs with the desired differences). The fourth column is surprising: many cases will also evaluate extremely few right pairs, you just don't know in advance which ones. For these cases, the computation cost (in this method called 'complexity') required is higher once we have found appropriate plaintexts, which shouldn't come as a surprise.

The first and last rows of the table are the most interesting. As mentioned in Section 4.1.4, product algorithms can sometimes have a 'sound barrier' for cryptanalysis to overcome. We can see clearly from the table that an 8-round DES is still vulnerable—we could imagine success in deliberately introducing 2^{14}, i.e., 16 384 plaintext pairs. In contrast, 2^{47} plaintexts correspond to a data

Number of rounds	Chosen plaintexts	Known plaintexts	Analyzed plaintexts	Complexity of analysis
8	2^{14}	2^{38}	4	2^9
9	2^{24}	2^{44}	2	2^{32}
10	2^{24}	2^{43}	2^{14}	2^{15}
11	2^{31}	2^{47}	2	2^{32}
12	2^{31}	2^{47}	2^{21}	2^{21}
13	2^{39}	2^{52}	2	2^{32}
14	2^{39}	2^{51}	2^{29}	2^{29}
15	2^{47}	2^{56}	2^7	2^{37}
16	2^{47}	2^{55}	2^{36}	2^{37}

Figure 4.12: Cost for differential cryptanalysis against DES.

set of more than one quadrillion bytes (more than one million Gbytes). That's beyond good and evil, not only technically. Nobody would ever encrypt such a huge data set with only one key. Certainly, no attacker could foist such a data set on a code writer ever.

So, if you read something along the lines of 'DES can be attacked by differential cryptanalysis', it is basically true but can't be realized in practice. Such claims create false doubts about this algorithm if they remain unqualified. DES is resistant to this attack thanks to the careful design of its S-boxes (and 16 rounds, a number certainly not chosen at will): attacking with differential cryptanalysis is not more effective than brute force even with known (but not chosen) plaintext.

This is why differential cryptanalysis enjoys a strong interest. In fact, it was the first method that worked faster than brute force. Moreover, the resources required might be reduced to practically interesting levels one day.

4.4.3 Attacking With Related Keys. Weak Keys

Thought experiments are always possible and interesting when they bring new findings. The attack with related keys was originally such a thought experiment.

The underlying idea is to look at the changed key bits rather than at the effect these changed plaintext bits have. For the time being, we are not interested in the practical realization of this attack. In theory, it looks like this: a known or perhaps chosen plaintext is encrypted with different keys, which naturally differ in certain bits. The key is reconstructed from the ciphertexts created.

Schneier [SchnCr, 12.4] writes that the irregular rotation of the DES keys in the single rounds frustrates this attack. The DES designers may also have thought about it! But 2^{17} (over 100 000) chosen plaintexts are sufficient for this type of attack if the key is rotated constantly. This was shown in a study by (well, guess who) Biham.

This attack was found to be independent of the number of rounds and, if feasible, effective also against Triple-DES, described in Section 5.2.1.

A related principle was exploited in a new type of attack that created a great stir. More about it in Section 4.4.5.

Weak Keys

As troubling as this heading may sound, the impact on the security of DES is negligible. The reason is that the algorithm is insecure to special keys. For

```
0000 000 0000 000 0000 000 0000 000    0000 000 0000 000 0000 000 0000 000

1111 111 1111 111 1111 111 1111 111    1111 111 1111 111 1111 111 1111 111

1111 111 1111 111 1111 111 1111 111    0000 000 0000 000 0000 000 0000 000

0000 000 0000 000 0000 000 0000 000    1111 111 1111 111 1111 111 1111 111
```

Figure 4.13: The four weak keys of DES (bitwise representation).

example, if all bits of the key are equal to 0, or perhaps all equal to 1, then rotating the half keys in each round changes nothing: all rounds use the same key. This holds true even if the left half key contains only 0-bits and the right one only 1-bits. Such keys are called **weak keys**.

Six pairs of DES keys consist of **semiweak keys**. The keys in such a pair are inverse to each other: things encrypted with one of the two keys are decrypted with the other key. Finally, there are 48 **possibly weak keys**: each one of them creates only four different round keys, which are each used four times in the 16 rounds.

If there were many weak keys, or if these four keys occurred frequently due to poor automatic key selection, then an attacker could test for them right away. This test could be an attack tailored to DES, for example, with equal round keys. If it is successful, the attacker has reached his goal; otherwise he has to try other methods.

Compared with the 72 trillion possible keys, these 64 potential risks are a ridiculously small number. In addition, it is very easy to discard such weak keys, or have weak keys automatically replaced by 'strong' ones.

In general, a key is said to be weak if the encryption method that uses it deteriorates into one that's easier to break. How about this for a blurred definition? Anyhow, when designing an algorithm, one also has to think of this type of attack. If an algorithm uses a fairly large percentage of weak keys in any respect, it earns a minus score.

4.4.4 Linear Cryptanalysis and Other Methods

Linear cryptanalysis was developed by Matsui in 1993; it is one of the most modern cryptanalytic methods. It seems that it will not be used to its full potential until a long time in the future.

When there is talk about linear cryptanalysis, you can often read: '... works with linear approximations, thus trying to recover the key', or perhaps: 'you XOR a few bits of the plaintext and the ciphertext, and there is a certain probability that you will obtain a value produced by XORing several key bits'. Such statements don't explain the background. A few theoretical comments will be useful before describing the method itself.

Linear Method

What does 'linear' mean? In algebra, a linear expression in variables, $x_1, \ldots, x_n$, has the form

```
a₁x₁ + a₂x₂ + ... + aₙxₙ
```

where a_i are constants. We are not looking at integer or real numbers in this discussion, but at the 'value range' of a bit, which is the numbers 0 and 1. We know that an addition is defined on this two-element number field, namely the XOR operation:

```
0 ⊕ 0 = 0
0 ⊕ 1 = 1 ⊕ 0 = 1
1 ⊕ 1 = 0
```

The commutative and associative laws hold, similarly to a normal addition:

```
a ⊕ b = b ⊕ a
a ⊕ (b ⊕ c) = (a ⊕ b) ⊕ c
```

There is also a multiplication in set {0,1} (or we couldn't call it a number field). This is the 'AND' link ('&' in C):

```
0*0 = 0*1 = 1*0 = 0
1*1 = 1
```

The usual arithmetic rules for real numbers apply here, too, though they may seem a bit odd. Analogous operations can be defined bitwise, e.g., on 64-bit blocks.

The term 'linear expression in bits $b_1, \ldots, b_n$' actually means nothing more than selecting a few bits (corresponding to a multiplication by constants, which can only be either 0 or 1) and subsequently XORing them.

Why are such linear expressions of interest? Because block methods that represent only linear expressions in the plaintext bits and key bits can be cracked by solving a system of equations. Assume the key consists of n bits, s_i. Further assume that the ciphertext bits, c_i, can be calculated from the plaintext bits p_i, as follows:

$$c_1 = p_{i_{11}} * s_{j_{11}} \oplus p_{i_{21}} * s_{j_{21}} \oplus \ldots$$

$$\ldots$$

$$c_m = p_{i_{1m}} * s_{j_{1m}} \oplus p_{i_{2m}} * s_{j_{2m}} \oplus \ldots$$

We know the indices, i_{kl} and j_{kl}, and if we additionally know p_i, then this is a linear system of equations in the key bits, s_i, except that it uses unusual arithmetic operations. Of course, 'knowing p_i' means that we carry out a plaintext attack. This is very effective: if the block length is N, and k is large enough so that $kN \geq n$ (where n is the key length) holds, then knowing k different plaintext blocks might suffice to recover the key.

We can see that linear methods are very sensitive to plaintext analysis. The Vigenère cipher is a trivial example of linear methods, but for cryptanalyzing them, we don't need that much theory, while still being able to mount successful ciphertext attacks.

The DES algorithm without S-boxes (but with a fixed compression permutation instead) discussed in Section 4.4.2 is more interesting. It is not too hard to derive from Figures 4.7 and 4.9 that each output bit can be represented as a XOR of plaintext bits and key bits. The indices of all these bits, i.e., their positions in the plaintext block or in the key, are known—that's the most important thing. One single known plaintext block may be enough for us to compute the key!

Now the comment that the S-boxes introduce a 'non-linear element' to DES is easier to understand. They are really decisive for the method's security.

Linear Cryptanalysis on DES

Schneier [SchnCr, 12.4] writes about linear cryptanalysis: 'This attack uses linear approximations to describe the function of a block cipher'. We know what linear mapping on the number field with the elements 0 and 1 is, but how can a linear approximation be defined where only two distances, 0 and 1, are possible? The meaning is taken from the theory of probability. For example, if we know there is a 90 % probability that the following equations hold between the key bits, s_i, the bits of the plaintext block, p_i, and the bits of the ciphertext block, c_i:

$$s_2 \oplus p_{15} \oplus s_6 \oplus p_7 = c_2 \oplus p_5 \oplus c_7$$
$$s_2 \oplus p_8 \oplus s_6 \qquad\quad = c_5 \oplus c_6$$

then, knowing p_i and c_i, we can recover the two key bits, s_2 and s_6, with equal probability for a statistically sufficient number of plaintexts almost for sure.

In general, when mounting a linear cryptanalysis, you exploit the fact that there is a linear relationship (which the attacker has to find) with a probability *other* than 50 %. This is a deviation from 'pure randomness' and can give clues on the key bits. In our example, once we have studied a sufficient number of plaintext–ciphertext pairs, we will have revealed the values for key bits that tend to occur preferentially (only with a probability of exactly 50 % we can't).

How does this look specifically with DES? First, we will only look at one DES round and omit the input and output permutations for the sake of simplicity (since they only cause more typing and don't change anything in the study itself).

S-box number 5 seems to offer the best vulnerability. That's the reason why this box was chosen for Figure 4.9. The thing is that, among the 64 possible inputs (corresponding to 6 bits), the second input bit equals the sum (i.e., the XOR) of the four output bits in only 12 cases—we would expect 32 cases. Shamir discovered this back in 1985, but wasn't able to exploit it.

The second input bit of S-box number 5 came into being by XORing bit s_{26} of the round's key with bit 26 of the expanded right half block which, in turn, was formed from bit r_{17} of the unexpanded half block. Due to the subsequent P-box permutation, the four output bits of the S-box land in positions 3, 8, 14, and 25. These are four bits in the functional value $f_{S,1}(R_1)$ in equation (1), Section 4.2. We can compute this functional value from the ciphertext:

$$f_{S,1}(R_1) = R_2 \oplus L_1$$

Denoting the four bits in the functional value as $c_3, c_8, \ldots$, then the equation

$$r_{17} \oplus c_3 \oplus c_8 \oplus c_{14} \oplus c_{25} = s_{26}$$

holds with a probability of 3/16. For a one-round DES (which isn't used), we can recover bit s_{26} of the round's key (which doesn't help much yet). To this end, we look at as many plaintext–ciphertext pairs as may be necessary to detect whether the right-hand side is equal to 0 or equal to 1 in about 3 out of 16 cases.

We proceed similarly with the 16-round DES, however, there won't be any more probabilities that deviate as significantly from 50 % as in the previous example. This is one of the reasons why a product algorithm with many rounds is normally more secure than one with few rounds or even just one. So, against DES, we have to work with minimum deviations from the 50 % probability.

Consequently, it won't come as too big a surprise to learn that, with linear cryptanalysis in the form described, 2^{47} known plaintexts are required to recover the key. So many items of input data are required for cryptanalysis. Though we are dealing with *known* plaintexts here, in contrast to differential cryptanalysis that uses *chosen* plaintexts (compare the second and third columns in Figure 4.12!), the result is merely one bit of the last round's key. A trick can help us recover another bit: we study the decryption, which is identical to the encryption except for the sequence of the keys. The key of the last round in the decryption is the first key in the encryption, and the 26 bits in the keys of the two rounds correspond to different bits in the original key.

But recovering two key bits by analyzing 1000 terabytes of text is nothing to write home about.

For the 14 rounds from 2 through 15, however, there is a better linear approach. We have to guess the 12 input bits of S-box number 5 in the first and last rounds, i.e., we have to run 2^{12} or 4096 linear cryptanalyses in parallel and then pick out the most probable among them. We obtain 13 bits, together with s_{26}, and this number will double to 26 bits if we apply the trick mentioned above—additionally studying the decryption instead of the encryption. To resolve the remaining 30 bits, we have to once more fall back on brute force (which corresponds to about one billion possibilities).

Results and More Methods

If we use linear cryptanalysis, we need 2^{43} *known* plaintexts to break a complete 16-round DES. That's 16 times less than the *chosen* plaintexts required in differential cryptanalysis, and even 4096 times $(2^{55}/2^{43})$ less than the *known* plaintexts needed in differential cryptanalysis. It is currently the most effective attack against DES. And how does all this look in practice?

The data volume to be analyzed is only 70 terabytes. This means that, if somebody sends DES-encrypted data (of course, assuming that the same key is used) over a 34-Mbit/s line, then an attacker needs to listen in on the communication for the better part of half a year. Subsequently, the attacker (similarly to what Matsui did in 1994) puts twelve HP-9735 workstations (which correspond roughly to very fast Pentium Pro computers for this purpose) to work and will retrieve the key within another 50 days.

You can see that even the time–memory tradeoff discussed in Section 4.4.1 has more chances, let alone hardware-based brute force (using *Deep Crack*).

In contrast to time–memory tradeoff and 'direct' brute force, however, the methods mentioned here can be expanded, which makes them more interesting. In 1994, Hellman and Langford introduced an attack against an 8-round DES using so-called **differential linear cryptanalysis**. With only 512 chosen plaintexts, this attack recovers ten key bits with a probability of 80 %—which increases to a 95 % probability with 768 chosen plaintexts. The computing power it required was amazing: a Sun-4 workstation, which is a rather slow computer by today's standards, took only 10 seconds. Our Web site includes a description of this method.

4.4.5 DFA and the Chip Crackers

There's actually only one important conclusion we can draw from the last few sections: no practicable attack against the DES *algorithm* has become known in public cryptological research. On the other hand, cryptanalysts also try to attack the *use* of DES. This book is not about spying out keys through vulnerabilities in an operating system or in an application. Another approach targeted to revealing DES keys hidden in chip cards has much more to do with cryptanalysis and is currently making headlines.

Biham's DFA Method

An article titled 'Hot chip cards leak code' appeared in *Computerzeitung* [CZ96] at the end of October 1996. The article referred to chip cards that do a

DES encryption. The key is said to be unreadable and built into hardware—the chips are referred to as **tamperproof**. However, heat, microwaves, ionizing radiation, and similar things can be applied to 'flip' some bits in internal registers. In contrast to attacks using related keys, this attack uses 'related keys of rounds'. Plausible probability-theoretical assumptions have it that this allows an attacker to reveal stored DES keys. To this end, the same plaintext is used over and over again to encrypt it by means of round's keys disturbed differently every time.

This method was first used by Boneh, Demillo, and Lipton (Bellcore) against RSA (Section 4.5.3), but not published. Only an article by Markoff in the *New York Times* of September 26, 1996, documented it. Again, the famed cryptanalysts Biham and Shamir emerged, claiming that the method can be transferred to complex block algorithms. They launched an attack against DES, in which 200 created ciphertexts were sufficient. Most interestingly, it is not necessary to know the plaintext. There's more to it—even the structure of *unknown* Feistel algorithms could allegedly be recovered in this way!

Biham calls this cryptanalysis **differential fault analysis (DFA)**. But it is still very new; I put a rough description of the method in a file on our Web site. I found the reference on Biham's homepage on the Internet. This topic had been fiercely discussed; visit `http://cryptome.org` and, searching for 'DFA', have a look around.

The chip card manufacturers naturally claimed that there was no way of purposefully influencing the key bits. Would you say otherwise in their place?

For one thing, what we learn from this attack are the unusual ideas cryptanalysts come forth with, and the many different things one has to think of when developing an algorithm. But if you think this was bad it will get worse.

A Sensational Improvement by Anderson and Kuhn

Anderson and Kuhn (article on the Web site) said the chip card manufacturers are not totally wrong. In reality, both the keys and the encryption program are stored in the same EEPROM. A randomly flipped bit normally influences the program, and what you get after exposure to radiation is just garbage rather than a slightly modified ciphertext—if anything at all will come out.

The authors thought that one should rather attack the *program code*. Pay-TV pirates have recently started using similar techniques, including techniques that interrupt the power supply to the chips for fractions of a microsecond, or, for example, send four 20-MHz pulses instead of a 5-MHz clock frequency. The effect is that though the program counter in the microprocessor jumps forward, the corresponding command is executed either faultily or not at all. By selecting a suitable point in time and a suitable interference, the attacker can select a command to be skipped purposefully. The attack hadn't been used for cryptanalysis to that date. That's where Anderson's idea came in.

In particular, an attacker can suppress the XOR of a byte in a round's key in the last or next to the last DES round. He encrypts an arbitrary plaintext with the properly working card and once more with the suppressed command. He then compares the two ciphertexts created to find clues on key bits, similarly to differential cryptanalysis. (However, this analysis is clearly less costly than the one by Biham and Shamir.) On average, five key bits result per ciphertext, and 40 key bits result after eight faulty encryptions. The last 16 bits are resolved by brute force. This means that *ten ciphering operations are sufficient to reveal the DES key in a chip card, without destroying the card.*

This attack is not theoretical at all, since Anderson and Kuhn virtually mounted it on a chip produced in series. It is indeed possible that a modified terminal would reveal keys by the dozen from cards inserted without the customers ever finding out. The effect would be as dangerous as breaking the algorithm itself. The Triple-DES introduced in Section 5.2.1 and a large number of other methods offer no protection against this sort of sneaky attack. The protection must come from the hardware.

No details were published out of consideration for the card manufacturer, to ensure that both the manufacturer and the bank customers can adjust to the situation. Such ideas are not totally new to card manufacturers, and they do undertake countermeasures; see [Koch.DFA].

Anderson's 'Parity Attack' Against Chip Cards and Memories

When things are bad they tend to get worse: Anderson [AndDES] found a much simpler way to recover DES keys in chip cards. Most people have come to think that the NSA pushed for reducing the DES key length from 128 to 56 bits. This corresponds to 8 bytes of 7 bits each; the 8th bit of each of these bytes can be used for parity check. (Nobody speaks of byte parity anymore today. But bear in mind when DES was developed.)

As a cruel irony, it is this very parity, which is often required still today, that Anderson exploited. It is known where in an EEPROM the internal key is stored—usually in the lowest address. It is astonishingly simple to open such a chip (also described by the author in [AndKuhn.tamp], since insiders have known this for a long time) and to localize the corresponding bits. Only reading the bits is not that simple.

But that's no problem. You can use simple means to *set* an EEPROM bit from the outside. You won't need an expensive UV laser for it. Two micro needles and an 18-V pulse over 10 ms will do and are much cheaper. Anderson suggests the following method: Set the lowest key bit to 1. If the chip complains about a parity error, then it should have been 0; otherwise 1 was correct. Next, set the second bit to 1. Depending on the previous result and the current parity displayed, you will get this bit, and so on. Once he has read the key, the attacker might burn another chip card himself to this key and use it to cause considerable damage.

That's cryptanalysis at the lowest level and independent of the ciphering method! You may reasonably assume that there are plenty of code cards out there on which this attack works.

This attack is also of interest against bank computers. In his article [AndDES], Anderson mentions a security module produced at the end of the 1980s that held twelve DES keys in memory. Every few years, the internal battery had to be replaced. The power went off as soon as a maintenance engineer opened the device, and the memory cells were deleted. With a fresh battery in place, the bank people stored the keys safely again.

However, memories (SRAMs and DRAMs) tend to 'burn in' bits after years. This is analogous to a picture tube: if you display the same block of letters in the same position over many months, then the internal coating of the picture tube will change at that place, and the letters will become indistinctly readable if the screen is equally gray (that's the main reason why we use screen savers). Similarly, a memory cell has an indefinite ('gray') state after voltage was fed, unless its content has been exactly the same over several years—then this content is preferred. Together with parity check, this allows an intruder to even attack Triple-DES (Section 5.2.1) using a 112-bit key. Anderson doesn't speculate in this respect; he actually studied a bank computer and recommends banks to observe the following:

1. have your maintenance engineers supervised during their work; and

2. thoroughly destroy the memory modules when scrapping computers.

The Chip Crackers

Though we've moved rather far away from mathematical cryptanalysis and landed on its 'physical' counterpart, the way that the two methods can be merged together seemed interesting enough for me to mention it. We will come across tamperproof chips several more times in this book, e.g., in GSM cell phones (the D- and E-networks in Germany), digital signatures, and the Clipper chip (Section 6.4). Even if you have only the slightest interest in this field, you should skim through the fascinating article by Anderson and Kuhn [AndKuhn.tamp] on the Web site. It will give you a rough idea of the guile involved in reading chips, which makes the trick used by pay-TV pirates look harmless; appropriate labs can reconstruct the design of an 80386 microprocessor within two weeks—that corresponds to several 100 000 transistor functions! Among other things, the authors explain in their article how nuclear weapons are protected; we will get back to this issue in Section 6.2.

4.4.6   Bottom Line

We have discussed DES in more detail than any other algorithm in this book. This corresponds to its historical significance. If you compare Chapter 3 with what you've read so far in this chapter, you will clearly see the difference between modern and classic cryptology. The specification of DES—the first time ever a good algorithm was published for the world to study—drove the theory forward by a quantum leap, particularly the theory of cryptanalysis. Five thousand years from now, an 'expert' might explain this big jump forward by the landing of aliens. We know better.

We can identify a new, interesting tendency for the years to come: differential linear cryptanalysis, differential higher-order cryptanalysis, progress in attacking with related keys—things might look really exciting.

From the perspective of the theory currently known, DES is remarkably good. Why should the NSA *not* have built in a backdoor? It is currently impossible to answer this question. It might really be true that the publication of DES was actually based on a misunderstanding between NIST and NSA.

Such a large number of talented cryptanalysts have cut their teeth on DES during the past twenty years or so that I personally don't believe in a simple backdoor. The weakness of DES is its key length. With 64-bit keys, brute force gets much more costly, but the end of the 56-bit era has already come. It may be reasonably assumed that many national intelligence organizations have DES crack machines. Nevertheless, DES has been confirmed as a secure standard by NIST repeatedly every five years. Schneier [SchnCr] wrote in 1996, 'Guess what will happen in 1998'.

Schneier was wrong in this respect. Already at the beginning of 1997, the NIST had begun searching for a DES successor, which turned out to be the **Advanced Encryption Standard** (**AES**). Meanwhile, this process was completed successfully. You will learn more about it in Section 5.5.

What we should take home from these lessons is that nobody should send valuable DES-encrypted information over the Internet, never ever again. And it's not necessary. There are DES variants, such as Triple-DES or DES with key-dependent S-boxes, that appear to be secure. Better yet, use more secure algorithms. We will get back to this issue in Chapter 5.

4.5 Asymmetric (Public-Key) Methods

DES was confirmed as a standard at the end of 1976 and, as you know, brought about a radical change to cryptology. In that same year, another path-breaking event occurred in this field: Diffie and Hellman introduced the first asymmetric encryption method ever at a conference, while Merkle submitted his work on the same topic at the same time. These methods introduced a new quality to the field: they widely solve the problem of key distribution. But before we can study this problem, we need to look at some more theory. Once you've understood some important basic terms and the practical uses, we will discuss three specific examples.

4.5.1 Symmetric and Asymmetric Methods

So far in this book we have discussed only **symmetric methods**: the receiver decrypts each message with the same key that the sender used to encrypt it. Notice that the symmetry refers to the keys rather than to the methods themselves: with a few exceptions (e.g., one-time pad, ROT13, stream ciphers), the encryption algorithm is different from the decryption algorithm. Encryption and decryption differ even in the Caesar and Vigenère ciphers: an amount (modulo 26) is added to each character during the encryption and subtracted during the decryption. More specifically, though they work with one key, symmetric methods almost always use two methods.

Asymmetric methods (also called *public-key methods*) also use two methods (which can be identical), but they always use two keys. One of them is the **private key**, and its algorithm is referred to as the *decryption algorithm*; the other key is the **public key**, and its algorithm is the *encryption algorithm*. This still looks pretty much symmetric. But the decisive point is:

The private key cannot[1] be derived from the public key.

In contrast, the reverse may easily hold. This is the actual asymmetry. It makes the following procedure possible, where the names used start making more sense.

We create a private key and a public key. We give the public key to somebody without having to fear that the security of the private key may be compromised. We don't show the private key to anybody. Everybody can now encrypt a message with *our* public key and send it to us; only we as the owners of the private key can read it. So we actually make public keys public to *receive* messages rather than to *send* them!

This means that asymmetric methods have to guarantee cryptological security in two ways: they must guarantee (i) that the plaintext cannot be derived from the ciphertext (encrypted with the public key); and (ii) that nobody can derive the private key from the public key. Again, this is meant in the sense of cryptology, i.e., they should prevent these things against available algorithms and justifiable cost and time.

There is a twofold reward in return: in addition to the security gained, there is a key that *cannot* be compromised since it is not secret. The real secret—the private key—never has to leave the owner's computer. That's a cute thing indeed. A practicable and more secure asymmetric algorithm would presumably drive symmetric algorithms quickly into a corner. Some magazine articles actually give you the impression that the golden times have already dawned.

Unfortunately, however, there are huge drawbacks. Only very few principles for secure and practicable algorithms are known to date. These algorithms are extremely slow and vulnerable to chosen-ciphertext attacks, which is critical when used for digital signatures (see Sections 4.5.3 and 6.3.3). This is why *asymmetric methods are currently used only to exchange session keys, but not to encrypt messages. Session keys are secret keys for symmetric methods.*

We will have a closer look at this use in the following section.

---

[1] 'Not' is meant in the cryptologic sense, i.e., you cannot derive it with the known means within a practically feasible time.

4.5.2   Exchanging Keys With and Without a Public Key

Exchanging Keys Without an Asymmetric Method

If you exchange encrypted messages with someone on a permanent or regular basis, you can often do without an asymmetric method. Asymmetric methods may only mean additional work. The installation of additional software, such as PGP, and the training required can quickly cost a company a couple of hundred dollars. Moreover, additional risks cannot be totally excluded; see Section 4.5.6.

So, if you exchange encrypted emails with your converser and the only thing you have to look out for is protection against *one* cunning competitor, just call your converser up and tell him the password on the phone. The competitor would have to both intercept your emails (which is doable) and listen in on your phone conversations (you really think he does?). If you wouldn't put it past him, send the key by regular mail. All right, he could have bribed the mailman if he knows your tactics. In that case, try to send half the key by mail (perhaps in several portions) and tell your converser the other half on the phone. Who on earth can monitor postal *and* phone traffic concurrently (well, guess who can)?

If you use three or four different distribution channels for the 'parts' of your key, a normal adversary won't stand a chance (let's define the other adversaries as 'abnormal'). Of course, you mustn't distribute a 64-bit key in four portions of 16 bits each (the broken magic amulet is only good for fairy-tale movies), for, in the unlikely event that somebody intercepts three key parts, then brute force will become a kid's game for them (as opposed to the magic amulet!). A better idea is to represent your 64-bit key as the sum of four 64-bit numbers, three of which are random. This way you can rest assured that an eavesdropper won't have a chance, unless he actually possesses all key parts. This is presumably the most reliable practical method for secure message exchange.

If you don't trust anybody other than your converser, why not make a trip, hand him the key over personally, and subsequently enjoy a short vacation?

There won't be many occasions for you to go through this procedure, though. Agree on a 'key encryption key' (KEK) with your converser that must never be compromised. For each message, you create a new separate **session key** (using a cryptologically good computer program; see Section 5.1.4) and use it to encrypt the message. You use the KEK to encrypt the session key and send it along with the message. This careful approach ensures that no single key is ever used to encrypt large amounts of data, thus significantly improving

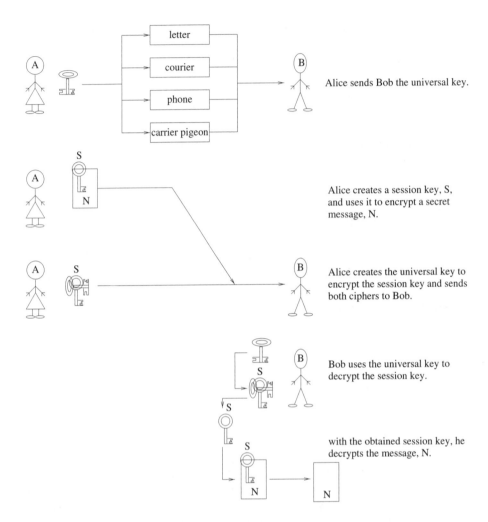

Figure 4.14: Distributing a secret key more securely.

the security. This is presumably the way people always work in critical areas. And it is the reason why a theoretically possible plaintext attack will become practically doable if it can make do with a few Mbytes of plaintext.

There's nothing new to all of this. The work regulations for the Enigma corresponded to it years ago! You probably remember Section 2.5.2: a universal key—the so-called 'ground setting'—was transmitted over cryptologically secure channels (in the code book); the radio operators set the message key themselves and encrypted it with the day key. The German cryptologists were well aware of the fact that a ciphertext attack would have been possible otherwise. In practice, however, operators worked under stress and inadvertently passed the ball to the adversary by selecting bad message keys (naturally other weaknesses of the Enigma played a role, too).

For the sake of completeness, I should mention that there is yet another possibility to distribute keys securely: through so-called centralized *key servers*. A universal key known only to the legitimate users is used to distribute a session key at one of these users' request. A good example is the so-called *wide-mouth frog protocol* described in Section 6.1.1.

Exchanging Keys With Asymmetric Methods

The method of distributing key parts separately, as described above, can become cumbersome and slow if you have to exchange encrypted messages with many conversers. It can also become costly, for example, if your converser happens to work in New Zealand; or it can become unnerving if your Japanese business partner writes English much better than he speaks it.

Things look much simpler when using asymmetric methods: everybody who wants to receive encrypted messages creates a corresponding key pair and publishes their public keys. To send an encrypted message (even without previously announcing it) to a 'key owner', we can use a similar approach:

1. We get the receiver's public key.
2. We create a random session key.
3. We use this session key and a *symmetric method* to encrypt the message; then we use the receiver's public key and an *asymmetric method* to encrypt the session key.
4. We send both ciphers to the receiver.
5. The receiver is the only one who can recover the session key, since he, and only he, knows the private key.
6. The receiver can decrypt the message using the session key and the symmetric method (Figure 4.15).

(As a sideline, the description of such an approach is called *cryptographic protocol*. Chapter 6 is entirely dedicated to this topic.) We generally speak of **hybrid methods**, because they use both symmetric and asymmetric algorithms.

Nothing can go wrong any more! In fact, a plaintext attack against the asymmetric method is not doable, since random session keys are encrypted (it would

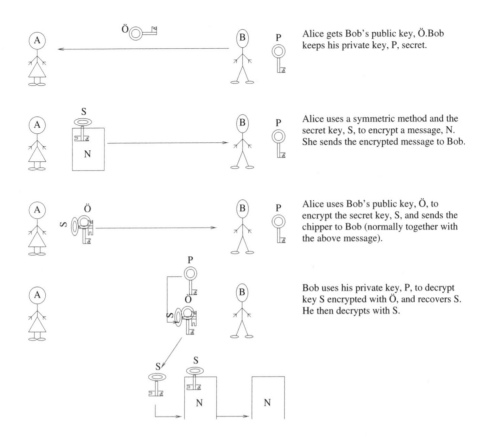

Alice gets Bob's public key, Ö. Bob keeps his private key, P, secret.

Alice uses a symmetric method and the secret key, S, to encrypt a message, N. She sends the encrypted message to Bob.

Alice uses Bob's public key, Ö, to encrypt the secret key, S, and sends the chipper to Bob (normally together with the above message).

Bob uses his private key, P, to decrypt key S encrypted with Ö, and recovers S. He then decrypts with S.

Figure 4.15: Hybrid method for transmitting encrypted messages.

be too hard to memorize them). The low speed of the asymmetric method is negligible thanks to the relatively short session keys (8 to 16 bytes). Or is there a drawback after all?

There is, and we will recognize it when looking closer at Point 1 above. What makes us so sure the public key we got really belongs to the person we think it does? Fraudulent maneuvering is possible, indeed, and we will discuss it below.

The Man in the Middle

As is customary in cryptology, we will call the 'good conversers' Alice and Bob, and call Mallory the 'malicious attacker'.[2]

---

[2]For the sake of simplicity, Mallory sometimes assumes the role of Eve, the eavesdropper, in this book.

Alice wants to transmit encrypted messages to Bob and sends him an email: 'Please mail me your public key.' Bob receives the mail and sends Alice the key. Alice gets the key, sends the encrypted message, and Bob can actually read it—without doubt a message from Alice, or so he thinks. In reality, however, Mallory, the intruder, listened in on everything. He is the administrator of the firewall computer, bribed by the competition, through which all emails flow in Alice's company. How did he do it?

First, Mallory read Alice's request to Bob to send her the public key. Then Mallory intercepted Bob's reply, i.e., Bob's public key. In its place, however, he sent his *own* public key to Alice. From then on, he could decrypt and read every mail from Alice to Bob, and then re-encrypt the session key with Bob's public key and send it to Bob. It is not difficult at all to have a computer program handle this procedure.

This attack is known as the **man-in-the-middle attack**. Mallory sits virtually in the middle of the line, pretending toward both conversers to be the respective other one.

The Interlock Protocol

There are several possibilities to prevent this attack. An easy-to-implement method that does without a trustworthy third party called **interlock protocol** was invented by Rivest and Shamir in 1984. When using this protocol, Alice and Bob have to send each other messages that allow each one of them to recognize that a message clearly originates from the other one. The protocol works like this:

1. Alice and Bob send each other their public keys. Like before, Mallory could use his own keys.

2. Alice encrypts an individual, but not too confidential, message with the public key she obtained (which might be Bob's or Mallory's). From this message, however, she sends only a part that cannot be decrypted to Bob. If the asymmetric method used is a block algorithm, then she could, for instance, send only the left half of each block. Or she sends only the bits or bytes in uneven positions within the message. Or she uses the CBC mode and leaves the initialization vector (will be explained in Section 5.1.1) out.

3. *After* he receives the first part, Bob proceeds similarly: he sends Alice a part of an encrypted message that cannot be decrypted.

4. Alice sends the second part of her message.

5. Bob puts the two parts of Alice's message together and decrypts it, using his private key.

6. If everything is correct, Bob sends the second part to Alice. Alice puts the two parts together and decrypts the message (Figure 4.16).

Since Alice's first message part cannot be decrypted, Mallory cannot 're-encrypt' it with his own or Bob's key. He would have to forward invented messages pretending to Bob that they came from Alice. This shouldn't be possible after this prerequisite; how Alice achieves it is not part of the protocol.

But why is Step 3 included in the protocol even if only Alice wants to send a message to Bob? Wouldn't it be sufficient for Alice to decompose her message into two parts? No, because Mallory could 'collect' the two halves and proceed as usual. Only the trick that both parties send parts that cannot be decrypted *alternately* and then complete these parts *alternately* makes the protocol secure. Moreover, both parties can discover a fraud and don't have to talk about it via email. For, Mallory could also have tampered with this email. Pretty clever.

The only downside is the prerequisite that Alice and Bob have to recognize that the messages received 'come doubtlessly from the converser'. While this is easy in personal contact, it is hard to automate. This point can become a problem when computers want to communicate securely among themselves and automatically over the interlock protocol.

Distribution of Public Keys

You can see that the sore point in using asymmetric methods is the distribution of public keys, as long as the methods themselves are secure, of course. The interlock protocol introduced above is a clever method, for instance, to exchange public keys individually and exclusively on the Internet. A public key can also be reliably checked over the phone—it's not easy to fake another person's voice *and* diction. But that means there will be additional cost with every new contact. It would be nice to have a way to publish the public key securely. We could publish it in a daily paper, but the costs of ads and handling newspapers are not ideal. We would like to use one single communication medium, e.g., the Internet.

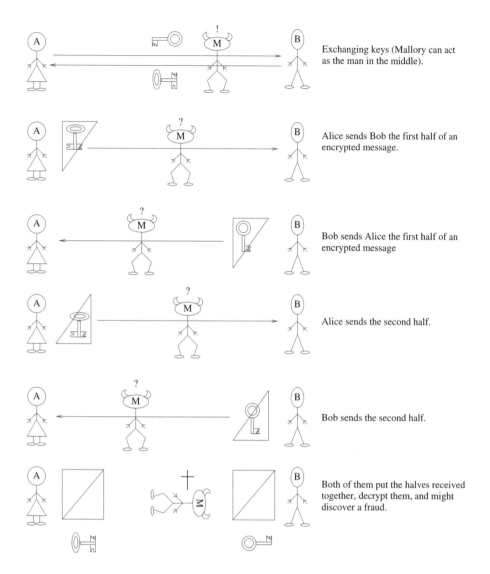

Exchanging keys (Mallory can act as the man in the middle).

Alice sends Bob the first half of an encrypted message.

Bob sends Alice the first half of an encrypted message

Alice sends the second half.

Bob sends the second half.

Both of them put the halves received together, decrypt them, and might discover a fraud.

Figure 4.16: Using the interlock method to avoid the man-in-the-middle attack.

This is an endless topic, so I will mention the solutions just briefly. There are two popular concepts related to two software packages: PEM and PGP (more in Chapter 7).

PEM (Privacy-Enhanced Mail) is a standard for sending encrypted emails on the Internet that manages public keys on certified computers arranged hierarchically in a tree structure (see also Figure 2.1). A trustworthy 'root computer' uses suitable cryptographic protocols to confirm that certain other computers are trustworthy. These computers, in turn, certify other computers, and so on. Leaving the details aside, it means that the entire security depends on the root computer. That's a point to worry about. But the interlock protocol can be used to periodically check a root computer.

PGP is the popular counterpart to PEM, but rather than using a centralized trust hierarchy, it works on a 'federal' principle: every PGP user (electronically) signs the public key for parties he personally trusts (electronic signatures will be dealt with in Section 6.3). According to the motto: 'my friend's friend is my friend too', PGP builds a 'Web of Trust', a network with pretty secure connection channels. This network is hard to disturb because it is irregular—similar to the Internet, the precursor of which was actually invented to guarantee secure transmission of messages in times of war. More about PGP in Chapter 7.

This section actually belongs to Chapter 6 since it deals exclusively with cryptographic protocols. But unless we are aware of such problems, dealing with asymmetric methods gets somewhat dry.

4.5.3   The RSA Method and Eight Risks

You have probably heard of the RSA method since it is the most popular asymmetric method. In contrast to the methods known up to then (knapsack algorithm and Diffie–Hellman key exchange), RSA was the first method to be suitable both for asymmetric encryption and digital signatures. The name is composed of the initials of its three discoverers, Rivest, Shamir, and Adleman, who published the algorithm in 1978 [RSA]. (Gardner quoted it in 1977 [GardRSA].)

The RSA method is based on a mathematically 'hard' problem, namely factoring very large numbers (currently 300 decimal places and more). The algorithm is quickly described, but as so often in mathematics, it wouldn't explain how they came by this idea. I will try to build such an idea in the following. What we need is some number theory, but really very little.

Congruencies and Fermat's Little Theorem

You have been confronted with congruence arithmetic several times in this book. You know that two natural numbers, a and b, are called **congruent**

modulo n (where n is a natural positive number), written as

```
a = b mod n     or     a ≡ b mod n
```

if a and b leave the same remainder when divided by n. The equivalent is that $(a - b)$ is not divisible by n without remainder, which can be written like this:

```
n | a-b
```

We can do arithmetic with such congruencies similarly to equations, e.g., we can add or multiply them:

```
a = b mod n
```

and

```
c = d mod n
```

are followed by

```
a+c = b+d mod n
ac = bc mod n        and
ac = bd mod n
```

In particular, the last equation results in

```
aᵏ = bᵏ mod n
```

for every natural number, k.

Finally, we conclude from

```
a = b mod n    (i.e., n | a-b)
```

that

```
nc | ac-bc
```

or

```
ac = bc mod nc
```

holds.

This means that we can multiply both sides of a congruence *and* the module (in this case the number n) by the same number. We will utilize this finding further below.

This subsection of mathematics is called **congruence arithmetic** or **modular arithmetic**. It works exclusively with integers, which is implicitly understood in the following.

Not all equations can be solved by this arithmetic. For example,

```
3x = 1 mod 12
```

has no integer solution x. And not all simple equations can be easily solved. While d can still be computed by

```
de = 1 mod n
```

for suitable numbers, e and n, at a reasonable effort (see below), equations in the form

```
aˣ = g mod n
```

for large numbers are extremely hard to solve for x. Without the 'mod n' at the end, we could simply write '$\log_a(g)$', but we are dealing with integers and remainders here—that's something totally different. Only the name of solution x is similar to normal numbers: x is the **discrete logarithm** from g to base a. We will get back to this in Section 4.5.4.

For the time being, we are interested in a number-theory theorem that is not proved here. You presumably remember from school that a number (greater than 1) is called a **prime number** if it is divisible only by 1 and itself without remainder. **Fermat's little theorem** applies to prime numbers and states that if p is a prime number and a cannot be divided by p, then

```
a^{p-1} = 1 mod p
```

holds. Euler proved an important generalization of this theorem, which applies also to non-prime modules:

A number, m, is **relatively prime** to n if there is no integer greater than 1, by which both m and n are divisible. So, 12 and 7 are relatively prime, while 12 and 8 are not. The amount of all numbers from the set $1, \ldots, n$, which are relatively prime to n, is called **Euler's function** of n, written as $\phi(n)$. Fermat's little theorem can now be generalized as follows:

```
a^{\phi(n)} = 1 mod n
```

holds for every natural number, n, and every a that is relatively prime to it.

When n is a prime, then $\phi(n) = n - 1$ holds. We can see that it is actually a generalization of Fermat's little theorem.

We can also use Euler's generalization to compute the modular reciprocal of a number, i.e., we can determine x that meets

```
ax = 1 mod n
```

for given a and n. The solution is $x = a^{\phi(n)-1}$.

This should do for a preparation.

Reaching the Goal With Ease

There is often no direct way to a solution in mathematics; instead, solutions are found by apparently aimless experimenting. We'll take good heed of this, and just see what we can do with Euler's generalization of Fermat's little theorem as we use it on products of two prime numbers. This is our basic idea: we know that it is extraordinarily difficult to calculate the prime numbers from a product, $n = pq$, of two large prime numbers, p and q. The problem is referred to as the **factoring** of n. The difficulty increases as numbers have increasingly more decimal digits. We might be able to build an asymmetric algorithm: n is known, and we could somehow encrypt something using this number, but we couldn't decrypt it without knowing p and q.

We will first consider that Euler's function looks like this for all prime numbers:

```
φ(pq) = (p-1)(q-1).
```

The proof is simple: there is a total of pq numbers, $1, \ldots, pq$. Out of these numbers, the following are *not* relatively prime to pq: the numbers p divisible by q, and the numbers q divisible by p, i.e., $p + q$. We have to bear in mind that we considered pq twice, since it is divisible by p and q. All other numbers divisible neither by p nor by q have got to be relatively prime to pq (since p and q are prime numbers). Thus

```
φ(pq) = pq - (p+q-1) = (p-1)(q-1).
```

Consequently,

```
m^(p-1)(q-1) = 1 mod pq    (2)
```

or

```
m^(p-1)(q-1) + 1 = m mod pq
```

holds for all m that are divisible neither by p nor by q. This could be the procedure we are looking for: we find two natural numbers, d and e, by

```
de = (p-1)(q-1)+1    and    d,e > 1
```

and publish e and n. Everybody can calculate the remainder for every number that is relatively prime to pq, $m < pq$, which m^e leaves when divided by pq.

Let this remainder be the ciphertext; m the *plaintext*; and $n = pq$ *and* e the *public key* (i.e., *two* numbers!). We are the only ones to know d, the *private key* (actually this also includes n, but it is not secret). When somebody sends us ciphertext m^e (or, more exactly, the remainder from the division by n), then we calculate plaintext m as follows:

```
(me)d = med = m(p-1)(q-1) + 1 = m mod pq
```

The calculation of d from e and n is done by factoring $n = pq$. Somebody who does not factor n (i.e., who does not compute p and q from n) cannot find d either. Is this correct? Isn't $(p-1)(q-1)$ all an attacker needs to find d? Well, if he somehow managed to compute $(p-1)(q-1)$ in any other way, then he also knows

```
pq - (p-1)(q-1) - 1 = p+q
```

so that he can easily calculate p and q from pq and $p + q$, i.e., he can factor n. Calculating $(p-1)(q-1)$ is not easier than factoring n. And the direct calculation of m from m^e means taking the eth root, which is not easier than computing the discrete logarithm of m^e to base m, or factoring large numbers. There might be another way to find d or m, but nobody has found such a way yet. The most recent work I know was presented at the EUROCRYPT '98; but it merely suggests that there could be such a way, without showing the direction.

All of this looks pretty good, doesn't it? The only thing is that we have left two problems unsolved.

Problem 1: Have you noticed the unproved prerequisite? The reason is that, in general, there are no two numbers, d and e, with $d, e < 1$ and

```
de = (p-1)(q-1) + 1.
```

For example,

```
(p-1)(q-1)+1 = 41
```

becomes a prime number for $p = 5$ and $q = 11$. This problem can be solved. If e is relatively prime to $(p-1)(q-1)$ (a number bigger than 1 can always be found), then there is a modular reciprocal, d of e, i.e., a d with

```
de = 1 mod (p-1)(q-1)
```

(This d is calculated by the so-called extended Euclidean algorithm.) This translates to

```
de = k(p-1)(q-1) + 1
```

for any natural number, $k > 1$, because

```
m^k(p-1)(q-1) = 1^k = 1 mod pq
```

follows from (2), and we will then still have

```
m^de = m mod pq    (3)
```

Problem 2: What happens with those $m < n$ that are not relatively prime to $n = pq$? A small calculation shows that the equation (3) we are interested in will nevertheless hold. Proving it is not difficult, so I will demonstrate it.

We know that

```
t^p-1 = 1 mod p    and   q^p-1 = 1 mod p
```

holds for each $t < p$ according to Fermat's little theorem, so it also holds for each $k > 0$:

```
t^k(p-1)(q-1) = 1 mod p    and    q^k(p-1)(q-1) = 1 mod p.
```

We multiply the two equations together and then multiply the two sides by t:

```
t(tq)k(p-1)(q-1) = t mod p
```

Now, we remember the above rule that both sides of a congruence and the module itself can be multiplied by the same number, in this case q:

```
(tq)k(p-1)(q-1) + 1 = tq mod pq.
```

Thus (3) also holds for all multiples of q. Analogously, we show the equation for multiples of p.

As a result, we have derived the RSA method and concurrently proved that it works.

Using RSA

All you have seen so far were variables, but natural numbers hide behind them, of course. How can all of this be turned into an encryption method? First of all, we have to create a key pair:

1. We define a key length; 1024 bits are currently thought to be secure. We create two different prime numbers, p and q, with a length of at least $1024/2 = 512$ bits each (more about this further below).

2. We define an exponent, e. Common values are 3, 17, and $65\,537 = 2^{16} + 1$ (m^e can be calculated particularly fast for these special values). e has to be relatively prime to $p - 1$ and $q - 1$. If it weren't, we would have to select e, or p and q, differently. But there won't be a problem using the three values above for e, since they are prime numbers and certainly not equal to p or q (for we want p and q to be extremely large).

3. We use the extended Euclidean algorithm (it won't be discussed here; you can find a C program in [SchnCr, 11.3]) to calculate a d by

```
de = 1 mod (p-1)(q-1).
```

The RSA Method

Creating keys:

- Choose two large prime numbers, p and q (e.g., 512 bits long).
- Compose $n = pq$, where n is N bits long.
- Choose an $e > 1$ that is relatively prime to $(p-1)(q-1)$.
- Use $de = 1 \bmod (p-1)(q-1)$ to calculate a d.
- n and e form the public key, d forms the private key.

Encryption:

- Decompose the plaintext into blocks of $N-1$ bits each (the last block may have to be padded).
- For each block with value $m < n$, calculate remainder c from m^e after division by $n.c$, this is the ciphertext block, and it is N bits long.

Decryption:

- Decompose the ciphertext into N-bit blocks.
- For each block with value $c < n$, the remainder from cd after division by n is the corresponding plaintext.

Figure 4.17: The RSA method.

d is the private key that we will never ever show to anybody. We can basically forget about p and q now. We will publish their product, $n = pq$, together with the exponent, e, as our public key.

As a result, we have created the key. The encryption looks like this:

1. If key $n = pq$ is exactly N bits long, then we divide the text into blocks of $N-1$ bits each (we may have to pad; see Section 5.1.2).

2. We take each block with numerical value m and calculate the remainder, m^e, from division by n. This produces the ciphertext block, but has length N (we can pad it to bring the ciphertext block and the plaintext block to the same length, if need be).

We proceed in reverse order for decryption:

1. We divide the ciphertext into N-bit blocks.

2. For each ciphertext block with numerical value c, we calculate the remainder, c^d, from division by n. This produces a plaintext block with a length of $N - 1$ bits (we delete the first bit—it has to be 0; otherwise, there is an error).

We can easily see that RSA is slow: multiplications and calculating remainders take time with 1000-bit numbers.

How to Create a Key

One question that has remained unanswered so far is very important for the method's security and speed: how do we find such huge prime numbers? You probably know Eratosthenes' sieve, the simplest method to compute prime numbers.

We write down all numbers, e.g., up to 1000, beginning with 2:

2	3	4	5	6	7	8	9	10	11	12	13	14	15	...

We delete all multiples of the first number (which is 2), except that number itself:

2	3	5	7	9	11	13	15

The smallest number greater than 2 is 3; that's the next prime number. We delete all multiples of 3, except 3 itself:

2	3	5	7	11	13

Now we look for the smallest number greater than 3 that's still left, and so on. The method works like a sieve: only prime numbers are caught. This is very effective, for example, if you want to calculate *all* prime numbers up to ten million. Though you'd need ten million storage locations (3 Mbits might be sufficient), that shouldn't represent a hurdle today.

With 512-bit numbers, however, you'd overtax all resources. The search can be simplified if we break away from our idea of 100 % security and make do with 99.9999 . . . % instead.

With huge numbers like these, it is generally most effective to randomly select a number in the desired order of magnitude and test whether or not it is a prime number. If it isn't, we choose the next number—whether randomly or deterministically doesn't matter.

Testing for prime numbers is also done with the help of chance. We will always get just statements in the form: 'There is a 50 % probability that the number in this test is a prime number.' After 50 independent tests, the error probability will drop to 2^{-50}, which roughly corresponds to one error in one quadrillion trials. I will use the test by Rabin–Miller as an example [Rabin]; its hit ratio is not 50 %, but 99.9 % and better. With long numbers, the error probability is supposedly smaller than 2^{-50} after only six tests.

In practice, prime numbers are created as follows:

1. We create a random number with a length of N bits, p (N is the given key length). We set the first and the Nth bits to 1 to make the number uneven and greater than 2^{N-1}.

2. We check to see whether p is divisible by a small prime number, e.g., by a prime number smaller than 256 or 2000. If so, then p is out, and we have to return to Step 1.

    This is faster than discarding, if needed, by the following test.

    We represent p in the form $p = 2^b m + 1$, where b should be as large as possible. It is pretty easy: we set the last bit of p to equal 0; the number of zero bits at the end is equal to b, and the previous remainder produces m.

3. We run the following Rabin–Miller test [Knuth2, 4.5.4] six times, for example:

    (a) We randomly select a number, $a < p$.

    (b) We compute $z = a^m \bmod p$. If z is equal to 1 or $p - 1$, then p passed the test for this a. Otherwise, we set a counter, $j = 0$, and enter into a loop.

(c) If $j > 0$ and $z = 1$, then p is a composite number, i.e., it won't pass the test. We start all over again from Step 1.

(d) We increase j by 1 and decide:

- If $z = p - 1$, then p passed the test for this a.

- If $j < b$ and $z \neq p - 1$, then we calculate $z = z^2$ mod p and return to (c).

(e) That leaves us with $j = b$ and $z \neq p - 1$: so, p failed the test and we start again.

Non-mathematicians will presumably find it hard to understand how this test can work: the residual classes modulo p form a field only for prime numbers p. In it, each square has exactly two roots; in particular 1 has the roots 1 and $p - 1$. As the test runs, number z is continually squared. When it first takes on the value 1 without previously having taken on the value $p - 1$, then 1 has to have a third root, i.e., the residual classes modulo p cannot form a field, and p cannot be a prime number in this case.

The above test will be rejected with a probability of at least 75 % if p is not a prime number [Knuth2, 4.5.4]. In practice, things look much more optimistic (see above).

The costliest operation in this test is computing a^m mod p in Step (b). According to [SchnCr, 11.5], finding a 512-bit prime number on a Sparc II takes about 24 seconds; with 1024 bits, this can easily increase to well over 5 minutes. Consequently, generating keys for the RSA method is not a matter of fractions of seconds, even when using modern, faster computers (aside from the fact that we have to create two prime numbers). But that shouldn't pose a problem since it is extremely seldom that we'd have to create keys.

As a sideline, we don't have to choose p randomly every time. After the first step, we can cleverly increase p in every step so that divisibility by small prime numbers, such as 2, 3, or 5, is avoided from the outset.

See [SchnCr, 11.5] for more tests and literature references.

We will now discuss the security of the RSA method. Of course, the security stands or falls with the possibility of factoring very large numbers; in this case computing these prime numbers from the product of two prime numbers at an acceptable cost. People have worked on this problem for decades. Before we get to it, we will have a look at several other security aspects.

Risk 1: Identical Prime Numbers in Different Modules

If somebody finds that his module n is not relatively prime to a third-party module (as we know, the modules are integral parts of the public keys, i.e., they are generally known), then this person knows a factor of the third-party's module, i.e., he can factor it without any problem. When millions of public keys have been published one day sooner or later, there will be trillions of pairs—there could at least be one pair with a common divisor, couldn't there?

Theoretically, yes; practically, no. The reason is that a well-known prime-number theorem in number theory says that $\pi(N)$, the number of all prime numbers smaller than number N for large N, is described as $n/\ln N$ by approximation. More specifically,

```
π(N)  lnN/N
```

tends toward 1 as N tends toward infinity. This means that, between 2^{512} and 2^{513}, there are roughly as many prime numbers as there are between 1 and 2^{512}, and that's approximately $7.5*10^{151}$, a number for which human languages don't have a suitable superlative to classify it. So, no risk whatsoever can emerge from the set of possible prime numbers.

It is much more likely (certainly not 'only' 10^{100} times) that several users will hit the same prime number due to poorly chosen random numbers. This risk has to be excluded by most careful implementation of the random number generation!

Risk 2: Chosen-Plaintext Attack

This brief discussion refers to a cryptographic protocol that will be covered in Chapter 6, namely digital signatures. Nevertheless, we have to jump ahead a little since the issue relates to RSA.

In digital signatures, a character string is 'decrypted' with the private key (naturally, gibberish comes out of it). The result can be re-encrypted with the public key to check it, which means that it has the function of a signature (only the owner of the private key was able to create this signature).

People who use RSA to decrypt third-party character strings and publish the results can be compromised. This happens as follows: Eve, the eavesdropper, intercepted one of Alice's encrypted session keys. From the mathematical perspective, she knows $c = m^e \bmod n$, where m is the session key and (e, n) is Alice's key. To recover m (and read the entire message encrypted with the session key), Eve uses the public key to encrypt any number, r, that is relatively prime[3] to n. Then she takes the ciphertext produced and multiplies it with the intercepted ciphertext, c:

```
y = cr^e mod n
```

Foisting this y on Alice, Eve asks her for a signature, i.e., decryption. So Alice computes

```
y^d = c^d r^ed mod n
```

and gives this result back to Eve. On account of

```
m = c^d mod n   and   r^ed = r mod n
```

Eve now knows the remainder from dividing mr by n, and can use it together with the extended Euclidean algorithm to compute m (using this algorithm, she first solves the equation $rx = 1 \bmod n$ and then multiplies $mr = u \bmod n$ by x: $m = ux \bmod n$).

Of course, Eve could have submitted $c = m^e \bmod n$ to Alice for signature right away. That would have been more obvious. In that case, however, though very costly, Alice could have caught Eve cheating if she'd kept all encrypted session keys and compared c with these keys. In the attack described here, Alice has no chance to see through Eve's intention.

Eve exploits a particularity of RSA, namely that the decryption of a ciphertext can be derived from the encryption of another ciphertext, though the two ciphertexts are apparently not related. This is not a weakness of RSA, but of the cryptographic protocol. With the protocols used in practice, there is no chance this weakness can be exploited. But knowing about it helps to prevent us from developing insecure methods.

---

[3]If it weren't relatively prime to n, Eve would have recovered a prime factor of n and reached her goal.

Risk 3: Attack Against Small Values of *e*

Choosing a small value for exponent *e* in the public key saves computation
time during the encryption, but there are inherent risks. If every user within
a group uses their own modules, but all use a common exponent *e*, then a
message, *m*, encrypted by *e* users, will suffice to reveal *m*. The same is true
when $e(e + 1)/2$ linearly dependent messages are encrypted [Hastad].

If there is a risk that this weakness might be practically exploited, then one
can disturb the messages with random bits. The probability that these bits will
prevent linear dependencies is high.

As a sideline, exponent *d*—the private key—shouldn't be too small either, but
this doesn't play an important role in practice.

Risk 4: Attack Against Common Modules

If you now think that all users could use the same module (the keys would then
have to be created centrally) after what was said in the section above, I have
to disappoint you—there are also powerful attacks where even the module can
be factored.

Risk 5: Attack Against the Protocol

At the CRYPTO '98, Daniel Bleichenbacher suggested an attack against a protocol called **PKCS#1** that is normally used for RSA encryption [BleichRSA].
This attack is practically doable, so it caught some attention, although the threat
is within limited boundaries. I will briefly explain the basic idea.

With the PKCS#1 protocol, an RSA plaintext has the following form:

```
00 | 02 | pad bytes ... | 00 | plaintext
```

Bleichenbacher's attack sends a 'ciphertext' to a server that decrypts it. The
server checks whether or not the 'plaintext' created has the described format; if
it doesn't, it returns an error message. And this is the information the attacker
is after. The attacker creates the next 'ciphertext' dependent on the previous
replies and sends it again to have it decrypted. We can easily see that this is
a typical adaptive-chosen-plaintext attack (see Section 3.1). Though the author
does not give an exact figure for the trials required, we can reasonably assume

that between 300 000 and two million ciphertexts will suffice, based on rough estimates and practical experiments.

Readers with some mathematical knowledge who are interested in learning the details of this attack find the well-written original article, *txt/cryptana/pkcs.ps*, on our Web site.

It is remarkable that Bleichenbacher exploits only the fact that the first two bytes have the values 00 and 02 when the server does not report an error! With symmetric algorithms, such a finding would not be a breakthrough, but RSA can't be compared with these methods. It was even proved that an attack which reveals only one single bit of an RSA key can be used to compute the entire key. It had been known for some time, but Bleichenbacher's was the first practicable chosen-ciphertext attack. Until then, such methods had been considered to be of theoretical interest in the RSA world.

In practice, the attack works on some sufficiently fast SSL servers. In theory, it can be used to crack even relatively slow servers: if you are lucky you need only 300 000 requests at 80 requests per second to reach your goal in about one hour.

The attack works even if the server does not report whether or not the plaintext created was correct. The reason is that, sometimes, it first checks the format and then looks for a digital signature. If it finds that the plaintext is not correct, it normally omits the signature check. Due to the relatively long computation times, this allows an intruder to mount a special type of *timing attack*, which will be described in Section 5.10.

Of course, the attack can be prevented. If the plaintext contains a checksum that is included in the test, then the attacker has a poorer hand. The requirement that the server additionally check the length of the data block and the SSL version is much simpler, without the need to change the protocol. This makes it less likely for the server to return error messages, and the number of trials the attacker needs to run increases from one million to one trillion. A yet cleverer approach would have the attacker prove somehow or other (perhaps by a hash value) that he knows about the existence of the plaintext. Version 2 of the PKCS#1 protocol thwarts the attack. The timing attack mentioned above can also be easily prevented, for example, by always including the digital signature in the checking procedure (or integrating an appropriate time delay).

Nevertheless, Bleichenbacher stirred things up quite a bit, especially among the developers of Secure Shell SSH, which will be discussed in Section 7.3.

Risk 6: Stealthy or Accidental Change to the Private Key

RSA signatures (Section 6.3) are normally determined by the so-called Chinese Remainder Theorem (CRT). Rather than having to calculate values modulo pq, they are calculated individually—modulo p and modulo q.

Now, if a bit of either p or q is changed due to a hardware or software error, the wrong signature thus computed can be used to compute p and q [BonRSA]. This is a dangerous attack. An unnoticed one-time bit error in a register can cause a disaster.

This can be prevented, for example, by subsequently checking the signature for correctness, but it requires some computation time. Stealthy changes to private keys (on smartcards, or if it is XOR-encrypted, as discussed at the end of Section 7.1) can be reliably detected by using suitable checksums.

Appropriate implementation allows us to prevent the six risks discussed so far, but not the following risks.

Risk 7: Private Key Stolen

Absolutely clear, you will think—the private key has to be protected as well as it possibly can. Everything is actually 'only' a matter of implementation, but it is so important that it is listed as a separate risk here. The problem is as follows: private keys are normally encrypted by their owners (e.g., using a passphrase like in PHP; see Section 7.1), so they are (hopefully) protected against unauthorized access. But some time sooner or later when owners will want to work with their private keys, these keys form a coherent area in the memory. On Web servers that establish secure connections over the SSL protocol, private keys are held in memory even permanently.

Until not so long ago, people thought that private keys were hidden well enough amidst all those many megabytes of data in memory. The trouble is that keys have a distinct feature: they look really random, while almost all program code and 'normal' data have a structure. Nicko van Someren and Adi Shamir robbed people of this illusion when they showed in [SomSham] that these keys can be found astonishingly fast. At the IHW '99 convention in Dresden, Germany, Someren demonstrated just how fast. In fact, searching for a private RSA key on a hard disk can even be as fast as physically reading the disk! This opens up ways for a specific attack: hacker methods are used to intrude a Web server, bring the server down, and analyze the core image created on the disk. The process can be automated.

A 128-bit session key can presumably not be found in this way. But 1024 or 2048 bits of 'real chaos' do stand out in memory.

As bad as this may sound, don't panic just yet. A private PGP key on a private computer is still safe, at least it will be if you are paranoid about disconnecting from the network as you encrypt it (just joking). With Web servers, however, the owner should know that a hacker attack can jeopardize the ciphering security even after the attack's traces were removed. Generating new keys is part of damage repair. Someren recommends to keep private keys in hardware only, and process them only there.

This attack doesn't actually belong in a book on cryptology, because it is closely related to computer security, a different (and endless) topic. Nevertheless, I think the method for finding private keys is closer to cryptanalysis than it is to computer security. Moreover, it is helpful to know that 1024 bits of randomness cannot be hidden coherently 'somehow' within 2 gigabytes of data.

Risk 8: New Methods for Factoring Large Numbers; Quantum Computers; Twinkle

The attacks discussed so far are directed against the procedure, i.e., the protocol, rather than against RSA itself. A cryptanalysis in the sense considered so far would be successful if we could factor module n. It is assumed that finding the plaintext from the public key is equivalent to the problem of factoring n, but it can't be proved (yet?) [BonVen]. We have seen earlier that finding the private key enables factoring. But perhaps it is also possible without the private key.

Research work in this field is running at full speed. You may have heard of the spectacular decryption of a 428-bit number (129 decimal places) in April 1994 [GarPGP, Chapter 4, 'RSA-129 Solved!'; SchnCr, 11.4]. A group of mathematicians under the supervision of Lenstra used a variant of the so-called **quadratic sieve** for factoring large numbers and coordinated huge computer capacities on the Internet: 600 users had 1600 distributed computers work for over eight months. This corresponded to between 4000 and 6000 MIPS-years. 'MIPS' is a very blurred unit; it roughly means 'one million computing operations per second'. This means that a total of 150 billion operations were executed (whatever that may mean). By the way... notice something about this number? A similar amount of decryptions is necessary to brute-force attack DES.

This 129-digit number had long been known. Rivest published it as a riddle in 1977; he estimated that 40 quadrillion years would be required to decrypt that text. Within a little less time, namely in 17 years, he could read his plaintext to his great surprise, as nobody had expected to ever see it printed:

```
THE MAGIC WORDS ARE SQUEAMISH OSSIFRAGE.
```

But this speaks against the theory rather than against Rivest. This success wasn't initially a real risk for the public keys in use. Factoring a 512-bit number would have taken a hundred times longer (for a key only 84 bits longer!).

However, the theory behind this attack was five years old. Meanwhile, another variant by the name of **number-field sieve** (**NFS**) was developed [Lenstra]. NFS would have made the attack ten times faster. For large numbers with many decimal digits, the cost for factoring a number, n, by NFS is roughly

$$e^{(1923\ +\ o(1))\ f(n)}$$

where f stands for

$$f(n) = (\ln\ n)^{1/3}\ (\ln\ n)^{2/3}.$$

(As usual in higher mathematics, $o(1)$ denotes a quantity the value of which gradually reduces as n increases.) If we were able to reduce the constant 1923 to 1.5 today, then factoring 1024-bit numbers, which are secure by current standards, would already be real. But it hasn't happened yet.

By the time this book goes to print new findings will have been published. Perhaps somebody may even have made a 'great breakthrough', or perhaps such a breakthrough is not even possible.

People also have great hopes of **quantum computers**, which will be discussed in Section 5.9. It is currently believed that, with their help, factoring very large numbers might become a 'kid's game'. Unfortunately, quantum computers have a serious drawback: they don't exist yet, and it is in the lap of the gods whether and when we will ever have one.

Conversely, an opto-electronic device called **Twinkle** (**T**he **W**eitzman **IN**stitute **K**ey **L**ocating **E**ngine) by Shamir appears to be much more realistic. Shamir introduced it at the EUROCRYPT '98; he estimates that the device can increase the length of breakable RSA keys by 100 to 200 bits. However, Twinkle accelerates only the first step (the 'sieving') within the factoring process. The second, much more memory-intensive step doesn't change.

An improved version of the device was discussed at the EUROCRYPT 2000 [Twinkle]; it is said to help factor 768-bit keys within nine months. Unfortunately, it requires about 5000 upgraded Twinkle devices and 80 000 standard Pentium-II computers . . .

Anyway, the example of the RSA method shows clearly how much direct influence current research has on cryptological practice, how much knowledge is buried in a good implementation, and how open the future of this algorithm actually is.

Multiprime

The heading of this section is the buzzword a company used at the RSA Conference 2000 in Munich, Germany, for their product—same security but dramatically increased performance! What's behind it? One can modify the RSA method by working not only with the product $N = pq$ of two prime numbers, but also by using several very large prime numbers: $N = p_1 p_2 \ldots p_n$. Everything runs analogously, and if the prime numbers used are large enough, security won't suffer either. But since the computation time for multiplication (or raising to power) grows quadratically in line with the bit length, things can be speeded up; for example, you can do things twice as fast when using four instead of two factors. That's all there is to it. Cryptologists had long been aware of this, they just might have forgotten to tell software developers about it. So, if a cryptocard takes 25 seconds to encrypt using a 'classic' key, then this might be reduced to 8 seconds when using six factors. It still remains slow.

Patents

RSA was patented in the USA in 1983, and the patent expired on September 20, 2000; it hadn't been patented elsewhere. RSA is the de-facto standard for asymmetric methods all over the world, except in the USA. Public Key Partners (PKP) handle all patents for such methods. This company is part of RSA Data Security, Inc. and Caro-Kahn. Though free licenses appear to have been granted, everything remained secret, and no law suit against PKP ended with a non-appeal judgment. This is probably the reason why much free software, e.g., PGP and SSH (see Chapter 7), prefer methods no longer patented, such as the

Diffie–Hellman or ElGamal method (see next section), which have not been covered by patents since 1997.

Fortunately, this is all history now; the only thing you should be aware of when using public-key algorithms in data communication with the USA are continually relaxing export regulations.

The ElGamal Method

While the RSA algorithm can presumably be cracked by factoring large numbers, the ElGamal method is based on the difficulty of computing discrete logarithms, i.e., determining the value of x from

```
y = aˣ mod n
```

with known base a and module n. This method has two distinct benefits versus RSA:

1. People who can compute discrete logarithms have also won an algorithm for factoring large numbers. Theoretically, it is not more insecure than RSA.

2. In contrast to RSA, ElGamal is not patented, but the PKP patent management thinks it is covered by the Diffie–Hellman patent in the USA. This patent expired on April 29, 1997. By the time you read these lines, ElGamal will presumably be the first non-patented asymmetric algorithm.

After the number-theory preparations above, it is no longer difficult to explain the algorithm.

We choose a prime number, p, as our module, and a base, g. Both are part of the public key. $(p - 1)/2$ should also be a prime number. The private key is a secret exponent, $x < p$. We also publish remainder y with

```
y = gˣ mod p.
```

So, the *public key* consists of three numbers: prime number p, base g, and remainder y. The *secret key*, x, is the discrete logarithm of y to base g with

---

The ElGamal Method

Creating keys:

- Choose a large prime number, p (e.g., 512 or 1024 bits long), for which $(p-1)/2$ is also a prime number. Let p be N bits long.
- Choose a base, $g < p$.
- Choose a secret exponent, $x < p$.
- Compute $y = g^x \bmod p$.
- p, g, and y form the public key, x forms the private key.

Encryption:

- Decompose the plaintext into blocks of $N-1$ bits each (the last block may have to be padded).
- Choose a $k < p$ that is relatively prime to $p-1$. k must remain secret. It can be created by a program and discarded after use.
- For each block, m, compute two numbers, a and b, as follows:

```
a = g^k mod p     and    b = y^km mod p
```

The two numbers, a and b, form two ciphertext blocks of length N.

Decryption:

- Decompose the ciphertext into N-bit blocks.
- For two consecutive a-and-b blocks, solve the equation

```
a^xm = b mod p
```

toward m (using the generalized Euclidean algorithm). m is the plaintext looked for.

Figure 4.18: Asymmetric encryption by the ElGamal method.

regard to module p. Though there is an effective algorithm to compute such logarithms, it only works if $(p-1)/2$ itself is not a prime number.

The encryption of a message, $m < p$, looks a bit unusual: the sender chooses a random number, k, which must be relatively prime to $p-1$, and computes

```
a = g^k mod p    and
b = y^km mod p .
```

The ciphertext consists of *two* numbers, a and b. The sender won't tell anybody the value of k and doesn't have to know it any more later on. Otherwise, anybody who knew k could solve the number-theory equation

```
y^km = b mod p    (4)
```

and find m. Conversely, we know x and can resolve the equation

```
a^xm' = b mod p
```

toward m'.

```
a^xm' = g^kxm' = g^xkm' = y^km' = b mod p
```

holds now, and when comparing it with (4) (and due to the unique solvability of this equation, modulo p) we can see that $m = m'$ in any event.

The fact that the ciphertext is twice as long as the plaintext doesn't matter, because we only want to encrypt session keys.

The ElGamal encryption is closely related to the **Diffie–Hellman key exchange**, the first method that used public keys (see Section 6.1.1). ElGamal methods are mainly used for digital signatures. We will not discuss them further here and refer to [SchnCr] instead.

4.5.4 The Knapsack Story

You may be surprised to learn that the asymmetric methods commonly used are solely based on the problems of factoring or computing discrete logarithms.

With *that* amount of inventive talent, you might think that cryptologists should certainly have found other methods! Well, they have, and one such story is worth being told.

Two years after the first asymmetric algorithm was published by Diffie and Hellman, Merkle and Hellman proposed another method, the so-called **knapsack algorithm**. It takes much less background knowledge than RSA to understand it.

The knapsack problem is mathematically formulated like this: let a number be a sum, where the summands are taken from a given set of summands. This can be expressed in more culinary terms: several yummy slices of different thickness and the same diameter are placed on a table. Pack some of the slices in a certain cylindrical knapsack (with the width of the slice diameter) such that the knapsack is filled up to the rim. Which slices have to be packed?

The problem is not always solvable, and when it is, the result is not always unambiguous. We are mainly interested in making its solution generally difficult for large knapsacks. We say purposefully 'general', because the summands are very easy to find for specific number sequences. One such number sequence is, for instance,

```
1, 2, 4, 8, 16, 32, ...
```

For example, the representation of 13 as the sum of such numbers can even be read from right to left from its representation as a binary number (dual number) in this case. The following holds:

```
13 = 1101₂
```

so we choose the first, third, and fourth members of the sequence above:

```
13 = 1 + 4 + 8
```

Solving the knapsack problem becomes generally simple if each summand in the ascending sequence of the given set of summands is greater than the sum of all previous summands. Such knapsacks are said to be **superincreasing**.

For the solution with such knapsacks, we only have to subtract the largest possible element from the sum to successively obtain the set of summands looked for.

How should we use it for encryption, or even for constructing an asymmetric encryption algorithm? The trick is to transform the superincreasing knapsack into a normal one. To this end, we choose a *secret* superincreasing number sequence, $(s_i)_{i=1,...,N}$, from N numbers. We then define a *secret* module, n, and a *secret* factor, k. The module should be greater than the sum of all s_i numbers, and k should be relatively prime to n. We multiply the given s_i summands by k modulo n. This results in different summands, t_i, $t_i = s_i k$ mod n. The t_i compose the *public* key.

If you want to encrypt, you represent your message as a bit sequence. You decompose this bit sequence into N-bit blocks. For each block, you compute the sum of all t_i, for which the ith bit in the block is equal to 1. This is the ciphertext.

But since we know n *and* k, we can use

```
kk' = 1 mod n
```

to determine a k'.

Multiplying the ciphertext by k' modulo n gives us those values that would have resulted had we used the superincreasing sequence for encryption. This problem is easy to solve. It's how we reveal the bits of the plaintext (Figure 4.19).

Except for finding k' and doing the modulo n multiplication, we need no number theory at all. The rest is almost school arithmetic, and the implementation is extremely easy, compared with RSA. Beautiful, isn't it?

Because of this question, you already may have a hunch that the algorithm is *too* beautiful. Though some flaws were found, nobody was initially able to crack the entire algorithm. At the CRYPTO '82 conference in California, however, several cryptanalysts claimed they had achieved it. Their attack might have consisted in transforming the 'public knapsack' into the superincreasing knapsack (this is actually jargon; we are talking of disks = summands that are packed in the knapsack rather than of the knapsack = sum itself).

In light of these claims, a ciphertext decryption challenge was published as early as on the first night. All lecturers expounded theoretical problems, but the riddle

The Knapsack Method

Creating keys:

- Choose a secret superincreasing number sequence with a length of N members, $(s_i)_{i=1,...,N}$, i.e., a number sequence in which each element is greater than the sum of all previous elements. N should be at least equal to 200; the s_i should be of the order of 10^{100}.

- Choose a secret module, n, greater than the sum of all elements of the number sequence.

- Choose a secret number, k, relatively prime to n.

- Compute k' by $kk' = 1 \bmod n$.

- Multiply all elements of (s_i) by k modulo n:

```
t_i = s_i k mod n    (i=1,...,N).
```

- Sequence $(t_i)_{i=1,...,N}$ forms the public key; k', n, and sequence $(s_i)_{i=1,...,N}$ compose the private key.

Encryption:

- Decompose the plaintext into blocks of N bits each (the last block does not have to be padded).

- For each block, compute the sum from those t_i, where bit i in the block is equal to 1. The sum is the ciphertext.

Decryption:

- Decompose the ciphertext into N-bit blocks.

- Multiply each ciphertext block by k' modulo n.

- Solve the knapsack problem for each number thus obtained with regard to (s_i) by successively subtracting the largest possible s_i from the sequence. If summand s_i occurs in the sum, then set bit i in the plaintext block to 1; otherwise set it to 0.

Figure 4.19: Asymmetric encryption using the knapsack method.

remained unsolved. Eventually, Len Adleman of MIT (we know him from the RSA method) took the biscuit. He had brought an Apple II computer along and solved the task in front of the spectators [GarPGP, Chapter 3, 'The Rise and Fall of Knapsacks']. That was tantamount to a sensation—the computer wasn't on the market yet, and 'real computers' came with power supply, ventilator, and line printers back then. And along came this cryptanalyst and solved a major task on a computer that a single man could *carry*, and what's more, with a neat and clean ciphertext attack!

To make the rest of the story short: improvements were 'handed in subsequently' over and again, and all of them were cracked every which way. Well, there are still some unbroken variants around. The question is, for how long?

Actually a pity for such a beautiful algorithm.

4.5.5   Bottom Line

The RSA method is the worldwide 'market leader' among asymmetric algorithms. It has been studied for almost as long as DES and except for the basic problem of factoring large numbers, all known flaws can be avoided by appropriate implementation. There are mature strategies for preventing intrusions like the man-in-the-middle attack. It is certainly easier to forge a 100-euro bill than to get hold of somebody's session key if this somebody knows a thing or two about security and cryptology.

But. I think this 'but' is very critical: The private key is a real 'universal key'. Compare it yourself (though all comparisons are known to be poor):

The German Wehrmacht published their code books with keys for rounds monthly. In the event that a code book fell into the adversary's hands, the Wehrmacht believed that they could send 'messages for listening in on' only for another month at most.

Public keys are generally changed much more seldom. An unbelievable amount of messages can belong to one key pair. If these messages include some that have to remain secret for years, then be careful. If somebody has listened in on your communication and a genius student discovers a factoring method after two or three years you are sunk. All your messages will be compromised at once in arrears, because all session keys will then be public (see Figure 4.15)!

Though this risk is perhaps extremely low, nobody knows. If you communicate with only one converser and use the symmetric universal-key splitting as shown in Figure 4.14, you are on the safe side. If Mallory missed listening in on one single channel, then he missed the train—you just have to carefully watch the computer that holds the universal key. All modern symmetric methods are vulnerable to plaintext attacks at best. Though a DES ciphertext (possibly encrypted in the CBC mode; see Section 5.1.1) can be recovered by brute force, methods with at least 64 bits make it much harder, and with 128-bit keys, it's an unrealistic venture. Apart from that, the risk mentioned last exists just as well when using public keys in hybrid methods.

In short: Current asymmetric methods offer a lot of comfort, very high security and enormous damage when they are compromised.

Chapter 5

Life After DES: New Methods, New Attacks

We have learned two important and modern encryption methods and know quite a few things about cryptanalysis. In this chapter, we will undertake an expedition through the colorful world of modern algorithms. It cannot be more than a short expedition though, and it shouldn't be. Moreover, our discussion will be limited to symmetric methods—you have already come to know the two popular asymmetric methods in Section 4.5. I refer readers who want to know about more algorithms and their analysis to the comprehensive and clearly written work by Schneier [SchnCr].

But before we start dealing with new methods, we will first have a look at very practical things. To be able to use cryptographic algorithms in programs, or—more frequently—to evaluate the security of cryptographic programs, you need to know a thing or two about the implementation of such algorithms.

5.1 Implementation of Algorithms

The best algorithm won't do any good if it is badly implemented from the cryptographic viewpoint. This section will discuss three things everybody needs to know before they embed a cryptographic algorithm in another program:

Cryptology Unlocked Reinhard Wobst
© 2007 John Wiley & Sons, Ltd

operating modes, padding, and key generation. Moreover, you will learn about an interesting cryptanalytic attack (the insertion attack against stream ciphers), and a useful trick.

5.1.1 Operating Modes: ECB, CBC, CFB, and OFB

Together with the DES standardization, four operating modes were defined for this algorithm. Rather than concerning DES in particular, they are applicable to all block algorithms. While a block algorithm per se can transform only *one* plaintext block into *one* ciphertext block (and vice versa), these operating modes specify how a *sequence* of plaintext blocks should be encrypted. While the ECB and CBC modes function as block ciphers, the CFB and OFB modes only use the block algorithm to define a stream cipher.

ECB: Electronic Codebook Mode

You've already come to know the ECB mode, just not by its name: plaintext blocks are transformed successively into the corresponding ciphertext blocks—that's all. The name is due to the fact that ciphering is done as if we were traditional spies using a codebook, and replacing the sensitive words by other words based on a rigid scheme. Except that, in our sense, these 'words' correspond to plaintext blocks, and the codebook would be rather extensive, for example, when using DES with 2^{64} (18 trillion) entries; in addition, we would use a different one for each key.

ECB is the simplest way of embedding a block algorithm into a program, but also the most insecure. Why?

Assume you want to send somebody a secret drawing. You don't know that your application works very weakly in this respect: it scans the drawing line by line and creates only the bit values 0 and 1 for 'white' and 'black', similar to a fax machine, but without compression. The rough manual drawing might be composed of relatively few strokes. The bit stream created would contain long sequences of zero bits, interrupted by few bits with value 1. You use, say, DES to encrypt this bit stream and send it over a channel, unaware of the fact that an attacker is listening. This attacker sees that one ciphertext block occurs much more frequently than all others. That's probably the encryption of 64 zero bits, he thinks instantly; the other blocks contain at least one 1-bit. With a resolution of 180 dpi (corresponding to a dot size of 0.14 mm), the attacker can easily make out the blackening in the drawing, except for a horizontal deviation of approximately 9 mm and a vertical deviation of 0.14 mm. That's very useful for the attacker!

You can use the best algorithm on earth, the only important thing for the attacker is to know that you encrypt in ECB mode. ECB doesn't blur patterns sufficiently in plaintext. There are other vulnerabilities. For example, somebody could stealthily replace ciphertext blocks by others, but the first vulnerability is bad enough. Nevertheless, many commercial programs are believed to use this mode. If the question of whether or not they encrypt in ECB or CBC mode doesn't mean anything to a vendor of cryptological software, they probably don't know much about cryptology.

CBC: Cipher Block Chaining Mode

The idea behind this mode is as simple as it is effective. Before encrypting it, a plaintext block is XORed with the ciphertext block created in the last step:

$$C_{n+1} = DES(P_{n+1} \oplus C_n)$$

(As before, P_n denotes the nth plaintext block, and C_n denotes the nth ciphertext block; 'DES' stands for an example of a block algorithm; see Figure 5.1). The decryption is analogous, we only have to put the ciphertext block aside for the duration of one encryption step and then XOR it with the created 'plaintext':

$$P_{n+1} = DES^{-1}(C_{n+1}) \oplus C_n$$

What happens in the first step? What about C_0? We choose C_0 randomly and send it as our first 'ciphertext' block! This won't cause any security risk at

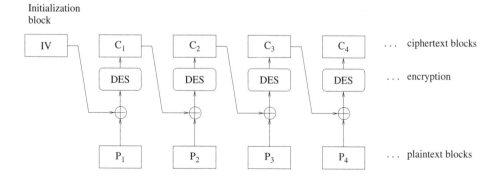

Figure 5.1: Ciphering in CBC mode.

all—C_0 won't mean anything to a potential attacker. This 'zeroth' plaintext block, C_0, is called the **initialization vector** (**IV**), a somewhat unfortunate name; it would be better called the 'initialization block'.

The CBC mode has several important benefits:

1. Plaintext patterns are destroyed. Every ciphertext block depends on all previous plaintext blocks.

2. Two identical plaintexts are transformed into different ciphertexts if they have different initialization vectors, C_0. This is normally the case when C_0 was well chosen (sufficiently random). This finally does away with a common ciphering error: sending an encrypted text repeatedly with almost no changes, and encrypting the same text with different keys.

3. A brute-force attack against time–memory tradeoff (Section 4.4.1) would take three times as long as normal because a fixed plaintext block occurs only with a probability so small it is negligible.

4. CBC can generally also thwart chosen-plaintext attacks. Only an algorithm vulnerable to normal plaintext attacks is not better protected by CBC.

   After all, an eavesdropper knows the ciphertext blocks and, if he learns the plaintext, he can also recover the input blocks for the algorithm (i.e., the sums $C_n \oplus P_{n+1}$). But modern (symmetric) methods should be resistant to plaintext attacks anyway.

Though each ciphertext block depends on the entire 'history', a block that was garbled during the transmission won't be disastrous: it will turn only two plaintexts into gibberish. This argument is not always important. The integrity of data transmitted over insecure channels is today normally ensured by checksums and redundancy. For example, the Internet Protocol (IP) resends garbled data packets; CD-ROMs encode 8-bit information by 14 recorded bits to ensure that bits missing due to data errors (which happen frequently in practice) can be computed from other bits.

CBC has several theoretical security flaws, too. First, it is vulnerable to the so-called **bit-twiddling attack**. The attacker knows the structure of the plaintext and wants to change it. For example, he wants to give himself a raise, say from 398 dollars to 16 782 dollars (and quickly disappear once he has received the pay check). If he can intercept and change the encrypted message before the receiver gets it, then all he does is change the correct bit *ahead* of the number in the ciphertext block, and the figure is raised by $2^{14} = 16\,384$. The block ahead of this block is decrypted correctly. But what users respond to errors?

An attacker could just as well append ciphertext blocks stealthily. Though he would produce meaningless plaintexts, it is a potential risk.

All these attacks are ineffective if plaintexts are sent with encrypted checksums (MACs) only. This is an important point to consider in the implementation.

However, CBC has another weakness: it is vulnerable to the **birthday attack**. You will learn more about it and its peculiar name in Section 6.3.3. This attack is normally used in connection with digital signatures. We are now interested only in the following consideration.

Assume that $C_2 = C_4$ in Figure 5.1. In other words, the following holds:

```
DES(C₁⊕P₂) = DES(C₃⊕P₄)
   C₁⊕P₂   =      C₃⊕P₄
    C₁     = C₃⊕ (P₄⊕P₂)
   C₁⊕C₃   = P₂⊕P₄
```

Since an eavesdropper knows C_1 and C_3, he can compute $P_2 \oplus P_4$. This is not much, but since Murphy usually has a hand in things, the attacker might make the right guess from the most important message of all messages ever sent, since he knows $P_2 \oplus P_4$. You might object that the probability for two blocks to coincide is negligibly low. Even with blocks only 32 bits long, the probability would merely be 2^{-32}, i.e., in the order of magnitude of 10^{-10}. Appearances are deceptive. With 32-bit blocks, about 2^{16} ciphertext blocks suffice for a likelihood that any two of them are identical. (We will get back to this issue in Section 6.3.3.) And with the assumed block size, this is only 256 Kbytes of text, not really much for today's circumstances.

The main reason for this weakness, at least theoretically, is not the CBC mode itself, because there are similar vulnerabilities in other modes, too. Too small a block size is the reason. People even mistrust 64-bit blocks, although two blocks coincide only within 32 Gbytes of ciphertext on average. The reason is that technologies normally evolve faster than we think. This is why we require 128-bit blocks for future algorithms to be on the safe side. The 'critical mass' would then be over 100 million terabytes, which should be sufficient for several years to come.

CBC got its name because the ciphertext blocks are XOR-chained with the plaintext.

CFB: Cipher Feedback Mode

To encrypt data traffic between a central computer and its terminals by means of a block algorithm, neither the simple ECB mode nor the better CBC mode can be used. Imagine you press the ENTER key at such a secure terminal and wait for a command to be executed. Like all characters, this ENTER is also subject to an encryption algorithm. But this algorithm works with 64-bit blocks, and your ENTER character is the second character in the block just started. You can quietly go get yourself a cup of coffee—nothing will happen. The only solution would be to append seven arbitrary bytes to each character and then send this block immediately. That would cause an eightfold increase of the data traffic, which is undesirable, of course.

The CFB mode comes in handy here, because it uses a block cipher as a stream cipher. It's also pretty simple: the ciphertext block produced in the previous section is re-encrypted and XORed with the plaintext block. The result is the new ciphertext block. Mathematically, it looks like this:

$$C_{n+1} = P_{n+1} \oplus DES(C_n).$$

(The names remain the same as with the CBC mode; as a reminder, 'DES' stands for a block algorithm; see Figure 5.2.) Again, we begin with a random initialization vector, C_0. But we can now encrypt every byte (and even bit) of P_{n+1} instantly, because $DES(C_n)$ is known. Once the eight plaintext bytes from P_{n+1} are read and encrypted, we compute $DES(C_{n+1})$, and start the game

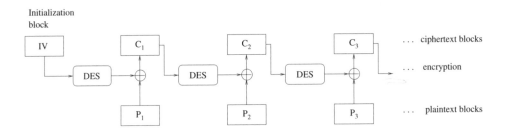

Figure 5.2: Ciphering in CFB mode.

all over again. In practice, something like this is implemented with a shift register, which is re-encrypted, for example, after each plaintext byte read (the ciphertext byte produced is pushed into the shift register from the right-hand side). Instead of 'bytes', we could also use 'a fixed number of bits'.

We won't deal with the details of using CFB as a stream cipher any further here, but instead direct our attention to two facts:

1. The block algorithm is used only to encrypt both when ciphering and deciphering in CFB mode; its reverse (denoted DES^{-1} in CBC) is not required. This is interesting for the hardware aspect when using algorithms other than DES, but also in the following respect: all UNIX systems have to have a DES encryption function, or logging into the system wouldn't be possible (see Section 3.3 and Figure 3.4). Conversely, the DES *de*cryption was not available in cryptological software outside the USA due to export restrictions. Those who use DES ciphering in CFB mode are not interested in it! This is an absurdity similar to the export ban of *UNIX-crypt* in view of the existence of CBW (Crypt Breaker's Workbench; see Section 2.5.3).

2. Similar to the CBC mode, initialization vector C_0 should be different for each data stream.

The name 'CFB' is due to the fact that the ciphertext created is fed back to the 'encryption unit', i.e., it is re-encrypted.

OFB: Output Feedback Mode

In CFB mode, the output of the block algorithm is XORed with the plaintext and then fed back to the block algorithm. If this feedback is done before rather than after the XOR, we obtain the OFB mode:

```
S_{n+1} = DES(S_n)
C_n = S_n ⊕ P_n
```

The initialization block is called S_0 here. The sequence (S_n) is used like a one-time pad (see Figure 5.3). This means that, rather than feeding the ciphertext back to the 'encryption unit', OFB feeds back the output of this unit itself—hence the name *output feedback*.

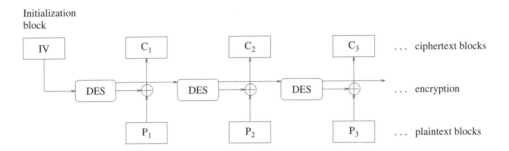

Figure 5.3: Ciphering in OFB mode.

Compared with CFB, this mode has an important benefit in some situations: the sequence (S_n) can be computed independently of the plaintext. This is interesting for online encryption over fast message channels, of course, but also for optional access: if all interesting S_n blocks are cached in main memory, or if they can be computed fast, we could pick out arbitrary ciphertext blocks, C_n, and decipher them immediately. This is exploited by the *crypted file system* (CFS) under UNIX (see Section 7.4); it also lets you encrypt databases.

However, the OFB mode is dangerous: when the same key and the same initialization vector, S_0, are used to encrypt two different texts, and an attacker knows parts of a plaintext, then he can use these parts and the pertaining ciphertext passages to easily XOR-compute the corresponding key blocks. The attacker can then learn parts of the remaining plaintext. This is the reason why every data stream must have a different S_0. This is necessary also to prevent a possible active attack; more about this in the following section.

Protection Against Active Attackers

It is well known that cryptanalysts try to get unauthorized hold of plaintexts and/or keys. Conversely, active attackers may not do any cryptanalysis at all (but have to have an understanding of it); they actively intervene in the data traffic, trying to exploit things to their liking.

For example, an intranet is often connected to the outside world over one single computer. This computer (often only the special software on it) is called a *firewall*, since it is supposed to protect the internal network against hacker attacks from the outside like, well, a firewall. The administrator of this firewall computer can use a program to stealthily intercept and modify data packets. The situation is totally different, for example, with cell phones in the German D- and E-networks. Phone calls are radioed to the next base station in encrypted form, and malicious swapping of data packets would be a technical masterstroke.

The modes introduced above are vulnerable to active attackers at different degrees. The ECB and OFB modes make it relatively easy to swap data blocks. In the CBC and CFB modes, only the first and last blocks can basically be swapped. Therefore, checksums appended to plaintexts should never be in the last block.

Similarly to all stream ciphers, where the key stream (which is called (S_n) in OFB) does not depend on plaintext, the OFB mode is prone to a dangerous active attack, referred to as an **insertion attack**:

The attacker intercepts the ciphertext, but doesn't initially know any bit of the key sequence and the plaintext. If he is successful in introducing a few bits or bytes into the plaintext and in intercepting the ciphertext encrypted with the *same* key sequence, then he can compute the key sequence and the plaintext from the insertion point onwards! This is relatively easy.

The first encryption produces ciphertext blocks C_i from plaintext blocks P_i, XORed with keys S_i:

$$
\begin{array}{ccccccc}
P_1 & P_2 & \ldots & P_i & P_{i+1} & P_{i+2} & \ldots \\
\oplus & \oplus & & \oplus & \oplus & \oplus & \\
S_1 & S_2 & \ldots & S_i & S_{i+1} & S_{i+2} & \ldots \\
= & = & & = & = & = & \\
C_1 & C_2 & \ldots & C_i & C_{i+1} & C_{i+2} & \ldots
\end{array}
$$

The attacker introduces a *known* block, $P*$, after P_i. The cipher looks like this now:

$$
\begin{array}{cccccccc}
P_1 & P_2 & \ldots & P_i & P* & P_{i+1} & P_{i+2} & \ldots \\
\oplus & \oplus & & \oplus & \oplus & \oplus & \oplus & \\
S_1 & S_2 & \ldots & S_i & S_{i+1} & S_{i+2} & S_{i+3} & \ldots \\
= & = & & = & = & = & = & \\
C_1 & C_2 & \ldots & C_i & C'_{i+1} & C'_{i+2} & C'_{i+3} & \ldots
\end{array}
$$

He uses this to compute the following, in this order:

```
Si+1 = P* ⊕ C'i+1 from the second scheme,
Pi+1 = Ci+1 ⊕ Si+1   from the first scheme,
Si+2 = Pi+1 ⊕ C'i+2  from the second scheme,
Pi+2 = Si+2 ⊕ Ci+2   from the first scheme
```

and so on. Since such a stream cipher actually works bitwise, the division in 'blocks' is arbitrary in this context. A block can be one bit long, or 8 or perhaps 31. Moreover, even changes to P_j for $j \leq i$ play only a secondary role; the only important thing is that bits are introduced deliberately.

This opens up ways for the following practicable approach: the attacker—let's call him Bond—had himself hired by a suspect company, knowing that an encrypted message he'd previously intercepted placed an order for hot goods with Gun Services & Partner. That company's contact, Müller, has been under surveillance by the secret service for quite some time. During a date with his company's attractive secretary, Bond mentions incidentally that he had recently put his foot right in it with him, because he had spelled Müller's name wrongly: it should actually read 'Mueller', and the man was known to be finicky about correct orthography. The following day, Bond promptly intercepts an encrypted message to Gun Services & Partner that coincides with the previous message, except in a certain place. He correctly assumes that the first differing byte came into being as the 'ü' was changed into 'u', and an 'e' was inserted after it. Since the name 'Müller' occurs only once in the plaintext—at the beginning of all places, Bond can decipher almost the entire order for an illegal weapons shipment, except for an addition in the second message, which was probably an apology for the wrong spelling.

The best methods are worth nothing to people who handle cryptology so laxly. They should also take more interest in whom their attractive secretaries date.

This attack was only possible because the same key sequence (S_n) was used in both bases. This shows how important it is to choose a different initialization vector for every message.

Other Problems

So much for active attacks. Another aspect is the potential *error propagation*. All modes discussed here are designed such that a transmission error (garbled blocks) can turn no more than two plaintext blocks into gibberish when decrypted. Synchronization errors, i.e., missing bits or blocks, are harder to deal with. In fact, only the CFB mode can handle these errors. It is presumably better to have a transmission protocol that excludes such errors from the outset, rather than leaving the consequences up to the ciphering mode.

Another problem relates to *parallelism*. It has enormous practical significance: network connections are getting increasingly faster, and encryption turns into a bottleneck during data transmission. Of the modes introduced above, only ECB supports the encryption of several blocks in parallel, i.e., it lets you operate several ciphering units in parallel.

There is an *interleaved CBC mode* that also allows you to run several encryptions in parallel. To this end, we decompose the data stream into about five smaller streams, for example, arranged by block numbers as follows:

```
1st data stream:    1,6,11,16,...
2nd data stream:    2,7,12,17,...
...
5th data stream:    5,10,15,20,...
```

We take each data stream and encrypt it with its own chip in CBC mode.

There is a large number of other ciphering modes, in addition to the ones mentioned above. For example, the security software Kerberos 4 uses a mode called **PCBC (Propagating Cipher Block Chaining)**, where the plaintext block, P_{n+1}, is XORed not only with C_n, but also with P_n. This mode guarantees text integrity, which is important because an error in parallelism propagates through all subsequent blocks. However, this feature is ineffective when two successive blocks are swapped. Due to this theoretical weakness, PCBC is no longer used in Kerberos 5—details of the other modes are found in [SchnCr] and [NISTmod].

Another unanswered question is the *cryptanalysis* of these methods. It is easy to understand that one cannot generally decide whether the use of CBC, for example, would make an encryption method more secure or more insecure. The latter is unlikely to be the case with modern algorithms. The purpose of ciphering modes is not to improve an algorithm, but to make its use more sturdy or possible at all: ciphering errors like the repeated sending of the same plaintext become ineffective thanks to careful CBC implementation; single bytes can be transmitted in encrypted form in CFB mode, although one uses a block algorithm.

5.1.2 Padding in Block Algorithms

When implementing block algorithms, we generally hit an apparent side problem relatively late: what should we do with the last block? If we use the block algorithm as a stream cipher (CFB and OFB modes), we work bytewise and have no problem. Things look differently with blockwise encryption, e.g., in ECB or CBC mode. In general, the length of the plaintext is not a multiple of the block length so that we *have* to pad the last block when using either of these modes. In doing so, we don't want to bargain it with cryptological insecurities, of course. This task is less simple than it looks.

If the structure of the plaintext is such that its end is uniquely marked, e.g., by ^Z in text files under MS-DOS, then we can pad the last block with random characters without running a risk. Unfortunately, the plaintext end is not always marked. We will often have to encrypt a binary file, and the end of such a file is determined only by the file length, for example, in UNIX. We also have to assume that arbitrary characters and patterns can occur in the plaintext, i.e., we cannot 'invent' an end identifier and simply append it.

Luckily, there is a very simple method recommended when a few bytes more in the ciphertext won't matter: we pad the last plaintext block with random bytes, and accommodate the number of filler bytes in the last byte:

```
Each_blo| ck_conta | ins_8_ch | aractersXX3
```

Here we have used 'X' for padding; there are three additional bytes, together with the 'count byte'. It is not important whether this last byte includes the *character* '3' or the *numerical value* 3 (corresponding to ^C)—the main thing is that the statement is unambiguous, and that the receiver program can handle it: it first decrypts all blocks, then looks at the last plaintext byte and truncates the number of bytes from the end.

Unfortunately, this method is inelegant when the plaintext just about fills the last block. In this case, we have to append a 'dummy block', the last byte of which has a value of 8 when using 64-bit blocks.

And here is another drawback of this method: the ciphertext is longer than the plaintext. This is undesirable, for example, when a subsection in the middle of a file (or a database) is to be encrypted.

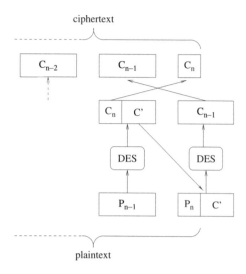

Figure 5.4: Ciphertext stealing in ECB mode.

To this end, Daeman [Daeman] developed so-called **ciphertext stealing** in 1995. I will explain this method for use only with the simple ECB mode (Figure 5.4): the last plaintext block, P_n, is shortened; let it be 11 bits long. We truncate the left 11 bits from the *last* ciphertext block *but one* (denoted C_n in the figure) and use them as the *last* ciphertext block. We append the remaining bits (C' in Figure 5.4) to P_n on the right-hand side and obtain a full plaintext block, and use its cipher as the *last* ciphertext block *but one*. This means that the last, short plaintext block 'steals' some ciphertext from the previous step, hence the name of this clever method.

Together with the CBC mode, ciphertext stealing is almost identical, except that C' is not appended to P_n. It suffices to use zero bits to pad P_n to the full block length—thanks to XORing with the previous ciphertext block ('$C_n|C'$' in Figure 5.4), C' appears nevertheless as if it were appended to P_n before the encryption.

From the programming point of view, ciphertext stealing is less cumbersome than the simple padding mentioned at the beginning of this section: we always have to have the last ciphertext block but one readily stored since we don't know in advance which plaintext block will be the last one. Moreover, the natural sequence of the ciphertext blocks is broken up in the last step.

We can see that ciphertext stealing allows us to substitute things 'in place'. With the CBC mode, however, we would have to accommodate the initialization vector (IV) elsewhere, or be able to compute it from the context any time (for databases, for example, from user and record numbers).

5.1.3 Integrating Checksums

When the encryption does not have to be done 'in place', i.e., when ciphertext and plaintext don't have to have the same length, it is recommended to append a checksum to the plaintext: it allows us to check the text integrity at any given time. This is certainly nothing new to you.

But there is another practical situation where encrypted checksums can come in handy: suppose you have an encrypted file many Mbytes long and you want to edit the pertaining plaintext. If you enter a wrong password, the deciphering algorithm will create a 'plaintext' all the same, though it will be anything but 'plain'. At the very end of the encryption, your program may find that the checksum is not correct and ask you to enter a new password. Meanwhile, it has created one more 'dead data body' and consumed considerable computer resources for nothing. Or perhaps the program works without checksums, and you will painfully notice your error when you first attempt to edit the plaintext.

This is annoying and user-unfriendly. Wouldn't it be simpler if your program were to refuse wrong passwords right away without risking the security? It is possible, and the trick is even very simple—you just have to first recognize the necessity.

We choose a random block, I_0, and encrypt it; we obtain a block I_1. We put both blocks—I_0 and I_1—in front of the plaintext and encrypt the plaintext thus expanded. I_0 becomes C_1, I_1 becomes C_2, and P_1 eventually becomes C_3, and so on (see Figure 5.5).

During the decryption process, we stop after the computation of plaintext block I_1 to check whether or not C_0 coincides with I_1. If it doesn't, the password has got to be wrong; if it does, then there is a high likelihood that it is correct. A theoretical drawback of this method is, however, that the plaintext block $I_1 = C_0$ is known. But resistance to plaintext attacks is taken for granted in modern methods anyway.

Numerous variants are possible here: with the CBC mode, we can use I_0 directly as the initialization vector. We encrypt the first two blocks, I_0 and I_1, as shown in Figure 5.5 in ECB mode, and then switch to CBC from the third block

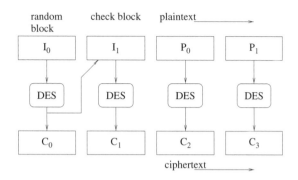

Figure 5.5: Fast password check during decryption.

(i.e., from plaintext block P_0) onwards. I find the trick to put two identical, random blocks in front of the plaintext and encrypt the product in CBC mode even more elegant. However, the statement 'the first two plaintext blocks are equal' can be similarly valuable for an attacker as the statement 'the first plaintext block consists of zeros'. This might actually be the reason why the PGP program discussed in Section 7.1 repeats only 16 bits of the first 64-bit block.

In my RC5a implementation, I use several input blocks, append a checksum, and have a block follow that contains only the release number of the algorithm. The actual plaintext begins only after that block. This arrangement facilitates a later migration to other algorithms or variants of RC5. More about this issue in Section 7.6.

When encrypting 'in place', however, such tricks are not easy to implement— the checksum and the initialization vector have to be accommodated in different places. Where exactly depends on the application.

5.1.4   Generating Keys

A particularly important aspect in implementing encryption methods is the careful choice of keys. We've already learned the risks inherent in reduced key spaces in Sections 3.2 and 3.3. In this section, we will look at another example and then discuss how such mishaps can be avoided.

The Netscape Story

A downright dramatic example of a reduced key space became public in mid-1995 when Ian Goldberg and David Wagner, then Berkeley graduate students, discovered a flaw in the popular Netscape Navigator Internet browser. For example, you can send encrypted credit card numbers through Netscape. To this end, the program creates 128-bit session keys and uses the symmetric RC4 method, which is probably still 'impermeable' (see Section 5.6). Within the USA, 128-bit keys may be used for RC4, while only 40 bits are effectively variable in export versions due to export regulations (the SSL standard used in Netscape ships 88 key bits along within the plaintext). Even 2^{40} is still a pretty large number—approximately 10^{12} or one billion. With so many keys, brute force won't presumably be worthwhile unless the plaintext is really interesting. Even with one million trials per second (which, I think, is not realistic on current computers in view of the required tests for plaintext), a computer would be busy for 11.5 days; but it might be busy even for six months...

As it appeared, the random-number generator for Netscape's session key was not random enough, at least under the Solaris and HP-UX UNIX systems. It was initialized with one quantity that depended on the system clock (with a microsecond accuracy) and on the identification numbers of the current process and the parent process (PID and PPID). This resulted roughly in a variation width of many trillion (10^{18}) possibilities. However, if somebody else had access to the same computer, then this other person could easily find the user's PID and PPID. In addition, that person had no problem determining the system time at least at minute's accuracy, which left a few umpteen million (10^7) possibilities. In other words, the variation width dropped by a factor of 10^{11}, i.e., 100 billion! The fact that Netscape actually used good ciphering algorithms didn't matter any more. Even if Netscape had done highly complicated computations with the initial numbers, 10^7 input values supplied 'only' 10^7 possible keys for trying. Even with only 1000 trials per second, a computer would have been through with them after three hours! But things were even 'better' in practice: often enough, the time in a computer cannot be measured exactly to the microsecond, e.g., only in 10-ms intervals. This will earn you another four orders of magnitude; the computer takes only 10 seconds. With that speed, a full brute-force attack would have taken over 30 years. I think there is hardly a better way to demonstrate more vividly what effect a reduced key space can have.

Since this specific case concerned credit card numbers, such an attack was worthwhile indeed. Netscape responded in exactly the way you'd expect from a manufacturer: rather than suing Goldberg and Wagner for illegal code reassembling, they admitted it was their fault and removed it immediately. This served the general public best. Except for large *and* experienced corporations, it is probably always best to have security studied publicly.

In general, there are two specific points where we have to be particularly careful when creating keys: when session keys are generated automatically, and when keys are entered manually. We will deal with the first point in the next section.

Creating Session Keys—ANSI X9.17

If you have a secret corner on your computer that really nobody can look into, then I recommend you to create keys based on ANSI standard X9.17 (published in 1985). Though this standard specifies DES only as block cipher, you can use any other block algorithm. As usual, we denote $E_K (E = \text{encryption})$ as the encryption with key K below.

Using this ANSI standard, we define a very secret key, K, and a secret initial value, V. We store the two values in that secret corner on our computer.

The procedure creates keys continually. In every step we have to determine a timestamp, T (more about it below), and compute a key, S:

$$S = E_K(E_K(T) \oplus V)$$

Subsequently, we determine a new V:

$$V = E_K(E_K(T) \oplus S)$$

and also put it away in the secret corner (Figure 5.6).

If the bit count of S does not coincide with the number of bits required for the key, we delete bits from S, or create several S keys and concatenate them.

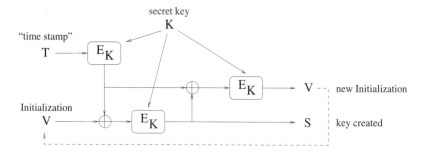

Figure 5.6: Creating session keys according to ANSI standard X9.17.

The result of either of the two equations depends on three quantities: K, T, and V or S. This means that, if we choose T for K and V 'very randomly', an attacker has no chance, even if he were to find K and V.

No question, the method was carefully designed and studied. But also no question excessive security can be effectively annihilated if the implementation is bad. For example, a programmer might take the term 'timestamp' too literally *and* make the set of possible secret keys K too small, thus producing a strongly reduced key space. It would be theoretically sufficient if the timestamp *or* the secret key were taken from a sufficiently large set of values.

The problem of finding a 'secret corner' on the computer is not a cryptological problem, but one that belongs to system security. K is normally created with a 'sufficient amount of randomness' when the program is started. More about this issue in the next section.

'Computer Randomness'

Randomness in a computer is usually not desirable, for example, when a Windows computer crashes purely by chance. On the other hand, you will find that creating randomness in a *targeted* way is not as simple as it may sound. This is not a matter of the statistical properties of randomness. We are only interested in preventing an attacker from anticipating or guessing the values created.

There are many ways to utilize pseudo-random events. However, this depends a lot on the operating system and the computer type used. We cannot discuss such programming techniques in generalized form. You will find some suggestions in Figure 5.7.

Password Selection—the Trick with Wait Times

If you program a password entry yourself, you should absolutely prevent users from entering 'bad passwords' in the program! Think of the experience people had with the Enigma: only the establishment of appropriate work rules made the radio operators think of keys better than 'aaa', 'asd', 'sdf', etc. Only an alarmingly small number of users I watched as they logged into a UNIX system typed long passwords. Older systems allowed users to use very short passwords and, well, many chose two-letter passwords. One single letter may have appeared to them to be too risky after all.

By the way, there is a trick that let's you live well with a one-letter password, but only in one special case. I wrote myself a program that locks the screen

- System time.

- Interrupt vectors or status information of the system: under UNIX V.4, for example, the output of *ps-elf*. Even more clever is the method by Wietse Venema, which he uses in his famous SATAN program (to check the security of UNIX systems); here modified for Linux:

```
#!/bin/bash
(ps axl & ps -elf & netstat -na & netstat -s & ls -1LRt
  /dev & w) 2>&1 | \
    md5sum |  { read word rest; echo $word; }
```

All six commands run concurrently in the background; the sequence of their outputs is not predictable. Each command describes a current system state. Error outputs (due to undefined switches) don't play a role.

- Values of non-initialized variables (this is an insecure and rather weak randomness, but it can be utilized: the values are sometimes hard to predict under UNIX).

- User keyboard entries. The time intervals between keystrokes are measured exactly as permitted by the computer. The keys pressed can also be included in the evaluation. For several dozen keys pressed, the value created will meet a high demand.

The method is well suited for one-time initializations. It is used, for example, in the PGP software package to create an initial value for searching prime numbers. Conversely, it would be cumbersome to have to chaotically clatter on the keyboard upon each program start. PGP stores values created in encrypted form.

- Air turbulences in hard disk boxes are believed to also have been utilized for random generation.

- External random sources such as speech input, Geiger counters, seismometers, and many more can also be used—but there is a drawback since additional hardware is required.

- Arbitrary mouse movements are suitable, too; but not every computer user works with the mouse.

Figure 5.7: Some pseudo-random events a computer could poll.

temporarily via password [Woblock]. I choose a different password every time myself. Anybody unauthorized who wants to work at my terminal waits three seconds after the first attempt fails, six seconds after the second attempt, then 12 seconds, then 24 seconds, and so on. Even if that person knew, for example, that I enter only one lowercase letter, the average brute-force attack against the 26 possibilities would take $3 * 2^{14}$ seconds or 13.5 hours on average—not a promising outlook, since by that time I'll have caught him. The main drawback of the program is that roguish or malicious colleagues could press a wrong button every now and then during my absence (though I took care that keystrokes are not recorded). Upon my return, there would be a wait time of just about 2^{13} seconds...

But let's get back to 'correct' passwords. You should test for the following:

- The password should not be too short (e.g., six characters minimum).

- It should contain not only letters, but also special characters.

- It should not have a simple structure (examples are X.X.X. or aaa,,,).

- And finally, it should not be a word (test against a big dictionary, or demand the occurrence of impossible or rare digrams).

Have a look at Figure 3.6: all these variations and many more can be tested automatically!

On the other hand, if you overstep the mark, you will most likely achieve the opposite: users will write down their passwords. This is a misery. There are two simple ways out of it:

1. If your system processes short passwords only (for example, often only eight characters under UNIX), then memorize a crazy sentence and use the first letters of its words and the punctuation marks. For example, I use the superuser password 'ImRbnje!' on all UNIX computers I administer; that's short for 'In meinen Rechner bricht nie jemand ein!' (Nobody breaks into my computer!). Well, don't take it literally.

2. I'm crazy about these things called passphrases in PGP, and Schneier [SchnCr] also uses that name, while GnuPG call them *mantras*. A **passphrase** is a simple sentence, like the one above, or a fraction of a sentence (a phrase). The program sees a passphrase simply as a long password. When using passphrases, a dictionary attack appears to

have no chance, unless you use a quotation from a book that has been stored electronically (there are even bible CDs and movie dialogs on the Internet!). The crazier the better; typos are allowed and even desired.

If you write the ciphering program yourself, you should allow for passphrases. Passwords would be possible anyway as a special case, for conservative users. If your algorithm wants a 128-bit key, then use the passphrase to build a suitable checksum. This is called **key crunching**.

The only problem with a passphrase is entering it. You normally type a password blindly. Unfortunately, blind typing of entire sentences is pretty hard for some people. PGP allows you to make your input visible in exceptional cases. It doesn't mean that somebody wants to look over your shoulder (there are telescopes!). It might be helpful to always display the passphrase in a small window pane (e.g., 5 characters) that scrolls horizontally. Should somebody watch you they won't be able to quickly read it as they pass by, and it helps people who have to look at what they type.

5.1.5 Bottom Line

This section has certainly showed you that the implementation of security software requires all kinds of tricks. Apart from purely cryptological criteria (such as modes or padding), you also have to bear in mind the entire security environment: password entry, managing secret data, key space size, and so on.

In general, you will probably not want to implement encryption programs yourself, but rather understand and evaluate their security problems. Well, now you have learned a few problems you should be aware of when buying such software. A software vendor should know how to deal with your questions. If they don't, or if they even keep the algorithm used hidden, then be as suspicious as you can afford in view of the market situation.

5.2 DES Modifications

Returning to our discussion of algorithms, we still remain in the DES environment. Based on current knowledge, brute force is still the only practicable attack against this method, i.e., its only exploitable vulnerability is its too short a key length. The slight suspicion whether or not the NSA built in a backdoor in DES remains, of course. There has not been a shortage of attempts to remove this drawback and concurrently utilize the careful design of DES. You will find two results of these attempts later in this section and a large number of additional ones in Schneier [SchnCr, Chapter 13].

5.2.1 Triple-DES

The most obvious means against short keys is multiple encryption with different keys. For example, using Double-DES encryption, we would choose a 112-bit key, and split it into two subkeys, K and K', and then encrypt each plaintext block, P, with K and then once more with K':

```
C = DES_K'(DES_K(P))
```

No brute force is possible against a 112-bit key. This method can be easily implemented in software, and it is slower than DES only by a factor of 2 (with a security 72 quadrillion times larger). To build a ciphering device, all we actually need to do is switch two DES chips in series and then feed them with subkeys separately—no problem at all.

These considerations are pretty obvious, and as usual in cryptology, obvious views are wrong—here too. Considering this generality, we cannot say that double encryption is more secure than simple encryption. First of all, it could well be that there is a (56-bit) key, K', so that the following holds for arbitrary plaintext blocks, P:

```
DES_K" = DES_K(DES_K'(P))
```

In that case, multiple encryption would not be more secure than simple encryption to fend off brute force; only dictionary attacks would get harder. Algorithms that *always* have such K' keys are said to have **group property** or to form a **group**. (Actually not a well-chosen name, because, in mathematics, there is always a single element that belongs to a group. In our case, this would be the identity. A key where the plaintext transforms onto itself doesn't have to exist in arbitrary algorithms with group property.)

DES does not form a group. Though an algebraic operation is defined on the set of mappings defined by multiple encryption as a result of consecutive encryptions, this set, together with this operation, does not form a mathematical group. It is quite possible that this algebraic structure offers vulnerabilities for cryptanalysis. To my knowledge, no such vulnerabilities are known; one doesn't probably even know whether or not consecutive encryptions can produce an identity (i.e., the original plaintext again)—except for the six pairs of semiweak keys from Section 4.4.3.

Let's not stumble about in the gray zone and instead look at a more substantial theory in the following section.

Man Meets in the Middle

There is a method to cryptanalyze double encryption. It is a brute-force attack combined with a known-plaintext attack. The cryptanalyst meets virtually in the middle between the two encryptions. On the one side, he encrypts the known plaintext with all keys; on the other side, he decrypts the ciphertext. The two results should coincide in the middle. This is the reason why this method is referred to as a **meet-in-the-middle attack**, not to be confused with the *man-in-the-middle attack*, where public keys are exchanged (see Section 4.5.2).

Two plaintext–ciphertext block pairs are basically sufficient for this attack. The idea is very simple:

Suppose a plaintext block, P, and the corresponding ciphertext, C, produced from a double encryption, are known:

```
C = DES_K(DES_K'(P))
```

We encrypt P with all possible keys, K', and save the results. We then decrypt C with all possible keys, K, and see whether or not the deciphered product occurs in the ciphers created. If it does, then we test the two keys, K and K', on a second (C, P) pair. If K and K' pass this test, then it is very likely that they are the correct keys. We can now run other, more elaborate tests.

Rather than trial-and-error testing all K for every K', i.e., working our way though $2^{56}*2^{56}$ possibilities like the wise men of Gotham, we save the results for all possible 2^{56} K' keys and test for possible Ks up to 2^{56} times, so that the time required is now only $2^{56} + 2^{56}$.

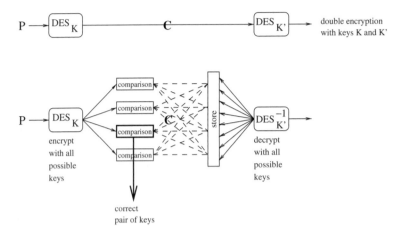

Figure 5.8: Meet-in-the-middle attack against double encryption.

Though our calculation is a bit cleverer than that of the wise men of Gotham, it is stuck on a naïve level. You know that 2^{56} plaintext blocks correspond to an order of magnitude of 576 million Gbytes. As mentioned in Section 4.4.1, this could be stored, for example, on 850 million CDs. (However, we would need a different set of CDs for every plaintext block, $P, \ldots$) This data record has to be looked up 2^{56} times, i.e., roughly 72 quadrillion times. There are very effective search strategies—arranged in a binary tree, we would find every entry in 56 steps at most—but these methods work at a snail's pace, unless the data is on fast hard disks or even in memory. Even if there were such as thing as a superfast, superdense optical memory that required only one square with an edge length of 1 μm for every bit and where every bit could be addressed directly, then the bits of this memory required would still fill a square with an edge length greater than 2 kilometers.

In short, the attack is totally unrealistic in practice. Nevertheless, double DES encryption is an unloved child. Of course, theoreticians get upset when the double cost theoretically yields only a tiny fraction of the effect intended. There might be other considerations. In any event, triple encryption is commonly used today.

Triple-DES

The DES developer Tuchman proposed a method called **Triple-DES**, or **3DES**, in 1979. Let us use two DES keys, K and K', again. We use the first key, K, to encrypt the plaintext, and then use the second key, K', to *de*crypt the result to finally encrypt it with K again:

```
C = DES_K(DES_K'^{-1}(DES_K(P)))
```

The receiver uses K for decryption, K' for encryption, and K for re-decryption.

The decryption in the middle part may be somewhat surprising, but the reason is obviously only the compatibility with the simple method: Triple-DES turns back into the usual DES cipher for $K = K'$. This allows a 'triple ciphering device' to talk to a 'simple ciphering device' without the need to change anything (except the key selection).

There are meet-in-the-middle attacks here, too, which are faster than brute force for 112-bit keys. Schneier suggests using a separate key in each of the three steps rather than the two keys, K and K', to prevent this type of risk.

However, *if* there were an effective attack against DES—the notorious 'backdoor'—it might well be that multiple encryption won't help either. Think only of the combined Vigenère cipher and transposition discussed in Section 2.2.5, which can be broken almost as easily as any one of the single methods.

But we are stumbling about in the gray zone again. To this day, there are no rational arguments against the security of Triple-DES—only irrational ones. But it's true that Triple-DES is rather slow, particularly in software, so that it is markedly inferior to more modern algorithms (especially the final candidates of the AES Initiative; see Section 5.5).

5.2.2 DES with Key-Dependent S-Boxes

In 1994, at the ASIACRYPT conference, Biham and Biryukov introduced a modified DES that can be easily implemented on certain DES chips and in software [Bih.biry]. The trick is to construct key-dependent S-boxes. Some DES chips support variable S-boxes so that these boxes can be created outside the chips and then be fed into them.

Now, it is well known that the original S-boxes are optimized against differential cryptanalysis. DES with random boxes is much easier to break. This actually means that an attacker needs to know the boxes, but let's not draw over-hasty conclusions.

The method is easily described:

1. The key is 104 bits long, which means that it contains 48 bits in addition to the 56 DES key bits.

2. We arrange the eight S-boxes in this sequence: 24673158.

3. We use the first 16 bits of the 48 additional bits of the key for swapping rows and columns in the S-boxes:

   – Two bits each modify an S-box: if bit 1 is equal to 1, then we swap the first two rows with the last two rows; if bit 2 is equal to 1, then we swap the first eight columns with the last eight columns.

   – From said 16 bits, we modify the first two of the first S-box, the next two of the second S-box, and so on.

4. This leaves us with $32 = 4 * 8$ extra bits. Using four bits each, we modify an S-box by XORing these four bits with every element of the box. This corresponds to a permutation of the elements.

5. Otherwise, the DES encryption method remains unchanged.

Without question this method is very hardware-friendly and not slower than DES. The number of (either chosen or known) plaintexts required for differential or linear cryptanalysis is 2^{51} and 2^{53}, respectively, based on current studies. Conversely, brute force requires 2^{102} encryptions. Everything is outside the technically feasible range. Moreover, it cannot be reasonably expected that a DES backdoor—if there is one—would still be open with the Biham–Biryukov method.

We may want to prefer this method over Triple-DES. Schneier [SchnCr, end of Chapter 12] gives a tip how to give the NSA a hard time: 'Therefore, I recommend the use of Biham's construction of key-dependent S-boxes. ... It strengthens the resistance of DES against brute-force attacks, makes differential and linear cryptanalysis harder, and ensures that the NSA has to think of a method that is at least as strong as DES, but different.'

5.2.3 DESX and Whitening

There is yet another extraordinarily simple method to make algorithms more secure based on current knowledge. The method is called **whitening** and it is of special interest for DES, because it increases its short key length. But it can also be applied to almost every other block algorithm.

The idea behind this method is simple: we use two 64-bit keys, *Kp* and *Kc*, in addition to the 56-bit DES key. Ciphertext *C* is computed from plaintext *P* as follows:

```
C = Kc ⊕ DES_Kd(P ⊕ Kp).
```

This means that, in addition to the DES cipher, the plaintext is XORed with additional keys before the encryption, and the ciphertext is XORed with additional keys after the encryption. It also means that an attacker won't have any plaintext–ciphertext pairs for DES, and brute force won't work either. The structure of DES suggests that the algorithm gains from this procedure (and should there really be a backdoor in DES, then this assumption might be wrong).

The method is attractively simple. It requires only minimum hardware expansion, while the gain in security is presumably very high. The fact that the USA once exported only ciphering devices with limited key length (here 40 bits) won't matter, since whitening compensates for this limitation.

The idea is a brainchild of Ron Rivest; the method is thoroughly studied in [DESX]. An algorithm called **DESX** computes *Kc* as a one-way hash value (see Section 6.3.1) from *Kd* and *Kp*. It has been used in *MailSafe* (since 1986) and *BSAFE* (since 1987). The effective key length of DESX is 120 bits, far too many for brute force.

One would actually expect whitening to have an effective key length of $64 + 56 + 64 = 184$ bits. But this is not so: it is 'only' 120 bits. That's not too hard to check; I'll just briefly outline it below.

We pick two plaintext–ciphertext pairs, $(P1, C1)$ and $(P2, C2)$, and set $dP = P1 \oplus P2$ and $dC = C1 \oplus C2$. The modified plaintexts, $P1 \oplus Kp$ and $P2 \oplus Kp$, still also have XOR difference dP. Also, the ciphertexts XORed with Kc produce a XOR difference, dC.

Now we brute-force all (P, S) plaintext-key pairs such that

```
DES_S(P) ⊕ DES_S(P ⊕ dP) = dC
```

holds. This search requires $2^{64+56} = 2^{120}$ DES ciphers each. In terms of the order of magnitude, only $2^{64}(P, S)$ pair solutions can be expected. We can try to compute *Kp* and *Kc* for each pair and test the result on a third and fourth plaintext–ciphertext pair. This effort is 'negligibly small' (namely about 72 quadrillion times smaller) compared with 2^{120} ciphers, but 256 times larger compared with the usual DES cracking.

Should anybody one day succeed in reducing the search for (P, S) pairs with a clever trick, then whitening would presumably not be of much use.

[DESX] shows that the cost to be expected for different *Kp* and *Pc*, too, would be in the order of magnitude of $2^{64+56-1-lg(m)}$, where *m* denotes the number of eavesdropped plaintext–ciphertext pairs.

Under this aspect, it appears reasonable to choose *Kc* as a function of *Kp* and *Kd* right away as is done in DESX.

5.3   IDEA: A Special-Class Algorithm

Despite Triple-DES and the modified DES with key-dependent S-boxes by Biham and Biryukov, there was an understandable wish to get away from this algorithm once and for all. In fact, this algorithm is more than a quarter of a century old, and it cannot be entirely excluded that somebody *might* know a more successful attack against this type of encryption than we do—after all, it is assumed that only the smaller part of cryptological research is public.

A joint project of ETH Zurich (under the supervision of famous cryptologists X. Lai and J. Massey) and Ascom Systec AG tried to find theoretically solid foundations for a new algorithm. Such an algorithm was published with the name **PES (Proposed Encryption Standard)** in its original form in 1990. This method was attacked successfully by Biham and Shamir using differential crypt-analysis. As a consequence, Lai and Massey protected their algorithm against this attack and put an 'I' for 'Improved' in front of its name. Since 1992, we have known the algorithm by the name **IDEA—International Data Encryption Algorithm** (see *algor/idea* directory on our Web site and [SchnCr, 13.9]).

5.3.1   This Time First: IDEA Patent Rights

IDEA is used for symmetric encryption in the very popular PGP software package, which is the main reason why it is well known. Unfortunately, it is less noticed that IDEA is patent-protected—in Europe until May 16, 2011, while the USA will enjoy its free use one year earlier. This fact is omitted so

Table 5.1 Patent protection of IDEA; source: company brochure (as of March 5, 1996)

Country	Patent number	Filed on	Granted on	Expiry
Europe:	0482154	5/16/1991	6/30/1993	5/16/2011
Austria,				
France,				
Germany,				
Great Britain,				
Italy,				
Netherlands,				
Sweden,				
Switzerland,				
Spain,				
USA	5'214'703	5/16/1991	5/25/1993	5/25/2010
Japan	508119/1991	5/16/1991	pending	

often that I will describe the legal issues before discussing the algorithm itself. Table 5.1 shows the details.

The current licensing terms and conditions can be obtained directly from Ascom Systec AG (`www.ascom.com`).

At the beginning of 1996, the license fees ranged between 2 and 15 dollars per user, where not all employees in companies are counted as users, depending on their type of classification.

As a sideline, the fact that algorithms cannot be patented in Germany or elsewhere doesn't matter: IDEA is patented in Switzerland, and this patent is effective in other countries, too.

Use of the algorithm is free for non-commercial purposes, but a copyright notice has to be included in the corresponding software, and the developer should contact Ascom prior to publication.

5.3.2 The IDEA Method

After this legal stuff, let's return to cryptology:

- IDEA works with 64-bit blocks and uses a 128-bit key. This key is used to create 52 subkeys of 16 bits each as follows.

  The key is first decomposed into eight subkeys of 16 bits each. These are the first eight subkeys.

Subsequently, the 128-bit key is left-rotated by 25 bits (i.e., the 25 most significant bits walk back in from the right) and once again decomposed into eight equally long subkeys. This produces the next eight subkeys.

In the seventh round, only the four subkeys with the most significant bits are chosen.

- The algorithm encrypts in eight rounds, so it is a product algorithm rather than a Feistel network. It uses six subkeys in every round.

- In every round, the blocks are split into four subblocks of 16 bits each and linked with three different, 'incompatible' operations; all operations process 16-bit numbers only.

  This facilitates implementing IDEA in hardware; better yet, it even works effectively on 16-bit microprocessors.

- Finally, the four subblocks are linked with the four remaining subkeys in an output transformation and composed into one single 64-bit ciphertext block.

Before having a closer look at the IDEA round, we want to briefly discuss the operations used to get a basic grasp of the design.

5.3.3 Three Algebraic Operations Cleverly Linked

With a set of 16-bit numbers at hand, we look at the following three operations:

- the known bitwise XOR operation, '$\oplus$';
- the usual addition, '$+$', which is a modulo 2^{16} addition due to the limitation to 16-bit numbers; and
- the modulo $2^{16} + 1$ multiplication, denoted '$\odot$' here; where zero represents the remainder, 2^{16}, i.e., if either of the operands a or b equals zero in the equation

```
a ⊙ b = c mod (2^16+1)
```

then we write 2^{16} in its place to compute c, and vice versa: if result c becomes equal to 2^{16}, then we write the value zero in its place. This is a pure issue of definition, but somehow unusual.

The definition mentioned last is normally quoted uncritically (and not explained), but it is apparently contradictory. The thing is, we only have 2^{16} numbers available to represent $2^{16} + 1$ remainders—the remainder zero is missing here, or is it? Well, zero can never occur as a remainder: since $2^{16} + 1 = 65\,537$ 'happens' to be a prime number, the product of two numbers is divisible only by $2^{16} + 1$, if this holds at least for one of the factors. In this arithmetic, however, we multiply only numbers between 1 and 2^{16} together, and none of these numbers is divisible by the prime number 65 537.

Expressed mathematically: together with '$\odot$', we have defined an algebraic operation within the set of numbers 0, 1, ..., $2^{16} - 1$, which is always executable within this set.

Before describing IDEA any further, we can already see why it calculates with 16-bit numbers rather than, for example, 32-bit numbers: $2^{32} + 1$ is not a prime number; rather the following holds:

```
2^32 + 1 = 641 * 6700417
```

We wouldn't be able to define this analogously to the '$\odot$' operation for 32-bit operands.

These three algebraic operations are 'incompatible'. This blurred statement needs some explanation.

We all know the distributive law

```
a(b + c) = ab + ac
```

from school. There is no pair of operations among these three for which the distributive law holds, i.e., for all 16-bit numbers, $a, b,$ and c. For instance, there is the counterexample

```
a = b = c = 1
a + (b ⊕ c) = 1 + 0 ≠ 0 + 0 = (a ⊕ b) + (a ⊕ c)
```

for the '$+$' and '$\oplus$' operations.

Moreover, no 'generalized associativity law' holds for any two of the three operations. As we know, the usual associativity law of addition for three normal numbers says

```
a + (b + c) = (a + b) + c
```

The 'generalized associativity law' for the '+' and '⊕' operations would read like this:

```
a + (b ⊕ c) = (a + b) ⊕ c
```

Again, $a = b = c = 1$ supplies a counterexample: the left-hand side is equal to 1, the right-hand side is equal to 3.

We can also prove the following: the algebraic structures defined by the three operations (formulated mathematically: they are monoids) cannot be transformed one into the other by some clever transformation or other in two cases (formulated mathematically: they are not isotopic). This holds for the two pairs of monoids that belong to the operations '⊕' and '⊙', and '⊕' and '+', respectively. Though there is isotopy between the monoids belonging to '⊙' and '+', it is as complex as a discrete logarithm, and we know from Section 4.5.4 that discrete logarithm is a 'hard' function.

These comments were aimed not only at furthering your mathematical knowledge, but also at emphasizing why Lai and Massey chose these operations: they are really a poor match. And now you know where the decomposition into 16-bit blocks stems from: the fact that $2^{16} + 1$ is a prime number (and not because they felt sympathy for owners of vintage 16-bit computers...).

5.3.4 The IDEA Algorithm in Detail

IDEA links these three operations within a network that looks desperately complicated at first. Figure 5.9 shows the description of a round.

As usual, each operation processes the operands that correspond to the incoming arrows. The result 'walks' alongside the outgoing arrow to the next operation, or forms a subblock. In six cases, however, a result is used in two additional operations.

Figure 5.10 shows the output transformation.

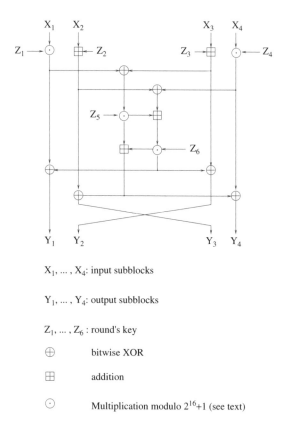

$X_1, \ldots, X_4$: input subblocks

$Y_1, \ldots, Y_4$: output subblocks

$Z_1, \ldots, Z_6$: round's key

$\oplus$ bitwise XOR

$\boxplus$ addition

$\odot$ Multiplication modulo $2^{16}+1$ (see text)

Figure 5.9: Description of the IDEA algorithm.

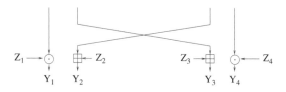

Figure 5.10: Output transformation in IDEA, using the same notation as in Figure 5.9.

A closer look reveals that the structure of this network is surprisingly logical. First of all, we will quickly notice that, *together* with the output transformation, the network is symmetric. The reason is that, if we were to swap the plaintext blocks with the ciphertext blocks, traversing the network from bottom to top,

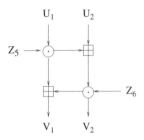

Figure 5.11: The MA transformation forms the 'core' of IDEA.

then the same computations would be executed! This explains the meaning of the output transformation in a very simple way.

Having made this discovery, we already know how to decrypt: we substitute each key by the key that currently reverses the operation during the encryption. These are the negative values of Z_2 and Z_3, and the reciprocals modulo $2^{16} + 1$ with the others. XOR operations are self-inversing, i.e., applying them once more to the same intermediate results produces the original result again. This is why subkeys stand explicitly ahead of the '+' and '⊙' operations, but not ahead of '⊕'!

That's cleverly designed indeed, but rather a technical question. We would certainly accept a separate decryption algorithm for the price of higher security.

In contrast, another feature of IDEA is more interesting: *the result of an operation never becomes the operand of an operation of the same type in any place.* No matter how we go along the arrows—two equal operations never follow one after the other on one path. This is an important property of IDEA that has caused *confusion*. But this confusion is 'more unfathomable' than with DES, at least subjectively.

There are more remarkable properties in IDEA. In its core is the **MA** (multiplication–addition) **transformation**, shown in Figure 5.11.

The MA transformation is responsible for *diffusion*. Computer experiments have shown that, with this transformation, *every bit of V_1 and V_2 depends on every bit of the keys and every bit of blocks U_1 and U_2*. And all this after one single round! Lai and Massey also showed that at least four operations are required to achieve this—so the MA transformation is even minimal in this sense.

5.3.5 Cryptanalyzing IDEA

After these impressive and theoretically underpinned properties of this algorithm, you'll not be surprised to hear that so far the most successful attacks against IDEA have become stuck after 3.5 rounds (where the output transformation is counted as half a round). The method is optimized against differential cryptanalysis; Lai thinks that it is resistant to this attack after only four rounds. And an attempted attack with related keys by Biham also failed.

There are **weak keys** in the sense that their use by foisting chosen plaintexts can be proved, which could be interesting for chip cards with a 'burnt-in key'. First of all, however, these keys can be easily avoided—one only needs to XOR all subkeys with the hexadecimal number 0x0dae—and second, the probability that such a key can be caught is 2^{-96}; that is about one out of 10^{29} randomly selected keys (this number even has a name: 100 quadrilliards).

An effective cryptanalysis was presented by Philip Hawkes at the EURO-CRYPT '98 [HawIDEA]. Hawkes discovered 265 weak keys for which roughly 20 chosen plaintexts would suffice to recover 72 bits of the key. The remaining 56 bits are then recovered by brute force—a cost comparable to cryptanalyzing DES. This means for an attacker that he can fire up his IDEA crack machine (which is slightly larger and slower than his DES crack machine) every 9 trillion (9 000 000 000 000 000 000) sessions he listened in on to compute the key. This doesn't sound particularly dangerous. Nevertheless, Hawkes recommends changing IDEA's key generation system. This is no paranoia—the next cryptanalytic improvement could be more effective.

Another attack was demonstrated by Borst, Knudsen, and Rijmen at the EURO-CRYPT '97 [BorstIDEA], but only against a 3.5-round IDEA (i.e., three rounds plus final transformation). In about 5/6 of all cases, this attack finds the key using 2^{56} chosen plaintexts (accordingly more than 500 000 terabytes of plaintext). Though the authors assume that this attack could be mounted more effectively, they doubt whether it would change the security of the full 8.5-round IDEA. In his work mentioned above [HawIDEA], Hawkes studied a 4-round IDEA. With a little less than 40 chosen plaintexts, he recovered 15 bits of the key, which is only of theoretical interest for the time being.

It would be absolutely hopeless to ever want to brute-force IDEA. With a key length of 128 bits, this belongs to the realm of science-fiction movies (see also 'Brute Force' entry in the Glossary and Section 5.9).

However, the IDEA algorithm has one big drawback: it is not scalable, which means that it cannot benefit from the growing processing width of modern computers (32 bits, 64 bits, ...) and is particularly fixed on 64-bit blocks. We know from the discussion of the CBC mode in Section 5.1.1 that too small a block size theoretically represents a vulnerability for birthday attacks. In fact, its small block size and its fixed key length were the only reasons IDEA disqualified as a candidate for the AES algorithm, the successor of DES (see Section 5.5).

Of course, IDEA has not been studied long enough to convince even the last doubter of its security. Even the theoretically underpinned design, over which one could go into raptures, doesn't exclude potential vulnerabilities. Crypt-analysts traditionally look for sore points and don't normally let themselves get carried away by the esthetic inner life of an algorithm. Anyhow, no successful attack has become publicly known, although cryptologists have busied themselves increasingly with IDEA.

5.3.6 Speed, Outlook

IDEA is about twice as fast in software as DES. Schneier [SchnCr, Section 13.9] mentions 300 Kbytes/s on a 66-MHz PC-486 (compare this with RC5 in Section 5.4). In hardware, however, IDEA is much harder to implement than DES, which is mainly due to the '$\odot$' operation. An IDEA chip developed at the ETH Zurich achieved about 22 Mbytes/s, but it is not produced in series. The major obstacle appears to be reservations by the industry on account of the license fees for the algorithm. Security has not yet reached the importance for an organization with 100 employees to pay 1000 dollars for encryption within their internal networks. For example, a software vendor would have to pay 2 % of their sales to Ascom Systec AG just for using IDEA in their products. This is obviously too much even for an attractive name like IDEA. In addition to its use in free software (for example, PGP and SSH; see Chapter 7) I know that it is commercially used in the *Brokat* software package, which has been deployed by at least four German banks since early 1997. Deutsche Telekom presumably purchased a large number of IDEA licenses for their own products.

5.4 RC5: Yet Another Hope for DES Replacement

This section discusses perhaps the simplest and most flexible of modern algorithms. **RC5** is a symmetric block algorithm introduced by Ron Rivest [RivRC5] in 1994 (you know Rivest from the RSA method). In designing this algorithm, Rivest pursued the following goals:

- RC5 should be equally suitable *for hardware and software*.

- RC5 should be *fast*. To this end, the algorithm uses only operations on words in the sense of hardware, i.e., operations on 32-bit blocks, for example, when working with 32-bit processors.

- RC5 should be *variable*. No word length, block length, key length, or number of rounds are defined. It should be up to the user to opt between higher speed and higher security.

- RC5 should be *simple*, which would not only simplify the implementation: the main idea is that a simple structure makes it easier for cryptanalytic study.

- RC5 should require *little memory*. This makes it interesting for chip cards.

- Finally and most importantly, RC5 should be *secure*.

5.4.1 Description of the RC5 Algorithm

For the sake of simplicity, we will limit our discussion in this section to 32-bit words, i.e., to the algorithm fastest for 32-bit processors. RC5 looks the same for 64-bit words, and it can also be implemented on 32-bit processors, but this makes it somewhat slower.

Figure 5.12 summarizes the original description of RC5.

We can represent the algorithm in an alternative form. Denoting A as L_i and B as R_i, each of the two equations looks like this in an RC5 round:

```
L_{i+1} = R_i
R_i     = ((L_i ⊕ R_i) <<< R_i) + S_i
```

This reminds us strongly of a Feistel network (see Figure 4.6), but it is not: first, the round function depends not only on R_i, but also on L_i; second, L_i is not XORed with the round function's result. Figure 5.13 shows a graphical representation of an RC5 round.

RC5 is really very fast: my own implementation on a 133-MHz Pentium and ESIX V.4.2 PC-UNIX achieved 1.5 Mbytes per second—i.e., 12 Mbits

The RC5 Algorithm

The algorithm depends on three parameters:

- the word size, w, in bits (in the following written as '$w = 32$');
- the number of rounds, $r(r \leq 1)$; and
- the key length of b bytes ($b = 0, 1, \ldots, 255$).

Plaintext and ciphertext blocks are each $2w$ bits long, for $w = 32$, i.e., 64 bits. Rivest recommends a key length of 16 bytes for $w = 32$ with 12 rounds, and denotes the method as 'RC5-32/12/16'.

Encryption

- From a key K of length b, create a field, $S_0, S_1, \ldots, S_{2r+1}$, of $2(r + 1)$ subkeys with 32 bits each (see below).
- Decompose every plaintext block into two 32-bit blocks, A and B.
- Set

```
A = A + S₀
B = B + S₁
```

- In the ith round ($i = 1, \ldots, r$) set

```
A = ((A ⊕ B) <<< B) + S₂ᵢ
B = ((B ⊕ A) <<< A) + S₂ᵢ₊₁
```

where $A <<< B$ denotes the left rotation of A by B bits. Since the left rotation by 32 bits is the identity for $w = 32$, you have to consider only the five least significant bits of B for computing $A <<< B$.

Decryption

Decryption proceeds accordingly in the opposite direction:

- Decompose the ciphertext block into two half blocks, A and B, with 32 bits each.

Figure 5.12: The RC5 algorithm.

- For $I = r, \ldots, 1$ compute

```
B = ((B-S₂ᵢ₊₁) >>> A) ⊕ A
A = ((A-S₂ᵢ) >>> B) ⊕ B
```

  where $>>>$ denotes the right rotation, analogous to the encryption.
- Set

```
B = B -  S₁
A = A -  S₀
```

  and put A and B together into the plaintext block.

Computing the Key

Initialize the key field (S_i):

- If w is the word length in bits, i.e., 32 in this case, then define two constants, P_w and Q_w, by

```
Pᵥᵥ = Odd(2ʷ(e-2))
Qᵥᵥ = Odd(2ʷ(φ − 1))
```

  where e is the basis of the natural logarithms $(2.718\,281\,8\ldots)$, ϕ is the golden ratio

```
φ = (√ 5 + 1)/2 = 1.681033...
```

  and *Odd()* is the nearest uneven number.
- Now set

```
S₀ = Pᵥᵥ    and
Sᵢ = Sᵢ₋₁ + Qᵥᵥ    for i=1,...,2r+1.
```

Figure 5.12: (*continued*)

Mixing with the Key

- Copy the *b*-byte key, $K_{i=0,...,b-1}$, into a word field, $L_{i=0,...,c-1}$. Choose as small a value for *c* as possible. This is similar to copying the character string *K* into field *L* on Intel processors; in general, *K* has to be shoved into *L* bytewise. Written in C, it looks like this:

```
for(i = c-1; i > = 0; --i) L[i] = 0;
for(i = b-1; i > = 0; --i) L[i/u] = (L[i/u] << 8) + K[i];
```

- For integers *i, j, t, m* and for words *A, B* set (again written as a C program):

```
i = j = 0;
t = 2*r + 2;
m = 3*max(t,c);
A = B = 0;
```

and compute

```
for(k=0; k < m; ++k)
  {
    A = S[i] = (S[i] + A + B) _ 3;
    B = L[j] = (L[j] + A + B) _ (A + B);
    ++i; i % = t;  /*, i.e., i = (i + 1) mod t */
    ++j; j % = c;  /*, i.e., j = (j + 1) mod c */
    }
```

Figure 5.12: (*continued*)

per second—when encrypting long files on the hard disk (so this is not a trimmed benchmark). Even on a 486-33 computer, the same RC5 implementation still yielded 240 Kbytes/s, corresponding to 1.9 Mbits/s.

5.4.2 Cryptanalyzing RC5

Similarly to IDEA, RC5 also links three different operations, but in a much simpler way. As you might expect, the *diffusion* is weaker than with IDEA; but RC5 has more rounds. The following simplified example shows the weaker diffusion.

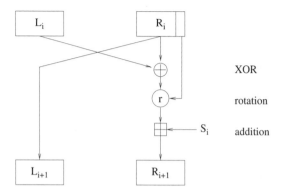

Figure 5.13: Alternative representation of an RC5 round.

Choose two plaintext half blocks, A and B, and all subkeys, S_i, such that the five least significant bits are each equal to 0. Then the last five bits of the ciphertext half blocks are also equal to 0, which means that they certainly won't depend on other key or plaintext bits. However, if the rotation occurs even in one single round, the diffusion grows explosively. This might be one of the reasons Rivest chose extremely 'odd' values for the initialization values, P_w and Q_w, and 'mixed in' the subkey field, S, extremely 'thoroughly'. With 12-round RC5 and random subkeys, the last five bits of all subkeys will be equal to 0 only once in 2^{130} cases. In mathematics, 2^{-130} is a positive number indeed; for us humans, such a probability simply means 'never'.

The *confusion* is essentially determined by the data-dependent rotation. Anyhow, the security of RC5 depends essentially on the data-dependent rotation. However, it has not yet been studied exhaustively.

RC5 was analyzed intensively at the RSA Laboratories. Statistically, the algorithm has excellent properties—as may be expected. After only four rounds, the single ciphertext bits depend 'equally' on the single plaintext bits (formulated mathematically: the correlation almost no longer depends on bit positions). During my own studies, I found no indication of statistically usable dependencies. But this doesn't mean much. An algorithm with obvious statistical dependencies is considered weak anyway.

According to information in [RivRC5], a trial with 100 million random plaintexts and random keys showed that every plaintext bit influences a rotation at least once (i.e., it influences the last five bits of a half block) after only eight rounds.

Among 100 million random pairs of 16-byte keys and 64-bit plaintext blocks tested, there were plaintext bits which, when changed, did not influence the rotations of RC5 ('influence' means the number of places that are rotated changes). Such cases were found as follows:

34 732 with 7-round RC5;

1915 with 8-round RC5;

104 with 9-round RC5; and

15 with 10-round RC5.

Up to the 11th round, every plaintext bit influenced a rotation (there were probably exceptions, but 100 million trials were obviously not enough to find them).

Figure 5.14: Modified plaintext bits influencing the rotations in RC5.

I cannot confirm the last statement. In my own trials, I created 100 million random pairs of 16-byte keys and 64-bit plaintext blocks. For each of these pairs, I initially stored the amounts by which things are rotated in each of the twelve rounds. Subsequently, I changed one bit one after another in all 64 bit positions in the plaintext and compared the rotations with the 'ground setting'. I found that there are still cases where a modified plaintext bit influences *no* rotation even after ten rounds. Figure 5.14 shows the specific results.

Differential Cryptanalysis

The first attack against RC5 by means of *differential cryptanalysis* was presented by Kaliski and Yin at the CRYPTO '95 Conference [KalisRC5]. The results spoke in favor of RC5: a 6-round RC5 required 2^{31} chosen plaintexts (i.e., approximately one billion, or 8 Gbytes); 8 rounds required 2^{39}; 10 rounds required 2^{50}; and finally 2^{62} were required for 12 rounds. The computation time grows as you would expect: a Sun-4 workstation (considered a rather slow computer today) worked for 10 minutes to attack a 5-round RC5, but it worked for not less than 12 hours against a 6-round RC5 (corresponding to 2^{25} and 2^{31} plaintexts).

For practical purposes, these values are not interesting. In theory, however, they represent progress: 2^{62} chosen plaintexts are clearly faster than brute force.

The background of this attack is interesting. The IDEA developers introduced so-called **Markov ciphers** [LMM.IDEA]. These are product algorithms where the probability for an arbitrary difference of two ciphertexts depends only on the difference in the pertaining plaintexts, and not on that difference's value, in every round. Such methods are resistant to differential cryptanalysis, because every ciphertext difference has about the same probability after a sufficient number of rounds with a fixed plaintext difference.

RC5 is not a Markov cipher. But every fixed plaintext difference creates a large number of possible ciphertext differences with about the same probability across several rounds, mainly thanks to rotation.

This attack was improved by Knudsen and Meier by a factor of up to 512, i.e., 2^9 [KnudRC5], at the CRYPTO '96. Their idea was to search for such plaintexts where no rotation occurs at the beginning in several rounds, i.e., where there is only a weak diffusion. They found these plaintexts by use of a special *key-detection* algorithm. Against a 12-round RC5, they 'only' needed 2^{53} chosen plaintexts to find special plaintexts where no rotation occurred in the first few rounds. Subsequently, they would need another 2^{54} chosen plaintexts to recover the key. As a sideline, 2^{54} plaintexts correspond to a data volume of 128 000 terabytes...

Another improvement was introduced by Biryukov and Kushilevitz at the EUROCRYPT '98 [BirKush]. They defined a pair of plaintexts where the rotation amounts coincided in all rounds to serve as a *right pair* (see Section 4.4.2) for differential cryptanalysis. (The exceptions found in Figure 5.15 may in this sense also be considered to be right pairs that differ only in one bit.) Rather than looking at the differences of 32-bit words, they studied only the five least significant bits. This is why they also call their method *partial differential cryptanalysis*. Its result is more dangerous by a factor of about 1000: 2^{44} chosen plaintexts suffice to recover the subkeys. So, the only thing left for the attacker is to foist 128 Gbytes of chosen plaintext on the code writer (or the chip card). That kind of volume is transmitted over a 34-Mbit data line within a little over one hour. As a sideline, RC5a, my modification introduced in Section 5.4.3, is resistant to this attack, just as well as to the attack by Knudsen and Meier.

Weak Keys

Knudsen and Meier additionally found weak keys in the sense that using such a key facilitates differential cryptanalysis. These keys—the S_i words in

Figure 5.13, and not the original key, K—have three subkeys, S_i, S_{i+1}, and S_{i+2}, with special values in their last five bits. This increases the probability of special differences over three half rounds by a factor of 4.7. However, a special test with chosen plaintexts is required here, too, to detect the use of such a key.

These weak keys have different 'risk classes'. The higher the risk class, the easier the attack, but also the fewer weak keys of that class there are. More specifically, only 2^{45} chosen plaintexts (270 Tbytes of text) are required to find the key to be weak with RC5-32/12/16 for a key group with frequency $2^{-32.2}$ (approximately one key out of five billion random keys). For these keys, differential cryptanalysis can make do with 'only' 2^{40} chosen plaintexts (8.2 Tbytes). For other keys with frequency $2^{-10.7}$ (one key out of 1663 random keys), you would need 2^{53} plaintexts for the key and 2^{49} plaintexts for the attack.

This doesn't represent a particular risk for practical purposes. But there might be faster methods to find weak keys, and there might also be other types of weak keys.

As you can see, the result is not as alarming as the Abstract in Knudsen's article may suggest: 'We also show that RC5 has many weak keys with regard to differential cryptanalysis. This weakness is in the structure of the algorithm and not in its key generation.' However, we should follow up closely on the development. It's certainly no mistake to use RC5-32/16/16, i.e., to work with 16 rounds rather than 12. This algorithm is still very fast. And, by the way, this cryptanalysis doesn't work for RC5a (see Section 5.4.3).

Linear Cryptanalysis and Linearly Weak Keys

The first known linear cryptanalysis on RC5 was done by Kaliski and Yin [KalisRC5]. They required 2^{47} plaintexts for a 5-round method (i.e., like with the differential cryptanalysis on DES!), but as many as 2^{57} with 6 rounds. Consequently, the 12-round method is secure in this respect. However, similarly to Knudsen and Meier, Heys [HeysRC5] showed that there are weak keys here, too, which facilitate linear cryptanalysis: using the 12-round method with a 128-bit key, there are 2^{28} (about one quarter of a billion) such weak (sub)keys, and only about 2^{17} plaintext blocks (corresponding to 1 Mbyte of plaintext) are required to recover the subkeys. This sounds more worrying than the result from differential cryptanalysis. Though the probability of catching such a key is only 2^{-100} (approximately 10^{-30}), what if Rivest's algorithm were to create preferably weak subkeys for generation? The counter-proof may not be easy.

There are no such worries rationally, but being careful has never hurt. RC5a, my modification introduced in Section 5.4.3, should not have differentially or linearly weak keys (Heys thinks so, too). The reason is that the probability that no rotation occurs in successive rounds is much smaller with RC5a (it can even be arbitrarily reduced if there is enough memory available). All attacks against RC5 discussed so far are based on the assumption that there is no rotation in several rounds.

The mod-3 Cryptanalysis of RC5P

Kelsey, Schneier, and Wagner introduced a new type of attack against a modification of RC5 in [Schnmod3]. I find this attack worth noting here since it was the first direct attack against data-dependent rotations. In fact, all cryptanalyses I know of try to find chosen plaintexts where nothing or little is rotated, and attack the algorithm, for example, by differential cryptanalysis. The underlying idea outlined in [Schnmod3] is different and so simple you once again have to ask yourself why nobody thought of it earlier.

We look at the remainders of 32-bit numbers, X, when dividing them by 3. If X is smaller than 2^{31}, then the cyclic left rotation by 1 is nothing but a multiplication by 2:

```
X <<< 1 = 2X  (X < 2^31)
```

Conversely, the following holds in the other case:

```
X <<< 1 = 2X + 1-2^32 (X • 2^32) .
```

But the following holds in general since 2^{32} leaves a remainder of 1 when divided by 3:

```
X <<< 1 = 2X mod 3 .
```

Consequently, this equation also holds for all $X <<< n$ rotations with uneven n. When n is even, the remainder of X modulo 3 does not change in the rotation. In particular, the divisibility by 3 is not lost in any rotation. If X and n are random, then the following holds with a probability of 2/3:

```
X <<< n = X mod 3.
```

In other words, the data-dependent rotation doesn't 'blur' information on X (namely the remainder from dividing by 3) sufficiently, and the confusion is 'weak' in this respect. The results of intermediate rounds differ from randomness in a definable way. That's the point where the authors mount their attack.

I will just discuss two details below (you can find the full article in *txt/cryptana/ mod3.ps* on our Web site):

1. In order for the 'beautiful number theory' to remain applicable, RC5P is analyzed rather than RC5. The RC5P modification emerges from the original RC5 when replacing the XOR operations by additions in every round. Kaliski and Yin studied RC5P back in 1998 (so the algorithm was not 'invented' especially for the mod-3 cryptanalysis) and assumed that the method was just as secure as RC5 itself. They were wrong as it turned out.

   It is easy to see without further explanation that additions are 'friendlier' towards residual classes than XOR operations.

2. The authors didn't initially succeed in providing a clean theoretical substantiation for their cryptanalysis, i.e., estimating statistical shifts mathematically. They replaced the theory by computer experiments and constructed their attack on this basis.

Something like this is generally disapproved of among theoreticians, but justified from the cryptanalytic point of view: the end justifies the means. If the attack works in practice, then it is irrelevant whether or not it was theoretically substantiated.

Nevertheless, the authors endeavor to close this gap. For cryptographs, i.e., from the algorithm development perspective, the current state is somewhat unsatisfactory: only when the background is fully understood can one start building algorithms that cannot be cryptanalyzed by such methods.

Kelsey, Schneier, and Wagner succeeded, after all, in attacking a 14-round version of RC5P in practice; a Pentium-133 took about 3 hours for this attack. They then turned their method against the **M6** algorithm, which is based on Japanese research and supposedly used in the FireWire standard. Against M6, a mod-5 attack and subsequently a mod-257 attack led to the goal. (Notice that 3, 5, and 257 all divide $2^{32} - 1$, i.e., 2^{32} leaves a remainder of 1 when divided by these prime numbers. This is decisive in this type of cryptanalysis.) The results are devastating: one single known plaintext suffices to find the 40-bit key 16 times faster than by brute force, and with a few dozen known plaintexts it can be found 512 times faster. A minor modification of the M6 algorithm might effectively help prevent such attacks.

The use of the XOR operation *and* the addition in both RC5 and RC6 (see Section 5.4.4) is also decisive for their security. Mixing operations with various algebraic structures still appears to be key for high security. Not without reason is this principle implemented in practice in IDEA.

Of course, we cannot exclude the fact that somebody might discover a totally new method to attack RC5. It might well be that RC5 in its current form will be considered to be insecure one day. If and when this happens, the algorithm will have advanced the theory. However, I think that an encryption with a sufficiently large number of rounds (e.g., 16) is secure against the known theory; at least the RC5a modification from Section 5.4.3 is.

Cryptanalyzing the One-Round RC5

You probably remember how we defined the product algorithm in Section 4.1.4: 'Simple, cryptologically relatively unsure steps are made one after the other.' How does this look with RC5? Is RC5-32/1/* (one round, optional key length) cryptologically insecure?

Even if nobody would use one-round RC5 in practice, the issue is a welcome opportunity for us to make an excursion into cryptanalysis. I can finally show you a real 'bit fiddling' attack in a reproducible way in this book. Being familiar with these considerations will perhaps help you to understand Section 5.7.1, which is more relevant for practice.

The differential cryptanalysis by Kaliski and Yin discussed above requires 128 *chosen* plaintexts for RC5-32/1/*. Of course, this is far from being optimal, because it's an attack against RC5 with many rounds. I found a plaintext attack against the one-round method, for which three (almost) *arbitrary* plaintexts

(24 bytes) normally suffice. This is quite interesting: RC5-32/1/* also supplies a statistically 'well randomized' text and uses 128 key bits in CBC mode.

The one-round RC5 is easy to describe:

Let the plaintext half blocks (each 32 bits long) be A and B, and assume the key consists of 32-bit words S_0, S_1, S_2, and S_3. To determine the ciphertext half blocks A_1 and B_1, we compute

```
A₀ = A + S₀
B₀ = B + S₁
A₁ = ((A₀ ⊕ B₀) <<< k₀) + S₂  (1)
B₁ = ((B₀ ⊕ A₁) <<< k₁) + S₃  (2)
```

Where k_0 or k_1 is the value from the five least significant bits of B_0 or A_1, respectively.

Assuming that both A and B (the plaintext) and A_1 and B_1 (the ciphertext) are known, we try to recover the keys, $(S_i)_{i=0,...,3}$, from as small a number of plaintexts and ciphertexts as possible. (We are not interested in the method used by RC5 to generate keys S_i from a byte field here. Once we know S_i we can decrypt.)

We begin with equation (2). Since our assumption was that we know A_1, we also know k_1, so that we can represent subkey S_1 as a function of S_3 that we can compute:

```
S₁ = (((B₁-S₃) >>> k₁) ⊕ A₁)- B(3)
```

From among the ciphertexts available, we find two with k_1 values that differ as little as possible, but are not equal. This prerequisite is almost always met in practice: with ten known 'random' ciphertexts, for example, the probability that all k_1 are equal is not more than 2^{-45} (approximately $3 * 10^{-14}$). Moreover, with four different ciphertexts at hand, there are two k_1 values that differ by $32/4 = 8$ at most. The more different ciphertexts we have the smaller the smallest positive difference of any two k_1.

Now, having picked out two such plaintext–ciphertext pairs, we turn to equation (3) for both pairs, writing the equation with the largest k_1 value first. We subtract the second equation from the first, which causes a zero to appear on the left-hand side. The right-hand side is the sum of the difference of the triple bracketed expressions and the difference of the Bs. To prevent us from getting lost in multi-step indices, we define the following terms:

$X = B_1 - S_3$ for the B_1 of the first equation;

$D = B_1$(2nd equation) $- B_1$(1st equation);

$P = A_1$(1st equation);

$Q = A_1$(2nd equation);

$K = k_1$(1st equation);

$L = k_1$(2nd equation); and

$R = B$(1st equation) $- B$(2nd equation).

The difference of the two equations will then look like this:

```
(X>>>K) ⊕ P-((X+D)>>>L) ⊕ Q = R (4)
```

(where XOR $= '\oplus'$ is executed prior to the subtraction). All quantities except X are known in (4). $K > L$ also holds based on our assumption. We set $n = K - L$.

We can use brute force on n bits to determine the value of X from equation (4) (the reason why n should be as small as possible). That's the difficult part of this cryptanalysis.

As a starter, we look at arbitrary values of the n bits $x_L \ldots x_{K-1}$ of X. Using (4), we can determine n bits $y_K \ldots y_{K+n-1}$ of the 32-bit number $(X + D)$, where y_{32} should be equal to y_0, y_{33} should be equal to y_1, and so on. From this, in turn, we obtain n bits $x_K \ldots x_{K+n-1}$ of X, but ambiguously—depending on whether or not the addition of X and D produced a carryover in bit L. Similarly, we compute the next n bits of X. This computation is unambiguous since a carryover can be determined if there is one. After $32/n + 1$ steps, we can compute known bits and check whether or not things work out. If they don't, we try our luck with the next n-bit combination, $x_L \ldots x_{K-1}$.

There has to be a solution for X. Perhaps only a few other solutions remain (the smaller the difference, n, of K and L, the fewer solutions are possible). For each $X = B_1 - S_3$ found, we compute S_3 (since B_1 is known as a ciphertext half block) from (2), then we compute B_0 and from this S_1 again. Consequently, we can use (1) to determine B_0 and k_0 for every plaintext–ciphertext pair. You can see that determining S_2 from (1) represents the same problem as determining S_3 from (2). We determine S_2 and S_0 analogously. Running a check based on other plaintext–ciphertext pairs eliminates wrong solutions for X. If several solutions still remain, we have to test with other methods, depending on the problem at hand.

I wrote a demonstration program to this end and ran tests under UNIX (see Appendix A.1, *algor/RC5a* directory). It is not even 400 lines long, including overhead. The critical function is *solve_X*, which solves equation (4) (as described above); it's only 50 lines long. I admit having worked at this short function for quite a while. Have a look at the source text and you will see why.

You don't need to understand *solve_X* when using this program. You can blindly feed it with some plaintext and the entire ciphertext—and the entire plaintext will come out in a flash. The result is impressive: in all cases tested, three plaintext–ciphertext pairs sufficed to find a unique solution, and the computing time on a 133-MHz Pentium under UNIX V.4.2 was only 2 ms (0.002 seconds)!

This attack doesn't make RC5 any weaker, though. It cannot even be mounted against the two-round RC5, nor can it be mounted against the one-round variant of the RC5a algorithm that will be discussed in Section 5.4.3. And yet, the entire thing is no dry run as you will see in the next section.

Attacking Chip Cards

Helena Handschuh first presented a *timing attack* against RC5 in the 'rump session' (where ideas and comments are suggested freely) at the EUROCRYPT '98: an attacker measures the execution times of encryptions and tries to recover information from them. I don't want to discuss the details here, because this method will be discussed in detail in Section 5.10.

The result sounds alarming at first: once you have access to a chip card with internal secret RC5 key, all you need is to encrypt about 8 Mbytes of chosen plaintext (i.e., approximately 2^{20} plaintext blocks); then you measure the ciphering times to get hold of all subkeys. However, this method is applicable only to certain 8-bit microprocessors, and even then, they can be thwarted with little effort.

I find another type of attack much more dangerous: while having access to such a card, why wouldn't one better use the 'hacker methods' by Anderson and Kuhn, as described in Section 4.4.5? As a reminder: you mess up the processor by interfering with the clock frequency at a clock time computed exactly. It is perhaps not too bold to assume that this might suppress the execution of the last RC5 round. Using the same plaintext, this supplies the ciphering result after $r - 1$ and r rounds, i.e., the plaintext and ciphertext for the one-round RC5! Now we can finally use the knowledge we gained in the previous section and compute the subkeys of the last round in three trials. Next we suppress round $r - 1$. Since we already know the last round's subkeys, we can decrypt this one round and analogously compute the subkeys of the last round but one. This means that 36 ciphering trials would probably be required for the 12-round method—a matter of fractions of seconds in any event. And all this without the parties concerned noticing anything.

Don't interpret this attack as a weakness of RC5. Such nasty methods can crack almost every algorithm—surely including the RC5a method introduced below, though I currently don't know how (you may have to suppress half rounds).

5.4.3 The RC5a Modification

Knudsen and Meier's attacks against RC5 exploit the fact that there is no rotation in some steps. Even the improved method by Biryukov and Kushilevitz studies only pairs where the same rotation occurs in all steps. Rotation introduces confusion and diffusion to the algorithm, which appears to still be hard to crack. In this respect, the results from Figure 5.15 are not entirely satisfactory. I propose a modification which I call **RC5a**. It deviates only slightly from the original. Moreover, it is just as fast as the original, except for the key generation, but increases the 'mixing' factor considerably.

The idea is as follows: keys S_{2i} and S_{2i+1} are added to the rotated words in the ith round. We denote the keys as $S[2*i]$ and $S[2*i + 1]$, like in the C programming language, for technical reasons:

```
A = ((A ⊕ B) <<< B) + S[2*i]
B = ((B ⊕ A) <<< A) + S[2*i + 1]
```

We modify these steps such that keys $S[2*i]$ or $S[2*i + 1]$, respectively, can each be chosen from a larger set of 2^K keys, depending on either B or A. Each $S[j]$ is 'replaced' by an *independent* set of keys; this set is called the **keybox**. It makes decryption possible.

What effect does this change have? If the last five bits of B are equal to 0 in the first equation, then ciphering the last five bits of A leads to an addition

of $S[2*i]$. A change to B in the remaining 27 bits has no impact on the last
five bits of A. With the modification, however, K additional bits now have an
impact. This means that the larger K the greater the diffusion. The value of K
is basically limited only by the memory available.

More specifically, algorithm RC5a-32/r/* (32-bit words, r rounds, optional key
length) with given K between 1 and 27 now looks like this:

1. Set $KB = 2^K$ and $KBSH = 32 - K$.

2. Create $(2r + 2)*KB$ subkeys, $S[i]$, as shown in Figure 5.13.

3. Encrypt the half blocks, A and B, from Figure 5.13 as follows:

```
A = A + S[B >> KBSH];
B = B + S[KB + (A >> KBSH)];
for i=1 to r do
    A =  ((A ⊕ B) <<< B) + S[2*i*KB + (B >> KBSH)];
    B =  ((B ⊕ A) <<< A) + S[(2*i + 1)*KB + (A >> KBSH)];
```

where $A \gg$ denotes the right rotation of A by n bits. In other words, the
five least significant bits of A or B, respectively, determine the rotation
of A or B, while the most significant KB bits determine the choice of
the key. RC5a turns back into RC5 when $K = 0$. I recommend $K = 4$.
With 12 rounds, this corresponds to a memory requirement of well over
1.5 Kbytes for the $S[j]$ subkeys.

Cryptanalyzing RC5a

As expected, RC5a has fewer random key–plaintext pairs in which changed
bits have no influence on the rotation. Figure 5.15 shows this clearly.

This modification might not be the philosopher's stone, but the improved differential cryptanalysis by Knudsen doesn't work on this algorithm any more,
since the probability for 'no rotation' drops considerably. Kaliski and Yin also
followed paths across the RC5 rounds, where ideally no amount of a rotation
changes due to changed bits. The point is presumably that the probabilities
of characteristics (see Section 4.4.2) for $K = 4$ are smaller by a factor of 16,
which makes differential cryptanalysis more ineffective than brute force with
less than 12 rounds. The weak keys discussed above—if there are any in RC5a
at all—are then no longer a threat either. The same applies to the linearly
weak keys of Heys and the partial differential cryptanalysis of Biryukov and
Kushilevitz.

Analogous to Figure 5.14, the following number of cases where no rotation is influenced results with the RC5a algorithm when using $K = 4$ ($2^4 = 16$ keys in one keybox):

5179 with 7-round RC5a;

220 with 8-round RC5a;

11 with 9-round RC5a; and

0 with 10-round RC5a.

Figure 5.15: Influence of changed plaintext bits on the rotations in the modified RC5a algorithm.

Of course, the 'meager' information of key K from Figure 5.13 in RC5a is 'distributed' over more bytes than in RC5. From the information-theory perspective, the subkeys are anything but independent. But you know this sort of discussion from other cryptographic algorithms: ciphering a lot of information (a long plaintext) by means of little information (namely the key) does not mean that the plaintext information is exposed entirely or in part—at least in practice that is.

We can probably handle successive keys $S[j]$ as we would handle independent random quantities with a clear conscience. I cannot imagine an attack that exploits some rule as to how the bits of $S[2^*i^*KB + j]$ vary in dependence on $j = 0, 1, \ldots, 2^K - 1$.

Can you use mod-n cryptanalysis to attack RC5a? I don't know, but I don't think so. I originally modified RC5 in this specific way to make finding subsets without rotation improbable. In view of mod-n cryptanalysis, I am no longer interested in this argument. But RC5a offers yet another security reserve: one has to reconstruct more subkeys for each round, e.g., 16 times more, than with RC5, an otherwise identical method. This probably increases the number of known plaintexts required so much that one wouldn't do better than with brute force, unless the number of rounds was heavily reduced.

Anyway, I hope that RC5 (and RC5a with it, of course) will continue to prove secure. The algorithm can effortlessly 'grow' with the hardware. Its security can be increased by the number of rounds at the cost of performance, just as well as the block size and the key length, which are actually limited arbitrarily (a 12-round method uses a total of 104-byte subkeys, i.e., 832 bits!). RC5 is very easy to program and to implement in hardware. The same applies to RC5a, except that you can trade not only 'computing time for security', but also 'memory requirements for security'.

5.4.4 Patents and the RC6 Successor

A US patent was filed for RC5. Rivest claims that the license fee will be extremely low and is intended only to finance further research at the RSA Laboratories. Similarly to IDEA, non-commercial use might even be free. Unfortunately, I don't have more details at the time of writing. The improvement named RC6 would have been available for free if it became AES. However, since Rijndael won the race (see Section 5.5), RC6 was also patented.

Rivest assumes that RC5a also falls under the RC5 patent. However, everybody outside the USA can use this algorithm for free in any event. It has been on an FTP server on the Internet (visit `ftp.cert.dfn.de/pub/tools/crypt/RC5-IFW/*` and have your search engine look for *rc5a.c*) since February 1996. I have not set any restrictions on its use, just the copyright has to be ensured. Due to the disclosure, there was no way for RC5a to obtain patent protection in Germany, provided the method is accepted as an independent algorithm. Section 7.6 will discuss an implementation that detects and considers the internal number representation (big endian/little endian) automatically, in contrast to others, as well as on the Web site to this book.

My RC5a implementation was ported to Windows NT by the Chile-based company S&I Chile, and it is used at EffCom GmbH, based in Ludwigshafen, Germany, in their *Treasury* asset management program. At the occasion of this porting, the code was thoroughly checked and a small error was found, luckily without impact. We are grateful to S&I Chile for making us the pertaining porting in addition to a small cryptolibrary available for free—you will find all these things on our Web site.

RC6 Further Development

Time didn't stand still at the RSA Laboratories, of course. RC5 didn't meet the requirements of the AES standard described in Section 5.5, since it specifies 128-bit block sizes. Considering that it uses 64-bit words, RC5 is not particularly fast on 32-bit processors. This motivated people to find out how the algorithm could be further developed, how it could work faster, remain as flexible as it was simple, and be harder to attack than RC5 at the same time.

The RC6 Algorithm

The algorithm depends on three parameters:

- the word size, w, in bits (in the following called $w = 32$);

- the number of rounds, $r (r \leq 1)$; and

- the key length, b bytes ($b = 0,1,\ldots, 255$).

Plaintext and ciphertext blocks are each $4w$ bits long, i.e., 128 bits for $w = 32$. Rivest recommends for $w = 32$ a key length of at least 16 bytes (128 bits) with 20 rounds and calls this method 'RC6-32/20/16'.

Encryption

- Take a key K with a length of b bytes and create a field, $S_0, S_1, \ldots, S_{2r+3}$, of $2(r + 2)$ subkeys with 32 bits each (see below).

- Decompose each 128-bit plaintext block into four 32-bit blocks, A, B, C, and D.

- Set

```
B = B + S0
D = D + S1
```

- In the ith round ($i = 1, \ldots, r$) set

```
t = (B(2B + 1)) <<< 5
u = (D(2D + 1)) <<< 5
A = ((A⊕t) <<< u) + S₂ᵢ
C = ((C⊕u) <<< t) + S₂ᵢ₊₁
(A,B,C,D) = (B,C,D,A)
```

(cyclic swapping of the four words), where $A <<< B$ is the left rotation of A by B bits. Multiplications and additions are done mod 2^{32}. To compute $A <<< t$, you need to consider only the five least significant bits of t. For word lengths of $2^6 = 64$ bits or more, generally 2^w bits, replace number 5 by the value of 6 (generally w).

Figure 5.16: The RC6 algorithm.

- After the last round, set

```
A = A + S2r + 2
C = C + S2r + 3
```

- Keys are generated exactly as in RC5.

Figure 5.16: (*continued*).

The product of this development work is called **RC6** and is very similar to RC5. You can find a description in Figure 5.16 and on our Web site, where you will also find the source code in C.

The decryption results quite easily from the ciphering rule.

How do RC5 and RC6 differ, and what do they have in common?

- The most important operation in both methods is the data-dependent rotation. It guarantees extraordinarily strong diffusion and confusion and cannot be attacked effectively at present.
- RC6 initially reminds you of two RC5 methods running in parallel, except that the cyclic swapping of the four words—A, B, C, D—'mixes' both methods after each round. This becomes even more striking if you compose an RC5 round from two 'half rounds' in the form

```
A = (A ⊕ B) <<< B) + Sᵢ
(A,B) = (B,A)
```

(i.e., swapping the two half words after each [half] round, similarly to a Feistel algorithm).

- The decisive improvement versus RC5 is the computation of two helper quantities, t and u, in each round. The transformation $t(B) = B(2B + 1)$ has the property that the five most significant bits of t depend on all bits of B (which is the main reason for the left rotation when computing t and u; in other words, the five most significant bits of $B(2B + 1)$ determine the rotation of $A \oplus t$).

Compare this with RC5, where only the five least significant bits of B determine how $A \oplus B$ is rotated. Cryptanalysts tend to 'kick in' at these last places, because these values are not 'disturbed' by carryovers from additions. In RC6, these are the five most significant bits of t, which additionally depend on B in a very complicated way.

As a sideline, the transformation of $t(B)$ is unambiguous, which means that all possible 2^{32} values of t are accepted even if B traverses all possible values (proving this is a moderately hard task for mathematicians). This is important, because it ensures, for example, that the $A \oplus t$ operation will not only link the word A with 'partial information' on B, which is critical for the diffusion.

- The (A, C) and (B, D) pairs mix even more than the cyclic swapping of the four words after each round in that the rotation amounts and the 'XOR' partners—t and u from B and D—are computed and applied to A and C concurrently.

The closer a look you take at RC6, the simpler and cleverer you will find this algorithm. It appears to be the one with the shortest description out of all AES candidates; this is the only reason I can describe it here fully.

However, there are two minor drawbacks. First, the integer multiplication suggests where the algorithm runs most effectively: on 32-bit processors. Things look less good with 8-bit smartcards, where the data rotation is costly. And second, while the usual cryptanalytic attacks against RC6 have failed so far, I agree with Schneier's comments on the mod-3 cryptanalysis (see Section 5.4.2): here too, an effective attack is prevented by XOR and addition. Moreover, the transformation $t(B) = B(2B + 1)$ produces only remainders 0 and 1 when dividing by 3. This type of 'distortion' could 'survive' the cleverly constructed round function if it weren't for said XOR.

In contrast, the mod-3 cryptanalysis seems to be less effective against RC5a, however at the cost of increased memory requirement. Apart from patent rights, as there may be, RC5a is still attractive indeed. Of course, RC6 could be similarly modified into an RC6a algorithm, but I don't see a need for the time being.

Nevertheless, no symmetric algorithm since DES has been cryptanalyzed as thoroughly and with such good results as the five AES final candidates, including RC6.

5.5 Rijndael Becomes AES and Replaces DES

Even before Deep Crack, the DES crack computer (see Section 4.4.1), was built, scientists, industries, and government authorities understood that the days of DES were numbered. The pressure from the business world to create and use secure algorithms is very strong today; we will see this particularly in Chapter 8. The AES Initiative of the NIST is an excellent example showing how the situation has changed during the past twenty years.

Remember how DES was born (Section 4.3.1)? Back then, the NBS had major difficulties in obtaining a usable proposal at all, and they had to involve the NSA due to a lack of internal competency. And today? Successor NIST challenged a new standard at the beginning of 1997; it was to be named **AES** (**Advanced Encryption Standard**). But this time it seemed that all the leading people in public cryptological research had participated in the challenge, submitted a large number of proposals, discussed and cryptanalyzed the algorithms submitted, until eventually they were spoilt for choice. Though it was primarily a matter of a new US standard, proposals and analyses were submitted from all over the world. Eventually, a Belgian algorithm was selected to become the new security standard in the USA. This alone shows almost symbolically how much cryptology has changed during the past twenty years.

Everything had actually run so smoothly that there was hardly a reason for criticism. Even the requirements to the new standard were not formulated by the NIST alone, but in an open workshop especially conducted to this end in April 1997. For defining the requirements was not an easy task—after all, AES was to be secure for long into the future so that it had to meet extremely strict criteria from the outset. You can read the result in Figure 5.17.

The required block length of 128 bits relates to the birthday attack discussed in Section 5.1.1 in connection with the CBC mode: having two equal ciphertext blocks, one can draw conclusions on the XOR product of the pertaining plaintext blocks, thus obtaining a (minimal) hint on the plaintext. The probability for such an event should be as small as possible. With 128-bit blocks, such a pair generally occurs with more than 100 million terabytes of ciphertext, which would seem to be sufficient for the next twenty years.

This meant that, for example, IDEA with its 64-bit block length was ruled out, among others. RC5 was not an eligible candidate either since it works most effectively with 64-bit blocks on 32-bit processors. Thus, RC6 came into existence, as described in Section 5.4.4. And the requirement for a key length up to 256 bits is by no means paranoid considering that quantum computers might exist (Section 5.9) within the next twenty years.

A worldwide search for candidates began as a consequence. The NIST presented 15 proposals at the first conference in August 1998. At the second AES

The requirements for AES specified by the NIST were formulated in public discussion, including a workshop on April 15, 1997. Here are a few selected criteria:

- AES shall be a symmetric block algorithm.

- The algorithm shall use a block length of at least 128 bits and be capable of using keys 128, 192, and 256 bits long.

- It shall be suitable for most different purposes of use, e.g., it shall be equally implementable in hardware and software.

- AES shall resist all methods known in cryptanalysis.

- It shall especially resist power analyses and timing attacks.

- It shall have excellent performance both in hardware and software.

- It shall have computational efficiency especially for use in smartcards (small code length, minimum memory requirement).

- The algorithm shall be free from patents and freely available to everybody.

Figure 5.17: NIST requirements for AES.

conference held in March 1999, these algorithms were studied and cryptanalyzed thoroughly. If there was even the slightest doubt about its security, a candidate would not be short-listed. The Magenta method submitted by Deutsche Telekom was one of the candidates that did not make it to the shortlist.

The most capable cryptanalysts in the world dealt with the five candidates that survived the thorough and numerous analyses, and ended up in stalemate: all the algorithms were found to be excellent and hard to compare. Each one of them could have become the new standard, and no flaws were found in any of them. Each had different benefits, but which properties should be considered to be the decisive ones?

In two of his contributions to the third AES conference, Don B. Johnson of Certicom asked: 'Does there have to be a best method?' After all, modern software implements a standardized crypto-interface anyhow, and normally offers several methods to choose from. None of the five AES candidates was that big a program that all of them together would blast the volume of crypto-software (this looks different in hardware).

January 2, 1997:	Solicitation for initiative; submission of candidates by September 12, 1997.
April 15, 1997:	A public AES workshop was held to formulate the exact requirements. Cryptographers all over the world began developing appropriate algorithms.
August 20, 1998:	First AES conference; NIST announced receipt of 15 candidates. Public study began.
March 1999:	Second AES conference; discussion of current results. 28 candidates from all over the world were submitted and made accessible on the homepage several weeks prior to the conference in order to hold the conference on as high a level as possible.
April 15, 1999:	End of public study of all candidates. Five candidates (MARS, RC6, Rijndael, Serpent, Twofish) were short-listed. Further work was then concentrated on these five algorithms.
April 13/14, 2000:	Third AES conference; the analyses of the five final candidates were presented and discussed.
May 15, 2000:	End of public discussion.
October 2, 2000:	Announcement of Rijndael as the "winner".
November 2000:	Publication of the FIPS standard as a manuscript; request for public comments.
February 2001:	End of public discussion on the standard.
April–June 2001:	Approval as FIPS standard.

Figure 5.18: Timeline of the AES Initiative.

Or better yet, a preferred field of use (smartcards, online encryption, ...) should be stated for each algorithm. This kind of flexibility would clearly have more benefits than drawbacks. Products fixed on a specific method would become insecure instantly if, against all odds, a weakness were detected in the method. A warning example is the use of DES in banking applications, which had bet on it exclusively for twenty years. The migration to 3DES took years and devoured huge sums.

The decision the NIST took turned out to be anything but the expected—only the **Rijndael** algorithm by the Belgian authors Joan Daemen and Vincent

Round 1:

- CAST-256: Entrust Technologies, Inc. (represented by Carlisle Adams).
- CRYPTON: Future Systems, Inc. (represented by Chae Hoon Lim).
- DEAL: Richard Outerbridge, Lars Knudsen.
- DFC: CNRS—Centre National pour la Recherche Scientifique, Ecole Normale Superieure (represented by Serge Vaudenay).
- E2: NTT—Nippon Telegraph and Telephone Corporation (represented by Masayuki Kanda).
- FROG: TecApro Internacional S.A. (represented by Dianelos Georgoudis).
- HPC: Richard Schroeppel.
- LOKI97: Lawrie Brown, Josef Pieprzyk, Jennifer Seberry.
- MAGENTA: Deutsche Telekom AG (represented by Dr Klaus Huber).
- MARS: IBM (represented by Nevenko Zunic).
- RC6: RSA Laboratories (represented by Burt Kaliski).
- RIJNDAEL: Joan Daemen, Vincent Rijmen.
- SAFER+: Cylink Corporation (represented by Charles Williams).
- SERPENT: Ross Anderson, Eli Biham, Lars Knudsen.
- TWOFISH: Bruce Schneier, John Kelsey, Doug Whiting, David Wagner, Chris Hall, Niels Ferguson.

Round 2:

- MARS, RC6, Rijndael, Serpent, Twofish.

Selected after Round 3:

- Rijndael.

Figure 5.19: The algorithms short-listed for AES.

Rijmen won the competition. The arguments why one single candidate was selected failed to convince everybody:

- If Rijndael had practically relevant weaknesses against all odds, then the larger key length required would provide sufficient reserve.

- In the worst case, 3DES is still available as an alternative, and it might continue to offer full security into the foreseeable future.

- It is cheaper to implement one single algorithm (however, this argument applies to hardware only).

- The costs would be less in the event that patent claims were brought forward by inventors of similar algorithms (I suspect this was one of the most important reasons).

However, nobody was to be disappointed: the entire process was entirely open and very fair. In the USA, where algorithms had been classified weapons only a few years earlier, an algorithm developed by Belgians and studied internationally had made it to become a foundation of national security! Though the field of use for governmental agencies is described as 'sensitive, not classified', the NSA made a rather sloppy statement, but Rijndael will presumably form the ciphering basis (as the NIST expects) for the next twenty years or longer in spite of it. There is currently no reason for doubt.

The Rijndael Algorithm in Detail

That much on the background of the AES Initiative. In view of its outstanding significance, Rijndael will be described briefly in this section. This is not particularly difficult, since it uses only bytewise substitution, byte swapping, and the XOR operation. The following discussion uses 128-bit blocks and 128-bit keys in the individual steps. You will find details and source texts in C and Java on the Web site to this book.

I will first describe Rijndael roughly for 128-bit keys.

1. A plaintext block consisting of 128 bits or 16 bytes is written into a 4×4 matrix column by column. Daemen and Rijmen call these matrices 'states'. The plaintext bytes are in the matrix before the first round. Each round changes the contents of the matrix; after the 10th round, the matrix holds the ciphertext bytes that are read column by column.

   Before beginning with the encryption, the 128-bit keys for 10 rounds are created from the 128-bit key and written in 10 matrices with 4 columns and 4 rows each (I will skip the key generation for reasons of space, you can find it in *algor/rijndael.ps* on our Web site). Next, the Rijndael algorithm runs the following steps in each round:

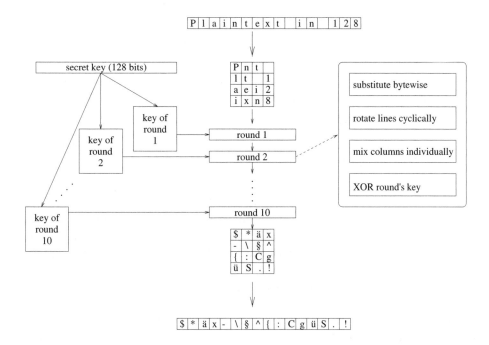

Figure 5.20: Basic representation of Rijndael.

– *ByteSub*: The single bytes of the state matrix are substituted by a fixed scheme. This transformation is deterministic and known, so it doesn't represent an encryption yet.

– *ShiftRow*: The rows of the state are cyclically left-rotated bytewise by 0, 1, 2, and 3 bytes. For example, if the characters

```
a b c d
```

are in row 2, then this row looks like this after the *ShiftRow* transformation:

```
b c d a
```

Naturally this transformation is deterministic and doesn't encrypt anything.

- *MixColumn*: The columns of the state are substituted by a deterministic principle. This rule is somewhat more complicated and uses transformations over Galois fields.

- *AddRoundKey*: The round key is XORed bitwise with the state. Only this process mixes a secret into the transformation so that one may speak of encryption.

2. Prior to the first round, an *AddRoundKey* transformation is executed, and the *MixColumn* transformation is missing in the last round.

Rijndael can also work with 192-bit and 256-bit blocks; it then uses 4×6 and 4×8 matrices, respectively, as states, and the *ShiftRow* transformation changes somewhat. The algorithm with 128-bit block and key lengths uses 10 rounds, while 12 and 14 rounds, respectively, are used for longer block or key lengths.

Cryptanalyzing Rijndael the Classic Way

Rijndael with only one round would offer extremely low security. Since *ByteSub, ShiftRow*, and *MixColumn* form only a fixed reversible transformation even when executed one after the other, the security would correspond to a 128-bit Vernam cipher. We know from Section 3.6 what kind of special treat this is for cryptanalysts.

But since Rijndael is a product algorithm, the security of such algorithms grows explosively as the number of rounds increases, as we know. The cryptanalysis of Rijndael known to date (see below) shows this rather impressively.

The *ByteSub, ShiftRow*, and *MixColumn* transformations are chosen such that they are simple (and thus easy to analyze) on the one hand, and that all cryptanalytic methods currently known will fail, on the other hand. The authors explain their motivation for choosing these transformations in detail in their publication (see the Web site: *algor/aes/rijndael.ps*. I just want to mention here that operations on Galois fields play an important role.

The most important factors in choosing the transformations are strong diffusion and confusion in every round:

- Diffusion means here that a change to even one single state bit (or to a round key bit) after as few rounds as possible influences all bits of that state. *ShiftRow* and *MixColumn* are mainly responsible for this in Rijndael.

- Confusion means that 'relationships are lost' so that one cannot draw conclusions on the input matrix from the result of one round. *ByteSub* and *AddRoundKey* are mainly responsible for this task.

Only the continual consecutive execution of these rounds (which are nothing but a deterministic substitution of 128-bit states with subsequent XOR addition of a secret key) represents (hopefully) an almost unsolvable task for cryptanalysts. Neither differential nor linear cryptanalysis (which works even against DES in theory), nor the so-called interpolation attack work in this case; there are no weak keys, and even attacks with related keys (interesting for smartcards) fail, in contrast to DES.

As for all five final candidates of the AES challenge, no effective attacks are known on Rijndael. If you reduced the number of rounds, you would obtain the following results (which become of interest only with 192-bit and 256-bit keys):

6 rounds: Using $6 * 2^{32}$ chosen plaintext blocks, you can compute the key with 2^{44} complex (i.e., approximately 17 billion) operations.

This means for practical purposes that about 400 Gbytes of plaintext given by the attacker have to be encrypted and analyzed. If one complex operation takes one microsecond, then this would take roughly 200 days (or 5 hours with one nanosecond).

7 rounds: Requires almost 2^{128} chosen plaintexts (corresponding to approximately $5 * 10^{39}$ bytes) and a computing effort of 2^{120}. With one nanosecond per operation, this would take $4 * 10^{19}$ (40 trillion) years.

Notice how tremendously the security grows by adding a 7th round! However, Rijndael runs at least ten rounds (depending on the key length).

Though theoretical weaknesses were discovered in the way the round keys are created, they may only be of academic interest. There is no practical impact based on current knowledge.

Algebraic Cryptanalysis

Several experts expressed their doubts about the security of Rijndael, arguing that the design was too simple to be secure. Though complex, 'hard-to-understand' methods (such as DES, among others) may be harder to attack mathematically, this is only an apparent benefit in an age of fast computers and high-performing software which can, for example, handle much more complex formulas than humans will ever be able to.

An 'alarmingly interesting' article by Niels Ferguson, Richard Schroeppel, and Doug Whiting of May 2001 [FergSchrWhit] shows vividly that this is far from being paranoia. The article describes how an astonishingly simple representation of the Rijndael transformation as a sum of continued fractions can be found. Though there would then be about 2^{25} five-step (well over 33 million) continued fractions on either side of the equation, if it helped to mount an attack, then such an attack would perhaps be practically feasible. However, nobody yet has any idea what this attack would look like.

Another work by Nicolas Courtois and Josef Pieprzyk that appeared in 2002 [CourtPiep] (see also *eprint.iacr.org/2002/044*) caused quite some hurly-burly. The so-called **XSL (Extended Sparse Linearization) method** exploits the fact that AES can be represented as a system of 8000 square equations with 1600 variables. A number of scientists (including Don Coppersmith, among others) heavily criticized this article. The main arguments were that the cost required was impossible to estimate, and that the method was not demonstrated in a practical example. It seems that the attack in the form *presented* does not represent a risk in practice. However, I find four points pretty alarming:

- Attacks always improve; they never deteriorate.

- In addition to AES, it would be Serpent, the AES final candidate estimated to be the most secure, of all candidates that would be vulnerable to this method, if it really works.

- This attack would require only few plaintexts, in contrast to differential and linear cryptanalysis. If the computational effort could be reduced to something realistic, then this would be the first practicable attack against a modern algorithm—and then AES of all algorithms!

- Also in contrast to differential and linear cryptanalysis, the number of rounds or keys does not play a significant role. This is alarming in view of the fact that increasing the number of rounds and/or the key length was thought to be a 'secure bank'.

Current and qualified information about this issue can also be found in Wikipedia at en.wikipedia.org/wiki/XSL_attack.

So it is understandable indeed that people justly worried about the strikingly simple structure of Rijndael. One should bear in mind that there are algorithms other than AES. My personal tip: Twofish.

Is AES Secure, Or Is It Not?

Authors Daemen and Rijmen explain the background of their design to the finest detail, which seldom happens in cryptography, unfortunately. For this reason, one may reasonably assume that the method has no backdoor built in. Considering its simple design, it is astonishingly secure! If AES can be attacked effectively at all, then it probably would be by algebraic means, but no success is in sight. So, there currently is no rational reason against betting on this algorithm.

Implementation Issues

It is easy for both insiders and outsiders to see that Rijndael can be implemented nicely in hardware; even written as a C program, Rijndael in its optimized version remains less than 500 lines of source code. Another important point is that Rijndael can be 'cast' in hardware such that timing and power analyses, which will be introduced in Section 5.10, are widely ineffective.

Unfortunately, decryption runs a bit slower than encryption on 8-bit processors (for smartcards)—up to 30 % slower, in fact. In the software version, there are minor time differences since the round keys for decryption are computed a bit differently.

Encryption and decryption are often identical in other algorithms. Conversely, in the hardware version of Rijndael, the ciphering hardware can be used only partly for deciphering, and the software version requires different code and different tables. However, deciphering is not always necessary, for example, when the CFB and OFB modes (Section 5.1.1) are used.

As expected, the strongest response to the AES choice came on October 2, 2000 from the business world: on October 10, Demcom GmbH announced the beta package of Stegano's Security Suite 3, which uses Rijndael. On October 16, Utimaco Safeware AG followed suit with their *SafeGuard Private Crypt*. Of course, the free software world didn't lag far behind—GnuPG, which will be discussed in Section 7.1.4, is one good example.

5.6 RC4: Stream Cipher for (Almost) Everyone

RC4 is an encryption algorithm that has little in common with RC5 described above: it is also a brainchild of Ron Rivest, and it is very simple and fast. Apart from that, everything is different: RC4 was developed in 1987 and kept secret for seven years. It has been used in many commercial products, including Lotus Notes, Oracle Secure SQL, and not least the popular Internet browser Netscape Navigator. In contrast to RC5, which is a block algorithm, RC4 is a typical stream cipher: a byte sequence is created dependent on a key of variable length and used as a one-time pad. The ciphertext results from simple bytewise XORing of the key byte sequence with the plaintext, and the reversion works similarly.

Up to September 10, 1994, this was basically everything people knew about this algorithm. On that date, a C program that produced the same results as the commercial software packages that used RC4 suddenly emerged in the Internet newsgroup *sci.crypt* anonymously (through the *cypherpunks* mailing list). That was it—RC4 was revealed. Part of the response was rather unfriendly. I quote the original posting by David Sterndark (NETCOM On-line Communication Services) in the same newsgroup on September 14, 1994, as an example:

I am shocked, shocked, I tell you, shocked, to discover that the cypherpunks have illegally and criminally revealed a crucial RSA trade secret and harmed the secu-rity of America by reverse engineering the RC4 algorithm and publishing it to the world.

I will join this ugly game that harms the security of America and present you with the algorithm in Figure 5.21.

The method is astonishingly simple and extremely easy to program (it is very software-friendly, but less suitable for hardware). Since index i traverses all values from 0 to 255 cyclically, each number, P_i, is swapped with another one every 256 steps at the most. How j changes obviously cannot be told unless one knows the key. To determine the key byte, RC4 uses the sum of two secret P_k as index. Therefore, a statement about a few P_k would probably not tell us much. The RC4 design is really simple and clever. According to comments by the company RSADSI, no attack using differential or linear cryptanalysis is known. More doesn't appear to be known. I am convinced that this will change, because such a simple and important algorithm will surely be studied thoroughly.

But bear in mind that RC4 is a stream cipher and as such is vulnerable to insertion attacks (see Section 5.1.1). If a software package uses RC4 without an initialization vector (which could precede the key in the simplest case), then this software is dangerous, no matter how good RC4 may be! You can read about other methods that implement this good algorithm in security-ineffective ways in *txt/cryptana/wlanrc4.txt* on our Web site.

Description of RC4

RC4 is a stream cipher, i.e., a secret key is used to create a secret byte sequence
(K_i), and simple XOR is used for encryption and decryption:

Ciphertext byte$_i$ = plaintext byte$_i$ $\oplus$ K_i

Plaintext byte$_i$ = ciphertext byte$_i$ $\oplus$ K_i

Internal Key

Two bytes, i and j, and a permutation, $(P_i)_{i=0,\ldots,255}$, of the numbers $0, \ldots, 255$ are
used as internal key, i.e., each of these numbers occurs exactly once in sequence
(P_i). The size of the key space is approximately 2^{1700} ($= 256^2 * 256!$).

Ciphering

A step to create a key byte, K, looks like this:

```
i = i + 1  mod 256
j = j + Pᵢ mod 256
swap Pᵢ and Pⱼ
t = Pᵢ + Pⱼ mod 256
K = Pₜ.
```

(A modulo-256 addition is simply a bytewise addition—in C adding two data of
the type *unsigned char*.)

Creating the Internal Key

Let the key entered consist of l bytes, $S_0, \ldots, S_{l-1}$. We set

```
i = 0
j = 0
Pₖ = k  (k=0,...,255)
```

and compute the following 256 times:

```
j = j + Pᵢ + Sᵢ mod 256
swap Pᵢ and Pⱼ
i = i + 1 mod l.
```

With this, i, j, and the P_k are initialized.

Comment: In [SchnCr, 17.1], i traverses all indices from 0 to 255, and the key
is iterated as often as needed until all 256 bytes, $S_0, \ldots, S_{255}$, are filled. I didn't
check whether or not the two versions are equivalent. My variant stems from tested
C programs.

Figure 5.21: Description of the RC4 stream cipher.

In the WLAN standard 802.11, it is easy to forge messages and even decipher them (see also below). You can find an overview of the current RC4 crypt-analysis at `www.wisdom.weizmann.ac.il/~itsik/RC4/rc4.html`. As it appears, the algorithm should be used only with some precautionary measures. For example, keys and the initialization vector should be generated by means of cryptographic hash functions (see Section 6.3.1), and a sufficiently large number of bytes at the beginning of the key stream should be discarded.

You can see that the name 'RC4' itself doesn't mean anything. A good example is the work described in *eprint.iacr.org/2005/007.pdf*, which points to the fact that the initialization vector in RC4-ciphered Microsoft Word and Microsoft Excel documents doesn't change when the documents are modified: you know how this vulnerability can be attacked! Also, when designing the WLAN standard WEP, people initially made almost all errors that can possibly be made in an RC4 implementation. Obviously not a single cryptologist was involved in the workgroups. With the related IEEE standard 802.15.4/802.15.4b and mainly with the ZigBEE standard derived from the former (which is interesting, for example, for self-connecting wireless sensor networks), things look better, but this is not the topic of this book.

Thanks to its proliferation in commercial products, RC4 is used by many users (mostly without their knowing it), and thanks to its simplicity, programmers could actually build it in their products themselves, of course, with the use of an initialization vector. That would be a stream cipher for everybody, well, if it weren't for the license fee to be paid to RSADSI for commercial use. Though this is rather doubtful, the license fees would probably be less than the cost of a legal action.

5.7   Other Interesting Methods

Many more ciphering methods are used than you have learnt so far in this book. In the rest of this chapter on modern methods, I won't even try to give an overview; you will find one in Schneier [SchnCr]. I have just picked the most interesting or practically important algorithms and will then introduce yet another very original cryptanalysis in Section 5.10.

5.7.1   The *pkzip* Cipher and How to Break It

As the heading of this section suggests, we will again be dealing with a 'weak' method. You probably know that 'weak' in cryptanalysts' lingo is everything that has been cracked or where breaking is imminent. In the present case, cryptanalysis is rather complicated. Astonishingly, there is a free program to break this code. But let's look at these things in turn.

The *pkzip* tool widely used in the PC world groups several files into a single one—an archive. The files are compressed using a suitable method, and the entire archive can be encrypted. We are interested in the latter feature, of course. Despite it being complicated, this section is important, since you will come to understand at least roughly how today cryptanalysts can disentangle complex things.

The *pkzip* Cipher

The *pkzip* encryption is a stream cipher. Similarly to RC4, it creates a key-dependent byte sequence which is XORed with the ciphertext or the plaintext. In *pkzip*, the key-dependent byte sequence depends additionally on the plaintext previously encrypted. For this reason, and because twelve partially random bytes, which serve as an initialization vector, among other things, are set prior to the encryption, an insertion attack won't work.

The method uses three secret 32-bit words, $key0$, $key1$, and $key2$, and a secret byte, K. Byte K is XORed with the plaintext for encryption, or ciphertext for decryption. Subsequently, the method computes new values for $key0$, $key1$, $key2$, and K, depending on the plaintext. This actualization procedure looks like this:

```
C = P ⊕ K
key0 = crc32(key0,P)                             (a)
key1 = (key1 + (key0 & 0xff)) * 134775813 + 1   (b)
key2 = crc32(key2, key1 >> 24)                  (c)
tmp  = key2 | 3                                  (d)
K    = (tmp * (tmp⊕1)) >> 8                      (e)
```

where P is a plaintext byte, C is a ciphertext byte, and *tmp* is a 16-bit number. Similarly to the C programming language, $A \gg n$ denotes the right shift of A by n bytes, i.e., $key1 \gg 24$ is the most significant byte of $key1$, and K is the most significant byte of $tmp*(tmp \oplus 1)$. The operation $key0$ & $0xff$ creates the least significant byte of $key0$, and the expression $key2 \,|\, 3$ just means that the two least significant bits of $key2$ are set equal to 1. Finally, *crc32()* is an easily computable CRC polynomial:

```
crc32(key,c) = (key >> 8) ⊕ crctab[(key&0xff) ⊕ c]    (5)
```

where *crctab[]* denotes an easily computable table, *key* denotes a 32-bit word, and *c* denotes a byte. The function *crc32()* is reversible, i.e., one can easily determine *key* for given values of *crc32(key,c)* and *c*. Using

```
Crc32 = crc32(key,c)
```

the solution looks like this:

```
key = (Crc32 << 8) ⊕ crcinvtab[Crc32 >> 24] ⊕ c       (6)
```

(again, *crcinvtab* is a computable table).

How does a secret key get in there? First of all, the words *key0, key1*, and *key2* are initialized:

```
key0 = 0x12345678
key1 = 0x23456789
key2 = 0x34567890
```

Then you run the actualization procedure described above for all key bytes. This corresponds to a cipher where the ciphertext is discarded. This means that there is no restriction as to the key length. The internal key consists of the three *key* variables, thus it is 96 bits long (corresponding to 12 bytes); far too many for brute force.

About the Security of 'Wild' Algorithms and How to Break the *pkzip* Cipher

This cipher was designed by Roger Schlafly[1] and looks pretty 'wild' at first. I don't know all the design principles of the algorithm. For example, I have no idea where factor 134 775 813 in the actualization procedure comes from (it is not a prime number, but is equal to the product 3*17*131*20 173). Perhaps it is as arbitrary as the initialization of the three *key* variables.

---

[1]Homepage on the Web: bbs.cruzio.com/~schlafly/; see also [GarPGP, end of Chapter 6].

I certainly don't want to suggest that Roger Schlafly designed the algorithm 'arbitrarily'. (The use of an initialization vector and the inclusion of the plaintext in the key stream generation show profound knowledge.) Gradually changing the *key* variables is also typical: *key0* changes *key1, key1* changes *key2*, and *K* is computed only from *key2*. But things will go as they went for Schlafly for everybody who builds a 'wild' algorithm on the off-chance: his method will be cracked, not only in theory. *pkzip* is instructive in this respect—cryptanalysts would probably proceed in the same way with other insufficiently protected ciphers, too.

In 1995, Biham and Kocher published a successful plaintext attack against the *pkzip* cipher [Bih.zip]. The article is available on the Internet. It is not easy to read, so we should take time to do some basic thinking and look at the results—they are interesting.

As usual with a plaintext attack, we assume that we know at least one byte of the plaintext and the corresponding ciphertext byte. We can then compute byte *K* from the key byte sequence:

```
K = P ⊕ C
```

The first exploitable point is equation (e) above. The multiplication is a strongly mixing operation, but we are not interested in it at all. We know from (d) that the two least significant bits of the 16-bit variable *tmp* are equal to 1. So *tmp* can be represented as follows:

```
tmp = 256a + b + 3
```

where *a* and *b* denote bytes, and the last two bits of *b* are equal to 0. We can thus write (e) alternatively as follows:

```
K = LSB((2b + 5)a) + MSB((b + 2)(b + 3))
```

where *LSB* stands for 'least significant byte', and *MSB* stands for 'most significant byte'. We can use both to unambiguously determine the lower-order byte of $(2b + 5)a$ for given *b* and *K*. But we can also compute *a* now, since the congruence

```
(2b + 5)a = c mod 256
```

is solvable toward a for known b and c, because $2b + 5$ is relatively prime to 256 (see Section 4.5.3).

Byte b can accept $2^6 = 64$ values at most. Knowing key stream byte K, a results from b unambiguously. So, there are only 64 possible values for tmp as well as for the 14 bits $2, \ldots, 15$ of $key2$! The 16 higher-order bits of $key2$ are undetermined for the time being; a total of 2^{22} (approximately 4 million) values can be considered for the 30 most significant bits $(2, \ldots, 31)$ of $key2$ with given K.

That's all we can get out of (d) and (e); the two least significant bits of $key2$ play no role in these equations. We can recover values of $key2$ that belong to successive plaintext bytes from equation (c). The same applies to (a) and (b). So we need several successive plaintext–ciphertext pairs, i.e., the values of K in successive steps. Now things get far more complicated.

Equation (c) won't help us further in the form stated, since we can see in (5) that the two least significant bits of $key2$ play an important role. But the reversion of $crc32()$ described in (6) shows us how to proceed: we represent $key2_i$ (the value of $key2$ for the ith step) as a function of $key2_{i+1}$ by means of (c) and (6), and compare the right and left sides bitwise: if $key2_{i+1}$ is known, then bits $10, \ldots, 31$ are given on the right-hand side, and the left-hand side can accept only 64 (2^6) values in the 14 bits $2, \ldots, 15$ of $key2_i$ anyway. Since the right and left sides have to coincide in the six bits, $10, \ldots, 15$, the 14 bits $2, \ldots, 15$ of $key2_i$ are given 'unambiguously on average'. Under this prerequisite, we can continue comparing the right and left sides to gradually determine all 30 bits of $key2_i$ and eventually all bits of $key2_{i+1}$. What remains are 2^{22} possible values for the entire sequence, $key2_{i+1}, key2_i, \ldots, key2_1$. This is a clever attack in my opinion.

However, we haven't reached our goal yet; we don't know the values of $key1$ and $key0$. We can use the values for $key2$ and the $crc32$ reversion (6) to compute the most significant bytes of $key1$ in successive steps. This would yield us 2^{24} (approximately 16 million) values for bytes $0, \ldots, 23$ of $key1$. We can now easily reverse equation (b):

```
key1ᵢ₋₁ + LSB(key0ᵢ) = (key1ᵢ − 1) * 134775813⁻¹ mod 2³²
```

(The reciprocal of 134 775 813 is formed modulo 2^{32}.) Since the most significant byte of $key1_{i-1}$ is given and $LSB(key0_i)$ concerns only the eight lowest-order bits on the left side (except for carryovers), the eight most significant bits on the left side are given. Consequently, this equation limits the value reserve for $key1_i$ to about $2^{24}/2^8 = 2^{16}$. We can now compute $key1_{i-1}$, except for the eight least significant bits, which are 'disturbed' by the least significant byte of $key0_i$, for each of these 2^{16} values. Next, we write the last equation once for $i - 1$ and put in all 256 (2^8) possible values for $key1_{i-1}$ there—this time on the right-hand side. Only every 2^8th value of $key1_{i-1}$ will result in the given most significant byte of $key1_{i-2}$ on average. Again, $key1_i$ is 'unambiguous on average'. We thus obtain the least significant byte of $key0_i$. A nice ending, don't you think?

Let's capture the intermediate state of affairs: we determined 2^{22} possible sequences for the values of $key2$, and about 2^{16} sequences of $key1$ values are possible for each of these 2^{22} sequences. Altogether, this results in approximately 2^{38} (or a quarter of a billion) possibilities.

Things get pretty fast from now onwards. We can determine the values of $key0$ from (a), (6), and the least significant bytes of $key0$ for four successive steps using the solution of a linear equation system. We take this result to compute the $key0$ values and compare their least significant bytes with the values given in 2^{38} lists for additional steps. This is basically the solution.

We can now decrypt the ciphertext backwards without knowing the plaintext. This is much easier than the approach above. We obtain the same initial values for $key2, key1$, and $key0$, i.e., the internal representation of the key. With this, we decrypt the entire archive.

About 12 or 13 coherent plaintext bytes, which don't necessarily have to be at the beginning of the file, will suffice for the attack. The complexity of the computation is around 2^{38}, i.e., we have to trial-and-error test roughly one quarter of a billion key lists. This complexity can be dramatically reduced if more plaintext is known.

When computing $key2_{i-1}$ from $key2_i$, we get double values. This reduces the number of possible $key2$ in every computation step. So, with 12 000 known plaintext bytes, about 2000 lists instead of 2^{22} (4 million) remain typically, reducing the complexity of the entire computation from 2^{38} (250 billion) to 2^{27} (about 100 million) lists.

Biham and Kocher even found a way to reveal the unknown key. Remember that it was initially used as 'plaintext', while the 'ciphertext' created was discarded. With a key length of up to 6 bytes, the key can be revealed unambiguously; the complexity of the computation increases by a factor of 2^8 with every additional byte. A maximum of 2^{48} tests are to be expected. This corresponds to a 12-byte key that contains as many bits (96) as the internal key. It is believed that there are cases where 13-byte keys represent the shortest solution to the problem. However, a value of 2^{48} strongly reminds us of DES cracking, and that's a case for special hardware. But the key entered does not *have* to be computed, it is just the icing on our cryptanalysis cake.

The *pkcrack* Program

It is a remarkable achievement to 'cast' this algorithm in a program and then make it available for free on top of it all. Many problems remain unanswered in the original work, too, and even understanding them all won't make the implementation any easier. I tend to think that this **pkcrack** program is the most difficult among all free cryptanalytic software. In fact, AccessData don't even have it in their product supply (see Footnote 1 in Section 1.2.2). Author Peter Conrad from Germany deserves all respect for this work. Version 1.2 of his program can be used as a 'black box'. It runs under UNIX (particularly Linux); a special compiler can be used to run it under DOS. It requires 33 Mbytes of virtual memory in the startup phase, but a physical 16-Mbyte memory is normally enough.

I used *pkcrack* on an encrypted archive, knowing that it included a file 728 bytes long. The computational effort was considerable: a DEC workstation with a 300-MHz alpha processor was busy breaking code for almost 6 hours. After all this work, only one password was output—it was the right one. Things would have been much faster had I used more known plaintext, though. The workstation's performance corresponds to a very fast Pentium-Pro.

Since *pkcrack* is easy to use, and its technical details and installation are well documented, I will spare you the details here. It is not excessively long (3000 lines in C) and written in a pretty compact way. Conrad uses the denotations of the original work.

All files are encrypted with the same password in a *pkzip* archive so that it is sufficient to know a bunch of 12 or 13 coherent bytes of *one* file from within the archive to decrypt *all* files! These 12 or 13 plaintext bytes don't have to be at the beginning of the known file; you only need to know their offset. However, an attacker has to overcome yet another obstacle: *pkzip* normally compresses each file by the best possible method. This means that 12 or 13 bytes of the *compressed* file need to be known to reveal the archive. Generally speaking, one has to know at least the first 40 bytes of a file and a suitable compression method (the method can be trial-and-error determined, if need be, usually from the length of the compressed file). This prerequisite is met often enough, particularly when only some of the archived files are sensitive. This is the reason why it is strongly advised not to use the *pkzip* cipher.

The 'license fees' for using *pkcrack* are rather interesting, if not amusing. No software developer can make a living from shareware in Germany. So they distribute it as 'cardware': everyone who uses the program and likes it is kindly requested to send the developer a postcard from their home country with some text of their choice (praise is preferred). It doesn't always take money to create incentives!

The commercial use of *pkcrack* is 'strictly forbidden in any form whatsoever'. Don't allow yourself to be led into accepting money for supporting companies in economic espionage—consider code breaking as voluntary assistance and cash in on respectable consultant fees instead. Joking aside: whoever protects corporate data with *pkzip* can't be helped. I appreciate Peter Conrad's program very much. It made the decisive step from theory to practice and, as a side effect, prevents a large number of people from pocketing dream commissions semi-legally. (There are enough opportunities to make money with software.)

Bottom Line

Cryptanalyzing the *pkzip* cipher is perhaps the most demanding part of this book, though merely outlined. If you are interested in the details, you should have a look at the original work by Biham and Kocher. It is included in the *pkcrack* program as a PostScript file. However, even the original text is not easy to understand. Perhaps the explanations given above will help you get started. Conrad's program also helps to better understand things, though the detail is not mentioned.

The *pkcrack* program can be seen as a realization of the 'threat' from Chapter 1: if you use a theoretically insecure method, you have to expect that somebody with no knowledge of the background but lots of money for fast hardware (a Pentium PC and Linux in this case) and an appropriate program (*pkcrack* in this case) will get hold of your sensitive information. It won't take more than a couple of hours on a PC, or maybe less.

The design of the *pkzip* cipher is not bad at all. But its single steps (a) through (e) are not secure enough. Each step can be cracked in itself without knowing the previous step. This is an important difference to product algorithms like the ones discussed in this book. The single steps in *pkzip* differ a lot, but without doing any good.

5.7.2 Classified Stuff in Air: The D-Networks and the A5 Algorithm

Cellular telephones are great as long as Mr Mallory can't listen in on them. Some owner of a C-network phone was obviously not aware of this problem. In the C-network, phones worked analogously, like radio senders and receivers. Though voice was scrambled, listening in on them wasn't a major problem for techno freaks more or less familiar with the matter. In short, if you made confidential phone calls within the C-network you might just as well have written the contents on postcards and given them to the next passerby to put them in a letterbox. That wouldn't be as fast as a phone call, but more secure if the passerby looked fairly trustworthy.

Things changed with the advent of the GSM standard. In Germany, these are the networks D1, D2, and E-Plus. These networks digitize, compress, encrypt, and broadcast voice in single 114-bit data packets to the next base station. Up to eight subscribers can concurrently use a frequency in one time slot based on timesharing—every one of them is 'on' for about half a millisecond. Moreover, the transmit frequency can be set anew over and again during the transmission. This is called *frequency hopping*. Theoretically, 124 frequencies are available in each cell; the practical number of frequencies used per cell seems to still be in the single-digit figure range. Frequency hopping enables broadcasting behind coarse grids like steel bridges, while making eavesdropping more difficult for attackers.

The base station receives the packets individually, decrypts them and forwards them via radio relay or fiberglass cables. If the receiver happens to be using a GSM handset, then his base station encrypts the data packets received, and the receiver's handset decrypts them, puts them together again, and converts them back into voice. Otherwise, this process happens upon the transition into a different telephone network. All this shows the following clearly.

Eavesdropping on D-network conversations is not meant for freaks with tuned broadband receivers. You need very expensive special hardware. If the information on frequency hopping itself is also encrypted (which I don't know), then the cost would multiply once more considerably.

Consequently, conversations in the D- and E-Plus wireless networks are much more secure, compared with conventional wireline networks, for several reasons. First, a 'hacker' can't get hold of the line as easily as they can get to your telephone distribution panel in the basement, since base stations are interconnected by radio relay or fiberglass cables. Second, he cannot run up your phone bill as easily as in a wireline network, because digital networks authenticate their users. We will get back to this issue in Section 6.1.3.

However, governments (and naturally all national intelligence agencies) can listen in on your conversations in spite of it all. The government may tap base stations. Though this was not possible when the D-networks were introduced, the software was meanwhile changed at high cost upon the government's request.

A weak ciphering algorithm could be a theoretical threat to the confidentiality of the communication within the D-network. And this is exactly the case. We will be dealing with the A5 algorithm in the following, because it concerns an important field: ciphering by means of shift registers.

LFSRs and the A5 Algorithm

All kinds of interesting rumors are woven around the A5 algorithm. I particularly refer to messages posted in the *sci.crypt* newsgroup on June 17, 1994, which you can read on our Web site (see A.1, *algor/A5* directory). In the mid-1980s, people discussed whether A5 should be strong or weak. Germany voted in favor of a strong algorithm, since the Iron Curtain was very close back then. Other countries feared an export ban to the Middle East due to the cryptography used. The outcome was a stream cipher designed in France, which is obviously weak. This very circumstance seems now to restrict its export.[2]

Though A5 was kept secret for a long time, it eventually leaked to the Internet over several channels (including Bradford University in Great Britain). Dr Simon Shepherd of Bradford University wanted to lecture on a cryptanalysis of this algorithm at an IEE colloquium to be held in London on June 3, 1994. However, his lecture was prevented at the very last minute. In 1997, Jovan D. Golic presented another analysis at the EUROCRYPT [GolicA5], but revealing the session key remained a costly enterprise, as it turned out. So there was something out there to get credit for after all! The reduction of the key length to 54 bits (see also Section 6.1.3), which wasn't discovered until April 1998, could not be used in his cryptanalysis, as Golic himself stated. But

---

[2]However, this is not a typically European problem—think of the 160-bit Vigenère cipher for US mobile phones (end of Chapter 3).

that's of no interest to anybody anymore. We will see further below how the algorithm can be cracked in a flash.

Apart from these dubious circumstances and the fact that A5 is one of the encryption algorithms most frequently used in the world, this algorithm represents an encryption class we haven't dealt with in this book yet: stream ciphers using **LFSRs** (**Linear Feedback Shift Registers**). This impressive name hides a rather simple method.

A *shift register* is nothing more than a memory location with n bits, where n does not have to be a power of 2; it can be an 'odd' number, for example, 9, 23, or 47. A special piece of hardware allows you to shift all bits concurrently by one position to the left and to fill the least significant bit with a given value. It would look like this in C:

```
R = (R << 1) | b
```

where R is a data type with n bits, and b is a value with all of its bits equal to 0, except perhaps the least significant bit. Registers of microprocessors can be shifted. However, microprocessors handle other tasks, too; conversely, shift registers are specialized and particularly fast pieces of hardware.

Linear functions on a shift register are defined exactly as at the beginning of Section 4.4.4: some bits are chosen from the register and XORed. *Feedback* means that, in a shift, the least significant bit of the shift register is the result of a linear function on that register. The most significant bit of the register pushed out on the left is reused. Figure 5.22 shows how this process works. (The shift could just as well run from left to right, and use the least significant bit; the names are arbitrary.) The positions of the bits that 'participate' in the

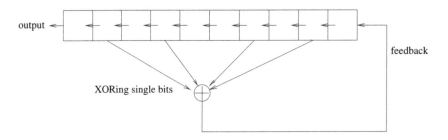

Figure 5.22: A 10-bit shift register with linear feedback (LFSR).

XOR in the feedback are referred to as a **tap sequence**. Such an LFSR is very easy to implement in hardware, of course.

What has all this got to do with cryptology? Well, we could fill an LFSR with a secret content—the key—and then use the bit sequence created for a stream cipher. That's far from being secure yet. First, LFSRs have a period, which means that, after a finite number of steps, a state repeats itself. If this period is too short and much of the ciphertext is known, we could mount an attack similar to how we would attack the Vigenère cipher. The period length can be maximally $2^n - 1$ for an LFSR n bits long (though the LFSR can accept 2^n values at most, value 0 is not applicable: once all bits are equal to 0, they will remain equal to 0). The period is maximal if the tap sequence corresponds to a so-called *primitive polynomial modulo 2*. Rather than explaining this term, I refer to [SchnCr] and the large number of literature references included therein.

LFSRs have been interesting for a long time and formed the backbone of military cryptography because they are particularly easy to implement in switching circuits, and because of the high ciphering speed. On the one hand, there is a mature mathematical theory of LFSRs. On the other hand, little is known about their use in devices, and most developments are secret [SchnCr, 16.4]. It is interesting that almost all Cray supercomputers process a strange machine command that determines the number of bits set in a register. This means that an LFSR can also be implemented very efficiently in software. It is believed that this command is a requirement in almost all computer contracts with the NSA. It has meanwhile become an open secret that Cray computers were initially built mainly for cryptanalysis.

Simple LFSRs don't offer cryptological security any longer; they are easily cracked. A plaintext attack with $2n$ successive plaintext–ciphertext bit pairs suffices to break an n-bit LFSR. For this reason, several LFSRs are linked in as complicated a way as possible. We will only look at a brief outline of A5 in this book.

The A5 algorithm uses three LFSRs with lengths of 19, 22, and 23 bits, i.e., 64 bits in total (and that's also the key length). The tap sequences (bits counted from 0 on) are:

```
18, 17, 16, 13 for the 19-bit register,
21, 20, 16, 12 for the 22-bit register,
22, 21, 18, 17 for the 23-bit register.
```

We look at the middle bit of each register (i.e., positions 9, 11, and 13). Every ciphering step moves a register forward exactly when either its middle bit is equal to 1 and the middle bits of the other two registers are equal to 0, or vice versa (the bit considered is 0, the others are equal to 1). The feedback bit—and not the bit pushed out in that step—goes into the key stream. That's all!

The points of departure for cryptanalyzing A5 are the register lengths and the tap sequences—both are too short. The register lengths allow you to mount a plaintext attack with 2^{40} trial-and-error encryptions on average: you guess the first two registers and compute the third from the key stream. Little plaintext will suffice, because one single 23-bit LFSR can be broken with 46 bits of plaintext. Ross Anderson estimates that the computing performance required can be handled by programmed Xilinx chips: if each chip trial-and-error tests two keys per microsecond and 50 chips are housed in a special computer, the key should be found in about 3 hours on average. The insufficient lengths of the tap sequences appear to have been exploited by Dr Shepherd.

Birkyukov and Shamir put an end to all the speculation around A5 in 2000. They showed how to crack A5 in their publication [BirShamA5]. You need a computer with two 73-GB hard disks. You fill them with data computed in advance. This is certainly costly, but you need to do it only once. You then *replay 2 minutes' worth of plaintext and ciphertext* of a communication and put the computer to work; it will compute for *1 second*, and you will have the session key. Alternatively, you need a 2-second plaintext and several minutes of computation time. This is more realistic for data transmission, if the beginning of the data stream is known. This method doesn't work for normal voice communication, though. You would proceed differently.

GSM handsets know an additional algorithm called **A5/2** (probably the reason why A5 is sometimes called 'A5/1'), which is much more insecure than A5. In 2003, Barkan, Biham, and Keller published an article (*cryptome.org/gsm-crack-bbk.pdf* on the Web site to this book) describing how to practically and effectively attack A5/2. They exploited an error in the protocol: the checksum of the data packets is a CRC, an algebraic function of the packet's bits, and this CRC is included in the cipher. Now, A5/2 is so weak that the algebraic dependency between CRC and data is not sufficiently blurred (insufficient confusion). You can reveal the key by *replaying a few hundredths of seconds* of the ciphertext within a *1-second computation time*. In practice, Mallory could use an IMSI catcher, play the man in the middle, and convince the handset at the beginning of the conversation to use A5/2 instead of A5/1. The cost amounts to a couple of thousand dollars and sufficient know-how.

However, somebody who can use an IMSI catcher and play the man in the middle is normally more nifty: he'd talk the handset into disabling the cipher (which often happens due to poor transmission conditions, since unencrypted messages require less bandwidth). Only very few handset models display this state, and if they do, users don't normally pay attention. Disappointed? That's espionage in practice: it's not the elegance that counts, but the result.

5.7.3 FEAL: The Cryptanalysts' Favorite

Read a lot about cryptanalysis and still not heard of the **FEAL** block algorithm? Just like every cryptologist should know the Enigma, they should have heard of the cryptanalytic successes against FEAL. For, whenever a new cryptanalytic method is discovered, FEAL seems to be the first victim, and the algorithm does 'lend' itself indeed.

FEAL was designed by the Japanese Shimizu and Miyaguchi in 1987 with the goal to replace DES by a faster and at least equally secure algorithm. Similarly to DES, it is a Feistel network with 64-bit blocks, but it uses a 64-bit key. The intended improvement was to be a more secure round function. Four rounds had originally been planned. FEAL-4 (4-round FEAL) is really much faster than DES; unfortunately, it is not more secure. Figure 5.23 shows the round function.

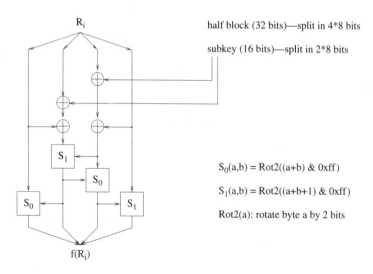

half block (32 bits)—split in 4*8 bits

subkey (16 bits)—split in 2*8 bits

$S_0(a,b) = \text{Rot2}((a+b) \,\&\, 0\text{xff})$

$S_1(a,b) = \text{Rot2}((a+b+1) \,\&\, 0\text{xff})$

Rot2(a): rotate byte a by 2 bits

Figure 5.23: The round function of FEAL.

The design goal was thoroughly missed. The first attack by means of differential cryptanalysis that was published at all was not the famous attack Biham and Shamir launched against DES, as you might expect, but the one by Murphy [MurFEAL] against FEAL-4 in 1990: the algorithm can be broken with as little as 20 chosen plaintexts. In contrast to DES, this is *very* practicable indeed!

The developers' response was FEAL-8. Biham and Shamir came along and showed that differential cryptanalysis is more effective than brute force against FEAL *with up to 32 rounds*. The number of chosen plaintexts for FEAL-4 dropped to 8 (!), and was 10 000 for FEAL-8, and FEAL-16 required 2^{28} chosen plaintexts or $2^{37.5}$ (corresponds to 1.5 Tbytes) known plaintexts.

The designers then came up with FEAL-NX which uses 128-bit keys. Biham and Shamir didn't fall down on showing that their attack works just as effectively against this algorithm.

In their linear cryptanalysis attack in 1992, Matsui and Yamagishi broke FEAL-4 using *five known* plaintexts (40 bytes)! FEAL-8 would have required 2^{15} (32 768) known plaintexts.

Meanwhile, differential linear cryptanalysis can be used to break FEAL-8 with only *twelve chosen* plaintexts.

FEAL is an impressive example of the progress modern cryptanalysis has made during the past few years: while 10 000 chosen plaintexts were necessary to attack FEAL-8 in 1990, that number was down to 12 five years later. The unsuccessful improvement of this algorithm shows that new ideas can turn a weak algorithm into a secure one only fundamentally.

Implementations of FEAL-8 and FEAL-NX are given on the Web site associated with this book (see www.wileyeurope.com/go/cryptology).

5.7.4 Other Algorithms: SEAL and Blowfish

In closing our discussion of known algorithms, I will briefly describe the SEAL stream cipher and the Blowfish block algorithm below.

SEAL

Similarly to RC5, **SEAL** is a relatively young algorithm—it was first introduced by Rogaway and Coppersmith [RogCoSeal] in 1994. (We know Coppersmith from the DES development; he is thought to be an excellent cryptanalyst.) SEAL is a stream cipher, i.e., it takes a key to compute a secret key sequence and XOR it with the ciphertext. The method has three outstanding features:

- The algorithm is one of the fastest ciphers in software that are currently considered to be secure: it achieves 58 Mbits/s on a 50-MHz PC-486 (that translates in 7 Mbytes/s, about five times faster than my RC5a implementation on a 133-MHz Pentium!).

- The computation of special tables about 3 Kbytes long from the key is much slower than the encryption. This prevents trial-and-error attacks, such as dictionary attacks or brute-force attacks, against a different subset of all keys.

- The key byte sequence does not have to be computed sequentially (as with other algorithms); you can skip an arbitrary number of bytes. This makes SEAL ideally suited for encrypting entire hard disks or single distributed database entries. In contrast to other stream ciphers, SEAL-encrypted messages can be sent over channels that lose data from time to time—there is no synchronization problem.

However, SEAL is patented by IBM and has not yet been publicly cryptanalyzed. But when Coppersmith designs an algorithm you may reasonably assume that it is well designed.

SEAL takes a secret 160-bit key, k, and creates a sequence $k(n)$ of pseudorandom character strings of length L for an arbitrarily given number L (not greater than 2^{16}, corresponding to 64 Kbytes), where index n is a 32-bit number. The details of this algorithm are rather complex; an implementation in C is included on the Web site associated with this book (see `www.wileyeurope.com/go/cryptology`).

Blowfish

The **Blowfish** block algorithm is also fairly new. It was introduced by Bruce Schneier, the author of the seminal cryptographic book [SchnCr], in [SchnBlow1] and [SchnBlow2] in 1994. In contrast to SEAL, Blowfish is free and has been cryptanalyzed. It is also used practically, namely in *FolderBolt* for MS Windows and Macintosh as well as in *Nautilus* and *PGPfone*. Because it's free, it is also used in many public-domain products, including SSH (Section 7.3) and *GnuPG* (Section 7.1.4).

Blowfish is essentially a Feistel network with 64-bit blocks, 16 rounds, and variable key lengths (up to 448 bits, i.e., 56 bytes). Figure 5.24 shows its round function.

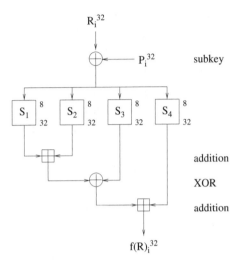

Figure 5.24: Round function of the Blowfish algorithm. The S-boxes are computed dependent on the key.

However, referring to Figure 4.6, R_i is also XORed with a subkey, P_i. Each of the four key-dependent S-boxes contains 256 values of 32 bits each. This reminds us a little of DES with key-dependent S-boxes (Section 5.2.2), but the round function is clearly more complex, and since it uses XOR and addition, its non-linearity is stronger.

The *cryptanalysis* of Blowfish showed no weaknesses in the algorithm. An attack with 2080 chosen plaintexts and about 2^{34} computations was found against the 3-round method. However, Blowfish uses 16 rounds. According to Schneier [SchnCr], there is a differential cryptanalysis by Vaudenay, which finds the subkeys of the Blowfish algorithm with r rounds using 2^{8r+1} chosen plaintexts. This does not mean that the attacker knows the S-boxes yet. Weak keys required 'only' 2^{4r+1} chosen plaintexts, so they don't give reason for concern.

Blowfish can be programmed very effectively on large microprocessors, such as Pentium or Power Chip (Schneier states 26 CPU cycles per byte; this would correspond to about 5 Mbytes/s on a Pentium-133!). It requires less than 5 Kbytes of memory and, not least, it's free. Altogether an interesting algorithm indeed. You can find an implementation in C on our Web site (see A.1).

5.7.5   NSA and Skipjack

In April 1993, the President of the United States started a Technology Initiative related to the **Escrowed Encryption Standard** (**EES**), the **Clipper chip**, and the **Capstone chip**, among other things. The initiative was intended to provide for cryptologically secure data and voice transmission, however, with some reservation: governmental agencies should have access to the secret key upon demand. This would be done by **key escrow** using a device-specific key, which can be used, in turn, to decipher the session key. We are only interested in the underlying symmetric algorithm called **Skipjack**.

Nothing was known about its structure for many years. The reason was that Skipjack was developed by the NSA and subject to secrecy. It was permitted for use in 'non-analyzable' hardware (tamperproof chips) only, more specifically in the *Clipper* chip (for telephone and telefax) and in the *Capstone* chip (for data communication; embedded in the *Fortezza* card for notebooks). Though a group of cryptologists were allowed to look at the algorithm [BrickDenn], their results showed no vulnerabilities whatsoever—neither statistically nor by means of differential cryptanalysis, and weak keys had obviously not been found either. Nevertheless, this is not very convincing since nobody else was permitted to have a look at the algorithm.

It is presumed in [SchnCr, 13.12] that Skipjack has a structure similar to DES. The presumption was substantiated: in the unlikely event that somebody manages to analyze either Clipper or Capstone, they should at least not be able to learn a novel cryptographic method of the NSA. Anderson and Ross mentioned in their remarkable article [AndKuhn.tamp] that the chip was read at the Sandia National Laboratories.

However, when Matthew Blaze showed how the Skipjack algorithm implemented in the Clipper chip can be exploited *without* key escrow, the EES Initiative was all of a sudden not pushed at full stream anymore. He may have hit a sore point, apart from hefty animosities against the Initiative by civil rightists and many cryptologists. More about this issue in Sections 6.4 and 8.2.3.

The Secrecy Concept Fails—Skipjack is Revealed

Skipjack was not supposed to become known, because nobody was supposed to learn anything about the level of knowledge at the NSA. As a consequence, only the NSA itself or suppliers under its strict supervision were permitted to produce the Clipper and Capstone chips. And this is exactly the point where the huge almighty authority made an elementary error, just as happens with such authorities: they forgot to allow for alternatives. Had the protocol additionally permitted disclosed algorithms like RSA and 3DES as alternatives, the chip could have been implemented in software, including key escrow, since the latter is an integral part of the cryptographic protocol and not the algorithm. But methods that are kept secret have to remain hidden in hardware.

So, Alice needed an NSA chip to be able to communicate with some equipment fitted accordingly, and she didn't have one. We don't know whether she found the chips too expensive, or whether there simply weren't enough chips around. Anyhow, problematic cases appeared to pile up. The only feasible way out was to implement the chips in software.

Now, the NSA knew that people would have started mounting their analyses on the very day such software was shipped, eager to closely inspect the first algorithm ever developed by the NSA. All that remained was to take the bull by the horns: the NSA disclosed the algorithm in mid-1998, along with its public-key method called **KEA** (which will be briefly discussed in Section 6.1.1). You can imagine (just as the NSA did back then) that cryptanalysts from all over the world plunged into it.

Skipjack is a product algorithm (a Feistel network) with 64-bit blocks, an 80-bit key, and 32 rounds. It differs from the 'civilian' algorithms mainly in that it uses linear feedback shift registers (LFSRs; Section 5.7.2), which are commonly used for stream ciphers, a traditional military field. The design is astonishingly simple, you can find the detailed description and source texts on our Web site. In his online magazine *Cryptogram* 7/98, Bruce Schneier wrote that Skipjack is very 'vulnerable', and that even the slightest modification would wreck its security.

A Spectacular Cryptanalysis

Biham, Biryukov, and Shamir, the cryptanalysts well known to our readers, appear to have put up a memorial to themselves as they cryptanalyzed a Skip-jack variant reduced by one round only. In fact, they invented a new variant of differential cryptanalysis, the method of impossible differentials, spiritually slightly related to the negative pattern search discussed in Section 3.4.1: roughly speaking, you look at differences that can currently *not* occur and exclude keys that create such differences. This method is ingenious and very strong—its successes include the best known attack against IDEA [Skipana].

The authors succeeded in attacking the Skipjack variant reduced to 31 rounds more effectively by this method than by brute force. However, this is irrelevant for practical purposes. You'd require 2^{34} (128 Gbytes) chosen plaintexts and 2^{78} steps. Even if you executed one billion steps per second on one million processors in parallel, this cryptanalysis would still take 9.5 years.

On the other hand, the result is enormously significant for self-confidence in public research. Take a minute and compare this with the cryptanalysis of the five final AES candidates: none of them can be attacked faster than by brute force, if you reduce it by only one round. What you usually do is consider some security reserve in your planning. Since the NSA didn't, the conclusion that they didn't know this attack suggests itself. Let's sum things up:

Biham, Biryukov, and Shamir presumably found a cryptanalytic method that the NSA didn't know.

Together with Matt Blaze's attack against the Clipper protocol and the consequential disclosure of the algorithm, the NSA no longer appears as almighty as you might be led to believe.

5.8 Probabilistic and Quantum Cryptography

This section will show you that cryptographic algorithms can sometimes come along in rather exotic shapes. What we will be dealing with are ingenious ideas rather than specific algorithms.

Probabilistic Cryptography

Probabilistic algorithms contain randomness, as the name suggests. They can generate many possible ciphertexts from one fixed plaintext; which one of them will be output is totally accidental. The reverse procedure—decryption—must remain unambiguous, of course.

'What's the point?', you may ask. For one thing, such an algorithm is useful as an *improvement of asymmetric methods*. If encryption with the public key is probabilistic, nobody can prove that a certain ciphertext belongs to a certain plaintext, unless they know the public key. Something like this can be desirable in many a situation!

Furthermore, the usual asymmetric methods are vulnerable to adaptive-chosen-plaintext attacks—after all, the public key is known. In probabilistic asymmetric encryption, the amount of information gained by encrypting a chosen plaintext is clearly smaller, it might even be zero. These are not more than diffuse threats. No such attack is known against RSA, for example.

The first probabilistic method was invented by Goldwasser and Micali as early as in 1982, but the method was not practicable. In 1984, Goldwasser and Blum [BBS] introduced a simple and applicable method that I will briefly describe below.

The basis is the *random-number generator by Blum, Blum, and Shub*, also referred to as the *BBS generator*. Similarly to the RSA method, two large prime numbers, p and q, form the secret key, and their product, $n = pq$, forms the public key. Here, however, it is necessary that p and q leave a remainder of 3 when divided by 4 (such prime numbers are also called *Blum numbers*). If you want to encrypt something, you choose a random number x that is not divisible by p or q and compute

```
x₀  =  x² mod n
x₁  =  x₀² mod n
x₂  =  x₁² mod n
x₃  =  x₂² mod n
. . .
```

Sequence $b_0, b_1, b_2, \ldots$ of the least significant bits of $x_0, x_1, x_2, \ldots$ is used as a one-time pad. Value x_{t+1} (if the plaintext consists of t bits) is appended to the ciphertext. This x_{t+1} value is useless for attackers. But if you know p and q, you can construct the sequence (x_i) and thus also (b_i) in reverse order (corresponds to calculating roots modulo n).

Since value x was chosen randomly, every encryption will normally produce a different ciphertext.

You can alternatively take several bits rather than the least significant bits. The algorithm would still be secure and faster than RSA (with the above-mentioned benefits versus RSA). Moreover, it would allow you to *prove* that cracking the method requires the factoring of n.

The only drawback of this method is its high vulnerability to chosen-ciphertext attacks (see Section 4.5.3). However, this is of no importance to the exchange of session keys.

Quantum Cryptography

The field of quantum cryptography suggests that the world of cryptology is much larger than one would expect from what has been discussed so far in this book. In fact, this is the field where cryptographic algorithms and protocols merge with modern physics, challenging cryptanalysts in their race with cryptography.

The decisive novelty of quantum cryptography is that it lets you detect or thwart potential eavesdropping on data lines with certainty. To this end, it uses the laws of quantum mechanics, which leave even the niftiest national intelligence organizations powerless over the foreseeable future. They will have to find another vulnerability. In critical cases, one-time pads can be transmitted over secure channels, thus offering a chance (using appropriate noise sources) to—hopefully—rid oneself of cryptanalysts for good.

Such ideas were first published and expanded by Bennet, Brassard *et al.* in 1982 (see [BBEQuant] with references for further reading). The principle is not really hard to understand. You already know the basics from physics at school.

We know that light can be polarized. You can think of a plane of polarization of light, for example, horizontal, vertical, or diagonal (and there are more planes to polarize light differently). You may even have used this phenomenon in a 3D slide show. The glasses used in the binoculars are polarization filters, i.e., they let light penetrate from one polarization level only. The level of the left glass is superimposed vertically on the right glass, similar to frames on a special screen (that does not scatter the polarization direction). Thus, each eye sees only the 'correct' frame.

However, things are a bit more complicated than the simplified analogy above. Say, one of your acquaintances has a 3D projector; have him cover one of the two objectives, then look at the frame through the corresponding binocular glass. Rotate the glass slowly by 90 degrees: the image turns gradually darker until it almost disappears. The model to see polarization as a polarization plane is not entirely correct. When using a filter to measure polarization, we measure the amplitude (intensity) of light in the direction determined by the filter—as shown in Figure 5.25.

If the filter looks onto the polarization plane, then the light intensity is maximal; if the filter is vertical to it, then the intensity is minimal (theoretically equal to zero). And if you hold the binocular glass rotated by 45 degrees to the polarization plane while looking at the screen with one eye, you will see both frames with equal brightness.

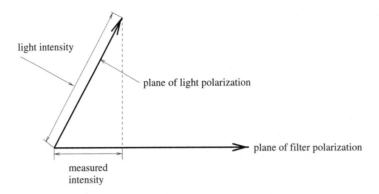

Figure 5.25: Measuring the polarization of light.

If one single polarized photon (light quantum, light wave train) hits such a filter, the term 'intensity' loses its meaning. We have to replace it by 'probability'. If a photon polarized vertically arrives at the receiver's end with a filter placed vertically, the photon passes this filter with a high probability. If the receiver filter is arranged horizontally, the photon can theoretically not pass it. However, if the receiver filter is rotated diagonally by 45 degrees, the photon will pass it with a probability of 50%, and the polarization is undetermined. An eavesdropper trying to detect the polarization cannot achieve this by the laws of quantum mechanics without changing the photon's polarization or even absorbing it.

This means that the polarization of a photon can be determined only once at most. This is the decisive physical principle of quantum cryptography.

Naturally, the technical details of the method are complicated. However, the considerations above should help you to understand the following cryptographic protocol:

1. Alice sends randomly polarized photons. Each photon is polarized horizontally, vertically, or in one of the two diagonal directions.

2. Bob has a habit of setting his receiver horizontally or diagonally slanted to the right, and arbitrarily for each photon. With each incoming photon, he can determine whether or not it passed the filter. He can decide from the filter set horizontally whether the photon was polarized horizontally or vertically. His finding will be random for photons polarized diagonally.

3. Bob tells Alice his settings over a non-tamperproof channel (but the message must not be vulnerable to manipulation). With this, Bob doesn't give away anything to an eavesdropper: the sentence 'I used a filter set horizontally in the 5th pulse' does not reveal the polarization he actually measured in the 5th pulse.

4. Alice tells Bob the numbers of the correct settings, for example: 'You measured the 1st, 3rd, 4th, and 5th pulses correctly'. Again, this won't allow the eavesdropper to understand *what* Bob actually measured. The measuring results for these pulses are pieces of *information* that Alice *transmitted securely* to Bob. 50 % of the settings should be correct on average. The intruder eavesdropping on the line would necessarily falsify the information. Alice and Bob could find this out, for example, by comparing hash values. They would also be able to notice forgeries as they exchange filter settings.

The last point shows us that quantum cryptography does not provide for a secure data channel, but it does allow the conversers to detect whether or not somebody listened in on them. For this reason, quantum cryptography is meaningful only for transmitting a random key (which does not contain important information), but less suitable for transmitting sensitive information.

The protocol can be expanded such that information can be transmitted securely despite a (necessarily active) eavesdropper. The only problem could arise in steps 3 and 4: man-in-the-middle attacks where an intruder pretends to both conversers to be the other converser must be prevented in these steps. Asymmetric methods can be used to reliably exclude such attacks. Notice that there is a difference to using asymmetric encryption in hybrid methods, where cracking would reveal the private key, and consequently all session keys and with them all secret messages. Conversely, in quantum cryptography, only the filter settings would be compromised, which are not secret anyway. For this reason, it is actually sufficient to exchange digitally signed messages about the filter settings. Mallory, in the middle of the line, would have to forge these messages as fast as Alice and Bob exchange them. To this end, Mallory would have to know their secret keys in advance, which can normally be ruled out.

Quantum cryptography is theoretically a heady approach. There is finally a *provable* security rather than the usual assumptions and speculation.

The fact that the entire thing works in practice is still cooler. Employees of British Telecom managed to transmit information over a fiberglass line 10 km long. Researchers at Los Alamos achieved 48 km in 1999. This is an outstanding achievement in view of the fact that *single* photons are transmitted.

Unfortunately, even such outstanding achievements don't remove all problems. If Alice and Bob are at a distance of 2000 km, then quantum cryptography won't work over fiberglass even if the most sophisticated technology were used. The solution could be airborne, at least partly: through the atmosphere to a satellite and back to earth again.

Is this doable? Isn't air an optically 'dirty' medium compared with superclean fiberglass? Richard Hughes of the Quantum Information Team at Los Alamos has been working at it for years and has achieved results that stun physicists with disbelief. A receiver with a diameter of a few centimeters, circulating the earth in 8 km/s at a height of 300 km, would have to be hit by one single photon that must neither be absorbed nor change its polarization as it travels through air. Hughes hasn't gotten there yet, but almost. He uses the following tricks:

- The selected wavelength is 770 nm (this is borderline infrared). The absorption is very low in this range, and turbulences (that could change the polarization) have a smaller impact due to their typical expansion of several centimeters.

- Light scatter is widely excluded by receiving only photons that ideally come exactly from the sender's direction. To this end, a special receiver unit was built at Los Alamos.

- A sharper frequency filter lets pass only photons of the transmitted wavelength.

- Nevertheless, many photons are still disturbed, though they do come from the right direction and have the right frequency. For this reason, a time window of only 5 nanoseconds is opened for reception in every microsecond.

- Other sources of interference are air turbulences. Though they don't absorb the photons, and they don't change their polarization noticeably, they provoke a change to the photons' traveling time due to density fluctuations in the air. However, this is not jerky. The time difference remains moderate within 1 microsecond.

To compensate for such differences in the time of flight, each 'sharper' pulse is preceded by a 100-nanosecond measuring pulse. This is how the current time of flight is determined, and the receiving window is kept open at exactly the right point in time.

- Yet another problem is that turbulences deflect the light ray. This is why the current deviation from the ideal is determined concurrently to ensure that the sender is always directed exactly to the receiver.

Such tricks helped Hughes and his team to demonstrate airborne quantum cryptography over a distance of 500 meters. 'Big deal', you will probably say, 'people covered 48 kilometers over fiberglass'. Well, let's not jump to conclusions yet! Once we have overcome a 2-km airway, we will reach 300 km into orbit somehow sooner or later! This is so for the simple reason that the density of air and turbulences decrease quickly as the height increases.

For the time being, however, we will stay on earth, where considerable progress has been made:

- The 67-km distance between Geneva and Lausanne has been overcome by fiberglass.

- Toshiba achieved a transmission rate of 15 bits/s over a 100-km fiberglass line in Cambridge.

- The most impressive achievement, however, is probably the bridging by telescope and laser of a 23.4-km beeline between the Wendelstein and Zugspitze mountains on the German side of the Alps. You can read all the details about this fascinating work by Matthäus Halder on our Web site and the Internet at `scotty.quantum.physik.uni-muenchen.de/ publ/matthaeusdiplom.pdf`.

  Nothing is impossible, so it seems.

5.9 Quantum Computers. What's Still In There for Brute Force?

If you think the last point above seemed like witchcraft, you will probably banish the following into the realm of utopia. You wouldn't be alone. Except for a group of theoretical physicists, nobody took the 'quantum computer' seriously for a long time. We had failed to understand that such computers could turn our ideas about information technology upside down radically. However, I have to take a run-up to explain this.

You'll probably remember from school that quantum mechanics does not speak of deterministic states, such as 'power on' or 'power off' (corresponding to bit 0 or 1); it works with probabilities. The last point above suggested this. It is hard to imagine in everyday life that something can have several states concurrently, based on a certain probability distribution.

But there are more inconceivable things: quantum particles can be in super-position to one another so that they are no longer independent. This is called *quantum entanglement*. If you influence one of these entangled quantum parti-cles, you also influence all others concurrently rather than with a minimal delay. It is easier to describe it mathematically (though complicated) than trying to imagine it.

All of this has been known since about 1920 and can be described by quantum mechanics. But around 1980, Bennett, Benioff, and Feynman hit upon the idea that one could build a computer on that basis. This computer would look totally different from the computers we are used to today, and it would also work in a totally different way:

- The bit of our times would be replaced by a **qubit** in such a computer. A qubit could take states 0 and 1 concurrently, with different probabilities.

- Operations change the state of all qubits concurrently. Though there are processes that correspond to the logical AND, OR, and NOT operations, they would merely change probability distributions in quantum computers.

- Computations are totally 'blind', i.e., there is no feedback on the system's state as the computer works. And it wouldn't be possible, since you can't 'read' quantum particles without influencing them (which is exactly what quantum cryptography in the previous point is based upon!), and a measuring process would destroy an entanglement immediately.

- The art of programming a quantum computer consists in, for example, changing probability distributions by continued operations such that the 'correct' state (i.e., the solution) has a higher probability than all other states in the end. Only then is the system of qubits read and destroyed as it is read. Moreover, quantum computers allow you to directly determine periods of functions. This is the principle that the Shor algorithm for factoring, which is explained in detail in [WillClear10], works by.

In sequential work, say, in iterations, quantum computers are not faster than conventional computers. But they can do things like determining the period of a function 'directly', which poses enormous problems for our classic sequential computers. Consider diffraction radiograms of crystals: the images give you a direct clue to the periodic crystal structure. The method works selectively, virtually filtering the periodic shares. Compare optical electron microscopy with scanning electron microscopy—this is roughly how you should think of the difference between conventional computers and quantum computers.

If you are interested to learn more, you can find other texts on this topic in *txt/quant* on our Web site. Furthermore, I recommend the excellent book *Ultimate Zero and One* [WillClear10], and the Web site `www.nsf.gov/pubs/2000/nsf00101/nsf00101.html` on Quantum Information Science (QIS), which some experts think is the most interesting or even strategically most important progress in information technology of the 1990s.

Fascinating Outlook

The quantum computer was initially a pure thought experiment: there was a logic, and this logic was used to build a hypothetical computer without considering its practical feasibility. Such a computer could not be compared with our current computers. 500 entangled qubits could take on 2^{500} states *concurrently*. You know that the number 2^{500} is beyond good and evil on conventional computers with regard to both memory capacity and number of operations. The number of atoms in the entire known universe is incomparably smaller.

The downside is that quantum mechanics has always been hard to understand. And because this fascinating new quantum computer appeared very hypothetical and hard to grasp on top of it all, these things were discussed within a small circle of specialists for fourteen years, until 1994. In that year, Shor developed an algorithm that allows you to factorize large numbers on quantum computers at a speed one can hardly imagine.

'Wait a minute', you will say, 'wouldn't that be sensational! One could easily break RSA and most encrypted messages sent around nowadays at one go!' That was exactly what jumped to the minds of militaries, national intelligence agencies, governmental agencies, and large organizations like IBM. With his purely theoretical work, Shor had woken sleeping giants. Since 1994, intensive research work on quantum computers has been underway, and all of a sudden financial means that physicists had never even dreamt of have become available. Rumors have it that the NSA sponsored nine universities for activities in this field.

Talking about dreaming: the discrete logarithm could also be computed by use of quantum computers. This would mean that *all known reliable public-key methods became insecure.* The computational speed versus algorithms currently known would accelerate exponentially. It is currently possible that a 512-bit RSA key could be broken on conventional computers, and 768 bits should be possible with the Twinkle device introduced in Section 4.5.3. Cracking 1024-bit keys is definitely utopian with such methods and current computing technology. If we had quantum computers, for example, 1024 bits would take only twice or four times as long as 512 bits. And that's thought to be fast, really fast—perhaps in the range of seconds or minutes.

Quantum computers could be useful for other tasks, too. For example, searching unordered data repositories is one of the most time-consuming tasks for current computers. It generally takes $n/2$ steps to find a specific record from a list of n records. In his article included on our Web site (*txt/quant/qc-grover.txt*), Grover explains an algorithm for quantum computers that needs only $\sqrt{n}$ steps. More specifically, while a conventional computer requires 500 billion steps to find a specific entry out of one trillion entries on average, a quantum computer with Grover's algorithm can do this in about one million steps—500 000 times faster. Grover even shows that it cannot be faster than that in general on a quantum computer.

Finding periods of functions is much faster on quantum computers compared with using classic algorithms. This is the special feature that methods for factoring and computing discrete logarithms are based on. Rather than working sequentially, quantum computers truly work in parallel.

Back to Reality

Unfortunately, there is no single quantum computer yet, at least not one that deserves this name. One of the large number of hurdles has been that quantum computers don't work deterministically, which means that they are error-prone. This problem was solved by Shor and Steane at the same time in 1995. They designed methods for error correction in quantum computers which obviously nobody had believed in.

In August 2000, Isaac Chuang of the IBM Almaden Research Center presented the most promising approach to that date in a cumbersome manner to the press: a glass tube with special molecules, in which atomic nuclei simulated a 5-qubit quantum computer, triggered and read by electromagnetic waves based on nuclear magnetic resonance (NMR) imaging. In effect, this computer can process a very short algorithm. Insiders will want to know that the qubits correspond to the spins of single atoms in specially constructed molecules coupled over electron sheaths (so the algorithm lies obviously in the molecular structure). The relaxation times are still within the range of seconds. Don't laugh: the first computers worked mechanically with punch cards and weren't much faster.

That was the state of affairs in summer 2000. Meanwhile, one arrived at 7 qubits and managed to factor the number 15 (`http://www.research.ibm.com/resources/news/20011219_quantum.shtml`). Many great developments began with a 'proof of concept'.

More results won't be long in coming considering the intensive research in this field. However, the way toward factoring 1024-bit numbers is extremely cumbersome. Solving the problem might indeed be more difficult than it appears. It wouldn't be the first time. For instance, people thought of nuclear fusion reactors as a future technology forty years ago, whereas things around this issue are very quiet today. Some researchers bet that the sun would extinguish before a quantum computer could factor 1024-bit numbers.

Cryptologists should be more careful because they have to invent algorithms that resist novel types of attack ahead of their time. Grover recalls a contribution to a discussion in 1949, which read that 'while a computer like the ENIAC is equipped with 18 000 tubes and weighs 30 tons, computers of the future might perhaps have only 1000 tubes and weigh only one ton'. Now just imagine how experts might laugh at our current ideas in 50 years from now...

Schneier said in an interview that 'quadratic acceleration' as in Grover's algorithm would be rather typical for quantum computers. This would mean that AES with 256-bit keys might still have the security of a 128-bit algorithm, i.e., it would still be invulnerable (see below). Quantum computers are exponentially faster for special problems only. Unfortunately, this includes the two problems all current asymmetric encryptions suffer from. And other secure methods are still not in sight.

So there is need for action. Some studies suggest that quantum computers could, for example, replace conventional semiconductor technology by the year 2020 once this technology has reached dimensions where quantum effects dominate. Though we have to be patient, only two mathematical problems identified in the past twenty years are suitable for public-key cryptography, namely factoring and computing the discrete logarithm.

And I wouldn't be so sure about symmetric methods. Quantum computers do not offer faster speeds when running successive operations. But who checks whether or not symmetric algorithms could be attacked somehow 'differently'? Hardly a cryptanalyst is in the habit of attacking such methods by means of quantum computer algorithms (aside from the fact that it cannot be tested practically yet). On the other hand, quantum computer specialists are not yet familiar with the shallows of modern cryptanalysis.

Quantum computers are often confused with quantum cryptography, but there is a huge difference: though both use quantum mechanics, they differ profoundly.

- Quantum cryptography serves to transmit data where eavesdropping can doubtlessly be detected in arrears, while quantum computers implement algorithms, i.e., they are actually computers.

- Quantum cryptography makes our world more secure, while quantum computers make it clearly more insecure.

- Quantum cryptography has progressed pretty far experimentally, while nobody can tell whether we will ever be able to build a reasonable quantum computer.

I personally tend to believe that cryptanalytic research will come up with a few whopping surprises before the first large quantum computer is built. Think only of unexpected methods like Shamir's impossible differentials (Section 5.7.5) or Schneier's mod-3 cryptanalysis (Section 5.4.2).

What's Still In There For Brute Force?

Let's stay with physics and speculation for another while. People claim over and again that brute force is only a matter of cost. That's nonsense! Of course there is no such a thing as an absolutely secure system, but that's a different story. I will compute a few simple examples that you can easily reconstruct yourself.

To start with, take an *80-bit key*. Brute-force cracking it takes 2^{79} trials, corresponding to about $6 * 10^{23}$ on average. The fastest processors reach a clock frequency of about 1 GHz nowadays. Assume we actually had a superprocessor that could really decrypt at this frequency. Though this is currently utopia, it could well happen several years from now. Let's further assume that we have 100 000 such processors in parallel at our disposal. It would cost us a huge amount of money, but it's not impossible. All right, so we would be able to run 10^{14} decryptions per second. This comes pretty close to the frequency of light! Nevertheless, the result is sobering: such a code would be broken in well over 190 years on average—not particularly relevant for practical purposes. Even one million or ten million such processors would overtax the attacker's patience.

However, if we were able to penetrate into the THz (terahertz, 10^{12} clocks per second) range by means of novel types of physical principles and to operate one billion (10^9) deciphering units in parallel with just as novel a miniaturization, then this ultracomputer would take only 10 minutes—a usable value indeed.

With these things in mind, I wouldn't want to guarantee a 20-year resistance of a Skipjack-encrypted ciphertext, for Skipjack (Section 5.7.5) uses 80-bit keys.

But while talking about such long periods of time, Skipjack is probably not the algorithm of choice; it would rather be AES with a minimum *key length of 128 bits*. What about security there? Our ultracomputer that can find 80-bit keys in 10 minutes would have to work on AES for over five billion years. You see that classic physics won't help solve this problem.

Even more reason to leave our current minds would be an attempt to attack *256-bit keys* by brute force. This would correspond to $2.3 * 10^{77}$ trials. Suppose we had a way to exploit quantum-mechanical effects of some sort that turn an electron into a deciphering unit and put each electron to work at a clock frequency of 10^{15} Hz (which corresponds to the frequency of hard X-rays!). The wonder computer thus constructed, which is supposed to solve this task within one year, would have to have a mass of 10^{28} grams (for each electron weighs roughly 10^{-27} grams). This means that it would be as heavy as the earth. If we replaced electrons by molecules, we would immediately land in an order of magnitude of 10^{33} grams, and that corresponds to the mass of a star. Thinking more realistically based on our current minds, the computer would be so heavy it would have to form a black hole, within which our task would perhaps be solved—but the result could never come back out of it, as things are with black holes.

You see that the key lengths of 192 and 256 bits additionally required for AES don't originate from the fear of ending up with keys too short to resist brute force. People wanted to have a large security reserve against future cryptanalytic methods.

More realistic appears the thought that quantum computers might be built one day, and that symmetric algorithms could also be attacked. If these computers really worked 'squarely faster', then a 256-bit security would shrink to 128-bit security. Well then, are 256 bits sufficient? Let's calculate things down: qubits are controlled by means of electromagnetic radiation (radio waves, light, or something similar), based on our minds. With a clock rate of 10^{15} Hz, something imaginable in the remote future, we would have to put $5 * 10^{15}$ (i.e., five quadrillion) quantum computers to work in parallel to handle the computation within one year. To make sure the monster won't get heavier than 100 tons, every quantum computer may weigh 20 ng (nanogram; a billionth of a gram) at most—a tiny silicon cube with an edge length of 20 μm, including control electronics and all other 'physics required'.

All the considerations above suffer a little from the fact that they are based on current knowledge and assumptions. Maybe quantum computers will be built one day, and maybe they will be able to attack symmetric methods using algorithms more elegant than we can imagine at present. But I can just as well imagine that quantum computers might be used one day sooner or later to finally help estimate the minimum cost required to break a certain encryption method.

However, you may laugh about people who claim that breaking a 128-bit key is but a matter of pure diligence for the time being. And you may laugh even more about the company (I'd better not mention the name here) that advertised 'totally new algorithms filed for patent with *key lengths of up to 200 000 bits*', would you believe, at the CeBIT 2001 trade fair. Such vendors understand neither cryptology nor the random generation required for creating such long (and useless) keys.

Developers of this kind of 'ultra-algorithm' are normally convinced and often even pretty aggressive. I came across arguments like 'Experts claim that all new algorithms were insecure while in reality they only want to protect their trades', or 'True novelties won't be noticed in the first place', on Web sites and in mails. I am sure that if you understood the cryptanalytic parts in this book only roughly you already know more than these pastime developers do. Once you discover a 'cryptanalysis' on such a Web site you will recognize the true level very quickly.

5.10   Surprise Attack From Behind: Timing and Power Analyses

As the last 'hit' in this chapter, I want to show you an entirely new, totally different cryptanalytic approach. At first, this approach does not appear practicable, but this was thought to be the case with attacks using related keys, too, until the first chip cards emerged. For example, the new method could

find a private RSA key or even IDEA keys illegibly hidden in a chip card
non-destructively and fast.

The method is called **timing attack** and was published by Paul Kocher at the
end of 1995 [Koch.Tim]. You will find the work in a PostScript file on our Web
site. Kocher's cryptanalysis requires an attacker to be able to measure the time
a program or chip needs to encrypt or decrypt a plaintext or ciphertext block.
We will look at the example of decrypting the RSA method (see Figure 4.16)
to see how this works. Suppose the attacker knows many ciphertexts and can
monitor the program or chip as it decrypts, i.e., the attacker can measure the
execution time. RSA decryption requires the computation of an $R = c^d \bmod n$
expression. This power can be computed as follows (all operations modulo n),
for example:

- Set R equal to 1 and traverse the bits of d, starting with the least significant.
- If the bit of d currently looked at is equal to 1, then multiply intermediate
  result R by c; otherwise leave R unchanged.
- Substitute c by its square and advance to the next bit of d.

The multiplication times in the second step now have a certain distribution
that depends on c and on the method used. For example, when using bitwise
multiplication, it will take longer the more bits you set in c. Suppose the
attacker already knows b bits of c ($b = 0$ at the beginning). He can determine
the computation time consumed for these b bits himself and deduct the result
from the total time. Depending on whether bit $b + 1$ is equal to 1 or equal to 0,
he can also deduct the computation time required for bit $b + 1$ and check in both
possibilities whether or not the distribution of the remaining computation times
thus obtained deviates from the theory. This way the attacker can determine
bit $b + 1$ and successively compute the entire exponent d.

The nice thing about this method is that mistakes are permitted. It can be implemented similarly to the tree search in my *vigc_crk.c* program (see Figure 2.1
and Section 3.6.4): even if you happen to end up on the wrong branch, you
will obtain a computation time distribution that clearly indicates an error at
some point in time, and you just walk back along that same branch.

Putting this train of thought more generally: it suffices to find that the computation time for b fixed bits of a secret key and random ciphertexts depends on
bit $b + 1$. What's more, these b bits don't even have to be the least significant
or most significant of the key.

More specifically, the computation of c^d with a 256-bit exponent d and a 512-bit module n takes between 392 411 and 393 612 CPU clocks on a 120-MHz Pentium computer under MS-DOS, which means that it fluctuates by 0.3 % at most [Koch.Tim]. About 2000 ciphertexts suffice to identify strong dependencies of the computation time distributions on the bits in the exponent.

Many vulnerabilities can be exploited by timing attacks, including the following examples:

- The computation times necessary to determine $(c \bmod p)$—where c is in the order of magnitude of p—depend on whether c is greater or smaller than p.

- Rotations can be time-dependent. This can play a role when computing DES subkeys (depending on the hardware used) and, of course, with RC5.

- IDEA also uses a multiplication, in this case modulo $2^{16} + 1$.

- When the internal tables are not always addressed in the same way, for example, with Blowfish, SEAL, or DES, then *cache hits* can represent a vulnerability, i.e., how often a looked-up table entry is already in the processor cache.

I'm sure you have long asked yourself this question: 'How does an attacker get hold of these times?' The most intuitive possibility is offered by chip cards with non-readable keys burnt in. Measuring clock times should be fairly easy. Imagine that your credit card would one day use an RSA cipher. Just like organized gangs can copy your ATM card stealthily, they can recover your credit card's key. Say an encryption took 0.3 seconds and required 1000 ciphertexts. You would have to let your credit card out of your hands (perhaps not voluntarily) for not more than 5 minutes to risk compromising your secret key with the legal force of a signature!

There are many more possibilities. Say you work on a secure multi-user operating system that sends encrypted messages to other similar computers and exchanges RSA-encrypted session keys. You can have somebody listen in on all ciphertexts at the cable, but you don't have access to other users' jobs. Never mind, the system has a flaw that allows you to measure the execution times of other users' work. Or even more likely, the system holds a valid private key that nobody can read for all users. That's no big deal, for you could send ciphertexts in separate (perhaps identical) blocks to other computers and measure the computation time. All of these scenarios are rather speculative, however, and depend a lot on the operating system and the applications. But where there is a flaw, it will be exploited for sure sooner or later. Eavesdroppers usually sit inside their own companies rather than attacking from the outside.

How can these attacks be prevented? Timing attacks are actually not directed against algorithms, but against their implementations. It would be ideal if every ciphering/deciphering process took exactly the same number of CPU clocks. The downside is that it would cause the performance to drop since all ciphering processes would have to run as slowly as the *worst case*. Rivest thinks that this does not represent a dramatic deterioration in RSA: he states that the computation time grows by 10 % to 20 % at most. However, it is rather difficult to create a corresponding implementation. As a sideline, randomly interfering with the computation time is ineffective because interferences can be filtered statistically.

Power Analysis and Differential Power Analysis (DPA)

We have learned that the novelty in the timing attack was to exploit side effects—varying execution times of operations in this case—rather than attacking the algorithm itself. An intuitive consequence was to exploit parameters other than the execution time. The first approach in this direction was the **power analysis**, also referred to as the **Simple Power Analysis (SPA)** in 1995. The SPA is an attack that measures the fluctuating power consumption of a chip card. This is helpful, for example, to distinguish multiplication and squaring on RSA cards based on the power consumption. This new method is yet another one invented by Kocher.

SPA is powerful; it can normally find secret keys in a matter of seconds. The method turns a smartcard that can be activated without a PIN into a security risk: it is pretty easy for somebody to non-destructively read the key, and you won't have the slightest idea later on how and where on earth this happened. On the other hand, it is not particularly difficult to protect smartcards against this attack. The only thing is that the manufacturers have to know about it first.

A much more powerful attack is the **Differential Power Analysis (DPA)**, also developed by Kocher, this time in cooperation with Jaffe and Jun. Though a DPA normally takes several hours, the authors found not a single smartcard then on the market that would have resisted it! In contrast to SPA, DPA statistically evaluates large data sets, which means that even a single bit flipped in the data stream can be identified. When they introduced the **High-Order DPA** in their work, the authors went even a step further. This method can process data streams from different measuring series concurrently (for instance, it additionally determines the electromagnetic radiation). For the time being, this attack is mainly interesting for designers, since current systems are not resistant to SPA. You can find details in *txt/cryptana/dpa* on our Web site.

Timing attack, SPA, and DPA all show how hard it is to build secure systems, even when using algorithms that are secure by current standards. Such 'side-effect attacks' are a marginal field of cryptology: in contrast to the usual cryptanalysis, they do not attack the algorithm directly, but they differ with regard to computer security by their typical cryptanalytic methods.

However, smartcard designers have not been idle either: visit `www.research.ibm.com/intsec/side-channel.html` for an overview of current research work.

5.11   What Is a Good Ciphering Method?

Five increasingly difficult chapters were necessary before we can finally ask this question. Only now is it clear how much a statement like 'algorithm XYZ is secure' depends on time and the state-of-the-art, i.e., officially published results. The race between cryptography and cryptanalysis gets increasingly faster, but we have to live with that. Though key lengths of 128 bits and higher are theoretically secure, future developments in cryptanalysis may have surprises undreamt of in store. *This* circumstance forces us to be careful, and *not* the increasingly faster computer technology.

In addition, cryptology has to struggle with the nasty problem that encrypted data can be stored. If you secure a money transporter based on the current state-of-the-art in both technology and logistics, the money will probably arrive at its destination, and you can forget about the matter. If you wire sensitive RC5- or AES-encrypted data, they will most likely not be jeopardized by an attacker. However, an attacker can store this data and cause unexpected problems many years later if and when RC5 or AES may have been broken. Perhaps one day, quantum cryptography will help create accomplished facts. So far, cryptanalysts have had new and unusual ideas anyhow. The timing attacks discussed in Section 5.10 are a typical example.

No single algorithm (except the one-time pad) known today can claim that it will be secure with absolute certainty in ten years from now. What we do know are the properties it should have as a *minimum* requirement. You should not expect a stronger statement than this in this section either.

So what does the 'ideal' encryption algorithm look like, and how should it be implemented?

1. It should implement *confusion*, i.e., the relationship between plaintext and ciphertext should not be discernible. (This property is so matter-of-fact that it is listed here for the sake of completeness only—it sounds so prettily scientific.) Plaintext and ciphertext have to be statistically independent.

2. It has to implement *diffusion*, i.e., structures in the plaintext should be blurred to the largest possible extent. For example, the CBC mode should be used when working with block ciphers.

3. The key length should be large enough to make brute force too costly compared with the value of the message (bear in mind that computers are getting continually faster!).

4. *Identical or similar plaintexts* should never create *identical or similar ciphertexts*. You should always use block ciphers in combination with a mode that uses a random initialization vector (Section 5.1.1); this is mandatory for stream ciphers to prevent insertion attacks.

5. A ciphertext must not be *statistically distinguishable from a sequence of random numbers*. This applies not only to the character distribution, but also to correlations between characters or bits, even when the plaintext is a constant character sequence (see Point 4 above).

6. *No exploitable cycles* should occur in constant, periodic, or otherwise strikingly structured plaintext, i.e., the ciphertext must not repeat itself from a point forward. Though iterations occur theoretically, except for the one-time pad, their period should be long enough to prevent exploitable cryptanalysis.

7. Block algorithms are required to support the *avalanche effect*: a change to an arbitrary plaintext bit must influence every ciphertext bit with a probability of exactly 50 %, when using a random key; otherwise, there might be a risk of linear cryptanalysis attacks. This is an aggravation of Point 1 above.

8. *Known-plaintext or chosen-plaintext attacks* should not be practically feasible.

9. In particular, the algorithm should not be vulnerable to *differential or linear cryptanalysis*.

10. The algorithm must not use *weak keys*, and if it does, then they should be easy to determine.

11. With a product algorithm, *one round must not be breakable if the other rounds are not broken.* Compare RC5 with the *pkzip* cipher. Though the latter is not a product algorithm, the individual steps can be broken one after the other; the attack against RC5-32/1/* is not usable on a method with several rounds.

12. The algorithm must not be attackable by *algebraic methods* (e.g., the ciphertext bits must not be linear functions of the plaintext bits). Good algorithms mix 'incompatible' operations, such as addition, XOR, and multiplication.

13. The implementation must guarantee a sufficiently *large key space*. This requirement is very important but hard to implement (Section 5.1.4).

14. Also, *initialization vectors must not repeat* themselves.

15. Try to find out whether *timing attacks or power analyses* could be a threat, and implement countermeasures accordingly.

An algorithm that meets all the points above is a good algorithm based on current standards. An *ideal* algorithm would also have to be *theoretically* secure, i.e., it must not be vulnerable to novel attacks or special hardware.

I currently know of only two methods that ensure both practically and theoretically secure message communication: one-time pad and quantum cryptography. The latter, however is not an algorithm in the strict sense, but rather a type of cryptographic protocol.

Chapter 6

Cryptographic Protocols

According to Schneier, a protocol serves to 'run a certain task and consists of a series of actions in which two or more parties participate' [SchnCr, 2.1]. Cryptographic protocols are aimed at securing secrecy or preventing fraud or sabotage. Such protocols sort of mediate the use of cryptographic algorithms in practice once they have been designed and implementation issues have been clarified. Exactly like algorithms, protocols can be broken by discovering a possibility for fraud that was unconsidered in the design. You can find a good example in Section 6.4.2. There are cryptanalyses for cryptographic protocols, too, but their formalization is not yet on the same level as with algorithms.

You already know a few cryptographic protocols. The distribution of a secret key over several channels (Figure 4.13), for example, is a simple protocol, and so is the key distribution by means of hybrid methods (Figure 4.14). The interlock protocol (Figure 4.15) is a bit more sophisticated. And the password check under UNIX (Section 3.3) is a cryptographic protocol, too.

Cryptographic protocols are primarily intended to map processes or objects related to processes from the real world to the digital world and protect them. Examples include

- signatures;
- non-repudiable agreements;
- personal identifications;

Cryptology Unlocked   Reinhard Wobst
© 2007 John Wiley & Sons, Ltd

- elections; and

- cash payments.

This is not as easy as one might think. So far in this book, we have dealt with the environment of one single activity, namely the transmission of secret messages. Securing this activity is difficult enough!

As it turns out, however, we can apply our current knowledge to fields other than message encryption. If you have read Section 4.5 and are familiar with one-way hash functions (these will be discussed in Section 6.3.1) you will easily understand, for example, how to create digital signatures.

Even better, cryptographic protocols can offer new functionalities. For example, it is not difficult to distribute a secret among several people such that all together can reconstruct the secret, but none of them can recover any information from their part alone. This is a way to secure secrets more reliably than keeping them in safes.

Cryptographic protocols are extremely complex in many cases. For example, people still work on digital elections, and protocols for electronic payment systems are subject to intense further development. Section 6.6.7 will introduce a protocol for electronic checks which, in turn, uses several other cryptographic protocols.

But I won't give you an overview of the most important protocols here (you will find a full overview, including references for further reading in Schneier [SchnCr]). I will limit this discussion to a few understandable and particularly important protocols for practical purposes to give you an insight into this field.

6.1 Key Distribution

Protocols for secure key distribution are probably the protocols most widely used today. We have dealt with several important key distribution methods in Section 4.5.2, but there are many more interesting possibilities.

6.1.1 Diffie–Hellman, SKIP, KEA, and the Wide-Mouth Frog

We know that keys for symmetric methods are distributed by splitting them over different channels, and how they are distributed in asymmetric cryptography. Neither of the two methods is always satisfactory.

Though splitting over several channels is secure in practice, it is hard to automate. For a government agency with important data to acquire daily that should reach the headquarters automatically in the evenings, the described splitting over several channels is not acceptable.

In contrast, there is a considerable risk inherent in public keys. As you know, a new and dramatically faster method for factoring the product of large prime numbers in the RSA method would reveal all session keys at once.

But there are other possibilities for key distribution. You will learn two of them in the following.

Diffie–Hellman Key Exchange

As mentioned in Section 4.5.3, this algorithm was the first asymmetric method ever. But it is not a cipher in the usual sense, and strictly speaking, there are two private and two public keys, which are used to generate a session key. That sounds confusing, but the method itself is astonishingly simple.

1. Alice and Bob together choose a large prime number, p, and a primitive number with regard to p, g (this means that all numbers $1, \ldots, p - 1$ can be represented in the form $g^i \bmod p$). These numbers p and g are not secret.

2. Alice chooses a large secret number, $x < p$, and sends Bob the remainder X from the equation

   ```
   X = g^x mod p
   ```

3. Similarly, Bob chooses a large secret number, $y < p$, and sends Alice the remainder Y from the equation

   ```
   Y = g^y mod p
   ```

4. Alice computes the remainder s $= Y^x \bmod p$.
5. Bob computes the remainder $s' = X^y \bmod p$.

The remainders s and s' are equal, for

```
s = s' = g^xy mod p
```

holds.

Value s serves Alice and Bob as their shared session key. Though Mallory can learn the values of p, g, X, and Y, to obtain key s, however, he has to compute the discrete logarithm, i.e., he has to determine x from remainder $g^x \bmod p$. As we know from Section 4.5.4, this is a hard mathematical problem and at least as difficult as factoring. To ensure that the Diffie–Hellman key exchange is secure, $(p-1)/2$ should also be a prime number.

This method is related to the asymmetric ciphering method of ElGamal. It is special because there is no secret key that has to be permanently protected against unauthorized access. Only when the keys are passed on are x and y secret; once Alice and Bob have obtained s from x and y, they can delete x and y. At the end of their ciphered communication, s is also destroyed.

This is an interesting advantage over asymmetric encryption. An attacker can only try to compute discrete logarithms in arrears, i.e., frontally approach the mathematical problem—and that's beyond his means for the time being. He cannot steal a private key in arrears.

The drawback of the Diffie–Hellman key exchange in the form introduced is that session keys have to be exchanged in pairs. With encrypted messages to be broadcast to, say, 100 people, this can become pretty costly! Moreover, Alice and Bob both have to become active before they can communicate. Alice cannot leave an encrypted mail for Bob while he happens to be on vacation (and then go on a trip herself).

This drawback can be removed as follows: Bob can send his value Y to Alice and then go on his trip. Alice would choose a different x for every message sent to Bob and send the public key X together with her message. This method is more elegant.

Finally, a small modification helps to enable communication between many conversers without the need for prior interaction. To this end, the public keys $(X, Y, \ldots)$ are stored in a generally available database. The protocol then looks like this:

1. Every participant chooses a random $w < p$ and deposits the remainder, $g^w \bmod p$, in a public database. They each keep number w to themselves and protect it against unauthorized access.

2. Alice fetches Bob's key Y from the database.

3. Alice selects a random $x < p$ and uses it to compute $X = g^x \bmod p$. (She could take her X from the public database, but our variant is more secure.) She then computes the session key, $s = Y^x \bmod p$.

4. Alice uses s to encrypt the message and sends Bob X and the encrypted message.

5. Bob computes $s = X^y \bmod p$ and decrypts the message.

However, there is a catch in this procedure: it now uses private keys again, and Mallory is interested in them.

Though this methods appears a bit awkward, it can be automated in software or hardware just like any other cryptographic protocol. It is not more insecure than RSA, and what's more, it had a considerable benefit over RSA for three years: since autumn 1997 it is no longer patented (while the RSA patent expired in September 2000). This is certainly one of the reasons why the Diffie–Hellman principle is used in the **SKIP** Internet protocol, which ciphers data packets without the need for users to change their applications. SKIP was a competitor of the IPsec protocol, which is much more complicated but eventually won the race.

However, there is a more important reason why SKIP uses key exchange rather than RSA. Using RSA means that a session key has to be generated, encrypted, and then distributed. This translates in an additional data packet for each session and each key exchange, which is not desirable in this context. SKIP solves this problem simply and elegantly: Alice and Bob choose their secret exponents, x and y, for good and deposit their certified public keys, g^x and g^y, in a public database. To ensure that they won't permanently use the same joint secret, g^{xy}, a timing mark and a sequential number are appended to this number. Both parties know the timing mark and the sequential number, so these two items don't have to be distributed separately. Now, a one-way hash function is applied to this conglomerate, creating the joint session key. This virtually excludes the possibility that somebody might guess the joint secret, g^{xy}. Furthermore, the session key changes often enough, and the procedure does not create additional data packets.

KEA, the NSA Variant by Diffie–Hellman

Together with the disclosure of its secret Skipjack algorithm (Section 5.7.5), the NSA published **KEA** (probably short for 'key exchange algorithm'), the public-key method used in the Clipper chip. In contrast to Skipjack, which would go beyond the volume of this book, KEA is quickly explained. We will have a look at how the NSA implements asymmetric cryptography.

Initially, everything runs like in Diffie–Hellman: both parties know (in this case) the 1024-bit module p, base g of equal length, and both possess a secret key 160 bits long: Alice has the number xA, Bob has the number xB. As before, Alice sends $YA = g^{xA}$ mod p to Bob, and Bob sends $YB = g^{xB}$ mod p to Alice. However, xA and xB are fixed, similarly to the SKIP example. Either one of them creates 160-bit random numbers, rA and rB, especially for that session and sends $RA = g^{rA}$ mod p and $RB = g^{rB}$ mod p, respectively, to the other party. Next, Alice computes

```
tAB = (YB)ʳᴬ mod p = gˣᴮ ʳᴬ mod p and
uAB = (RB)ˣᴬ mod p = gʳᴮ ˣᴬ mod p.
```

Analogously, Bob computes $tBA = (RA)^{xB}$ mod p and $uBA = (YA)^{rB}$ mod p, i.e., the same numbers: $tAB = tBA$, $uAB = uBA$. Next, both parties create

```
w = (tAB + uAB) mod p
```

where w is the joint secret. It is created by the fact that each party links its *random* secret key, xA (xB), with the *fixed* public key, YB (YA), of the other party, and links its *fixed* secret key with the *random* public key of the other party.

The two parties can now take the same bits from w to get their session key. The NSA obviously found this to be too risky. Using Skipjack, it derives the session key by a relatively complicated method:

- First of all, the 80 most significant bits are taken from the 1024 bits of w; they form the number $v1$; the next 80 bits form $v2$.

- $v1$ is XORed with a fixed 80-bit number, *pad* (*pad* has the value 0x72f1a 87e92824198ab0b). The result, kv, serves as key for Skipjack.

- Skipjack and key kv are used to cipher the most significant 64 bits of $v2$ twice, producing the 64 most significant bits of the session key.

- The 16 least significant bits of the session key are equal to the 16 least significant bits of $v2$, XORed with the 16 most significant bits of the result produced by the first Skipjack cipher.

Figure 6.1 shows a schematic view of this procedure.

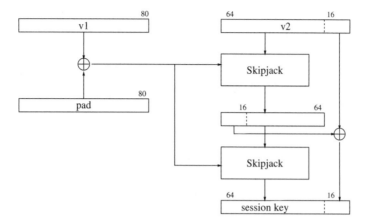

Figure 6.1: Generating the session key from $v1$ and $v2$ in KEA.

But how does this work in email where the receiver does not communicate with the sender directly? In this case

$$\text{uAB} = (\text{YB})^{\text{xA}} \mod p = g^{\text{xB xA}} \mod p$$

is computed instead of

$$\text{uAB} = (\text{RB})^{\text{xA}} \mod p = g^{\text{rB xA}} \mod p$$

and the number RA is attached to the mail.

Of course, KEA has the drawback that it computes twice as long as the usual Diffie–Hellman key exchange. On the other hand, it really creates random session keys. Though the SKIP protocol can handle this more simply, it requires a separate hash function, which would first have to be implemented in the Clipper or Capstone chips. Furthermore, the NSA doesn't seem to trust in the direct use of bits from $tAB + uAB$.

The Wide-Mouth Frog Story

There are protocols where the security depends essentially on one single centralized computer—a server. This has benefits and drawbacks versus distributed

security. We will look at an example and discuss it. The protocol by the catchy
name of **wide-mouth frog** we are looking at uses one single symmetric method.

1. Using a trustworthy server, Alice and Bob independently of one another
   agree on secret keys; Alice picks Sa while Bob picks Sb. Only the server
   knows both keys.

2. Alice generates a session key, Ss, and creates a timestamp, T_A (which
   is a unique byte sequence showing the current time). She concatenates
   Bob's name, B, and the timestamp and the key, and encrypts the byte
   sequence thus created using the secret key, Sa. She then sends the cipher
   together with her name, A, to the server:

```
A,  E_Sa (T_A,  B,  Ss)
```

   (As usual, $E_{Sa}()$ denotes the encryption by use of key S_a.)

3. The server decrypts Alice's message. The server can do this, because
   Alice's name readably precedes the message, and because it also knows
   Sa. The server creates a new timestamp, T_B, and sends the following to
   Bob:

```
E_Sb (T_B,  A,  Ss)
```

4. Bob can decrypt this message and recognize both Alice's name and the
   session key from it. Their secret communication can now begin.

You will probably ask: 'If both Alice and Bob agree on secret keys with a
server, why don't they agree on a key directly?' There are at least two reasons.
First, such a server can secure the communication of perhaps 100 users. If each
pair of communicators were to directly agree on keys, then there would be 5050
different keys, 99 per user. This is impracticable, and the consequence is that
each converser would use only a few keys. The second reason actually results
from the first: *one* negligent user storing other people's keys readably on his
disk would be enough to compromise many others. Within the wide-mouth frog
protocol, one negligent user would compromise only himself.

Another thing: timestamps seem to be unnecessary with this protocol. Though
the method can certainly do without them, Mallory could exploit this situation
and mount a **replay attack**:

- Mallory intercepts the message the server sends to Bob in Step 3 above. Though he can't decrypt it, he knows from snooping on the server activities that it came on Alice's request.

- At a later point in time, Mallory pretends to be the server and sends the intercepted message once more to Bob. For example, Mallory waits until Alice wants to communicate again with Bob and replaces the server message in Step 3 by the old message. Similarly, he can send the message regardless of Alice's activities.

- Bob doesn't check whether or not session key Ss had been used before, since that would be pretty cumbersome. He assumes that Alice wants to tell him something and unsuspectingly starts sending Ss-encrypted messages to Alice. Or he waits for a note from Alice.

At this point, Mallory has several options: he can send some junk data to Bob; he can have Alice and Bob 'communicate' with different session keys (which won't work, of course); he can snatch one of Bob's requests and pretend Alice had been kidnapped. Any of these options would perhaps make both of them panic, which is absolutely in Mallory's interest.

This form of disturbing a channel (without anybody being able to identify the initiator) is a **denial-of-service attack** at the same time. The main goal of this attack is to impair or bring down a system without being able to identify the initiator rather than intercepting or forging data.

Naturally, the protocol also has drawbacks:

- If Alice happens to create bad keys, she can cause threats to Bob.

- If the centralized server is compromised, then all users are compromised at once.

- Using timestamps means that the clocks of all computers have to run synchronously. This is not a trivial problem: programs used by time-announcing services, of all programs, often have security flaws. A radio clock for each computer is normally too expensive. The administrator could forget to manually adjust the clock, or it may be too costly.

The problem of choosing keys is handled better by other protocols. In *Kerberos*, for example, two trustworthy services create and distribute session keys, among other things. Kerberos is rather complicated and will not be discussed here any further.

6.1.2   Merkle's Riddle

The key distribution method discussed below is presumably not used in practice, but it is interesting for several reasons. It is a method that Ralph Merkle, famous for the knapsack algorithm (Section 4.5.4), among other things, invented in 1974. Back then, the method obviously did not mean anything to anybody—public cryptological research was still in its infancy (as you know from Section 4.3.1 in connection with the DES design).

So Merkle's method is of historical interest. Moreover, it is easy to understand, and it uses symmetric encryption only:

1. Alice tells Bob that she wants to send him an encrypted message. Bob creates 2^{20} (approximately one million) messages in the form: 'The key with identifier x is called y.' The values for both x and y have to be different in each message. Bob uses a known symmetric method to encrypt these messages individually, and he also uses 2^{20} 20-bit keys, a different one for each message.

2. Alice uses brute force to cryptanalyze a message picked out randomly (this won't generally take long for 2^{20} keys). She obtains a value pair (x,y).

3. Alice uses key y to encrypt her message, and sends the cipher together with x to Bob.

4. Bob can easily determine the correct y from the value x sent, and decrypt Alice's message.

An eavesdropper who wants to find y has to decrypt 2^{19} messages on average to find the one that contains the x sent. Using brute force, the eavesdropper needs 2^{19} ciphers, i.e., a total of 2^{38}, for each decryption, while Alice has to run only 2^{19} ciphers on average. This means that an attacker would require a computing technology that is about one million times faster than Alice's to be able to listen in on the data communication.

Even though the method is probably not used in this form (there are thought to be more effective variants), it is worth noting because its security is based on one single encryption algorithm, and the cost for breaking the protocol can be sized up.

6.1.3   Key Management and Authentication in GSM Networks

Another example of encrypted data communication that uses session keys, but doesn't use an asymmetric method, are the cell phone networks based on the GSM standard (D1, D2, and E-Plus in Germany) mentioned in Section 5.7.2. You already know the A5 ciphering method—but how are keys agreed upon?

Each GSM handset uses a SIM card that contains a chip. This chip stores a fixed serial number and a secret number, *Ki*. This number can presumably not be read, but remember what was said in Section 4.4.5, and consider the remarkable article by Anderson and Kuhn [AndKuhn.tamp] on the security of tamperproof chips.

Furthermore, the chip implements two algorithms, A3 and A8. The GSM standard does not specify these algorithms. The network providers keep them secret, and they build them into their chips and into the computers of their networks themselves. A3 serves for authentication, A8 serves for key distribution. The method works as follows.

Secret number *Ki* is also stored in the network provider's computers. When a subscriber initiates a call, the chip on the SIM card sends its serial number. This identifies the subscriber. The network looks up the corresponding secret number, *Ki*, and sends a random number, *SRAND*, to the subscriber. The chip on the SIM card uses A3 to compute a 32-bit response, *SRES*, from *SRAND* and *Ki*, and returns it to the base station. Since the base station also knows *Ki*, A3, and *SRAND*, it can compute *SRES* itself. The computer in the base station compares the value computed with the value received. If the two values match, then the call is admitted. This prevents unauthorized use of the network at somebody else's cost.

Furthermore, both the SIM chip in the handset and the computer in the base station compute a 64-bit session key, *Kc*, from the *Ki* and *SRAND* values, using the A8 algorithm. However, this key *Kc* is used by both parties for A5 encryption and decryption only; it is *not* transmitted. Thanks to the previous authentication by means of *SRES*, the two parties can be sure to be using the same key, *Kc*.

GSM networks in other countries could use different A3 and A8 algorithms, while subscribers can still use their cell phones. The reason is that the other country's GSM network recognizes that a phone is not registered with it, and

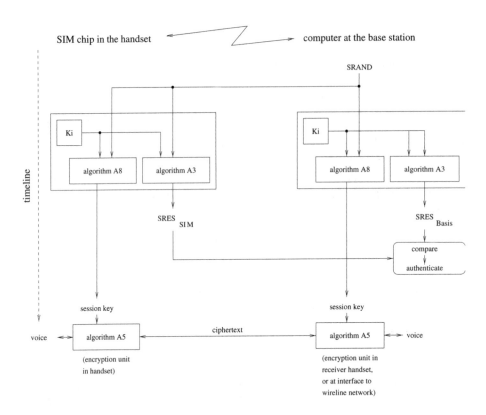

Figure 6.2: Authentication and creating session keys in GSM networks.

has the phone's home network send it sets of *SRAND, SRES*, and *Kc* for authentication and encryption, referred to as **triplets**, in advance. This explains why roaming contracts have to be stipulated among GSM providers in several countries before you can use their networks. Roaming contracts are signed for billing reasons, but also for cryptological purposes: if a subscriber switches on his German cell phone in Italy, the Italian network must be able to see that it needs to fetch the *SRAND, SRES*, and *Kc* triplet from Germany (triplets are normally kept in stock after the first call).

You may have noticed that the first logon abroad takes much longer than the connections you established afterwards. The reason is clear now: for the first call, the network abroad has to procure triplets, while it will have some in stock later on. As a sideline, in all these activities, the secret *Ki* never flows over a network; it remains in the network provider's database computer and in the handset.

Cloned Cell Phones

Authentication, generation of session keys, and exchange of encrypted data together represent a rather complex cryptographic protocol. Is it secure? Up to April 13, 1998, the answer was generally 'yes'. On that day, a spectacular successful attack against the GSM authentication was published jointly by Marc Briceno, Director of SDA (Smartcard Developer Association) and the two Berkeley graduate students, Ian Goldberg and David Wagner. (The same Goldberg and Wagner who discovered the weak key generation in Netscape, as you will recall from Section 5.1.4.)

In some way that cannot be reproduced, as usual, the standard versions of the A3 and A8 algorithms kept secret had somehow 'escaped'. The two algorithms together are sometimes also called COMP128. Goldberg and Wagner discovered a flaw in COMP128 that could be exploited by a so-called **chosen-challenge attack**: a SIM card is 'fed' with many chosen $SRAND$ values and its replies are then studied. After a sufficient number of trials, the secret value Ki can be computed, and with it both the response, $SRES$, and the session key, Kc, for any request, $SRAND$. Now, if an intruder stealthily analyzes somebody else's SIM card, he can use a regular computer (that knows Ki and has A3 and A8 implemented) to simulate the SIM card without the mobile network provider noticing it. In other words, the intruder can make phone calls at another customer's expense. You can find details on our Web site in the *txt/gsm* directory (in addition, *algor/A5/a3a8.c* contains the COMP128 implementation in C).

The attack mentioned above is real. It was demonstrated by Chaos Computer Club (CCC) in Hamburg, Germany, using a D2 card (see [SpiegClon]). But let's not panic just yet. The attack is not that simple in practice. Computing Ki requires roughly 150 000 $SRAND$ requests, and since a SIM card is no supercomputer, it will take about 8 hours. This is the time somebody needs to have your cell phone and card without you noticing it. Only then would they be able to run up your account. If you notice that your phone's gone earlier and have your card and/or phone locked, nothing could actually happen.

That's not all. The SIM card is protected by a four-digit to eight-digit PIN, as we know. The handset normally locks after three faulty PIN entries, and to access the network, you have to enter your eight-digit super-PIN. You can try it with this number ten times at most. If all of these attempts fail, all you can do is visit your phone dealer, taking all your documents along. So it's really useless to steal a GSM cell phone!

Somebody with the requisite knowledge and lack of morals can still get hold of the super-PIN as things stand currently, but I am convinced that this way will have been barred by the time this book goes to print. (As a sideline, some cell phones in rental cars have no PIN—for how much longer?)

Finally, I should mention that Mannesmann was the only D2 provider who used the COMP128 algorithm unchanged; D1 and E-Plus used variants. But we know that this won't be a security edge for long, because these variants will also be compromised one day.

Incomparably more dangerous would be an 'air raid' on the SIM card. This attack forces an unsuspecting user's cell phone to constantly authenticate itself while it is switched on. Network providers have denied this vulnerability, and meanwhile people are careful about such allegations.

Another method to reveal the secret, Ki, compromises the computer in a base station. However, this would probably not remain unnoticed. Network providers surely have taken appropriate precautions.

Together with the considerable technical problems involved in eavesdropping on GSM mobile communications, the system is still moderately secure, based on current knowledge. Nevertheless, network providers have underestimated and obviously even ignored the threats described above. Only very few of them have responded to the attacks discovered so far. There were more details at `www.research.att.com/~janos/3gpp.html`, but this Web site is no longer accessible. This is why I put the text version in *txt/gsm/3gpp.txt* on the Web site to this book.

Conclusions and One 'Side Effect'

Let's briefly return to the attack described above. It exploited an obvious and presumably unintended vulnerability of the COMP128 algorithm. A public study of the method would have found this vulnerability immediately—it took Goldberg and Wagner only one day! With a uniform, but cleanly designed and thoroughly analyzed algorithm, we could probably still make secure phone calls. Unfortunately, all GSM users, currently more than one billion worldwide, are potentially at risk (though there is currently little reason to worry). Modifying the algorithms would be extremely expensive. There is probably no better way to show you how little mystery-mongering in designing algorithms helps security.

The real sting got lost in the media hype. It 'incidentally' turned out that the 64-bit A5 key, Kc, is only 54 bits long; the ten remaining bits are always zero. This means that a brute-force attack would be faster by a factor of 1000. In cryptanalyzing A5, however, this flaw cannot be exploited easily, according to Golic (see [GolicA5]).

The official statement of the GSM providers on this 'short key' (you can read it in *txt/gsm/gsm_press.txt* on our Web site) seems somewhat strange: on the one hand, it mentions only the authentication code (but not the A5 cipher); on the other hand, the free bits allegedly enabled a 'more flexible response to technical security threats'. It can't be taken seriously...

However, there is general agreement on the fact that only national intelligence organizations have an interest in such an intentional reduction of security. Marc Briceno told me that, up to the end of April 1998, there had been no single SIM card worldwide in which the A3/A8 algorithm had *not* produced 54-bit keys. We can only sense dimly how much national intelligence organizations, first and foremost surely the NSA, can influence the business world and the security of all of us. You can find more hints in Section 6.7 in connection with the Swiss company Crypto AG, and in Section 8.2.1.

6.1.4 UMTS: People Learned Their Lessons

GSM was the first wireless communication system that used cryptography in a mass-market product. In view of the fact that there are several hundred million cell phone owners worldwide (the widespread SMS hype not included), the number of encrypted messages per year might be in excess of a trillion. Considering this number, the weak A5/1 algorithm has left the much securer DES far behind.

The network providers themselves hadn't anticipated such a success, so it appears even more important to point to the system's weaknesses:

- A3/A8, the algorithms used for authentication, and A5 used for encryption, are weak, as we saw in Sections 6.1.3 and 5.7.2. I think the main reason is that the algorithms had been kept secret. Officially, the ban on strong cryptography in some countries (like France, for example) and export regulations played an important role.

- The concept envisions only one algorithm for encryption, namely A5.

- Encryption always ends up in a base station. This means that unencrypted phone conversations also traverse non-tamperproof relay networks.

- A cell phone within GSM has to identify itself only toward the base station, but not vice versa. Nobody seemed to have thought of *active* attacks—the equipment required was too expensive, so they argued.

Meanwhile, the prices for such equipment are in the range of less than 10 000 dollars, and it is no longer hard to find.

- This means that man-in-the-middle attacks against cell phones are no longer utopia, just as message forgery isn't.

- The last point above addresses *replay attacks*, where data packets previously sent are resent to a cell phone or a base station. In a particularly malicious attack, for example, the pretended base station sends a command to the cell phone asking the owner to send packets in unencrypted form. The existence of this command emerged 'incidentally' during discussions on UMTS, by the way.

A GSM cell phone cannot defend itself against this type of active attack, since signalization messages are not sufficiently protected. The base station can check whether or not a cell phone is legal only at the beginning of a communication, while all further packets are protected by the cipher only. For example, a malicious attacker could prolong a victim's 0900 call (at exorbitant rates per minute) for hours by copying the data packets in the first minute and then sending them to the base station over and over again at a much higher transmission rate than the cell phone.

Nevertheless, almost nothing has been changed in the GSM system to my knowledge. But things are bound to get better with the advent of UMTS. The ban on strong cryptography is no longer an issue, i.e., the algorithms will be getting better and made public.

The UMTS security concept is very extensive and complicated, as you will see when reading the text *txt/gsm/UMTS_sec.pdf* on our Web site. I will mention only a few differences here:

- The authentication mechanism is identical with that of GSM, because the basic principle was good, only the algorithms were too weak. The new methods are essentially based on **KASUMI**, a variant of the hardware-friendly **MISTY1** algorithm, developed by Matui (Mitsubishi) in 1996; it is resistant to linear and differential cryptanalyses. KASUMI differs from MISTY1 in that its key generation is simpler, its cryptanalysis is harder (we know that this is not quite easy), featuring 'statistical improvements', and higher speed as well as simpler hardware implementation. KASUMI has been studied by expert teams, including famous names like Knudsen, Preneel, Rijmen, and Vaudenay.

- The 54-bit encryption of GSM was replaced by a 128-bit encryption. As long as there are no serious weaknesses in KASUMI—and it doesn't look like there are—there will be no practically effective attacks like that of Biryukov and Shamir (see Section 5.7.2).

- At the base stations **quintets**, rather than triplets, arrive. The three values—*SRAND, SRES*, and *Kc*—remain in place (with different names though), while an *integrity key, IK*, and an *authentication key, AK*, were newly introduced. Similarly to the encryption key, *Kc*, these two 128-bit numbers never traverse the airway, but are computed from *SRAND* and *Ki* at the network provider and in the handset.

- *IK* is used to encrypt 64-bit checksums (so-called MACs; see Section 6.3.1), which have the function of digital signatures. A base station can use the MAC to identify itself to the cell phone (and vice versa), particularly for important signalization messages ('disable encryption' as an easily remembered example). A sequential number and a *direction flag* that specifies the direction a data packet flows, i.e., from the cell phone to the base station, or the other way round, are appended to the computed MAC. Both pieces of information prevent special types of replay attacks, where an active attacker reuses packets previously sent.

- The *AK* key serves to hide the sequential number, which could be used by an attacker to discover the sender's identity and cell. *AK* is set to zero if this preventive measure appears superfluous.

- The MACs mentioned above enable 'signed' (authorized) signaling messages. In contrast to GSM, this enables fast local authentication, i.e., without the need to request or consume new quintets every time a connection is established. This is important in UMTS, because connections have to be continually established and torn down, for instance, when surfing the Web, to release unused frequencies quickly. The lifetime of a key is agreed upon at the beginning of a connection and written to a special field in the signaling message.

- Encrypted packets are not always decrypted in a base station; they may also be decrypted in a *Radio Network Controller* (*RNC*). An RNC is used to securely overcome non-tamperproof network sections.

The wireless communication is encrypted by means of KASUMI, which is operated in OFB mode, but with two minor modifications. While you would write

```
Sn+1 = KASUMI(Sn)
Cn   = Sn ⊕ Pn
```

in standard OFB mode (P_n = plaintext; C_n = ciphertext; see Section 5.1.1), you compute

```
Sn+1 = KASUMI(Sn ⊕ S0 ⊕ n)
Cn = Sn ⊕ Pn
```

in this case, where n is the block number, and S_0 is computed by KASUMI-encrypting connection-dependent data. The block number is involved to prevent cycles, while S_0 is used to prevent special chosen-plaintext attacks.

Obviously people learned their lessons from the errors in GSM. Though the investment costs will strain our wallets over the next cell phone generation for quite some time, and the user demand seems to be scarce, there is good news as far as security is concerned.

6.2 Sharing Secrets

Cryptographic protocols serve more purposes than key distribution. For example, they help us distribute sensitive data such that they are protected against both loss and unauthorized access. Simple sharing is called **secret splitting**, and the more universal method is called **secret sharing**. The two methods are described in the following sections.

6.2.1 Secret Splitting

In its simplest form, *secret splitting* can be built by means of a one-time pad (see Section 2.6): you have a message, P, and encrypt it using the one-time pad, S, to produce ciphertext, C:

```
C = P ⊕ S
```

Now you give key S to Alice and ciphertext C to Bob. Neither Alice nor Bob can do anything with their data. Only when the two of them get in touch and use their information jointly can they reconstruct the plaintext:

```
P = C ⊕ S
```

This can be easily generalized for an arbitrary number of persons. You create $n-1$ one-time pads, $S_1, \ldots, S_{n-1}$, and XOR them; the result should be S_n. You use S_n to encrypt the plaintext, creating ciphertext C. You give $S_1, \ldots, S_{n-1}$ and C to your n conversers—one file to each one. Only XORing the data of *all* conversers will reveal the plaintext.

For a very large amount of data, you can split plaintext P into n equally long parts, $P_1, \ldots, P_n$, of length 1 (you may have to pad the bits). Moreover, you create n one-time pads, $S_1, \ldots, S_n$, of length 1. Each bit sequence, P_i, with all S_j is then XORed with $j \neq i$. Each one of the n conversers gets ciphertext C_j thus created, together with key S_j, which had *not* been used when encrypting P_j.

Secret splitting is an excellent method of establishing and maintaining secrecy, much better than safes. Split your secret into five parts and give each part to five trustworthy persons who lock it away in their safes. Even if these safes were of Franz Jäger (Berlin), Egon Olsen would be powerless, because at the latest when breaking the third safe, he would surely end up in prison. And even if you were wrong about the trustworthiness of your partners, it suffices that *one* of them remains trustworthy, and the probability for this is sufficiently high. Moreover, you can make sure that your partners know nothing about each other.

However, the method has a flaw. If one single safe of your partners is robbed or the contents destroyed in a fire, then the entire information is lost. The probability for one single such event may not be high, but with five partners, it is five times as high. Backup concepts double the cost. To overcome this problem, secret sharing was invented.

6.2.2 Secret Sharing

If you fear that two of the five safes of your partners might burn down, then you have to split your data by the *secret sharing* method: three arbitrary partners together can reconstruct your data, while two can't. The reason is related to error-correcting codes, which you may make ample use of: when listening to a CD, the computation of 8 bits of information out of 14 bits of data is played back several ten thousand times per second. The physical recording method of CDs is so unreliable that every byte has to be 'expanded' to 14 bits. If a few bits are lost during the reading process, they can be computed from the remaining bits. If too many are lost, nothing can be computed anymore.

I want to show you at least one such secret sharing method in this section. You know that a square polynomial (corresponding to a parabola) is defined by its values at three different points. Two points are not sufficient, because there are infinitely many parabolas that traverse these points. The same applies to residual classes. From this we construct a *polynomial method* [Shamshare]:

Let your secret message be a number, M. Choose a non-secret large prime number, p, which is greater than all secret messages and their subsets. Define arbitrarily two integer coefficients, a and b. Take the polynomial

```
ax² + bx + M
```

and compute the values for $x = 1,2,3,4,5$ and distribute their remainders modulo p among your five partners, who also have to know p. You can forget the values of a and b forever. No two of your partners will even theoretically be able to determine M from their pieces of information, while any three of them, in contrast, need to solve only a linear equation system in the residual class modulo p. This is not excessively hard.

By computing in residual classes, by the way, all messages M become possible only with two known subsets of the secret. This means that the method is provably secure!

If your secret is several Mbytes long, you can encrypt it using a random session key and then distribute this key by the secret sharing method.

Unfortunately, the protocol described above is still vulnerable to denial-of-service attacks: if one partner cheats as the secret is reconstructed, then a wrong secret is created, and what's more, the cheater cannot be identified. The problem can be solved by using **robust secret-sharing protocols**, which work with zero-knowledge proofs. You can find details about this protocol in [SchnCr, 3.7] and [Gemmel].

There is a more general secret sharing method. For example, you could demand that among three partners who can reconstruct the secret, one out of two must always be particularly trustworthy. Or two of the participants should be fierce enemies. (You could make a list of corresponding pairs.) Arbitrary logical schemes are conceivable, and intensive research has been done in this field since 1979. You can find more theory in [Shamshare], [Stins], and [Blakshar; with further references] and in [SchnCr, 3.7].

Secret Sharing in Practice

Ferguson and Schneier write in [FergSchnPract, 22.9] that secret sharing is hardly used because both its implementation and use are too complex. I don't share this opinion. While the protocol is surely an overkill for everyday purposes, it does solve an important problem for critical secrets that is often overlooked: it can handle the fluctuation of employees. When employees leave their company, they can take along passwords, and they might have procured encrypted data from outside the company. In this case, changing the passwords in arrears is of little help! Secret splitting would help in such a case, though with the drawbacks we already know: no subkey must ever be lost, and if a key has to be changed (due to termination of employment), then all other keys have to be changed, too.

Secret sharing could be used to implement the following concept.

- Critical data are encrypted with a session key generated automatically, and this key, in turn, is encrypted with a universal key, which is created, for example, by three out of five employees on a computer via secret sharing, but only in the memory of one computer.

- If one of these five employees leaves the company, then the session key is decrypted on that computer (which is doable because there are still four bearers of the secret), a new universal key is generated and re-encrypted together with the session key (and added to the encrypted files).

- The new universal key is split into five subkeys via secret sharing, and these subkeys are distributed among the four previous employees and one new bearer of the secret. From this moment onwards, the subkey owned by the former employee becomes worthless.

More measures are required in practice, though. I implemented the following additional measures in a contracted project.

- Subkeys are divided into number groups and printed, and checksums are added. The resulting number sequences were relatively long, and only memory artists can memorize such numbers (I didn't test for this capability, though).

- The printouts were packed in sealed envelopes in the presence of witnesses and handed out to different persons who kept them in different places (safes).

- A sealed computer without network access at a secure location was used for activation. A script was used upon each startup to check that swapping was disabled and only one user logged on to the system. A modified live CD with a Linux system would be even more secure.

- The persons handed their sealed envelopes to third parties, who sat at this computer one after the other, opened their envelopes only there, and typed the subkeys (an asterisk as an echo on the screen is helpful here). A supervisor observed the entire procedure from some distance, where he could not recognize the numbers printed.

- Once each subkey had been entered, the printout was put back in the envelope, freshly sealed and returned to its owner.

- When a sufficiently large number of subkeys had been typed, the computation of the universal key was initiated, followed by the decryption of the data (where the data can be transferred on diskette or USB stick), and the computer was then switched off. With this, the created key was lost, because it was only in the memory.

The astonishing thing about this apparently cumbersome procedure was the seriousness with which the employees dedicated themselves to the matter. It seemed that the very typing of checksum-secured number sequences under observation, and individually entering that computer room had something especially important about it. Even designers need to know that security has to do with psychology.

So there are practical uses for secret sharing after all; it is not too complex. But what about the implementation? The interface was not extremely hard to design, only the algorithm itself didn't seem to be available in free software. Though there are plenty of demo programs, they included only a little serious stuff. I'm grateful to Sebastian Mozejko, a young cryptologist from Poland, who drew my attention to one of these few products. However, it used IDEA—not really an option for commercial applications.

For this reason, I sat down and developed an easy-to-use class in *Python*, which can be used to create and use arbitrary K-of-N schemes (i.e. K keys out of N are needed for decryption). By default, it serves for encrypting and decrypting data held in memory, files, and data streams. The encryption itself is handled by an external C program that uses Blowfish-128 or AES-128 (as well as the OpenSSL library *libcrypto*). As usual, the shared secret serves only as a master key (KEY, key encryption key), while the actual encryption uses random session keys. Furthermore, the integrity is checked by means of an MD5 hash sum (which is secure in this context).

The Python script language is ideally suited for such applications, since it has fast long-number arithmetic built in. Moreover, it is a modern and extremely easy-to-learn language with interfaces to C/C++ and other languages (visit www.python.org for more information). Thanks to its large number of modules, hardly a wish remains unfulfilled (it doesn't always have to be Perl—Python programs are generally much easier to maintain and understand).

The software is covered by the usual PSF license for Python scripts, which means that it may also be used commercially. It has been tested under Linux only to date. The software and documentation area the Web site under *PD/secshare*.

6.2.3 Shared Secrets and Nuclear Fission

There is a very serious motivation behind the development of secret splitting and secret sharing: these methods served to secure nuclear weapons. Following the Cuba missile crisis, there was concern that a world war could start by accident—for example, by a rogue or hysterical commander feeling that 'if only they knew in Washington how bad things were here, they would let us use the bomb'.

President Kennedy's response was to order that almost all nuclear weapons[1] should be brought under 'positive control'. This meant that missile warheads could be activated with a secret code only. But it would have been far too dangerous to use the same key for all warheads; a maintenance engineer could have recovered it. So they needed a group key for smaller quantities of weapons. At the same time, nuclear weapons were not to be used without the President's approval.

This was the point where secret splitting came in handy: local commanders knew part of the group key. Together with the universal key made known by the President, the group key produced a key valid for a specific batch of weapons (now you have a vague presentiment of what's in Putin's famous little suitcase).

If a Soviet 'surprise raid' were to destroy the US army's top echelon, it would presumably no longer be possible to learn the universal key. The solution in

---

[1]Except for the 'nuclear demolition munition', which is taken from its storage depot to its target and detonated using time fuses.

this case, you might guess, is secret sharing. Only a certain group of people in joint action would be able to activate warheads. This is certainly not a matter of a simple 'three out of five' scheme.

It is probably clear to you as it is to me: if cryptological work is done to perfection, then this is an extremely sensitive area. Another fascinating detail shows how far this can go: of course, all nuclear warheads are optimally protected against espionage and sabotage. An attempt to get unauthorized hold of the nuclear charge or the electronics causes the immediate destruction of the warhead. Gas bottles are used to deform and chemically change the plutonium body, targeted demolition charges destroy neutron boosters, tritium charges, and the secret code, of course. After tests showed that 1-mm chip fragments survived the protective detonation, the software was rewritten so that, based on secret splitting, all key material was stored as two separate components, which were kept at addresses more than 1 mm apart on the chip surface.

All these security measures have been successful to date. Not a single warhead has been reported stolen, nobody has spied out *and* used the universal key, to public knowledge. With this background, James Bond movies appear even more absurd, but this is what makes them so attractive.

You surely wonder where such interesting information can be found. I neither interviewed militaries nor national intelligence agents; I just read the fascinating article [AndKuhn.tamp] that formed the background for Section 4.4.5. You can find it on our Web site.

6.3   Digital Signatures

Currently the most popular cryptographic protocol in German politics and jurisdiction is the **digital signature**. In line with the increasing migration of information flows to electronic media, it has simply become a necessity to develop an electronic equivalent for traditional signatures. This is not a problem cryptologists couldn't handle, but it is a double-edged sword with regard to law and risk. However, before we can create and study signatures, we have to deal with *one-way hash functions*.

6.3.1   One-Way Hash Functions

Common hash functions are something IT experts have long been familiar with; they represent a simple and genial idea. Imagine the following situation: you create a large database with customer names. The company is doing well, so you have to continually add new names and have no time to sort things (or your computer would be busy sorting all the time). On the other hand, you have to continually search for names previously entered. Though searching through the names is much faster than sorting them, it has to be done so often that your computer lags behind.

The way out of this dilemma is pretty simple. As you enter names, you calculate the 'sum of the digits' for each name, i.e., you simply add all the bytes in a name. In addition to the database, you create a **hash table** with 256 entries—one entry for every possible sum of digits. This entry contains references to all database records in which a customer name matches the given sum of digits. So when searching for a name, you first calculate its sum of digits, then you look up that entry in the hash table and search only for the references given there. Since all sums of digits will occur roughly equally when there are many names, searching based on the hash table is 256 times faster!

Calculating the sum of digits is a very simple example of a **hash function**. The sum of digits itself is called a **hash value** or **hash sum**. The most important properties of hash functions are:

1. It takes an extensive piece of information (a name) and computes a compressed piece of information (a one-byte sum of digits).

2. The values of the hash function for different names should differ with a sufficiently high probability (to make the rows in the hash table about equally long).

   The **one-way hash functions** used in cryptography differ considerably from the hash functions used in information technology. Though they also meet the requirements 1 and 2 above, they add at least a third property:

3. With a given hash value, it is not possible to construct a byte sequence that produces this hash value at reasonable cost.

   So the difference between common hash functions and one-way hash functions is as big as the difference between a simple conversion of character sets and a cryptographic algorithm.

   For example, if a one-way hash function is applied only to readable texts, then it should basically suffice to ensure that no readable text can be constructed from a given hash value. However, this demand can hardly be checked in practice. So we try to stay on the safe side and ask for more. One-way hash functions should generally not be 'reversible'. But these three properties are still not sufficient. Many cryptographic protocols using one-way hash functions additionally require the following prerequisite:

4. With a given byte sequence, it is not possible to find a second byte sequence with the same hash value at reasonable cost. A pair of byte sequences with an identical hash value is also called a **collision**.

This relates to the birthday attack, which will be discussed in Section 6.3.3.

One-way hash functions are sometimes also referred to as *compression functions, concentration functions, message digests, cryptographic checksums, message integrity checks* (*MIC*), and there are more names. You can see quickly from the context what each one is about.

One-way hash functions do not use secret keys. This corresponds to their purpose of use—they should be computable for everybody. We will see this in the following section. However, there are non-reversible hash functions with secret keys. They are called **MACs** (**message authentication codes**) and serve for creating signatures that can be verified only provided one knows the secret key. Such signatures are useful, for example, to detect virus infection or other manipulations to your software with certainty. We won't discuss MACs any further here; you can find all the details in [SchnCr, 18.14] and [MenOoVan, 9.5].

Research on one-way hash functions began only around 1990. With one-way hash functions, cryptanalysis concentrates on different goals than it does with encryption algorithms. The reversion of a hash function (Property 3) has been successful only once so far, namely for a reduced variant of MD4 (see below). One tries instead to compute collisions, i.e., to find different byte sequences with the same hash value (Property 4).

Examples of One-Way Hash Functions

The structure of one-way hash functions appears very complicated at first, and their design is not easy to understand. I spare you the detailed description of such difficult hash functions as MD5 and will present only the most simple (MD2) which is, however, pretty outdated. The important things to remember are statements on the cryptanalysis of these functions. The following list mentions several known one-way hash functions.

- *Snefru*: This function was developed by Merkle in 1990 (it was probably the first algorithm of this type). Its major drawback is that, if SneFru is to be secure at all, it gets extremely slow.

- *N-Hash*: This function originates from Japan, from the inventors of the FEAL symmetric method. It is just as insecure as FEAL itself (see Section 5.7.3).

- *GOST*: Insiders will know immediately that this has to be a Russian standard (they are generally called GOST). According to Schneier [SchnCr, 18.11 and 20.3], the GOST function is probably secure, though its description is somewhat confusing.

- *MD2*: This function was developed by Ron Rivest and published in RFC 1319 in 1992. It computes a 128-bit hash value and is shown in Figure 6.3. ('MD' stands for 'Message Digest'.) The only cryptanalytic attack against MD2 currently known to RSA Laboratories was found in 1995: when the checksum appended to the text (Step 3 in Figure 6.3) is omitted, you can construct a collision [RogChMD2]. That already suffices to advise you against long-term use of MD2. The major benefit of MD2 is its simple implementation, its major drawback is the relatively slow computation of the hash value (Schneier [SchnCr] mentions 23 KB/s on a PC-486SX/33 MHz). This shouldn't come as a surprise since it was designed for 8-bit computers, while the MD4 and MD5 functions mentioned below were designed for 32-bit computers. MD2 is (still) used together with MD5 in PEM (see Section 7.2.1).

- *MD4*: MD4 was designed by Ron Rivest in 1990; it creates a 128-bit hash value. Successful attacks had been known against the first and last two rounds of the algorithm for some time. Later on, Dobbertin computed a collision on a regular PC [DobMD4] within one minute. He even managed to compute the reversion of a 2-round MD4. In [DobMD4inv], he states the archetype of hash value 0, i.e., he constructs a byte sequence with a hash value of 0. Together with the successful cryptanalysis of MD5 (see below), MD4 was attacked very successfully: collisions can meanwhile be calculated by hand. This is why I strongly recommend not to use this function any more. Nevertheless, its design serves as a template for many other hash functions.

- *MD5*: This is one of the best known one-way hash functions. It is supposed to remove the weaknesses of MD4, and was also developed by Ron Rivest (in 1991). MD5 is the hash function exclusively used in PGP up to Version 2.6, and produces a 128-bit hash value, like MD4. You can find an implementation in C on our Web site.

  Serious flaws were found in MD5, too. In 2004, somebody even succeeded in computing collisions (see below). This function should, therefore, no longer be used for critical purposes.

1. Compute a permutation of numbers $0, \ldots, 255$ based on the decimal places of π. Let this permutation be $S_0, \ldots, S_{255}$.

2. Pad the text with i bytes of value i such that its length is a multiple of 16. (For example, if the text is 6 bytes long, you append 10 bytes of numerical value 10.) The bytes of the text thus created are called T_i.

3. Append a 16-byte checksum to the text.

4. Consider a group of 48 bytes: $X_0, \ldots, X_{47}$. Initialize $X_0, \ldots, X_{15}$ to 0 and set $X_{i+32} = X_{i+16} = T_i$ for $i = 0, \ldots, 15$.

   Set $t = 0$.

5. Compute new X_i according to the following symbolic C program:

```
for(j=0; j < 17; ++j)
    {
        for(k=0; k < 47; ++k) {t = Xk ^ St; Xk = t;}
        t += j; t &= 0xff;
    }
```

6. Allocate the next 16 bytes T_i to $X_{16}, \ldots, X_{31}$ and compute

```
Xi+32 = Xi ^ Xi+16    (i=0,...,15).
```

   Go back to Point 5 where the old value of t is reused.

7. Once all T_i are used up, $X_0, \ldots, X_{15}$ form the 128-bit hash value.

Figure 6.3: Computing the MD2 one-way hash function.

- *RIPE-MD160*: This algorithm is an integral part of the European project RIPE and is also based on MD4. RIPE-MD160 creates a 160-bit hash value. Together with SHA-1, it is currently thought to be one of the algorithms against which no practically effective attacks are known. An implementation together with a description can be found on the Web site. RIPE-MD160 didn't gain acceptance versus SHA-1.

- *SHA-1*: SHA stands for 'Secure Hash Algorithm'. This function creates 160-bit hash values. It was developed jointly by the NIST and the NSA in 1993 and published in 1994. One year later, the NSA submitted an improved version without stating any reasons. This new version rotates by one bit during expansion, which is a minimal change with a big effect, as we will see further below. It is called SHA-1 and has meanwhile become the most frequently used hash function. To distinguish it, the older version is now called SHA-0. But even in SHA-1, the first theoretical vulnerabilities have been found (see below).

- *SHA-256*: Hash functions are also used for generating session keys, among other things. Since AES optionally processes key lengths of 192 and 256 bits, SHA-1 is not suitable for it. This was presumably the main reason why the NIST published other hash functions, including SHA-512, in August 2002. As the name suggests, SHA-256 creates hash values of 256-bit length. Though the function is slower, it is easier to program than SHA-1. And in contrast to SHA-1, no theoretical weaknesses have become known to date. A description and C program (from GnuPG) in *algor/SHA* is on the Web site.

Minor Earthquake: Collisions Found!

With all due respect for the successes in cryptanalyzing MD4, MD5 collisions have continued to be wishful thinking for cryptanalysts. Conversely, Chabaud and Joux introduced a theoretical attack against SHA-0 with complexity 2^{61} at the CRYPTO '98, which means in the worst case that 2^{61} SHA-0 values have to be computed to find a collision (a totally unrealistic number for practical purposes). The basic idea was derived from differential cryptanalysis: messages are 'disturbed' in single bits, and one tries to do this in such a way that the effect of the disturbance is removed in the subsequent compression ('corrective pattern').

Based on this work and the lecture by Biham and Chen at CRYPTO '04, Joux succeeded in reducing the cost to 2^{51} calculations. A supercomputer with 256 Itanium2 processors was busy for about 13 days (80 000 CPU hours), and the outcome was the first collision of SHA-0 ever found. You can check it out using my Python script *algor/SHA/sha0coll.py* from our Web site. This was a sensation indeed: not even an MD5 collision had been computed up to that time despite many years' effort. Nobody had even expected something like this could happen to the SHA-0 algorithm. In contrast to MD4 and MD5, SHA-0 uses each message bit more than 20 times. But the authors exploited the fact that the bit positions don't 'blur' during expansion of the message ('stretching' it from 16 words to 80 words)—in contrast to SHA-1! When left rotated, this single bit in SHA-1, the only difference between the two SHA versions, has an astonishingly strong effect. How much did the NSA know back then, considering that they submitted this correction in 1994?

Staying with SHA: Xiaoyun Wang, Andrew Yao, and Frances Yao presented an attack against SHA-1 with a 2^{63} complexity at CRYPTO '05, which cannot be tested in practice, of course.

But the sting at CRYPTO '04 was a lecture in the rump session, when the Chinese Wang and Feng and others presented a full MD5 collision. It consisted of two 512-bit blocks. Calculating the first block took an IBM P960 supercomputer about one hour. The second block was worked at on a regular PC within from 15 seconds to 5 minutes. (Meanwhile, a notebook computer can do all this in about 8 hours [Klima] read the article at *algor/SHA/MD5_collisions.pdf* on the Web site.) This earned a standing ovation, an extremely rare thing to happen at a scientific conference. It gets even better: MD4 collisions were said to be computable by hand; even HAVAL and RIPE-MD (but not RIPE-MD160) were said to be breakable, the authors explained, and collisions in SHA-0 could be found with 2^{40} function evaluations—2000 times faster than Joux's attack.

The eagerly awaited work appeared much later, but no doubts arose about the correctness of the result. The Python script *algor/SHA/md5coll.py* on our Web site demonstrates the MD5 collision. Remarkably, the two blocks differ only in six bytes, and then only in the most significant bit of them. A book cannot be completely up to date by nature. Expect to hear of new exciting results by the time you read this.

Practical Impact of Cryptanalysis

The question is whether these theoretically important successes are significant for practice. The answer is, unfortunately, yes. But many said 'no' initially because one cannot yet change checksum-protected documents by calculating collisions. Some examples show what is possible in spite of this:

In [LenstraMD5], the authors constructed two different valid **X.509 certificates** (we will discuss them later), of which only one was legal. More specifically, they constructed two official RSA keys with an identical MD5 hash sum. In practice, a fraud could look like this:

- Bob creates two different public RSA keys, *A* and *B*, with an identical MD5 sum. He has *A* signed digitally by VeriSign (see next section). Since this signs only the MD5 sum, the certificate is automatically valid for *B*, too.

- Subsequently, Bob uses the private key of *B* to sign a loan receipt with Alice. She checks the signature using public key *B*, which she received from Bob, and checks the VeriSign certificate for the key. Everything appears in order.

- Bob refuses to pay his debts, stating that he had not signed. In court, he shows key *A* with the valid certificate. An inquiry with VeriSign shows that *A* had actually been there for verification. However, *A* does not verify the signature on Alice's contract, which meant that it was invalid.

If the judge had read this book, he would have understood immediately that Bob must have cheated, because the two keys, *A* and *B*, could have been constructed only together—it is still not possible to calculate *B* for a given *A*. Furthermore, the parameters of *B* are unusual (different bit numbers of the two prime factors). But I wouldn't rely on such knowledge in court. The consequence is that one should make sure X.509 certificates are not signed using MD5, but at least using SHA-1 or even better SHA-256.

Another practical example is the creation of pairs of **self-extracting archives** with identical MD5 checksums, as demonstrated in [Mikle]: a malicious employee creates two such archives. The collision is hidden in a part of the data not used otherwise. A modified code for extracting the archive tests which of the two versions is present, and unpacks different archives or files, depending on the version found. Version 1 is deemed in order and to be published on the Web. The malicious employee, however, publishes Version 2 on the Net (which only appears to be the one tested because it creates the same MD5 sum), and this version proliferates malicious software. The consequence is that you should trust only SHA-1 checksums, or better yet SHA-256, if you cannot trust the creator of the archive.

The new findings discussed in the previous section have no impact on **HMAC** checksums. These are special MACs (i.e., checksums protected by secret keys), which are computed by the following scheme [MenOoVan, 9.5.2]:

```
HMAC(msg) = hash(key || pad1 || hash(key || pad2 || msg))
```

where '||' denotes the bitwise appending, and *pad1* and *pad2* are fixed bit sequences. Other sources state XOR instead of '||' (search the Net for 'RFC 2104'). *key* is the secret key. You can find more information on how to build hash functions and about the impact of cryptanalysis in [Wobhash] and in Wikipedia articles.

What Next?

So far, one can only compute collisions, i.e., create pairs of messages with identical hash values. If you create an MD5 hash sum of a document, the content of which you want to protect against forgery, then don't be sure that nobody can derive a second document with this checksum. In the **Tripwire** program that checks system files regularly for changes on UNIX/Linux computers, the fastest of all commonly used hash functions, i.e., MD5, is still sufficient. You can also protect messages by MD5-HMAC. With MD5 sums for documents of unknown origin, however, you should consider whether or not the creator could have an interest in bringing two different versions with identical sums into circulation.

In contrast, pseudo-collisions where two equally long messages, N and N', for given different equally long messages, M and M', can be found by,

```
hash(M || N) = hash(M' || N')
```

which would allow you to forge digital signatures for practical purposes. But this is currently out of the question (you can find details in [Wobhash]). And in particular, you cannot invert a hash function, except if MD4 were reduced to two rounds. For creating **one-time passwords** (Section 6.5), MD5 is probably still acceptable. In contrast, you shouldn't use MD4 for this purpose any longer, though the full function has not been inverted yet.

With regard to new or updated hardware and software, you would do best to follow the NIST recommendation and migrate to **SHA-256**. Though this hash function is the slowest, it has a more compact code and should be resistant to new types of attacks for a reasonably long time. However, nobody can tell what surprises we may expect in the next few years, since cryptanalysis of hash functions has only just started intensively. Rivest said once that 'it's not hard to design a secure cryptographic hash function. Things get hard when it is supposed to be fast, too.'

6.3.2 Creating Digital Signatures

Digital signatures are intended to replace signatures on paper. Let's see what characteristics are important.

1. The signature cannot be forged.
2. The signature was put on a document out of free will.

3. It cannot be transferred to another document.

4. The document cannot be changed in arrears (the document is printed, and hand-written changes have to be signed separately or initialed).

5. The signature cannot be repudiated later on.

There are several possible solutions to meet these criteria for electronic signatures. We will try to develop gradually better solutions in the following.

Using Symmetric Cryptography

Any of the symmetric encryption methods offers the simplest way to electronically 'sign' documents. Agree on a secret key with your converser and use it to encrypt your documents. That's sufficient for the simplest purposes. Your converser knows that only you could have created the document. If you use a good block algorithm in a secure encryption mode (such as CBC with checksum, for example), then nobody can change the document during the transmission.

Naturally, this has not much to do with a signature. The decrypted document is not protected against subsequent changes, and the 'signature' can be verified only by people who know the secret key. If your converser is dishonest, his knowing the key can be a risk for you—he could perfectly forge your 'signature'.

Using Asymmetric Cryptography for Signatures

The following method can do much more.

We know that, in asymmetric methods, a plaintext is *encrypted* with the public key and *decrypted* with the private key. The new idea is now to use the private key first. We simply define the plaintext as 'ciphertext' and *decrypt* it with the private key. Of course, this produces gibberish. But everybody can *encrypt* this 'product' again with the public key, only this time, the cipher is readable.

It is often wrongly stated that the private key is used for *encryption* in digital signatures. This definition can be tolerated only with the RSA method, because it runs the same mathematical operation (computing an exponent modulo n; see Figure 4.16) for encryption and decryption. In principle, we *decrypt* with the private key and *encrypt* with the public key.

It is important to make this distinction when encryption and decryption use different algorithms. However, you can also see why not every asymmetric method is suitable for digital signatures: first of all, it has to be able to decrypt

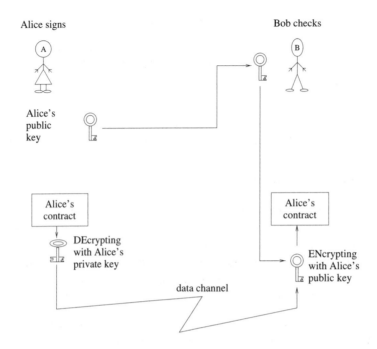

Figure 6.4: Using RSA for key exchange and signature.

an arbitrary text; second, the 'encrypt' and 'decrypt' operations have to be interchangeable. RSA was the first asymmetric method well suited both for key distribution and creating digital signatures.

This method meets Points 1 through 5 above. The security of the signature is entirely based on the fact that the private key is never made known. However, this method still has serious drawbacks.

- Asymmetric methods are extraordinarily slow. This means that they cannot be used to sign extensive documents.

- The signed document is initially gibberish; it first has to be encrypted with the public key—a time-consuming process. In practice, the signed text will, therefore, normally be used as readable text where the signature can no longer be checked. The risk of subsequent manipulations is high.

- When signing third-party documents, a chosen-ciphertext attack against RSA is possible (see Section 4.5.3). For this reason, a key pair different from the one used for key distribution should be used for signing.

Signatures with Asymmetric Cryptography and One-Way Hash Functions

The three drawbacks mentioned above can be avoided if we apply a one-way hash function to the text and subsequently decrypt only the hash value with the private key rather than applying the method to the entire text. Figure 6.5 shows how this method can be used to create a digital signature.

You can easily see that the five criteria for digital signatures mentioned above are met and that the three drawbacks listed above are gone.

- Hash values are short, generally about 20 bytes long. This means that the application of RSA for these 'compressed' texts costs less time.

- Hash values of one-way hash functions are not predictable, which means that chosen-ciphertext attacks are not possible.

- The document can be read by everybody, and it can be checked at any time by those who know the public key.

Many other methods are commonly used for digital signatures [SchnCr, Chapter 19], but we won't discuss them here. I think discussing the security of such signatures is more important.

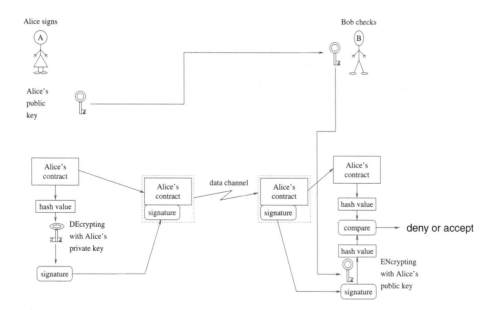

Figure 6.5: Using a one-way hash function and RSA for digital signature.

6.3.3 Security of Signatures

In his attacks against Alice's signature, Mallory is interested in putting her valid signature on a different or modified document. He has two possibilities.

1. Mallory finds a second document to his liking; it supplies the same hash value. (Anybody can calculate the hash value by means of the hash function from the document, i.e., it is not secret.) This is an attack against the one-way hash function.

2. Mallory finds Alice's private key. He can now sign any document he wants in Alice's name.

Attacking the Asymmetric Method—The Remote-Future Problem

Let's look at the second possibility. The following threats arise from using an asymmetric cipher.

1. Alice's private key is spied out. There are many ways to do this, but Alice could be more careful and destroy her private key once she has signed all important documents. But that doesn't matter, because her public key remains known and can still be used to check the signature. I'm afraid, however, that Alice will not be as careful in practice, and she wouldn't be able to—nobody changes their public key as often as they change their shirt.

2. Mallory could pretend his public key is Alice's public key and sign a document himself. We discussed this threat in Section 4.5.2. It can be excluded with sufficient certainty.

3. Mallory breaks the asymmetric method, in this case RSA. It is generally thought that this is currently not possible for sufficiently large prime factors.

4. Finally, Mallory could mount the chosen-ciphertext attack described in Section 4.5.3. In the simplest case, he puts a faked hash value on a document and has Alice sign it.

In a narrower sense, this is not an attack against the signature itself, but Mallory could recover one of Alice's session keys in this way. This is worth something indeed.

Let's hope that Alice's signature program computes the hash value itself. The probability that this value represents a ciphertext to Mallory's liking is not negligible. If Alice is very careful, she changes every document submitted to her for signature just a little. Appropriate care can help exclude the threat described.

Moreover, Alice should use a different private key for signing and for decrypting session keys, as mentioned earlier.

However, if Alice digitally signs a favorable lease contract for a 20-year period, then the prime factors (i.e., her private key) have to remain hard to compute over this period of time. Who can tell what methods mathematics will use in 20 years from now?

This problem is much more critical for digital signatures than it is for key exchange. When encrypted information becomes worthless after only one year, then hybrid methods would be our choice. Conversely, we often sign documents that are supposed to remain valid over long periods of time.

I can currently think of only one solution: all digitally signed documents with long-term validities should be countersigned by a trustworthy party periodically based on the latest state-of-the-art in cryptology. You probably can imagine what kind of cost this means. Perhaps there are already usable cryptographic protocols that can handle the 'aging' of digital signatures. Perhaps the fail-stop signatures mentioned in Section 6.6.5 could be a suitable approach. I think that this problem will play a major role in the future.

In practice, however, public keys remain valid over long periods of time. The Web of Trust in PGP (see Section 7.1.2), for example, even prevents frequent key changes. The risk that Alice's private key could be compromised one day is, therefore, not to be neglected. Theoretically, all her signatures would then become worthless at once. If you compare this risk with how conventional signatures are handled, cold shivers will probably run down your spine.

The trouble is that we will need digital signatures in the near future. In Germany, the first set of regulations for legal recognition of digital signatures have already been ratified (see Section 8.2.5). Cryptologists simply *must* develop and offer secure protocols and methods for digital signatures; otherwise, insecure methods will make the race.

Attacking the One-Way Hash Function—The Birthday Attack

A 'softer' forging method is to outsmart the hash function. This can look like this: Alice and Mallory sign a work-for-hire agreement. Mallory fabricates a second contract with financial terms more to his liking, which supplies the same hash value so that Alice's signature is valid for this contract, too. Canting Mallory goes to court. Alice cannot prove that Mallory's contract is forged.

How does Mallory fabricate such a contract? Suppose the hash value is only 20 bits long. Mallory is not at all interested in the complicated structure of the hash function; instead he replaces the agreed amount of 10 000 dollars by five times that amount. Then he marks 20 or more places in the contract which may be changed without influencing the content: there could be eleven or twelve blanks at one place, or another place could either read 'this' or 'that', or there could be one or two blanks in another place, and so on. Twenty variable places result in 2^{20}, or about one million, possibilities. He calculates the hash values for this million easily modifiable text parts. The hash value sought is among them with high probability. Otherwise, Mallory will just have to keep changing some more harmless places.

Sufficiently long hash values can protect you against this. However, there is a method that can break 40-bit hash functions as easily as 20-bit hash functions. The method is called **birthday attack**, and its original name comes from a technique often used in statistics. The question is: how many people do you need in a group before the probability of having two people with the same birthday exceeds 50 %? You may think of $366/2 = 183$ people or something along that line. Wrong: it takes only 23 people. If you look for somebody with his birthday on the same day as yours, this will be the case with about every 365th person on average. But in a group of 23 people, there are $22*23/2 = 253$ pairs so that the probability for said duplicity is much higher. This is what Mallory exploits in an attack against a 40-bit hash value: he constructs 2^{20} benign and 2^{20} malign contracts in the manner outlined above, i.e., by introducing small variations. The probability is then high that there is one pair of a benign and a malign contract that have the same hash values. Now Mallory (who is in reality female and Alice's secretary) foists the benign contract on Alice. Alice unsuspectingly signs the contract, and Mallory sends it out by email before her eyes—naturally just pretending. After work, Mallory puts Alice's signature on the malign contract and then really sends it, perhaps even with a falsified timestamp.

This birthday attack works even when the benign and malign contracts have nothing to do with one another, and Mallory uses them to create 2^{20} variations of each version separately.

It is apparently very easy to protect yourself against this type of attack: Alice inserts a blank in a trivial place before Mallory's eyes. Mallory has great trouble not to lose her temper at that, because the probability is 1 to 1 000 000 that the hash value now produced occurs in *none* of the malign contracts. Also, Alice should modify the contract in one of the first lines to ensure a strong impact on the hash function.

In practice, however, you cannot expect such prudent behavior; in the real world, people tend to 'always' be negligent. Furthermore, the person who changes the contract last always has a possibility for forgery. So, we might as well forget about this solution. This is the reason why hash functions create sufficiently long hash values, e.g., 160 bits.

If somebody discovers a way to compute collisions at reasonable cost, then the one-way hash function is insecure, even if its hash value may be as long as it can get. The reason is that the collision can consist of two readable texts with short random character strings at their beginnings—'to protect us against

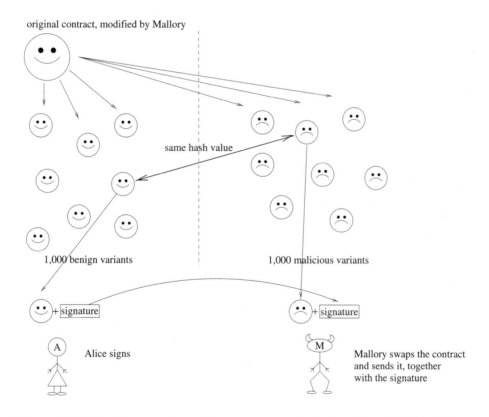

Figure 6.6: Birthday attack against a one-way hash function with 40-bit hash values.

fraudulent maneuvers', as Mallory hypocritically says [DobMD4]. Now you understand why we required Property 4, no collision in hash functions, in Section 6.3.1.

Subliminal Channels

For signatures, *subliminal channels* can be thought of as 'true steganography': together with her signature, Alice sends additional information, the existence of which can be proven only if one knows a certain secret key. This secret key can be Alice's private key, but not for all signature methods.

Notice the difference to steganography: steganography does not use a key, and it hides information in a way similar to a picture puzzle. Those who know the trick can easily recover the hidden information (unless it is encrypted). In contrast, subliminal channels in signatures hide information cryptographically well. A signature with additional information is still innocuous, even after most thorough analysis. Only the use of a secret key opens up the treasure box, showing its inner life.

Subliminal channels were first designed by Simmons in 1983 [Simmsubl]. They are used in several signature methods. Simmons even showed that such channels can be constructed in every signature method. The DSA signature algorithm designed by the NSA, of all methods, offers channels that can be read without knowing the private key. Allegedly nobody knew about it. 'Is that so bad?', you will ask.

Yes, it is. If you buy a program for digital signatures and the signature algorithm has such subliminal channels, then the program vendor can feed a few bits of your secret key into the subliminal channel together with each of your signatures. You can look at the program's output—nothing provable there. However, the program vendor or their allies record your signatures regularly. Only they know the secret additional key for the subliminal channel. After a sufficiently large number of signatures, they will have your private key on their desk. Now they can perfectly forge your electronic signature, compute all your session keys, read all your secret messages . . . that's a fine prospect! Section 6.7 deals with such fraudulent maneuvers.

DSA allows you to 'plug up' the channel using a suitable cryptographic protocol between Alice and Bob. However, Bob can then set up his channel in a manner that's named *cuckoo channel*. Luckily, there are ways to prevent this, too.

To protect yourself from this kind of espionage, use the freely available PGP program. You can then be sure that it has been studied and analyzed as to such fraud by many experts. Not for nothing is its source text digitally signed! However, PGP is not usable for every purpose, and it was subject to license fees for commercial use in connection with IDEA (Section 5.3.1). But there is also GnuPG, which will be discussed in Section 7.1.4.

Known channels can be 'plugged up'. Perhaps somebody will discover new ones that will also be plugged up. Here we are again: the eternal race between cryptography and cryptanalysis. However, there is the additional problem that plugging up channels is hard to check in software. We will discuss this issue further in Sections 6.7 and 8.3.

Bottom Line

Let's briefly return to conventional signatures. They cannot be forged to perfection. 'Wait a minute', you will say, 'there are enough con artists who master this!' True, but never entirely perfectly. You can have a modern graphologist study things like the geometry of a signature, the writing pressure and the writing speed, the ink, and perhaps even one day microscopic palm-sweat traces. In short, more and more characteristics of a signature can be determined as the state-of-the-art in criminal-investigation techniques grows.

Let's sum things up: as perfectly as a conventional signature may be imitated, there will always be one little detail the forger just won't get right. They can never be sure their forgeries might be provable one day.

It is a fact from the outset that digital signatures cannot offer this kind of 'dynamically expandable' security. There will never be sweat traces on electronic files. If somebody manages to get your private key by computation, or trickery, or extortion, then he can forge *all* your digitally signed contracts, and you *cannot* prove it no matter how hard you try.

It is not sufficient to use cryptologically secure methods and protocols. Also, the problem of determining whether or not a public key presented really belongs to Alice has to be solved safely. PGP and PKI show two possible solutions (Chapter 7). The private key has to be protected securely enough. Your capability of signing in a certain way cannot be stolen from you. The 'theft' of two large prime numbers, in contrast, can be a kid's game. It is not sufficient to PIN-protect them. In the near future, biometric methods will surely emerge—we will deal with this issue in Section 6.6.9.

And there is yet another problem: when manually signing you see the document you sign. Whether or not the text on the screen is really the text you sign is doubtful if a hacker has visited the system.

Digital signatures mean that we have to deal with a new quality of threats. The probability of compromise may be smaller by several orders of magnitude than the probability that conventional signatures can be forged perfectly by current standards. Conversely, the potential damage is higher by orders of magnitude one can hardly estimate. We discussed something similar in Section 4.5.6.

This is a real dilemma. How insecure we become with our ethical value system when we have to decide in such a situation can be seen in the example of the dispute about the threats emanating from nuclear power. In the case of signatures, in contrast, we can expect a certain amount of help from cryptology, provided we don't ignore the potential threats and look for ways out.

As a minimum requirement, you should use different pairs of private and public keys for signatures and key distribution.

6.4   Key Escrow. Matt Blaze's Attack Against the EES Protocol

We will be dealing with a totally different field in this section. It has been (and hopefully never will be again!) fiercely discussed in the USA and Germany. It concerns key escrow. More specifically, it concerns the US standard EES (Escrowed Encryption Standard) briefly mentioned in Section 5.7.5. In that section, we had just looked at Skipjack, the symmetric algorithm EES uses. In this section, we want to have a closer look at the underlying cryptographic protocol. Later, in Section 8.2.3, we will discuss the legal and political consequences and backgrounds of key escrow.

As you know, two chips currently implement EES: the Clipper chip for encrypted phone calls and the Capstone chip for data communication. In addition to encrypting, Capstone can also sign digitally (using DAS, the standard developed by the NSA), handle key exchange by means of an asymmetric method, compute hash functions (using SHA, which belongs to DSA), and many more things. Clipper is virtually a subset of Capstone. Nevertheless, the hot debate on EES in the USA is conducted by the buzzword 'Clipper', because listening in on phone calls seems to still agitate more people than insecure data communication.

6.4.1   How Clipper and Capstone Work

As mentioned earlier, most details of Skipjack and its implementation are secret and hidden in non-analyzable hardware. The main reason for this hide-and-seek game is officially that Skipjack may be used only together with key escrow. How does this work?

Each chip contains:

- a serial number (*unit ID*);

- a secret chip-specific key (*unit key*); and

- another secret key, the so-called *global family key*. It is identical for all chips in communicating devices.

All chips are *tamperproof*, which means that their secrets cannot (allegedly) be read. During the production of the chips, the unit keys are split into two subsecrets via secret sharing, as described in Section 6.2. Together with the unit IDs, the manufacturer hands the two lists of subsecrets over to two trustworthy authorities, in this case the NIST and the Department of the Treasury.

In a communication, the chip at the sender's end uses the unit key to encrypt the session key and then accommodates it in a 128-bit field, the so-called **LEAF**, an acronym for *Law Enforcement Access Field*. Together with an initialization vector (IV), this LEAF is created at the beginning of a communication session and transmitted. A chip begins to work only once it has received a valid LEAF–IV pair. The session key and the IV can be loaded into the chip registers only after they have been submitted together with the pertaining LEAF. This prevents modified software from feeding the chip with old LEAFs and then continuing to work with a different session key–IV pair.

Now, if a court wants to listen in on somebody, they first record an encrypted conversation. They then determine the unit ID of the sender chip from the LEAF. Subsequently, they use this number to request the 'halves' of the unit key from the two authorities via the FBI, and then XOR the two pieces. Using the unit key thus produced, they can compute the session key and decrypt the conversation. For more calls from the same chip, they can continue decrypting without checking back with the two authorities. Once the sender has been busted, they delete the key . . .

What does a secret communication look like with the Clipper chip?

1. Alice wants to call Bob. The two of them agree on a session key (e.g., by means of an asymmetric method).

2. Alice has her Clipper chip create a LEAF and an IV from the session key, and has the chip load both the key and the IV into its registers concurrently. She must not create the IV herself—it would mess up the way the chip works.

3. Alice sends the LEAF together with the IV to Bob. Bob feeds in the session key, activates his Clipper chip with the value pair obtained, and the communication can begin.

6.4.2 How to Undermine the Protocol

At first, the method looks watertight. Provided the hardware is 'untouchable', there is no way to use the chips without transmitting valid LEAFs, which automatically forwards the valid session key to the two authorities.

Matthew Blaze of AT&T Bell Laboratories published an analysis of how to outsmart the EES protocol at the beginning of 1994. He used the Clipper or Capstone chip together with easily modifiable software, which means that he used the Skipjack algorithm *without* the government being able to eavesdrop.

Rather than analyzing some software or unauthorized opening of a chip, Blaze looked at the reactions of the chip to different inputs and used known information, i.e., he used absolutely legal methods only. The report [Blazeskip] landed like a bomb.

Blaze's considerations are not as complicated as you may think. We will have a closer look at them below.

LEAF Under the Magnifying Glass

First of all, Blaze found out more about the structure of LEAF in various experiments. Figure 6.7 shows the scheme.

The most important detail is the calculation of the 16-bit checksum. It depends at least on the IV and the 80-bit session key, probably also on the encrypted session key. Together with the 32-bit unit ID—the chip's serial number—this produces a block of 128 bits. This block is encrypted using the global family key. The cipher is the LEAF. Since the global family key cannot be read, an eavesdropper can't even recover the serial number from the LEAF. Anyway, this cipher works in a mode that seems to 'mix' all 128 bits.

We can easily understand from the figure why Alice cannot come up with a false LEAF to a session key and an IV. Blaze took all of this to launch two possible attacks.

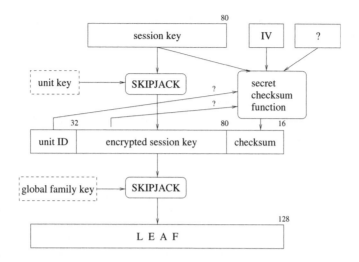

Figure 6.7: Creating a LEAF in a Clipper or Capstone chip. The numbers above the rectangles denote the width in bits.

Inventive Impostors

In the first attack, named **LEAF feedback** by Blaze, Alice and Bob agree to outsmart the investigators. To this end, they slightly modify their software. The following consideration shows them the way: even before a LEAF arrives at Bob's, his chip already knows the session key, since it had been agreed upon with Alice. Bob can now create a LEAF with this session key himself. He thus gets an IV different from Alice's. Bob terminates the process and switches to reception.

Alice doesn't send her LEAF along; Bob feeds his chip with the LEAF he created himself instead. This LEAF is valid, since it belongs to the session key, and the IV matches, too—so Bob's chip starts decrypting the session key and Bob's IV.

But there is a problem: Alice's and Bob's IVs are different. The solution depends on the ciphering mode used, which can be set in the Capstone chip. You know the four most important ciphering modes from Section 5.1.1.

- If Alice and Bob use the ECB mode, the IV doesn't matter, but this mode is too insecure.

- If they both use the CBC mode, then a faulty IV can cause only the first 64-bit block to decrypt wrongly. So Alice and Bob agree that the first

block is 'garbage' and start their actual communication from the second
block onwards.

- Things are similar with the CFB mode; it also recovers after a few blocks
  encrypted wrongly.

- Only the OFB mode causes damage beyond repair due to a wrong IV. If,
  for some reason, Bob can receive in OFB mode only, then Alice has to
  operate her chip in ECB mode and implement the OFB cipher externally
  via software.

Surprisingly simple, isn't it? Cryptological knowledge is actually required only
for the handling of faulty IVs. Nevertheless, one has to get on to the idea first!

Now you might say that all of this can be easily prevented: Bob's chip can use
the global family key to decrypt the LEAF and find that the LEAF originates
from himself. It shouldn't be a big deal for the chip to reject its own LEAFs.
That's exactly the remedy Blaze suggested.

But even Blaze underestimated Bob's slyness. The thing is that Bob bought
himself two chips, feeding the second with the LEAF that the first chip created.
There is no way for the second chip to know that the first chip is also Bob's.

You might end up thinking that data or phone communication without LEAF
should be punished. Well, even that won't bother Alice and Bob much. They
precede their message with another valid LEAF. The fact that the eavesdropping
investigator hears noise instead of voice can be easily explained; they simply
say that their devices are running a test (or has some key escrow center made
a mistake? Let's hope not!).

The fact is that as long as Clipper and Capstone don't use better protocols
(at least with cleverer ciphering modes), you can exchange Skipjack-encrypted
messages without the government learning the keys you use.

Unnoticed Fraud

The second attack against the protocol is launched from a different situation:
Bob works under third-party control so that he cannot use Clipper or Capstone in a way that allows him to mount the first attack (LEAF feedback).
Bob is supposed to receive Alice's message with a LEAF that belongs to the
session key and the IV, but that doesn't actually contain an encrypted session
key yet.

In this situation, Alice exploits the shortness of the checksum. She doesn't know how to calculate the checksum. But she knows what information Bob's chip can use to check Alice's LEAF: it knows neither Alice's serial number nor her unit key. It can compute itself a checksum only from the session key, the IV, and the LEAF. It will then decrypt the LEAF using the global family key and compare the resulting checksum with the one it calculated.

Alice proceeds as follows: just like in the first attack, she creates a session key and an IV on her chip and terminates. She then switches her chip to reception and feeds it with the session key, the IV, and a *random* LEAF. The chip takes these pieces to compute a checksum. It then decrypts that nonsensical LEAF diligently and, from the result, takes a checksum that will naturally not match the one it computed.

But the checksum is only 16 bits long. 16 bits correspond to $2^{16} = 65\,536$ possibilities. On average, the two checksums will match after $32\,768$ trials, i.e., the LEAF will be accepted. Alice sends this LEAF instead of the correct one along with the rest. Bob's chip will accept it and decrypt Alice's message with the session key previously agreed upon. (The chip has to load the session key directly; it cannot compute it from the LEAF since it doesn't know Alice's unit key.)

The next thing Uncle Sam hears is perfect noise, for its 'session key' is a random number.

A Capstone chip requires about 38 ms to check a LEAF. This translates to a mean time of 42 minutes for finding a random but valid LEAF. This much time passes between negotiating the session key and starting the communication. It's too much for a telephone conversation. Bob's software could have a timeout set to a couple of seconds so that Alice's chance to outsmart Uncle Sam fades to improbable.

Alice can solve the problem by buying many chips and paralleling her brute-force attack. The NSA who designed the chip could easily defend itself from this: it suffices that one Capstone or Clipper chip refuses its service for one minute after every 50th wrong LEAF (and apart from that, it should take a minute to start up; otherwise, Alice might briefly disconnect the chip from the power source after each failed attempt).

And what does the NSA do? They have the chip reset itself after every tenth failed attempt. This extends these 42 minutes to 46 minutes. In his article, Blaze thanked the NSA staff for their extensive help in his analyses.

A Practical Application

This heading is not totally serious. I just want to hint what consequences breaking the EES protocol could have.

Bob works undercover in the drug-trafficking underworld. He is excellent at reading people, he is a first-class shooter and fighter, and he is extremely wary at the same time. Though he doesn't know much about cryptology, he knows that Alice (presumably the big boss) sends him encrypted messages that can be wiretapped by the FBI. He thinks that Alice is also aware of that. She encrypts nevertheless, because it prevents her major competitor Carol from listening in on her.

Alice knows a cryptologist who modifies her Clipper software as described above. When she discovers Bob's identity, she sets up a trap for him: Bob is to show up at a certain location at a certain time.

Bob has a dim feeling but eventually relies on the fact that Alice's communication is wiretapped. He thinks: 'After all, Alice knows that they listen in on her. So she won't be as naïve as to lure me into a trap over the phone.' Bob has no way of knowing that Alice's LEAF was forged (and he cannot know theoretically either, because he doesn't know her device's serial number). He shows up at the location agreed upon and, trusting that his colleagues will help him out if need be, gets shot.

Court Evidence

Schneier [SchnCr, 24.16] lists more objections to Clipper. This chip should only work in OFB mode, i.e., as a stream cipher. When plaintext and ciphertext are known, then both can be used to reveal and reuse the key sequence. This means that an OFB-encrypted data stream does not necessarily have to have been constructed by the owner of the secret key. This is why a Clipper conversation (or a Capstone-encrypted file transmitted) cannot be attributed to Alice in court for the simple fact that it was encrypted with Alice's key (or more exactly, because the session key encrypted with Alice's unit key is contained in the LEAF). Alice can at least say that a dishonest investigator tampered with the recording.

In cases of doubt, the LEAF cannot be recognized as a legal authentication. We can think of enough scenarios where fraud is possible. For example, Alice could mount a *squeezing attack* to have Bob call her and conduct a harmless conversation with him. In reality, however, she is after his LEAF with the pertaining session key–IV pair. With these data and a couple of tricks, she calls Carol pretending to be Bob (since she uses Bob's LEAF) and tells her in Bob's voice about the most recent criminal activities that are pure imagination. You can read the details of this and other attacks in [Frankcl]. These possible compromises are another reason why the unit ID must not be recognized as authentication.

Bottom Line

The EES protocol has many weaknesses. It is not just a matter of the fraudulent maneuvers described above; the protocol does not supply any additional evidence. This is unfortunate, because cryptology could be very helpful. Furthermore, the protocol often causes the keys of uninvolved people who happen to call a wiretapped criminal to be revealed.

You saw how problematic key escrow can be from the cryptological perspective, let alone legal and political issues. The serious doubts about the use of Clipper and Capstone are of both a subjective and technical nature. You now have a rough idea of the dreadful consequences cryptologically weak hardware or software used in masses can have. This is important in Europe, too, even though there is logically not much interest in buying EES devices.

6.5 One-Time Passwords

You can lean back in the next three sections for they are easier than the previous ones.

The protocols described in this section are intended to allow Alice to identify herself unambiguously by use of a password, though Mallory is back to his old habits. This is not a negligible threat, for example, when Alice logs into a UNIX computer over the Internet. Though the password mechanism in modern UNIX computers is cryptologically secure, the best password won't do much good when it runs across the data line in the clear as you log in.

6.5.1 The Trick with One-Way Hash Functions

Key exchange using asymmetric cryptography is out of the question for the problem mentioned above, because Alice will probably have no computing capacity at her disposal yet before logging on.

There is a similar—much more frequent—situation where the user has no computer at hand either. It relates to *home banking* by phone. In this case, Alice as the bank's customer has to authenticate herself via password, but Mallory mustn't be able to use the same password and pretend to be Alice later on. This wording already contains the solution: the customer is given many passwords and uses each one only once.

One-way hash functions enable a particularly simple and secure implementation of this principle. The protocol was proposed by Leslie Lamport [Lamport] in 1981 and looks like this.

1. The computer creates a random key, S_0.

2. It uses a one-way hash function, H, to encrypt this number over and again, thus obtaining, for example, 100 numbers, S_i:

```
S₁   = H(S₀)
S₂   = H(S₁)
. . .
S₁₀₀ = H(S₉₉)
```

3. It sends numbers $S_0, \ldots, S_{99}$ to the customer/user and then deletes them. The computer itself stores only S_{100}.

4. A customer who wants to identify himself to the computer sends S_{99}. The computer checks whether $H(S_{99}) = S_{100}$. If so, the customer is deemed to have been authenticated; otherwise, the customer will be rejected.

5. Next, the computer replaces S_{100} by the value S_{99} obtained, and the customer deletes S_{99} from his list.

6. All further authentications work analogously: the customer sends a password not yet deleted with the largest index. The computer computes the hash value for the customer password and compares it with the value stored. If the value is accepted, the computer replaces the password value stored.

7. When all 100 passwords have been used up, the computer creates a new list and sends it to the customer.

This method can be highly appreciated from the cryptological viewpoint. Similarly to UNIX, no password is stored in plaintext on the computer. Each password is used only once, so that no attacker can get unauthorized access to the computer. And cryptanalysts have a hard time: they have to invert the hash function, in addition to computing a collision.

One-time passwords also protect you against **replay attacks**. Up to 1994, this had been a weakness of Novell NetWare, which transmitted passwords in encrypted form, but used a cipher without an initialization vector. This allowed Mallory to pretend to be Alice and to replay Alice's password. This sort of flaw (including copying of encrypted passwords) must have been exploited in masses in the hard real world.

Security Problems

In practice, however, one-time passwords have a few inherent problems. First, these passwords are random, i.e., they are hard to remember. So every user of this system has to constantly watch their walking sticks in the knob of which is hidden the password list. Second, the average user is *always* careless and forgetful (if you want to believe system administrators). They forget to bring their lists along or to print the new one. The system administrator has only 'additional trouble with this'. Third, Mallory only needs to take S_0 from a list lying around openly for unauthorized login, theoretically as often as he wants. But don't panic just yet—these drawbacks can be widely excluded in many situations. All it takes is to memorize only S_0 and have a locally used program compute S_{49} out of it (which is done, for example, in the OPIE program; see Section 7.5). But as things are in the real world, most users will write down their S_0 anyway. So this risk remains.

Mallory can theoretically exploit this until he is filthy rich; plus he has an almost perfect alibi: suppose Alice has to pay a rather large bill to him. Late payment would entail a hefty collection fee. Meanwhile, Mallory has spied out Alice's key S_0 and knows that Alice's 47th password has just been polled. He computes S_{46}, logs himself on as Alice several times, but every time just very briefly. Alice's next connection to the computer fails. It doesn't occur to her that somebody might know her password. She reacts like a typical user: 'The computer is down.' It's a weekend and new password lists won't be issued before Monday—and Alice has to pay the collection fee.

Hardly anybody will be able to prove that Mallory disturbed the synchronization. If he has a clever system for spying out the passwords of his customers, then he can do such maneuvers as often as he wants and continually pocket collection fees. Nevertheless, his work is absolutely legal toward the outside, as opposed to illegally fabricated money transfers: up to the day when the bank notices that all of Mallory's customers seem to have problems authenticating themselves all the time.

This type of attack is also a *denial-of-service attack* (we came across it in connection with the wide-mouth frog protocol). This attack doesn't steal or forge information; it disturbs or frustrates an activity. Good cryptological protocols should prevent such attacks or at least identify the initiator.

6.5.2 Attacks Against Your Bank Account

In this short section, we will make a trip into harsh reality and study an attack against Internet home banking that has become known. The result came to me as a surprise and I hope it will give many readers cause for thought.

Nice Theory . . .

In general, one-time passwords don't prevent man-in-the-middle attacks. On January 28, 1997, the German TV channel *ARD* demonstrated in its popular *Plusminus* program how hackers can get to people's online bank accounts pretty easily. Like so many others within this program, the report was presented spectacularly, without, however, giving exact information. I initially had the following thoughts (don't believe what you will be reading now).

Certainly no hacker ever cracked one-time passwords, because they are not cryptanalysts in the closer sense (i.e., they don't crack complicated encryption algorithms). The freaks[2] in that TV program might have exploited security flaws in the application program and in the operating system, and pretended to a customer that their computer is the bank's. What would something like this look like? Normally, the communication between the bank and its customers proceeds as follows.

1. The customer fills in an electronic transfer slip and sends it to the bank, together with a valid one-time password (in the banking trade more elegantly called a **transaction number (TAN)**).

2. The bank checks the password. If it is valid, the bank accepts the transfer and stores the customer password (Step 5 of the protocol for one-time

---

[2]I call them 'freaks' rather than using the infamous term 'hacker', because they made the public aware of potential threats and wanted to prevent damage rather than cause it.

passwords above). After some feedback to the customer, if applicable, the customer will delete the password used.

The hack could be mounted in Point 1:

1. The hacker computer pretends to the customer it is the bank computer. This is possible, because the bank computer does not authenticate itself, and because network software, application program, and operating system (mostly an insecure Windows system) do have security flaws.

2. The customer fills in his slip on the hacker computer without being aware of it, and sends his one-time password to the hacker. The hacker can confirm acceptance of the slip for the sake of good appearance.

3. The hacker changes the account number and the amount to values more to his liking and sends both to the bank. In doing so, he may pretend his computer is the customer's.

4. The bank finds no error and accepts the transfer.

It is not too difficult to find a countermeasure. The attack can be prevented if the bank computer were to identify itself using a digital signature. The pertaining protocol could look like this.

1. The customer fills in an electronic transfer slip and sends it to his bank without a password.

2. The bank signs the slip and returns the signature together with a transaction number.

3. The customer checks the signature (he obtained the bank's public key directly from his branch) and sends his one-time password.

In this scenario, the hacker has no chance to cheat anymore, even if he could modify the entire data communication between the customer and the bank. The transfer is accepted only if the password is correct, and the customer comes out with the password only after he holds the tamperproof bank signature on the *correct* slip in his hands.

The only way a hacker could interfere with this scenario is a denial-of-service attack. To this end, the hacker would have to disturb the password in Step 3. Naturally, this attack could be prevented, too, if the bank were to send their regular case:

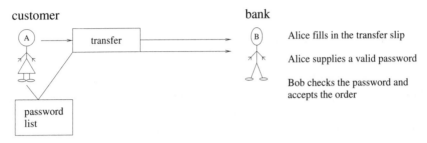

fraudulent maneuver:

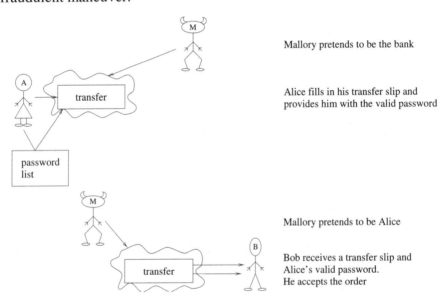

Figure 6.8: Home banking with one-time passwords and man-in-the-middle attack.

signature on the correct, accepted password to the customer in a fourth step. But in practice, a denial-of-service attack would be much harder than pretending to be a bank computer anyway.

There are effective countermeasures even without digital signatures: if you are doubtful of something, you simply write a transfer order for a non-existing account and pass a wrong password along with it. No hacker can find this out. Even if he knows your habits well and discards one attempt to be on the safe side, he doesn't know whether you are still bluffing next time. Upon consultation with the bank, an attempted fraud can be detected with sufficiently high probability.

This means that the damage can be kept within boundaries in the existing system. But once again, it showed the shockingly low level of 'cryptology' in some practical applications, totally in contrast to the impression advertising tries to give.

The entire issue makes a pretty miserable impression. The user and the bank blame each other. Both are even right in their own ways.

- The bank protected itself properly. Only the customer uses insecure operating systems and insecure software, allowing hackers to steal his password.

- The customer can demand that the bank let only cryptologically secure software access their accounts. Those who work with one-time passwords count on being wiretapped anyway. In that case, they should make another small step to include *mutual* authentication. After all, the bank knows more about security than an inexperienced customer!

It is not the 'anarchic Internet' that is to blame but insecure cryptographic protocols and insecure software. It's about time both were brought to the state-of-the-art level.

From the cryptological viewpoint, encryption by means of hybrid methods would certainly be a better choice. In practice, this is sometimes required for non-readable chip cards and perhaps additional biometric systems. Until we get to this point, however, we make do with one-time passwords, perhaps additionally protected by digital signatures.

...and Cruel Practice

Those were my thoughts. They are important for systems with one-time passwords in any event, but they remained gray theory. Because later I heard the truth about the attack demonstrated in that TV program.

The customers used Microsoft Internet Explorer, which activates so-called *ActiveX controls*. These controls let you dial up a suitable page on the Web to load and start an application on your local computer (similar to Java applets, but with less protection). It used to be customary under DOS and Windows that this application would then have access to the entire computer. This is a design error. The customer virtually gets his virus himself over the network. [Donnhack] describes in detail how this is done. The attacker offers a nice colorful page on the Web and hopes to lure bank customers visiting it, and that's it basically.

This security hole (you can't speak of a 'flaw' anymore in this case) basically allows a hacker everything, but the *Quicken* software used in the example above made it even easier for them: home banking programs normally store orders to the bank rather than handling them online. To save phone costs, the customer may perhaps store his one-time passwords on the disk. A program that somehow sometime sneaked in via Internet Explorer just needs to fit in the attacker's 'additional order', or it modifies an order stored on the disk to the attacker's liking. You can imagine that such an attack is not very hard to program. Once they've 'collected' enough transfer orders, the attacker's cute Web site disappears mysteriously, and with it the attacker and the money from all these transactions.

So what is the banks' point in supplying one-time passwords in printed form when users offer the passwords with their software de facto to the whole world? Considering this case, we cannot but exonerate the banks from any fault. Whoever uses such 'open' systems has to be made responsible for damage incurred. This security hole has virtually nothing to do with cryptology, but we cannot deal with theory while ignoring the real world.

Many a Windows user may feel offended by a UNIX freak. The fact is the security concepts of many household computers are simply insufficient for critical tasks such as banking. And the number of critical areas increases as more and more services are offered on the Internet.

Certainly UNIX systems (and others) have security flaws, too. A large number of users are dealing with them intensively and they are aware of the risks. There is still a long way to go until we'll see acceptable security in computer technology, considering that there wasn't even an elementary security awareness until recently. I only hope software vendors will not succeed in continuing to downplay the threats. If they do, the consequences cannot be foretold.

6.5.3 Password Tokens

The protocols discussed so far are not always satisfying. Either Alice knows a secret password, S_0, that Mallory can spy out, or she carries a password list around, which Mallory could copy. And all this while one-time passwords are particularly useful when Alice moves about in an 'insecure environment'. Commercial uses normally demand a higher security.

To this end, several vendors introduced devices the size of key tags or pocket calculators that automatically generate one-time passwords to the market. Such a piece of hardware is referred to as a **token**. I will introduce the RSA products as the first example in this section. RSA named their password token **SecurID** (see Figure 6.9).

Some tokens are additionally protected by PINs. This splits Alice's secret by the principle of 'possessing and knowing': to authenticate himself as Alice, Mallory has to not only spy out her PIN (i.e., the knowledge component), but also steal her token (the possession component). Mallory will have a hard time if Alice always carries her token with her and never lets it out of her hands.

Figure 6.9: RSA SecurID for generating one-time passwords in hardware.

However, the way these tokens work is different from what was described in Section 6.5.1. Why? Suppose the secret password, S_0, were stored in the token RAM. At the push of a button, a one-way hash function would be applied to it n times, and the result would be displayed. The number n would have to be taken from a counter running backwards. Since a token may be used many thousand times, the counter would have to be initialized to a very high startup value, e.g., 10 000. In other words, the startup time would apply the hash function to S_0 about 10 000 times at each push of a button. The computing times would be unacceptably long. Moreover, the number of uses would be limited from the outset. This may not always be desirable. To solve both problems, value S_0 could be changed in a defined way when $n = 0$ is reached, and the counter would be reset. And finally, the pushbutton should be protected against inadvertent activation.

Users find the SecurID tokens more convenient. These tokens create new passwords (in our case six-digit numbers) by the minute. RSA produces two types of tokens: with and without keypad. In the first version, you type your PIN on the token keypad and enter the number read in the computer upon request. In the second version, you put your PIN ahead of the number read and type this conglomerate. Though this variant is cheaper, it is more insecure, of course. More about it further below.

But how are the passwords created? One approach accommodates a secret DES key in every token, and repeatedly encrypts a known or secret 64-bit startup block with this key. It does not necessarily have to be DES. If you continually encrypt two 64-bit blocks using IDEA and compute a hash value from the 128-bits of ciphertext produced, you can certainly forestall cryptanalytic attacks. The server (as we call the computer Alice logs on to for reasons of simplicity) naturally also knows the key and can check the password for correctness.

In contrast, RSA uses a hash algorithm that has been made public (they trust in the abilities of Ron Rivest who checked the method). A built-in clock and a token-dependent secret value called *seed* are used to code a hash value every 15 seconds. The key-tag variant uses four such values to compute numbers that change every minute. This is a clever idea. One could simply compute a hash value from the seed and the clock every minute and display it. But if Mallory knows that two successively displayed values are computed from numbers that differ by 1 (or by 60), then he might be able to calculate parts of the seed, if the hash function is vulnerable to such an attack. (I don't think that one-way hash functions have to be resistant to this type of attack.) However, the four subvalues mentioned above will differ in many bits so that such 'differential cryptanalyses' can be prevented.

And the PIN? In tokens with keypads, it is simply XORed with the hash value computed. That's secure. As Mallory listens in on the data channel, he has no chance to get hold of the PIN. Doubtlessly, transmitting the PIN in plaintext ahead of the password is much more risky. But to use such a wiretapped PIN, Mallory first has to steal the token. And if Mallory steals the token, he first has to have listened in on the PIN. So this variant is more secure, even in plaintext.

There is another problem we haven't considered yet: how does the server learn the password currently created on Alice's token? Clocks tend to be either fast or slow, as we know, particularly when a token is exposed to blazing sun or sharp frost. The solution is relatively simple: the server stores the current 'time shift' for each token and additionally works with a time window for the token, i.e., it also accepts passwords, for example, that would have been valid two minutes earlier, or which should have come up three minutes later. Based on these deviations, the server can correct the time shift, if needed. Only when the deviation grows too large will it request the next password, which introduces additional security. Experience has shown that this case occurs very seldom.

How Secure Are SecurID Tokens?

There are two attacks against all types of tokens: the first is the man-in-the-middle attack—Mallory intercepts Alice's password and talks to the server alone from that moment onwards (this includes mainly *phishing attacks*). This sort of attack is not up for discussion here, because one-time passwords can't protect you from them either. The other attack is somewhat more subtle: Mallory cannot interfere in the connection between Alice and the server, but he monitors the first five places of the six-digit password. He then sends all ten possible last digits over ten parallel channels faster than Alice can, thus obtaining a connection on one channel. This is only possible if Alice uses a badly configured *telnet* program that sends each character individually. The server can make this attack harder, for example, by permitting not more than two or three faulty attempts before it requests the next password (it may even use an 'out time').

Things get easier for Mallory if Alice uses a token without a keypad. Mallory listens in on the PIN at the network, and then steals the token. However, theft is 'manual work' and is normally soon discovered. I think a scenario where Alice forgets her token somewhere and Mallory finds it is more realistic. This is the reason why tokens are never distributed with the vendor's corporate logo on them; only with an anonymous serial number. Without diving into this scenario any further, it is clear that the probability of an illegal login is low in this concept.

On the other hand, users might see reasons to mistrust the token vendors themselves. After all, they store the seeds in the token RAMs. What if they ship the secret number to the NSA at the same time? What stands in the way of such a scenario is the fact that the user himself agrees on the PIN; the manufacturer does not know it. While the NSA could certainly replay a PIN from tokens without a keypad, it could just as easily log the unencrypted data communication. A national intelligence agency normally has little interest in faking authentications.

Probably the most scary scenario would be if Mallory succeeded in reading the seeds from the server. That's tantamount to a masterpiece. The devices are shipped to the users in encrypted form. On the server's hard disk, the seeds are RC4-encrypted using a 128-bit key. And to get them from the memory, you first need to grab the security blocks of the *Progress* database, which is a true challenge even for a superuser.

A brute-force attack against the 64-bit seed might be possible. This would correspond to a capacity of 256 DES crack machines working in parallel. So, cost and benefit are far beyond a reasonable ratio! Much more interesting would be attacks using DFA, as described in Section 4.4.5; vendors don't like to talk about this. But to launch DFA, one has to first own the token, and then probably open it without deleting the RAM.

Theoretical cryptanalyses work faster than brute-force attacks; read about them in *PD/skey/SecurID/securid_attack* on our Web site. My impression is, however, that this is not really significant for practical purposes. Cost and benefit have to be in a reasonable ratio, even in espionage.

Meanwhile, special SecurID tokens work on an AES basis, but the details are not public at the customers' request. But there are alternatives, as we will see in the following section.

Open Authentication, Federated ID, and the VeriSign Idea

RSA deserves respect for having developed password tokens to series maturity; there is no question that these devices dominate the market (it is estimated that about 16 million devices were in use in 2006). Since other vendors wanted to have a share in this business, they joined in the **Open Authentication Initiative (OATH)**. This is an open standard you can download from their Web site

at `www.openauthentication.org`. The core underlying this standard is the
HOTP algorithm, which is described in RFC 4226; you can download the
PD/skey/OATH/rfc4226.txt file from the Web site to this book. The basic idea
is very simple: a counter is increased with every step (pushbutton at the token),
and SHA-1 is used to compute an HMAC. The key that is used to calculate the
HMAC assumes a role similar to the seed in an RSA token. Synchronizing the
counter between token and server is a separate problem (time could also assume
the role of the counter, similarly to the SecurID token). The major benefit of
such an open algorithm is that token vendors compete, being independent of
server software. Burt Kaliski, Chief Scientist at RSA Laboratories, expressed
doubts though: relying on one single algorithm like SHA-1 was unwise, because
nobody can anticipate future cryptanalyses. While this argument appears to be
reasonable, an SHA-1–HMAC would be far from being at risk even when
SHA-1 collisions were easy to calculate. There certainly does not seem to be a
threat in the years to come. Kaliski would like to see a standard that includes
many algorithms and methods. It may evolve some day, but OATH represents
important progress.

OATH can solve another problem: if you have to token-authenticate yourself
at five different servers, you normally need five different tokens. This is cumbersome, and the probability of forgetting exactly which token you need at
the moment increases. This argument is not negligible: when asked who ever
forgot their tokens at the RSA Conference Europe 2006, a large number of
participants raised their hands.

It would be nice to have one single token for all vendors. In this context, we
speak of **federated ID**. On the other hand, such a concept can cause mistrust:
would the token cleanly separate the set of identities? What identity is actually
sent, and can the user control it? What can the vendors that the token serves
learn from one another? Does a different algorithm have to be implemented
for every vendor?

The answer to the last question is 'no', thanks to OATH. The other problems
can be solved by an approach of VeriSign, the most renowned and mighty
company that creates certificates and handles DNS requests for the two most
important Internet domains, *.com* and *.net*. Its concept is called **VIP** (VeriSign
Identity Protection) and is actually pretty simple.

- VeriSign hosts the secret keys of independent vendors contained in the
  tokens and the (non-secret) serial numbers (IDs) of the tokens.
- The tokens are sold freely, independently of the user's merchants, such
  as eBay.

- If a user wants to authenticate himself with eBay, for example, he sends the token ID and a one-time password generated on the push of a button, together with his personal data to eBay. eBay, in turn, strips the personal data, sending only the token ID and the one-time password over a secure line to VeriSign. Finally, VeriSign checks the password for validity and returns the result.

I think the model is pretty secure based on the interests of the parties involved: eBay will not send personal user data to VeriSign, or it would disclose its customer data and buying activities. The token vendors don't know where buyers will eventually use their devices. They no longer participate in subsequent transactions. For this reason, they have no interest in passing secret keys on to others than VeriSign.

The obvious drawback of the method is that it binds you to a company as mighty as VeriSign. There are certain doubts. But eventually, we always have to weigh the advantages and disadvantages. If VeriSign demanded unacceptable conditions for the checkup, the system would not survive in the market, and token vendors might look for another host.

Bottom Line

The tokens discussed above appear to be a reasonable compromise in situations where secure authentication is most important. The data communication between terminal or client and server can still be encrypted. The important thing is that attacks will generally not go unnoticed, because the loss of an object is more evident than stealthily listening in on a password. Tokens are cheaper and easier to handle, compared with challenge–response methods (where servers ask questions).

6.6   Other Protocols

Cryptographic protocols are too extensive and complicated a field to be represented in this book, even in an overview. There is ongoing research in this field so that new scenarios—both of practical relevance and theoretical interest—are continually studied. Readers interested in further reading are referred to the literature and the Internet.

The next sections briefly describe several ingenious and practically interesting protocols. Similar to the cryptographic algorithms, the choice was made at will.

6.6.1 Timestamps

I'm sure I don't have to explain that the age allocated to a file by the operating system is helpful, but proves nothing. For practical purposes, however, it is often necessary to have timestamps that have evidential value. This means:

- The timestamp cannot be changed stealthily in arrears.
- The document cannot be changed stealthily in arrears either.
- The document cannot be fitted with another timestamp in arrears.

The first two requirements are no problem. Alice writes 'created on February 29, 1996, 17: 30' in plaintext on her document, adding her digital signature to the document. If it is doubtlessly known that this document originates from Alice, and a wrong time would only be damaging, and her public key is also known, then this protocol is absolutely sufficient. Nobody other than Alice can add a different timestamp to it and digitally sign it in Alice's name as long as her signature is secure.

Unfortunately, this is not always enough. First of all, we could think of cases where Alice herself has some fraudulent idea. Second, a governmental agency that will receive ten thousand virtual documents per day in our golden electronic future cannot procure the public key of every user to check the time. Third, it should generally be possible to check the authenticity of the document–timestamp relationship, regardless of the author.

Notarized Timestamps

An intuitive solution to the problem is to use a trustworthy timestamp service. Alice has to submit her document to this service, and will get it back with timestamp and signature included. The public keys of the timestamp service are published regularly in a daily newspaper.

To ensure that the transmission capacities on the Internet will suffice for audio mail and cool images, Alice should only send the hash value to the stamp service. The service would then return the signed 'timestamp–hash value' pair. A short random character string appended to the timestamp by the stamp service will remove all doubts about a potential ciphertext attack (see Section 4.5.3).

This protocol is pretty good. Though minor drawbacks could be slight delays, and that it will cost money, it would hardly be feasible without such minor drawbacks.

Nevertheless, Alice has a possibility for fraud: she can bribe the operator of a stamp service, or put the wrong date on her document. An audit of the service is not included in the protocol. So we need a better protocol for mass use.

Auditing the Service

There are several ways to prevent the timestamp service from being bribed. For example, one protocol has the service sign not only the timestamp and hash value, but additionally an identification number of Alice as well as name, time, and signature of the last customer—everything concatenated—and then return this conglomerate duly signed to Alice. Moreover, it will tell her the identification number of the next customer in line after Alice.

Depending on the auditor's persistence, this protocol can be used to determine an arbitrary number of customers ahead and after Alice. Grossly forging a timestamp within such a chain would be noticed immediately, since the times stated have to be sorted in ascending order. To be able to backdate a complaint by only one day, Alice would have to find a service that had not been used for an entire day, and then she would have to bribe it. Not much reward in such an undertaking.

The only problem with this scenario is that some customers could disappear from within the chain after some years. This problem can be solved, for example, by using distributed timestamps. To this end, Alice has her document signed with a timestamp by many other persons. Exactly which persons from a large set these are is determined by the hash value of her document. This variant is secure, but costly and time-consuming.

In addition, there are protocols where the timestamp services are arranged in a tree structure and monitored from top to bottom. Surety Technologies (an affiliate of Bellcore) has such protocols patented in the USA.

You see that the problem is not quite as easy to solve as it appeared in the beginning. But the security level achieved with good protocols is far beyond a signed sheet of paper despite all doubts with regard to the security of digital signatures. This is yet another case where cryptology can truly improve security, rather than restoring old securities in the new world.

6.6.2   Bit Commitment

Bit commitment is an important protocol for everyday life: you need it, for example, if you want to deposit your will on the Internet. But more about this later.

The scenario is as follows: Alice wants to sell Bob some piece of information, but disclose it only once Bob has paid for it. Though Bob buys a pig in a poke, he wants to have a guarantee that he will get this information once he has paid, and that Alice does not replace the information stealthily by some worthless information once she has received payment, which would mean that he couldn't prove anything.

Without a cryptographic solution, you would have to use sealed envelopes. A cryptographic solution is much simpler.

1. Bob sends a random bit sequence, R, to Alice.

2. Alice appends her information, I, to R, and uses a secret key, S, to encrypt it. She sends the cipher to Bob.

3. Bob pays for the information.

4. Alice tells him the key she used, namely S.

5. Bob decrypts Alice's message and checks whether or not his bit sequence, R, is at the beginning. Then he reads I.

The random bit sequence, R, prevents Alice from decrypting the cipher after Step 2 with all possible keys until a plaintext to her liking results. She would then send Bob the false key found in Step 4. Such a fraud can be realized only if the information is very short (particularly if I is only one bit long, and if it can be revealed from the least significant bit of the plaintext block). But what if Alice knew special plaintexts which, if calculable with a second key for a second calculable plaintext, would produce the same cipher? Random bit sequence R prevents Bob from having to worry about such vulnerabilities with this algorithm. It suffices if the algorithm is resistant to plaintext attacks.

Other possibilities use one-way functions and random-number generators. However, the protocol introduced above is practicable and secure. Now, if you want to deposit your will without having to pay notary fees, you proceed as follows: have each of your potential heirs send you a random bit sequence, R, and run Step 2 for each heir. Each heir deposits his R value and the cipher with the other heirs. In turn, you use the same key for all of them for the sake of simplicity. This key is kept in a sealed envelope at a secure location and opened after your death. No heir will then be able to say that the envelope had been replaced, or that he had received a forged testament.

6.6.3   Blind Signatures

Blind signatures are signatures where the signer is not supposed to know the contents of a document in whole or in part. In the former case, such signatures are also referred to as **completely blind signatures**. The most important aspect of such signatures is that the document in question existed at a specific point in time. Such signatures were developed by Chaum for implementing digital money at the beginning of the 1980s. We will see under what circumstances blind signatures are meaningful in connection with a similar protocol (Section 6.6.7).

Without cryptology, completely blind signatures are easily possible. A notary signs page by page with 'document no.: ... submitted on: ... signature: ...', where each page is disguised by the document's author. Using cryptology, the scheme could be such that Alice sends only a long one-way hash value of her document to Bob, and Bob signs it. In the simplest case, Bob decrypts the hash value with his private key. To prevent a chosen-ciphertext attack, he had better calculate a hash value from the hash value and then decrypt this one.

Unfortunately, the method has a flaw. Bob can memorize all hash values given to him, so he can learn the time and place when each document was signed. This may be undesirable in some situations. Moreover, Bob could use a subliminal channel to infiltrate a document number in the signature, together with his signature, and correlate these numbers with additional information in a secret list.

The protocol first introduced by Chaum used the following idea: Alice can multiply her document by a random number. This makes the document indecipherable so that she can give it to Bob for signature without worrying. Once Bob has signed, she computes the random number out of it, converting Bob's signature into a valid one for the original document. Since multiplication and signature have to be 'compatible', it is best to use the RSA method. However, the multiplication cannot be removed from the hash function for certain. The following method suggests itself (for the RSA method; see Figure 4.16).

1. Alice calculates the hash value, m, for her document.

2. She chooses a random number, k, which is relatively prime to module n, and computes

```
t = mk^e mod n
```

3. Bob receives t for signature. He computes

$$t^d = m^d k^{de} \bmod n$$

Now, decryption with the RSA method was just based on the equation

$$M^{de} = M \bmod n$$

for all $M < n$. In particular, $k^{de} = k \bmod n$. This means that Bob actually computed

$$t^d = m^d k \bmod n.$$

4. Since k is relatively prime to n, Alice can resolve the equation

$$uk = t^d \bmod n$$

toward u, thus revealing Bob's signature, $u = m^d$, of m.

Based on this protocol, k^e is sometimes referred to as the **blinding factor**, and Step 4 is said to *remove the blinding factor*. Later on, Bob can no longer recover t from m. As a minimum, if Alice used only primitive roots, k of n, then there is a k with

$$mk^e = t \bmod n$$

for each t and each m. This means that hash value m could belong to every t that Bob memorized.

That much about completely blind signatures. Blind signatures (better termed as 'semi-blind signatures') should grant Bob an insight into the document in general, but not reveal too much. For example, Bob wants to protect himself against signing horrendous claims. For this situation, there is no intuitive solution, neither in the physical world nor in cryptology. One possible protocol was described by Schneier [SchnCr, 5.3]:

Alice works on a top-secret assignment and needs a forged diplomatic passport in her cover name. Home Secretary Bob has to sign her passport, but must not learn her valid cover name. Alice sends him ten passports, each issued to a different name. Bob randomly selects nine and checks whether they are in order. He signs the tenth by the completely blind signature method. If Alice submits a passport with illegal authorities, then the chances are 9:1 that she will get caught.

Intensive research work on blind signatures is being done, and some are patented by Chaum in the USA. Section 6.6.7 describes a practically relevant use for blind signatures.

6.6.4   Zero-Knowledge Proofs

Similar mystery-mongering as with blind signatures is involved in a type of protocol called **zero-knowledge proof**. Alice would prove to Bob that she owns certain information without telling him what this information is. Naturally, the protocol depends on the specific problem. Alice could even publish hints about her secret so that every doubter will eventually be convinced of her knowing the secret, whereas Alice doesn't disclose a single bit of that secret. This variant is called **non-interactive zero-knowledge proof**.

As unbelievable as this may sound, you know an example: Alice wants to make believe she knows the two prime factors of a 1024-bit number. To this end, she constructs a public–private key pair and uses her private key to decrypt a text *not* selected by her, similar to digital signatures. She publishes the 'plaintext' thus created together with the public key. Everybody can do reverse ciphering to convince themselves that Alice knows the private key and with it the two prime factors, as we saw in Section 4.5.3.

We will see a practical use in Step 5 of the authentication protocol of Secure Shell SSH in Section 7.3: Bob gives Alice a 256-bit random number he had encrypted with her private key. Only Alice can reverse-calculate this number. To prove it, she sends Bob a hash value from this number (and not the number itself to make sure Mallory won't get a chance).

However, zero-knowledge protocols normally work **interactively**. In a challenge–reply scenario, the probability that Alice really knows a secret tends towards 1 as the number of her replies grows.

There are much more sophisticated protocols; you can find some in [SchnCr, 5.1], but you have seen what we are talking about.

6.6.5   Fail-Stop Signatures

The idea behind this type of signature is related to probabilistic cryptography (Section 5.8), where encryption is ambiguous, while decryption is unambiguous. With fail-stop signatures, decryption is ambiguous, while encryption is unambiguous. More specifically, many private keys should exist for each public key. In the first case, nobody can blame Alice for having created a certain session key. In the second case, Alice can prove that her signature was forged. The reason is that, even if Mallory cracked the asymmetric method and reconstructed *one* private key, the probability that he has not found the one Alice used (these keys are actually equally probable; there is no cryptological assumption behind it) is extremely high (e.g., 2^{100}:1).

This means that Mallory's signature will virtually always be different from Alice's. Alice can demonstrate in court that she created a different signature, using officially certified documents signed by her earlier as evidence.

The first fail-stop signatures were introduced by Birgit Pfitzmann and Michael Waidner in 1990. In her book [PfitzFSS], the author explains also how the name came about: in the event of a cracked public key ('fail'), Alice can prove the fraud and revoke ('stop') all her signatures, for which that key was used.

Fail-stop signatures are based on cryptological assumptions, similar to regular digital signatures, such as: the factoring of extremely large numbers is hard, one-way hash functions are cryptologically not reversible, and so on. Fail-stop signatures are not more 'durable' than regular ones. But they remove the largest part of uncertainty: has somebody forged signatures or not? If Mallory decides to apply his secret super crack algorithm after all, then at least he'll most likely get caught.

In case of damage, Alice has to first notice the fraud, of course (this is the biggest problem in my opinion). She'd revoke all her current signatures, which even increases the damage. She'd then reduce the damage again by checking every single one of her old signatures that are still important (and accessible at all), and replacing them by a new one that's more secure. Not bloody likely! What's more, Mallory's forgery may by then have caused damage beyond repair.

There might be a way to avoid this crazy repair effort after all, since digital signatures are actually as secure as we hope them to be. Fail-stop signatures will at least offer more certainty. This new technology may help solve the 'durability problem' satisfactorily. For the time being, this protocol is rather costly. There are no usable implementations, but let's hope there will be in the near future.

The downside is that fail-stop signatures are ineffective in preventing attacks against the one-way hash function. And if Alice's private key is stolen, then the catastrophe is preprogrammed, regardless of the protocol used, unless cryptologists can find a trick to limit this damage, too.

6.6.6 One-Way Accumulators

A **one-way accumulator** is a protocol that allows Alice to prove to important people that she is a member of a secret intelligence organization without having to disclose its member list.

This is nothing new, you might think, there are IDs after all. In the digital world, she only needs to show an appropriately signed document.

Unfortunately, no trustworthy authority willing to sign the electronic member IDs was to be found. Or more likely, the members fear that a national intelligence agency is trying to infiltrate members. Headquarters would notice this, but the ordinary members don't carry lists around with them for security reasons, so they cannot see whether or not an ID is forged (intelligence agencies can forge). Nobody from within the organization is sufficiently immune to extortion that his signature would be good for the member IDs.

Cryptology comes in handy here, too. A one-way accumulator can serve as a one-way hash function defined for sequences of member names, and the results are independent of the order computed. This means that they are similar to a commutative sum. However, the function must not be reversible in the cryptological sense: it should not be possible at an acceptable cost for a given result, R, to construct two names that supply result R when using the one-way accumulator. So calculating a sum is a poor example.

Benaloh and De Mare introduced better functions in 1994 [Benal.acc]. The authors demonstrated a simple example based on the security of discrete logarithms:

All members agree on a product, m, of two very large prime numbers and an initial value of x_0. The one-way accumulator from the values $y1, \ldots, yn$ then has the following value:

$$x^{y1 + \ldots yn} \bmod n$$

Every member obtains an identification sequence composed of his name and a confidential character string. Alice learns the value W_{Alice} of the one-way accumulator, composed of the identification sequences of all members except her own. This value is not secret; it can be published to third parties in advance, if need be. Moreover, the value W_{all} of the accumulator, composed for *all* members, is published by a third party. If somebody has doubts about Alice's membership, they can ask for her identification sequence and compute the accumulator from that sequence and W_{Alice}. If the result is W_{all}, then Alice has to be a member; otherwise she is a spy. Since identification sequences are made known upon request only, no member list can be revealed by trial and error.

The security of this protocol can be compared with that of digital signatures using a centralized service, except that it can do without the latter. It is a nice example of showing that cryptology can still discover simple and useful things even today.

6.6.7 Electronic Money

Just hearing the buzzword 'electronic money' will cause many people to think: 'Yet another technical gadget that no one needs!' It is understandable since nobody wants to move our daily payment system to the Internet for the time being, even though advertising has been going into raptures about electronic malls.

Information has become merchandise, and this merchandise is shipped increasingly over the Internet. It would be natural to also be able to pay for it on the Internet. There is certainly a lot of speculation going on about the vision of teleshopping and customers paying electronically. I'd rather not forecast whether and how fast this vision will gain acceptance in the real world.

But long before electronic money is widely used, cryptologists need to have appropriate algorithms and protocols ready. Otherwise it could happen that poor protocols are sold as the latest craze and the 'real' (bad) hackers celebrate for there's real money to be made.

There is a large number of approaches and products concerning electronic checks or coins. To keep within the scope and volume of this book, I will introduce and discuss one single protocol, namely one by Chaum, Fiat, and Naor [Chaum]. This protocol itself uses several of the protocols previously introduced, and it is pretty clever. We will only look at checks, not coins, since we don't want to deal with the additional problem of change.

Requirements for Electronic Money

Let's first consider several requirements electronic checks have to meet in any event.

- Checks have to be *covered*. This is easier for electronic checks than it is for paper ones: all electronic checks are signed by the bank and auditable by everyone, since it will issue only covered checks.

- Checks have to be *tamperproof*. With electronic checks, this means in particular that they cannot be used more than once, since copying cannot be prevented.

The second requirement is not as easy to fulfill as the first. If we take the wording literally, it means: any attempt to pay once more using the same check shall be declared to be invalid. No matter how the protocol is handled—the merchant has to have the check verified by a centralized party, which is generally the bank itself. Such protocols are called **online-payment protocols**. They can cause extremely high network loads. Moreover, every merchant has to be able to quickly establish a connection to many or all banks, and every bank has to be able to process its entire electronic payment traffic in real time.

This is unrealistic with the current state-of-the-art in technology, so people developed **offline-payment protocols**. With an offline-payment protocol, the merchant collects checks as usual and submits them to his bank or several banks in 'bundles'. In this case, submitting copied checks cannot be prevented, so there has to be a way to detect this type of fraud beyond any doubt. The Chaum–Fiat–Naor protocol is such an offline protocol. But there is another important requirement:

- The payment traffic must be *anonymous*. This means that the merchant learns the customer and the bank. When the merchant submits checks, however, the bank may see that they are their checks and that they are submitted by that merchant, but the customer must not be revealed.

Why is this so important? The bank always knows both the issuer and the presenter of every clearing check! True, but only in theory. A considerable part of the payment traffic still involves anonymous cash money and bills and other hand-written papers that are not completely scanned so that they are not completely back-traceable.

In contrast, gapless logging is no problem for digital checks and coins. 'So what,' you might say, 'let the bank know where I buy my stuff.' That's a dangerous mistake. Payment systems can reveal behavioral patterns, such as your preparedness to take risks, punctuality, personal preferences, contributions to political parties, cash reserves, employment relationships, alimonies, and many more things. Transparent humans can be manipulated and extorted, particularly if Mallory gets hold of your personal data. Greetings from Orwell. We will get back to this issue in Section 8.2.2.

Part of it is (hopefully) pie in the sky, but still, we should consider these threats today: once a non-anonymous protocol has been accepted it will be hard to suppress it. The only thing that will be suppressed is our threat-awareness.

The protocol introduced below is anonymous.

The Chaum–Fiat–Naor Protocol

We will first have a look at the protocol and then discuss its effects.

1. Alice wants to use an electronic check to pay Bob 978 dollars. She represents the information 'I am Alice in Wonderland, customer number 44322 with Second Reality Bank' unambiguously as number I, as agreed. I could be a hash value of her personal information, for example.

2. She wants to buy a check for 978 dollars from her bank. To this end, she creates a random number, R, which is so long that there can never be two checks with the same number R in the world. She writes R and the amount on the check.

3. Next, Alice creates three random number sequences, (a_i), (b_i), and (c_i), for example, with 40 numbers in each sequence. These numbers have to be of the same data type as information I in Step 1. She takes these numbers and a suitable generally known one-way hash function, $h()$, to calculate two sequences, (x_i) and (y_i):

```
xi = h(ai,bi)
yi = h(ai ⊕ I,ci)
```

She also writes sequences (x_i) and (y_i) on the check.

4. Alice has her bank sign the check by means of a *blind signature* (see Section 6.6.3).

To this end, she produces N such checks with the same amount (number N is specified by the bank). For example, she submits the hash values of these blinded checks (see Section 6.6.3). The bank randomly selects $N - 1$ of these checks and requests their complete disclosure. Alice has to submit these checks, together with the blinding factor and the pertaining number sequences, (a_i), (b_i), and (c_i). The bank verifies whether these numbers really result in the sequences (x_i) and (y_i). The bank signs the hash value of the non-disclosed check, returns its signature to Alice, and debits Alice's account with the amount of 978 dollars.

If Alice were to cheat here, it would be discovered with a probability of $(N - 1)/N$.

5. Alice puts the following together:

   - the amount;
   - the check number R;
   - the hash sum she had submitted to the bank (without the blinding factor); and
   - the bank's signature with the blinding factor removed (see Section 6.6.3).

   She sends this check to Bob.

6. Bob asks Alice for the name of her bank, the bank's public key (unless he knows it already), and then verifies the bank's signature.

7. If it's all right, he gives Alice a random 40-bit number, Z, consisting of bits z_i. Alice has to give merchant Bob

```
a_i, b_i, and y_i, if z_i = 1, or
a_i ⊕ I, c_i, and x_i, if z_i = 0.
```

   In the first case, merchant Bob can calculate value x_i from a_i and b_i, since he knows hash function $h()$. In the second case, he can recover y_i. This means that he knows x_i and y_i for every i so that he can verify the hash value (blindly signed by the bank) stated on the check.

8. Bob ships the merchandise to Alice and sends the check number, the amount, and all data he obtained from Alice to the bank. The bank stores these data and credits 978 dollars to his account.

How Secure is this Protocol?

This protocol protects Alice's anonymity. Though the bank gets the check number from Bob as well as the amount and the data mentioned in Step 7, it cannot recover Alice's identity. We can think of the two numbers a_i and $a_i \oplus I$ as a subset of secret I. The protocol uses secret splitting (Section 6.2) in this case. The bank learns from Bob only a subset of the secret, so it's not much good for them. The check number won't help them either, because they hadn't seen it when signing in Step 4 (which was the reason why Alice had to create R herself in Step 1). Finally, the hash sum was covered by the blinding factor upon signing.

However, if Alice cheats, i.e., uses the same check twice for different merchants, then her identity will be disclosed to the bank. This is the trick with this protocol, and the most important step is the seventh. The bank verifies each check submitted to see whether or not its number was already stored. If so, then numbers Z in Step 7 are identical with a probability of 2^{-40}, i.e., roughly one trillionth. This is seldom enough so that, at least in practice, there is at least one i in which bits z_i differ on the checks given to the two merchants. The bank recovers Alice's identity number I by simple XOR from a_i and $a_i \oplus I$. Should check numbers R for different persons happen to be identical, then different i would most likely produce different I, or I would be nonsensical.

On the other hand, if Bob submits one check twice, he gives himself away immediately. Identical checks (with the same data sequences from Step 7) are even rarer than one in a billion checks.

Finally, Bob cannot 'invent' checks himself since the bank can verify their own signature on the check.

'Remainder Problems'

We saw that the Chaum–Fiat–Naor protocol is cryptologically secure, and it is anonymous as long as Alice, the bank, and Bob are the only participants. However, if Mallory manages to wiretap the line, he can do things worse than theft: he can intercept Alice's check and issue it instantly, making Alice an impostor. He can listen in on the communication between Alice and Bob and submit the check faster than Bob, making Bob an impostor. Either way, there would be lack of evidence. For this reason, all data communications have to be cryptologically secure, and additional measures have to be taken in the event Mallory breaks into Alice's or Bob's computer.

In the procedure above, Alice remains anonymous, but some income is recorded at Bob's end. This is actually nothing exciting. Every merchant accepting checks discloses their income to their bank.

Alice incurs interest lost during the time from when the check is signed to when it is submitted to the bank. This shouldn't be a major problem since such transactions can be handled much faster on the Net than by current accounting methods.

In contrast, the load on the network is a big deal. Every payment transaction requires a multi-step dialogue between Alice and her bank, between Alice and Bob, and between Bob and the bank. Not all of this has to be done online though. Another downside is that this protocol doesn't allow for change. This means that Alice has to create a separate check for each 'odd' amount and have it signed blindly by her bank. Interferences in the line to the bank, or in the bank itself, will have an immediate hindering effect on the sales transaction, which is currently not the case with ATM cards or clearing checks.

A popular topic in magazine articles seems to be the catastrophe that Alice's hard disk 'goes up in smoke'. I even came across the argument that companies that restore data from destroyed disks will enjoy a strong boom. That's computer-technical nonsense. Electronic payment systems will initially be handling small amounts for which such an expensive operation wouldn't be worthwhile. By the time amounts get bigger users will probably have learned that every once in a while they should back up their data—even immediately when writing checks for 10 000 dollars and more. Also, it shouldn't be a problem to have one's bank stop payment of a check with a particular number, provided one has memorized that number.

Bottom Line

Let's leave it at that. You probably haven't paid for this book by e-cash, and you are likely to pay for the next in the same manner. I find it more interesting to look at how sophisticated cryptographic protocols can be. The protocol introduced above uses three other protocols: digital signatures, blind signatures, and secret splitting. The structure of digital coin protocols is even more complicated since they have to remain completely anonymous, and coins have to be divisible. The first protocol of this type required a transfer of about 200 Mbytes per payment. There is intensive ongoing research on practicable and secure protocols. At the EUROCRYPT '98, Chan, Frankel, and Tsiounis [ChanFrTsi] introduced a practicable and mostly anonymous method that can be done with 300 bytes per payment and requires only small computation times.

At any rate, the Chaum–Fiat–Naor protocol guarantees Alice's anonymity. That's a new feature that conventional check-clearance systems cannot offer.

Whether or not it is still desirable in view of the current terror-fighting hype
might be doubtful.

6.6.8   The PIN on an ATM Card

Probably the most frequently practiced cryptography in everyday life is PIN-
authentication at an automatic teller machine (ATM). It is understandable that
the question about the security of this system is on many card owners' minds,
and not without reason, as Figure 6.10 (though admittedly not current) shows. A
daily paper reported a yearly increase of 40 % in computer crime in 2001. Such
figures are not always reliable, of course. For one thing, the term 'computer
crime' is sloppy (some investigators may also use it for ATM card theft), and
second, nobody can estimate the number of unrecorded cases. But the trend is
there, and it's real.

Since this is a book about cryptology, we won't discuss popular methods to
steal PINs in detail. These methods include, for example:

- Using mounted mirrors to monitor the keyboard of an ATM (this has
  happened at gas stations).

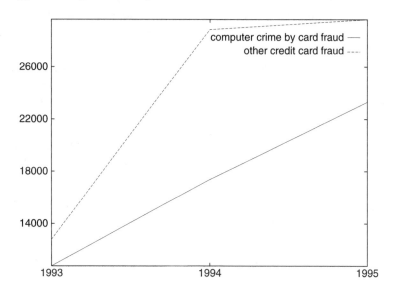

Figure 6.10: Criminal development of ATM card and credit card fraud.

- Trial-and-error recovering the four-digit number customers write on their ATM cards (that's always the PIN).

- Exploiting modified ATMs that pass the typed PIN on to third parties (this has happened particularly often in Italy, where it was estimated to account for 0.5 % of total sales loss).

- Analyzing the electromagnetic waves an ATM emits.

- Violence in any form.

The Hairspray Attack

Cryptologically more interesting is the method of impregnating ATM keyboards with talcum powder or hairspray. Once a customer has withdrawn money from the ATM, the 'sprayer' can reveal the digits the customer keyed in. 'This won't do much', you might say, 'since the thief won't get far without knowing the sequence of the digits. After all, the card is swallowed after the third failed attempt.'

Correct, but not entirely. With a four-digit PIN, there are $4! = 24$ possibilities of how the four digits are arranged. Somebody who stole eight bankcards has $8*3 = 24$ random attempts for free, which produces one winner on average. This estimate is too pessimistic, for not all PINs consist of four different digits. If you get 2222 as the PIN for your ATM card, you should be careful. (I recommend the impostor to pull a carnival mask over his head in this type of undertaking, perhaps with the face of the Secretary of the Treasury: you will certainly be filmed while at it.)

What we have here basically is a dictionary attack launched in parallel against several systems. (For each card, the dictionary consists of all four-digit numbers with the given digits.)

I am perfectly aware of such attacks, because they are done for real. There are simple countermeasures. Once I have typed my PIN, for example, I generally wipe over all the number buttons and hold an object in my hand as I type. That's easy to make a habit of, sending the fraudulent attempts described above into the realm of wishful thinking.

However, I cannot see what happens inside the teller machine. Ideally, I use only the teller machines in the branches of my bank. But that doesn't actually belong to cryptology.

How Does the PIN Work?

This section will first of all bring you to the technical state-of-the-art up to 1997. I will then discuss the migration at the turn of 1997/1998 further below in an effort to represent the differences in a simpler way.

How does the bank create a PIN? Banks most frequently use a system developed by IBM called the **MM protection method** (see Meyer and Matyas [MM]).

The bank takes

- the last four digits of the bank code;
- the customer's account number padded to 10 digits; and
- a one-digit card sequential number.

These 15 decimal digits together produce a theoretical result of 10^{15} or approximately 2^{50} possibilities, i.e., the customer data easily fits in a 64-bit block. The bank DES-encrypts this block with a strictly secret key, the so-called **PIN key**. The bank takes two bytes from the cipher to deterministically produce the PIN; sometimes (or always, I don't know), the bank adds an offset. In [Wcf], Anderson states that this offset serves to produce a more easily remembered number.

In Germany, all ATMs are online-connected to the corresponding bank computer. This means that the PIN key does not leave the high-security tract. The security module that contains this key can be opened only in the presence of two persons.

The PIN key is the vulnerability in this method. This is presumably the reason why it is secret-split and fed into the system by at least two employees independently of one another.

However, this is not quite sufficient. What happens when you withdraw cash at an Italian ATM using your ATM card from a German bank? This ATM is not online-connected to the pertaining computer.

To this end, every bank generates three **pool keys**. These pool keys are used to create three additional PINs. The difference to the 'basic PIN' is included in the card's magnetic strip. The foreign ATM knows only one of these three pool keys of that German bank. So it can verify the PIN the customer types in without having to be connected online to the German bank.

These three pool keys are changed regularly; entries that became invalid in the meantime will be deleted from the card by the ATM.

How Secure is the PIN?

From the cryptological viewpoint, the PIN is pretty secure. There is no mean-ingful chance for brute force at the ATM: for some reason or other, no PIN was to begin with a zero up to the end of 1997 (probably because they thought customers wouldn't type it); but that still leaves 9000 possible values. The chances are 1 to 3000 that money can be made with stolen ATM cards. That's not rewarding. If only every 3000th attempt succeeds, then the statistical profit per card is only 1/3000 of the amount maximally achievable. To make sure the impostor makes some profit from his undertakings on average, the statistically minimum earnings should be 24 dollars to cover the cost for the carnival mask mentioned above, even in one single theft, i.e., a thief would have to make more than 24*3000 = 72 000 dollars per guessed PIN. With *this* sort of calcu-lation, the mask manufacturer might subsidize the banks' loss even at a ratio of five to ten cards per thief. (Unfortunately, there are more effective methods, including cryptanalytical methods.)

Otherwise, there is a good reason why the PIN is created from the cipher. Compare this method with the verification of UNIX passwords (Section 3.3) where the password is part of the key. Here, this is out of the question, because the PIN is limited to four digits, and brute force would be a kid's game. Based on current knowledge, the PIN can only be recovered by brute force. If you hear to the contrary, don't believe it. Whoever publicly claims to be able to calculate the PIN without brute force (i.e., on a conventional PC, for example) would have to exploit a DES vulnerability. As it happens, the most capable cryptologists in the world (in the publicly accessible area) have not found it in twenty years.

Consequently, the entire system's security depends on keeping the four DES keys secret. If you know the PIN key you can *calculate* the PIN. This means that any ATM card or credit card turns into a gold mine, and based on the current legal situation (which will hopefully change), banks even blame their defrauded customers.

But brute force is no longer impossible, as the special *Deep Crack* and *Copa-cobana* computers introduced in Section 4.4.1 showed. Most ATM cards get stolen abroad (where the ATMs work offline with our cards). Whether or not the thieves owned a DES crack machine might never transpire.

On the other hand, you need to know the PIN of four or five ATM cards to mount this brute-force attack, because one PIN alone isn't enough to reveal the PIN key. This is not a barrier for organized crime syndicates.

Perhaps several programmers and engineers inside the bank can get hold of the DES keys. Perhaps they have the keys read out from offline ATMs (e.g., in Italy). Finally, a small explosive charge will remove finger prints and scratches (at least that's what the criminals hope).

We could continue spinning the thread. There are just too many possibilities to get hold of the DES keys. Though every ATM card is fitted with a tamperproof 'modulated machine-readable characteristic' (readable by infrared to my knowledge), it can currently be read by only about a third of all ATMs out there. So this data is not included in the PIN calculation; it only requires more care in handling forged cards. Mind you, magnetic strip cards and card readers are cheap and available at the computer store round the corner...

There is no reason to panic just yet. But we should handle our ATM cards and credit cards as if they were a thick bundle of cash. And we now know a good reason why we shouldn't tell anyone that our accounts are nicely filled up.

Things are worse with credit card numbers, by the way. I came across detailed instructions on the Internet how to evaluate these numbers and what tricks to use to make a handsome profit. It didn't come close to instructions on 'how to build bombs'; they simply wanted to remind everybody to be careful. I think we all have a hunch about how much criminal energy people sniffing the network put into their job. This is a good reason to transmit credit card numbers over the Net only in encrypted form to have more security against attacks, at least statistically.

Migration of PINs in 1997/1998

At the beginning of 1998, all European ATM cards migrated to a new system, and their owners received new PINs. As it happened, 0 is now admissible as the first digit. All of this raises hopes. Furthermore, it was said that 128-bit keys would be used from then onwards. Had they migrated to using IDEA?

People jumped for joy too early: they had merely replaced DES by Triple-DES. The good news is that this frustrates brute-force attacks, at least based on current knowledge. The somewhat strange arithmetic '2*56 = 128' used to specify the key length might be due to the fact that they included the parity bits.

Unfortunately, further details were not officially revealed. I know only that every bank now has its own PIN key, and that this key never leaves their computer center. In other words, all ATMs have to be connected online to the bank; the PIN is verified only there, never in the ATM itself. This is why one needs the plaintext from which the PIN is calculated; it cannot be calculated from the card data alone, and (hopefully customer-specific) secrets can be mixed in. This is actually done as a banker told me. Moreover, our cards can be used at ATMs abroad. Do they all have online connections to our country?

Remedies

The current PIN method appears theoretically secure enough, but vulnerable in practice. If breaking into the system increases faster than shown in Figure 6.10 in the coming years, then banks should consider migrating to more reliable methods. This won't be cheap; we won't like paying for it indirectly, but it will be necessary.

The first step towards improvement was made in 1998 when the key length was extended. Whether or not it would have been cheaper to use the whitening method described in Section 5.2.3 is hard to say. If there were doubts about Triple-DES, then migrating to whitening would still have been possible: one bit on the card could tell the ATM whether or not whitening should be activated.

In addition to other cryptographic modifications, all ATM cards and credit cards will be chip cards in the future. This is desirable at least for one reason: they would be more robust. Not without reason are magnetic cards read several times and the results compared in some bank. Security also increases: the article mentioned earlier [AndKuhn.tamp] describes clearly that chip cards are not a secure hiding place for keys, but protected chips can no longer be read out without destroying the chip. This represents a considerable barrier for attackers; bank chip cards can't be bought at the store round the corner.

Details on PIN generation, including literature references, can be found in the *pin.txt* and *wcf.txt* files on our Web site.

6.6.9 Biometric Methods

You have seen how many problems PINs, passwords, and passphrases can cause, and there will be more examples. Bad passwords and PINs written down noticeably are security problems that should not be underestimated; they increase as the number of chip cards and magnetic cards and logins on various computers rises. And to date, I don't see any improvement in software, whereas it could easily deny bad passwords, for example. So what next?

One intuitive way out of this dilemma is biometrics. How intensely this field is being researched can be observed at trade fairs, like the CeBIT: the number of vendors grows from one year to the next. As you can see in Figure 6.11, the wealth of ideas seems to be unlimited.

- **Fingerprint:** A fingerprint is taken as the finger is placed on, or moved past, a sensor. Fingerprint sensors can be found in keyboards, mice, and special USB sticks. *utimaco Software AG* even developed a crypto-smartcard with a built-in fingerprint sensor.

  Older systems could be fooled by using fingerprints printed on scotch tape. In modern systems, expensive sensors additionally check the temperature and some even the pulse beat and the pigmentation of the finger cup on the print. Some people might be cruel enough to cut somebody's finger off to use it for identification. Modern impostors are more humane (and still very successful) using simpler means, as the German Chaos Computer Club demonstrated: you need a digital camera, a simple image editing tool, a printer, and some liquid plaster to create a thin skin with the desired (stolen) fingerprint pasted to your finger. The funny thing is that this system passes all live tests (for finger authenticity). And with some extra talent, it even works under observation. You can find the article and the link in *txt/biometric/fingerprt_gelatine.txt* on the Web site.

  Dirty or injured fingers cause problems. Some systems compensate for injuries by accepting different fingertips. Also, the sensors themselves can be dirty. In addition, about 2 % to 5 % of all people don't leave usable fingerprints (e.g., carpenters or masons). Those who use fingerprints as a replacement rather than an addition haven't understood the concept of biometrics. It is a system mistakenly believed to be highly reliable, especially since it is used as legal evidence. But fingerprints in criminal investigations are taken differently (by rolling all ten fingers on a sort of ink pad), and the problem of liveness-checks doesn't exist in this field.

  Excessive use of fingerprint sensors and careless data protection can even cause fingerprints to be worthless as legal evidence, because it is too easy to forge them and, above all, they are not secret anymore.

- **Facial recognition:** Outstanding points or the three-dimensional shape of a face are detected and measured. If you select points the distance of which does not change, then the system would recognize you even after a night's carousing. Problems can be caused by eyeglasses, beards, injuries, anti-wrinkle creams, aging, and photos held in front of the camera in older systems.

Figure 6.11: Examples of biometric systems.

The use of these systems can be very convenient. One company (www.
cognitec-systems.de) showed me a screen saver that locks the screen
automatically after a set time of inactivity. To unlock the screen, the right
person either sits down and briefly looks into the camera or enters a password. This is a huge step forward against 'sloppy daily routines' at work!
In addition, this system cannot be fooled by showing it a photo, because it
detects changes in the perspective and shadows that always occur in the real
world. The two error values FAR and FRR (see below) can achieve about
1 % with this system.

Nevertheless, this screen saver was not well accepted. A decent technical
concept alone does not convince users; there has to also be a demand for
using it (this is why the company prefers to use their *FaceVACS* system in
airports). Problems in facial recognition are the high demand in computational
performance, aging, and lighting conditions (outdoor recognition can reach
error rates of up to 50 %).

- **Iris scan:** The pattern of the iris, just as unique as a fingerprint, is captured
  by a camera. Problems can arise from its uncomfortable use, in its present
  form, and due to eye or eyelid injuries, cataracts, eyeglasses, and contact
  lenses. Iris scanning is not cheap. This alone seems to be barring it from
  wide use despite its excellent FAR and FRR values.

- **Retinal scan:** This system scans the retina via infrared. The same problems as
  with iris scan systems can arise here, too, and the wait times are considerable
  (I know of systems with roughly a 1-minute wait time).

- **Signature recognition:** This system electronically detects a signature. You
  probably know of a simple system: the one used by UPS where you have to
  use a special pen to sign for receipt in a small screen.

  A much more sophisticated system appears to be **Smartpen** (www.
  smartpen.net). It lets you use a special pen to write on a regular sheet
  of paper on a regular base. Sensors in the pen acquire all sorts of writing
  characteristics, such as trait, dynamics, pressure, and pausing as well as the
  angle of tilt. Signature forgers would get nowhere with data acquired like this.

  Such pens would be ideally suited for ATMs if it weren't for the problem
  that they can be easily stolen, which is certainly significant considering their
  rather high price. A less elegant but cheaper system is offered by **Softpro**
  (www.softpro.de), for example, where a simple graphics tablet serves as
  the writing base.

Figure 6.11: (*continued*)

Nevertheless, signature recognition has considerable problems. First, the reject rate (FRR) is high if the system is to be moderately secure. You will have noticed that your handwriting changes, for example, after physical efforts or under stress. Another problem is that though you obtain a huge amount of data from a Smartpen, you have to know how to evaluate them: there is an obvious lack of theory. On the other hand, due to data privacy in some countries, including Germany, it is not possible to use arbitrary words instead of signatures since graphologists can learn pretty much about a personality from the handwriting.

- **Hand geometry:** This is a relatively old method. The geometry of hands differs individually. There are forging possibilities similar to fingerprints (but the hand geometry is easier to 'steal'), and I can imagine that swollen hands cause problems. Nevertheless, the method is the second most frequently used system after fingerprint recognition, particularly for admission control, e.g., in nuclear power stations, or in the students' dining hall at Georgia University, to reduce counterfeiting.

- **Vein patterns:** Similarly to retinal scan systems, these systems acquire the extremely individual arrangement of veins in a hand. The method appears to be robust and pretty secure against forgery, but it is not widely used yet.

- **Combined methods:** At the CeBIT 1998 trade fair, a system by the name of **BioID** (www.bioid.com) was introduced, which acquires facial traits, voice, and lip dynamics concurrently. It was remarkably insensitive to eyeglasses, beards, heavy tongues, and new face wrinkles. While achieving a good FAR with this system, however, you have to put up with a very high FRR. The system has meanwhile disappeared.

- **Methods of the future:** In addition to ongoing research in voice recognition, which is currently still unreliable (at least for civilian uses), intensive research work has been put into acquiring other individual characteristics. A particularly original system was introduced in the *New Scientist* dated December 12, 1999: every human has a different **gait**. This research work was motivated by the desire to identify masked bank robbers on video clips. Also, shoplifters pretending to be pregnant while smuggling stolen merchandise out of stores could be identified by their gait (genuinely pregnant women walk differently). These are promising prospects. However, I could also imagine that there is a potential for surveillance of people from considerable distances, and I'm afraid this won't remain utopia. More about this in Chapter 8.

Figure 6.11: (*continued*)

Another individual human characteristic is the dynamics of **keystrokes**. The major advantage of this method is that it can continually check whether or not the 'right' person is still working at a computer. The major downside is that the error rates are high. A practical use for this method comes from an entirely different angle: one can derive typed passwords from the keystroke echo—it works in practice. I don't know whether it would work for mouse movements, though, considering our keyboard-hostile world.

Figure 6.11: (*continued*)

Unfortunately, biometric authentication systems have a few problems. Schneier lists three critical points in his online magazine *Cryptogram*.

1. Biometrics are unique identifiers, but they are not secrets. You leave your fingerprints on everything you touch, and your iris patterns can be observed anywhere you look.

2. Biometrics also don't handle failure well. Imagine that Alice is using her thumbprint as a biometric, and someone steals the digital file. Now what? This isn't a digital certificate, where some trusted third party can issue her another one. This is her thumb. She has only two. Once someone steals your biometric, it remains stolen for life; there's no getting back to a secure situation.

3. And biometrics are necessarily common across different functions. Just as you should never use the same password on two different systems, the same encryption key should not be used for two different applications. If my fingerprint is used to start my car, unlock my medical records, and read my electronic mail, then it's not hard to imagine some very insecure situations arising.

These points are not arguments against biometrics in my opinion. There's a solution to every problem.

- First, at least the manufacturers I spoke with know very well that biometrics is not based on secrets. The security concept has to consider this fact. To use a specific example: suppose the BioID system (the one that concurrently recognizes face, voice, and lip dynamics) serves for admission control. In this case, it is hardly possible to feed the computer with stolen data, for you will never get to it.

- Biometrics can be combined with other controls, e.g., with owning a smartcard and knowing a PIN. In such a system, biometrics would strongly reduce the probability that somebody can sneak in with a stolen smartcard or PIN. In this landscape, biometrics makes classic authentication more secure. If it is used for authentication, it must not be the only measure. A computer that let's you log in via fingerprint only uses the wrong concept. There should always be another (more cumbersome) authentication control.

- This knocked off the second point. The thing is, if Alice's digital thumbprint file was stolen (which hopefully doesn't happen too often), the fingerprint recognition system could have been combined with a PIN and/or another method. The proper concept guarantees, here too, that critical cases can be handled.

In contrast, there are two critical parameters in every biometric system: the **false accept rate** (**FAR**) and the **false reject rate** (**FRR**). The FAR is the percentage of unauthorized people passing the control, while the FRR is the percentage of authorized people who were erroneously rejected by the device.

In the ideal case, both FAR and FRR would both be zero. Unfortunately, the real world is not ideal; only 1 % for either value are considered excellent. This number doesn't appear high, but imagine an organization with 1000 employees, where ten employees stand protesting behind the factory gate yelling for the security inspector day in day out, while industrial spies hired by the competitor are admitted.

Biometric systems (or better, their recognition software) can be tuned. Depending on the purpose, you select either a lower FAR or a lower FRR; keeping both values very small doesn't normally work. In high-security tracts, one has to put up with wrongly rejected employees more often than not (low FAR, higher FRR), while at the main entry there should only be a pre-selection with low FRR (and higher FAR). The overall concept will decide here, too.

I think the most promising is the concept of **variable biometrics**. By my definition, these are biometric characteristics that users can change themselves. The two outstanding examples in Figure 6.11 are the BioID system, where the user can say a spoken word (or an entire sentence) himself, and the analysis of handwriting dynamics. (Unfortunately, two points work against practice: first, BioID does not exist anymore; the reject ratio was too high. And in the second case, the system checks only for signatures due to data privacy and acceptance reasons.) Variability would actually be important: imagine that Bob gets hired by the competitor and logs himself in with the same word he used at the BioID system. His old company would be very tempted to gain access using his known BioID record. But certainly the old company is unable to calculate a record for newly spoken words from the old one.

Also, when using Smartpen, a user can choose *what* he writes on paper. Mnemonically advantageous would be something related to the purpose of authenticating: for example, the name of your bank, followed by the last three digits of your account number.

I see the future of biometrics in variable characteristics, or at least combined methods, and *not* in either fingerprint, gait, or facial geometry alone. Such data should not be used exclusively, and the concept should consider that a fingertip can be cut, or a face can change due to many things, such as a swollen eye.

Biometrics can doubtlessly make our lives somewhat simpler and more secure at the same time, provided it is applied properly.

If you are interested in learning more about this topic, I recommend the fascinating book [WoodBiom].

6.7 Trojan Cryptography

In this section, you will be presented with a new trend in cryptographic development that might represent a great risk for users of encryption systems, but which has earned little notice in practice, as things typically are with cryptology. I felt this personally: 'positive' articles in magazines like [Wobsymm] received a vivid echo, while nobody responded to [Wobtroja].

What is Trojan cryptography about? First of all, you won't find this term in the literature. *It is a name I use for cryptographic software or hardware that has a backdoor built in knowingly and without the users being aware of it.* (More specifically, Trojan cryptography denotes the algorithms and/or protocols such software or hardware uses.) The analogy with the Trojan horses used by hackers is obvious: Trojan horses are apparently harmless programs but undermine the user's security with fraudulent intention. The same purpose is pursued with Trojan cryptography. Presumably the first scientific study of such methods is relatively recent. The authors are Adam Young and Moti Yung who presented their results at the CRYPTO '96 and EUROCRYPT '97 conferences.

Strictly speaking, weak cryptography also belongs to this field. For example, I encrypted a Microsoft Word document with the primitive password 'AAA' and studied it under UNIX. I was shocked to find that the text was still easy to recognize (in hexdump, for example). The 'encryption' changed only a few bytes in the preliminaries, which leads the mouse-bound user to believe that the text wouldn't be readable without a password. I may have caught an 'unfavorable' case, for according to [SchwartzOLE], a particularly easy to crack variant of the Vigenère cipher was used; there are plenty of crack programs out there. Is this irresponsible marketing or fraud? The miserable encryption in WordPerfect does little better: it seems to be solely based on lack of knowledge.

Dubious Features in SESAME

A good example of doubtful cryptography is **SESAME**, an extended European variant of Kerberos. As we know, the Kerberos protocol protects a local computer network by encrypting the entire data traffic. The entire security relies on one or two particularly protected computers. The European SESAME project (the source text is on the Web site) came about within the RACE Initiative and is intended to represent a more flexible further development of that initiative.

However, a posting by Michael Roe in the *sci.crypt* newsgroup dated August 1, 1996, shows that SESAME is a truly 'open' system: whoever knows the internals can eavesdrop almost effortlessly. The cipher used is a 64-bit Vigenère method, which can be cracked in a fraction of a second, rather than the still relatively secure DES. To make matters worse, the method is used in CBC mode so that only every other block is encrypted. This naïve cipher hides behind misleading names like *xor_des_loop, des_encrypt_func*, and so on. The reason might be that they'd initially planned to use DES but changed the code again when the French protested. Schneier [SchnCr, 24.7] describes more weaknesses in this project.

Somebody who simply wanted to replace this XOR cipher by DES would nurture false security: line 339 of the code in *src/lib/csf/csf_encr.c* tests whether or not the method used is self-inverse, i.e., whether it supplies plaintext upon repeated use. XOR has this property, DES doesn't (like many other methods). If the test fails, the program does no encryption at all. The user, thinking he is particularly secure, is cheated in a particularly mean way. After all, who checks whether or not the data traffic in a LAN is encrypted?

Though the test can be bypassed, utmost mistrust is recommended. Why was such a test embedded in the first place without giving any warning? How many more backdoors might there be in SESAME?

This discovery is shocking in view of the project's significance. I wouldn't be surprised to hear one day that the designers caused the software's strange behavior for lack of qualification.

Sending Passwords, and a Shocking Story

The examples given above are not exhaustive and basically nothing new for cryptologists, and such a product is called *snake oil*. A 'more innovative' software or hardware product would mix the password into the ciphertext in some way or other. There are no limits to imagination. The bits can be hidden in the header, or you somewhat 'extend' the ciphertext. Or you compress the ciphertext to make plenty of room for sending the password along. In addition, the vendor could encrypt the password together with a known sequential number (using a fixed key) and mix the ciphertext created into the output. This makes it extremely difficult for others to detect the fraud. Large-scale surveillance of encrypted data communication would be easy in any event.

This fraud—you can't use a more harmless name—would probably not be detected. Ask around how many users know about the ciphering in Microsoft Word mentioned above. And yet, its 'quality' is easy to check. How much harder would it be in the current example where fraud can hardly be proven by analyzing the ciphertext alone!

However, the method has a disadvantage for the vendor: if a hacker eventually succeeds in discovering this hide-and-seek game, fraud can no longer be denied. Woe betide the vendor who is not the market leader!

There is a practical example for such an approach. During the preparation of the second edition, I came across the text you will find in *txt/policy/madsen.txt* on our Web site. The author thinks this might be the biggest secret-service scandal of the past century—but as often happens nowadays, most material about it is found on the Internet.

In March 1992, the Iranian military counterespionage arrested Hans Bühler, an honorable salesman of the Swiss firm Crypto AG, a leading supplier of ciphering devices, accused of spying for Germany and the USA. Bühler was interrogated for five hours daily for nine months, but he knew nothing about backdoors allegedly built into the devices. Eventually, Crypto AG paid one

million dollars to bail him out. To everybody's surprise, he was fired after
he got back home and was requested to pay back the ransom. Obviously,
former and current employees got cold feet and told reporters that the allegation
against the firm might not have been totally unjustified after all. They hinted
that members of the NSA and the BND had designed and obviously 'reworked'
these machines 15 years earlier. Investigations in Switzerland yielded no results.
When the Swiss media brought the matter up despite Crypto AG suing against
it, the parties agreed on an out-of-court settlement just a couple of days before
witnesses were to be heard.

Crypto's reputation was largely damaged, of course. When rumors had it that
Crypto AG was an affiliate of Siemens AG, and that the ransom for Bühler
was said to have come from Siemens, Siemens were also pulled into the affair.
The impact was devastating. These ciphering machines had been used in the
diplomatic community in about 120 countries. Had the NSA eavesdropped on
everything? Restlessness spread everywhere, from Saddam Hussein to the Pope.
A spokesman of the Vatican even called the brains behind the affair 'bandits'.
Libya switched to products of the Swiss firm Greta Data Systems AG. They
were believed to also have been approached by the NSA...

Anyway, this is how the NSA obtained (presumably via Israel) background
information on the aircraft bombing over Lockerbie, Scotland, as well as papal
secret messages, and Irish diplomatic messages during the British–Irish negotiations in 1985 (in this case via the British GCHQ). But read the story; it is
as thrilling as only the real world can be.

I'm not telling you fairytales—an acquaintance of mine spoke with a former
employee of Crypto AG about the matter and heard more or less the same story
as reported. I know from that same source that keys had actually been hidden
in headers.

The consequences and implications caused by an encrypted key secretly infil-
trated can hardly be illustrated more dramatically! By the way, I find it rather
worrying that this Trojan cryptography was revealed by employees of Crypto
AG themselves only after a very long time, and not by analyzing the machines
sold. How hard must it be then to reveal the methods described in the following?

A Refinement By Means of Asymmetric Encryption

The method described here has another drawback theoretically, namely for
the intelligence agency that had this cute feature built in by the manufacturer. If the manufacturer encrypts the user password, then the key has to be

contained in the software/hardware, which means that it is basically accessible. The hacker mentioned above could sit in another country and work for that country's national intelligence agency. He would be listening in on everything and nobody would know!

The manufacturer would appropriately use an asymmetric method to hide his malicious intentions, and encrypt the user password with his own public key. That would add yet another eavesdropping party—the manufacturer himself. If hybrid methods were used, one could additionally send along the user's private key rather than the session key every time, for example, piece by piece together with the position in the key.

This is an extraordinarily enticing method! It mightn't be used yet; the more important it is to know it now. It is similar to steganography, discussed in Section 1.3, in some respect; it is *steganography versus cryptography*, so to speak. But the implementation is simpler in the case discussed here: while the steganographer has to mix in complete ciphertexts, we could do it with a 128-bit key, for example.

There are countermeasures, as the term 'steganography' suggests: you have to take capacity in the data stream away from the manufacturer, preventing him from stealthily sending a key along. What it takes are cleanly defined network protocols, fully described headers, disclosed algorithms, access to the user's session key (unless it is predefined), and finally a defined padding in block algorithms (see Section 5.1.2).

Of course, as a practitioner you know that things will never get to this point; such requirements remain pious hopes. The best countermeasure I can think of might be an external crypto-interface that would allow the user to procure the entire ciphering and key management from a different manufacturer, or perhaps program it himself. But even this proposal might hit resistance. The concept is possible for software (though not in all cases). For hardware in general and chip cards in particular, however, this separation might not be possible. The Crypto AG story above shows how sad the real world can be.

The Perfect Fraud: Cleptography

Not meaning to be entirely serious, Young and Yung [Young] used this name for a further perfection of the method described here. Nothing is hidden by steganographic methods any more; *cryptography versus cryptography* is used instead.

Cleptographic software or hardware uses asymmetric methods. By cleverly choosing free parameters—during random generation, for example, in

RSA—the manufacturer can hide parts of the private user key in his public key such that it cannot be proven by analyzing the public key. From the outside, the software or hardware cannot be distinguished from a correctly working one. The authors call them a bit clumsily **SETUP (Secretly Embedded Trapdoor with Universal Protection)** systems.

Young and Yung define three types of SETUP systems: *weak, regular*, and *strong*. I briefly mentioned an example of a *weak SETUP system* in the last example above: though the system apparently works all right, the fraud can be detected by analyzing the outputs, but it cannot be used by third parties (since they don't know the manufacturer's private key). Conversely, *regular SETUP systems* don't manifest whether or not a fraud is built in, even after thorough ciphertext analysis.

It might be desirable to have a SETUP system make use of its secret capabilities only sometimes, for example, to make it harder to prove the fraud. We speak of a *strong SETUP system* when 'honest' and 'dishonest' outputs cannot be distinguished either in the future or in the past.

The authors implemented SETUP systems for a large number of algorithms and protocols (RSA, ElGamal, DSA, Kerberos) and demonstrated their practical use: computation times were only slightly longer, the costs remained within a reasonable range.

The fact that the specific implementation is rather complicated doesn't matter, for once it is programmed, the attack works automatically, enabling extensive automated eavesdropping activities.

Potential Impact

SETUP systems enable particularly clever data espionage. I hope they are not in use yet: the more reason to think about the potential impact such systems as well as the countermeasures may have.

First of all, a hairsplitting thought about the impact: the signature law of 1997 discussed in Section 8.2.5 said that the private keys created for users must not be stored in a trust center. An embedded SETUP trap would bypass this law by nature (which is not in the law's sense, of course). The thing is that, especially with RSA key generation, the two secret prime numbers required, p and q, can be chosen such that they allow the manufacturer to easily compute them from the public key created (more specifically, from the pq product). Naturally, trust centers have to meet particularly strict requirements. But the centers and the software they use can be audited for cleptographic attacks only provided one knows of the existence of such attacks in the first place.

Furthermore, nobody can discount the fact that there is a potential for unnoticed modification of trust-center software. The sheer mention of such an attack might fill some people in charge with outrage. However, they had better consider that the stealthy conversion of public-authority software in SETUP software is extremely attractive, for example, for national intelligence organizations of all flavors. Such a 'transformation' would doubtlessly be executed with utmost criminal energy, for the reward is unusually high against relatively little cost and minimal risk.

We should pay attention to the fact that keys created by trust centers are used for signing and never ever for ciphering!

I can think of yet another use for SETUP systems: they could serve for elegant key escrow (more about it in Section 8.2.3). In this case, the government, or the firm itself, would be the official owner of the 'universal key for all universal keys'. While this might be of theoretical interest, the formulation alone points to the risk: all, but really all, security depends on one single universal key. Once this key is compromised (i.e., known to unauthorized parties), changing it will be of little use. All messages of all users intercepted by eavesdroppers up to this point can be decrypted, and nobody can prevent it. This is one of the very big risks in cryptography; it is where it differs from the other system-security terrain.

Some Ideas About Countermeasures

How can SETUP systems be prevented or, at least, how can their use be made more difficult? Considering that the research work of Young and Yung stands more or less alone in the world, there are only a few ideas about possible countermeasures.

- An idea more inclined to the safe side uses freely available *and* popular cryptographic software. I can think of PGP 2.6, which will be discussed in detail in Section 7.1, or SSH, or mainly OpenSSL. For the sake of security, if you opt for this approach, you'd better check the checksum shipped with the product (it's the only thing that proves that you got the 'real software', unless it's an MD5 sum...).

  For example, the PGP source code was studied by so many programmers on the Internet that Trojan cryptography would have been discovered long ago. However, it is not always possible to use free software, so that it's no remedy for all cases.

- Where asymmetric methods can't help, one might try to use symmetric methods and distribute the key as described in Section 6.2.1.

- Cryptographic software should be able to combine modules of several—ideally competing—vendors. In particular, random generation should be detached from the program or hardware, because SETUP systems always use 'disturbed randomness'. However, the user should be able to see how randomness is processed. All this is possible only if all internal interfaces are completely disclosed. The more a manufacturer remains silent about his product's innards, the more mistrustful we should be about it. I know perfectly well that this requirement is rather utopian.

- The risk of Trojan cryptography is higher in cryptographic hardware by definition. You would best create private and public keys outside the device using publicly checked software (PGP might serve the purpose) and test for correct processing of the keys in the device based on its outputs. This might be sufficient when using the RSA method. Suitable industry standards can be helpful during the test.

- And finally, an interesting and doable countermeasure is the cascading of several devices from different manufacturers, similar to the software modularity mentioned above. Drawbacks are higher costs and perhaps lower performance.

Like I said earlier, these are just ideas about countermeasures. I hope that more solutions will be published in the years to come, and I mainly hope that this potentially very serious threat will be perceived on a broad level.

Chapter 7

Practical Applications

So far in this book, we have learned a number of algorithms and discussed problems in their implementation. In the previous chapter, we looked at cryptographic protocols as a theoretical basis of their application, so to speak. In this chapter, we will go a step forward, discussing the actual use, in this case, of cryptographic programs. As before, we are interested mainly in understanding the background rather than trying to achieve completeness. This is why we will be dealing with only a few free programs in this chapter. The source texts of all of these programs can be found on the Internet and on our web site.

Also, you shouldn't expect operating instructions for these programs in the following. There is plenty of documentation out there, and piles of books, especially on PGP (I recommend [GarPGP]). What these books and documents don't discuss extensively, though, are cryptological implementation details. This is what you will find in this chapter. For this reason, it doesn't really matter that some of the programs, or the protocols used, discussed in this chapter are outdated. The important thing is to understand the principles.

7.1 PGP—A King Among Cryptographic Programs

You've probably heard of the free program PGP (Pretty Good Privacy). I don't know of any other software that has stirred up so much dust, and that has apparently been a thorn in the flesh of so many national intelligence agencies.

Cryptology Unlocked Reinhard Wobst
© 2007 John Wiley & Sons, Ltd

Why? It took the crypto-monopoly they believed to have owned away from them. I will first discuss the 'classic' PGP 2.6 in the following sections, and start dealing with OpenPGP, the currently popular standard, in Section 7.1.4.

7.1.1   Phil Zimmermann, the NSA, and US Laws

The motivation for PGP was the insight that though email is very convenient, it is also very insecure. Most users cannot imagine that the security of email messages corresponds to that of postcards at most. I'd even claim it's less. Anyone, like nosy mail sorters or postmen, who can touch the postcard can read what's on the back, which is not too scary since they all are honest people, or mostly. In contrast, nobody can say what paths email messages may take on the Internet. Your mail may be transported across countries with lots of bribable system administrators—perhaps paid by their secret service—who knows?

I think you know the problem, so I don't have to make an effort to convince you. You also know that there is only one way to secure information in insecure networks: by encrypting it.

That's exactly what Phil Zimmermann, a computer engineer from Boulder, Colorado, thought, too. Not all business people are conservative. Phil Zimmermann had even done time for activities against the nuclear race in the early 1980s. These sorts of practical experiences may have aroused a certain dislike of overly mighty governments. At the same time, he very well saw the large number of surveillance possibilities that the quickly evolving Internet brought along. As an enthusiast cryptologist, he felt a need to counter 'Big Brother'.

Zimmermann thought of a cryptographically secure program that should allow *everybody* to send encrypted emails. The name PGP for 'Pretty Good Privacy' was probably intentional—it was a matter of protecting people's privacy against the government.

PGP Was Born

Zimmermann put enormous effort into the development of PGP for about ten years and almost ruined himself financially. In addition to his intensive dealing with cryptology and the development of PGP, he was confronted with the law rather unexpectedly. And what's more, at a time when he thought he was ready to make some money from PGP.

First of all, there were patent-law problems. He didn't get a free license for the RSA method. This meant that he couldn't sell PGP, and he couldn't distribute it as shareware either (money can be made with shareware in the USA). Furthermore, a law passed in 1991 bound all vendors of communication devices and services to supply the plaintext of data streams flowing though their devices and networks to governmental agencies upon request. That went far beyond the then current export regulations. It also limited potentially good cryptography dramatically within the USA.

Zimmermann panicked. He had just replaced DES as the symmetric method used (and which he didn't trust any more) by his own algorithm, called *Bass-O-Matic*. Though this algorithm hadn't been studied thoroughly yet, he quickly put together PGP Release 1.0 and gave it to a friend. This friend publicized it in the Usenet, which meant the Internet. No matter what else was bound to happen, PGP was no longer to be stopped. In 1992, Release 2.0 was published. It was developed with contributions from all over the world, and implemented the secure IDEA algorithm instead of *Bass-O-Matic*.

Now Zimmermann had not only patent-law problems on his back, but he was accused of having violated the strict export regulations, which means that, in addition to RSADSI, he now also had the FBI, the NSA, and other agencies turned against him. However, it is unknown who actually put PGP on the Internet.

Patent Problems

The patent issue had eventually been clarified. From 1993 onwards, Zimmermann had cooperated with *ViaCrypt*, a company that owned a legal RSA license. This is why the commercial PGP version was sold by *ViaCrypt* in the USA. On the other hand, he got unexpected assistance from the MIT, where RSA was originally developed. The MIT had created a software library called RSAREF, which could be used freely for non-commercial purposes. This is how PGP Version 2.5 came about in 1994. It was the first legally sold version. Though it still allegedly violated the PKP patents (see Section 4.5.3), the conflict ended in a tradeoff: Zimmermann implemented a cosmetic change that made the new Release 2.6 incompatible with all former illegal versions. The patent custodians could then prosecute only users of PGP Release 2.5 and lower, while the whole world used PGP 2.6.

The Security of the USA at Stake!

As it happened, the violation of export regulations turned out to be much more serious, for it served to 'preserve the national security'. US Customs started a criminal investigation on Zimmermann for allegedly violating the Arms Export Control Act. People all over the world started donating for Phil to finance his law suit. The publicity of the case led to enormous pressure on the government. If it weren't for PGP, the discussion around the Clipper chip (see Section 6.4) would probably have taken a different turn. Phil Zimmermann became a celebrity.

The investigation lasted three years, but the government dropped its case without indictment on January 11, 1996. However, the laws that had caused all this stir had still not been entirely done away with.

PGP had changed the world. For the first time, everybody had a tool to protect their information effectively against third-party access. Phil Zimmermann received loads of messages from enthusiastic users all over the world, including countries like Latvia and even underground movements. Governmental reactions, not only in the USA, hint that PGP seemed to also have stopped intelligence activities. At least this would explain why the MIT was *not* sued for violation of the export regulations, in contrast to Phil Zimmermann, although they had the cryptologically high-quality RSAREF software on an ftp server available for the whole world to download. However, this comparison made by Garfinkel in [GarPGP] is a bit lame, because RSAREF did not directly serve for the encryption of messages. By the letter of the law, however, exporting RSAREF from the USA was also illegal.

Certainly, many influential people had been stirred, because the worldwide proliferation of PGP could no longer be stopped, no matter what law.

We have anticipated a little of the topics we will discuss in Chapter 8. But it is impossible to talk about PGP without mentioning its political impact. If you are interested in more details about this adventurous story, I recommend you to read [GarPGP].

7.1.2   What PGP Can Do

It can be frequently read or heard that PGP uses asymmetric methods to send encrypted mails (meaning that the symmetric methods were 'out'), and that everybody can use it for free.

That's simply nonsense! Firstly, PGP is not a mail program. It processes files that a mailer can send, or has received. Secondly, PGP is certainly not 'RSA-encrypted'; it uses hybrid methods: it encrypts a session key using RSA, and the mail file itself using IDEA.

And thirdly, which is often overlooked, PGP is released only for private use due to the IDEA patent. We discussed this extensively in Section 5.3.1.

Even if all of this is not breaking news to you, help rebut such misleading allegations, because they can be damaging (partly also for OpenPGP). So, what does PGP really do? It offers all functions required for you to cryptologically secure your email traffic.

- PGP creates pairs of private and public keys for the RSA method.

- PGP creates random session keys, uses them to encrypt files by the IDEA method, and adds the session key encrypted with the receiver's public key.

- Upon request, the program also creates ASCII text to prevent the mailer from having problems, and converts the text formats of different operating systems (UNIX, Mac, DOS/Windows) into a uniform intermediate format, and vice versa.

- PGP makes incoming encrypted mail readable again: it removes the session key, decrypts it using your private key, and opens the file you received.

- You can use PGP to digitally sign a file and check signatures. PGP offers all functions required for key management:

  - It keeps the public and private keys separate, where the private keys can be kept in encrypted form, of course.

  - You can use PGP to sign third-party public keys, add them to existing keys, or delete or revoke keys.

  - You can use PGP to check the trustworthiness of a public key.

- And finally, PGP can encrypt and decrypt regular files.

That's a whole lot of functions. Nevertheless, PGP has 'only' 30 000 lines of code. The complexity of a program does not always have to show in its length.

The Web of Trust

The interesting and typical part of PGP is how public keys are managed. If no super algorithm is found for factoring large numbers (or quantum computers become reality one day; see Section 5.9), preventing man-in-the-middle attacks is probably the only security problem in the RSA method (see Section 4.5.3). It is a matter of proving that Bob's public key is really Bob's and not Mallory's.

Using a hierarchy of certified key servers like in PEM/SMIME (see Section 7.2), where every user can fetch public keys, would have contradicted Zimmermann's philosophy. His intention was to protect PGP from excessive governmental access. So the entire security of the system was not to be concentrated in a few points that could be audited by the authorities only.

Instead, Zimmermann invented the **Web of Trust**: every PGP user checks the keys of other trustworthy users. The principle is relatively simple:

Alice creates a public key and has it digitally signed by friends and acquaintances. Together with these 'credentials', she passes it on. Now, when she adds Bob's public key to her collection, her PGP will ask the following question: *do you accept a certification of third-party public keys by Bob's signature?* Alice can answer in either of the following ways:

1. Yes, always.

2. Sometimes.

3. No.

4. I don't know.

If Alice receives a third-party public key that was signed by one level-1 signature or two level-2 signatures, PGP will add it automatically as a trustworthy key. Of course, she could also use non-certified keys, but PGP would warn her. She could also change the levels of participants in either direction.

Alice can also check a public key directly. To this end, she creates a **fingerprint** of the public key received in PGP. This is the MD5 hash sum of the key, written as a readable sequence of 16 hexadecimal numbers, for example:

```
24 38 1A 58 46 AD CC 2D AB C9 E0 F1 C7 3C 67 EC
```

(This example represents the electronic fingerprint of Phil Zimmermann.) Alice calls the key's owner, Carol, and has her read the fingerprint she computed. If things match, there is no doubt—assuming that MD5 is secure: unfortunately, we saw in Section 6.3.1 that one can actually construct public-key pairs with identical MD5 hash sums (though these are not yet keys from prime-factor products with an equal number of digits; the construction may only be a matter of time, provided one would still be interested in it). This problem was done away with in OpenPGP: from Version 4 (1998) onwards, it computes SHA-1 fingerprints.

It's always a good idea to accommodate the fingerprint on calling cards or publish it in another print form, because it virtually excludes man-in-the-middle attacks.

Eventually, this is how a web of trustworthy partners is built. Sooner or later, all PGP users will be interconnected by at least one 'path of trust'. A test showed that the longest of these paths was only 14 steps long, considering that there are hundreds of thousands of users!

The theoretical strength of this concept reflects Zimmermann's intentions: it is virtually impossible for 'Big Brother' to destroy this web, as it is impossible to totally control the Internet, because the links are established and torn down locally and dynamically.

At the same time, this structure causes a major vulnerability: keys cannot be securely revoked. If a private key is stolen, then the web's landscape is disturbed, and even uninvolved users can be compromised. However, the vulnerability cannot be exploited to attack the entire Web of Trust itself.

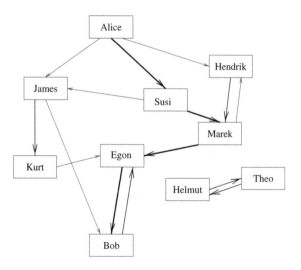

Figure 7.1: The 'Web of Trust' of PGP. Thick arrows show full trust, whereas thin arrows denote restricted trust.

Meanwhile there is a large number of **key servers**, i.e., computers that mutually certify themselves. They are used to deposit people's public keys in a more or less tamperproof way (for example, `www.de.pgp.net/pgp`, `www.keyserver.net`). The only drawback of this large number of servers is a potential for denial-of-service attacks. But you can deposit your key, against a fee, on a 'public' server less exposed to these risks.

That much about the theory. You will read in Section 7.2.3 what things with the Web of Trust look like in the real world.

Portability

One of the important and nice traits of PGP is its portability between various operating systems. It runs on all UNIX variants as well as DOS, OS/2, Windows, and on Macintosh, Amiga, Archimedes, and Atari computers, and even on VMS. Encrypted messages can be exchanged among all these systems. Ascom Systec AG, the owner of the IDEA license, even offered a commercial mail system (Ascom Mail), which understands and creates the PGP format. I find this approach remarkable: rather than bulkhead themselves from the free software domain with commercial products, they coexist. This will certainly not reduce the sale of Ascom Mail, because commercial systems also have benefits.

In any event, this covers the domain of privately used computers. This portability is important, because email generally connects all kinds of different systems, which is often forgotten. Only when PGP can be used by most users all over the world will it stand a chance to become a standard. The price to be paid for this is that PGP cannot be operated with the favorite mouse—it is command-line controlled. Though this is simpler and faster in many cases, it's mega-out. Users who don't want to work without graphics will find a sufficiently large number of graphical user interfaces and mailers that can be installed on top of PGP. More about this topic in Section 7.2.3.

Let's not dwell on the operation and functionality of PGP. You can read all about it in the literature or the product documentation as well as on the Web site.

7.1.3 How PGP Works

We will be looking at cryptologically interesting details of the PGP implementation in the following, and dealing with this product much more than with any other program. In view of its wide proliferation, quality, and functionality, PGP deserves this in every respect. I'm not looking for completeness, and it wouldn't be possible even if I wanted it. All information discussed here refers to PGP 2.6.3.

Algorithms

PGP uses three cryptographic algorithms:

- IDEA for symmetric encryption of messages and files.
- MD5 for the creation of digital signatures and initialization vectors, for computation of passwords from passphrases and fingerprints from public keys, and for internal random generation.
- RSA for the encryption of session keys, and for the creation and verification of digital signatures.

Passphrases

PGP uses passphrases with a maximum length of 253 characters rather than short passwords. You will recall that we talked about passphrases in Section 5.1.4. They are much more secure than passwords, and easier to remember. PGP takes a passphrase and uses the MD5 one-way hash function to create a 128-bit value that is then used as an IDEA key.

Normally, the passphrase is not displayed as you type it. But you can set the keyboard echo in the configuration file to enable it if you want to see what you type. Of course, this is a security risk. The scrolling window I suggested in Section 5.1.4 might be a suitable solution.

Moreover, you can accommodate your passphrase in the PGPPASS environment variable. That's very risky. Under UNIX, for example, it can be read by the *ps* command with suitable options (normally $-f$). However, *ps* shows only the beginning of the command line; more information can be recovered only by the superuser. If you are the only user of your computer, you can write pretty comfortable scripts using PGPPASS.

Phil Zimmermann implemented this option at the request of many users. He warns against using PGPPASS with a script, though. You should assign a value to the variable only via keyboard entry.

General Security

The entire security of PGP relies on one single passphrase. It is used to encrypt the private key, and this key, in turn, serves to verify all signatures and compute session keys of incoming encrypted messages. Finally, the signatures are eventually used to secure the integrity of files using public keys.

Since the use of PGP on multiuser systems is a somewhat insecure matter in any event (UNIX at least allows the superuser to theoretically always read the data from a running process), all sensitive data are overwritten by the *burn()* function immediately upon their use.

In the product documentation, Zimmermann points to the fact that all systems with virtual memories (basically all real multitasking systems and Windows) can swap sensitive unencrypted data to the disk. Once the program is exited or aborted, the private key might be found in the swap area in unencrypted form. This problem can be solved by a better security concept of the operating system, or by disabling or encrypting the swap. There is a number of security concepts available in UNIX, where the superuser is not almighty (SELinux is probably the best-known example). This is the only reliable way, because a malicious or sly administrator can run a daemon that automatically analyzes the PGP sessions of users. If you count on all superusers being malicious, then what you can do is to find out whether or not they are logged in during your PGP session (mind you, that's not easy, and it's not part of the topics of this book). A 100 % security can never be achieved, if only by the fact that analyzing the swap area can hardly be prevented. But a 95 % security is better than a 30 % security.

Generating Randomness

PGP puts a lot of effort into secure random generation when looking for large prime numbers. It uses a pretty reliable method: the user has to continue doing wild keystrokes until the program tells him it's enough. It then uses the time intervals between the keystrokes, together with the computer-internal time and the codes of the keys pressed to generate randomness. This is done by XOR-ing the byte sequence with parts of a 'random buffer', and then 'encrypting' this part with MD5 in CFB mode. PGP already uses random numbers for this last operation. A closer look at the functions *randPoolAddBytes()* and *randPoolStir()* in *randpool.c*, and at the comment at the beginning of *random.c* shows how much effort and care have been put into the program (these parts were presumably implemented by Colin Plumb). That much care is required;

Version 2.6 had an error in the XOR operation mentioned above, which weakened the randomness.

The wild keystrokes mentioned above are needed only once. In all subsequent uses, PGP securely falls back on the 'old randomness'—more about this in the section about the session keys.

Generating Prime Numbers

PGP initially uses these random bits to generate large prime numbers by statistical tests, as usual. The random bits determine the position where searching for prime numbers should begin. However, rather than using the very effective Rabin–Miller method (see Section 4.5.3), it uses simple tests for Fermat's little theorem, i.e., it checks whether or not the tentative prime number, p, in equation $a^{p-1} = 1 \mod p$ holds for a sufficiently large set of numbers, a (*slowtest()* function in *genprime.c*). PGP previously checks for divisibility by all prime numbers smaller than 8192 (2^{13}) (*fastsieve()* function in *genprime.c*), and then runs the Fermat test five times. Outputs in the form of

```
. . . . . . . . . . . . . . . . . . . . . . . . . .++++. . . . . . . . . .+++. . . . . . . . . . .+++++
```

appear during these tests, where each dot denotes a failed attempt in *fastsieve()*, and each + sign denotes a Fermat test passed in *slowtest()*.

Creating RSA Key Pairs

The program takes the two prime numbers, p and q, created above to compute module $n = pq$ and search for an exponent, e, for the public key. This exponent has to have at least 5 bits, i.e., it has to be at least equal to 17, but it may be longer. This means that no attack against RSA with a small exponent can be mounted (in addition, RSA is applied only to random numbers or hash values, respectively).

Generating Session Keys

The session keys and the initialization vector (IV) are generated based on the information in the *random.c* file and ANSI standard X9.17 (see Section 5.1.4), however with some slight modifications. The *randseed.bin* file is used as 'secret corner', where this data is 'washed' before and after each use (see comments on 'prewash' and 'postwash' in *random.c*):

The 'random pool' *randseed.bin* as well as the MD5 hash value from the first two Kbytes of the plaintext, a time marker, and non-initialized data are used to generate a session key. Subsequently, the pool is encrypted once more with the key just used and the IV so that no conclusions can be drawn from the content of *randseed.bin* on the keys and the IV.

The first two Kbytes of the message should actually be held in memory and not be read from the disk. But this way, PGP cannot encrypt data streams (i.e., work as a filter), as is customary in UNIX, for example, helping to save resources. Though PGP works like such a filter when the $-f$ switch is set, in reality the entire input is written to the disk, as in MS-DOS, and then read by PGP. Compared with a real filter, this is much slower, especially with long files, and a serious and unnecessary security risk.

But there is another reason why PGP cannot work like a filter; more about it in a minute.

Compression and Filter Mode

A message is compressed before it is encrypted by default for reasons of higher security and lower phone costs. (You recall from Section 3.6.4 that compression doesn't necessarily introduce more security. But as long as not even a *chosen-plaintext* attack against IDEA is known, we don't have to worry.)

The compression algorithm has to be able to jump back and forth within the input data. This is the second reason why PGP cannot be used as a real filter. Again, this reason is not mandatory. The highly efficient, popular, and free compression program *gzip* (available for many operating systems) can work as a real filter. Sure, PGP will determine whether or not compression is worthwhile, and leave it if it isn't. But it wouldn't be a problem to suppress this test if the user so wishes.

At least for the event that a user disabled compression, PGP should work as a real filter.

IDEA Encryption

PGP uses IDEA in CFB mode (see Section 5.1.1). This means that it can do away with padding, and what's more, it prevents insertion attacks (which are actually prevented by the random IV and the random session keys anyway). As a reminder, this mode basically re-encrypts the last ciphertext block and XORs it with the next plaintext block. This often looks slightly different in practice.

For example, blocks are 8 bytes long in IDEA. What you do is shove the ciphertext bytes into an 8-byte shift register and XOR one byte each with one plaintext byte. The shift register is newly IDEA-encrypted every eight steps.

Nobody prevents you from encrypting the shift register more often, it just takes more computation time. This is exactly what PGP does, only the distances between encryptions can be irregular. This is one of Zimmermann's interesting ideas. You can find details in the comment ahead of the *ideaCfbSync()* function in the *idea.c* file.

The IV is put right in front of the encrypted message, as usual. In addition, the last two bytes of the IV are ahead of the *unencrypted* message, which is then encrypted together with these bytes. This allows you to easily check whether or not the correct key is used during the decryption, as described in Section 5.1.3. The *ideaCfbSync()* function mentioned above seems to be intended for better security. But even without this trick, an attacker would have two bytes of plaintext to go with a ciphertext at most, which won't do him any good.

Traffic Analysis

National intelligence agencies are often not interested in the contents of messages at all, while being very interested in finding *who* sends a message *when* and *to whom*. Regularly recording these data supplies insightful information about a user. You can read how this is done at

```
ftp.cs.colorado.edu:/pub/cs/techreports/schwartz/Email.Study.txt.Z
```

(This article is also included on our Web site: we will discuss this further in Section 8.2.1.)

An encrypted PGP mail includes no information whatsoever about the receiver or the sender. Of course, the mailer attaches such information, but it can be easily forged. Some anonymous remailers let you blur the traces, albeit not secret-service-proof. In contrast, PEM mail (see Section 7.2) contains a rather large heap of information in the clear inside the header.

7.1.4 PGP Versions—OpenPGP and GnuPG

There is no question that PGP has become a standard. Though the design leaves a couple of wishes unfulfilled (see below), it represents a cryptologically clean implementation. That's much harder than designing pushbuttons and shift registers.

Release 2.6.3 even supports 2048-bit keys, thus implementing asymmetric cryptography on the current state-of-the-art. No vulnerability of IDEA is still officially known, and, well, PGP made IDEA popular in the first place.

A large number of key servers all over the world deposit public keys, and the number of users has grown to hundreds of thousands. Many mail programs have PGP interfaces nowadays, and there is a large offer of separate user interfaces for PGP available anyway.

Unfortunately, PGP uses MD5 as a one-way hash function. This is why signatures created in PGP 2.6 are not worth much nowadays. Here is a conceptual weakness of the program: the cryptographic modules are permanently built in and cannot be replaced easily. (But there is a way out of the dilemma; see Section 7.3.)

Other PGP Versions and OpenPGP

Further development of PGP and the emergence of compatible products had been rather confusing for many people. PGP 2.6 was progressive cryptologically, but less as a program:

- The algorithms it uses are 'permanently burnt in'; it doesn't give you a choice.
- Its DOS origin cannot be denied. As mentioned above, it cannot work in a UNIX pipeline, but instead swaps intermediate results to the disk.
- It uses the same key for encrypting and signing. This is an outdated and risky concept.
- The key management is generally in need of improvement.

The further developments it required were introduced mainly by Colin Plumb (cryptography) and Derek Atkins (key management) with the participation of thousands of programmers worldwide. The new release was completely rewritten and named PGP 3.0 in the announcement, but PGP 5.0 upon completion.

As usual, PGP 5.0 was not to be exported from the USA. However, this didn't concern its paper format; the lawmakers had obviously waved it off as of little interest. This is how it happened that the source text of PGP 2.6.2 was printed pro-forma in the appendix of a book, accidentally in an easily machine-readable font and with page numbers within C comment characters:

```
/* 131 */
```

As I wrote this section for the first edition, I received roughly the following message on detours: '...and if you want PGP 3.0—the only place to download it from is currently my desk. There are 2000 sheets of bound paper in the form of four books, which will soon be cut into single sheets and fed into a scanner...'

The 'cutting' part took longer than expected, though. What came out of it wasn't really convincing. There was still only one library for UNIX and no ready-made application, despite disclosure of the source text. PGP 2.6 was no longer supported. That cut off the secure communication of Windows users and owners of older releases using PGP 5. Rumors had it that PGP was no longer secure, and that it contained 'picklock keys'. Yes and no. PGP is still secure, and picklock keys were available only upon 'special request'. The thing is that, meanwhile, a company called NAI had taken over further development of PGP, and Phil Zimmermann had become an advisor to that firm. And commercial users sometimes need key escrow, for example, to monitor corporate communications, or to get hold of sensitive data in case a user lost his key.

Based on the description of PGP 5 the **OpenPGP** standard emerged, which has become the foundation for all PGP products. (However, PGP 5 itself wasn't fully OpenPGP-compatible then.) As a sideline, Phil Zimmermann was no longer with NAI, but supported other firms in implementing the OpenPGP standard.

The release numbers of PGP grew quickly, having meanwhile arrived at 9.5. NAI disclosed the source texts of some older releases. Currently (end of 2006), PGP Corporation develops and sells the software (www.pgp.com). It's best you have a look around on the Net to see where PGP is currently at home.

Since the confusion that PGP 5 created, the number of PGP-encrypted emails has decreased heavily, at least within my personal circle; I've been receiving almost all mails in the clear. Has data security in the private domain fallen out of fashion? More about this in Section 7.2.3.

GnuPG

Amidst this awkward situation, the German programmer Werner Koch began to create free software by the name of **GnuPG** (**GNU Privacy Guard**), which cleanly implements the OpenPGP standard. As happens to all designers in every software project, the product has grown out of its spiritual father's hands. Meanwhile, programmers all over the world had started working on its further development, its test, or its compilation. In fact, the project had become so significant and popular that the German government began to financially sponsor it. Amazing how policies can change over time! Not many years earlier, there had been hefty discussions about banning cryptography, at least with regard to key escrow.

GnuPG was born under Linux, but it also runs on many other UNIX derivatives (though the installation is cumbersome in some cases), and on Windows, of course, but with German documentation (*gpg4win*) only. Visit `www.gpg.org` for more details.

How does GnuPG differ from PGP 2.6 (and partly from its successors)?

- GnuPG is a free software without patent claims so that it can be used by everybody, including commercial use.

- GnuPG implements several algorithms, and the embedding of additional methods is easy. For example, Rijndael had been included in GnuPG immediately after it became the new AES standard.

  GnuPG 2.0 was announced in November 2006 (more about it below); but the current release is still 1.4.5. It supports the asymmetric algorithms ElGamal, RSA since its patent expiry in September 2000 (i.e., from GnuPG Version 1.0.3 and higher), and DSA (for signing). GnuPG knows several hash functions, including MD5, SHA-1, SHA-256, and RIPE-MD160 as well as symmetric algorithms including AES (with 128-bit to 256-bit key lengths), CAST5, Twofish, Blowfish, Triple-DES, and IDEA.

- GnuPG has a strongly improved security concept. For example, it continually collects randomness and uses it when creating session keys. This makes attacks against GnuPG much harder than against PGP 2.6. Also, sensitive memory locations where private keys are located are kept before swapping them to the hard disk (under UNIX for the time being). That removed a critical security flaw in the old PGP.

- The key management was expanded and improved considerably. Different keys are used for encryption and signature. There are keys with a finite lifespan, and keys can be revoked. A 'universal key' can be kept locally on a notebook, and 'work keys' with a finite lifespan can be used for signing and separate use later on in less secure landscapes. Keys can be sent to key servers or fetched from them directly from within GnuPG.

- Similarly to PGP 5.0 and successors, GnuPG can be embedded in mailers and graphic user interfaces. This is important for the program's acceptance. A uniform graphic interface (GPA) has been worked on for several years, but is still unsatisfactory.

However, I constantly quarrel with the program. Its installation and first-time use simply overtax inexperienced users. It certainly overtaxed me when I tried to test GnuPG 2.0 under time pressure: I was supposed to download four additional libraries from the GnuPG homepage, then compile and install them, or the program wouldn't run. Well, who has that time to waste other than somebody who likes to play with the program?

There is a tutorial, plus there are FAQs, a long user manual, and an extensive ManPage under UNIX. But the tutorial goes into lengths describing the background of email security as well as asymmetric and symmetric encryption before it deals with commands. When you finally make it to that part, however, you won't be able to use it, because you'll first have to create a key. Even the mini How-To (still in its 1999 edition) is not much better; it is designed for experienced Linux administrators rather than for the average user. And it is the average user, after all, who is supposed to use GnuPG for mail encryption on their household computers!

All in all, there are many small tripwires that can unnerve users as they try to get things done with the program. For example, it is almost impossible to find out what symmetric method is actually used, and how the configuration file is to be expanded. The ManPage of GnuPG 1.4.5 lists almost 300 optional switches for calling the program in alphabetic order. Which ones are the most important? All right, GnuPG is conceived as a plug-in for mailers, but mailers use only a tiny part of its capabilities.

Another critical point is that it accepts lousy passwords, like passwords only a single letter long. Though improvement had been promised, Release 1.4.5 is still as 'tolerant' as ever.

There is a conflict I'm particularly interested in: Alice has GnuPG 1.0.4, which supports AES, installed, and sends Bob an encrypted email. Since Bob uses GnuPG 1.0.3, which doesn't talk AES, he cannot decrypt the message. Now what? With SSH (see Section 7.3), the server and the client could negotiate the algorithm they want to use, but that doesn't work for mail! There is a solution:

Alice's software can learn the methods that can be used from Bob's public key. However, for Bob to know which ones these are, he has to call GnuPG with the $-v$ switch set (apart from knowing how to set switches), and he cannot change the methods in arrears once the key has been generated.

Nevertheless, the project is positive, mainly in connection with the OpenPGP standard, which is implemented in commercial software. GnuPG could make the old PGP dream come true, namely secure communication for everybody in a heterogeneous world, well, if it weren't for real-world conditions (see also Section 7.2.3).

Anyhow, all the criticism of the current or earlier versions doesn't change anything of the extraordinary stir PGP caused worldwide: for the first time ever, cryptography found general acceptance and can really be used by everyone. The cost involved is not high—I show in [Wobpgp] how to get ready within one hour to encrypt your mails and read them. You can find a similar text in *PD/PGP/pgp2.6.3/pgptut.txt*, and for GnuPG in *PD/PGP/GnuPG/microhowto* on our Web site. (The latter text is of the sort that I'd actually have expected to get shipped with the GnuPG package.)

PGP Cracked!

This was the breaking news around the beginning of 2001 all across the Web and eventually in the *New York Times*. It wasn't entirely correct, though, because what really happened was an attack against the OpenPGP protocol, but it was a critical attack indeed. You can read about this on *txt/cryptanalopenpgpattack.txt* on the Web site.

The attack required that Mallory had access to Alice's computer, for example, to stealthily modify her private RSA signature key. From then on, if Alice sent him a message signed with the modified key, he could actually calculate her private key and sign in her name!

You might object that Alice's private signature key was encrypted, and how would Mallory modify it? Well, it touches on a point where the OpenPGP protocol has a flaw (and thus PGP as well as GnuPG): private keys are encrypted in CFB mode only. This means that it shouldn't be a problem to change a certain bit. This allows an attacker to mount the attack described as Risk 6 in Section 4.5.3. Had the key been encrypted in CBC or ECB mode, the attack could be prevented as long as the factors p and q were not stored in separate locations, but, for example, in alternating byte sequences. But the OpenPGP standard dictates both the ciphering mode and the format to ensure that you can exchange private keys between different products.

In the event of a DSA signature based on the discrete logarithm, Mallory only needs to modify the public signature key: he changes the logarithm base such that it can be easily computed. This is how he reveals the secret exponent to arrive at his goal.

Fortunately, this security flaw can be fixed. One simple solution would carry encrypted key-dependent checksums (such as HMACs) in a separate file and then have this file evaluated by 'secure' implementations. The most secure solution is, however, to subsequently have the signature checked by its creator. Though this costs additional computation time, it is negligible in view of the time it takes to enter a passphrase. That's the solution GnuPG voted for.

In general, the attack wasn't considered to have been 'that bad' after all, because while Mallory had gained access to Alice's computer, he could just as well have swapped her PGP program for another one more to his liking. But things are not quite that easy. Alice might have noticed the swap. And listening in on her passphrase isn't that easy either. Mallory would have to be replaying at the very moment she typed it in, or he could install a program that listens in on it and sends him the result later. This program could also be discovered. In contrast, if Mallory changes a bit of the private key, intercepts a signature, and then undoes the change, what we'll then have is an (almost) perfect crime. Alice would never be able to prove that he can forge her signature. Meanwhile, all PGP and OpenPGP products are secured. By the way, this example shows how farsighted it was never to use the same keys for signature and encryption; otherwise Mallory could even have read Alice's communication traffic.

The actual cause of the entire trouble was once again lack of cryptological knowledge: the CFB mode enables 'bit-flipping attacks', similarly to stream ciphers, so that there has to be some integrity protection built in. This integrity protection should not be a CBC checksum (that was the mistake in WLAN encryption and GSM), but a cryptographic hash sum (best is an HMAC with the passphrase as the key).

7.1.5 A Tip for Working with Keyrings

I have warned on different occasions in this book that the private key is sort of a universal key: if it is compromised somebody can listen in on your encrypted traffic almost effortlessly—even in arrears. This makes a costly attack reward-ing. For example, if Alice encrypts her messages with DES, and if Mallory has access to a Deep Crack machine (see Section 4.4.1), it will take him about 4.5 days to read an intercepted message. That's not worth his while. However, if Alice uses an asymmetric method for encryption and secures her private key by DES only, Mallory will steal the key and then has to run Deep Crack only once. Even if Alice suspects there is a threat and switches to 256-bit AES, it's too late.

This risk can be reduced considerably, but it takes some work. Alice creates a 'good' key pair and has the public key certified. She stores the private (encrypted) key on external data media and on a secure computer, perhaps one without network access. She then creates a 'work key' and signs it using her 'good' key. She uses this work key for daily mail traffic and changes it every now and then, perhaps monthly. In the event that Mallory guesses her 'work passphrase', or steals the decrypted private key from the storage medium (as described as Risk 7 in Section 4.5.3), then the most he can do is read the mail traffic of one month in arrears. GnuPG supports this work by use of keyrings.

Of course, all of Alice's mail conversers need to know that they have to get a new public key every month. But this effort is negligible in security-critical applications. In practice, one can have two key pairs and need to change the work key only if one thinks it might have been compromised, or if one wants to use an algorithm that wasn't supported when the key was created. However, the cost should be in a reasonable ratio to the required security.

7.2   PEM/RIPEM, the PGP Rival, and S/MIME

PGP had only one rival to my knowledge, namely PEM. Since this was the first concept that used a certification hierarchy, we will discuss it here, though PEM is insufficient and doesn't play a role today (see also [Schmeh]).

7.2.1   The PEM and S/MIME Standards Contra OpenPGP

PGP is a true child of the Internet, similar to Linux: a programmer put an infinite amount of work into it, then other people helped improve his product. PGP succeeded despite massive animosities from governmental authorities, as we saw in Section 7.1.1.

The situation was totally different with **PEM (Privacy Enhanced Mail)**. As the name suggests, PEM pursued a goal similar to PGP. However, PEM didn't start out as a program, but as a standard that was elaborated by many experts. The standard was initially described in RFCs 1113 through 1115; more current versions are RFCs 1421 through 1424 of February 1993 (you will find these on our Web site).

The encryption method PEM dictates is DES in the form of an MD5 hash function, which shouldn't come as a surprise since it is a US standard.

Key Management

An important difference between PEM and PGP is how public keys are managed. Rather than using a Web of Trust, PEM relies on a centralized server hierarchy that is compatible with the X.509 protocol (see Figure 7.2).

When Alice wants to send a message to Bob, Bob first sends his certificate to Alice. This certificate was signed by Egon. Alice uses Egon's public key to check his signature. Egon's public key was signed by Kurt. Kurt's public key was signed by both Helmut and James. James's key was signed by Marek, and Marek's key was signed by Alice herself. So Alice can verify that Bob's certificate is authentic.

Each computer underneath the root server makes a generally readable **certificate** available, which was signed by the computers above *and* below that computer within the hierarchy, and which contains the certified public key (as well as an expiration date, the algorithms, the name of the issuer, etc.).

The construction of such hierarchies is related to **PKIs (Public Key Infrastructures)**. There was an enormous hype about these PKIs, especially toward the end of the 1990s. Difficulties with the organization and acceptance had been totally underestimated; you may compare this with the 'dotcom bubble'.

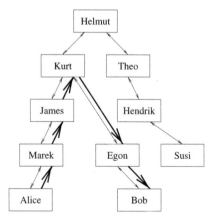

Figure 7.2: Hierarchical model of PEM. Superimposed computers mutually sign their certificates; the thick arrows show the path along which Alice checks Bob's certificate.

In his online magazine *Cryptogram*, Schneier referred to them as a failure. You can find more details in [Schmeh].

Potential for Fraud

The server hierarchy requires that a third-party public key *always* be checkable by definition. This is a clear advantage over the Web of Trust of PGP. This auditing ability can be easily implemented, and certificates can also be stored in easily accessible databases. Mallory cannot mount a man-in-the-middle attack as long as he can't forge digital signatures or compromise servers.

Another advantage over PGP is that it enables key revocation. However, this is not so simple: the validity has to be checked for every certificate newly received. To this end, a remote or local database that stores invalid certificates can be queried. This database could be compromised. However, in any event key revocation in the PEM protocol is more secure than within the Web of Trust.

A theoretical weakness of the server hierarchy is its potential to be compromised. For example, Kurt could be working for a national intelligence agency and have sold his private key to them. The agency intercepts Bob's certificate and instead of it sends their own with a different key signed by EgonII, who in reality is a computer inside the agency. EgonII and Kurt seem to be certifying each other. Since the agency knows Kurt's private key, they can do this even without Kurt knowing about it. The agency can intercept mails exchanged between Alice and Bob, decrypt them and re-encrypt them to forward them to whoever.

Helmut's signature can't prevent this fraud either, since nothing about Kurt has changed toward the outside: his public key remains the same, only his signatures are 'reconstructed' by the agency.

I gave a black-and-white depiction: PEM is supposed to protect its users from private attackers, while PGP is supposed to protect them from governments or national intelligence agencies. More specifically:

- PEM fully relies on the immunity of the server hierarchy, thus reliably excluding the usual man-in-the-middle attack. On the other hand, fraud is potentially possible by compromising the server. Furthermore, PEM requires continual access to the network.

- PGP cannot reliably exclude a man-in-the-middle attack, but it can with a rather high probability, because compromising *one* computer within the network doesn't normally do an attacker any good, and the network can even repair itself.

The optimum is probably somewhere in the middle. It would be desirable to have a hierarchy that cannot be compromised, or where a few compromised servers couldn't put the security at stake. I can think of an approach similar to the timestamp protocol discussed in Section 6.6.1, where several computers secure themselves.

It would be helpful if the PEM hierarchy was not a tree structure, but every server had to be certified by *several* servers above it. The ANSI standard X509.3 represents an improved development in this direction, but discussing it would go beyond the scope and volume of this book.

Traffic Analysis

PEM headers contain a whole range of information, particularly about senders and receivers. This allows an intruder to easily determine who communicates with whom, even if people use anonymous remailers. Though this might not be important in practice, it may have played a role for some people to vote for PGP and against PEM.

S/MIME Contra OpenPGP

PEM is hardly used anymore; S/MIME is the only thing people talk about in addition to (or preferred over) OpenPGP nowadays. A full discussion of the standard would go beyond the scope and volume of this book. And it doesn't really matter, because there is a wealth of literature on this popular mail encryption format developed by RSA (see, for example, [Schmeh; KirPGP]). Similarly to PEM, S/MIME uses a hierarchy (PKI), and it is compatible with PEM, at least its older versions are. The fact that it was embedded in MIME mail and has been supported by major manufacturers, including RSA and Microsoft, actually speak in favor of this standard rather than for OpenPGP. Moreover, S/MIME let's you encrypt large attachments. Meanwhile, PGP followed up on it with the *PGP/MIME* standard (which is supported by several products, including the *Mutt* mailer).

However, things took a different turn. According to [KirPGP], about 60 % to 70 % of all encrypted mails were exchanged in OpenPGP format in 2001. One of the reasons could have been the large number of platforms that support OpenPGP—and OpenPGP simply has a more flexible structure. For example, in contrast to S/MIME, OpenPGP supports several signatures and user IDs for each key. Furthermore, OpenPGP already has a working key-server network that people can easily access to fetch public keys. This makes it relatively easy, for example, to exchange OpenPGP-compliant encrypted mail with a new converser, while the strict certification hierarchy of S/MIME can cause problems if two conversers are not embedded in the same structure. Perhaps all these problems are only apparent, but I seldom found an S/MIME signature among the mails I received; I found OpenPGP-compatible signatures more often.

7.2.2 RIPEM

Insiders know that paper is unusually patient in the electronic data processing landscape. In particular, a standard formulated by theoretical considerations can exist for a long time without having an impact worth mentioning on practice, because there are no suitable implementations.

PEM is undoubtedly one of these standards. The best-known implementation was called **RIPEM (Riordan's Internet Privacy Enhanced Mail)** by Mark Riordan (you can find two articles about it on the Web site). RIPEM runs on many UNIX variants as well as DOS, Windows, OS/2, Macintosh, and Windows NT.

However, RIPEM was not a full implementation of PEM; in particular, it had no key management. More specifically, RIPEM didn't process PEM certificates yet, except the Macintosh version. An expansion was planned. Public keys were fetched using the *finger* command directly from the computer concerned. Moreover, RIPEM was able to create fingerprints, like PGP, for easy key verification.

RIPEM served primarily for email authentication and secondarily for encryption, while it is rather the other way around with PGP. RIPEM processes only simple text files (and no Microsoft Word files, for example), and the line length is limited to 1023 characters.

Riordan emphasizes two important benefits he thinks PEM has over PGP (in two articles on the Web site in the FAQs): The first is that PEM was an official standard while PGP is compatible only within itself. The second benefit is that PGP violated patent rights and was exported illegally. (That's not bad for the users, don't you think?)

Both arguments have become irrelevant. OpenPGP and S/MIME have become the de-facto standards on the Internet. In particular, the security concept of

OpenPGP is likely to be found more attractive by the average user. Though the Web of Trust doesn't fit well into corporate structures, OpenPGP doesn't ban certification hierarchies. The PEM concept might be better suited for commercial use, particularly within corporations, because there doesn't need to be privacy for emails. Also, while not everything has to be kept secret within corporations, authentication is of utmost importance. Corporations are more likely to use S/MIME.

7.2.3 Email Encryption in Practice: Disillusionment

This book is intended to help you to better understand cryptological concepts and to get a feel for why algorithms and protocols come in the form they do, and where pitfalls are hidden. I think this justifies looking at a totally outdated piece of software like PEM, or to discuss an encrypted file system called CFS (further below).

Nevertheless, I don't think I should be discussing mail encryption from the solely technical perspective without taking a closer look at the sad practice. My mail conversers amount to a three-digit number, but only a handful of them encrypt their mails. Take it literally: they are less than five. Typically, there is no 'real' business partner among them.

Following the slogan, 'don't trust statistics you haven't forged yourself', I decided one day to do a little poll among acquaintances and business partners at the CeBIT 2002 trade show: 'How many encrypted mails did you receive and how many did you send last year?' Since the people I asked were IT security experts without exception, I expected an untypical, even prettified result. But it was rather as I had feared: 9 out of 23 people I addressed hadn't encrypted anything at all, 9 others exchanged less than 20 encrypted mails (out of several thousand), including two for 'experimental purposes' only. Even PGP and GnuPG promoters encrypted on a strictly selective basis, i.e., only messages that they classified worth protecting (and how do you classify this?). The representative of the then PGP owner used an expired key. Another person signed all mails (without encrypting them), three persons encrypted many mails, and one single person actually protected about 5 to 10 mails per day to fend off eavesdropping. Interestingly, this very person had nothing to do with the development or sales of encryption software. Another person remembered having heard that only about 4 % of all companies were said to use mail encryption at all. Unfortunately, the source of this statement is unknown.

Excluded from these 'statistics' were a few cases of symmetric encryption where keys are distributed by phone, for example. If you are interested in reading more about disillusionment, read the magazine article [Wobmail2] (also online at `www.lanline.de`).

The Technical Side of the Problem...

When PGP emerged, computer users were real gurus, and the Internet was used by a restricted 'elite'. People had a permanent email address, and attachments were unheard of. Without wanting to make it sound like a reproach—this concept still sticks on OpenPGP.

For example, I think it's a conceptual mistake *to permanently bind a mail address to a public key* (there is no logical reason for it). The mail address can be changed, but only by its owner, and then she has to ensure that the changed key is distributed somehow or other. This is as difficult and unreliable in the Web of Trust as key revocation. In practice, Alice wants to send a PGP mail to Bob's private mail address, but her mail program says that it cannot find a key for that address. This is in order, because mail programs manage identities on mail addresses and not on the key-IDs of public keys. It is not in order that many mailers cannot handle this simple problem. From the mailers tested on Linux (Pine, Mutt, Kmail, Mozilla with Enigmail), only Kmail handled the task reasonably: it let me store the 'mail address-to-key' allocation. However, I had to put the key on the highest trust level within the Web of Trust to be able to encrypt at all, which is a conceptual error.

Another problem relates to the *incompatibility between Inline-PGP and PGP/MIME*. The first of these two formats is the one used in PGP 2.6, which encrypts only the mail body itself. The second of these two formats is the 'answer' of OpenPGP to S/MIME. It also encrypts attachments. However, only very few mailers can handle PGP/MIME, or they understand only one of the two formats by default. For example, Pine (as well as the WinPT plugin of Windows) can process only Inline-PGP, while Mutt deals only with PGP/MIME and gives the average user who wants to use Inline-PGP a hard time.

Things look a little better when it comes to the *compatibility between GnuPG and PGP*. GnuPG users should set -*openpgp* for encryption to make sure they won't use algorithms and other extras that only GnuPG knows. Mail traffic will then work nicely, at least it did with one of my readers of the Polish edition of this book. The thing is you first have to notice the problem.

Much more critical is the *incompatibility of the two OpenPGP and S/MIME worlds*. GnuPG 2.0 emerged at the time of writing this; it is the first tool to process S/MIME. However, the installation is cumbersome and the documentation is incomplete. There seems to still be a long way to go to get a mailer plugin that optionally handles OpenPGP and S/MIME, depending on the incoming mail.

You can read more about typical problems with encrypted mail in the article [Wobmail].

I turned back to the command line for receiving encrypted mail (not for sending, though), because that takes me to the goal fastest. I took that decision when I received a mail from a sender with a slightly faulty release of Squirrel Mail. A blank at the end of the marker line

```
-----BEGIN PGP MESSAGE-----
```

brought up the error message 'no valid OpenPGP data found', and guessing at riddles began. As it happens, I use a script that controls the *vim* editor to remove known errors in advance. My command line doesn't really speak in favor of a successful integration in mailers.

...and the 'Human' Side

Bruce Schneier wrote in his book [SchnCr] that if the average Web surfer clicks on a button that promises dancing pigs on his computer monitor, and instead gets a hortatory message describing the potential dangers of the applet, he's going to choose dancing pigs over computer security any day. In email terms, if a user doesn't see an urgent reason to encrypt mail he won't. You cannot expect a user to understand why he should encrypt mail, or what happens when he does. And things are still cumbersome in practice, as we saw in the previous section. Linux designers favor the *Mutt* mail program, which is believed to excellently integrate GnuPG. But to configure *Mutt*, you have to read the ManPage of *muttrc*, which is about 4000 lines of text. Who has that kind of time to waste? What's more, you have to know that Mutt obstinately prefers the PGP/MIME format, while the sender of an Inline-PGP mail has no idea what mailer the receiver uses.

Even if you eventually let yourself be talked into using your pal's favorite mail encryption tool, there is yet another problem: you left your private key in another location, so you still can't read his mails (it happened to me in three distinct cases). As things like these normally happen especially when mails are really important and things are urgent, I decided I'd rather sign them, but leave them unencrypted to get things done.

All right, so what's left of the pretty concept of the Web of Trust? I interviewed several dozen qualified and highly security-aware Linux users to find out which of them verified a key using the Web of Trust. Only one of the interviewed people did so, and he wasn't even totally sure about it. The lesson I took home was that, unofficially, people admit that the popular 'key-signing parties' are hardly suited to build a web of trust, but rather they are sports: the one out of many key owners who can be reached over as short a path as possible wins the trophy.

Those who doubt the authenticity of a public OpenPGP key are advised to better check the fingerprint over the phone. I have done it once in ten years.

Admittedly, all of this sounds pretty pessimistic, but it shows vividly how little a pretty theory is worth if you forget to consider the actual target group.

7.3   Comfortable and Secure: SSH and OpenSSH

PGP could cryptographically secure the worldwide email data traffic. **SSH** (**Secure Shell**) encrypts the data traffic in local area networks. Again, we will first have a look at the outdated Version 1 of SSH, before we discuss the current OpenSSH package. We are interested in the background rather than in the application. To understand what Secure Shell can do, we make a short excursion into the world of networked UNIX computers.

Working Within the Inhouse Net

Computers can be used as standalone machines, but they are generally networked over the TCP/IP network protocol—now for over a quarter of a century, by the way. You know this network in its worldwide form—it's the Internet. In contrast, a local area network (LAN) is an 'inhouse network', also referred to as a 'TCP/IP network'. Later on, a LAN went by the name of *intranet* and was advertised as a 'revolution', while it was simply an Internet with the plug to the world pulled.

A large number of standard helper programs ensure in every UNIX system that this network can be used transparently. Here, 'transparent' means that the user should be able to use a service without impairment, ideally without even noticing anything. For example, the **Network File System** (**NFS**) lets users embed files residing on remote computers into their own directory hierarchy and use these files as if they were on their own computer; even the application programs won't notice anything. We will get back to this issue in Section 7.4.

NFS has certain drawbacks, but it is not always necessary. *rlogin* (*remote login*), *rsh* (*remote shell*), and *rcp* (*remote copy*) are important for internal use. These three tools are used like those by the same name, but without the leading '*r*': you can log on to a remote computer (*rlogin*), or just execute a command there (*rsh*), or copy files between remote computers (*rcp*). A special file by the name of .*rhosts* in the user's home directory on the target computer is even more useful: if it contains the name of the calling computer together with the user name, then that user can log in without a password (and only then will *rsh* and *rcp* work, by the way). If the .*rhosts* file is missing, then the target computer will ask for a user password.

The security philosophy behind this concept is as follows for *rsh* and *rcp*: logged in on one computer—access to all 'friend' computers. *rlogin* without .*rhosts* is not much more secure: the password runs across the network in the clear, and everybody within the organization can basically listen in on it.

This doesn't make UNIX an insecure system. There is a clean separation between running programs, their data, and the operating system. Nobody can access third-party files without permission, nobody can use their program to simply bring UNIX down. But those who want to work comfortably in the network do normally give way to an eavesdropper. *rlogin* is hardly more secure than *telnet*, the open barn door.

If you try to log on to a remote computer from your home computer over an Internet provider, the *rhost* mechanism will refuse its service, because the provider normally assigns a dynamic (i.e., variable) Internet address, and the target computer doesn't know you by that address. You will learn the solution to this problem below.

Stuffing Up Security Holes

The solution for the three standard tools—*rlogin, rsh,* and *rcp*—is **Secure Shell (SSH)**: it provides for cryptographically secure authentication, and uses a hybrid method to encrypt the data traffic. This means that it reliably thwarts IP- or DNS-spoofing attacks (where Mallory pretends to be Alice), and the interception of passwords and data. SSH was developed by Tatu Ylönen of the University at Helsinki, and was not intended to be freely used for non-commercial purposes. You can find the source text of version 1.2.26 for analytical purposes on our Web site.

This SSH version is one of the programs you would like to see more often. It probably worked on all UNIX systems (and OS/2, while the Windows world used something else, for example, *Putty*). What's more, it was easy to install, well documented, and easy to use. Unfortunately, all of this applied to the version mentioned here only; more about this further below. We will then call it **SSH1**.

Of course, we are interested in the cryptography of this software package.

SSH1 can use five different methods for symmetric encryption:

- IDEA (in CFB mode);
- Blowfish (in CBC mode);
- DES (in CBC mode);
- Triple-DES (in CBC mode); and
- RC4 (the stream cipher discussed in Section 5.6; called 'arcfour' here).

You can select a method by configuration or switch on the command line. The interface is very simple and visible from the program code. For example, it is up to the user to integrate their own algorithms and to check the encryption functions based on reference implementations. I'd like to see this in every piece of cryptographic software.

Authentication and Key Exchange

The Secure Shell uses the RSA algorithm as its asymmetric method. The protocol it uses is interesting; it serves to authenticate computers and users, and for secure session-key distribution. In detail, it looks like this:

1. Upon installation, the program creates a fixed pair of 1024-bit keys on every participating computer. The public key is called 'public host key' in an ASCII file that everybody can read. The private key is in a file that only the superuser can access.

2. When starting the SSH daemon *sshd* (a program that should be started up on system startup), an additional pair of 768-bit server keys is created. The public part of it is the 'server key', while the private component is not stored anywhere, but kept in memory. This key pair is changed at hourly intervals.

3. The user, say Alice, additionally creates a 1024-bit 'user authentication key'. Both components are saved to files, where the private key is IDEA-encrypted with a passphrase, like in PGP.

4. When Alice tries to log herself into Bob's computer, Bob sends her two public keys: the server key and the public host key. Alice checks whether or not the public host key matches the locally stored key.

5. If it does, then Alice creates a random session key, and encrypts it using the *two public keys* of Bob's computer *consecutively*, and sends the cipher to Bob. From then onwards, the entire message traffic is encrypted. This has interesting consequences:

   Bob needs *two* private keys to decrypt the session key. If Mallory succeeds in breaking into the server (Bob's computer) and stealing both private keys, he can decrypt Bob's network traffic of the last hour at most, because the server key is changed every hour. The public host key is still required, because only this key authenticates the server.

   This method is an important improvement versus the usual hybrid methods. But it can be used only in direct network contact. This is the reason why it is not a choice for PGP, since the mail end nodes don't have to be continually connected. Email can be 'buffered', sometimes even for days in earlier times.

6. Now Alice knows almost for sure that she is communicating with Bob's computer. But Bob wants to be sure Mallory is not pretending to be Alice: Alice has to be authenticated. That's where the user authentication key comes into play.

   Bob uses Alice's user authentication key to encrypt a 256-bit random number. He sends this number to Alice. Alice knows the corresponding private component and can compute the random number and return it. This authenticates her.

   Here too, Ylönen recognized a potential risk: if Mallory broke into the server, he could mount a chosen-ciphertext attack against RSA (see Section 4.5.3). For example, he could do the following:

   - Alice tries to log into Bob's computer, but actually communicates with Mallory's computer. While Alice is busy doing Steps 4 and 5.

   - Mallory starts a session on Carol's computer. He pretends to be Alice and waits to get the 256-bit random number encrypted with Alice's public key from Carol.

   - He sends this number to Alice, who has no idea what's going on, and

   - Returns the decrypted value to Mallory. Mallory forwards the value to Carol and authenticates himself as Alice.

From then on, Mallory can read Alice's session on Bob's computer and sniff about in Alice's directories on Carol's computer at the same time!

To prevent such a scenario from happening, Alice doesn't send the decrypted number, but only its hash value to Bob. Mallory can't do anything with this.

7. Now, the two parties have authenticated themselves, and the actual session can begin.

However, if Mallory broke into Bob's computer and managed to become a superuser, he'd still read everything. No protocol can prevent this.

SSH is usually configured such that the *.rhosts* files mentioned above can be read and evaluated by SSH, but leads to an additional authentication by means of RSA. Since insecure tools like *rlogin* work nevertheless, every user should rename *.rhosts* to *.shosts*: SSH will handle this file like *.rhosts*, whereas *rlogin* will look around in vain. The RSA authentication should be admitted only in risky computer environments.

If you start the *ssh* command with the $-v$ switch set, you can see in detail how this authentication runs. Figure 7.3 shows an example. The average user won't notice anything.

Comfortable Use is Imperative

Security is generally uncomfortable. Ylönen knows that, too. Consequently, he tries to make the installation and use as simple as possible. To compile and install the UNIX version that comes with this book, it normally suffices to execute just four commands:

```
configure
make
make install
/usr/local/sbin/sshd&
```

Remember that SSH can be used on different hardware and all kinds of different UNIX variants. This installation cannot be compared with Windows programs that normally come in turnkey packages. Their installation is usually limited to copying files, and perhaps automatically updating a few configuration files.

```
txt/addis/book>ssh -v~$pf
SSH Version 1.2.17 [i386-univel-sysv4.2MP], protocol version 1.5.
Standard version. Does not use RSAREF.
Reading configuration data/home/wobst/.ssh/config
Reading configuration data/etc/ssh_config
ssh_connect: getuid 100 geteuid 0 anon 0
Connecting to ESIXV4Wo [88.0.0.1] port 22.
Allocated local port 1020.
Connection established.
Remote protocol version 1.5, remote software version 1.2.17
Waiting for server public key.
Received server public key (768 bits) and host key (1024 bits).
Host 'esixv4wo' is known and matches the host key.
Initializing random; seed file/home/wobst/.ssh/random_seed
Encryption type: idea
Sent encrypted session key.
Received encrypted confirmation.
No agent.
Trying RSA authentication with key 'wobst@SHL'
Received RSA challenge from server.
Enter passphrase for RSA key 'wobst@SHL':
Sending response to host key RSA challenge.
Remote: RSA authentication accepted.
RSA authentication accepted by server.
Requesting pty.
Requesting shell.
Entering interactive session.
Last login: Thu Feb 13 12:52:06 1997 from shl/home/wobst>date
Thursday, 13 February 1997, 14:09:00 MET
/home/wobst>exit
/dev/pts001
times:0m0.32s 0m0.39s
0m0.26s 0m0.92s
type ENTER
Connection to ESIXV4Wo closed.
Transferred: stdin 2, stdout 136, stderr 32bytes in 71.0 seconds
Bytes per second: stdin 0.0, stdout 1.9, stderr 0.5
Exit status 0txt/addis/book>
```

Figure 7.3: Trace of an ssh login on a remote computer. The details are output when using the '−v' switch; normally nothing appears, except the prompt. Only the 'date' command was used in this example.

The *ssh* daemon *sshd* should execute automatically upon system start, which represents a routine task for the administrator. I won't describe how public keys are distributed here. They are normally distributed upon the first attempt to establish a connection, or perhaps automatically.

The user normally has to type only one command, which is *ssh-keygen*. If there is a risk, even just theoretically (which is always the case), that somebody might break into your computer, you should encrypt your private key with a passphrase (the program pops up an opportunity). But you will then have to enter this passphrase every time you use SSH, which is unacceptable for some users. While users don't normally notice when they are given more security, they get upset when requested to enter passwords.

This motivated Ylönen to write another program called *ssh-agent*, which keeps the private key in memory, and can be executed within a regular UNIX session. It speeds the connection establishment up considerably. (You can see in Figure 7.3 that *ssh-agent* wasn't running when I logged the prompts: it requests a passphrase.)

SSH can be easily configured such that every user can continue working in the familiar way, except for the one-time entry of a password when they log in. When communicating with computers that don't have Secure Shell installed, SSH outputs a warning and automatically falls back on the customary tools, i.e., *rlogin, rcp*, and *rsh*.

Even the X-protocol is encrypted by default, and an integrated, undocumented compression (switch $-C$) comes in handy for slow transmission lines (mainly when using the PPP network protocol over a modem). And finally, SSH can also be used as a secure transmission channel for other applications.

Unfortunately, there is a painful drawback: security costs computation time. The IP protocol slows down considerably on a regular PC (which you won't notice on a Pentium-100 and better), and computations on 1024-bit keys are time-consuming. On the configuration I used back then, the remote execution of the *date* command took about 0.7 seconds (the IP connection has to first be established and then torn down even for such a tiny command). When I used SSH (and *ssh-agent*), this time increased to between 4 and 5 seconds.

This delay plays a subordinate role on modern computers when you log in or copy long files. But it is a big deal when you use SSH and bad shell scripts that transport 500 small files individually using *scp*. Regardless of the cryptographic program you use, there are only two solutions: either you get yourself a multiprocessor machine with eight kernels, or you improve the application by packing all of these files into an archive and ship the archive across the network.

You should use SSH to log on to remote computers in any event, because short additional wait times won't play a role there. And if encrypting the data traffic does take a lot of time, whereas you are mainly interested in an interception-proof login, then you can always enter 'ssh -c none *hostname*': in this case, the current data traffic is not encrypted. However, at least the Blowfish cipher (use the *blowfish* option) is fast enough to pull an interception-safe backup over the network.

SSH Everywhere: Proliferation and Licenses

SSH1 was once in use in about 10 000 organizations across roughly 50 countries, according to Ylönen's own statements. What I particularly like about SSH is its simple interfaces to the cryptographic modules, and the well-designed security concept.

The private use of SSH1 used to be free. For commercial use, there was a bunch of license terms and conditions for third-party contributions, which are stated in the COPYING file, among others.

Unpleasant Development

The protocol was changed with Release 2.0: it's now called **IETF SSH Secure Shell protocol**. The new SSH2 was available only for commercial use and didn't support the SSH1 protocol any more. That was extremely disappointing. All those people who wanted to communicate with servers that ran SSH2 were supposed to buy the software, even for private use. Compared to SSH1, that was a step backwards, no doubt: imagine you have to quite often log on to your work computer from home over an Internet provider. No problem over SSH1. As mentioned earlier, there wouldn't be any other way anyway, because the company computer can't possibly know your IP address, since it is normally assigned by the provider. Now, your company would have to migrate to SSH2, and you've got a problem.

Ylönen himself (who participated in the commercial development) recommends in several mailing lists to use only the new protocol since the old was insecure. One reason might be the Bleichenbacher attack discussed as Risk 5 in connection with RSA in Section 4.5.3, where I mentioned simple countermeasures. SSH1 would make this attack harder in any event, because changing the keys on an hourly basis would mean that an attacker would have one hour at most. With one million requests, this would result in a rate of about 300 requests per second, which generally requires additional expensive hardware on the server side. In addition, the attacker himself would have to do a lot of computations and need special hardware. You can read in *PD/SSH/ssh1_insecure.txt* on the

Web site about the fact the attack isn't even realistic in the opinion of people who spread the warning themselves.

This suggests that the propagated migration to the SSH2 protocol must have had a different reason. Bleichenbacher's work is quoted, but the countermeasures he suggested were left out. Perhaps sound financial interests played the most important role. That wouldn't be all that bad if SSH2 supported the old protocol, of course, with the countermeasures suggested by Bleichenbacher in place. Unfortunately, this was not so.

The public domain responded by developing free products compatible with SSH2. A shell by the name of **LSH** wasn't very successful. Meanwhile, the **OpenSSH** program (www.openssh.com) is widely used. It was born on the free UNIX variant FreeBSD and is further developed there. The current versions of OpenSSH support both SSH protocols. It can be ported to most UNIX systems.

Among other things, SSH2 offers a password-free authentication over RSA, and DSA keys that are kept on the local computers. This is clearly more secure than password-logins, the more so since the keys can also be kept on external data media, such as USB sticks. All the details would go beyond the scope and volume of this book, and wouldn't introduce any cryptological novelty anyway.

I'm not really happy with the new SSH in spite of it all. The versions change faster than the weather in Iceland, the configuration is extremely complicated and holds a large number of pitfalls. Nothing remained of the fast and comfortable way SSH1 secured your data traffic. Fortunately, OpenSSH is at least an integral part of all Linux distributions, and it is used instead of *rlogin*, etc., by default. Yes, no kidding: you even have to separately install and activate *rlogin* and *telnet* to be able to use them. The password-login works right off the bat. You don't have to learn anything. That's how security should be: always activated in the regular case, whereas everything else requires your intervention.

Still, I can't help criticizing it a bit: if you try to log in without a password and happen to make only a tiny wee mistake, you are in for it: you'll be looking for the cause infinitely. Since I don't usually configure such a login, it happens to me over and again. Together with the change from Version 3.6 to Version 3.7, the so-called 'X-forwarding' was disabled in the configuration file without any comment. What this means is that, if you want to open an X-terminal on a target computer, you now have to enter 'ssh -X', while the documentation still tells you how it was done previously. These are little things that aggravate. However, compared with GnuPG, OpenSSH is definitely friendlier. And don't forget: the Windows world still uses the totally insecure *telnet* standard.

7.4 CFS-Encrypted Hard Disks

The software products discussed so far helped secure the local and remote data traffic between computers, but how is a computer's local security ensured? UNIX users, for example, set corresponding access privileges for sensitive directories. This means that other users cannot change to these directories and read the files they contain.

This doesn't fend off nosy superusers (i.e., administrators) though. Their access privileges are not limited. Security holes in UNIX systems are usually due to the fact that somebody can become an unauthorized superuser. Which users know whether a security hole has been discovered in their system and whether or not it is already being exploited? And even if it isn't, if somebody has somehow physical access to your computer (which should always be assumed for notebooks), they can use a Linux-Live CD, such as *Knoppix*, and easily delete the superuser password, copy at will, and then reset everything back to normal.

The only thing that helps in these cases is to encrypt sensitive files. This is cumbersome and insecure. Application programs don't normally work with encrypted files. As long as they aren't open, they are normally on the disk in the clear. Only once the program is exited can you encrypt them. Even if your word processor offers good cryptography, nobody can guarantee that the data haven't been stored on the disk in the clear in the meantime.

Crypto-file systems put an end to this type of worry. Such files are accessed as usual, but the data on their way between the disk and the application are encrypted and decrypted transparently. In multiuser systems like UNIX, crypto-file systems wouldn't protect your files from an administrator accessing either the memory or the swap area, but they help: dismantling and analyzing the hard disk after work (or stealing the notebook) won't help James Bond much despite the modern analyzer in his wrist watch, at least in general. However, it would be desirable to have operating systems that would reliably delete data no longer required from the swap area from time to time. No administrator can do this; it's a system task. Clever users use crypto-file systems for the swap area, too, but it can significantly reduce the performance.

CFS and NFS

I'll be talking about some totally outdated software in this section once again! Crypto-file systems are used under Windows as well as under Linux and UNIX today, but there is rather complex software behind them. It is instructive to analyze a simpler package that also shows the typical problems.

CFS (**Cryptographic File System**) was developed by Matthew Blaze from 1992 onwards. We know Blaze from the attack against the Clipper chip protocol (see Section 6.4). CFS Release 1.3.3 can be found on our Web site. CFS Release 1.3.3 consists of roughly 8500 lines of source code and is used on some UNIX systems, mainly BSD and SunOS variants, but also AIX by IBM, HP/UX, Irix, Solaris, and (with problems) Linux. Its quality lags behind that of SSH: it is not written in a particularly portable and efficient way, its installation is cumbersome, and the encryption methods used are fixed on 64-bit block algorithms. I couldn't test it myself, but I know that CFS reduces performance considerably. This is the price to be paid for security, which sometimes appears to be higher than that for SSH.

CFS uses the Network File System (NFS) mentioned in Section 7.3 from within UNIX. The latter embeds file trees in remote computers such that they virtually reside on your own hard disk. With CFS, the file trees actually reside on your own disk, except that the data on their way from and to the file system are encrypted. That doesn't change anything, either for the application or for the user. The only thing is that the user has to use the *cattach* command to 'attach' a file tree into the current hierarchy before starting to work. To 'detach' the file tree, he uses *cdetach. cattach* requests a password. Outsiders won't even recognize file names, let alone file contents. That's not all, but we are interested in cryptology rather than in UNIX.

Encryption with Some Particularities

Things are not as simple as they may appear. Disks cannot be encrypted as you would encrypt files: they need to remain freely accessible. For example, a program has to be able to read the 34th, the 666 231st, and then the 11 004th byte from a file without getting into trouble. However, encryption is generally sequential, except in ECB mode and stream ciphers. But the latter don't allow you to hold a sufficiently long key stream in spare. For one thing, this stream would have to be at least as long as all confidential data together—that causes capacity problems. Second, computing it in advance would cost much time. And the simple ECB mode is too insecure. Now what?

Blaze had a simple and good idea to solve this problem [BlazeCFS]. Though he creates a key stream, that stream has a length of only 256 Kbytes (rather than 128 Kbytes as stated in the README file). After XORing the entire stream

with the data, you start all over again. Theoretically, this is a Vernam cipher
(see Section 2.4.2), but with a period of 4 Mbits. Though this blurs internal data
structures, it is not resistant to plaintext attacks. For this reason, he encrypts
the output once more using a 64-bit block algorithm in ECB mode. This makes
the method secure.

This combination of quasi-stream cipher and block cipher is effective. Free
access to the encrypted file won't pose any problem.

To read the 666 231st byte from a file, we first compute the offset in the key
stream:

256 Kbytes are 262 144 bytes, so the offset is $666\,231 - 2{*}262\,144 =$
141 943.

This byte is included in the 64-bit block, which is formed from bytes 141 936
through 141 943.

To decrypt things, we XOR the eight bytes 666 224 through 666 231 of the
encrypted file with the eight key bytes 141 936 through 141 943, decrypt the
result using the block algorithm, and pick the 7th byte from there.

While humans may find this hard, it is a kid's game for computers.

CFS Cryptography in Detail

The cipher looks a bit different in the program than it is described in the
article [BlazeCFS]. Instead of a single cipher stream, CFS creates two cipher
streams, here denoted $S1$ and $S2$. A key $K2$ (the *secondary* byte field in the
program) is used to create these two streams. A second key $K1$ (the *primary*
byte field in the program) is used with the block cipher. An 8-byte field called
vect (described as *perturbation vector* in the program) takes the place of the
initialization vector. This field has a different value for each file. The cipher
looks symbolically as follows:

```
C = S2 ⊕ DES_K1(P ⊕ S1 ⊕ vect)
```

DES is used by default, as the formula suggests. Other possible methods include
Triple-DES and SAFER-SK128, which is described in [SchnCr]. This is basically a more complex variant of whitening (see Section 5.2.3).

To calculate the *vect* field, you fill the four least significant bytes with the file's Inode number (a number that serves for unique identification of files) and the four uppermost bytes with the file's modification time. Everything is then taken and DES-encrypted using the 56-bit key (stripped of the most significant bits) that was constructed from the *fixedkey* character string.

This little trick guarantees that no files with identical contents can produce the same ciphers. Furthermore, the cipher of a slightly modified file never resembles the file's previous version. From the cryptological point of view, the DES encryption using *fixedkey* is even superfluous. The code apparently had been changed in this place (*fhmkfileent()* function, *cfs_fh.c* file), but not in a consistent way. By the way, modern 64-bit UNIX systems wouldn't evaluate the modification time, only the Inode number. This would be a critical security flaw (slightly modified files can be recognized as such).

The important XORing with *vect* can be suppressed using the −*l* switch for *cattach*. This is not a wise thing to do. This operation consumes minimal resources, compared with the DES encryption, but its cryptological effect is considerable.

The computation of the key streams $S1$ and $S2$ appears to be strange at first. CFS encrypts the numbers 0 through 32 767 ($2^{15} − 1$) in hexadecimal representation in the ECB mode, where the highest digit is set equal to 1 when computing $S2$:

```
S1 = {DES("00000000")| DES("00000001")|...| DES("00007FFFF")}
S2 = {DES("10000000")| DES("10000001")|...| DES("10007FFFF")}
```

This simple structure of $S1$ and $S2$ is certainly a welcome test condition for owners of a DES Crack machine. With good algorithms, however, the risk is smaller than it looks: this is the so-called **counter mode** we didn't discuss in Section 5.1.1, but which is still considered to be secure. It is used in UMTS and ZigBEE (and in the IEEE standard 802.15.4), among others.

CFS runs a continuous loop, which is aborted several times after a given time for cryptographic random generation. Since more or less unexpected events can occur in a multiuser system, there can be hardly predictable events (*truerand.c* file). The CFS author says that this method is pretty secure but slow, and it has to be tested separately for every computer. This is risky, because errors introduced from porting can remain undetected. There is a note in the documentation about the *esm* Session Manager.

Can CFS Be Recommended?

The defects mentioned above refer to the innards and probably don't decrease the value of CFS. It is important *not* to call *cattach* with the $-l$ switch (see previous section). The relatively poor portability is not nice but understandable (CFS sits deep within the operation system) and acceptable, because CFS runs locally. Users of other UNIX systems can look around for something else. More critical is the loss in performance, in my opinion. While the fastness of a file system doesn't play a role for a word processor, CFS can be extremely disturbing when processing long records in a database. I don't consider it wise to use DES of all things (or even Triple-DES, which is three times slower in software), because this algorithm was primarily conceived for hardware. SAFER-SK128 would be about five times faster, but utmost caution is advised, according to Schneier [SchnCr, 14.4]—not least because the NSA could have its hands in it. How about Blowfish, RC4/5/6, Twofish, or even AES?

However, cryptographic file systems are good concepts. They separate cryptography from applications and make things easier to audit. Only the swap area should be cleaned up by the system from time to time...

7.5 OPIE, S/Key, and Logdaemon: Secure Login

Three free software packages, namely **S/Key** (which probably means 'Secure Key'), **OPIE** (**One-time Passwords In Everything**), and **Logdaemon**, use one-time passwords for authentication (or, more exactly, for login) in UNIX systems. S/Key was developed by members of Bellcore in the early 1990s, representing presumably the first of this type of program. OPIE came about on the basis of S/Key in the US Naval Research Laboratories (NRL) and is downwards compatible with S/Key. It was renamed because S/Key is a brand name, whereas OPIE is the unprotected name of free software. Logdaemon was developed by Wietse Venema, the author of the popular SATAN security program; it can do a lot more. We are interested in the implementation of one-time passwords in this package. The following section discusses OPIE representatively for the other two programs.

How to Use OPIE

As long as you move about on known computers within the Internet or an intranet, you should use SSH for the required protection. However, if you work on a third-party system and want to log in to your computer at home, it is almost mandatory to use one-time passwords. The reason is that nobody knows whether the administrator of that third-party system has a replay daemon running. Furthermore, SSH won't help you much on third-party systems.

All three programs optionally use MD4 or MD5 as a one-way hash function. Even though MD4 was inverted in reduced form, and MD5 will probably suffer a similar destiny in the near future, it is still suitable for computing one-time passwords, because the cracking of MD5 modifications was based on collision computations, which means that it doesn't put the use of digital signatures at stake.

OPIE and Logdaemon replace the usual login mechanism with *rlogin, ftp*, and *su* (as opposed to S/Key). The latter is important for the situation described above, where you log in to your own computer from an external computer and have to act as a superuser.

In practical work, OPIE is slightly different than explained in Section 6.5.

First of all, the entries are only 64 bits long. The right 64 bits of the 128-bit hash value are XORed with the left 64 bits. This has ergonomic reasons that will be explained further below. This is not likely to jeopardize the security.

Second, you always begin with the startup password, S_0 (see Section 6.5 for denotations). A local 'OPIE calculator' requests S_0 and takes it to compute S_{49}, for example. The result is to be transferred to the password entry. If you use OPIE in a window system, you can easily use its cut-and-paste function; otherwise, the entry has to be manual. The password S_0 is calculated from a sequential number (called *seed* here), and a secret password that you enter when initializing the password list and which is easier to memorize than one-time passwords. Both the password and the seed are 'made into' S_0 in the *keycrunch()* function (called *opiekeycrunch* in OPIE talk) via MD4 or MD5. So, when having an OPIE calculator program handy, you don't have to memorize a secret password.

Since the manual entry of numbers (including hexadecimal numbers) is inconvenient, OPIE translates the hash sum into six readable words. That's pretty easy: you will find a list with 2048 entries of English words each at most four letters long in *libopie/btoe.c*. Each word stands for a piece of 11-bit information ($2^{11} = 2048$), so six words stand for 66 bits. These are 64 bits for the actual password and 2 bits for the checksum. All you need to do is to enter a passphrase, for example,

```
GILL HUED GOES CHUM LIEU VAIN
```

Of course, you can print the passwords if there's no computer around, but you'd have to watch the list carefully.

What you'd normally do is you'd create 100 passwords in spare (or more if you plan on going on a long trip). A shell script called *opieremind* that nice administrators have running regularly reminds all users concerned by email that less than 15 passwords are left. This means that it's about time to run *opiepasswd* again to create a new password list. Otherwise, OPIE warns you upon login when less than ten or five passwords are left.

Some Doubts

One-time passwords are very secure from the cryptological point of view. A new password list should be created only directly at the computer concerned or over a secure connection (e.g., using SSH) to ensure that eavesdroppers at the network can never intercept a valid password. Still, a few weaknesses remain:

- The password verification is only based on a required minimum length. This is 4 with S/Key and Logdaemon, and 10 with OPIE. That's not strong enough a protection. It gives way to dictionary attacks, for example. Ciphering errors shouldn't play a role in modern software anymore.

- OPIE and Logdaemon let you specify 'trustworthy' networks from where you can log in (using the usual password). If you work at your own computer you won't be working with one-time passwords. But it is impossible to activate OPIE for dynamically assigned IP addresses—you'd have to state the network address. This is hindering in practice. Logdaemon is more flexible in this respect and should be preferred over OPIE and S/Key.

- OPIE borrowed special data structures from the UNIX system, which means that it is not particularly portable (except for *opiekey*, the 'OPIE calculator', which is a pure computing program). The program comes from the BSD world, and you can tell. Porting it to non-BSD and non-Sun systems is difficult. Logdaemon seems to be doing better in this respect.

- There are several inconsistencies (e.g., 'OPIE' in the program, 'OTP' in the documentation) and plenty of typos, leaving a bad impression.

If you are not allowed to use the login program on your system, have a look at *skeysh*, a program that belongs to Logdaemon. It is similar to an S/Key login once you've logged yourself in, and has to have superuser privileges (called *suid root*).

If you can't get any of the three programs running on your system, or if your administrator is not nice, you can write yourself a C program (or there might already be one) that verifies one-time passwords, and is then invoked instead of the shell. Only if the test passes does this C program invoke the right shell. The benefit is that this program could test whether or not the login is via modem and, if not, skip the password verification. The administrator only needs to register this new shell for the user and won't have any other additional work. If he doesn't even want to do this wee bit, you can invoke the program from within *profile*. Watch for potential interrupts—execute the *trap* command first—and set an environment variable so that you won't end up in a continuous loop. This could look like this for the Bourne and Korn shells:

```
trap '' 1 2 3 15
[ "$MY_OPIE_WAS_CALLED" ] && exec my_opie
...
```

The *my_opie* program allocates a value to the environment variable MY_OPIE_ WAS_CALLED, for example, 'yes', and invokes the shell with leading '−' sign if the password verified successfully, so it becomes the login shell. More details would go beyond the scope and volume of this book.

With this, the UNIX password will lose its significance. However, this still doesn't provide you with a secure *ftp* access.

Unfortunately, you will have to enter two passwords in every login from now onwards: first the 'right' one, then the one-time password. Before going on a trip, you may want to change your 'right' password and activate the login via one-time password. Upon your return, you can undo everything. That's only a makeshift solution. But you saw that one can always try to build a solution from the tools available.

7.6 An RC5a Implementation

In closing this discussion, I will introduce the shortest program in this chapter, namely my own implementation, *rc5a*, of the RC5a algorithm described in Section 5.4.3. It is a C program about 650 lines long and primarily designed for the encryption of data streams, which means that *rc5a* works as a filter. The user interface is Spartan: the command line

```
rc5a <plaintext >ciphertext
```

suffices for encryption. For decryption, you just add an optional argument:

```
rc5a a <ciphertext >plaintext.
```

The password is requested interactively, but it can also be told by using the CRYPTKEY environment variable (which is a security risk, of course).

You can find shell scripts for easy encryption of single files and for the creation of encrypted archives on our Web site. In general, *rc5a* is conceived as a helper program to be embedded in other programs. The *main* function, which is responsible for the Spartan interface, is only a few lines long. It is best to have a look at the function *rc5a()* to see how components of the program, such as password entry, key management, and the actual encryption and decryption, are built into other software.

I tested the program on a number of different UNIX platforms (UnixWare 2.0, ESIX V4.2MP, HP-UX 9.0, Sinix 5.42, SunOS 4.1, OSF/1 3.0, Ultrix 4.3, SuSE-Linux 6.4...9.0,...), and no problem arose when porting it to Windows NT either (see Section 5.4.4). Using *unsigned long* as the data type for the WORD macro (see below), I even managed a DOS porting of the decrypted part for 16-bit compilers, though the input/output detour required some tricks. The terminal control upon entering a password requires POSIX compatibility, but the few machine-specific routines at the end of the program are marked as such and easily replaced anyway.

The speed of *rc5a* ranges from 240 Kbytes per second on a PC 486-33 to about 1.5 Mbytes per second on a 133-MHz Pentium PC (both computers running ESIX V4.2). The two macros ROTL and ROTR, which are responsible for rotating 32-bit words, make the performance drop. The speed improves slightly when using assembler commands instead of these macros, but not dramatically. Notice that the speeds measured are gross indicative values, i.e., they correspond to times *actually* required for encrypting files on the hard disk. Many such benchmarks state only a theoretical data throughput!

By default, the *rc5a* program works with 32-bit words, 12 rounds, a keybox size of 16 (= 2^4), and passphrases with lengths of up to 255 bytes. This means that it implements an RC5a(32,12,*) algorithm (the asterisk stands for passphrases of virtually unlimited length). The number of rounds can easily be increased; it is passed when *main()* invokes the function *rc5a()*. The program can easily be ported to 64-bit machines. You just need to edit the following macros in the program header:

```
#define WORD    unsigned long

#define WEXP    6

#define P32     0xb7e151628aed2a6b
#define Q32     0x9e3779b97f4a7c15
```

(The names P64 and Q64 would be better.) The last two constants are equal to $2^{64*}(e-2)$ and $2^{64*}(\sqrt{5}-1)/2)$, where e denotes the base of natural logarithms: $e = 2.718281828\ldots$

With RC5a(64,*,*), however, you can no longer evaluate encrypted texts on 32-bit machines. I therefore recommend to use this modification only locally. The 64-bit algorithm is twice as fast as the 32-bit algorithm with the same number of rounds under OSF/1 on an Alpha machine. (I recommend 16 rounds for RC5a(64,*,*); the effective speed increased only by 75 %.)

Byte Order

You probably know that different processors have different *byte orders*. This means that the four bytes of the 32-bit hexadecimal number

```
0x04030201
```

can have this order inside a machine, but they could also be 0x01020304, or even 0x02010403 on PDP-11 computers. This makes clear that the left rotation of this number by, say, 17 bits, produces a different value on each machine. An important feature of RC5a is that this program tests the byte order, and always writes the cipher in the byte order of Intel processors (the so-called *little-endian* representation).

The practical consequence is that RC5a-encrypted texts can be exchanged between Intel computers and Sun workstations, for example. The reference implementation in [RivRC5] does not use a binary input and output, which means that it doesn't solve the byte-order problem.

Cryptographic Details: Passphrase and Ciphering Mode

When entering a passphrase, the *check_passphrase()* function currently only verifies whether it contains both letters and numbers, and whether it is at least six characters long. It is very easy to modify this function.

The ciphering mode is more interesting. If you set the macro SIMPLE_CBC (compiler switch *-DSIMPLE_CBC*) during the compilation, then *rc5a* works in CBC mode. By default, however, it doesn't XOR the plaintext with the last ciphertext block, but instead carries two 32-bit words, *CBC_A* and *CBC_B,* along in parallel for the encryption. In every ciphering step, *CBC_A* is increased by the left half ciphertext block rotated, and *CBC_B* is decreased by the right half ciphertext block rotated. The rotation amounts are determined from the right or left *plain*text half blocks, respectively:

```
CBC_A += ROTL(A,B0)
CBC_B -= ROTR(B,A0)
```

(*B*0, *A*0 are the plaintext half blocks.) Admittedly, this is a willful ciphering mode and very much tailored to RC5. But I haven't discovered a vulnerability yet. In the event that you need a self-synchronizing mode, you can convert '+ =' and '− =' into simple equal signs, while still using a novel type of mode (meanwhile I'm doubtful of such experiments, but keep the mode for compatibility reasons).

If you want to use RC5 instead of RC5a, you simply set

```
#define KEYBOX_BITS  0
```

to make each keybox consist of one single element only, and RC5a will turn into RC5. A good compiler will then create a code that's just as short as if you compiled RC5 directly. The use of RC5a won't have measurable performance losses anyway.

The Header Structure

The CBC mode requires a random initialization vector that can be accommodated in a header. I used this in RC5a for building in a checksum (as described in Section 5.1.3) and the version number in this header. Again, this is programmed a little willfully:

The header of an encrypted file consists of six plaintext blocks (i.e., 48 bytes). The first four blocks are random (more about this in a minute); the fifth block contains the version and release numbers (the version in half block A and the release in B); and the sixth block contains a checksum.

The first four blocks are filled in the machine-dependent function *make_random()*. I use the output of the UNIX command *ps* with those options that list the largest amount of information about all processes running in the system (start time, process number, addresses, owners, states, etc.). Even if you are the only user of a UNIX system, many processes can be active so that the output of the command cannot be predicted. Though the execution of the command costs some time, I didn't find this to be a disturbance.

The *make_random()* function compresses a long field, $B_{0...n}$, to four blocks, $F_{0...3}$, by the formula

```
F_k%4 = F_k%4 ⊕  A
A = A ⊕ (B_k <<< A)
```

where $k\%4$ is the divisional remainder when dividing k by 4, B_k is a 32-bit word from the field (the output of *ps*), and A is a 32-bit word. Neither A nor F is initialized.

The background is a sufficiently strong mixing of the bits of B. Careful cryptographers would use a hash function at this point, but I think that's just introducing unnecessary overhead. The computation of the checksum is just as easy (see the *check_head()* function). Its main purpose is also to provide a sufficiently probable pretest for a password rather than cryptographic security—and it does meet this requirement.

The header is encrypted in ECB mode. During the decryption, RC5a first checks the checksum and then the version and release numbers. In the event that the ciphering mode or the algorithm change, then future versions should be able to decrypt all previous versions based on the version and release numbers. It might even help to increase the security by simply decrypting and subsequently encrypting with the same program.

Padding

RC5a pads the last block, as described in Section 5.1.2, using a simple 'count byte' at the end. The fact that it might append up to eight bytes doesn't matter in view of a 48-byte header.

A Treacherous Friend: Variable Number of Rounds

Taking a closer look at the program will reveal that RC5a already comes in Version 2.0. This is because I discarded Version 1.0 (which implemented 'only' RC5, by the way) pretty soon. The main reason was a variable number of rounds, for example, depending on the last ciphertext block. I thought back then that it would be particularly secure, because cryptanalysts usually focus on algorithms with constant numbers of rounds. As it happens, variable numbers of rounds are actually a welcome vulnerability for cryptanalysts.

Suppose we know a few plaintext–ciphertext pairs, and that the ECB mode is used for encryption, for the sake of simplicity. When encrypting in step k with r rounds, and then later on the same plaintext in step k' with $r+1$ rounds (which is known to the cryptanalyst), then he knows the input for the last round in step k': the ciphertext from step k. We saw in Section 5.4.2 how the one-round RC5 can be broken.

In CBC mode, though the encryption of identical plaintexts in successive steps is very improbable, it is better, and we don't have to worry about these types of attacks. This is why I recommend a constant number of rounds. You can use RC5a in ECB mode, too (it just takes a simple change to the program).

7.7 Bottom Line

Hopefully you have realized that you have to look *behind* the scenes in cryptographic software (as opposed to other much praised, colorful and easy-to-use applications). I realize that this is diametrically against the current trend. However, unless we do a sound evaluation, the probability to get *snake oil* is simply too high: products that make bizarre pseudo-scientific claims of amazing new breakthroughs in technology are almost certainly snake oil. I haven't found a doable way out of this situation. Vendors of poor software should be pilloried, and users should be made aware of the risks and damages incurred. But try to get a security person to admit that vulnerabilities in their software have been exploited.

We have only dealt with a tiny part of existing software in this chapter. I doubt whether the evaluation of the most important programs would even fit into one book. But I'm sure you saw the things I wanted to make a point of.

Among the programs discussed here, SSH is probably the best in terms of user friendliness, security, and functionality. That doesn't hurt PGP, though: it was the first really popular cryptographic program, offered users all over the world security across all operating systems, and even had an impact on political affairs. It is still unprecedented in its field—the exchange of secure email.

What's missing is perhaps the most important and best free cryptography software: **OpenSSL**. It can be used both as a library for C programs and in scripts thanks to its command-line interface. The reason I mention this thoroughly tested and very secure software only in this section is very simple: there is an excellent book on it, namely *Secure Programming Cookbook for C and C++* [ViegaMess]. Although it is a cookbook for programmers, as the title suggests, it belongs on your bookshelf, just as does [FergSchnPract], if you want to design on your own.

Finally, I spare you a discussion of snake-oil products. The cryptanalysis of such programs is rather an issue that belongs to Chapters 2 and 3, i.e., historic cryptography.

Chapter 8

Cryptology, Politics, and Business

We arrive at the end of this book and get back to its beginning: what role does cryptology play today and in the future? We know more about this fascinating field than we did at the beginning. So we can be more specific and try to propose solutions to the problems.

8.1 The End of the Crypto-Monopoly

When our notion of values was essentially connected to material goods, it was primarily a matter of protecting *them* against theft and destruction. Our entire security technology and laws are still oriented to this: locks, doors, alarm systems, estate regulations, deed registrations, and so on. In contrast, the protection of knowledge, such as by patents or copyrights, is much more complicated.

Really sensitive information that had to be kept secret was in the hands of diplomats, intelligence agencies, and militaries. No wonder these were the home of cryptology. According to [KahnCode], who consulted many militaries and members of intelligence agencies, cryptanalysis helped win more information about the adversary than the entire espionage activities in World War II. Better

Cryptology Unlocked   Reinhard Wobst
© 2007 John Wiley & Sons, Ltd

yet, cryptanalysis was decisive for the outcome of the war. Some examples from this era and the time after show this rather dramatically.

- The landing of the allied forces in World War II would have been delayed considerably if the Enigma code of the submarines hadn't been broken. It is assumed that nuclear bombs would have fallen over Europe.

- The battle near the Midway Islands stopped the Japanese in the Pacific. This battle would surely have taken a different turn if the Japanese had introduced their new secret code in May 1942, as planned, and not in June—the battle took place at the beginning of June. Cryptanalysis had an important part in the success of the USA.

- The German Wehrmacht threatened to land in Great Britain. After a few disasters for the British navy, which indicated the fact that the German radio reconnaissance listened in on them, the code was finally changed, and the tide turned suddenly.

- The fall of a French fortress in Vietnam was believed to have happened because of cryptology.

You can find a large number of historical events in the book by Kahn mentioned above.

Cryptology was once a power factor and a monopoly of governments. This changed quickly when a demand for secrecy of information emerged among firms and then increasingly among individuals. The turning point in public cryptological research was probably triggered by the publication of DES in the mid-1970s. The entire matter may really have been caused by a misunderstanding between the NSA and the NIST (see Section 4.3.1). Nevertheless, the demand for a generally accessible secure method had become urgent by the development of computer technology anyway. In cryptological research work from those times I know about, DES (in addition to asymmetric methods) played an extraordinary role. Finally, a good algorithm had become known and could be analyzed.

Meanwhile, cryptology has become an everyday matter for everybody. It will hardly protect anybody from business-secret theft. The most you can do is to sue the thief if you find him. By then it is normally too late in our fast-paced world. Interception-proof transmission channels will remain exceptional cases, if only for cost reasons. Furthermore, theft of information can seldom be proved. What remains is cryptography as a means of protecting against theft. The way toward a phase where protection of information will be a matter of course will probably be painful, but we have to go this way. Books like [SchnFear] show how difficult the entire security issue is, but this would go beyond the scope and volume of this book.

8.2 The Role of Politics Today

We don't know what non-public cryptological research looked like in the past and what it looks like today. The figures about the NSA mentioned at the end of Section 3.1 suggest that a considerable part of this research is still secret. We also don't know what the NSA can decrypt and how fast. There isn't even more than speculation about the computer technology it uses.

But I'm convinced that even the NSA cannot eavesdrop everything. It may be in a position to capture *and evaluate* communications. To underpin this daring statement, I will deviate briefly from cryptology to the question: how real is the anonymous threat by national intelligence agencies really?

8.2.1 A Look Into the World of Intelligence Agencies

This heading intentionally sounds a bit sensationalistic: I think this section is important and I want to draw the attention of many readers to it. Some things discussed in the following are based on speculation, for a well-known reason: since I don't work for an intelligence agency, I know only a little for sure. If I worked for such an agency, I would also know its methods (which is by no means the same). But then, I wouldn't be allowed to write about it in this book.

Anyhow, the sure facts, paired with obvious assumptions and the knowledge of technical possibilities, render a scary picture. This section alone would be enough motivation to write a book about cryptology. If you want to know more, I recommend you to read the book [WinkSpy] written by the former NSA employee Ira Winkler, who was out on spying assignments for firms to find security holes. In Section 1.1 of his book, he describes how an intelligence agency works, which is much more prosaic than Joe Average might think—and yet much more dangerous than we want to believe. The following is targeted in exactly this direction.

Traffic Analysis

As mentioned earlier, national intelligence agencies are often not interested in *what* a message contains, but *who* sent the message to *whom* and *when*.

The evaluation of this type of information is referred to as *traffic analysis*. The article by Schwartz and Wood, (on our Web site *www.wileyeurope.com/ go/cryptology*) is very illuminating in this respect (see also the end of Section 7.1.3). This article was written in 1992 when the Internet was 'small'. The authors collected data crossing 15 mail nodes over a period of two months. At the end, they had about 1.2 million emails of about 50 000 users on 17 000 computers in 31 countries. The significant growth of information happened in the first few days; the daily information yield then dropped by a factor of 10. Based on their analysis, the authors could clearly make out single groups of interest without previously having searched for specific topics. Also, it didn't matter if one email user belonged to several such groups.

The remarkable thing about this analysis is that Schwartz and Wood weren't interested in the email contents at all; they only acquired who mailed to whom how often.

You might think: 'So what, let the NSA know who I converse with!' Unfortunately, things are not that harmless. I will show this in another example.

There were once 'eternal phone cards' that reloaded themselves after use. Early in 1997, a case reported in Dresden had it that three users of such cards were busted while still in the phone booth. Of course, nobody would tell us how the trap the three fell into worked. But this example shows that card phones must be somehow online-connected to some center. It is also known that each phone card has a unique serial number, and that this number is reported to a center (together with all connection data) upon each call.

From the purely technical point of view, we have to assume that the owner of a phone card, though initially anonymous, can be identified perhaps after 20 or fewer calls made with this card thanks to his calling structure, at least in theory. This also means that he can be allocated to calls he conducted earlier. If this type of information harvesting does actually take place (I'm afraid it does), then it will certainly not become public in the next ten years.

More speculation: owners of cell phones tell their networks pretty good movement patterns, and the data acquired are forwarded to the center at intervals of about 10 to 15 minutes. Theoretically, cell phones would even allow somebody to do a highly precise radio position finding, though it appears to be too expensive yet, at least for the network operators. However, based on the rough radio cells, it is often possible to clearly determine when you have used which railway route or highway. Together with other information about you, this can produce your travel destination or the length of your trip.

Though network operators say that movement patterns are not yet acquired comprehensively, and that they delete the connection data after 80 days at the latest, we don't know what copy is meant. Once gathered without the users' consent, this type of data remains available forever. If what the Swiss paper *Sonntagszeitung* once wrote is true, then the Swiss police logged the movements of about one million cell phone users over a half-year period. In the name of the fight against terror, this type of data acquisition is likely to be legally enforced in Europe. The discussion about the technical feasibility has already begun.

Within the scope of so-called **locally based services** (**LBS**) of cell phone providers, the business world even wishes for an exact location finding of all users to be able to inform them of their special offers in time. Since October 1, 2001, a law in the USA requires providers to locate each handset two-thirds of the time to a 125-m accuracy. Data privacy laws in the USA are less restrictive than they are in Europe in general: if you give your personal data to a merchant (e.g., when acquiring a customer card), then the merchant owns your data, and he can sell it or do whatever he deems fit.

With the technical means available today and in the near future, you can collect incredible amounts of interesting information easily to keep 'in stock'. At the appropriate time (when the person concerned becomes of interest or falls out of favor for some reason or other), 'one' can fall back on it. Research work on national intelligence agencies showed that this takes only little personnel cost. It is estimated to amount to a few dozen or hundred employees per country.

Imagine an investigator telling you where you had been at a certain time after many years. You don't even remember yourself, and threw out your appointment book years ago. Greetings from Orwell.

You think this is gray theory? The text of the Telecommunications Surveillance Directive (Fernmeldeverkehr-Überwachungs-Verordnung; FÜV) of May 18, 1995, valid in Germany, is primarily about traffic analysis of monitored subscriber lines (including cell phones). However, considering the large variety of information to be supplied, the text suggests that authorized government agencies have access to connection details, too. There is currently a fierce dispute about the passing on of position-finding information to government agencies.

There is more evidence on the evaluation of the phone traffic mentioned above. In 1997, a reference application of a supercomputer concerned the so-called *call records analysis* in the telecommunications area, which is nothing but traffic analysis. More specifically, it relates to two Sun Ultrasparc 10000s with 64 processors each and a total disk capacity of 8.5 Tbytes (i.e., 8500 Gbytes) and 56-Gbyte memory. A Sun representative argued that this gigantic hardware deployment was required, for example, to grant discounts for preferred phone numbers. Well, businesses seem to do everything to keep their customers happy. By the way, this is possible thanks to the thorough digitalization of the telephone network.

Similar computers were produced by other manufacturers, including DEC, SGI, IBM, and Hewlett-Packard. And we are talking only of the civilian area here.

The NCR corporation shipped a *data-warehouse* application to Mannesmann; that's a huge database with a capacity of about 1.2 Tbytes [InfWeek]. To my knowledge, the biggest data warehouse with a data capacity of 24 Tbytes is in use at Wal-Mart. How these data are evaluated is not disclosed, 'because data warehousing allows you to be very close to the core of corporate strategy' [InfWeek]. It is less likely to know whether or not a national intelligence agency is granted access.

The bad thing about traffic analysis is that we cannot prevent it. Schwartz and Wood recommend the 'ethical use' of such algorithms. No comment. Also, so-called *mix servers* that anonymize Web access and have been used successfully (see anon.inf.tu-dresden.de) catch only a small part of our broad data trace and are hardly used, compared with the usual Web traffic. Meanwhile, it is believed that mix servers supply all data upon the request of investigative agencies.

Noticed something about the years mentioned? Everything is history! Today, in the name of the fight against terror, data about us that accrue somehow somewhere are openly requested to be made available. Including in Germany, the homeland of data privacy. The technical possibilities have greatly evolved, and meanwhile people have started to publicly become aware of the problem. I ask myself whether it isn't already too late. Read about the megalomaniac project named 'Information Awareness Office' (**IAO**) in Wikipedia (and is included on the Web site under *txt/policy/Information_Awareness_Office.html*). You will be amazed just how hungry for data they all are out there. This project, formerly called **TIA** (Total Information Awareness) and probably going by the name of **Tangram** in the near future, tries to acquire simply everything about all citizens of all countries to (initially) support the fight against terrorism.

Topic Analysis

Traffic analysis is still a current topic, but there are meanwhile much better surveillance methods. Traffic is out, topic is in—contents are already being acquired automatically. Of course, this doesn't mean that computers have already evolved to being able to understand contents, but they can classify them automatically. One of the most important technologies in this respect seems to be the *N-gram Analysis* developed and patented by the NSA. Computers can use this method to quickly sort large quantities (several million) of messages by author, language, content, writing style, and so on. There is no longer a programmer at his desk wracking his brain about sorting criteria. For example, the computer is fed with 100 emails from a range of interesting topics or circle of authors, and then filters 'suspect' emails all on its own. You see how naïve it is to believe that intelligence agencies' computers could be overfed by appending words like 'coke' or 'bomb-building instructions'. The remarkable thing is how insensitive the N-gram Analysis is to errors: according to the NSA research workgroup, about 10 % to 15 % of all characters can be faulty. You can easily imagine where this is important: in writing recognition for automatic evaluation of telefaxes.

This technique is also doubtful in that it has been commercially available since 1994. Businesses are also highly interested in classifying by contents. I knew a product (Xtra Secure, `www.thunderstore.com`; which didn't use N-gram Analysis though) that assigned security not only by access privileges, but also by the contents of files or emails. This means that a trainee wouldn't have unauthorized access to sensitive data even if the administrator forgot to set his access privileges right. Or she can read files, but cannot pack them into email and send them to somebody. This is major progress, but the same technique can be used to achieve a new quality of corporate internal surveillance.

An Octopus by the Name of Echelon

Yet another sensational heading—and one that has a good reason, because we are talking of widely proven findings about global interception activities.

The technically most interesting forms of eavesdropping by major Western intelligence agencies appeared to have arranged themselves in the strictly secret worldwide espionage network known as the **Echelon system**. This system appears to mainly work out of one single gigantic power center—the NSA, as you might have guessed.

There is quite a lot of information on Echelon on the Internet. One interesting starting point is to launch your favorite search engine to look for +*NSA* +*UKUSA* (in this spelling). Another source of information is looking for 'Echelon' in Wikipedia. It is rewarding. However, a large amount of information seems to be from the same source: the book *Secret Power* by Nicky Hager, which appeared in New Zealand in 1996 [Hager]. It must have been shocking for the intelligence agencies concerned to see the word 'Echelon' printed at all (ask around who knows it in Germany). When Hager's book appeared, intelligence agencies were said to have held crisis meetings where they considered withdrawing the book from the market right away. Eventually, it was found that this would have given the book even more publicity (it was reprinted in the same year, by the way). Figure 8.1 shows a rough overview of the system.

The **Echelon system** is organized and realized by the NSA (National Security Agency). It serves for worldwide surveillance of email, fax, telex, telephone, cell phone, and other wireline and wireless communication types.

Echelon monitors primarily non-military targets: governments, organizations, firms, and individuals. From the entire communications (including phone calls) eavesdropped, the system filters and sorts interesting messages automatically, which may then be classified manually, and finally archived.

Echelon is implemented within the **UKUSA alliance**, which is an intelligence agencies' alliance, and its members include the USA (NSA), Canada (CSE), Great Britain (GCHQ), Australia (DSD), and New Zealand (GCSB). The system has interception stations in other countries, such as Germany, Japan, South Korea, and Turkey. There are stations even in countries like China, but they won't profit much from the information won there. Every member country selects by the criteria of the others concurrently. The five UKUSA organizations are the largest and least known intelligence agencies in their own countries. But the NSA is behind all of them. It is believed to be the only one that has access to all information.

Echelon includes a large number of subsystems, which are known only in part:

- Interception stations for international communication satellites (particularly for the US Intelsat series).

- Interception stations for local message satellites.

- Relay stations for espionage satellites.

- A system for wiretapping radio-relay paths (terrestrial and from orbit), which concerns most phone connections.

Figure 8.1: A few basic facts on the Echelon system.

- Dozens of listening and position-finding posts eavesdrop the short- and long-range radio traffic (mobile radio, marine radio, microwave radio, diplomatic communications).

- Lines are said to be tapped directly, but little is known (see below).

There are five stations to eavesdrop *Intelsat communications*:

- Near Morwenstow in Cornwall (Great Britain) for the Atlantic, Europe, and the Indian Ocean.

- An NSA station near Sugar Grove, about 250 km south of Washington, DC, for communications of Atlantic satellites to North and South America.

- An NSA station in Yakima in the state of Washington, 200 km south of Seattle, for the Pacific and the Far East.

- Waihopai in New Zealand (was important in the Falkland and Vietnam wars).

- Geraldton in Western Australia for the rest of the Pacific region.

A station of the British GCHQ in Hong Kong disappeared in time before the city came to China.

Local satellites are eavesdropped, among others, in:

- Menwith Hill in northern England (the largest station with 22 satellite terminals; played an important role in the Gulf War).

- Shoal Bay near Darwin in northern Australia (for Indonesia communications).

- Leitrim south of Ottawa in Canada (for Latin America).

- Misawa in northern Japan.

The known NSA station in Bad Aibling near Rosenheim in southern Germany presumably served to receive signals from (and control) ground-level flying espionage satellites which, in turn, scan the radio and relay traffic in western Europe (?). The white balloons are intended to hide the direction of the antennas, by the way.

It is estimated that there is a total of about 120 active ground stations. An analysis of the antennas suggested that about 40 stations wiretap the message communications

Figure 8.1: (*continued*)

in Western countries, 50 additional stations wiretap the countries of the former
Soviet Union, and the remaining 30 stations serve for addressing their own espionage satellites.

An example of direct wiretapping of lines is an anonymous brick building in London (8 Palmer Street), which eavesdrops on all telexes within the city, both inbound
and outbound. The existence of this station became known because a former GCHQ
employee broke his silence and said to the *Observer*: 'This has got nothing to do
with security. One simply mustn't listen in on every telex. And they replay everything: embassies, businesses, even birthday greetings—they record everything. And
they filter all that stuff with the dictionary.'

Figure 8.1: (*continued*)

Whether the largest station in Europe at Gablingen with 100-m high antenna
grids with a diameter of 300 m (where huge computer equipment on twelve
underground floors is said to be working) also belongs to Echelon is not known.

Even embassies are utilized for data espionage. In 1980 (!), the existence of an
'extraordinarily clever technology' that fills an entire embassy room and which
can be used to track any arbitrary phone conversation in the town became
known.

Every UKUSA intelligence agency filters concurrently for the other agencies,
but again: the NSA seems to be the only one which can access all, really all
information. It also accounts for the largest part of hardware and know-how
within the alliance.

These details are really 'hot'. Even politicians have been fooled by intelligence
agencies. For example, David Lange, New Zealand's Prime Minister from 1984
to 1989, calls it a scandal in the foreword to *Secret Power* to have been told so
little about the things described in the book. When New Zealand declared itself
a non-nuclear weapon zone in 1984, it was officially banned from the UKUSA
alliance. In reality, however, all listening posts continued working happily and
supplied the NSA with strategic information. As a sideline, the UKUSA alliance
was founded in 1948, and its existence is denied, according to Hager.

You are probably asking yourself how Hager got hold of that kind of information. He says how in his book. For example, he compared the internal telephone
directory of the Department of Defense with the official list of employees. All
the people not listed there must be working for an intelligence agency. The
author did more than ten years of research work and interviewed about 50

ex-employees of intelligence agencies. In his book, he describes the structure and top echelon of New Zealand's GCSB (which is even less known there than the NSA is in Germany), including the layout of rooms in the headquarters and a few interception stations. You actually get the impression that an intelligence agency was spied out by use of intelligence-agency methods.

There was something about these issues in the media at regular intervals, and an **EU Echelon Committee** had even been founded to especially deal with commercial and industrial espionage (see further below). They had hardly any doubt of the existence of this interception system, they even knew a couple of technical possibilities, and they classified the role of cryptography as a 'defense measure'. On the Web site to this book, read *txt/policy*, which is a report by Gerhard Schmid to the European Parliament on this issue, or the official report, which is very detailed.

It has become clear meanwhile that even Echelon is just one of many activities concentrated on global communications traffic. In mid-2006, for example, it transpired that the NSA monitors the network traffic independently without the assistance of the telecom groups: up to 16 servers in every interception unit analyze data in the amount of up to 2 gigabytes per second. I spare myself the details and sources, since there is plenty of material on these issues on the Net. Furthermore, such reports will have been replaced by more spectacular ones by the time this book goes to print. Let's rather talk about the theory of how such data volumes can be processed and what role cryptology plays or can play.

Stifling the Information Flood?

The most frequent response to my Echelon narration is this: 'Well, that can only concern a very small part of messages; the NSA can't possibly replay or evaluate everything.' This seems logical in view of the huge and continually growing data traffic.

Sure, the rosy years when it was possible to control a large part of all messages are over. But it would be dangerous to underestimate the technical possibilities of intelligence agencies. The so-called STOA report entitled 'Interception Capabilities 2000' of the EU gives a highly interesting insight. However, it is 140 Kb long and not easy to read. This is probably why it is not well known. Much information contained in this chapter originates from this report.

Interception is comprised of two steps: one, wiretapping the data line; and two, evaluating the data stream. As it happens, the technologies in both fields are further advanced than is generally assumed. Figure 8.2 shows examples of hardware used but long outdated.

- A firm called AST offers SONET OC-48 computers; it has a module which can record and analyze a data stream of about 2.5 gigabits per second. A memory of 48 Gbytes of RAM ensures the required buffering as the load changes. This hardware feeds a so-called *trail mapper*, which automatically recognizes and processes all common US and EU standards (including ATM).

- The FDF (*Fast Data Finder*) chip by TRW supports topic analysis and can filter several gigabytes of data daily based on ten thousands of interest patterns in online operation.

- The Model 132 by AST is a *voice-channel demultiplexer* that can scan 56 700 phone channels in parallel, and pick out 3000 arbitrary ones for further evaluation.

- The firm IDEAS offers systems the size of credit cards that fit in a laptop and can evaluate eight cell phone channels in parallel (probably including decryption). Meanwhile that's outdated, too. Special laptops are believed to be able to scan all active cell phones in the environment automatically for 'interesting' numbers.

Figure 8.2: Examples of hardware that can be used for wiretapping data channels.

That's not all, of course. It is known that radio-relay paths, satellites, and submarine cables are also wiretapped. We shouldn't assume that the data traffic of the entire Internet would be too big a mouthful for the NSA: a large part of the international communication runs over eight nodes where the interception capacity is sufficient, at least in theory.

We already know a little about the second interception level: topic and traffic analyses are extensively used in any event. The data traffic is certainly filtered at several levels to master the data flood. Former NSA Director Studeman confirmed this and commented on the monitoring of fast data traffic: 'A certain system outputs one million messages for further processing within half an hour, for example. Filters leave 6500, and then maybe 1000 really interesting ones. Ten of these messages are selected, and one single report is written at the end.' This is roughly how one can think of the monitoring of the Internet. In Great Britain, a 1-terabyte database stores the entire Usenet postings of the past 90 days for further evaluation. Important Web sites are continually checked for changes. For example, the popular site www.jya.com has been visited by the NSA every morning.

As a sideline, the German Internet providers set up the central node DE-CIX intended for routing about 80 % of the data traffic in Frankfurt. And in Frankfurt of all places, where the NSA once rented the main post office to wiretap a central switching node of the telephone network (the official tenant was the BND; see [SchHad]).

However, illegal interception activities no longer appear to be the backbone of national intelligence agencies. It is estimated that 80 % of the information is from publicly accessible sources. Our privacy shrinks, and we can't prevent it even with the best data protection. More about this further below. The information edge of the national intelligence agencies in general and the NSA in particular might be on account of their capabilities for evaluating this information better than anybody else.

An unknown percentage of interesting messages are surely missed by systems like the Echelon. But as long as we don't know better we have to assume that potentially no phone conversation, no fax, no data transmission over intercontinental networks (e.g., the Internet), and certainly no email is secure against this system. Though the encryption of email doesn't prevent traffic analysis, it does prevent a more detailed analysis of the content (if it is good).

What Can't Be Done

To spare you sleepless nights (though it gets worse!), I list a few problems the NSA doesn't seem to be able to solve below.

- While the evaluation of non-encrypted emails and printed faxes (using OCR software for writing recognition) is very easy, handwriting recognition seems to cause big headaches. One reason might be that bad handwriting is deciphered in context, and computers don't understand contexts.

- Voice recognition is even harder. When a Berliner and a Bavarian talk on the phone they'll probably have problems the first time. This is true more so for computers which don't even know what dialect and context people are talking in. Many unclearly articulated words can eventually be understood only in context. Computers don't know how to do this. It is believed that several research contracts assigned by the NSA to solve this problem have failed. One can conclude from this that listening in on spoken telephone traffic is still hard physical work, requiring enormous intelligence manpower input, despite digitalization. What makes you worry though is the article on the **Oasis** computer program, which is believed to transform voice to text. You find more about it in *txt/policy/oasis.txt* on the Web site.

- It is believed that there is already some sort of automatic voice recognition. But according to vendors of biometric systems, they still have a high error rate. In any event, intense research work is done in this field. In my opinion, it is conceivable that small Webcams in telephone booths for (still also unreliable) face recognition could identify a person more or less reliably, combined with voice recognition, in the near future.

- Naturally, the NSA cannot read emails encrypted in PGP or GnuPG if you've properly protected your private key, unless the NSA already has quantum computers, which I don't believe. In a real-world case, it was much easier to get hold of the content of PGP mail: a hardware keylogger had been built into the keyboard of the person concerned; it revealed the passphrase that protected the private key.

What's All This For?

Though this section almost goes beyond the scope and volume of this book, we should ask ourselves what the motives are behind these obviously highly important activities.

The espionage targets that became known originally related to the Cold War, as you might have expected. For example, the radio traffic of Soviet trawlers and Soviet Antarctic stations were located and tapped out of New Zealand. All information about the French nuclear tests in the South Pacific was tracked in detail. This already touched strategic military information about allies. National intelligence agencies also provide the business world with important information from industrial espionage. For example, the New Zealand agency GCSB is said to have spied on the Japanese negotiating meat prices in the early 1990s. The financial gain from this information was said to have been so high it might have paid for New Zealand's Tangimoana station. The STOA report mentions a 1.2-billion-dollar contract for the SIVAM surveillance system for the Brazilian rainforest. In this case, the NSA wiretapped phone calls between Thomson-CSF and Brazil in 1994, and the US corporation Raytheon was eventually awarded the contract (since it knew its competitor's price offers). Incidentally, Raytheon was the supplier of important equipment for Echelon ground stations. The European Airbus Consortium lost a 6-billion-dollar contract for Saudi Arabia to McDonnell Douglas since the NSA had stored all phone calls and faxes between the negotiating parties via wiretapped telephone satellite.

As expected, there has also been abuse. For example, Margaret Thatcher had two unpopular ministers tailed by the Canadian intelligence agency CSE (to make sure the British GCHQ would officially remain clean in the event it was disclosed). It won't take you by surprise to hear that organizations such as *Amnesty International* are under surveillance by the UKUSA agencies.

Without question, the use of intelligence information is extremely important for the business world. This can even be behind an apparent investigation of illegal weapon trafficking (Nicky Hager mentions such an example). But even if this kind of 'intelligence service' is really of national interest because it's good for national business, there is a fly in the ointment: only the big global corporations have access to these sources, which necessarily promotes monopolization. This is presumably the scope of the activities of the small but not unimportant US **FinCEN** intelligence agency, which is believed to be responsible for insufficient encryption of financial transactions.

8.2.2 Privacy Shrinks

Joe Average sees the biggest threat in that potentially everybody can be spied on in view of current technologies, even in arrears, as opposed to old spy thrillers. Intelligence agencies collect data illegally and keep it in stock, and the storage and (continually improving) evaluation of these data are no longer a problem today. Expect to be asked in the year 2011 what you did on March 13, 2008 at about 15.00 hours in front of 27 Garden Street in Forest Town. You might have long forgotten where this place was at all. Schneier [SchnLie] even thinks that in a few generations from now we will record our entire lives, and that everybody not carrying his 'recorder' on him will be a suspect. I am slowly starting to think so, too.

Some strategists may think the transparent humans from Orwell's book *1984* will become feasible in the foreseeable future. They may find this possibility too enticing to let even the slightest scruple spring up. This is evidenced by agreements on a global 'interception system' between the EU and the FBI. Specifically, a resolution was passed at a conference of the European justice and home ministers in Brussels at the end of November 1993. Among other things, this resolution foresees an expert group to define single steps in the construction of this interception system. A declaration made in 1994, but publicized only in 1996, requests that telecommunication providers decrypt all messages for intelligence agencies. And not only that: they are to supply all connection data (including failed dial attempts), and decode and decompress all messages! In doing this, network providers have to ensure that their customers don't know anything about these activities. German readers will recall the Telecommunications Surveillance Directive mentioned earlier. You find more details in the file *feb97_state.txt* on the Web site. Countries not participating in such agreements are involuntarily eavesdropped, as already happens with the Echelon system.

Outdated Ideas

What I have said above underpins the cliché of almighty intelligence agencies. While they certainly have comprehensive access to your data, there are many other organizations that know a lot about you. For example, do you have a customer card for your favorite department store? It might not worry you if this store knows that you bought a huge pack of diapers for 14.95 pounds at 11.47 on September 23. But the more buying transactions are recorded, the more information can be won about you.

- Do you prefer hot sales or brands? Do you respond to price reductions? Do you look for a good price–performance ratio?

- Do you pick articles from the front shelf, or do you discover 'hidden' stuff?

- Do you buy regularly or on certain days of the month? (Aha, that's probably when you get your paycheck.)

- What books, perfumes, and clothes do you prefer?

- Has your buying pattern changed over the past few years?

You see that appropriate software can help build a personality image from 'totally harmless' buying activities. You will now better understand why you get discounts on your customer card. I recall the data harvesting at Wal-Mart mentioned above, that comprises at least 24 TB. This is 24 times more than all postings in Usenets (newsgroups) of the past 90 days. (By the way, these Usenet postings are stored in Great Britain and are presumably regularly evaluated by the GCHQ [Wobghm].)

If you now think that this can't happen in Germany, believing that things like this aren't allowed, I have to disappoint you. Apart from the fact that information has no national borders anymore, I want to briefly tell you something about a cashier slip I got in a renowned clothing store in March 2001. I paid with my bank card and accidentally signed that the firm is authorized to ask my bank for my name and address in case the debit cannot be honored. That's all right. But then there was some small print: 'I agree that in the event of dishonoring the bill, then this fact may be added to a bad-credit file and transferred to other companies who also use this debit system.' We aren't talking about trade-protection associations here! It might be enough for my account to just happen to be in the red due to a fraudulent access when the store tries to debit this amount. My name will then be 'going around', while I haven't done anything wrong. Such information cannot be 'undone'.

The technical possibilities already available today go far beyond our imagination. For example, the Racal systems were introduced at a price of 2000 pounds per unit in Great Britain in 1994. These are cameras that acquire and pass on vehicle license plates automatically. These systems form the *Ring of Steel* around London: no single car can enter or leave London without being reported immediately. These activities had originally been motivated by the tracking down of Northern Irish terrorists. The telephone surveillance in the EU is said to be on account of crime prevention.

Great Britain seems to be at the front when it comes to the surveillance of individuals. Statistics have it that every Londoner is acquired and stored in 300 cameras per day on average. So-called stroboscopic cameras (like the Danish *Jai* camera, for example) can acquire several hundred faces in a few seconds. Though face recognition is still relatively flawed, it will perhaps help to filter suspect persons in a crowded stadium much faster than humans could in the future. NeuroMetric, a firm based in Florida, says it can compare 20 faces against a database with 50 million records per second. Luckily, there is still a big gap between wish and reality: the error rate in face recognition in an outdoor area can be 50 %.

Another characteristic that could be used for identification is the human gait, as we know from the section on biometrics. Already today, microphones can be integrated in chips, directional microphones can listen in on conversations from a distance of hundreds of meters, and relatively cheap laser microphones can make you understand conversations behind window panes from several kilometers away. Does anything remain private?

Almost nothing. However, the methods mentioned last show only what can be achieved using *unlawful* means. One has to know them, because data privacy isn't as well protected in all countries as it is in Germany. If you take a connecting flight at London Heathrow airport, your face is likely to be stored, and who knows where it will land next? Data privacy at home won't help you much there.

But *lawful* means also help to continually create better and better profiles, because the data track we leave behind grows continually wider. Whether you make a speech somewhere, or see a medical doctor, or get books from a lending library, or pay for your purchases by bank card, or write letters to newspaper editors—nothing will be lost, and some will even land on the Internet.

Personal data are increasingly managed by private organizations, often beyond any control, because customer lists are corporate secrets. Nobody outside these organizations knows what happens to these data (and whether some are illegally sold). So let's be matter-of-fact and limit ourselves to the discussion of technical possibilities.

A security expert once said at a conference in 2000: 'It's correct that they know all about you. It's wrong to think they all cooperate.' This is the current state of affairs (in Germany!), but it might be totally different tomorrow. See Professor Cochrane's homepage (`www.labs.bt.com/library/cochrane/index.htm`). We won't be permanently able to prevent a lot of personal data from 'starting to walk'. The extent of the illegal address trade suggests what the practice looks like. Trading with data is legal in other countries. In the USA, individuals don't own the data about themselves. They belong to the businesses that collect them. A merchant might sell them. If you are interested in these issues, I recommend the book *Secrets and Lies* by Bruce Schneier [SchnLie].

It seems that nobody actually knows how to handle these problems. The article in *txt/policy/globueberwachung.txt* shows how fateful data gathering can be when it falls into the wrong hands by using the example of Norwegian Jews in World War II. On the other hand, we shouldn't try to stubbornly 'stonewall', but instead think of how to live in a world with meager privacy. Some protests seem stilted. After all, car license plates are there for publicly showing who a car belongs to. Is it really that bad if their registration is automated? Could you prevent it? I don't think so. We have to learn to accept it.

There is a much harder problem: our communications are increasingly electronic, which means that they can be stored forever, as opposed to the volatility of traditional voice communication. A silly joke you mailed out to your pals five years ago can all of a sudden make you a target in a terror investigation. How do we handle this?

For one thing, I think there is plenty of catching up to be done. Also—an issue that would easily make a separate chapter—we have to ask ourselves how far the protection of information can or may be carried. The reason is that, in contrast to material goods, the value of information doesn't increase as it becomes scarcer. Readers interested in this issue should read the fascinating book [DRM]; it only appears to be dry reading matter at first.

So this is the background on which we have to see the benefits of cryptography. Cryptography should be a matter of fact for firms, and individuals should be responsible for their own data protection. While politicians are still trying to set up fortresses ('the passing on of data is strictly forbidden'), practice undermines the walls in several places.

These kinds of considerations spoil the joy about 'revolutionary' changes upon the release of hard cryptography in some countries. In France, for example, secure encryption is now also permitted to individuals. The nasty US export regulations (limiting key lengths to 40 bits in export versions, with a few exceptions) seem to have been removed. This is certainly a loss for eager eavesdroppers. In the meantime, however, a large number of other possibilities for espionage have emerged, and increasingly more insecure computer systems can be cracked, some even automatically. Also, the pressure of the business world to permit secure cryptography grew considerably in the 1990s. With their restrictive export policies, the USA even harmed their own cryptographic software manufacturers, because European (including German) manufacturers meanwhile happily jumped into this 'market gap'. We will get back to this issue in Section 8.2.4.

8.2.3 Key Escrow

As mentioned in the last section, demands for more data protection in the business world have increased strongly. Something has to be done. But influential circles that appreciate the role of cryptology won't have their power restricted voluntarily. Zimmermann's PGP slogan, 'encryption for everybody', must have been a thorn in their sides back then.

On the other hand, politicians in many countries confirm that the protection of secrets is necessary for individuals, too, because this is the only way the information society will work. The bridge to overcome this conflict of interests is referred to as **key escrow**. Everybody may encrypt, but the 'government' should be allowed to read it upon demand. It should be given the secret key somehow. As usual in such matters, organized crime has been stated as the reason for this key escrow. If we can't get hold of the communications of these criminals, so the argument goes, they will turn into a huge threat.

The consequence was a hefty discussion in many countries, including Germany. People shouldn't look only at their own countries. I recommend studying the *Crypto Law Surveys* by Bert-Jaap Koops, which you find in the *txt/policy/claw 1996.txt* directory on the Web site. Which give an overview of the legal status in many countries as of 1996. Compare this with the content of *claw2001.txt*!

This is why key escrow continues to be utopia. We already saw this in the discussion about the Clipper chip. Figure 8.3 lists some substantial arguments.

This kind of insight apparently made it all the way to the highest circles. The wish for key escrow has certainly not disappeared, but when uninformed and suspicious citizens eventually boycott e-commerce because of this, then that's beyond a joke. Law-abiding people suffer from key escrow (and use the new media insufficiently, so they are not profitable for the future industry), while criminals have no problem in bypassing the laws. That's absurd.

It is more meaningful in my opinion to focus more on catastrophic insecurity of software and hardware used currently, see, for example, the attack against home banking described in Section 6.5. The consequential damage can hardly be estimated!

Key escrow is wishful thinking and just fighting the symptoms. When it first emerged, the telephone also opened up totally new options for criminals. Back then, people used codewords to protect themselves from being eavesdropped. This didn't lead to banning the telephone, of course. As a sideline, a request to submit codeword books and the ban on using own codebooks would have corresponded to key escrow.

Nevertheless, there is a legal field of application for key escrow: internal corporate use. Sensitive encrypted data need to be decrypted even if the key was lost by carelessness, or in case of software or hardware failures. Furthermore, the management of a corporation is entitled to check outgoing mails for confidential data. But that's a technical rather than a political problem and, as such, doesn't belong in this chapter.

Feasibility

A ban on secure cryptography becomes necessary. This is hard to control and unacceptable for firms. No national key escrow is possible in international data traffic.

Bypassing Potential

Cryptologically secure steganography (similar to subliminal channels for digital signatures) will be developed and used. Algorithms implemented in hardware can be slightly protected against key escrow by whitening. The use of secure algorithms will be camouflaged in many different ways.

Figure 8.3: Arguments against key escrow.

Risks Due to Abuse

A stolen 'picklock' (perhaps only after its generation, similar to eavesdropping on the Clipper chip) is related to a much smaller risk for the investigators, compared with the theft of other information. The risk of corruption and bribing is very high.

Both individuals and businesses are almost defenseless in the event of a political overthrow.

Relativity

Key escrow is expensive. Huge amounts of data have to be searched to filter a comparatively small amount of interesting information that merely complement other data harvested in a traditional way. The major part concerns information on law-abiding citizens. The protection of these data (which is never perfect anyhow) against misuse and abuse causes costs not to be underestimated.

Harmfulness

The information society needs strong cryptology. Key escrow would hinder or even stop the required public research in this field. Limitation to a few algorithms is a basic risk. *Cryptography needs diversity; otherwise it is too dangerous.*

Acceptance

When the public is informed about the matter, strong resistance has to be expected, which increases the creativity in finding bypasses.

Figure 8.3: (*continued*)

8.2.4 Export Regulations and Patents

This section discusses two other obstacles hindering the development of cryptology: export restrictions for cryptographic software and hardware, and patent-law issues. This discussion will be short, because both issues have come up several times in this book already.

Export Restrictions

Export restrictions are usually mentioned in connection with the US export laws, which turned into a barrier for many US firms. These laws allowed them to export only software and hardware with an effective key length of up to 40 bits. With the SSL protocol used in the Netscape Navigator browser, for example, an additional 88 key bits were shipped in an unprotected way. The following concept would probably have been better: the user sees a 128-bit key, but the key space comprises only 2^{40} elements due to secret dependencies between the bits. These dependencies would be known only to the manufacturer, and surely to the NSA. However, the question is how long such a dependency could be kept secret. One would have to implement it in a cryptologically secure and variable way. This would certainly be a challenging task for research.

How much would it cost to brute-force break such a key? Suppose a very fast implementation of the algorithm (e.g., in assembler language) on a Pentium chip manages the decryption of one million plaintexts in one second. 2^{40} keys correspond to about 10^{12} possibilities, i.e., the Pentium Pro chip would take about 500 000 seconds on average. That's almost 6 days. Using the time–memory tradeoff and several computers, the cost can be arbitrarily reduced. In short, this key space is already much too small for current and privately available computer technology, let alone special hardware. The only protection could be the secret bit dependencies within an externally longer key, as mentioned above.

Netscape didn't use such dependencies, and what's more, in software that was supposed to handle credit card numbers. However, the attacks that became known were much less clever than one would expect: hackers stole credit card numbers directly from Web servers, since they had been lying around there with almost no protection in place. This shows impressively that good cryptography is only part of comprehensive security.

Toward the end of the 1990s, even politicians and intelligence agencies apparently realized that secure cryptography 'cannot be avoided'. I assume that the business world had its share in arriving at this realization. Export regulations changed so quickly that I couldn't keep up, and I have to refer you to the Internet to learn the current status. Meanwhile, products using 128-bit keys may be exported from the USA within corresponding approval procedures. It is probably more rewarding to turn one's interest away from algorithms and key lengths and instead to look at backdoors built in application software, or better yet, to automated hacker techniques.

There has also been much speculation about the **Wassenaar accord** that includes export regulations for 33 countries, including the EU countries. As usual, the last meeting of the Wassenaar countries took place at a secret location near Vienna, Austria, and we know accordingly little about the agreements made there. Rumors have it that public-domain software was not concerned.

Let's stick to the facts: the German government financed a project in connection with the **GnuPG** mail encryption software (see Section 7.1.4) and supported its proliferation. Doesn't that speak for itself?

Patent-Law Issues

Things are slightly different when it comes to patents. Somebody who develops software knows how much money and time is involved. Good cryptographic algorithms are even harder to develop and to study. So, the question as to who is supposed to pay for this work is justified.

One solution could be publicly financed research. That's one reason why all software developed at universities is *a priori* free in the USA. This is how a considerable part—if not the largest part—of free UNIX software came about, and subsequently has had a positive effect on developments all over the world. I just mention two buzzwords: 'Linux' and 'Open Source'.

However, not all research is publicly financed. Shareware would be a good concept: users voluntarily pay a one-time fee for using the program, and proliferation of the software itself would be unlimited. (Experience has shown that shareware doesn't work in Germany, though.) But only *programs* can be shareware, *algorithms* can't. Imagine you work in a bank's procurement department, and you've just bought a novel type of ATM from IBM with the following note: 'This ATM implements the cryptographic shareware algorithms and protocols SDETY, XPKKL, and ACS-15. Please transfer the amount of 200 dollars each to...'

I guess there are currently only two ways to make money with algorithms.

- One, you can keep your algorithm secret and charge license fees for its usage. This was the case with RC4 for seven years until this algorithm was disclosed in an unauthorized way (see Section 5.6). Now basically everybody can use it legally, though RSA might sue.

  That's the big disadvantage for designers: once your product is disclosed, the source of money starts drying up. The disadvantage for users is that the algorithm cannot be studied globally. Nobody knows whether it has become known to good cryptanalysts, and whether they have found a backdoor. This should ideally cause acceptance problems among users so that they will reject this algorithm. The real world is far from being ideal, though. Imagine RC4 had been cracked before it was disclosed. A large number of programs use this algorithm.

- Two, you can have your algorithm patented. This is (fortunately) not possible in Germany, but it is in other countries, including the USA and Switzerland.

  Trying to get your algorithm patented can often backfire. For example, the Swiss IDEA patent is applicable in Germany, too. Many people thought the fees for commercial use were too high. According to a vendor of cryptographic products, he would never pay such an amount just for an algorithm. The consequence was that people held on to DES, even in critical banking applications. The vendors of IDEA apparently hurt themselves with too dashing an attempt to make money. Also, an IDEA chip found little attention in the industry. Apart from *Brokat*, the banking software mentioned in Section 5.3 and used at Deutsche Telekom, I haven't heard of IDEA being commercially used in a long time.

  The claim made by PKP (Public Key Partners) to cover all asymmetric methods with their patent led to a temporary preference for the Diffie–Hellman method from autumn 1997 onwards, because that method's patent was the first to expire after 17 years. RSA can also be used without restrictions since September 20, 2000. These patents apply only in the USA and in Canada.

The RC5 patent was to bring its owner, RSA Laboratories, small and perhaps one-time license fees for using this algorithm commercially (private use remained free). The patent's purpose—financing other research work at RSA Laboratories—was acceptable in any event. Would it have been a meaningful concept? RC6, the improved successor, would have had to remain free from patent, according to the AES challenge, had it won. It didn't, and RC6 is now patented nevertheless. But Rijndael, the AES winner, is free and commonly used. What does the patent for RC6 bring? The question about RC5 licenses has also become less interesting. It will certainly not be enough to finance the RSA firm.

I'm not the only one who thinks that patents and cryptographic algorithms don't go well together.

8.2.5 Digital Signatures

Germany passed a law for legal acceptance of digital signatures (**signature law**) in August 1997. This initiative was initially seen as progress (I thought so, too, as you can read in earlier editions), and people hoped it would have a positive effect.

We can see by the example of fax machines what can happen to an unregulated development: faxes cannot be used as legal evidence, but still, you can order merchandise, or make reservations, or whatever by fax. People simply think that the convenience of using faxes is much greater than the loss due to forged orders, and the business world bets on an insecure system.

But forged digital signatures can have more fateful consequences than faxes; it depends on the field of use. A legal framework would, therefore, be welcome.

Unfortunately, the effect of the signature law evaporated. Where are the certification entities, where are the applications that were to make everyday life easier? Though the law regulated the practical use, it failed to create spaces of freedom for it. Digital signatures weren't put on an equal footing with handwritten signatures. A decision to this effect would have been left up to the court in specific cases. What's more, the BSI (the German Federal Office for IT Security, which is part of the BND) published technical specifications for the methods to be used. Many businesses didn't like this at all, arguing that 'we're not going to let them tell us what technology to use'. The requirements on certification entities entitled to generate and certify public keys were extremely high. The effect was that there are almost no certification entities.

Eventually, the EU brought this nasty matter back on track. It demanded uniform and more liberal regulations, which the Germans initially didn't like at all. But eventually, the House of Parliament passed a new signature law in February 2001. Digital signatures are now supposed to be applicable across all states concerned, and there are (almost) no technical provisions. In turn, the certification entities are responsible for damage incurred.

The new law didn't bring about a decisive breakthrough. Similarly to the sad story about theory and practice in mail encryption, described in Section 7.2.3, wish and real world are poles apart. Bruce Schneier once said: 'The economic barriers to security are far greater than the technical ones.' Except in emails, I only use digital signatures on my electronic income-tax returns. Apart from the huge problems in the startup phase, I can't get rid of the impression that it worked much faster, simpler, and was less erroneous with paper and pen.

8.3 What Next?

Now that you've read this book you will better understand what was said in Section 1.2.2: cryptology is only a member in a long security chain, but a special one. The potential risks from bad cryptology are higher than the risks from poorly secured material assets.

- Communication intruders don't usually leave traces, and data theft can often not even be proved.

- Cracked algorithms have retroactive consequences: encrypted messages intercepted at an earlier date can perhaps be decrypted and used later on when technology marches on.

- With too strong a proliferation of one single weak encryption algorithm, or a program using it, there is a risk of massive compromise with unpredictable consequences. Suppose 70 % of digital signatures were created using the program of one single commercial vendor (which expressly excludes PGP), and the asymmetric method used would be RSA.

  None of the users would presume that the program doesn't use real randomness when generating RSA keys; instead, it uses prime numbers from a set consisting of a few million elements. When deemed necessary, a government agency could quickly factor these keys, collect global information, and pay considerable amounts of money to the dishonest vendor for his kindness.

In general, the current information security landscape looks rather gloomy, mainly in the private area. Apart from the totally insufficient security of the widely used Windows systems and a large quantity of PC software, security doesn't rank high in firms either, because it is (still) too expensive and doesn't increase operational profits. Denying vulnerabilities (I like to recall the overly used claim of '100 % reliable technology') is cheaper. All it takes is to keep secret the innards of an operating system and application software as well as the encryption algorithms used, and hope that hackers won't find these vulnerabilities. By the time they do, one would long have the next release ready, which would naturally be *much* better and *more* secure, though not totally for free.

No Reason to Panic

Nevertheless, there is actually no reason to be downcast; on the contrary, there is a lot to do. Cryptology gives us the tools that can make our world more secure. We have learned several interesting approaches in this book to dispel the concerns expressed above.

- The hourly change of the *server keys* in the Secure Shell (SSH1 (Section 7.3) limits retroactive damage caused by somebody breaking into a computer.

- The *Web of Trust* of PGP almost prevents even intelligence agencies compromising large parts of email connections. The decisive property of this network is that even a clever attacker would initially compromise only small parts of the network, which would be discovered. Even better, 'insecure customers' can be 'circumvented'. I guess power-securing works that way. Unfortunately, this beautiful concept plays almost no role in practice, as we saw in Section 7.2.3, but the Internet is based on the same philosophy and has successfully resisted all attacks to date. Perhaps this kind of error-tolerance should be planned into security more often than it is?

  The timestamp time series from Section 6.6.1 is another example of a mutual protection that can hardly be broken.

- Supporting several encryption algorithms as in SSH reduces the risks related to blindly using cryptography. Clean interfaces to the algorithms improve the situation further: suspicious users can embed their own algorithms, or compare the outputs of the methods implemented with those used in reference implementations. Moreover, it is not a problem (rather a cost issue) to use modified or stronger algorithms from other vendors, or to combine them with the algorithms built in. Problems can arise with ciphering hardware.

  My ideal is that cryptologists would find a 'component kit' of algorithms, where any combination of its parts produces a method roughly equally secure and, on the other hand, one could plausibly show that no uniform cryptanalysis of all of these methods would be possible.

- Fail-stop signatures offer at least a possibility to discover fraud, probably even to prevent it.

- Variable, combined biometric methods and two-factor authentications close dangerous security holes, which are caused solely by using weak passwords or many PINs.

In our buying decisions, in negotiations with vendors, and in product reviews, we will all be able to contribute to convincing software vendors to disclose the security-critical details of their programs provably as a matter taken for granted one day. This is currently utopia, but a quarter of a century ago when IBM and DEC dominated the market nobody would have believed that a largely vendor-independent system like UNIX (and today Linux) would proliferate so strongly (and that, over such a long period of time, an insecure and unstable system like Windows would dominate one day).

In closing, Kahn writes in his book [KahnCode] that cryptographers are about to win the race over cryptanalysts. Compared with the state of affairs up to World War II, this may be true, but we should beware of too much optimism—or do you happen to know what state non-public cryptological research has reached meanwhile? (If you do, let me know, by all means!)

In any event, cryptologists have to do a lot of research to make security compromises provable or even prevent them, and at an acceptable cost. It is theoretically even possible that cryptology will help make the information society more secure than it is today, but the way to get there is long.

Glossary

AES Advanced Encryption Standard. The successor of DES accepted in 2001. It is the Belgian **Rijndael** algorithm discussed in Section 5.5.

Altavista Popular Internet search engine (`www.altavista.com`). Though Google has meanwhile 'taken' the market, its search syntax is weaker than Altavista's. Another place to find material on cryptology is Wikipedia.

Anonymous remailer A computer (or better, a mail node) used for forwarding emails, which automatically strips sender information. There are pseudo-remailers that keep the true sender address stored locally (so that it can be given to the police), and real remailers, which prevent the path from being traced back, even if the remailer operator is extorted.

Asymmetric encryption (aka **public-key method**) An encryption method that uses two keys. The public key is used for encryption, whereas the private key is used for decryption. Asymmetric methods are used for encryption in general, *and* for session-key exchange in symmetric methods, *and* for authentication, especially for digital signatures (Sections 4.5 and 6.3).

Attacker A person who uses a software program and/or corresponding hardware to eavesdrop on communications, forge data, or pretend to be somebody else. A conventional attacker replays an encrypted message and decrypts it later. An attacker can also be a program running in the background, which collects passwords within a local network automatically for somebody to evaluate them.

Cryptology Unlocked Reinhard Wobst
© 2007 John Wiley & Sons, Ltd

Authentication A cryptologically secure method to verify the originator of a message, trying to prevent the sender from pretending to be somebody else. For example, by keying in a PIN at an ATM, the ATM authenticates the customer, because only he is assumed to know the PIN to an account. The receiver of a message *identifies* the sender, whereas the sender *authenticates* himself (proving his identity).

Avalanche effect Particularly strong diffusion of a block algorithm: every changed bit of the plaintext block should change every bit of the ciphertext block. If the probability of changing a ciphertext bit deviates from 50 %, then this is a vulnerability differential cryptanalysis could exploit (see Section 4.4.2).

Bletchley Park A strictly fenced-off area in Great Britain, where during World War II, encrypted messages of the German Wehrmacht were decrypted in masses, especially from the Enigma. At the beginning of 1944, about 7000 people worked at the Park, decrypting up to 90 000 messages per month (see Section 2.5.2).

Block, block algorithm A plaintext or ciphertext section that is encrypted or decrypted as a whole. Algorithms that encrypt only blockwise are called *block algorithms* (see 'stream cipher').

Blowfish A block algorithm developed by Bruce Schneier, which can be freely used; it is thought to be secure to date (see Section 5.7.4).

Breaking a method Using an approach to decrypt messages encrypted with a given encryption method without knowing the secret key. A method is deemed *not* to have been broken if it resists the most effective attack known by trial-and-error testing all possible keys (see 'brute force').

Brute force Trial-and-error testing all possible keys to reveal a plaintext. With 40-bit keys (e.g., in the international version of Netscape Navigator), brute force takes several computation hours on an extremely fast general-purpose computer (depending on the algorithm and the type of test). 56-bit keys (DES) require special hardware, such as the *Deep Crack* computer (see Section 4.4.1). In contrast, 80-bit keys (Skipjack) are secure into the near future. Brute force is basically impossible against 128-bit keys (IDEA) with the current technology. (One billion computers working in parallel, doing one billion decryptions per second each, would take ten million years; see Section 5.9.)

BSD Important UNIX variant, mostly popular in academic fields (representatives include SunOS and Free BSD). Large parts of it were integrated in SystemV.4 (see 'System V').

Caesar cipher Probably the simplest ciphering method (Section 2.1); no longer used.

Capstone chip A chip produced by Mykotronx for encrypted data communications with key escrow (Section 6.4.1).

CBC (Cipher Block Chaining) A ciphering mode used in block algorithms (Section 5.1.1).

CFB (Cipher Feedback) A ciphering mode used in block algorithms (Section 5.1.1).

Character coincidence Two characters coincide in the same positions when comparing two texts, which is important for computing the index of coincidence (see 'kappa').

Cipher A gibberish text (aka 'ciphertext') produced by ciphering (encrypting) a plaintext.

Ciphering error An error made in the encryption, impairing the security of the cipher. These errors often depend on the encryption method used. A typical example is selecting bad passwords (Section 3.1 and Figure 3.1).

Ciphering mode An operating mode that specifies how single plaintext and ciphertext blocks are computed in block algorithms (Section 5.1.1). The four commonly used modes are ECB, CBC, CFB, and OFB.

Ciphertext (aka 'cipher') The result of an encryption.

Ciphertext attack A cryptanalytic method that exploits only the ciphertext.

Clipper chip A variant of the Capstone chip for encrypted telephone communications.

Codebreaker A person who breaks encryption codes (as opposed to a cryptanalyst who develops the underlying theory).

Complexity theory A subsection of mathematics that tries to estimate the cost involved in solving a problem. It is very important for cryptology, because it is thought that only complexity theory can make reliable statements about the security of current encryption algorithms.

Compromise A successful cryptological attack against an encryption method or a cryptographic protocol.

Confusion The act of blurring the relationship between a plaintext and the corresponding ciphertext in the same text positions, as opposed to diffusion (Section 4.1.2).

Congruence In number theory, a subsection of mathematics, the term denotes equations with remainders when divided by integers: $a \equiv b \pmod{n}$ (also written as '$a = b$ mod n'), which means that the integers, a and b, leave the same remainder when divided by the integer module, n (see Section 4.5.3).

Cryptanalysis The art of decrypting an encrypted message without knowing the secret key, or, more generally, bypassing the secret-key defense without knowing this key (e.g., by forging a digitally signed document). This is the counterpart of cryptography.

Cryptographic protocol Cryptography implemented in practice, where several parties walk through a well-defined sequence of actions. Cryptographic protocols can be broken, just like cryptographic algorithms; their formalization is difficult (see Chapter 6).

Cryptography The art of designing encryption algorithms; the counterpart of cryptanalysis. Cryptography without knowing cryptanalysis is not meaningful (but that doesn't hold for the opposite!).

Cryptology Term used for cryptanalysis and cryptography together.

Daemon A program in UNIX that runs continually in the background, even when no user is working at the computer. For example, a daemon listens in on a network and establishes a connection when it hears a request. Other daemons adjust the system clock, or monitor the mouse port, or handle print jobs, or restrict user access to certain software, and some intercept passwords!

Denial-of-service attack A special type of attack against digital communication aimed at disturbing the traffic of messages in an untraceable way, or using cryptological means to prevent communication (e.g., by maliciously swapping a key to prevent further communication, but not by physically cutting a cable between two computers). Section 6.5.1 uses an example.

DES (Digital Encryption Standard) Still one of the most widely used encryption methods (Sections 4.3 and 4.4). DES is a product algorithm using 56-bit keys and 64-bit blocks.

Dictionary attack An attack against a reduced key space, where the structure of this key space can be described by a known basic set of keys (a *dictionary*), and by possibly modifying these keys. The most insightful example is the *Crack* program (Section 3.3).

Diffie–Hellman key exchange A cryptographic protocol for session-key distribution based on discrete logarithms (see Section 6.1.1).

Diffusion A property of block algorithms which ensures that information about parts of a plaintext block influence the entire ciphertext block (see also 'confusion'). A particularly strong diffusion is the avalanche effect (Section 4.1.2).

Digital signature A character string in a digital document that allows a person who knows the author's public key to verify whether that document really originates from this author, and that it hasn't been changed (see also 'authentication', 'integrity'). It cannot be forged without knowing the secret private key of the author.

Digram In the general sense, a pair of consecutive letters in a text. Digrams are important in classical cryptography (see Section 2.3).

Discrete logarithm See 'primitive root'.

DSA (Digital Signature Algorithm) A very secure method for creating digital signatures developed by the NSA. DSA is an integral part of DSS (Digital Signature Standard), and uses SHA (Secure Hash Algorithm) as a one-way hash function.

DSS See 'DSA'.

e-cash (electronic cash) Digital money; Section 6.6.7 discusses a protocol for e-cash.

ECB (Electronic Codebook) A ciphering mode used in block algorithms (Section 5.1.1).

Echelon A worldwide surveillance system of the NSA that monitors most international communications, and parts of national civilian communications (Section 8.2.1).

EES (Escrowed Encryption Standard) US standard for devices in connection with key escrow (see 'Clipper', 'Capstone', and Section 6.4).

Encoding The deterministic conversion of a text for the purpose of adapting it to special transmission channels (e.g., Morse code, base64, MIME). This conversion does not depend on keys. Encoding is often confused with ciphering. The difference is that encoded text can be easily read if the encoding method is known, whereas ciphering requires the knowledge of a secret key.

Enigma Famous German ciphering machine that was used to encrypt a considerable part of German communications (particularly those of German submarines) during World War II (Sections 2.5.1 through 2.5.3).

Exhaustion method See 'brute force'.

Fail-stop signature A special type of digital signature where many private keys belong to one public key. This helps to make provable successful attempts to break the underlying asymmetric method and the forgery of a digital signature (Section 6.6.5).

FEAL A block algorithm that was originally conceived as a DES substitute, but later proved to be extraordinarily insecure (Section 5.7.3).

Feistel network A particularly simple structure of a product algorithm that uses only one key-dependent function. The reversion of this function does not have to be computed during encryption (Section 4.2).

Fingerprint The MD5 checksum of a public key, which is used, for example, to verify the authenticity of this public key by phone. Fingerprints have become known mainly from the PGP software package.

Firewall A computer (or program) used to protect an intranet from external attacks based on some well-defined method. For example, a firewall may accept only specific types of data packets, check on senders, etc.

Flat or non-linear key space All keys in a *flat* key space are equally strong. The opposite is a *non-linear* key space. While the existence of weak keys is an undesirable side effect, algorithms with non-linear key spaces are aimed at ensuring that people unaware of the technique use only weak keys, making their ciphers particularly easy to decrypt. Only people knowing the internals of the algorithm can encrypt securely. This concept is even riskier than key escrow. Cryptologists are, therefore, interested in proving that the key space is flat.

GnuPG (GNU Privacy Guard) An email encryption program available for free and without license fee that implements the OpenPGP standard, in contrast to PGP Version 5.0 and higher (Section 7.1.4).

Half block The left or right half of a block, i.e., the least significant or most significant 32 bits in a 64-bit block. Half blocks are important in Feistel networks.

Hash function A sort of mapping that calculates checksums for data streams such that all possible function values occur roughly equally. The checksum is also called **hash sum** or **hash value**. Hash functions are important in search algorithms, and special hash functions are the one-way hash functions used in cryptography.

Hybrid method A cryptographic protocol where messages are encrypted by use of a common symmetric method, whereas the corresponding (random) session key is distributed by means of an asymmetric method. Hybrid methods have become very popular, e.g., in PGP (Section 4.5.2).

IDEA A product algorithm mainly used in PGP; works with 128-bit keys and 64-bit blocks, and is considered to be very secure.

Identification The act of identifying the author of a message. The receiver *identifies* the sender, whereas the sender *authenticates* himself (proves his identity).

Initialization vector ('IV' for short) A random block required in many ciphering modes as the first block. The IV causes the encryption of identical or almost identical plaintexts to produce totally different ciphertexts. Furthermore, it prevents various cryptanalytic attacks (e.g., pattern recognition).

Integrity A state proving that a (digital) document has not been tampered with, which is often guaranteed by digital signatures.

IV Short for 'initialization vector'.

Kappa (Character coincidence) A statistical quantity produced from two ciphertexts, which can be used to determine the period length in a Vigenère cipher (Section 3.6.1).

KEA A public-key algorithm used by the NSA in Clipper chips (Section 6.1.1).

Kerberos A protocol for authentication and encryption in local area networks (LANs), which relies on one or two trustworthy computers rather than using an asymmetric method. Nevertheless, it has several flaws. Kerberos is not discussed in this book.

Key escrow An attempt toward governmental regulation of cryptography: people can continue encrypting their stuff, but the government must be given the keys somehow upon request (see Sections 6.4 and 8.2.2).

Key stream See 'stream cipher'.

Left rotation See 'rotation'.

Linear expression In algebra, an expression in the form of $a_1x_1 + \cdots + a_nx_n$, where x_i are variables and a_i are constants. In cryptology, for example, 64-bit numbers take the place of real numbers, an addition corresponds to bitwise XOR, and a multiplication corresponds to bitwise AND. This turns a linear expression into a XOR sum of bits selected from integer data types (e.g., machine words; see Section 4.4.4).

MAC (Message Authentication Code) A one-way hash function the hash sum of which can be calculated only provided one knows the secret key. The simplest example is the encryption of a hash sum by means of a symmetric method. A secure and generally used method is the HMAC checksum (see [MenOoVan, 9.5.2]). MACs are used in tamperproof checksums (e.g., as a defense against viruses), but also in certain protocols for digital money (MilliCent).

MARS IBM's proposal for the AES challenge; it is very secure, effective, and fast, like all five final AES candidates.

MD2, MD4, MD5 Three important one-way hash functions (see Section 6.3.1).

Multiple encryption The repeated encryption of a text using the same or different encryption algorithms. In most cases, this is believed to increase the security, but cryptanalysis doesn't seem to have made much progress in this field (at least in public research). The best known example of multiple encryption is Triple-DES (see Section 5.2.1).

NBS (National Bureau of Standards) Former name of the NIST.

Negative pattern search Some encryption methods (e.g., Enigma, ciphering cylinders) do not transform any character onto itself. This helps exclude certain patterns that could be exploited in the plaintext (see Section 3.4.1). It is important in classic (character-oriented) cryptology, but not significant for current algorithms due to the avalanche effect.

N-hash A cryptographically insecure one-way hash function (see Section 6.3.1).

NIST (National Institute of Standards and Technology) A Department of the US Secretary of Commerce which, among other things, specifies cryptographic standards (including DES, EES, and DSS). Cooperates closely with the NSA.

NSA (National Security Agency) A US authority dealing intensively with cryptology and worldwide surveillance. Estimated to employ 40 000 people (including at least 2000 mathematicians); disposes of extremely fast computation technology (being the single largest buyer of hardware in the world), and also produces computers itself. Though the NSA was founded by Truman in 1952, its existence became publicly known in connection with the development of DES in the early 1970s.

OFB (Output Feedback Mode) A ciphering mode used in block algorithms (see Section 5.1.1).

One-time pad A random byte or bit sequence that is at least as long as the plaintext. Encryption and decryption are done by simple XORing with the plaintext or ciphertext, respectively. One-time pads are currently the only method with proven security (Section 2.6).

One-time password A cryptographic protocol (Section 6.5) enabling authentication over insecure lines, used without asymmetric methods. A password is used only once so that intercepting one-time passwords is worthless. One-time passwords are important in home banking or when somebody works at their own computer from third-party computers.

One-way hash function A sort of mapping that creates checksums for data streams, where no data can be reconstructed from a given checksum at a reasonable cost. An additional requirement is non-collision (Section 6.3.1).

OpenPGP A standard developed on the basis of PGP Version 5.0 and higher for secure email communication. Other than in PGP, it is also implemented in GnuPG and other products (see Section 7.1.4).

Passphrase A long character string used instead of traditional passwords six or eight characters long. Passphrases can be sentences (including punctuation marks and blanks), or phrases. Passphrases should be preferred over passwords since they offer more security. Passphrases are used, for example, in PGP.

Permutation Mathematically, the mapping of a biunique (one-to-one transformation) mapping of a finite set onto itself. Colloquially, an arrangement of a finite number or character set. Transposition ciphers (Section 2.2.4) are actually block algorithms, where plaintext blocks are encrypted by permutation. Extremely vulnerable to differential cryptanalysis, if used by itself (Section 4.4.2).

PGP (Pretty Good Privacy) The most popular free program used to encrypt files and email (see Section 7.1).

Plaintext A piece of readable text to be encrypted.

Plaintext attack A cryptanalytic method where a small part of the plaintext is normally known.

Playfair method A special digram cipher (see Section 2.3).

Polyalphabetic substitution A special substitution cipher, where the substitution rule depends on the position in the text. Examples are the Enigma and the Vigenère cipher.

Polygraphic substitution A special substitution cipher, where several characters together are substituted based on a large table. Corresponds to current block algorithms with a typical block length of two characters (then called *digram substitution*) or three characters (then called *trigram substitution*).

Primitive root A number g is the primitive root modulo of a prime number, p, if the $p - 1$ numbers, $g^0, g^1, \ldots, g^{p-2}$, produce all possible $p - 1$ remainders, $1, 2, \ldots, p - 1$, when divided by p. In other words, the number-theoretical equation $y \equiv g^x \pmod{p}$ can always be solved in x for each y that differs from 0 (x is the discrete logarithm of y to base g). Primitive roots are required in asymmetric methods that are based on the discrete logarithm, e.g., the Diffie–Hellman congruence (see Section 6.1.1).

Private key A secret key known only to its creator and used in asymmetric encryption methods, where it can also be used for decryption, as opposed to the public key.

Probabilistic method A special asymmetric method, where many public keys belong to one private key. A well-known representative is the method by Blum, Blum, and Shub (see Section 5.8).

Probable word A character string that is assumed to occur in a plaintext (often a specific word). Pattern search or negative pattern search can be used to find the position of a probable word, which means that a plaintext attack was successful. Probable words are relevant mainly in classic cryptanalysis (see Section 3.4.1, for example).

Product algorithm A special block algorithm, where the same key-dependent encryption function is applied to a block several times in a row. The use of this function is referred to as a **round**, and **round's keys** are derived from that key. The encryption function is applied in every round, depending on the pertaining round's key (see Section 4.1.4).

Public key A publicly known key used in asymmetric encryption methods; it is used only for encryption.

Public-key method See 'asymmetric encryption'.

Quantum computer To date, a hypothetical computer that works by the laws of quantum mechanics. If quantum computers existed, they could be used to quickly break all currently secure public-key methods (see Section 5.9).

Quantum cryptography A field involving physics and cryptographic protocols that enables you to safely prove an eavesdropping attempt. Quantum cryptography enables secure exchange of information (e.g., key exchange), but it is extraordinarily hard to implement in practice and, if achieved, considered a technical masterpiece (see Section 5.8).

RC4 A fast encryption method that is very easy to program and apparently secure to date. It is a stream cipher (see Section 5.6).

RC5 A very simple and fast block algorithm that uses variable parameters (block length, key length, number of rounds); see Section 5.4 as well as Section 5.4.3 for a discussion of RC5a.

RC6 The successor of RC5 (see Section 5.4.4), and one of the five final AES candidates.

Reduced key space We speak of a reduced key space when a potentially good algorithm uses only relatively few keys out of the theoretically possible number of keys due to poor implementation. It represents a vulnerability to dictionary attacks. Good examples are older versions of Netscape Navigator (Section 5.1.4); see also Section 3.3.

Replay attack A special cryptanalytic attack. Though the attacker may not be able to decrypt an intercepted message, he can copy it and replay it later, perhaps authenticating himself by mimicking somebody else. The idea is to intentionally disturb or forge data traffic, or to break into a third-party system. This was exploited in Novell Netware (encrypted passwords had no sequential number or timestamp).

Residual class Any set of all integers that leave the same remainder with regard to a given module (see also 'congruence').

Reversing drum A stationary rotor used in the German ciphering machine, the Enigma, which permutes the output and returns it backwards across the rotors (see Section 2.5.1).

Right rotation See 'rotation'.

Rijndael The Belgian algorithm that won the AES challenge and the accepted DES successor. It is very fast, very small, and very simple. No vulnerability has become known to date (see Section 5.5).

RIPE (RACE Integrity Primitives Evaluation) A collection of European security standards proposed within the RACE (Research and Development in Advanced Communication Technologies) Initiative.

RIPE-MD, RIPE-MD160 One-way hash functions used in RIPE. In addition to SHA (see 'DSA'), RIPE-MD160 is considered to be very secure and preferred over RIPE-MD.

ROT13 A Caesar cipher (used in news readers) where each letter is substituted by its 13th successor. Applying the method twice reproduces the original text. ROT13 does not allegedly offer cryptological security, but makes the undesirable reading out of character strings from program texts harder.

Rotation A computer operation where a word (consisting, for example, of 32 bits) is shifted to the left or right by a few bits, and the bits pushed out are shoved back in again at the other side. In this book, rotation is mainly relevant for RC5. Example: right-rotating the binary number 00001011 by 2 bits produces 11000010.

Rotor A rotating disk with 26 (or more) sliding contacts each on its outer sides, which are internally wired such that each contact on the left side connects exactly with a contact on the right side. This means that rotors implement a substitution in hardware that depends on the rotor's position. Rotors were used in **rotor machines**, with the Enigma being the best-known representative (see Section 2.5.1).

Round, round's key See 'product algorithm'.

S-boxes Special substitution tables used in the DES algorithm; they are the most important component for the security of this algorithm.

Serpent The proposal submitted by Anderson, Biham, and Knudsen to the AES challenge. It is presumably the most secure algorithm among the five final candidates, but not the fastest.

SESAME The European project initially conceived as the Kerberos substitute. The software had serious cryptological weaknesses (see Section 6.7).

Session key A random key created by a computer for use in a symmetric method. It is valid only for the duration of the transmission of a single message and often distributed by means of asymmetric encryption (see 'hybrid method').

SETUP system (Secretly Embedded Trapdoor with Universal Protection) A term introduced by Young and Yung to refer to Trojan cryptography, where parts of the private key are hidden in the public key in software or hardware such that the fraud cannot be proved by analyzing the output (see Section 6.7).

SHA See 'DSA'.

Skipjack algorithm A secret encryption algorithm developed by the NSA for the Clipper and Capstone chips (see Section 5.7.5).

Snefru Probably the first one-way hash function (see Section 6.3.1).

Stream cipher In contrast to block algorithms, a continuous (symmetric) encryption, where a byte or bit stream is created in dependence on a secret key, and that stream is XORed with the plaintext or ciphertext. The bit stream is also called **key stream** and used like a one-time pad (see Section 4.1.3).

Substitution A way of encrypting by systematically substituting the plaintext characters based on a given permanent table. The substitution encryption is very vulnerable to statistical cryptanalysis. It can be cracked by a ciphertext attack with known text structures on a computer within fractions of seconds.

Symmetric encryption The common type of encryption, where one single secret key is used for both encryption and decryption. These methods are secure when used in combination with session keys. A problem is normally the key distribution.

System V A UNIX variant mainly used in the commercial area (examples include SCO UNIX, UnixWare, and Irix). It was extensively unified with BSD from Release V.4 and higher.

Topic analysis A new type of interception method that classifies documents automatically by their contents so that huge amounts of data can be searched in a targeted way. This is mainly significant for national intelligence organizations, but it can also be used within security concepts of commercial or industrial organizations (secret information is automatically encrypted, and access privileges are regulated by contents). The method is based, among others, on the **N-gram analysis** developed by the NSA.

Traffic analysis A type of analysis that logs parameters of a message, such as sender, receiver, time and date, length, etc., rather than its contents (because it is encrypted, for example). Someone can collect huge amounts of such data and yield an astonishing amount of insightful information.

Transposition A special permutation, namely the transposition of two elements (each permutation can be represented as a sequence of a finite number of transpositions). In cryptology, a **transposition cipher** is an encryption method that permutes fixed-length blocks.

Trigram See 'polygraphic substitution'.

Triple-DES A variant of DES that does triple encryption, but uses only two DES keys:

```
ciphertext = DES_key_1(DES⁻¹_key_2(DES_key_1(plaintext)))
```

This method is intended to solve the problem with the DES key length that had been found to be too short, while ensuring optimal hardware compatibility (see Section 5.2.1).

Trojan cryptography A term used by the author of this book for implementations of cryptographic software or hardware that allow the vendor to unsurveillably listen in on encrypted messages.

Twinkle A yet hypothetical device based on an idea by Shamir, which could be used to factor large numbers faster than currently possible. This is important for the security of the RSA method (see Section 4.5.3).

Twofish A further developed variant of Blowfish, one of the five final AES candidates. It is a very secure, flexible, and fast algorithm.

Unicity distance A concept that measures the amount of ciphertext required such that there is only one reasonable plaintext. This number depends both on the characteristics of the plaintext and the key length of the encryption algorithm. The unicity distance for standard English ASCII text is 5.9 characters (approximately 47 bits) when using 40-bit keys. However, practical cryptanalysis requires much more ciphertext. The unicity distance has information-theoretical significance.

Vernam cipher A bitwise Vigenère cipher, i.e., a bitwise stream cipher with one periodic key stream. Vernam cipher is sometimes used synonymously for one-time pads (see Section 2.4.2).

Vigenère cipher The simplest polyalphabetic substitution, where a keyword is repeatedly written over a plaintext. The ciphertext is produced by adding superimposed characters. This book mainly discussed XORing rather than addition (which is a Vernam cipher in the closer sense). However, both methods can be treated equally (see Section 2.4.1).

Weak keys Special keys which, when used, reduce the security of the encryption method. An unusual example: every sequence of zero bytes is a (very) weak key in the Vigenère cipher since it leaves the plaintext unchanged during the encryption. If there are many weak keys in an encryption method, then it is worthwhile for an attacker to assume that a weak key was used to achieve his goal faster. If the attempt fails, the attacker might additionally use other methods (see Section 4.4.3).

XOR A basic computer operation between two binary numbers: bits in the same positions are XORed (exclusive XOR):

```
0 XOR 0 = 0, 1 XOR 1 = 0, 0 XOR 1 = 1, 1 XOR 0 = 1.
```

This is usually denoted as $\oplus$: $a \oplus b$.

Appendix A.1

Sources of Information

The Web site to this book at *www.wileyeurope.com/go/cryptology* is not a
'crypto Web site' in the usual sense. People familiar with the matter will miss
several things, or criticize the fact that the world has meanwhile switched to
using the next-but-one release of a popular program. The software and texts on
this Web site are merely intended to help you find further reading and references. For example, you will find the popular PGP Release 2.6.3, whereas PGP
9.50 had already been available when this book went to the print. However, I
selected all software primarily to give you a chance to look inside the source
code and understand how it works.

Some programs (such as *book/vigenere/vig_crack.c* or *book/trans/trans.c*) are
demonstration programs to allow you to experience cryptanalysis, or (as with
trans) see the weaknesses of an algorithm.

Also, there is a large number of texts, including sources for this book and
further reading sources. I'd have liked to fully explore many highly interesting
texts (e.g., *txt/chipcrack/andkuhn.html* or *txt/enigma/hinsley.txt*) in this book,
but that would have gone beyond its scope and volume.

You won't find programs of less cryptologic interest, such as dictionary attacks
against Vigenère-encrypted files or *pkzip*, or programs to break the Microsoft-
Word encryption. Good Internet addresses to look for cryptologic software,
include:

Cryptology Unlocked   Reinhard Wobst
© 2007 John Wiley & Sons, Ltd

- `www.jya.com/crypto.htm`

- `www.cryptome.org`

- `ftp.cert.dfn.de`, */pub/docs/crypt* and */pub/tools/crypt* directories

- `ftp.funet.fi:/pub/crypt`

- `www.rsasecurity.com/rsalabs`

Everything about the AES algorithms can be found at

- `www.nist.gov/aes`

Other interesting addresses are:

- `www.cs.auckland.ac.nz/~pgut001/links.html` (a very extensive link collection by Peter Gutmann)

- `www.cl.cam.ac.uk/users/rja14` (homepage of Ross Anderson with many details of technical interest)

I particularly recommend this address:

- `www.counterpane.com/crypto-gram.html` (where you can read and subscribe to Bruce Schneier's online-magazine *cryptogram* —an incredible source of current and interesting information!)

You should also take note of the following points:

Copyright and Liability

All files on our Web site are either programs I wrote myself—you can pass them on for free or use them freely, observing the copyright—or procured directly from the Internet. Though you may pass on the latter, you cannot use them freely—observe the copyright to each of those programs. Also pay attention to the import and export regulations for cryptologic software in force in the countries concerned.

As usual with free software, you use it at your own responsibility; nobody will provide support for it, or guarantee for that software's proper working.

Sources

Internet addresses tend to change from time to time. I couldn't always state them. Considering the quality and availability of current search engines (I mainly had to use Altavista back then), it is probably easiest to launch your favorite search engine and find the addresses on the Internet.

Data Formats and Language

Texts are available in one or several formats: PostScript (.ps), PDF (.pdf), HTML files (.html), or simple ASCI (.txt or no extension). Almost all texts are in English. I do not share some critics' comments that all texts should be supplied in one single format: Some texts are available in PostScript format only; searching for them is hardly possible. But exactly this can be important in research work.

Most programs are available in C source code.

Operating systems

Most programs and program packages are from the UNIX/Linux world. You find portability notes in the corresponding README files. I tested my own programs exclusively under UNIX and Linux, but some of them surely run on any systems and any C compiler (more comments further below).

A.2   Web Site to This Book

Our Web site includes five directories on the highest level:

book   The programs I created, and which are discussed in this book.

algor   Cryptographic algorithms.

cryptana	Cryptanalytic software.
txt	Text from the Internet.
PD	Free software packages, such as PGP.

book directory:

WP directory:

newwpcrack.c	C program to break the WordPerfect 5.1 encryption. It was discussed in Section 3.5.2.
wph.c	Short helper program to determine constant parts in the headers of WordPerfect files; it is invoked as follows:
	wph file1 file2 . . .

vigenere directory:

vigenere.c	This C program executes a Vigenère cipher of a data stream (XORing with a periodically repeated password). It is invoked on the command line:
	vigenere keyword <plaintext>ciphertext
	Repeated use turns the ciphertext back into the plaintext. The program is intended only to create ciphertexts for cryptanalysis.
vigcrack.c	For cryptanalysis of Vigenère-encrypted files. Its operation is discussed in the source code. The program was discussed in Section 3.6.3.
distr.c	Helper program for *vigcrack.c*; see there.
vigc_crk.c	For cryptanalysis of Vigenère-encrypted compressed files; see Section 3.6.4. Its invocation is explained in the source code.
_C,_eng,_wp	Frequency profiles for C programs, English texts, and a German WordPerfect file, determined by *distr*. You can easily create such files yourself.

trans directory:

escher.c, trans.c	*trans* is the 'pseudo-encryption' of an image, included as an *include* file *escher.c*. (You can also use other images in the X11 pixmap format, but you have to edit the dimensions in *trans.c*.)

	To run this program, you need Tcl/Tk and a UNIX system, because *trans* requires 'real pipelines' (they are merely emulated in DOS/Windows). The invocation is explained in the program and in Section 4.1.5. The images reappears after 72-fold encryption. The effect is amazing.

fcrypt directory:

| **fcrypt.c** | This is the *fcrypt* encryption program discussed in Section 3.7. There is no documentation; you find a description in [Wobfcrypt]. Don't use this method! The program is included for analysis only! |
| **secshare directory:** | Includes the Python script (plus C program) for secret-sharing implementation, as discussed in Section 6.2. |

algor directory:

A5 directory:

a5-article.txt	Description of the A5 algorithm for cell phones in the digital D- and E-networks (see Section 5.7.2).
a5.c	Implementation of the algorithm in C.
a3a8.c	Implementation of the secret A3 and A8 algorithms as they are used in the D2-network (see Section 6.1.3).
gsm.txt	Description of the security mechanism of cell phones (see Section 6.1.3).
AES directory:	The AES implementations from *www.nist.gov/aes* (see Section 5.5).
blowfish directory:	The implementation of the Blowfish algorithm from Section 5.7.4; including test data.
idea directory:	An implementation of the IDEA algorithm (5.3) by De Moliner (Zurich, Switzerland).

DES directory:

| **karndes directory:** | DES implementation by Philipp Karn; a very small and simple implementation of the algorithm. |
| **osthes directory:** | A much more extensive DES implementation by Stig Ostholm, including built-in ciphering modes, different key formats, etc. |

enigma directory:	A simple Enigma simulation; you can use it to study how this machine works in detail.
FEAL directory:	
feal8.c, feal8.h	The 8-round FEAL from Section 5.7.3.
fealnx.c, fealnx.h	The improved (but not secure) FEAL-NX version (see Section 5.7.3).
MD2 directory:	An implementation of the MD2 one-way hash function (Section 6.3.1).
MD5 directory:	An implementation of the MD5 one-way hash function (Section 6.3.1), together with some articles about MD5 cryptanalysis.
MD160 directory:	An implementation of the RIPE-MD160 one-way hash function (Section 6.3.1).
RC2 directory:	Description and implementation of the RC2 algorithm, which has been disclosed meanwhile.
RC5a directory:	This includes my RC5a implementation, discussed in Section 7.6, together with some shell procedures and the crack program for the one-round RC5 (Section 5.4.2); see README file. Moreover, this directory includes **sirc5a.cpp**, my implementation ported from S&I to Windows NT (in C++), as discussed in Section 5.4.3. The source code is intended for analysis; to use it, you should fall back on the crypto-library in *PD/S+I*.
RC6 directory:	Source texts and documentation of RC6 (Section 5.4.4).
SEAL directory:	Implementation of the SEAL algorithm from Section 5.6.4.
SHA directory:	
MD5_collisions.pdf	Articles by Klima [Klima].
md5coll.py	Python script to verify the correctness of a special MD5 collision. The value of the *msg* variable is arbitrary—the collision works always (incremental behavior of the hash function).

sha0coll.py	Similarly to *md5coll.py*, a Python script to verify SHA0 collisions. You need OpenSSL (as a command-line tool) to start, since SHA-0 is not supported by any of the modules that comes with Python.
sha256-384-512.pdf	Description of the SHA-256, SHA-384, and SHA-512 algorithms.
sha256.c	Source text from GnuPG for SHA-256; I slightly modified it so that it can be compiled and used on its own. You find a use example at the end of the source text.
Skipjack directory:	The Skipjack algorithm from `www.nist.gov/encryption/skipjack-kea.htm` discussed in Section 5.7.5. The PostScript and PDF files can be found on the homepage in this rather poor quality.
cryptana directory:	
crack directory:	The dictionary attack against UNIX passwords discussed in Section 3.3.
pkcrack directory:	The program to break the *pkzip* cipher by Peter Conrad discussed in Section 5.7.1. It requires 33 MB of virtual memory and a lot of computational power!
subscrack directory:	The Python script to automatically break substitution code, discussed in Section 2.2.1, including German and English documentation. Dictionaries are not included, but the documentation describes how to create them.
txt directory:	
biometric directory:	
fingerprt_gelatine.txt	Description by Chaos Computer Club (CCC) how to forge fingerprints for sensors (in German).
FAQ directory:	The FAQ (Frequently Asked Questions) lists on cryptology often found on the Internet; good educational material.

	You also find **memo.txt**, an important essay by Bruce Schneier, which you should absolutely read if you are interested in designing your own algorithms.
	The file **cryptanalysis.ps** is an introduction by Schneier into modern cryptanalysis with practical exercises. If you are shocked by how difficult the article is, particularly compared to this book, you are right...
PEM directory:	Three RFC files on the PEM standard and two on RIPEM (*RIPEM.Questions, RIPEM.Vulnerabilities*).
wpcrack directory:	The crack programs for the WordPerfect encryption (see Section 3.5.1) widely found on the Internet; they differ considerably from my *newwprcrack*.
chipcrack directory:	
andkuhn.html	The fascinating article by Anderson and Kuhn on hardware analysis, mentioned in Section 4.4.5, among others. Must read!
crpanahard.html	Considerations on the design and security of hardware for cryptologic purposes; authors: Goldberg and Wagner, known by their exploitation of the small key space in an older Netscape version (see Section 5.1.4).
dfa10.txt	Improvement by Anderson and Kuhn of the DFA method by Biham from Section 4.4.5.
rossdes.html	Attack against DES by means of parity and 'burnt-in' memory modules by Anderson (4.4.5).
winnemr.html	Study on the eavesdropping possibilities by electromagnetic radiation.
cryptana directory:	
biham.html, biham.ps, biham.txt	Description of the DFA attack by Biham (4.4.5).
dpa.txt, dpafaq.txt	Two articles by Kocher, including one on 'differential power analysis', mentioned in Section 5.10.

netscape_broken.txt, **netscape_answer.txt**	Report by Goldberg and Wagner on the small key space in the Netscape Navigator and the reply by Netscape Communications Corporation.
mod3.ps	Schneier's mod-3 cryptanalysis of RC5P from Section 5.4.2.
openpgpattack.txt	A discussion of the attack against the OpenPGP protocol published in the beginning of 2001, including links (see end of Section 7.1.4).
pkcs.ps	Bleichenbacher's attack against the RSA protocol PKCS#1; see Risk 5 in Section 4.5.3.
pkdfa.html	Article by Kocher on the above mentioned attacks against secure hardware: The problems are known and considered!
rc5_linear.ps	Heys' attack against RC5 (see [HeysRC5]).
shamirA5.ps	The cryptanalysis of the GSM algorithm A5 by Biruykov and Shamir (see Section 5.7.2).
timing_attack.ps	Description of Kocher's timing attack (Section 5.10).
viscrypt.ps	Shamir's 'visual cryptanalysis' (Section 4.4.1), as proposed at the EUROCRYPT '98.
wlanrc4.txt	Article on huge security holes in the RC4 implementation in the WLAN standard (*wireless LAN*, the alternative to Bluetooth).
des directory:	
attack-on-8-round- **des.txt**	Description of the attack against an 8-round DES by means of differential linear cryptanalysis; authors: Hellman and Langford (Section 4.4.4).
des56.txt	Report on the DES Challenge II, a successful brute-force attack against DES in January/February 1998 (Section 4.4.1).
ec directory:	
pin.txt	Description of securing PINs of EC bank cards (see Section 6.6.8) (in German; an FAQ list of the *de.comp.security* newsgroup).

wcf.txt   Description of adventurous malfunctions in securing the PINs of ATMs in Great Britain (by Anderson). Must read!

enigma directory: Nine text files about the history of the Enigma; must read: *hinsley.txt* (copy of a seminar by Sir Harry Hinsley on the impact of the Enigma on World War II, dated October 19, 1993. Hinsley is the official historian on the work of the British intelligence agency in World War II).

gsm directory:

gsm_secur.txt   Detailed technical description of the functionality of GSM telephones, and authentication and encryption methods (see also *algor/A5* directory.

                                Source: `www.10pht.com/~drwho/cell/gsm/` `gsm-secur/gsm-secur.html`.

gsm_press.txt   Press release of SDA (Smartcard Developers Association) dated April 13, 1998, on cloned GSM phones and security flaws (see Section 6.1.3).

gsm_faq.txt   Detailed information about the attack described in *gsm_press.txt*.

gsm_offic.txt: Statement of the GSM operators that the attack described is ineffective and the shortened A5 key was to serve only to increase 'flexibility'.

UMTS_sec.pdf   Speech by Mike Walker on UMTS security at the EUROCRYPT 2000. A good introduction to the field; mentions the weaknesses of GSM at the same time. However, you may never have seen so many abbreviations in so small a space. This style seems to be common in the telecommunications industry.

3gpp.txt   Overview of UMTS security documents.

gsm_crack_bbk.pdf   Work by Barkan, Biham, and Keller on breaking the A5/1 algorithm of GSM telephones (see Section 5.7.2).

policy directory:

Email.Study.txt	The article by Schwartz and Wood on traffic analysis mentioned in Section 8.2.1. This material is still current though it is of October 1992!
Privacy.txt	A statement by Professor Cochrane (British Telecom; see www.labs.bt.com/library/cochrane/index.htm) on disappearing privacy in the information age; radical, but interesting (also in connection with Section 8.2.2).
bbhitech.txt	A discussion on how intelligence agencies can exploit modern technology for surveillance of large groups of people, already practiced in some countries, e.g., Thailand. It is interesting to read about the 'data traces' US citizens leave behind already today.
cdt_policy.txt	Discussion of the Clipper chip, export restrictions, key escrow, etc.
claw1996.txt	This is the *Crypto-Law Survey* by Bert-Jaap Koops mentioned in Section 8.2.3. It gives an overview on crypto-laws in many countries (as of July 1996). The list is merely indicative, since the laws change constantly.
claw2001.txt	The version of *claw.txt* in 2001—a lot has changed since then!
crptlawwirt.txt	Statement of the business world on the draft law for digital signatures and regulations of the use of cryptography (favoring the first law, while criticizing the second draft). Must read!
cryptverbot.html	Statements of several political parties and organizations on the regulation of cryptography.
echelon_schmid.pdf	Detailed report of the Echelon Commission of the EU Parliament on the Echelon surveillance system.
eml.txt	*Fortune* report dated February 3, 1997, on the practices and possibilities of replaying e-mail, breaking into computers, etc., in the USA; includes huge amounts of interesting facts, and deals intensively with the hacker scene.

feb97_state.txt	Report on the negotiations between the FBI and the EU on a global telephone monitoring system. Rather shocking!
fuev.txt	Telecommunications Surveillance Directive (Fernmeldeverkehr-Überwachungs-Verordnung; FÜV) of May 18, 1995.
globuberwachung.txt	Discussion of modern surveillance possibilities based on the Schengen Treaty and the Sirene System. The example of the destiny of Norwegian Jews in World War II is used to show how 'useful' data harvesting in stock can be in such cases.
ic2kreport.txt	The STOA report of the EU, mentioned in Section 8.2.1, which deals in detail with the technical possibilities of intelligence agencies.
Information_ Awareness_ Office.html	Wikipedia page of November 2006 on IAO, formerly TIA, the extensive surveillance system planned for fight against terror.
kahn.txt	David Kahn's backing of key escrow; author of the fascinating book [KahnCode].
madsen.txt	A highly interesting contribution on the obvious involvement of the NSA in Crypto AG (Switzerland). The affair became public in 1992 when an alleged Swiss spy was bailed out from Iraqi prison. This is the only use of 'real Trojan cryptography' I know of (see Section 6.7). The article is a must-read for every cryptologist who is interested in more than mathematics!
nsa-hersh.txt	Text on the discussion in Section 8.2.1 as to how 'fatal' cryptography and modern data-transmission methods might have become for intelligence agencies—certainly useful to prevent becoming paranoid, but one shouldn't underestimate the NSA.
nsaabout.txt	Presentation of the NSA on itself on its homepage; among other things, it mentions that the NSA produces hardware, and that it is the largest employer of mathematicians.

nsasec.txt, nsasec.ps	Text on the security manual for NSA employees that somehow 'leaked'. I recommend this reading if you are interested how large intelligence agencies work.
oasis.txt	An article on the *Oasis* program, which is said to be able to convert audio files (e.g., phone-conversation replays) automatically into plaintext. This can be very significant for interception technologies.
schmid_bericht.html	Speech by Gerhard Schmid on Echelon at the EU Parliament; good overview.
quant directory:	
matthaeus-diplom.pdf	The work by Matthias Halder on optical data transmission by means of quantum cryptography between the Zugspitze and the Wendelstein mountains in the Alps (Section 5.8).
quantumcon.txt	An interesting and popular article on quantum cryptography as discussed in Section 5.8. It mainly describes the enormous technical problems.
qc-grover.txt	A well-written introduction to the theory of quantum computers; easy to understand.
stego directory:	
mimic.txt	Description of the so-called *mimic functions* by Peter Wayner (see Section 1.3, Figure 1.2).
PD directory:	
CBW directory:	*Crypt Breaker's Workbench* by Robert Baldwin that breaks the old UNIX encryption, *crypt* (see Section 2.5.3).
CFS directory:	The cryptographic file system by Blaze discussed in Section 7.4.
PGP directory:	
pgp2.6.3 subdirectory	PGP Version 2.6.3 (see Section 7.1).
inpgp50.txt	The innards of PGP 5.0 (see Section 7.1.4).

GnuPG directory:

microhowto.txt, microhowto.eng	Strongly simplified instructions for getting started with GnuPG. These instructions help you to send and received encrypted mails on the command line within one hour of learning.
pgp2x.html	Instructions for migrating from PGP 2.6 to GnuPG.
SESAME directory:	The European SESAME project, which is supposed to replace Kerberos. This software is highly insecure (see Section 6.7). I just included it for readers to perhaps find more vulnerabilities.

S+I directory:

SICryptLib11OS.zip	The rudimentary crypto-library, which includes my RC5a algorithm ported to Windows NT, by the courtesy of S+I.

SSH directory:

ssh.tgz	Secure Shell SSH, Version 1.2.26, discussed in Section 7.3 (this is a compressed. tar archive).
ssh1_insecure.txt	Text warning of the insecurity of SSH1.
skey directory:	Three program packages for one-time passwords in UNIX; see Section 7.5; and algorithms for authentication.
OPIE subdirectory:	OPIE Version 2.22.
logdaemon subdirectory:	Logdaemon Version 5.6.
skey subdirectory:	S/Key Version 1.1.

OATH subdirectory:

rfc4226.txt	Description of the HOTP algorithm based on OATH.

SecurID subdirectory:

securid_attack	Description of a cryptanalysis of the RSA SecurID Token.

Appendix A.2

Bibliography

[AndDES]   Anderson, R., *A Serious Weakness of DES*, manuscript dated Nov. 2, 1996; included on our Web site.

[AndKuhn.tamp] Anderson, R., Kuhn, M., *Tamper Resistance—A Cautionary Note*, 2nd USENIX Workshop on Electronic Commerce Proceedings, Oakland, CA, Nov. 18–21, 1996, pp. 1–11, ISBN 1-880446-83-9. The manuscript is included on our Web site, or found on the Internet: `www.ft.uni-erlangen.de/~mskuhn/tamper.html`. This is one of the most interesting texts from this list. It shows impressively that there is a race between chip designers and chip crackers, similar to the race between cryptography and cryptanalysis. Some of the methods used for analysis are adventurous.

[BBEQuant]   Bennett, C. H., Brassard, G., Ekert, A. K., *Quantum Cryptography*, Scientific American, Vol. 267 (1992) H.4, pp. 50–57.

[BBS]   Blum, M., Goldwasser, S., *An Efficient Probabilistic Public-Key Encryption Scheme Which Hides All Partial Information*, Advances in Cryptology: Proceedings of CRYPTO '84, Springer, 1985, p. 289.

[BauerDS]   Bauer, F. L., *Decrypted Secrets, Methods and Maxims of Cryptology*, Springer, 1997, ISBN 3-540-60418-9.

Cryptology Unlocked Reinhard Wobst
© 2007 John Wiley & Sons, Ltd

[BauerMM]   Bauer, F. L., *Kryptologie—Methoden und Maximen* (2nd edn),
                   Springer, 1994. If you are interested in the history of the
                   Enigma, in addition to cryptology, you should read one of
                   these two books. Even though some simple things are
                   formulated strictly mathematically, and finding things is
                   cumbersome—it is still an entertaining and informative work.
                   However, it deals only briefly with modern cryptology.

[Benal.acc]   Benaloh, J. C., de Mare, M., *One-Way Accumulators: A
                   Decentralized Alternative to Digital Signatures*, in:
                   EUROCRYPT '93 Proceedings, pp. 274–285, Springer, 1994.

[Bih.biry]   Biham, E., Biryukov, A., *How to Strengthen DES Using
                   Existing Hardware*, in: Advances in
                   Cryptology—ASIACRYPT '94 Proceedings, Springer, 1995.

[Bih.diff]   Biham, E., Shamir, A., *Differential Cryptanalysis of DES-like
                   Cryptosystems*, in: Advances in Cryptology—CRYPTO '90
                   Proceedings, Springer, New York, 1991, pp. 2–21.

[Bih.zip]   Biham, E., Kocher, P. C., *A Known Plaintext Attack on the
                   PKZIP Stream Cipher*, K.U. Leuven Workshop on
                   Cryptographic Algorithms, Springer, 1995.

[BirKush]   Biryukov, A., Kushilevitz, E., *Improved Cryptanalysis of RC5*,
                   Advances in Cryptology—EUROCRYPT '98, Springer, 1998,
                   pp. 85–99.

[BirShamA5]   Biryukov, A., Shamir, A., *Real Time Cryptanalysis of A5/1 on
                   a PC*, Proceedings of the 7th Workshop on Fast Software
                   Encryption, Springer, New York, 2000.

[Blakshar]   Blakley, G. R., Kabatianski, G. A., *On General Perfect Secret
                   Sharing Schemes*, in: Advances in Cryptology—CRYPTO '95,
                   Springer, 1995.

[BlazeCFS]   Blaze, M., *A Cryptographic File System for UNIX*, Proc. 1st
                   ACM Conference on Computer and Communications Security,
                   Fairfax, VA, Nov. 1993.

[Blazeskip]   Blaze, M., *Protocol Failure in the Escrowed Encryption
                   Standard*, in: [Hoff], pp. 131–146 (2.3).

[BleichRSA]   Bleichenbacher, D., *Chosen Ciphertext Attacks Against
                   Protocols Based on the RSA Encryption Standard PKCS#1*,
                   Advances in Cryptology—CRYPTO '98, Springer, 1998,
                   LNCS 1462, pp. 1–12.

[BonRSA]   Boneh, D., DeMillo, R. A., Lipton, R. J., *On the Importance of Checking Cryptographic Protocols for Faults*, Advances in Cryptology—EUROCRYPT '97, Springer, 1997, pp. 37–51.

[BonVen]   Boneh, D., Venkatesan, R., *Breaking RSA May Not Be Equivalent to Factoring*, Advances in Cryptology—EUROCRYPT '98, Springer, 1998, pp. 59–71.

[BorstIDEA]   Borst, J., Knudsen, L. R., Rijmen, V., *Two Attacks on Reduced IDEA*, Advances in Cryptology—EUROCRYPT '97, Springer, 1997, pp. 1–13.

[BrickDenn]   Brickell, E., Denning, D. *et al., SKIPJACK Review: Interim Report*, in: [Hoff], pp. 119–130 (2.2).

[ChanFrTsi]   Chan, A., Frankel, Y., Tsiounis, Y., *Easy Come—Easy Go Divisible Cash*, Advances in Cryptology—EUROCRYPT '98, Springer, 1998, pp. 561–575.

[Chaum]   Chaum, D., Fiat, A., Naor, M., *Untraceable Electronic Cash*, in: Advances in Cryptology—CRYPTO '88 Proceedings, Springer, 1990, pp. 319–327.

[CourtPiep]   *Cryptanalysis of Block Ciphers with Overdefined Systems of Equations*, in: Advances in Cryptology—Asiacrypt 2002 Proceedings, Springer, Dec. 2002.

[Crutch]   Crutchfield, J. P., Farmer, J. D., Packard, N. H., Shaw, R. S., *Chaos*, Scientific American, Vol. 255/6 (1986), pp. 38–49.

[CZ96]   *Heiße Chipkarten geben Code preis* (Hot Chip Cards Leak Code), Computer-Zeitung, No. 44, Oct. 31, 1996, p. 1.

[Daeman]   Daeman, J., *Cipher and Hash Function Design*, PhD Dissertation, Katholieke Universiteit Leuven, March 1995.

[Denn83]   Denning, D. E. R., *Cryptography and Data Security*, Addison-Wesley, Reading, MA, 1983. This book is considered the precursor of Bruce Schneier's seminal work [SchnCr]. It discusses cryptology in a mathematically compact form, and computer security. Due to the publication date, many modern methods are missing, of course.

[DESX]   Kilian, J., Rogaway, P., *How to Protect DES Against Exhaustive Key Search*, in: Advances in Cryptology—Crypto '96, Springer, 1996. This article is included on our Web site.

[Ditt]   Dittman, J., *Digitale Wasserzeichen* (Digital Watermarks),
                          Springer, 2000. The author discusses problems in creating
                          truly tamperproof and destruction-proof digital watermarks
                          (see Section 1.3). Her analysis is profound, and her
                          conclusions give hope for the future.

[DobMD4]   Dobbertin, H., *Cryptanalysis of MD4*, Proceedings of the 3rd
                          Workshop on Fast Software Encryption Cambridge, Springer,
                          1996, LNCS 1039, pp. 53–70.

[DobMD4inv]   Dobbertin, H., *The First Two Rounds of MD4 are not One-way*,
                          in Proc. Fast Software Encryption, Springer, 1998. This work
                          calculates the archetype of hash value 0 of a one-way hash
                          function reduced (from three) to two rounds (MD4). This was
                          probably the first time the reversion of a hash function was
                          computed.

[Donnhack]   Donnerhacke, L., Peter, S., *Vorsicht, Falle! ActiveX als
                          Füllhorn für Langfinger* (Watch for Traps! ActiveX is a Horn
                          of Plenty for Thieves), iX, 3/1997, pp. 90–93.

[DRM]   *Digital Rights Management*, Springer, Berlin-Heidelberg,
                          2003, LNCS 2770, ISBN 3-540-40465-1. Only apparently dry
                          literature: it discusses basic issues, such as: Is information
                          ownership meaningful and possible at all? What are the
                          chances for Digital Rights Management, and what technical
                          barriers are there? You should have a look at this work to
                          better understand some of the problems of our information
                          society.

[EFF]   Electronic Frontier Foundation, *Cracking DES, Secrets of
                          Encryption Research, Wiretap Politics & Chip Design*,
                          O'Reilly & Associates, 1998, ISBN 1-56592-520-3.

[Feistel]   Feistel, H., *Cryptography and Computer Privacy*, Scientific
                          American, Vol. 228 (1973), No. 5, pp. 15–23.

[FergSchnPract]   Ferguson, N., Schneier, B., *Practical Cryptography*, Wiley,
                          2003, ISBN 0-471-22357-3.

[FergSchrWhit]   Ferguson, N., Schroeppel, R., Whiting, D., *A Simple Algebraic
                          Representation of Rijndael*, in: Proceedings of Selected Areas
                          in Cryptography (SAC '01), LNCS 2259, Springer, 2001,
                          pp. 103–111.

[Frankel]   Frankel, Y., Yung, M., *Escrow Encryption System Visited:
                          Attacks, Analysis and Designs*, in: Advances in
                          Cryptology—CRYPTO '95, Springer, 1995, pp. 222–235.

[GardRSA]   Gardner, M., *A New Kind of Cipher That Would Take Millions of Years to Break*, Scientific American, Vol. 237 (1977), No. 8, pp. 120–124.

[GarPGP]   Garfinkel, S. *PGP: Pretty Good Privacy*, O'Reilly & Assoc., 1995, ISBN 1-56592-098-8. This book has become known as the 'PGP bible'; written in an entertaining style, it includes a large amount of interesting information about the author and the PGP landscape. However, it does not always go into the cryptologic details.

[Gemmel]   Gemmel, P. S., *An Introduction to Threshold Cryptography*, CryptoBytes, No. 3, Vol. 2 (1997), pp. 7–12; also available at `www.rsa.com/rsalabs/pubs/cryptobytes.html`.

[GolicA5]   Golic, J. D., *Cryptanalysis of Alleged A5 Stream Cipher*, Advances in Cryptology—EUROCRYPT '97, pp. 239–255, Springer, 1997, LNCS 1233.

[Hager]   Hager, N., *Secret Power*, Craig Potton Publishing, Nelson, New Zealand, 1996, ISBN 0-908802-35-8. This is the first and probably the only book that describes the Echelon system of the NSA in detail (see Section 8.2.1). There is presumably no other work as comprehensive and current as this on communications intelligence. Despite some dry passages, the contents read like a thriller. Unfortunately, the book is hard to get (the first edition had to be reprinted in the year of publication).

[Harris]   Harris, R., *Enigma*, Heyne-Verlag, Munich, 7th edn, 1995, ISBN 3-453-09077-2 (English original: Random House, London/New York). A well-written and thrilling book about the atmosphere at Bletchley Park (where the Enigma was decrypted during World War II). The story is closer to reality than you'd believe.

[Hastad]   Hastad, J., *On Using RSA with Low Exponent in a Public Key Network*, in: Advances in Cryptology—CRYPTO '85 Proceedings, Springer, 1986, pp. 403–408.

[HawIDEA]   Hawkes, P., *Differential-Linear Weak Key Classes of IDEA*, Advances in Cryptology—EUROCRYPT '98, Springer, 1998, pp. 112–126.

[Hell.troff]   Hellman, M. E., *A Cryptanalytic Time–Memory Trade Off*, IEEE Transactions on Information Theory, Vol. 26, No. 4 (1980), pp. 401–406.

[HeysRC5]   Heys, M. H., *Linearly Weak Keys of RC5*, IEE Electronic Letters, Vol. 33 (1997), No.10, pp. 836–838. This article is included on our Web site (*txt/cryptana/rc5_linear.ps*).

[Hinstrip]   Hinsley, F. H., Stripp, A., *Codebreakers*, Oxford University Press, 1993, ISBN 0-19-285304-X. The authors write about the innards and cryptanalytic methods at Bletchley Park, where the Enigma was cracked during World War II (see Chapter 2). An important piece of original literature.

[Hoff]   Hoffmann, L. J., *Building in Big Brother—The Cryptographic Policy Debate*, Springer, 1995, ISBN 0-387-94441-9. A collection of contributions to the key-escrow/Clipper-chip issues, including contributions by PGP-author Phil Zimmermann and Matthew Blaze (see Section 6.4), and contributions from *The Times*, and former US Vice-President Al Gore.

[Humm]   Hummelt, R., *Wirtschaftsspionage auf dem Datenhighway* (Industrial Espionage on the Data Highway), Hanser-Verlag, Munich/Vienna, 1997, ISBN 3-446-19070-8. This is a highly interesting and informative book, despite some negative critique. The author used to work with a 'competitive analysis' firm and knows what he is talking about. He describes many specific practical cases, and the practical use of PGP.

[IHK]   Wetjen, B., *Know-how zum Nulltarif* (Know-how for Free), Wirtschaftsdienst, Monthly Magazine of the Chamber of Commerce (IHK), Dresden, No. 2/96, pp. 15–17.

[InfWeek]   'Ein Data-Warehouse muss skalierbar sein' (A Data Warehouse has to be Scalable), Interview in *Information Week* 4/19, February 1998, p. 26.

[InfWeekDES] *Information Week* 17/98, p. 12.

[KahnCode]   Kahn, D., *The Codebreakers: The Story of Secret Writing*, 1st edn, New York, MacMillan, 1967; 2nd edn, New York, Scribner, 1996, ISBN 0-684-83130-9. Perhaps the first book that summarizes the history of cryptology. The author thoroughly researched among first-hand sources, militaries, and intelligence agencies (and nevertheless didn't know in 1967 that the Enigma had been broken). Despite its scaring volume (about 1000 pages, including references), everybody should have a look at this book. You will learn about a large number of authentic James Bond stories, surprising historical interrelations, and classic ciphering methods. The coverage of the period from 1945 to the present is a bit short in the second edition, but the respective chapter is still interesting and informative.

[KahnEnig] Kahn, D., *Seizing the Enigma*, Houghton Mifflin, Boston, 1991. This book can perhaps be seen as an intensification of [KahnCode]. You will learn interesting details about the history of the Enigma, and the way it was handled in the Wehrmacht, and all the dramatic circumstances under which secret material was yielded from German submarines, and much more. There is only one downside to this book: it is currently unavailable.

[KalisRC5] Kaliski, B. S., Yin, Y. L., *On Differential and Linear Cryptanalysis of the RC5 Encryption Algorithm*, in Advances in Cryptology—CRYPTO '95, Springer, 1995, pp. 171–184.

[KirPGP] Kirsch, C., *S/MIME versus OpenPGP: Eine Entscheidungshilfe* (A Comparison of the two Products), KES, 1/2001, pp. 60–65.

[Klima] Klima, V., *Finding MD5 Collisions—a Toy for a Notebook*, *cryptography.hyperlink.cz/md5/MD5_collisions.pdf*. Description of how to compute MD5 collisions on a notebook (included on the Web site to this book).

[KnudRC5] Knudsen, L. R., Meier, W., *Improved Differential Attacks of RC5*, in Advances in Cryptology—CRYPTO '96, Springer, 1996.

[Knuth2] Knuth, D., *The Art of Computer Programming*, Vol. 2, Seminumerical Algorithms, 2nd edn, Addison-Wesley, 1981.

[Koch.DFA] Kocher, P., *Fault-induced Crypto Attacks and the Risks of Press Releases*, News article; included on our Web site.

[Koch.Tim] Kocher, P. C., *Cryptanalysis of Diffie-Hellman, RSA, DSS, and Other Systems Using Timing Attacks*, preliminary manuscript; the final version appeared with the title 'Timing Attacks on Implementations of Diffie-Hellman, RSA, DSS, and Other Systems', in Proceedings of CRYPTO '96, Springer, 1996, pp. 104–113.

[Kunz.ct] Kunze, M., *Netz-Razzia* (Network Raid), c't, 7/95, p. 22.

[LMM.IDEA] Lai, X., Massey, J. L., Murphy, S., *Markov Ciphers and Differential Cryptanalysis*, in Advances in Cryptology—EUROCRYPT '91, Springer, 1991, pp. 17–38.

[Lamport]   Lamport, L., *Password Authentication with Insecure Communication*, Comm. ACM, 24 (1981) No.11, pp. 770–772.

[Lenstra]   Lenstra, A. K., Lenstra, H. W., *The Development of the Number Field Sieve*, Lecture Notes in Mathematics 1554, Springer, 1993.

[LenstraMD5]   Lenstra, A., Wang, X., Weger, B., *Colliding X.509 Certificates*, eprint.iacr.org/eprint/2005/067/.

[MM]   Meyer, C., Matyas, S., *Cryptography: A New Dimension in Computer Data Security*, Wiley, 1982.

[MenOoVan]   Menezes, A. J., van Oorschot, P. C., Vanstone, S. A., *Handbook of Applied Cryptography*, CRC Press, 1997, ISBN 0-8493-8523-7. A very extensive and mathematically sound work on modern cryptography. In particular, it contains the tables of contents of all proceedings of the ASIACRYPT/ AUSCRYPT, CRYPTO, EUROCRYPT, and Fast Software Encryption conferences, as well as the tables of contents of the *Journal of Cryptology*. One of the most important sources for cryptology, but only for readers with mathematical knowledge.

[Mikle]   Mikle, O., *Practical Attacks on Digital Signatures Using MD5 Message Digest*, eprint.iacr.org/eprint/2004/356/.

[Müpf]   Müller, G., Pfitzmann, A. (eds), *Mehrseitige Sicherheit in der Informationstechnik* (Multi-sided Security in Information Technology), Addison-Wesley, 1997. In addition to a large number of technical problems, this work also discusses legal issues, in particular the German signature law.

[MurFEAL]   Murphy, S., *The Cryptanalysis of FEAL-4 with 20 Chosen Plaintexts*, Journal of Cryptology, Vol. 2 (1990), No. 3, pp. 145–154.

[NISTmod]   `http://csrc.nist.gov/CryptoToolkit/modes/ModesPage .html`

[PetAndMark]   Petitcolas, A. P., Anderson, R., Kuhn, M., *Attacks on Copyright Marking Systems*, 2nd International Workshop on Information Hiding, Portland, OR, April 1998, Springer, LNCS.

[Peters]   Peters, T., *Das Tom Peters Seminar. Management in chaotischen Zeiten* (Management in Chaotic Times), Campus Verlag, Frankfurt/New York, 1995.

[Pfitzfinger]	Pfitzmann, B., *Anonymous Fingerprinting*, Advances in Cryptology—EUROCRYPT '97, pp. 88–102, Springer, 1997, LNCS 1233.
[PfitzFSS]	Pfitzmann, B., *Digital Signature Schemes, General Framework and Fail-Stop Signatures*, Springer, LNCS 1100, 1996.
[Pfitzstego]	Franz, E., Pfitzmann, A., *Ableitung eines neuen Stegoparadigmas mit Hilfe empirischer Untersuchungen* (Deriving a New Stego-Paradigm by Empiric Studies), 2nd International Workshop on Information Hiding, Portland, OR, April 1998, Springer, LNCS.
[RSA]	Rivest, R. L., Shamir, A., Adleman, L. M., *A Method for Obtaining Digital Signatures and Public-Key Systems*, Comm. ACM, Vol. 21 (1978) No. 2, pp. 120–126.
[Rabin]	Rabin, M. O., *Probabilistic Algorithm for Testing Primality*, Journal of Number Theory, Vol. 12 (1980), No.1, pp. 128–138.
[RivRC5]	Rivest, R., *The RC5 Encryption Algorithm*, in: Fast Software Encryption—Second International Workshop, Leuven, Belgium, Springer, 1995, LNCS 1008, pp. 86–96.
[RogChMD2]	Rogier, N., Chauvaud, P., *The Compression Function of MD2 is not Collision Free*, introduced at the Cryptography '95 conference, Ottawa, Canada, May 18/19, 1995.
[RogCoSeal]	Rogaway, P., Coppersmith, D., *A Software-Oriented Encryption Algorithm*, in: Fast Software Encryption, Cambridge Security Workshop Proceedings, Springer, 1994, pp. 56–63.
[SchHad]	Schulzki-Haddouti, C., Ruhmann, I., *Abhör-Dschungel* (The Eavesdropping Jungle), c't 5/98, pp. 82 ff.
[Schmeh]	Schmeh, K., *Safer Net. Kryptografie im Internet und Intranet* (Cryptography in the Internet and intranets), dpunkt.verlag, 1998, ISBN 3-932588-23-1. An easily readable introduction to cryptography and its use in networks. Though the author doesn't deal with things in depth, the book discusses many issues. Also available in English.
[SchnBlow1]	Schneier, B., *Description of a New Variable-Length Key, 64-Bit Block Cipher*, in: Fast Software Encryption, Cambridge Security Workshop Proceedings, Springer, 1994, pp. 191–204.

[SchnBlow2]	Schneier, B., *The Blowfish Encryption Algorithm*, Dr. Dobb's Journal, Vol. 19 (1994), No. 4, pp. 38–40.
[SchnCr]	Schneier, B., *Applied Cryptography*, 2nd edn, Wiley, 1996, ISBN 0-471-11709-9. This is still *the* seminal work on cryptography, unique in its completeness and easy readability. This book is a must for every cryptologist (and accordingly quoted often in this book).
[SchnFear]	Schneier, B., *Beyond Fear*, Copernicus Books, New York, 2003, ISBN 0-3878-02620-7.
[SchnLie]	Schneier, B., *Secrets and Lies*, Wiley, 2000. In addition to [SchnCr], this book on computer security is another bestseller of this author. Schneier shows, among other things, that cryptography cannot be a panacea, and that security involves much more than we think. It gives you an idea how much we still have to rethink to get things right in information society.
[Schnmod3]	Kelsey, J., Schneier, B., Wagner, D., *Modern Cryptanalysis, with Applications Against RC5P and M6*, Proceedings of 6th International Workshop on Fast Software Encryption, 1999, Springer, pp. 139–155. This article is included on our Web site (*txt/cryptana/mod3.ps*).
[SchwartzOLE]	Schwartz, Martin, *Aus dem Allerheiligsten* (On the Inner Sanctum), iX, 5/98, pp. 163–166.
[Shamshare]	Shamir, A., *How to share a secret*, Communications of the ACM, Vol. 22 (1979), No.1, pp. 612–613.
[Shamvis]	Shamir, A., *Visual Cryptanalysis*, Advances in Cryptology—EUROCRYPT '98, Springer, 1998, pp. 201–210. This article is included on our Web site (*txt/cryptana/visualcr.ps*), courtesy of the author.
[Simmsubl]	Simmons, G., *The Subliminal Channel and Digital Signatures*, EUROCRYPT '84, Springer, 1985, pp. 364–378.
[Sinkov]	Sinkov, A., *Elementary Cryptanalysis. A Mathematical Approach*, Random House and L.W. Singer Company, New York, 1968. This book deals with really elementary algorithms, the ones discussed from Section 2.4 onwards in this book. The theory is clearly explained, and examples are carefully cryptanalyzed. It also includes a nice tutorial. However, it deals only with the status of before World War I (and then only in part).

[Skipana]   Biham, E., Biruykov, A., Shamir, A., *Cryptanalysis of Skipjack Reduced to 31 Rounds Using Impossible Differentials*, Proceedings EUROCRYPT '99, Springer, LNCS 1592, pp. 12–23.

[SomSham]   Someren, N. V., Shamir, A., *Playing 'Hide and Seek' with Stored Keys*, Proceedings of 3rd International Conference on Financial Cryptography '99, Springer, LNCS 1648.

[SpiegClon]   *Aussichten eines Klons* (The Prospects of a Clone), Der Spiegel, 18/98, pp. 98–99.

[SpiegDat]   *Lauscher im Datenreich* (Eavesdroppers in the Data Realm), Der Spiegel, 36/96, pp. 198–211.

[Stins]   Stinson, D., *Cryptography: Theory and Practice*, CRC Press, 1995, ISBN 0-8493-8521-0. An important and modern work on cryptography; very mathematical and yet easy to read.

[Twinkle]   Lenstra, A. K., Shamir, A., *Analysis and Optimization of the TWINKLE Factoring Device*, Proceedings EUROCRYPT 2000, Springer, LNCS 1807, pp. 35 ff.

[ViegaMess]   Viega, J., Messier, M., *Secure Programming Cookbook for C and C++*, O'Reilly, 2003, ISBN 0-596-00394-3.

[Wcf]   Anderson, R., *ATM Security—Why Cryptosystems Fail*, Proceedings of the First ACM Conference on Computer and Communications Security (11/93), pp. 215–227.

[Welch]   Welch, A. T., *A Technique for High-Performance Data Compression*, IEEE Computer, 17(6) (1984), pp. 8–14.

[Westf]   Westfeld, A., *Steganografie am Beispiel einer Videokonferenz* (Steganography by the Example of a Video Conference), in: [Müpf], pp. 507–525.

[WillClear10]   Williams, C. P., Clearwater, S. H., *Ultimate Zero and One*, Copernicus/Springer, New York, 2000, ISBN 0-387-94769-8.

[WinkSpy]   Winkler, I., *Spies Among Us*, Wiley, 2005, ISBN 0-7645-8468-5.

[Wobfcrypt]   Wobst, R., *Schnell & geheimnisvoll, Ein neues Verschlüsselungsverfahren* (Fast & Mysterious, A New Encryption Method), UNIX-Magazin, 7/92, pp. 86–95. This is the *fcrypt* method discussed in Section 3.7.

[Wobghm] Wobst, R., *Begrenzte Allmacht* (Omnipotence Limited), UNIX open, 10/99, pp. 33–39. This article shows fascinating technical possibilities of major intelligence agencies, mainly based on a STOA report of the EU.

[Wobhash] *New Attacks on Hash Functions*, International Security Bulletin (ISB) 3 (10)/05, pp. 85–94.

[Woblock] Wobst, R., *Dringendes Bedürfnis* (Urgent Need), UNIX open, 4/93, pp. 32–34.

[Wobmail] Wobst, R., Hartmann, D., Kirsch, C., Seeger, J., *Vorwiegend sonnig* (Mostly Sunny), using GnuPG for mail encryption, iX, 3/2004, pp. 126–131.

[Wobmail2] Wobst, R., *Der lange Weg zur sicheren E-Mail* (The Long Way to Secure E-Mail), Lanline Special, III/2002, pp. 45–49. Also available at www.lanline.de > full text search.

[Wobpgp] Wobst, R., *Nicht abschrecken lassen* (Don't Let Yourself Be Put Off), an introduction to the use of PGP, UNIX open, 10/97, pp. 38–41.

[Wobrump] Wobst, R., *Plaintext Compression Helps the Cryptanalyst*, contribution to the Rump Session at EUROCRYPT '97.

[Wobsymm] Wobst, R., *Wissen ist Macht* (Knowledge is Power), Part I, UNIX open, 4/96, pp. 94–100, *Starke Abwehr* (Strong Defense), Part II, UNIX open, 5/95, pp. 118–124.

[Wobtroja] Wobst, R., *Trojanische Kryptografie* (Trojan Cryptography), UNIX open, 12/97, pp. 42–47.

[WoodBiom] Woodward, J. D., Orlans, N. M., Higgins, P. T., *Biometrics*, McGraw-Hill/Osborne, 2003, ISBN 0-07-222-227-1.

[Young] Young, A., Yung, M., *Cleptography: Using Cryptography Against Cryptography*, Proceedings EUROCRYPT '97, Springer, LNCS 1233, pp. 62–74.

[ZimmPGP] Zimmermann, P., *Pretty Good Privacy: Public Key Encryption for the Masses*, in: [Hoff], pp. 93–107 (1.9).

Index

Cryptology Unlocked Reinhard Wobst
© 2007 John Wiley & Sons, Ltd